Street by Street

BRISTOL, BATH

AVONMOUTH, BRADFORD-ON-AVON, CHIPPING SODBURY, CLEVEDON, TROWBRIDGE, WESTON-SUPER-MARE

Bradley Stoke, Congresbury, Keynsham, Kingswood, Mangotsfield, Midsomer Norton, Nailsea, Portishead, Radstock, Thornbury

Ist edition May 2001

© Automobile Association Developments Limited 2001

This product includes map data licensed from Ordnance Survey® with the permission of the Controller of Her Majesty's Stationery Office. © Crown copyright 2000. All rights reserved. Licence No: 399221.

Published by AA Publishing (a trading name of Automobile Association Developments Limited, whose registered office is Norfolk House, Priestley Road, Basingstoke, Hampshire, RG24 9NY. Registered number 1878835).

Mapping produced by the Cartographic Department of The Automobile Association.

A CIP Catalogue record for this book is available from the British Library.

Printed by G. Canale & C. S.P.A., Torino, Italy

The contents of this atlas are believed to be correct at the time of the latest revision. However, the publishers cannot be held responsible for loss occasioned to any person acting or refraining from action as a result of any material in this atlas, nor for any errors, omissions or changes in such material. The publishers would welcome information to correct any errors or omissions and to keep this atlas up to date. Please write to Publishing, The Automobile Association, Fanum House, Basing View, Basingstoke, Hampshire, RG21 4EA.

Ref: MX061

Key to map pages	ii-iii
Key to map symbols	iv-1
Enlarged scale pages	2-17
Street by Street	18-131
Index – towns & villages	132
Index – streets	133-154
Index – featured places	154-158

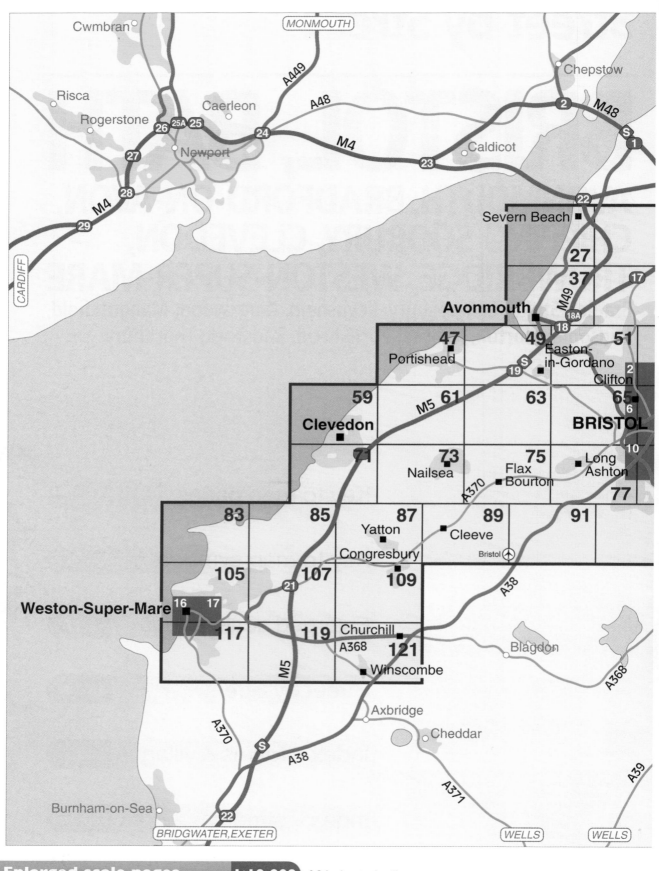

MONMOUTH

Cwmbran

Chepstow

A449

Risca

A48

Caerleon

M48

Rogerstone

A48

26 25A 25

24

M4

Caldicot

2

S

1

27

Newport

23

22

28

M4

29

Severn Beach

CARDIFF

27

37

17

M49

Avonmouth

18A

18

47

49

51

Portishead

S

Easton-
in-Gordano

2

19

Clifton

59

M5

61

63

65

6

Clevedon

BRISTOL

71

73

75

Long
Ashton

10

Nailsea

Flax
Bourton

A370

77

83

85

87

89

91

Yatton

Cleeve

Congresbury

Bristol

105

107

109

A38

21

Weston-Super-Mare

16

17

117

119

Churchill

Blagdon

M5

A368

121

A368

Winscombe

A370

Axbridge

Cheddar

S

A38

A371

A39

Burnham-on-Sea

22

BRIDGWATER, EXETER

WELLS

WELLS

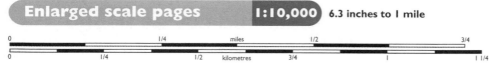

Enlarged scale pages   1:10,000   6.3 inches to 1 mile

0   1/4   miles   1/2   3/4

0   1/4   1/2   kilometres   3/4   1   1 1/4

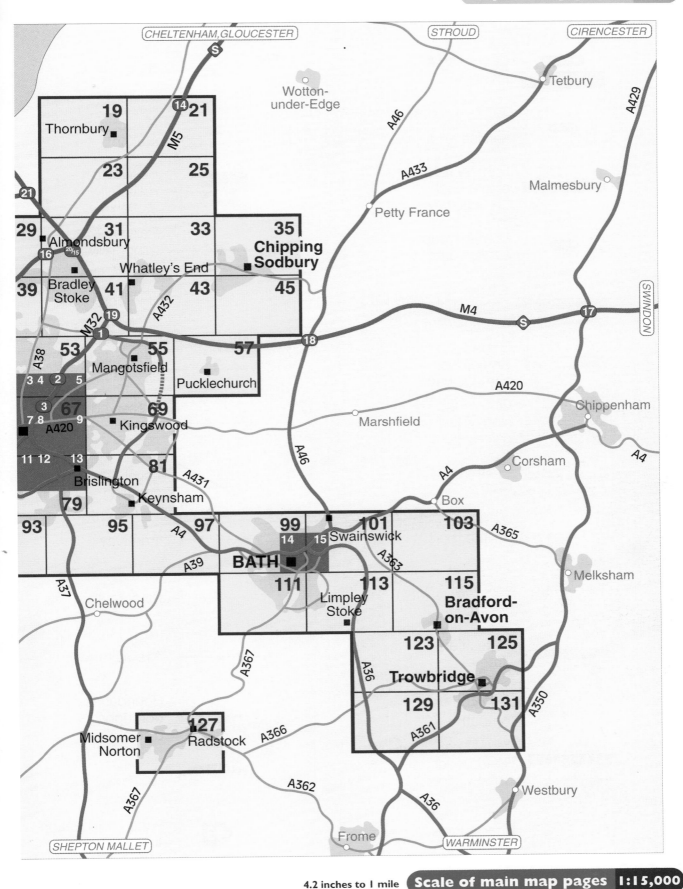

Junction 9	Motorway & junction
Services	Motorway service area
	Primary road single/dual carriageway
Services	Primary road service area
	A road single/dual carriageway
	B road single/dual carriageway
	Other road single/dual carriageway
	Restricted road
	Private road
← ←	One way street
	Pedestrian street
	Track/ footpath
	Road under construction
	Road tunnel
P	Parking

P+	Park & Ride
	Bus/coach station
	Railway & main railway station
	Railway & minor railway station
⊖	Underground station
⊖	Light railway & station
++++++++++	Preserved private railway
LC	Level crossing
•—•—•—•	Tramway
-------------	Ferry route
....	Airport runway
—·—·—·—	Boundaries- borough/ district
▼▼▼▼▼▼▼	Mounds
93	Page continuation 1:15,000
7	Page continuation to enlarged scale 1:10,000

River/canal
lake, pier

Aqueduct
lock, weir

465
▲
Winter Hill

Peak (with
height in
metres)

Beach

Coniferous
woodland

Broadleaved
woodland

Mixed
woodland

Park

Cemetery

Built-up
area

Featured building

City wall

A&E   Accident &
Emergency
hospital

Toilet

Toilet with
disabled facilities

Petrol station

PH   Public house

PO   Post Office

Public library

Tourist Information
Centre

Castle

Historic house/
building

Wakehurst
Place NT   National Trust
property

Museum/
art gallery

†   Church/chapel

Country park

Theatre/
performing arts

Cinema

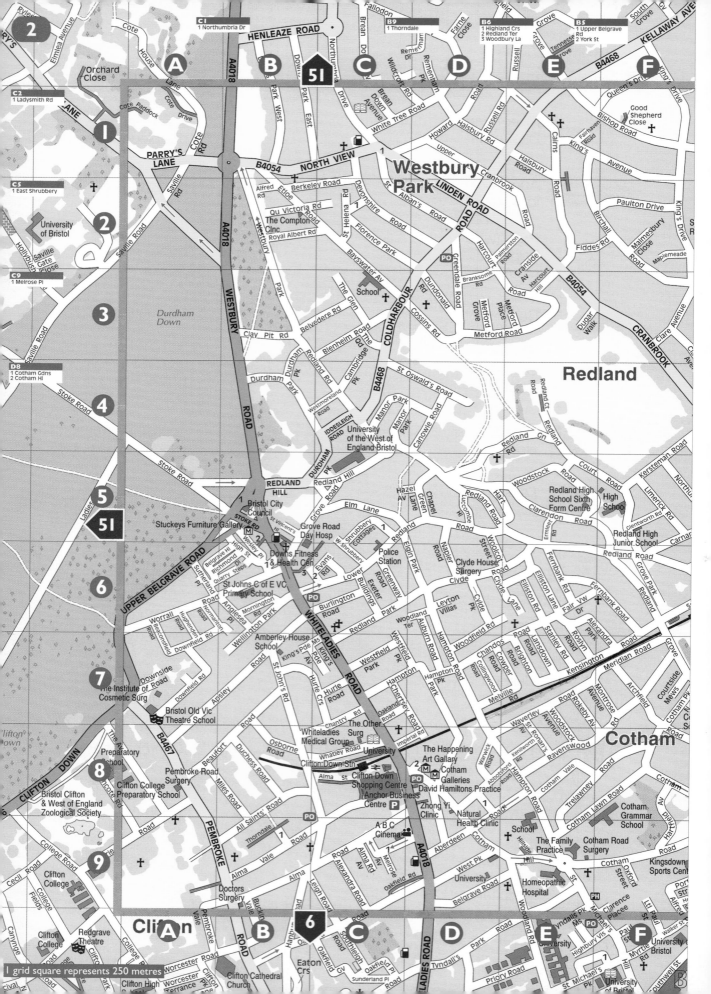

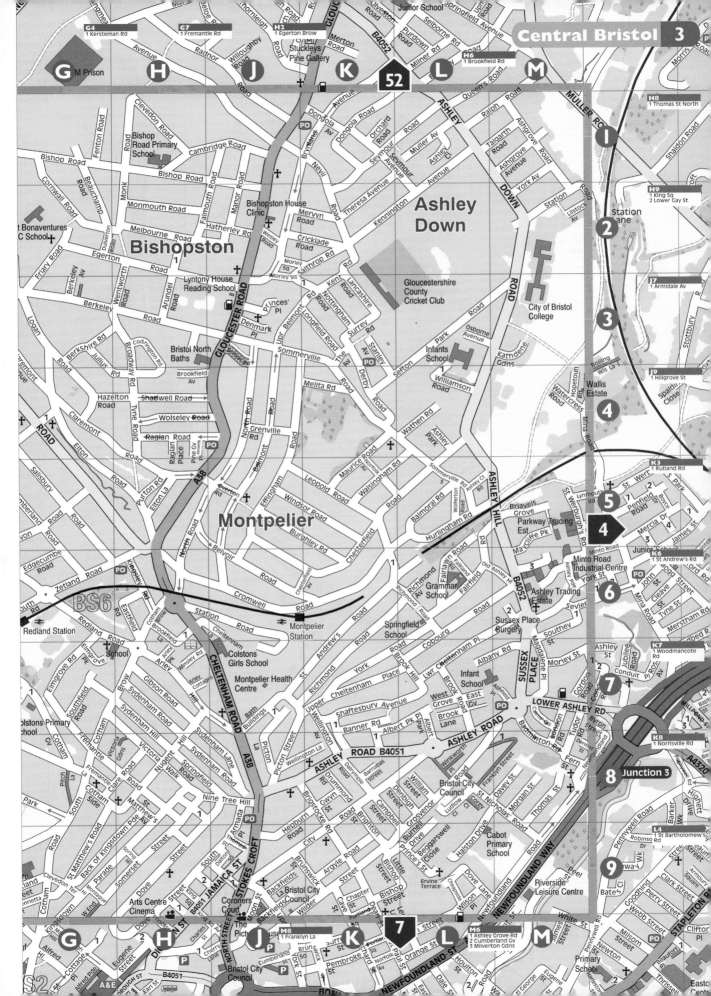

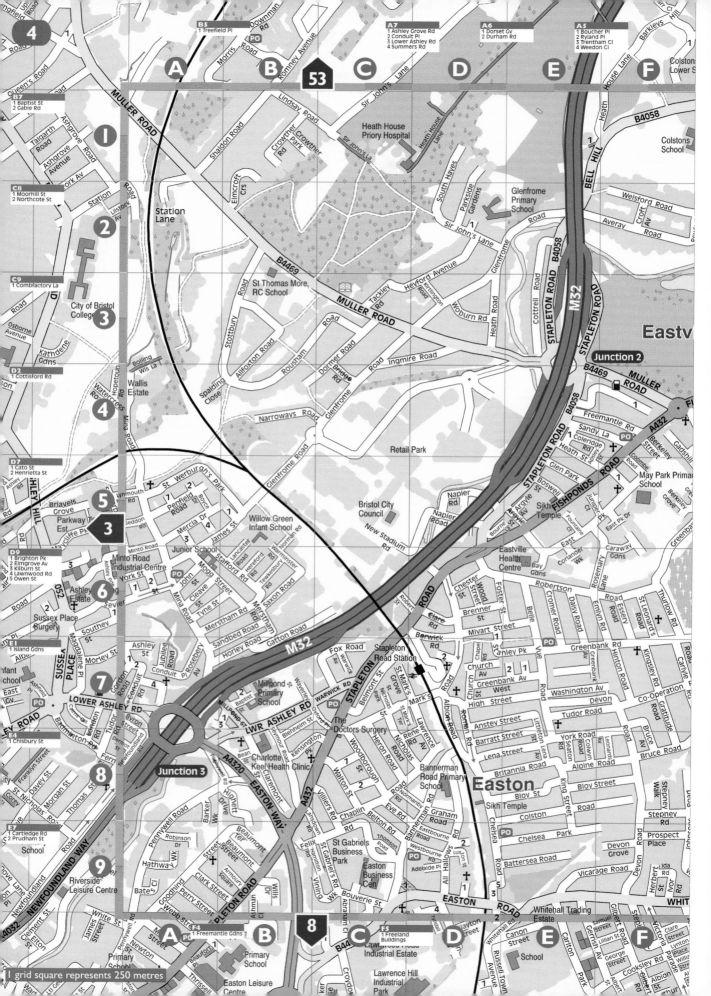

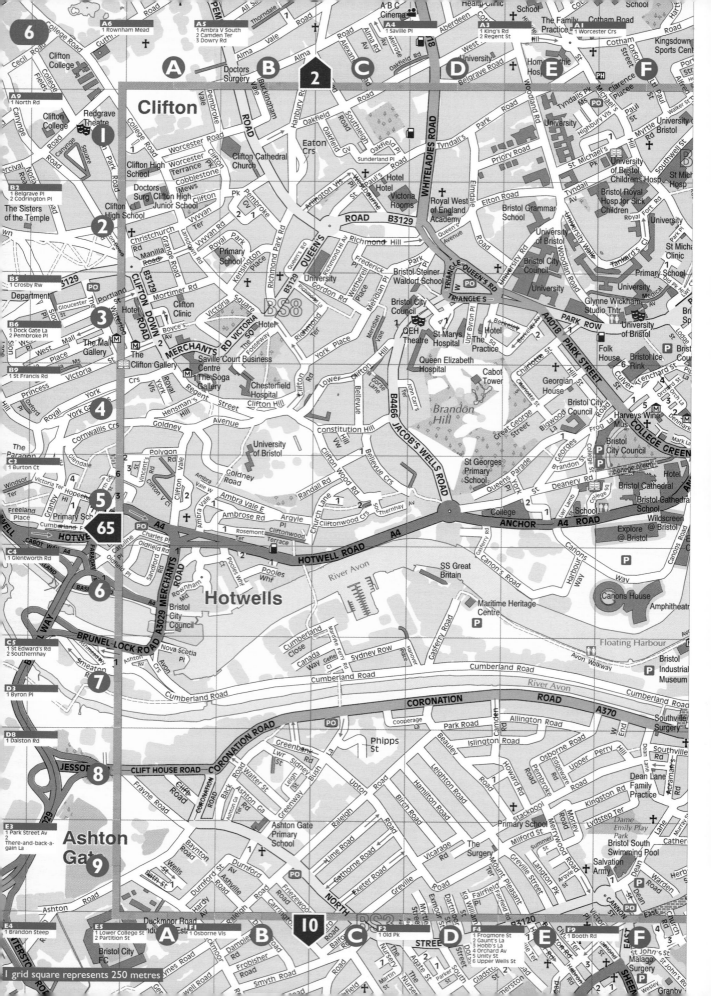

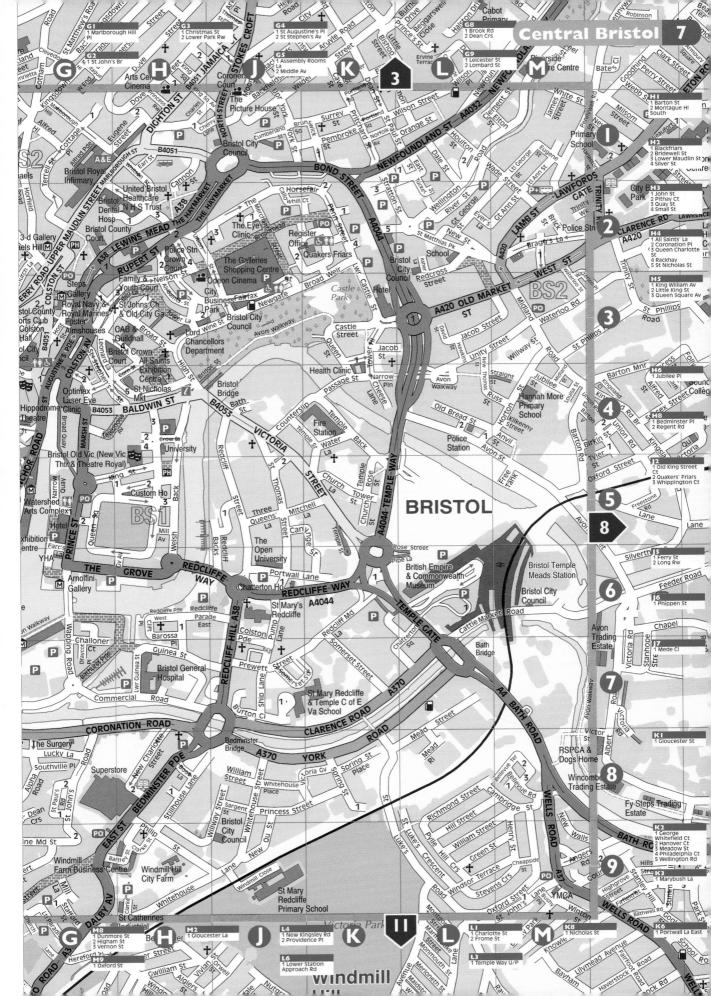

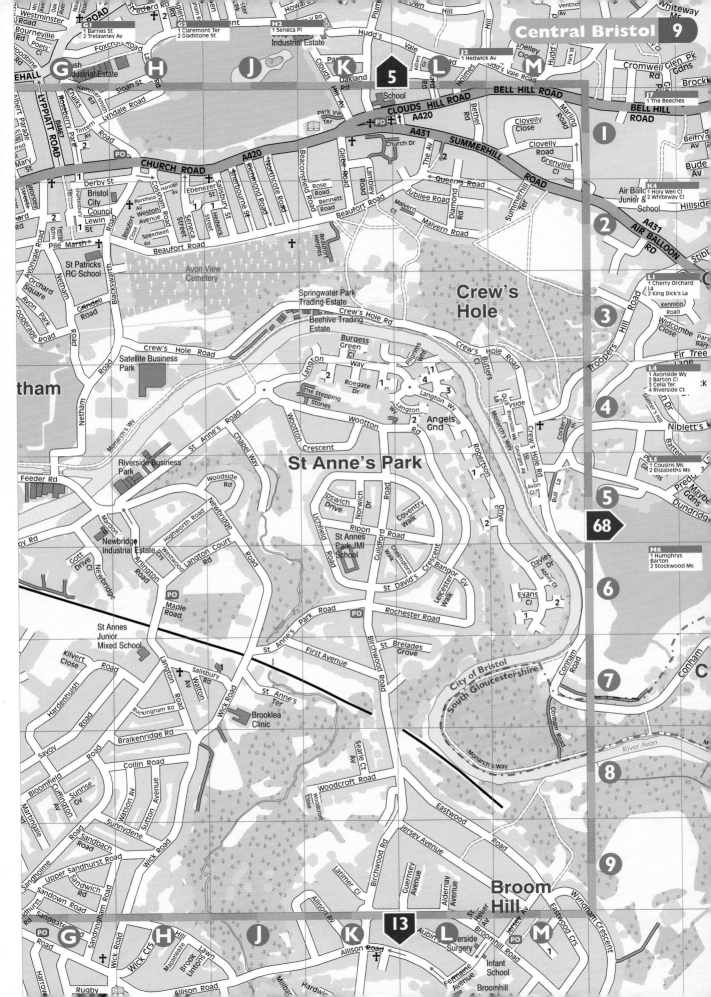

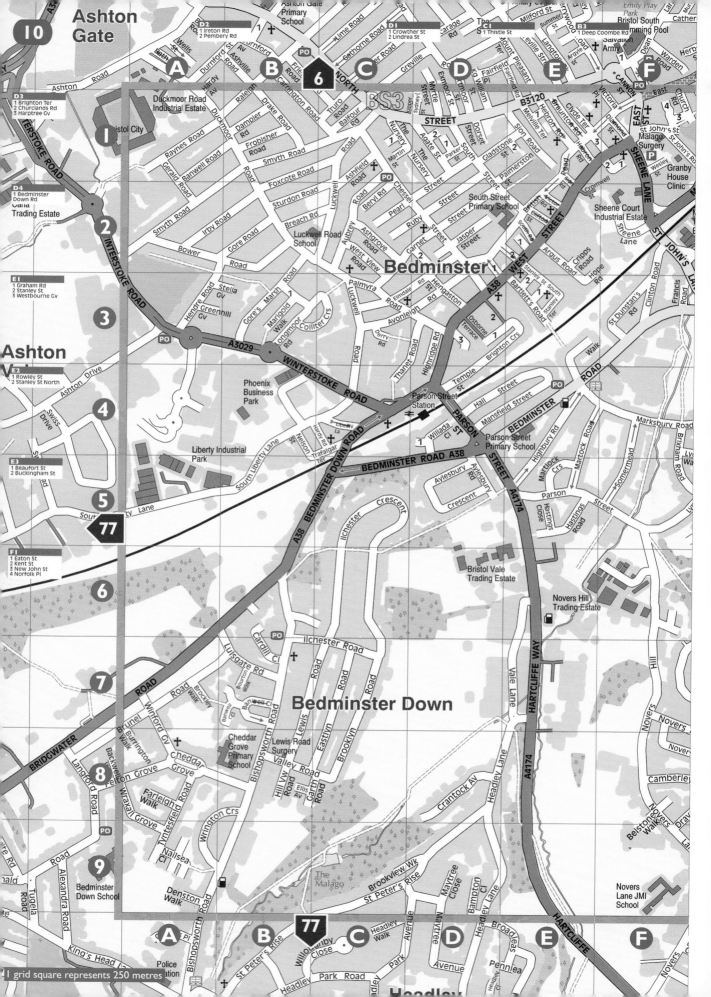

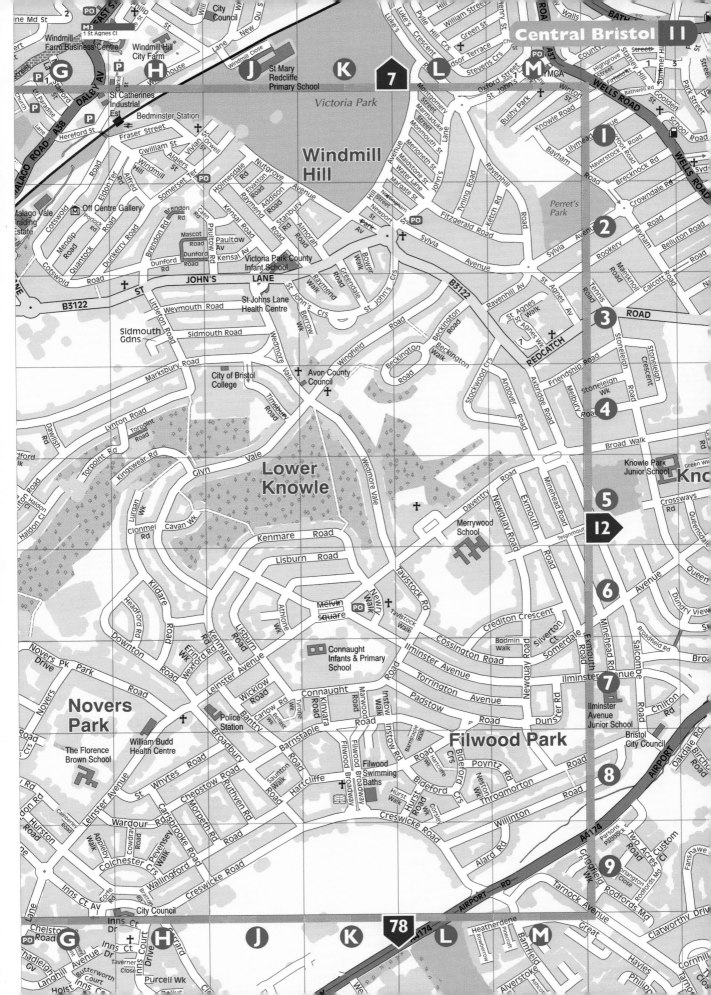

Brislington

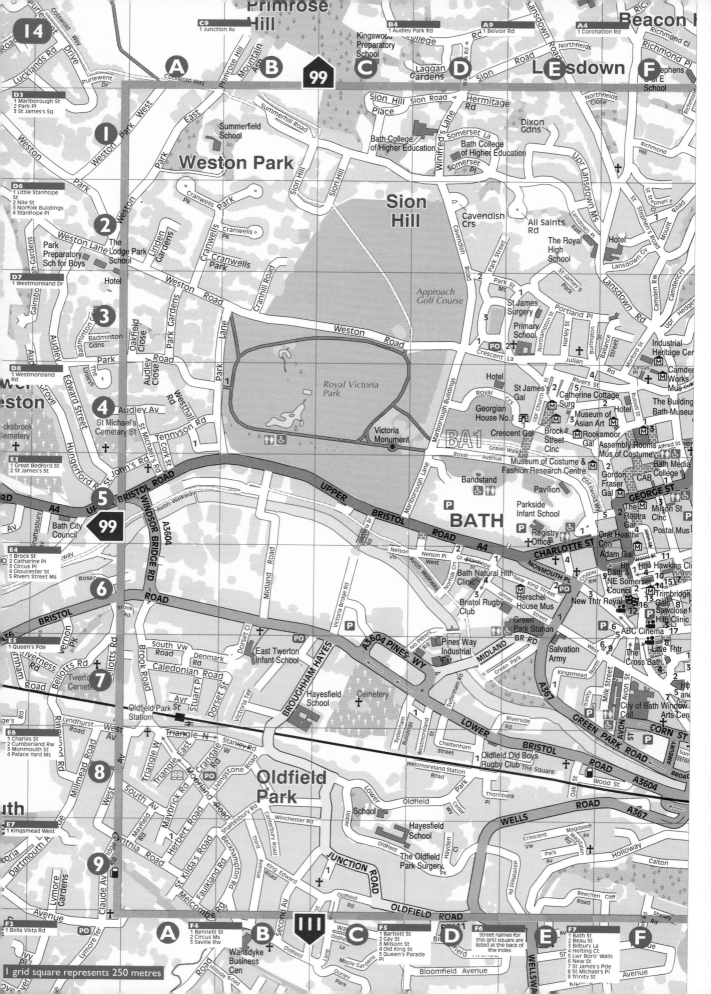

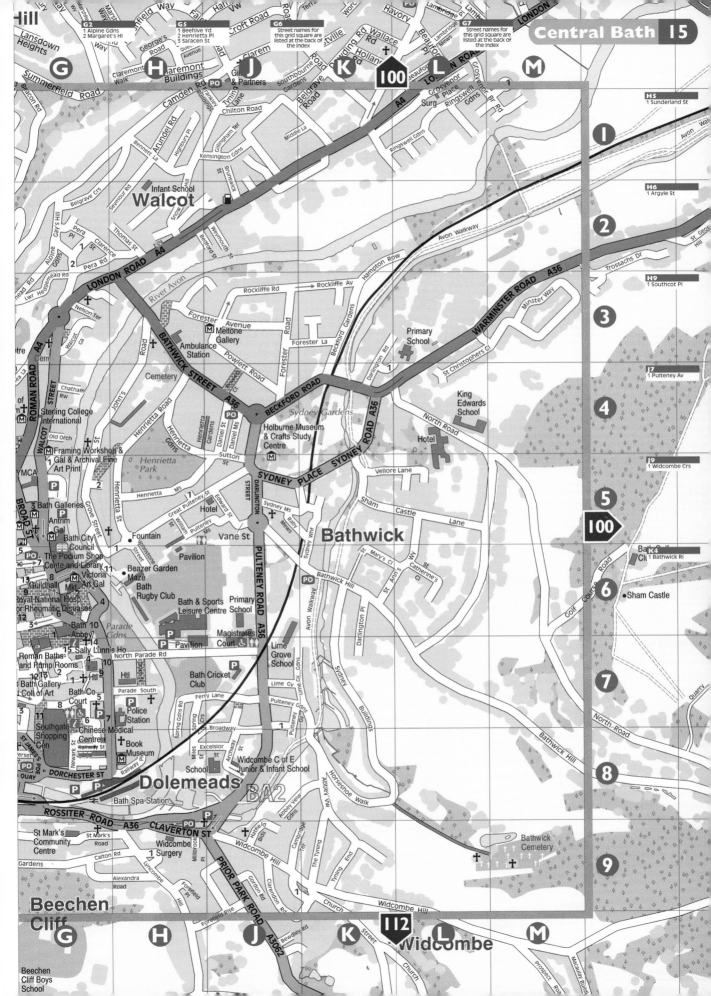

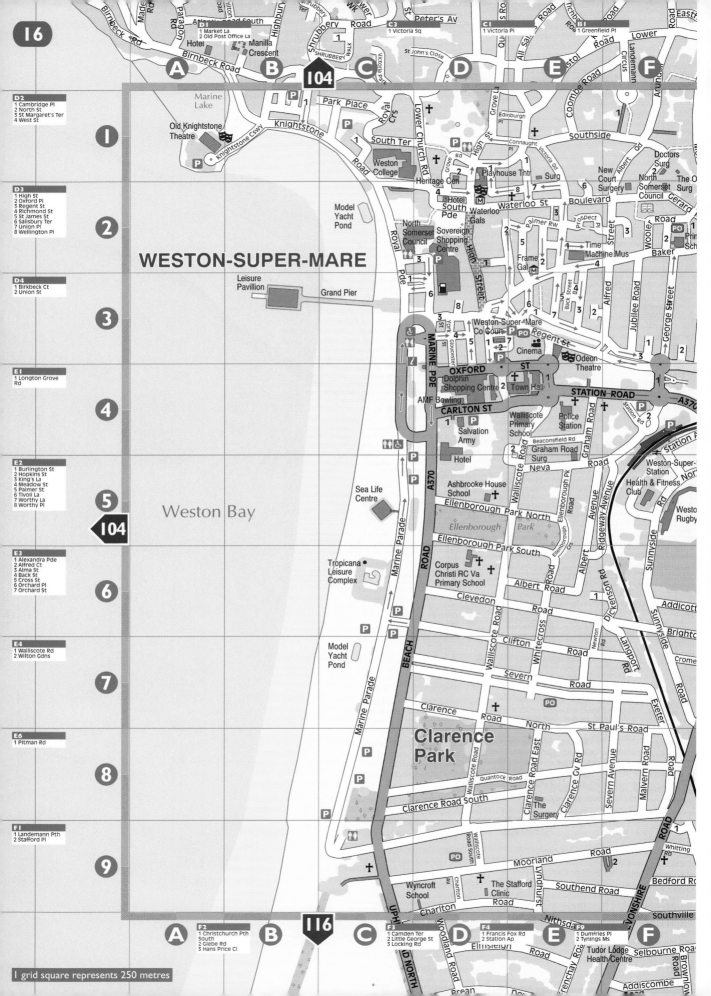

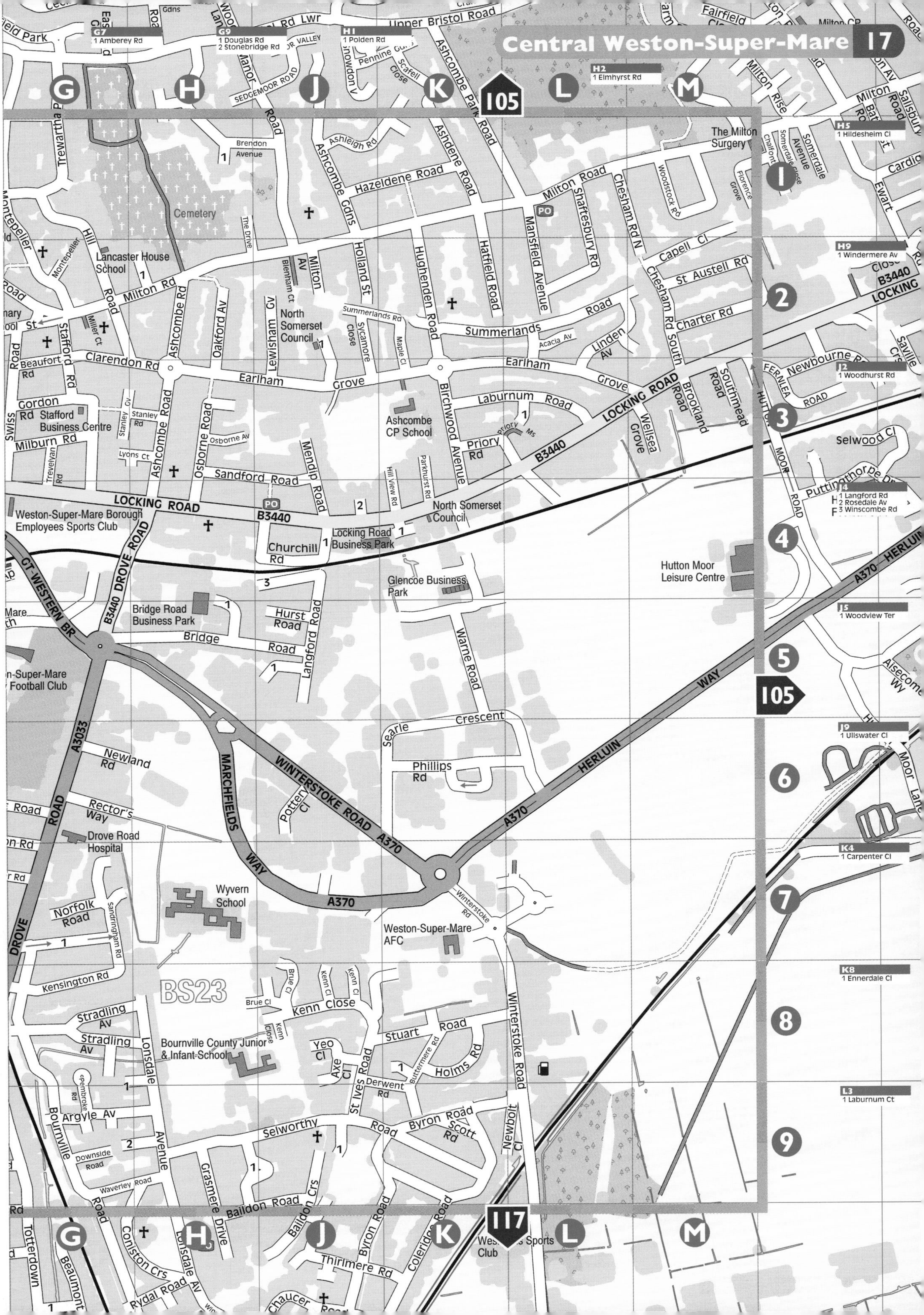
G7 1 Amberey Rd
G9 1 Douglas Rd 2 Stonebridge Rd
H1 1 Polden Rd
H2 1 Elmhyrst Rd
H5 1 Hildesheim Cl
H9 1 Windermere Av
J2 1 Woodhurst Rd
J4 1 Langford Rd 2 Rosedale Av 3 Winscombe Rd
J5 1 Woodview Ter
J9 1 Ullswater Cl
K4 1 Carpenter Cl
K8 1 Ennerdale Cl
L3 1 Laburnum Ct
105
117
G
H
J
K
L
M
2
3
4
5
6
7
8
9
Upper Bristol Road
Ashcombe Park Road
Sedgemoor Road
Pennine Gdns
Scafell Close
Ashleigh Rd
Hazeldene Road
Ashdene Road
Brendon Avenue
Trewartha Park
Cemetery
Milton Road
The Milton Surgery
Woodstock Rd
Florence Grove
Somerdale Avenue
Somerdale Close
Chalfont
Ewart
Cardigan
Salisbury
Milton Rise
Milton Road
Fairfield
Montpelier
Lancaster House School
Milton Rd
Milton Av
Blenheim Ct
Holland St
Hughenden Road
Hatfield Road
Mansfield Avenue
Shaftesbury Rd
Chesham Rd N
Chesham Rd South
Capell Cl
St Austell Rd
Charter Rd
Summerlands Road
Summerlands Rd
Sycamore Close
Maple Cl
Acacia Av
Linden Av
North Somerset Council
Lewisham Gv
Oakford Av
Ashcombe Rd
Stafford Rd
Miller Ct
Beaufort Rd
Clarendon Rd
Earlham Grove
Newbourne Rd
Fernlea Road
Hutton Moor Road
Locking Road
B3440
Gordon Rd
Stafford Business Centre
Stanley Gv
Stanley Rd
Ashcombe Road
Osborne Road
Osborne Av
Lyons Ct
Milburn Rd
Trevelyan Rd
Sandford Road
Mendip Road
Ashcombe CP School
Laburnum Road
Priory Rd
Priory Ms
Birchwood Avenue
Hill View Rd
Parkhurst Rd
Wellsea Grove
Brookland Road
Southmead Road
Selwood Cl
Puttingthorpe Dr
Weston-Super-Mare Borough Employees Sports Club
Locking Road Business Park
North Somerset Council
Churchill Rd
Drove Road
Hutton Moor Leisure Centre
Glencoe Business Park
A370 Herluin Way
Gt Western Br
Bridge Road Business Park
Hurst Road
Langford Road
Bridge Road
Warne Road
Weston-Super-Mare Football Club
Aisecome Wy
Searle Crescent
Phillips Rd
Newland Rd
Rector's Way
Potter Cl
Winterstoke Road
Marchfields Way
A3033
Drove Road Hospital
Moor Lane
Wyvern School
Norfolk Road
Sandringham Rd
Winterstoke Rd
Weston-Super-Mare AFC
Kensington Rd
BS23
Brue Cl
Kenn Cl
Kenn Close
Stradling Av
Bournville County Junior & Infant School
Lonsdale Avenue
Yeo Cl
Axe Cl
St Ives Road
Stuart Road
Buttermere Rd
Holms Rd
Derwent Rd
Pembroke Rd
Bournville Road
Argyle Av
Downside Road
Selworthy Road
Byron Road
Scott Rd
Newbolt Cl
Waverley Road
Grasmere Drive
Baildon Road
Baildon Crs
Coleridge Road
Coniston Crs
Lonsdale Av
Totterdown
Beaumont
Rydal Road
Thirlmere Rd
Chaucer Road
Weston Sports Club
PO

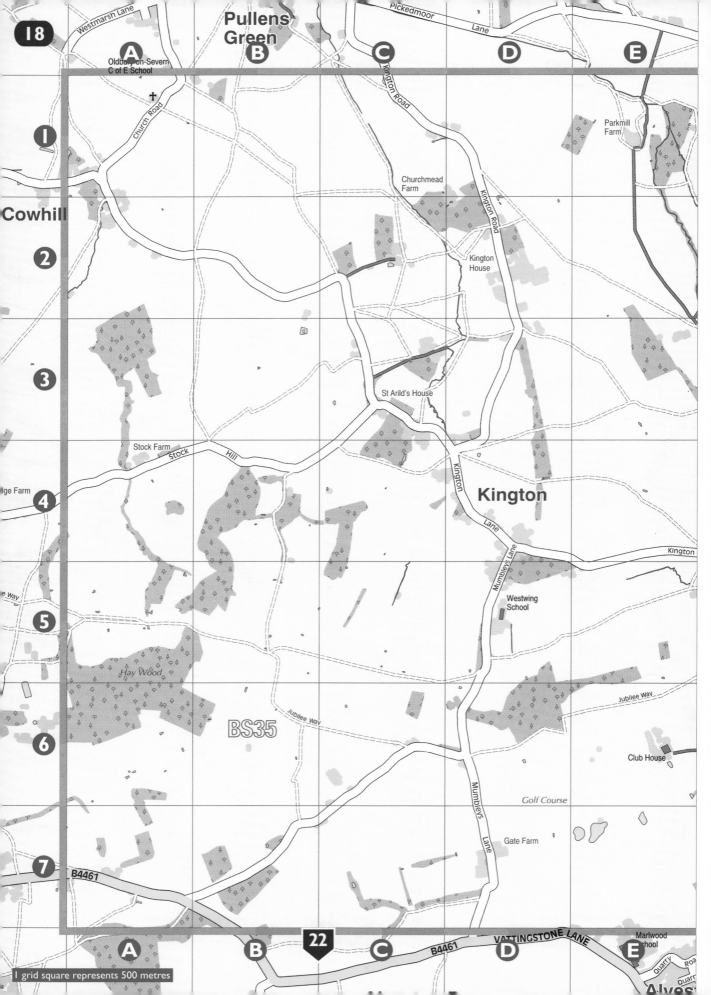

A B C D E

I

Pound House
Farm

Morton
Farm

pper
lorton

GLOUCESTER ROAD

B4061

Whitfield

Iron Hogg La

D B4061

2 The Knapp

Knapp Road

Buckover
Farms

OLD GLOUCESTER ROAD

Buckover

Brinkmarsh Lane

M5

3 Crossways

B4061

A38

Whitewall

Lane

Milbury Heath

Horseshoe
Farm

Chapel
La

ane

4

Lane

19

Green La

The Hacket

Hope Farm

Hacket

Hacket Hill

Cuttsheath
Road

5

Lane

Corbets

6

Road

M5

Grovesend

New Road

7

Itchington Road

Tytherington

Road

Stow
Hill
Road

Baden Hill Road

Stidco

Stowell Hill Rd

A B C D E

24

The
Cas

+

The Orch

Duck

ot Lane

Itchin
Roa

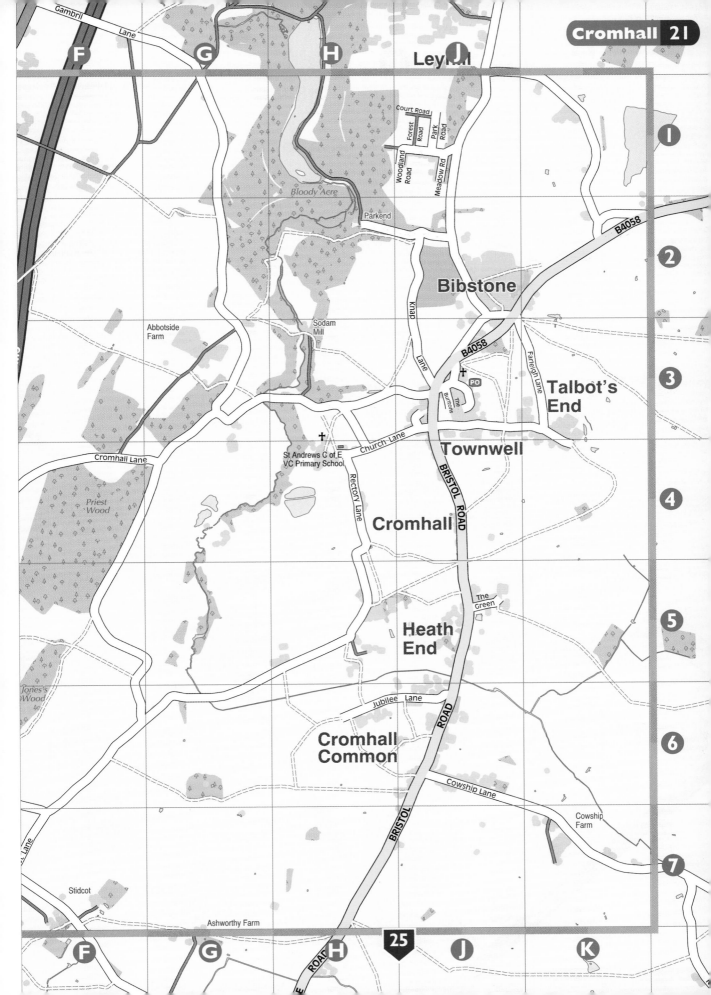

Gambril Lane

F

G

H

Ley Hill

J

Court Road

Forest Road

Park Road

Woodland Road

Meadow Rd

Bloody Acre

Parkend

Bibstone

B4058

1

2

Abbotside Farm

Sodam Mill

Knap Lane

B4058

Farleigh Lane

PO

The Burtons

Talbot's End

3

Cromhall Lane

Townwell

Church Lane

St Andrews C of E VC Primary School

Rectory Lane

BRISTOL ROAD

Cromhall

4

Priest Wood

The Green

5

Jones's Wood

Heath End

Jubilee Lane

ROAD

6

Cromhall Common

Cowship Lane

BRISTOL

Cowship Farm

7

Stidcot

Lane

Ashworthy Farm

25

F

G

ROAD

H

J

K

B4461

A   B   18   C   D   E

E2
1 Hazel Gdns
2 Olive Gdns

1

B4461   VATTINGSTONE LANE

Marlwood
School

Alves

Alveston Down

Quarry Road
Quarry

Strode Gdns
Strode Common
Rosewood AV
The Down
Wolfridge
Lime Grove   Holly Close
Greenwood Drive   Birch Cl   Wolfridge Dr
West View

Hazel Farm

Stroud Common

2

Bridle Way
2   7

Oldown
Country
Park

Foxholes   Lane

Greenhill Lane

Pump Lane

Road   The Down
Hazel Lane

**Old
Down**

The Inner Down

& Elberton
School

Vicarage   Lane

Alveston

**Lower
Hazel**

3

Olveston

Laxton Cl   Russet Cl
ard Rise

Haw Lane

Hill

Down

GLOUCESTER ROAD

Briarleaze

e Surgery

4

Sheepcombe
Farm

Gloucester Rd

Tockington
Road

Pool Cnr

Old

Tockington Manor
School

Washingpool   Hill

Road

Rudgeway

Hardy

Lane   Mill Lane

Tockington

Manor   PK
Manor Cl

Rudgeway Park

5

Silverhill
Brake

Oakleaze

Lane

Tockington   Rd

The
Roundabout

**Woodhouse
Down**

Tockington Park
Farm

6

Lower   Tockington

Fernhill

Tockington Lane

Tockington   Park   Lane

Harts

A38

7

M4

Fernhill Farm

Woodhouse Avenue

GLOUCESTER ROAD

**Woodhouse
Down**

Woodhouse Close
South Road

*Hortham
Wood*

A   B   30   C   D   E

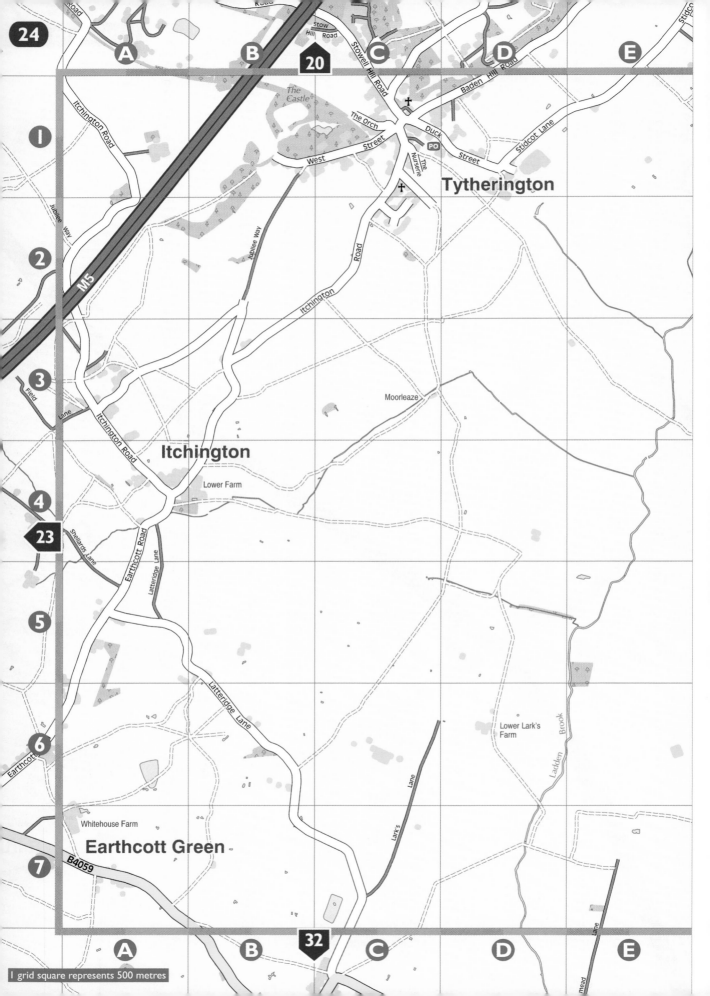

A   B   **20**   C   D   E

1

The Castle

Stow Hill Road

Baden Hill Road

The Orch Street

Duck Street

PO

The Nurserie

Stidcot Lane

Tytherington

Itchington Road

Jubilee Way

2

M5

Jubilee Way

Itchington Road

3

Field Lane

Moorleaze

Itchington

Itchington Road

Lower Farm

4

23

Shellards Lane

Earthcott Road

Latteridge Lane

5

Latteridge Lane

Lark's Lane

Lower Lark's Farm

Ladden Brook

6

Earthcott

Whitehouse Farm

Earthcott Green

7

B4059

A   B   **32**   C   D   E

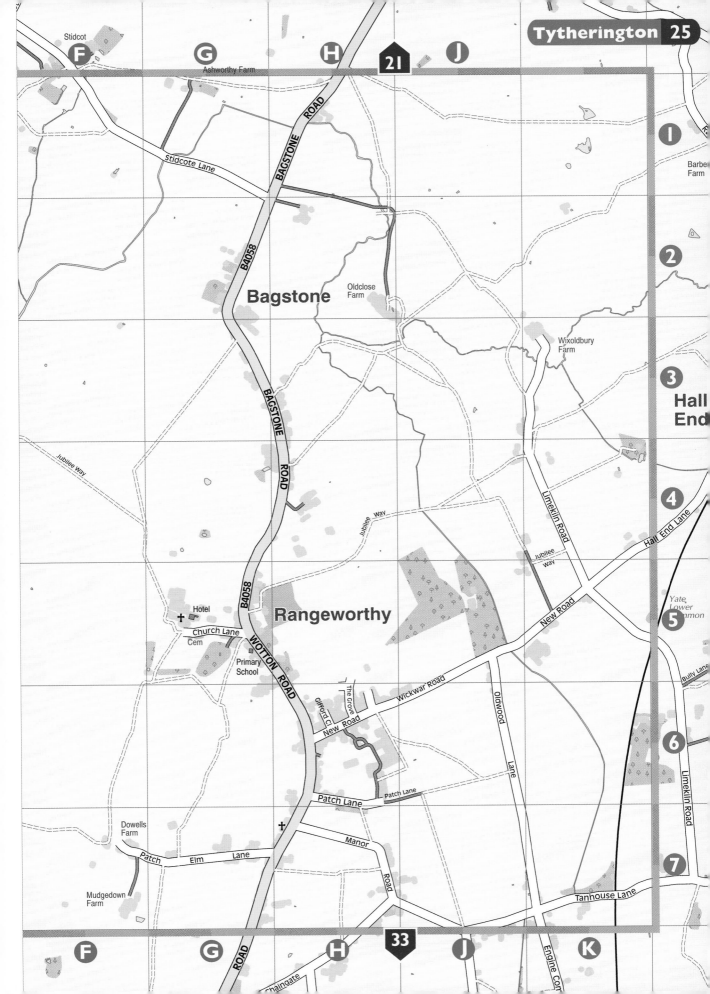

F
Stidcot

G
Ashworthy Farm

H
21

J

I
Barber Farm

Stidcote Lane

BAGSTONE ROAD

B4058

Bagstone

Oldclose Farm

2

Wixoldbury Farm

3
Hall End

BAGSTONE ROAD

Jubilee Way

4

Limekiln Road

Jubilee Way

Jubilee Way

Hall End Lane

B4058

Hotel

Rangeworthy

New Road

5
Yate Lower Common

Bully Lane

Church Lane
Cem

Primary School

WOTTON ROAD

The Grove

Wickwar Road

Oldwood Lane

6

Limekiln Road

Gifford Cl

New Road

Patch Lane

Patch Lane

Dowells Farm

Manor Road

7

Patch Elm Lane

Mudgedown Farm

Tanhouse Lane

F

G
ROAD

H
33

J

Engine Com

K

Chaingate

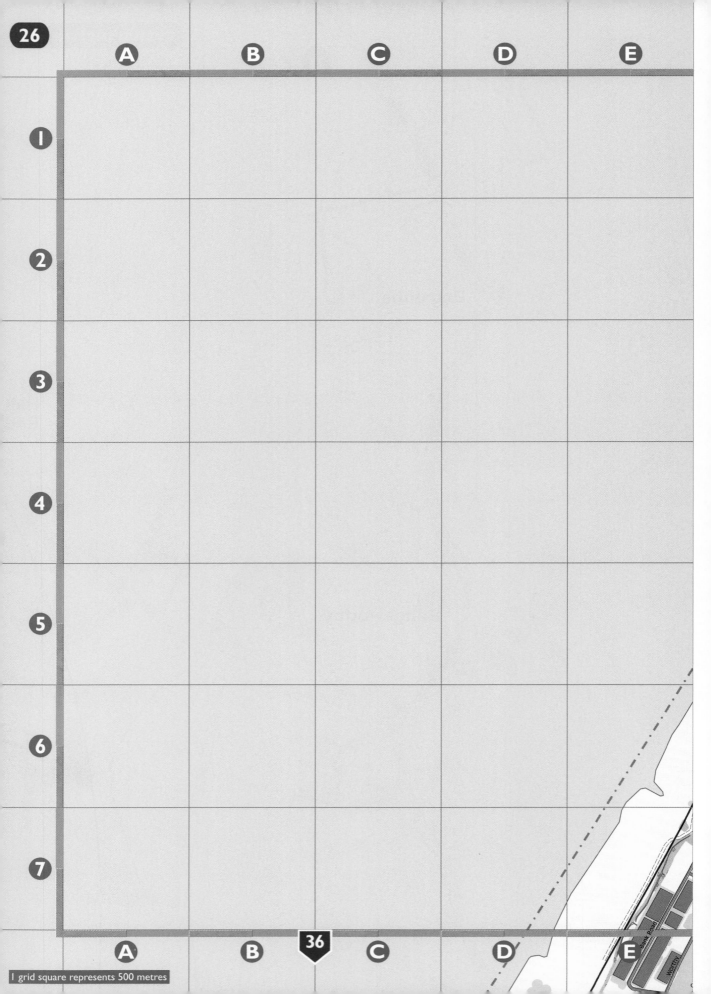

1 grid square represents 500 metres

F

G

H

J

I

2

3

4

28

5

6

7

PO

Severn Wy

Beach Rd

Station Road

Riverside Park

Severn Beach Stn

Albert Rd

Victoria Crs

Ableton

Denny Isle Dr

Prospect Rd

Lane

Abbott Rd

Severnwood Gdns

Severn Beach CP School

Church

Cover Rd

Gorse

Beach

Cover Rd

Little Green Lane

BEACH AVEN

Road

Osborne Rd

Road

Church Road

Severn Beach

M49

A403

SEVERN ROAD

Whitehouse Farm

So Glo Co

Wainbridge Crs

CROSS HAN

Ableton Lane

Central Avenue

Avlon Works

Dyer's Common

Farm La

Severnside Works

A403

SEVERN ROAD

South Gloucestershire
City of Bristol

Ableton La

Crook's Marsh

Green Lane

Philblack Works

Minor's

Ableton La

Severn Road

Lane

Gas Works

Elmington Manor Farm

Docks Ind Est

CHITTENING ROAD

Road

Greensplott Road

F

G

37

H

J

K

Niatts

J6
1 Newnham Pl

K2
1 Chestermaster Cl
2 Walnut Tree Cl

K7
1 Thirlmere Rd

F   G   H   J

I

Tockington Lane

Cemetery

Marshwall Lane

Lower
Court Farm

Lower Court Road

Court Vw

2

Scop

Church Road

Hotel

The Pound

Glebe Fld

Surgery

Lower Knole Farm

Monmouth Hill

Townsend

Almondsbury C of E
VC Primary School

Hollow

Road

Red House Lane

3

GLOUCESTER ROAD

Knole Cl

Church Vw

Sundays Hill

Over Lane

Oaklands Dr

JU

Town Football
Club

North Bristol
Rugby Football Club

Cattybrook
Farm

Knole Pk

Knole Pk

Over Lane

4

30

PO

Park Avenue

Hotel

5

Ash
Lane

Badger's
Lane

Lane

Over

Aztec
West

Park Avenue

Hempton Lane

Waterside Dr

Patchway
High
School

6

Over Lane

Coniston Primary
School

PATCHWAY

Chillington Court

Blakeney Road

Epney Cl

Elmore Road

South
Gloucestershire Council

PO

Coniston Road

Coniston Road

Windermere Road

7

PO

Bevington Wk

Bevington

Bevington Close

Bevington Drive

Arlingham Way

Tidenham Road

Longney Place

Derwent Cl

M5

Falcon Cl

Falcon Wk

Falcon Drive

Swallow Dr

Stroud Road

Bradley Road

Durban Road

Worthing Road

Pretoria Road

Cavendish Road

Rodway Road

Eagle Dr

Kestrel

Linnet Close

Martin Close

Brighton Rd

Lee Close

Infant
Sch

Patchway
Town
Council

Patchway
Health Clinic

Patchway
Trading Estate

Callicroft
Junior

Hawthorn Close

Rodway Road

Cranbourne Rd

Cedar Close

Southsea Road

Ashford Rd

Hazeldene Rd

Camcroft Road

Grove-In
Estate

on 17

F

Superstore

G

Olympus Road

Britannia Road

Willow Cl

Larch Wy

Sycamore Dr

39

H

J

K

Highwood
Lane

nwood Lane

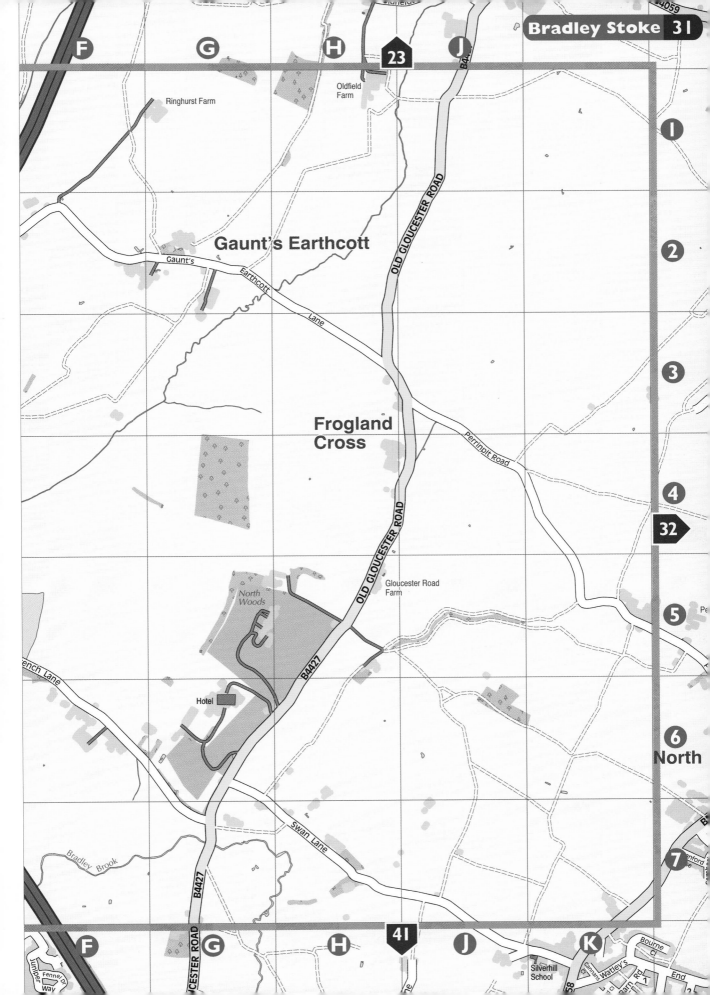

Ringhurst Farm

Oldfield Farm

Gaunt's Earthcott

Gaunt's

Earthcott

Lane

OLD GLOUCESTER ROAD

Frogland Cross

Perrinpit Road

Gloucester Road Farm

North Woods

B4427

Hotel

ench Lane

B4427

Bradley Brook

Swan Lane

CESTER ROAD

North

Silverhill School

Bourne

Watley's

Fennel Way

Juniper

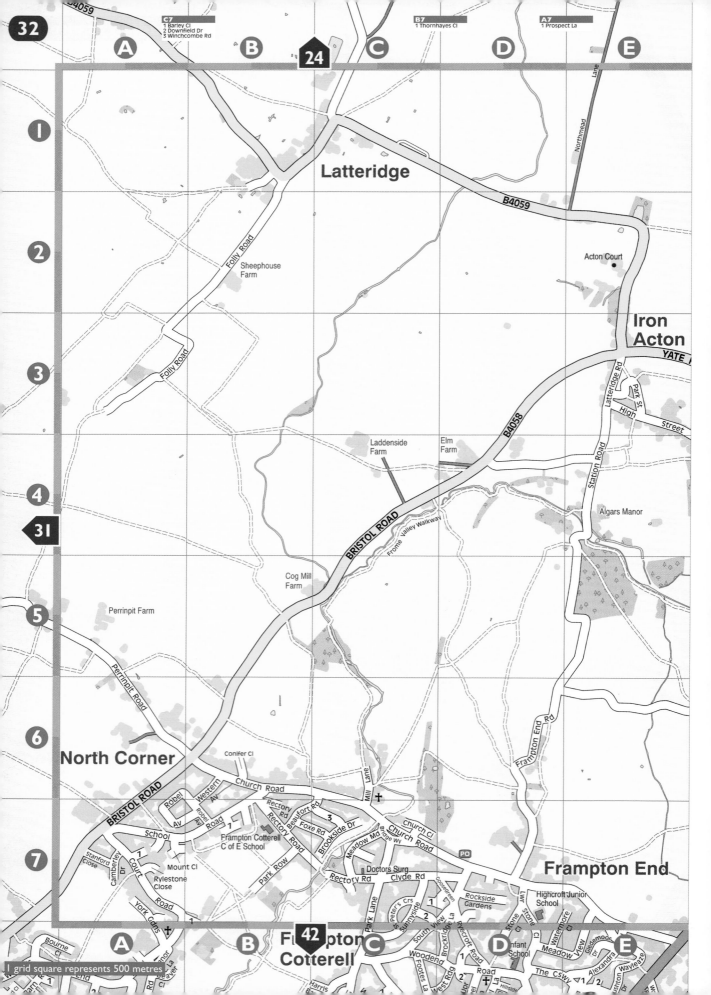

A   B   24   C   D   E

1

Latteridge

B4059

2

Folly Road

Sheephouse
Farm

Acton Court

Iron
Acton

3

Folly Road

YATE

B4058

Laddenside
Farm

Elm
Farm

Latteridge Rd

Park St

High
Street

4

31

Bristol Road

Frome Valley Walkway

Station Road

Algars Manor

Cog Mill
Farm

5

Perrinpit Farm

Perrinpit Road

Frampton End Rd

6

North Corner

Conifer Cl

Church Road

Mill Lane

Bristol Road

Robel
AV

Western
AV

Robel Road

Rectory
Rd

Beaufort Rd

Foxe Rd

3

Brookside Dr

Church Cl

Church Road

PO

Frampton End

School

Frampton Cotterell
C of E School

7

Rectory Road

Park Row

Meadow Md

Bridge Wy

Doctors Surg

Rectory Rd

Clyde Rd

Stanford
Close

Camberley
Dr

Court

Mount Cl

Rylestone
Close

Road

St Peter's Crs

Sunnyside

Goose Green

1

Rockside
Gardens

Highcroft Junior
School

York Cans

Bourne
Cl

A   B   42   Frampton   C   Infant School   D   E

Cotterell

South View

Woodend

Brockridge La

Footes La

West Rdg

Ryecroft Road

Road

Hillside

La

Meadow
View

Watermore
Cl

Stone Stone

Gledemoor
Dr

The Cswy

Alexandra
Dr

Rushton
Dr

Wayleaze

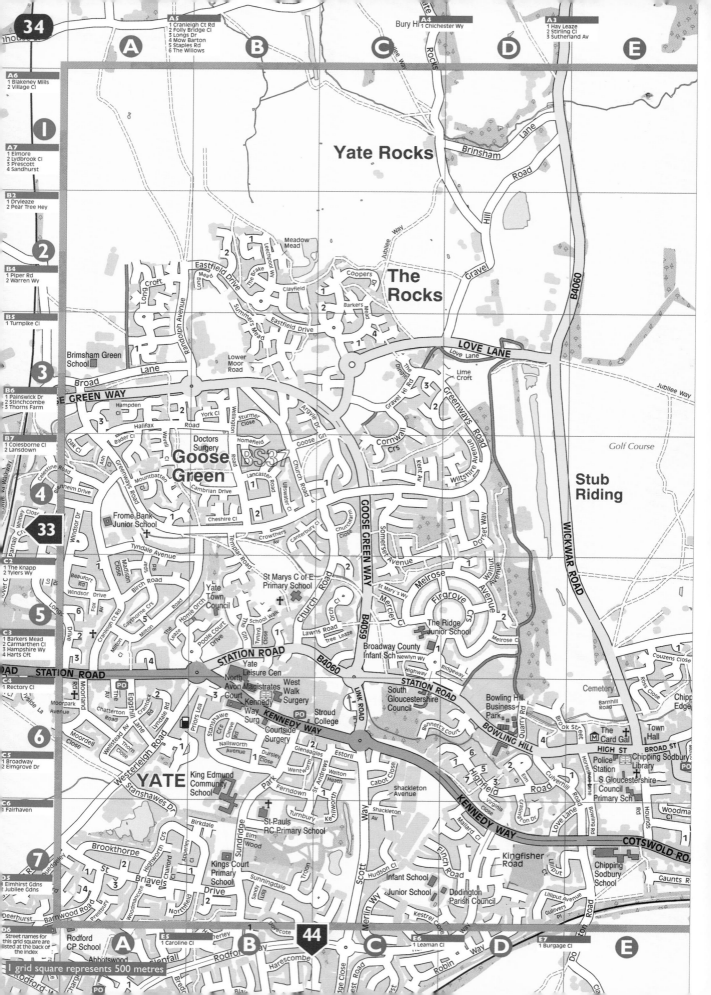

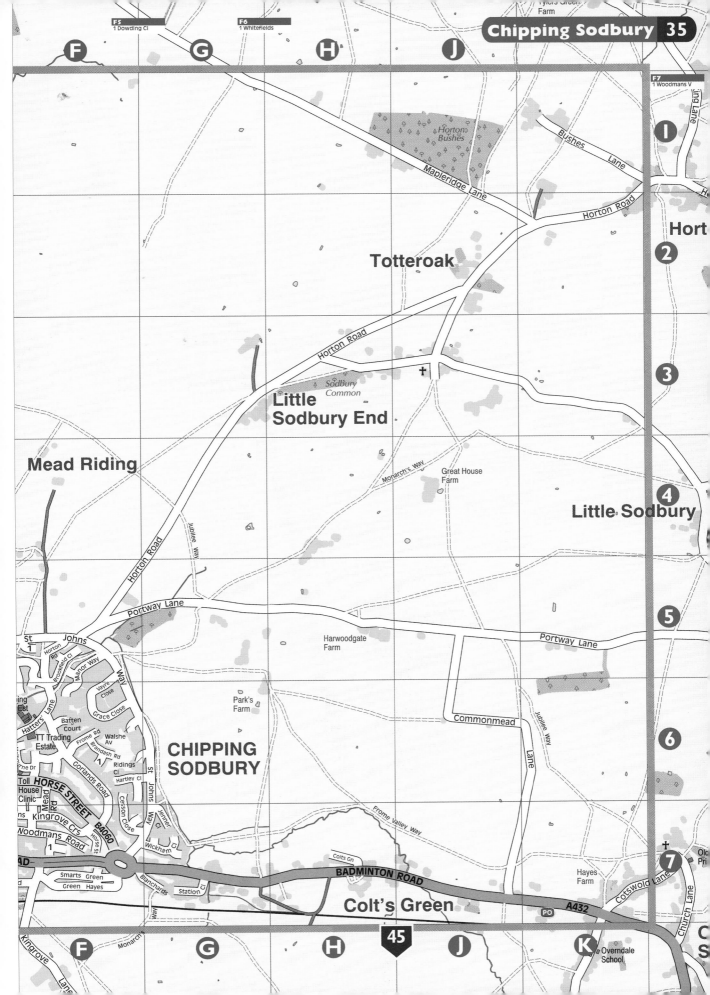

F5
1 Dowding Cl

F6
1 Whitefields

F7
1 Woodmans V

F **G** **H** **J**

Horton Bushes

Mapleridge Lane

Bushes Lane

Horton Road

I

Hort

2

Tyler's Green Farm

Totteroak

Horton Road

†

3

Sodbury Common

Little Sodbury End

Mead Riding

Monarch's Way

Great House Farm

Little Sodbury **4**

Jubilee Way

Horton Road

5

Portway Lane

Portway Lane

St Johns

Harwoodgate Farm

Horton Rd

Brookfield Cl

Manor Way

Vayre Close

Grace Close

Batten Court

Way

Hatters Lane

TT Trading Estate

Frome Rd

Walshe AV

Brandash Rd

Ridings Cl

Hartley Cl

Commonmead

Jubilee Way Lane

6

Park's Farm

CHIPPING SODBURY

ne Dr

Gorlands Road

St Johns Way

Cesson Close

Jenner

Toll House Clinic

HORSE STREET

Mead Rd

B4060

Kingrove Crs

Horse St

Woodmans Road

1

Wickham

†

Old Pri

7

Frome Valley Way

Hayes Farm

Cotswold Lane

Church Lane

Smarts Green

Green Hayes

Blanchards

Station

Cl

Colts Gn

BADMINTON ROAD

PO

A432

Colt's Green

F **G** **H** ▼**45** **J** **K**

Kingrove Lane

Monarch's

Overndale School

C S

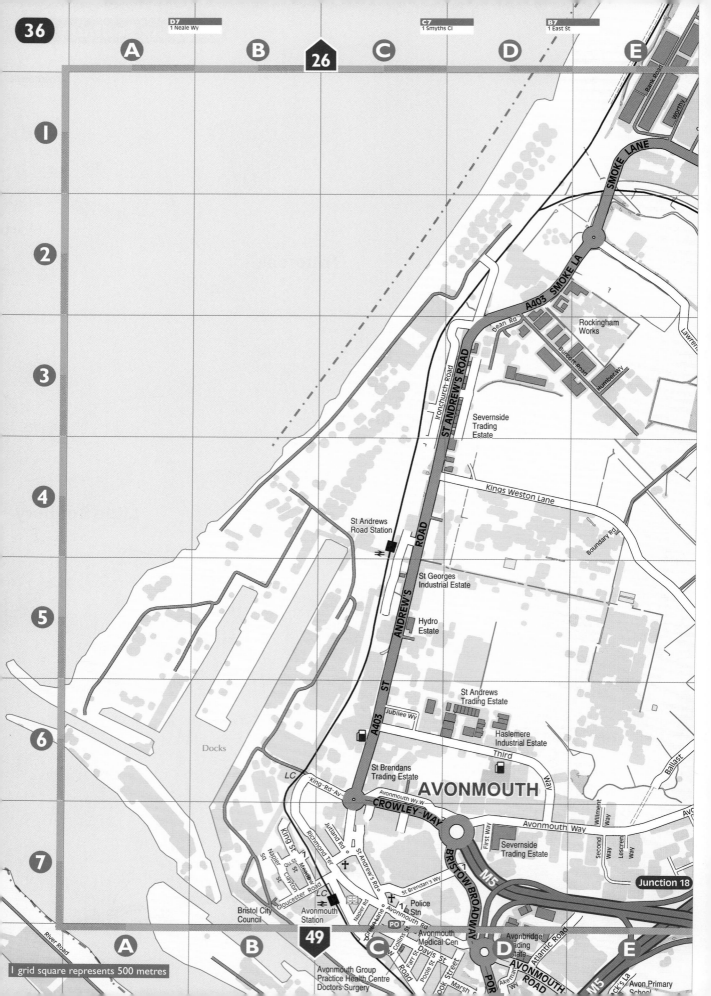

A B 26 C D E

I
2
3
4
5
6
7

SMOKE LANE

A403 SMOKE LA

Smoke La

Bank Road

Worthy

Lawren

Rockingham
Works

Dean Rd

Burcott Road

Humber Wy

Ironchurch Road

ST ANDREW'S ROAD

Severnside
Trading
Estate

Kings Weston Lane

Boundary Rd

St Andrews
Road Station

ST
ANDREW'S
ROAD

St Georges
Industrial Estate

Hydro
Estate

St Andrews
Trading Estate

Haslemere
Industrial Estate

Jubilee Wy

A403

Third
Way

Ballast

Docks

LC

King Rd Av

St Brendans
Trading Estate

AVONMOUTH

Avonmouth Wy.W

Avonmouth Way

Severnside
Trading
Estate

CROWLEY WAY

BRISTOW BROADWAY

First Way

Willment
Way

Second
Way

Lescren
Way

Avo

M5

Junction 18

King St

Sq

Napier
St

Clayton
St

Qu
St

Meadow
St

Richmond Ter

Jutland Rd

St Andrew's Rd

St Brendan's Wy

Avon
bridge
Trading
Estate

Bristol City
Council

LC

Avonmouth
Station

Gloucester Road

Napier Rd

Police
Stn

Avonmouth Rd

PO

Avonmouth
Medical Cen

AVONMOUTH
ROAD

Akeman
Road

Atlantic
Road

ck's La

Avon Primary
School

POR

M5

River Road

Avonmouth Group
Practice Health Centre
Doctors Surgery

Davis St

Collins St

Parr St

Poole St

Cook St

Marsh St

Green Lane

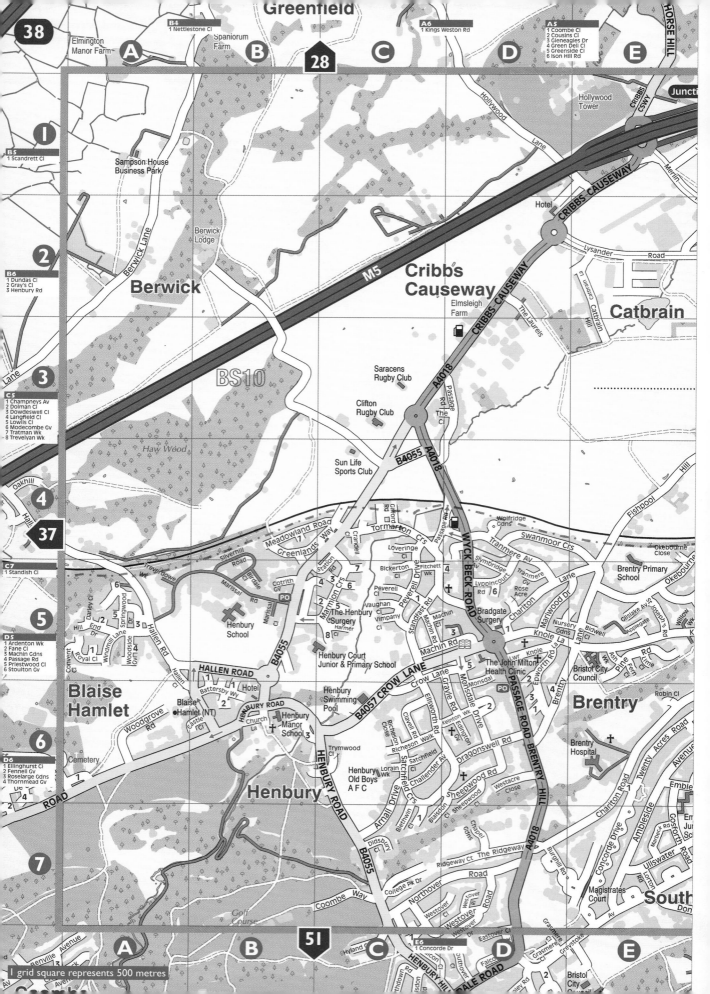

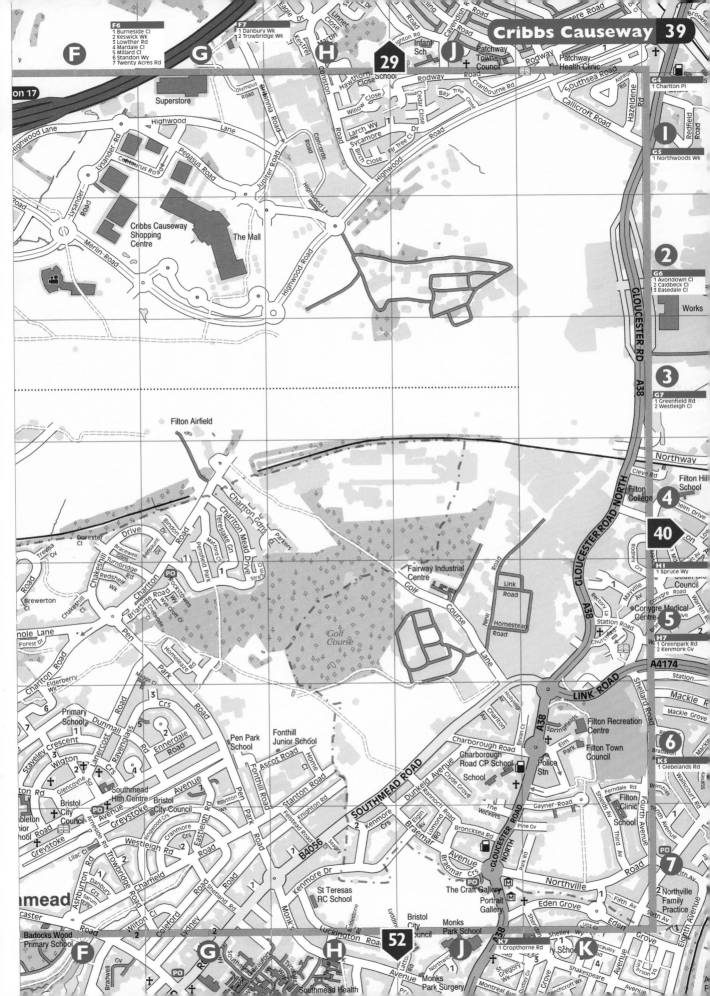

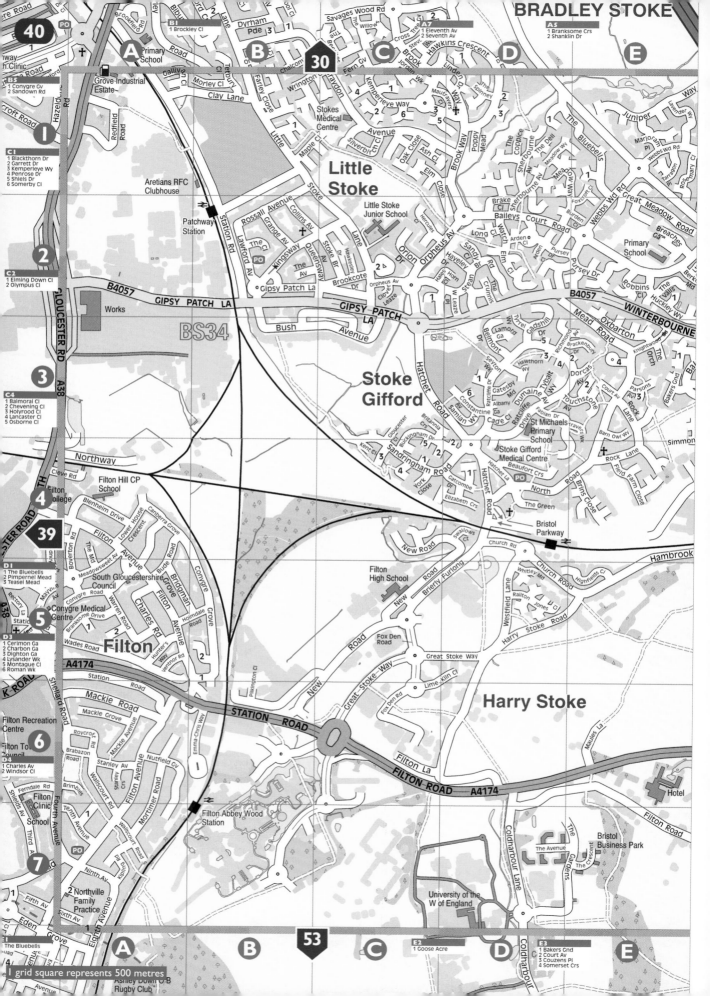

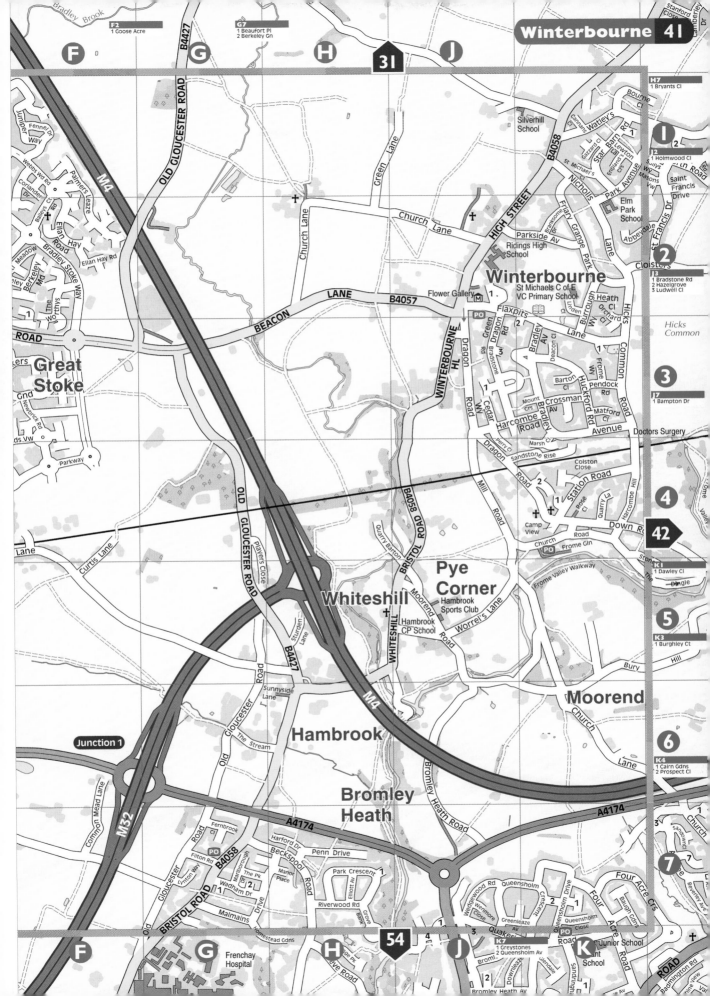

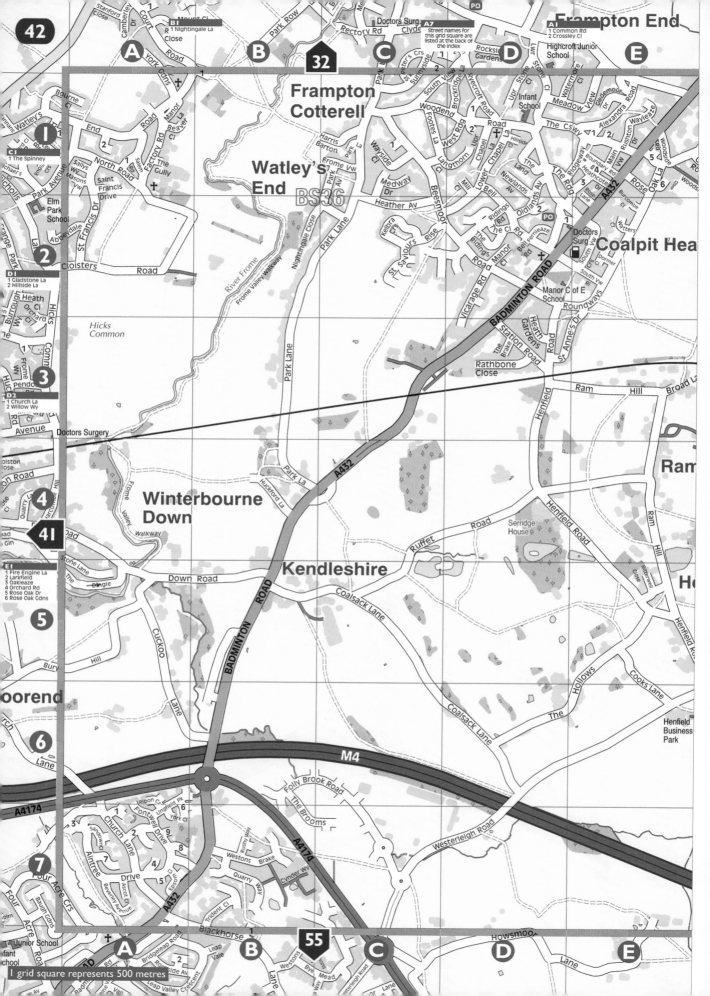

K1
1 Cranham
2 Pitchcombe

F

G

Says Court
Farm

H

33

J

Deerhurst
Barnwood Road
Prestbury
Bisley
Infant
School
Rodford
CP School
Abbotswood
Surg
Chedworth
Rodford Way
PO
Rodborough
Witcombe
Brockworth
Westerleigh Rd
Shire Way
Badgeworth
School
Edgeworth
Kingscote
Abb
Infa
Kelston
Frog
Lane
Coalville
Road
Road

1

2

Westerleigh Road

†

Besom Lane

3

Jorrocks
Estate

n Hill

Broad Lane

Westerleigh

Newman
Close
Westerleigh Road
The Quadrangle
Mill Crs
PO
†

Beanwood
Farm

4

44

enfield

Boxhedge Farm Lane

Old Mill
Close
Shorthill
Road

5

Wester
Hill

Westerleigh Road

Cliff Farm

B4465

6

Folly Brook

Leigh
Lane
Leigh Lane

7

Leigh
Farm

F

G M4

H

56

J

K

Lyde

WESTERLEIGH ROAD
Batchfield

D4
1 Down Cl
2 Ivy Ct
3 Meadow Cl
4 Norwood Gv
5 Severnmeade

C6
1 Chesle Cl
2 Homestead
3 Redcliffe Ci

B5
1 Waterside Pk

A B C D E

I

D5
1 Bedwin Cl
2 Gaunts Cl
3 Hill Gay Cl
4 Kingsway
5 Monmouth Cl
6 Newport Cl
7 Ranchways

2

3

E4
1 Blackdown Rd
2 Bruton Av
3 Cabot Ri
4 Denny Cl
5 Frobisher Cl
6 Polden Rd

Black Nore

4

5

Redcliff Bay

6

7

A B **60** C D E

1 grid square represents 500 metres

Weston-in-

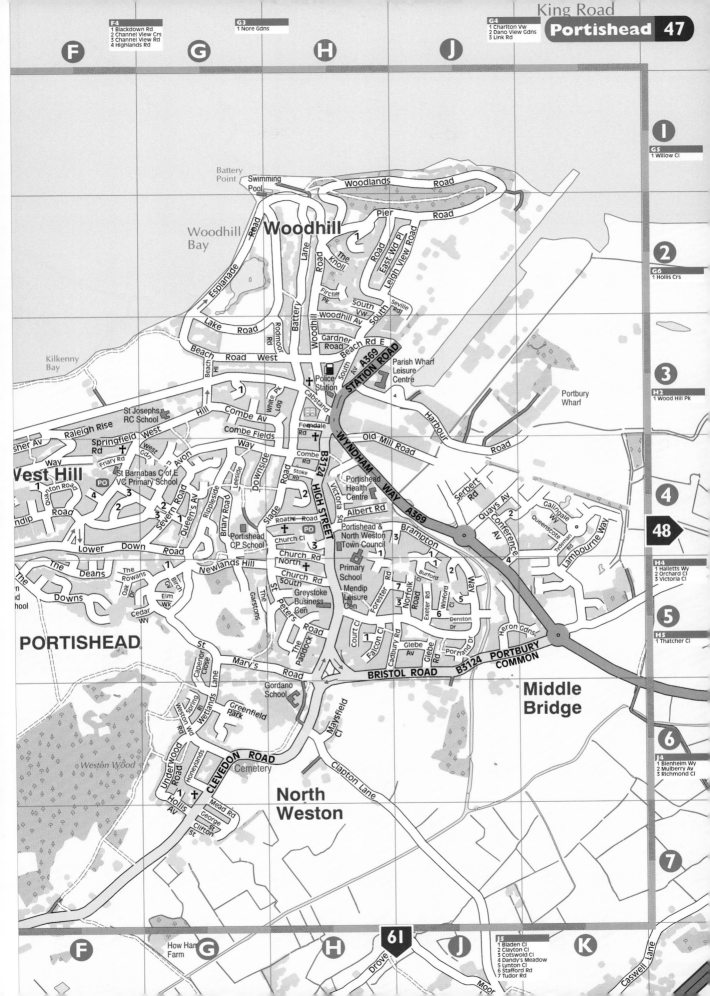

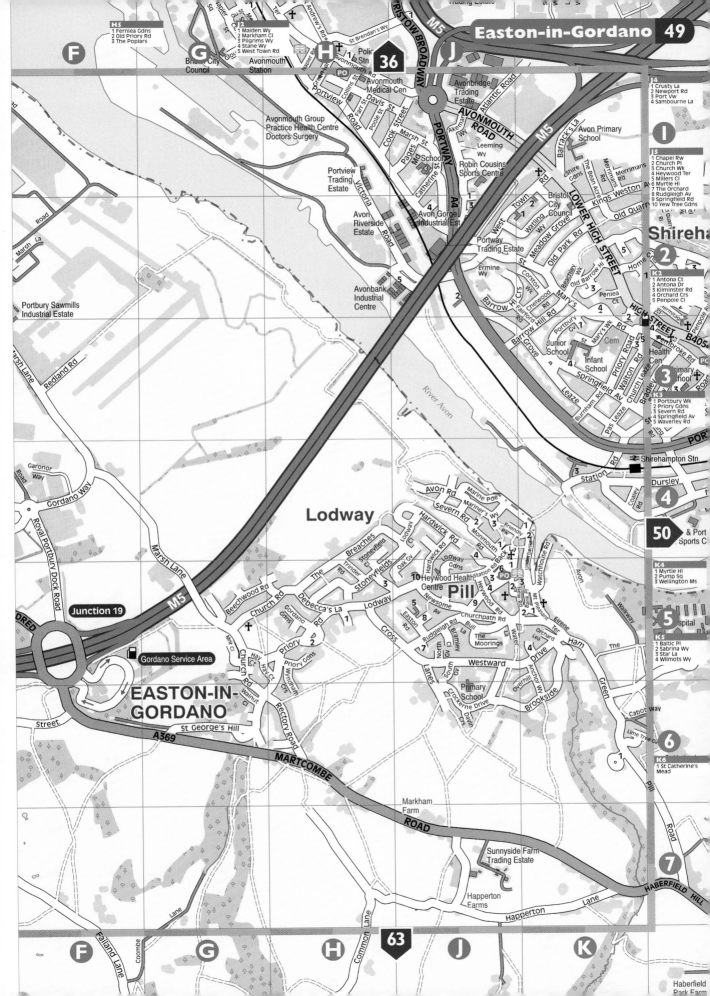

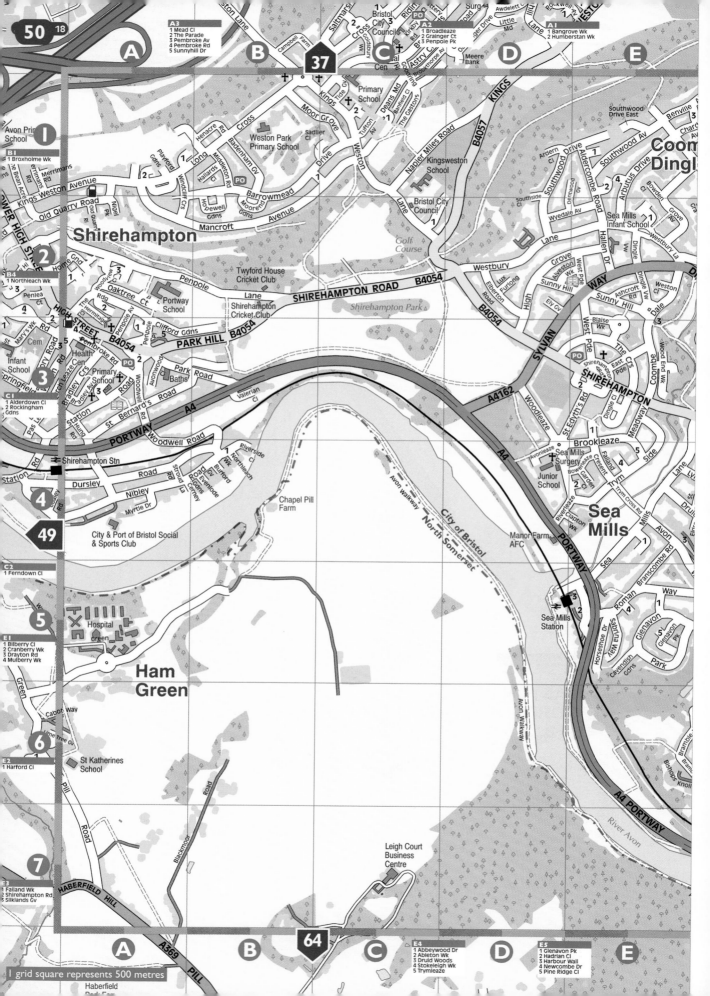

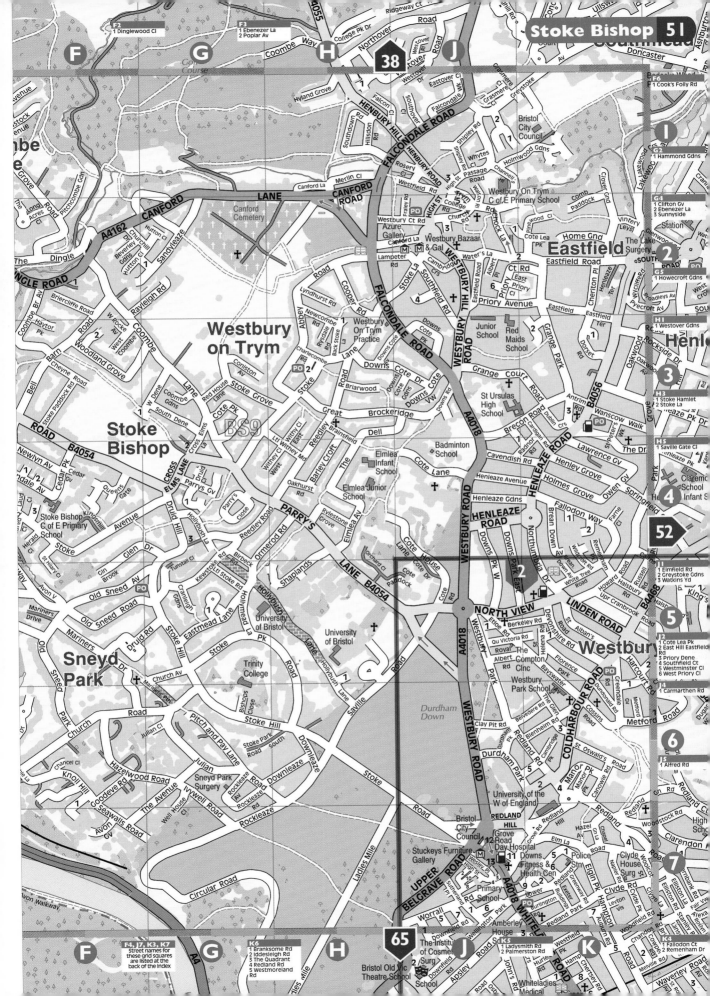

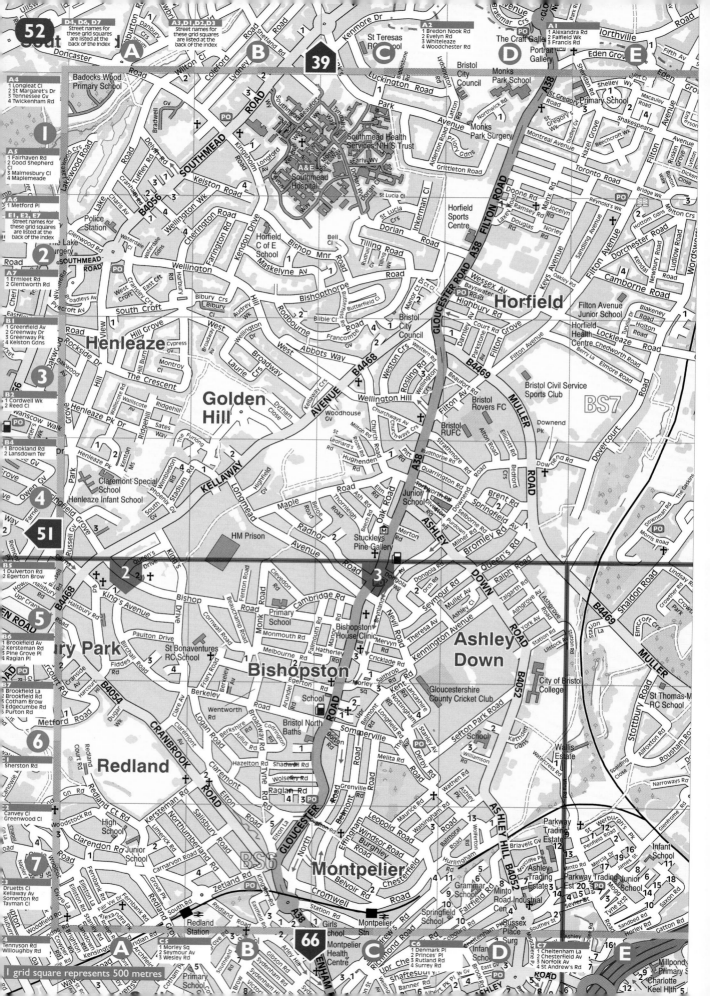

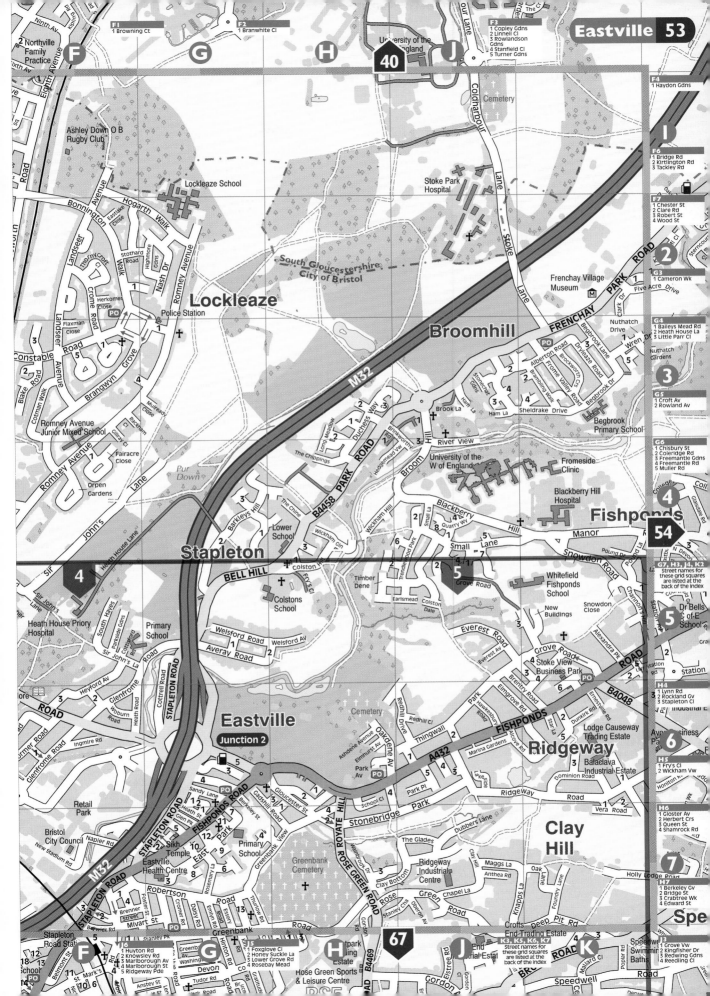

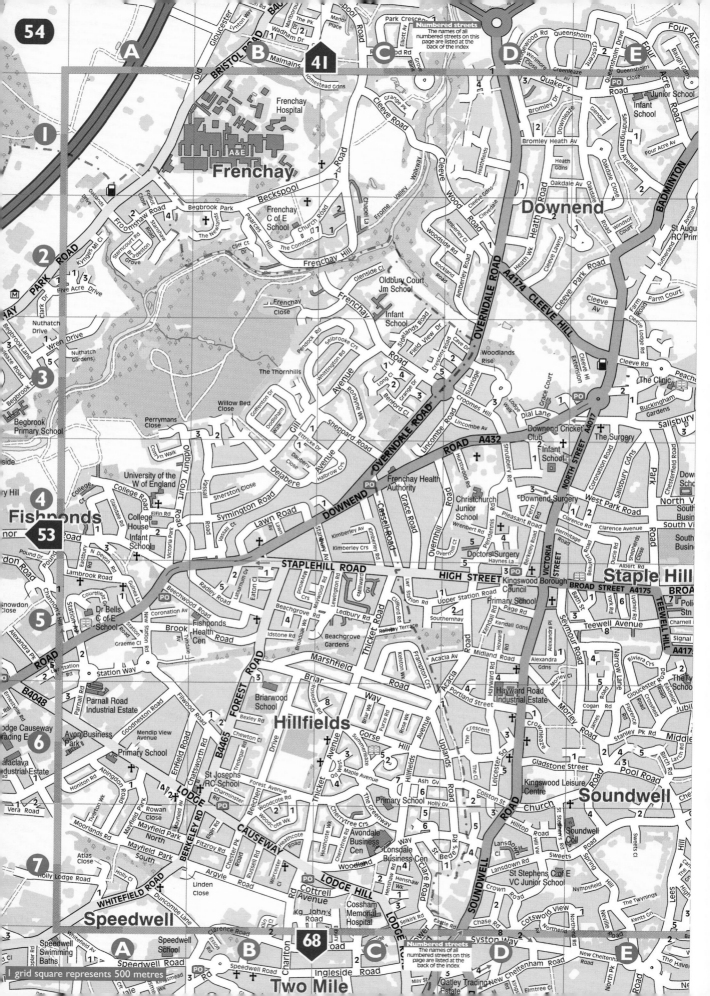

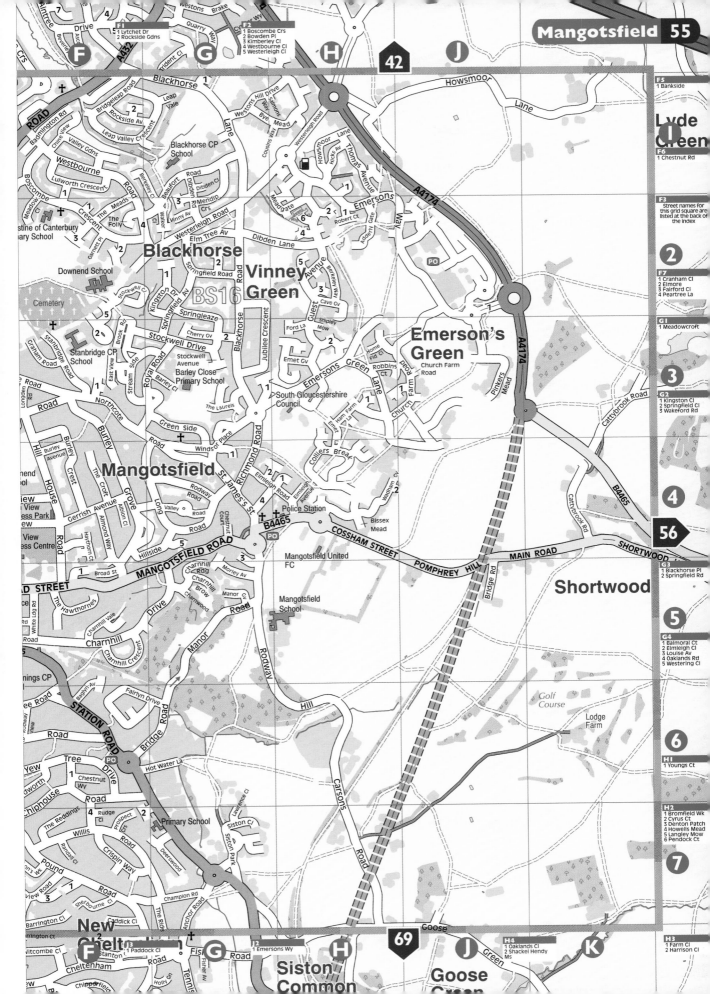

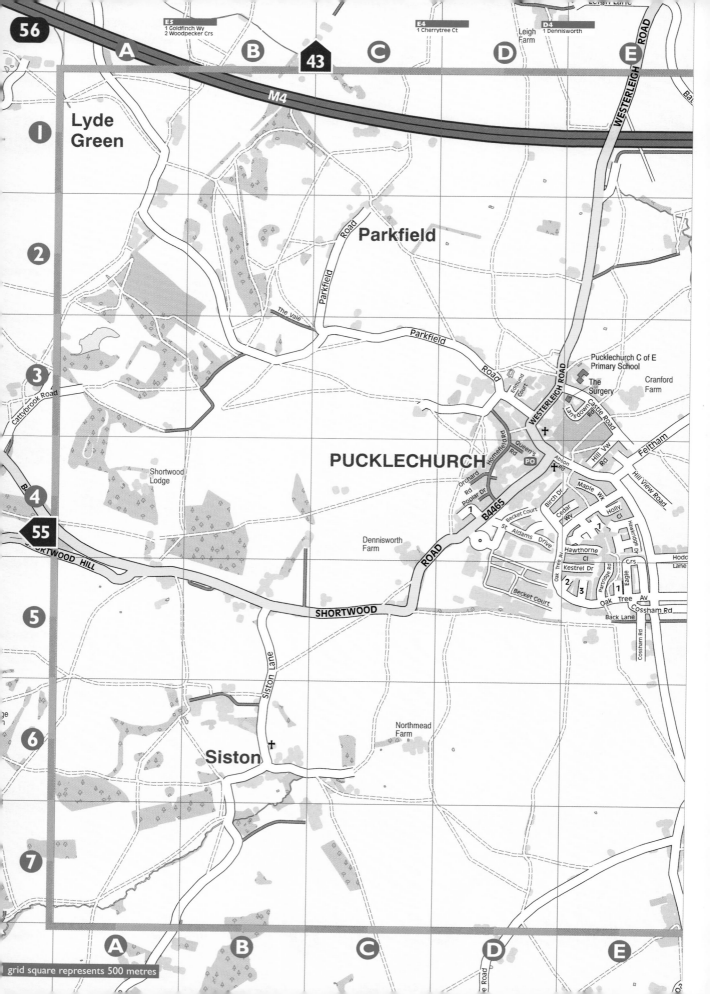

A **B** **43** **C** **D** **E**

E5
1 Goldfinch Wy
2 Woodpecker Crs

E4
1 Cherrytree Ct

D4
1 Dennisworth

Leigh Lane

Leigh
Farm

WESTERLEIGH ROAD

M4

1 Lyde
Green

2 Parkfield

Parkfield Road

The Vale

Parkfield

Parkfield Road

Pucklechurch C of E
Primary School

The Surgery

Cranford
Farm

3

Cattybrook Road

Edmund
Court

WESTERLEIGH ROAD

Castle Road

Lansdown

Hill Vw
Rd

Feltham

Hill View Road

Shortwood
Lodge

PUCKLECHURCH

Orchard
Rd

Homefield Rd

Queen's
Rd

PO

Abson Rd

Maple
Wk

Holly
Cl

4

55

SHORTWOOD HILL

7

B4465

Poplar Dr

Becket Court

Birch Dr

Cedar
Wy

7

Hawthorne
Cl

Hawbridge Dr

Partridge Rd

Dennisworth
Farm

St Aldams Drive

Oak Tree Av

Kestrel Dr

2

3

1

Eagle
Crs

Hodd
Lane

5

SHORTWOOD ROAD

SHORTWOOD

Becket Court

Oak Tree Av

Cossham Rd

Back Lane

Cossham Rd

6

Siston Lane

Northmead
Farm

Siston

7

grid square represents 500 metres

F   G   H   44   J   Barleyclose Farm

Monarch's Way

chfield   Lane

M4

I

St Aldam's
Ash Farm

2

Hint

Lower Fields
Farm

Ring 'O' Bells
Farm

3

Road

Marsh
Farm

Monarch's Way

4

Ta
Fa

Hoddon   Lane

ion

Redford   Lane

River Boyd

5

Doynton Lane

Rookery Lane

6

Rookery
Farm

Abson

7

Bottoms
Farm

Monarch's Way

F   G   H   J   Woodmead   Lane   K

Mill Lane   Road

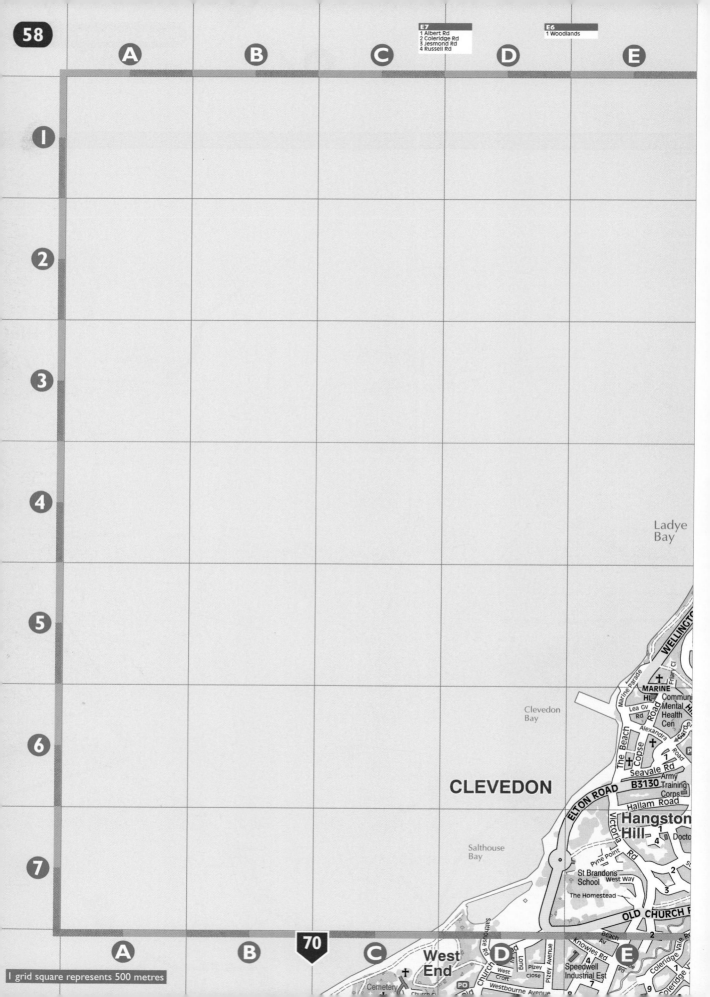

F

F7
1 Lower Queen's
2 Madeira Rd
3 St John's Av
4 Station Rd
5 Sunnyside Crs

G

G7
1 Meadow Rd
2 Somerset Rd

H

J

H7
1 Broadlands
2 Greenway Pk
3 Hollyman Wk
4 Maynard Cl
5 Streamside
6 Woodview

Pigeon
House
Bay

Farley

1

Walton
Down

Hack's
Wd

2

Margaret's
Bay

3

Walton-in-Gordano

Golf
Course

Walton

Ladye Bay

Ladye
Point

Bay Road

Linkside

Edgehill
Rd

CASTLE ROAD

Clynder
Gv

B3124 **HOLLY LANE**

Brackenwood Rd

Drove

4

No's Wood

60

B3124

Hotel

B3124

Channel

Argyle Rd

PO

The Av Road

Cambridge Gv

Orme Dr

Edward Road

Edward Road

Wayside Dr

Clevedon
School

**Walton
St Mary**

Conygar Cl

Nortons Wood Lane

5

Durbin Park Rd

Robin Lane

King's

Castle Vw Rd

Old

Road

Park

Woodside Road

Ripplefield Road

Woodland
Glade

Bennetts Way

B3124

The
Croft

Norton's
Wood

Castle Wood Cl

Birch Av

Strawberry Hill

WALTON ROAD

East
Clevedon VC
Primary School

The
Warren

Court Wood

Esmond Grove

Thackeray Av

Chestnut Gv

Ash Gv

All Saints La

Carey's Cl

Clevedon
Court (NT)

6

Linden Rd

Rydal
School

Thackeray
Rd

Old Park Road

Park Rd

St Nicholas
Chantry Primary School

TICKENHAM **ROAD**

Herbert Rd

Prince's Road

Highdale

Road

East Clevedon

7

rs Surgery

Sunnyside Rd

Police Stn

Chapel Hill

Lime Kiln Rd

Lwr Linden

Clevedon
Hospital

Highdale Av

B3130

Clevedon Health
Centre

Freshmoor

Kingston Av

Sumerlin Dr

Daniel
Way

Court Lane

Clevedon
Moor

John's Road

Marson
Rd

North
Somerset
Council

OLD STREET

PO

ROAD

Parnell

Seymour

Northern

Way

Clover Cl

Brookfield Wk

B3130
Clevedon
Fruit Mkt

KENN RD

Griffin Rd

Teignmouth Road

Beaconsfield

Willow
Cl

Saw

Cherry Av

Kelting Gv

F

WESTERN **MOOR LA** **B3133**

G

Hither

ETTLINGEN WY

H

71

J

K

Craft
Centre

Oldville Av

Avenue

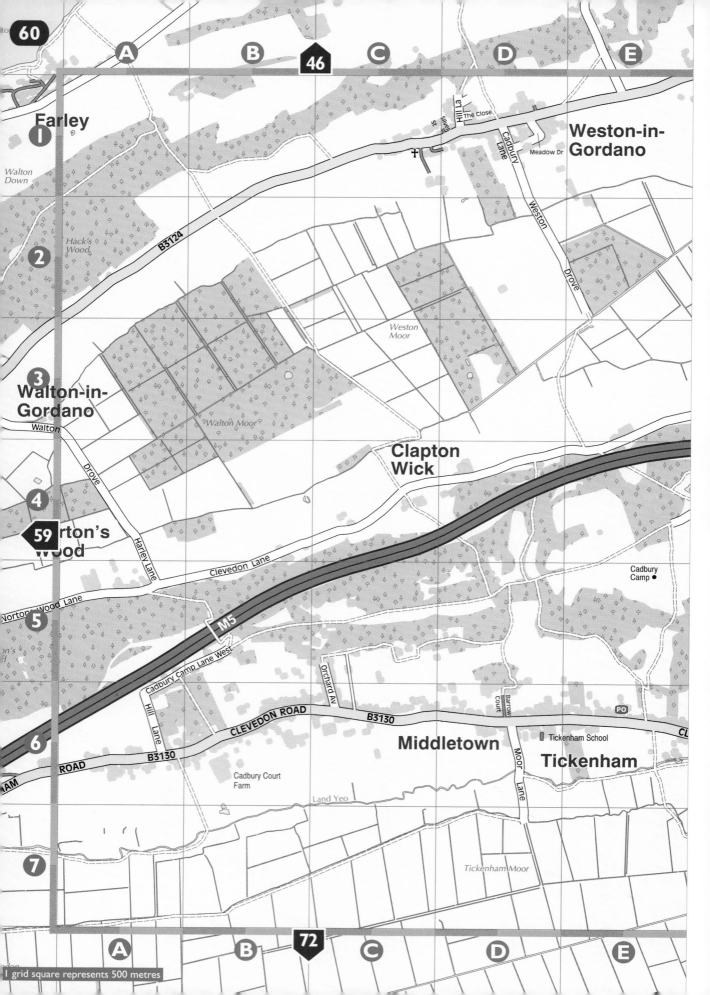

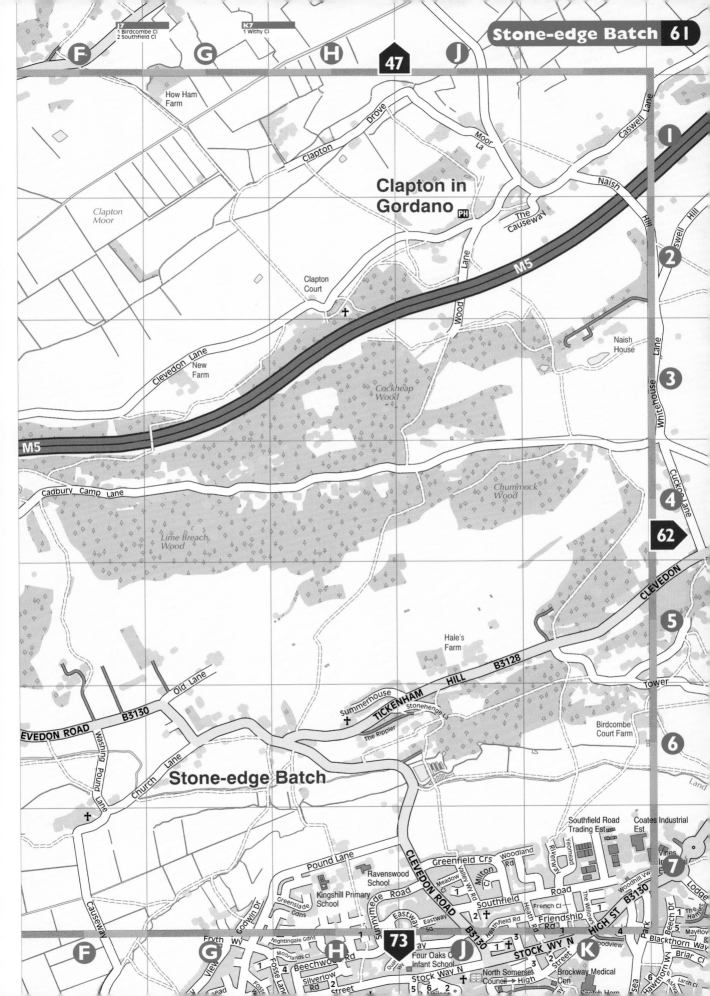

F G H J

47

I

2

3

4

62

5

6

7

K

73

Clapton in Gordano PH

How Ham Farm

Clapton Drove

Clapton

Clapton Moor

Moor La

The Causeway

Caswell Lane

Naish Hill

Caswell Hill

M5

Clapton Court

†

Wood Lane

Clevedon Lane

New Farm

Naish Lane

Naish House

Whitehouse Lane

Cuckoo Lane

M5

Cockheap Wood

Cadbury Camp Lane

Chummock Wood

Lime Breach Wood

CLEVEDON

Hale's Farm

TICKENHAM HILL B3128

Tower

Old Lane

B3130

Summerhouse

stonehenge La

†

The Rippler

Birdcombe Court Farm

EVEDON ROAD

Washing Pound Lane

Church Lane

Stone-edge Batch

†

Causeway

Godwin Dr

Fryth Wy

View

Pound Lane

Greenside Gdns

Ravenswood School

Kingshill Primary School

Nightingale Gdns

Moorlands Cl

Fosse Lane

Beechwood Rd

Silverlow Rd

Fosse

Sunnymede Road

Quar Wy

Eastway

Eastway Sq

Four Oaks Cl Infant School

Stock Way N

North Somerset Council - High

CLEVEDON ROAD

Greenfield Crs

Meadow Cl

Valley Vw Rd

Milton Cl

Woodland Rd

Southfield

Heathfield Rd

B3130

Friendship

STOCK WY N

†

Southfield Road Trading Est

Rivermead

Yeomead

Road

French Cl

Brockway Medical Cen

Scotch Horn

Coates Industrial Est

The Willows

HIGH ST B3130

Woodhill Vw

Woodview

Vines Ind E

Park

Beech Dr

Blackthorn Way

Lodge

Larch Cl

Ash Wk

Mayflower

Briar Cl

sea

Hawthorn Cl

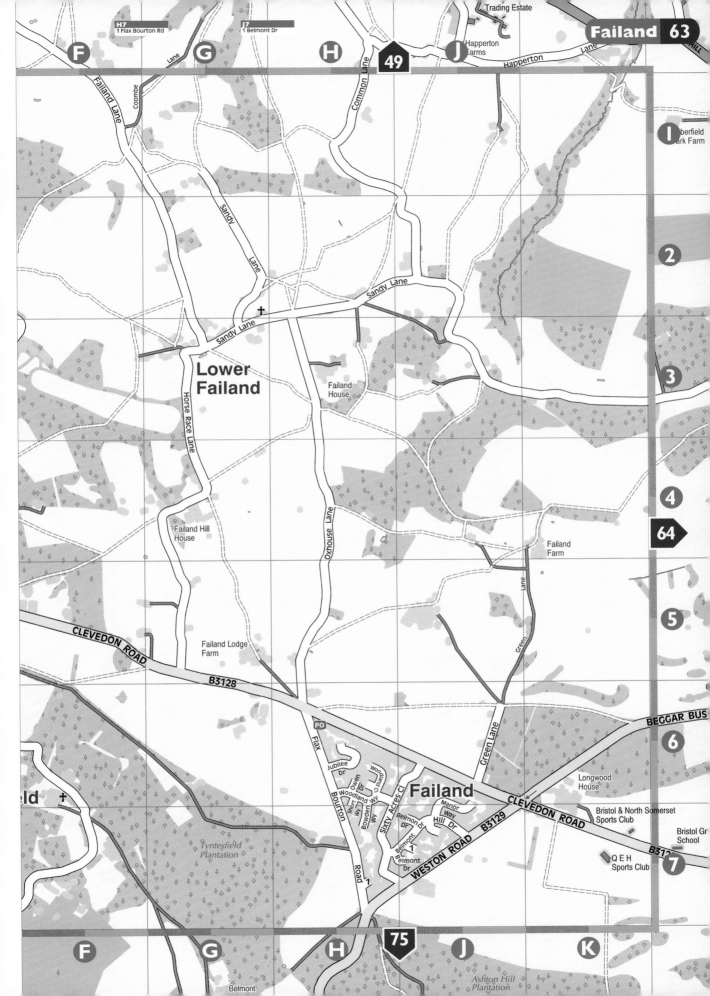

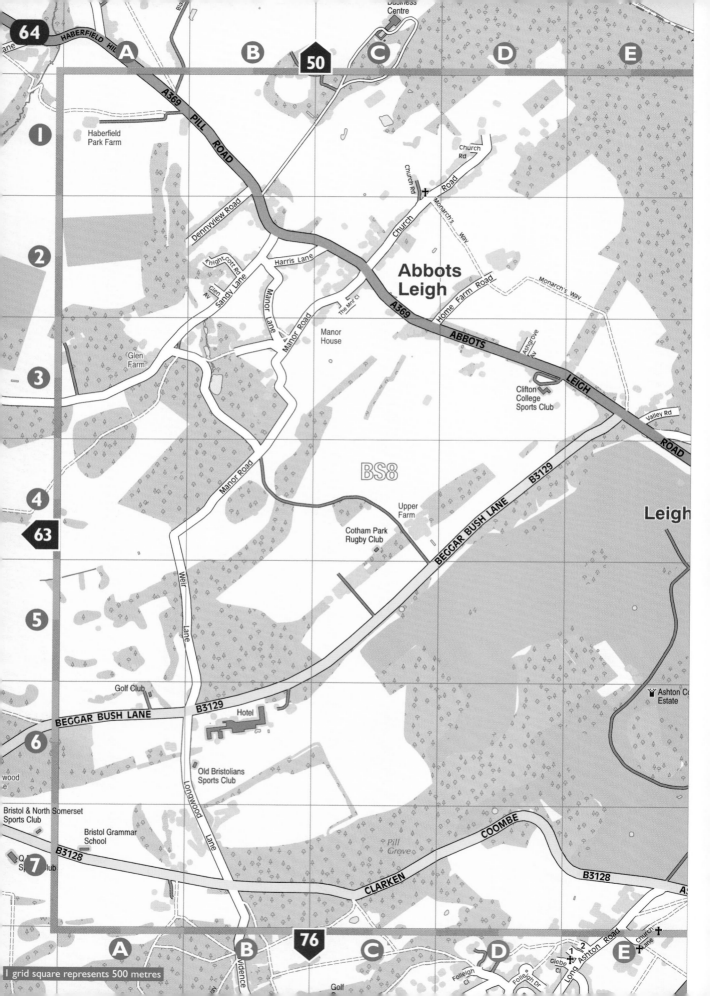

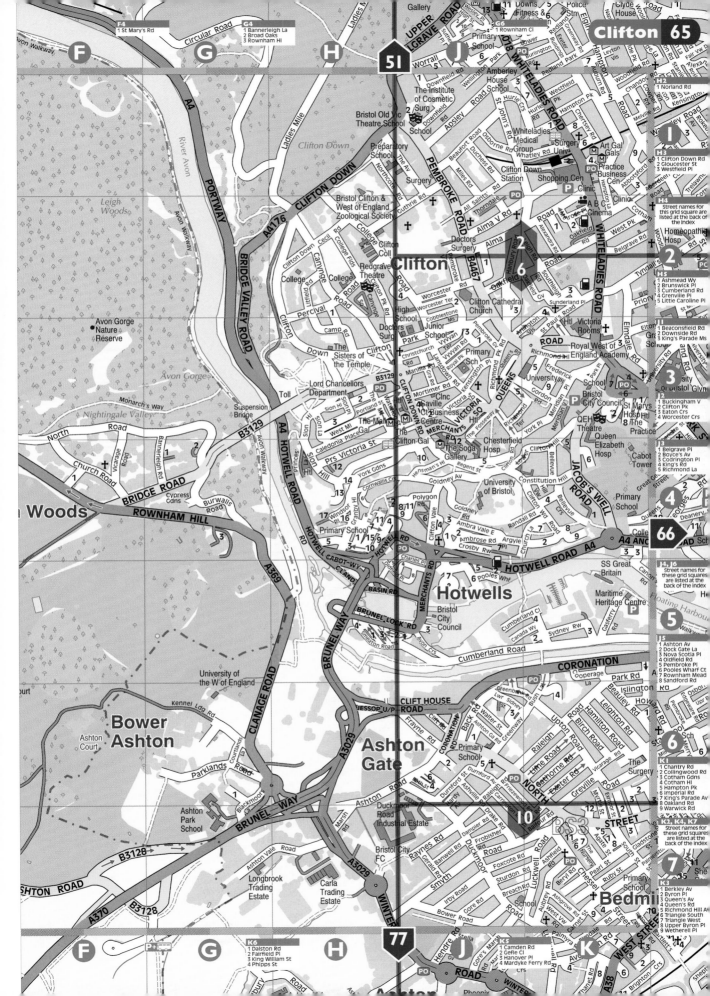

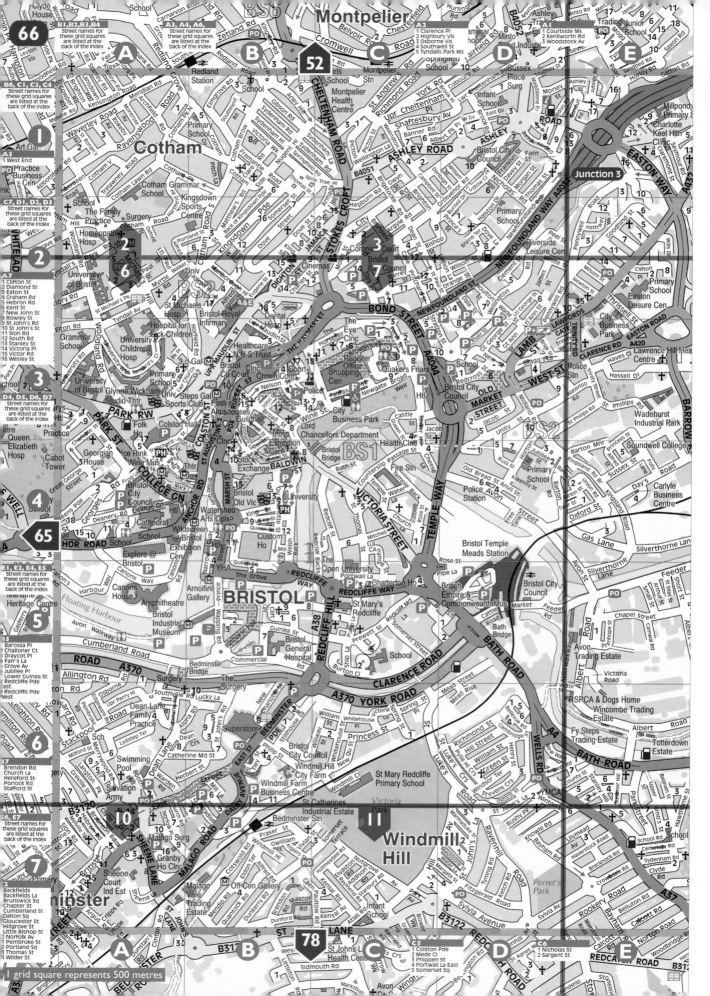

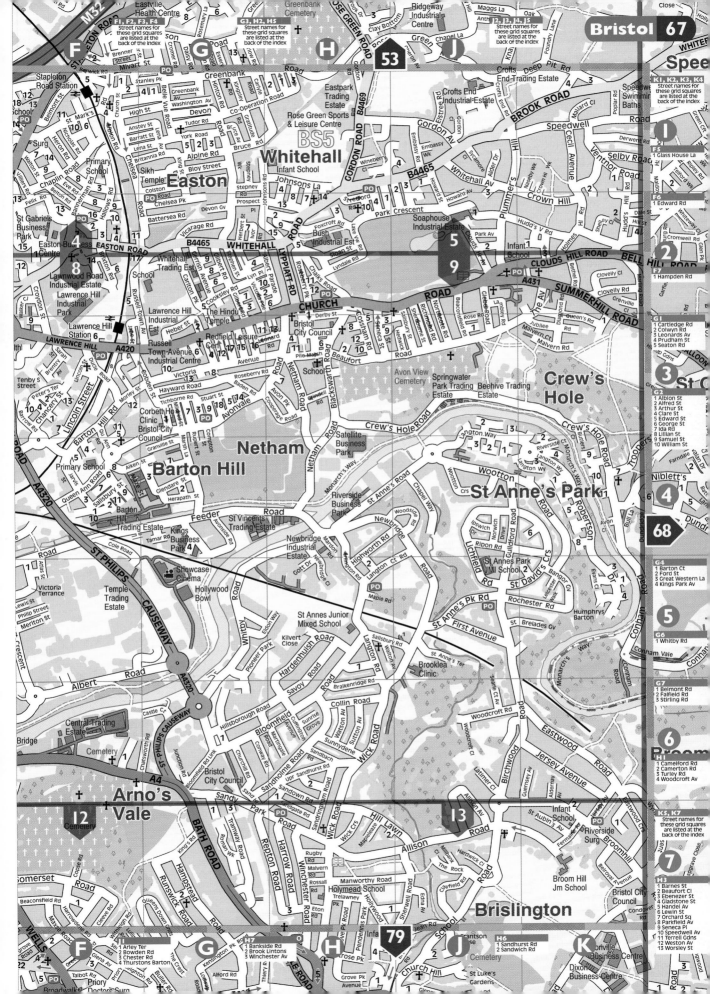

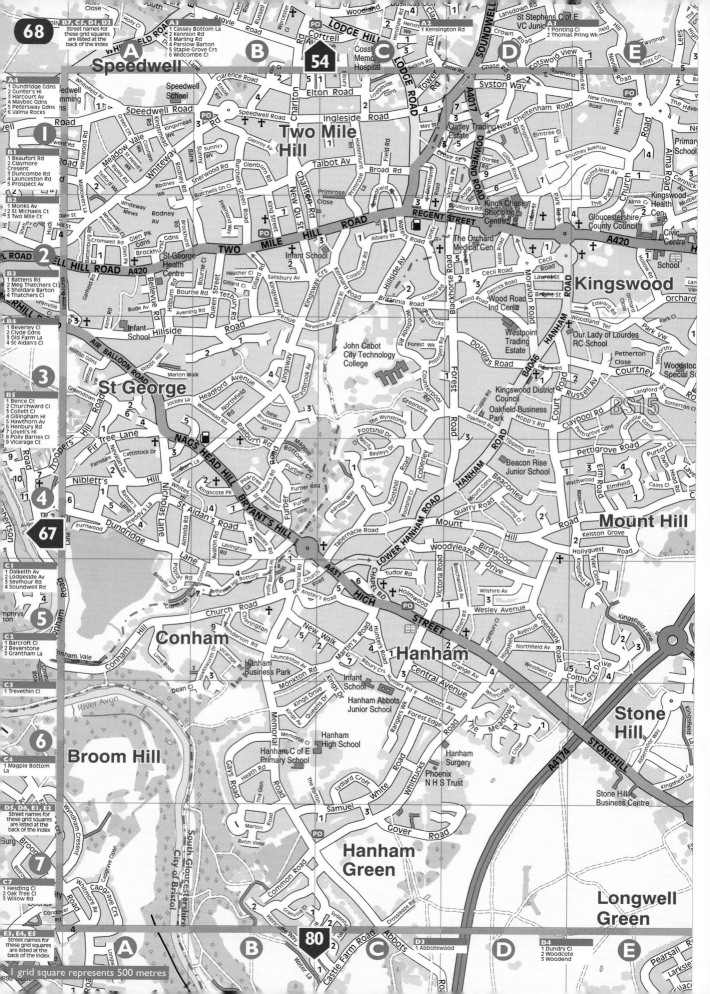

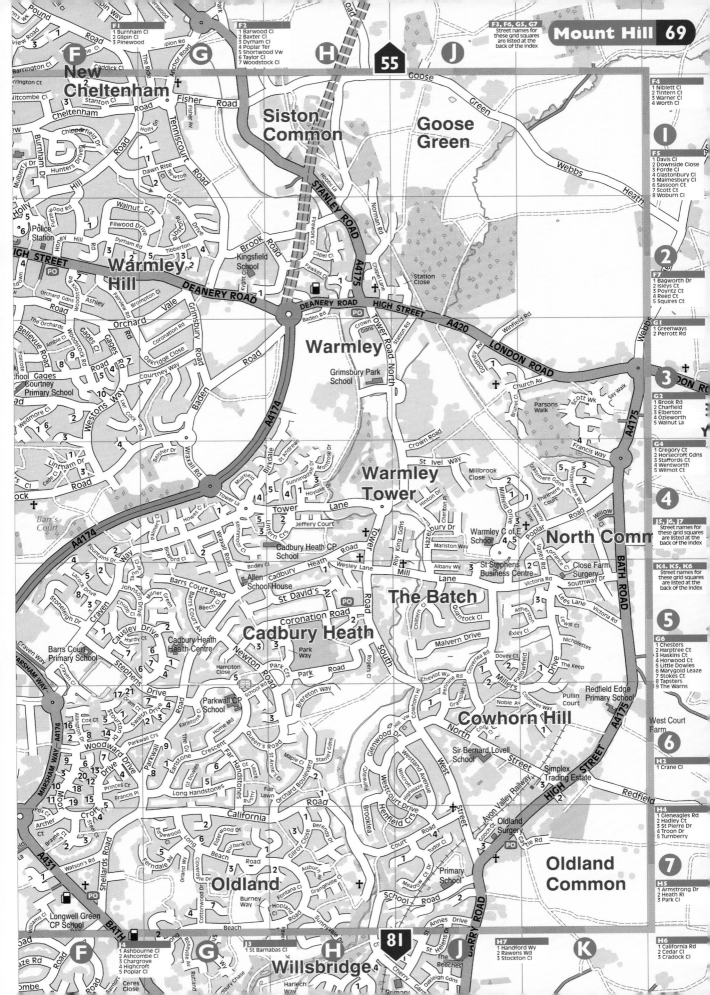

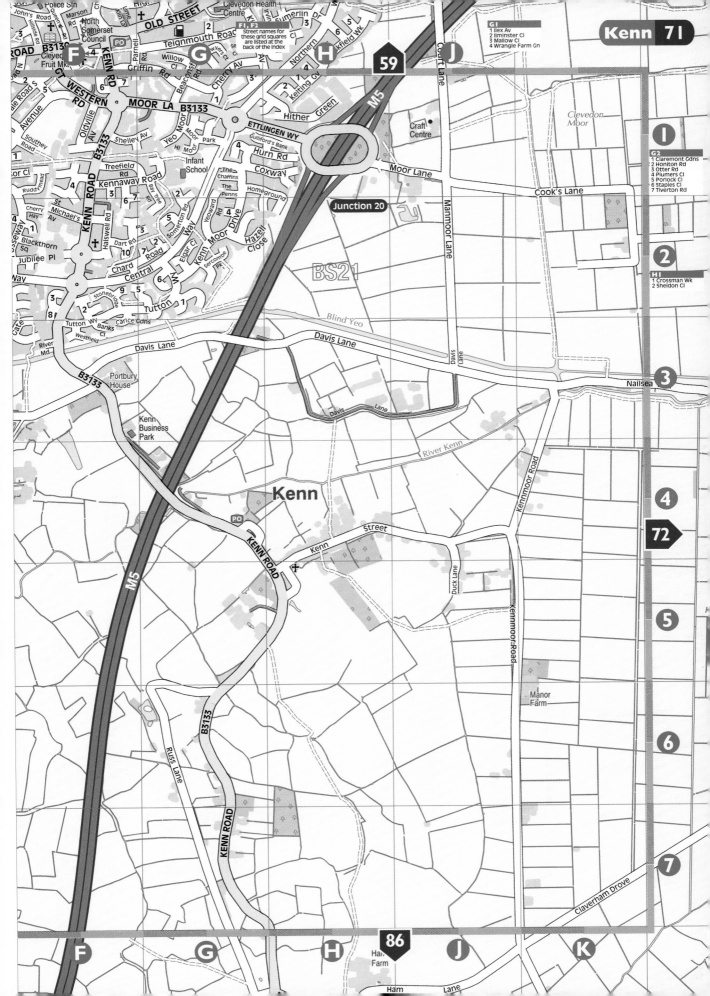

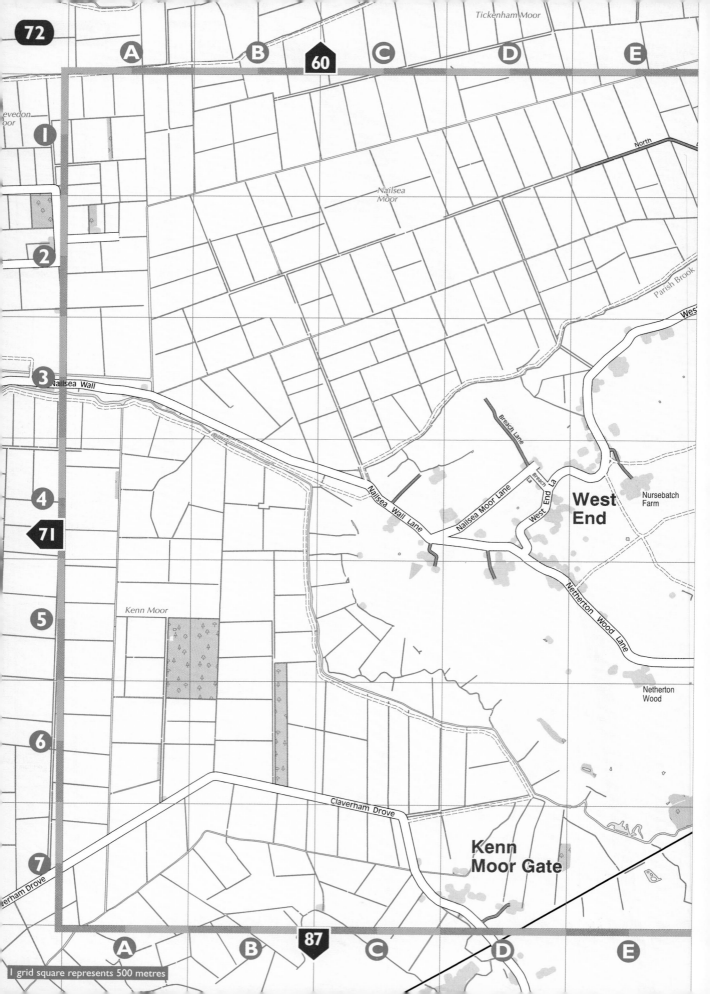

72

A   B   **60**   C   D   E

I

Tickenham Moor

evedon oor

Nailsea Moor

North

2

Parish Brook

3 Nailsea Wall

West

Breach Lane

Nailsea Wall Lane

4

Nailsea Moor Lane

Breach La

West End La

West End

Nursebatch Farm

71

Netherton Wood Lane

5 Kenn Moor

6

Netherton Wood

Claverham Drove

7

erham Drove

Kenn Moor Gate

A   B   **87**   C   D   E

I grid square represents 500 metres

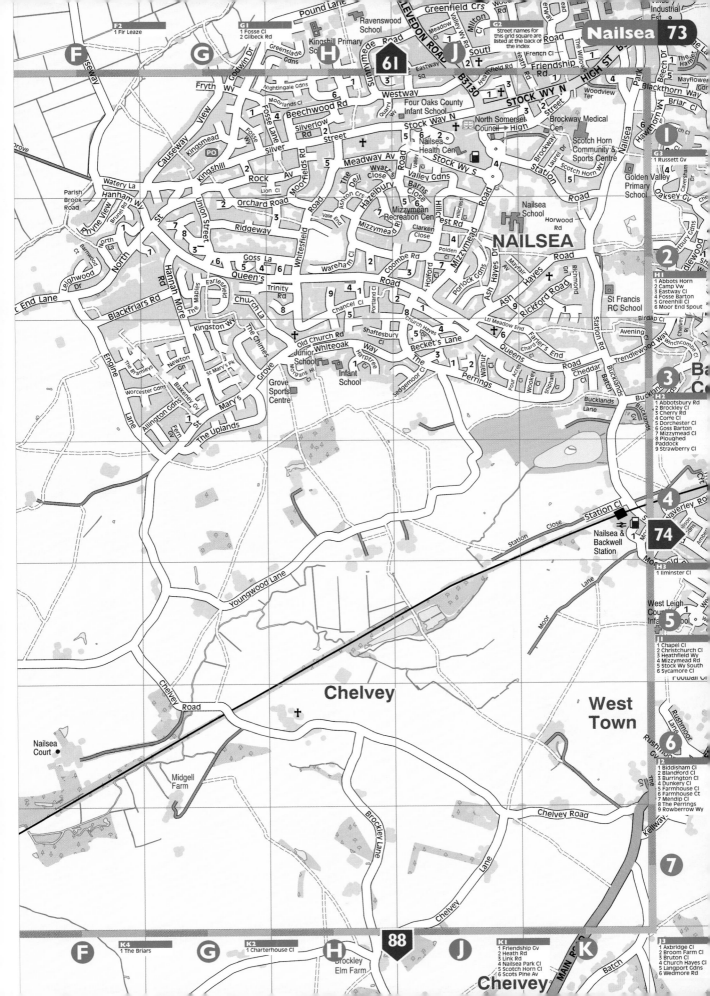

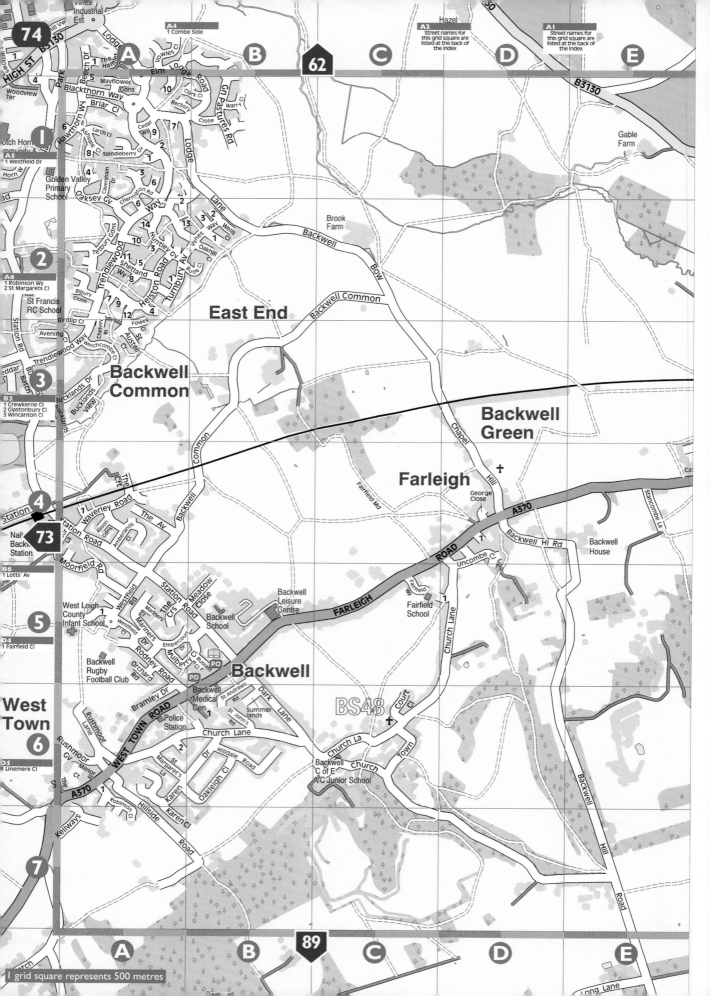

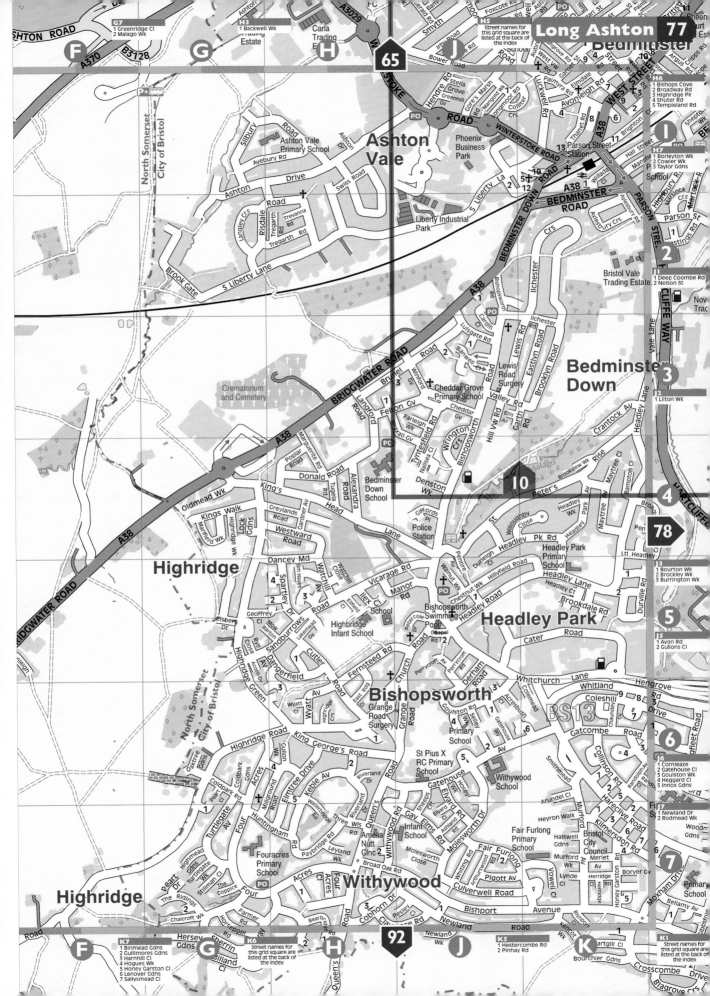

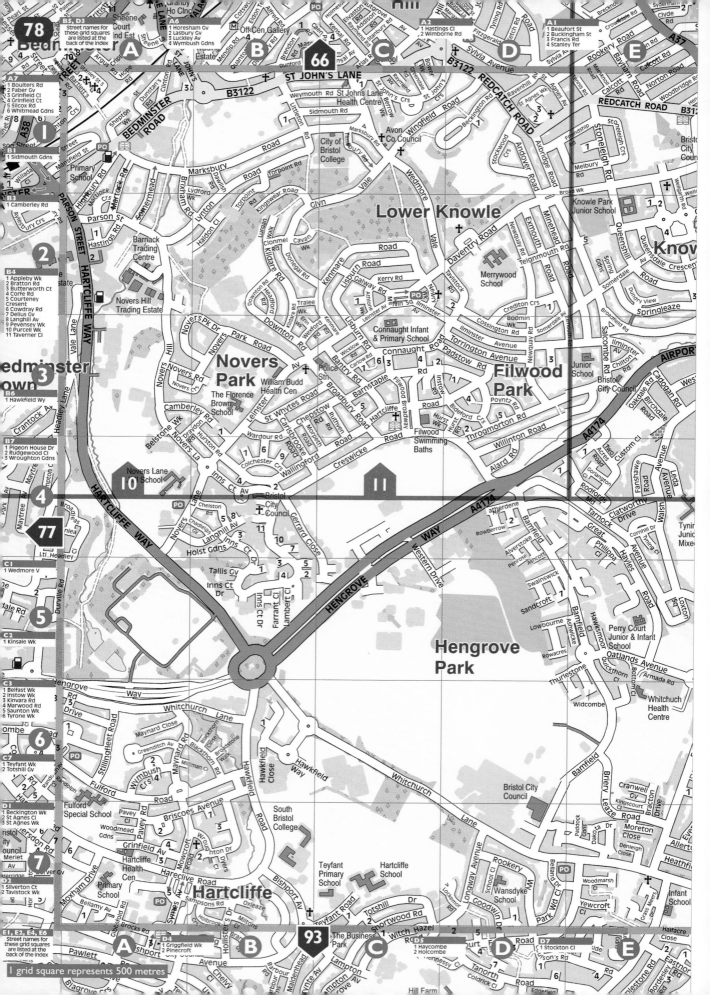

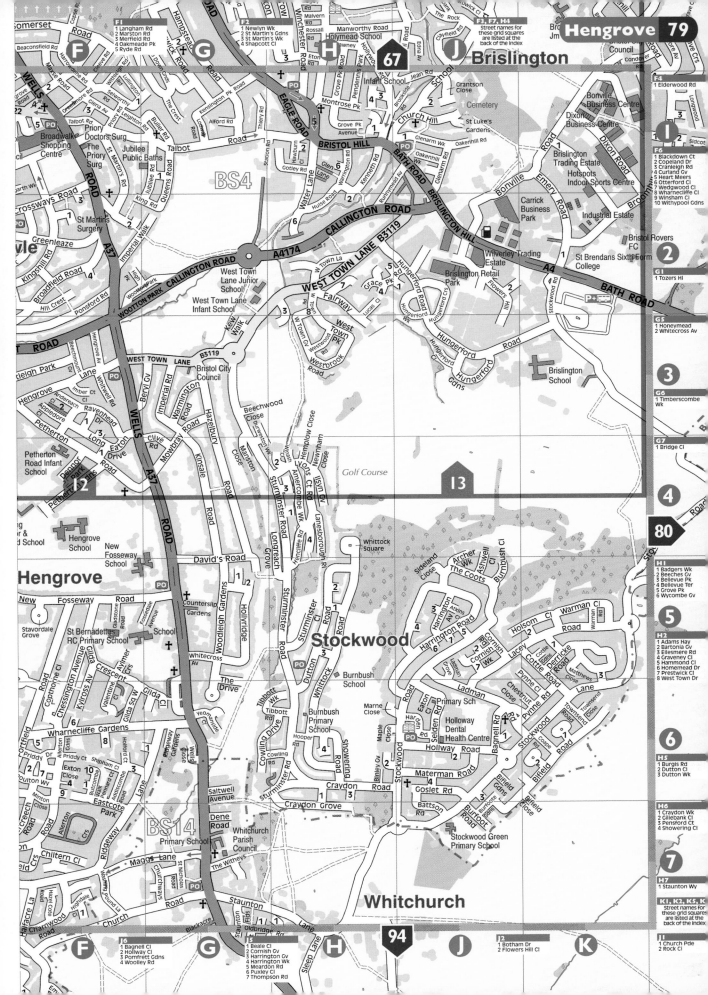

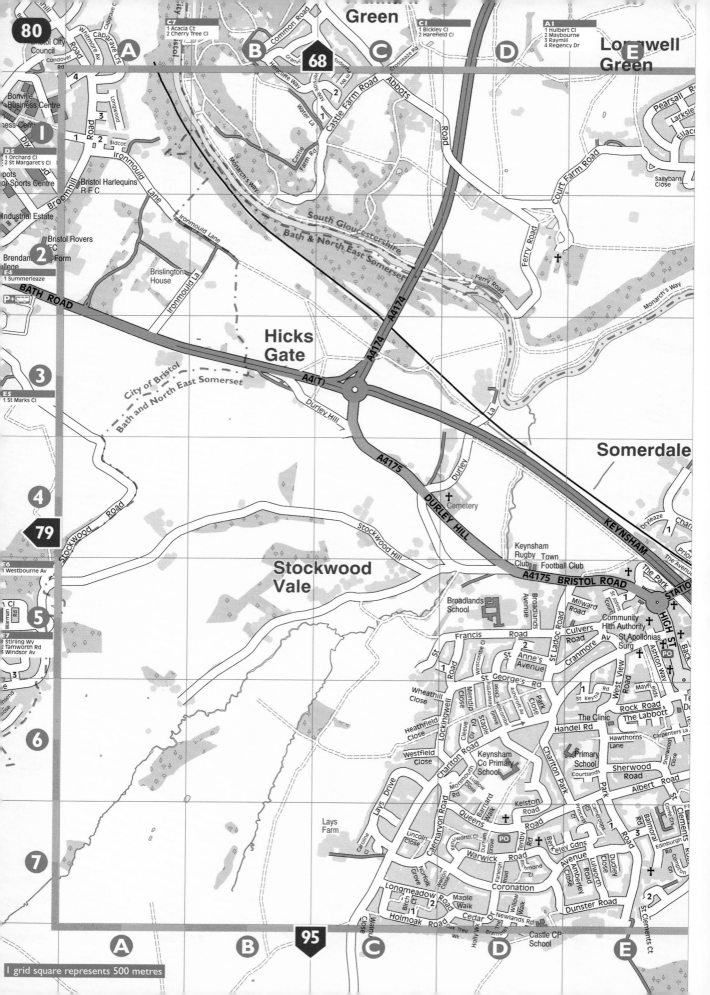

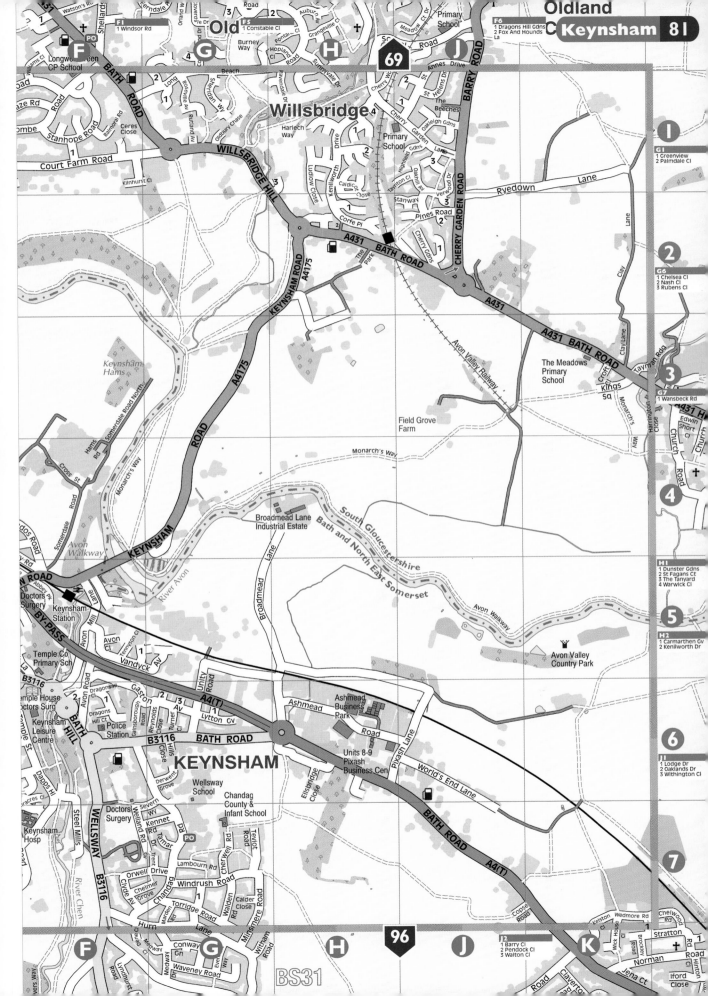

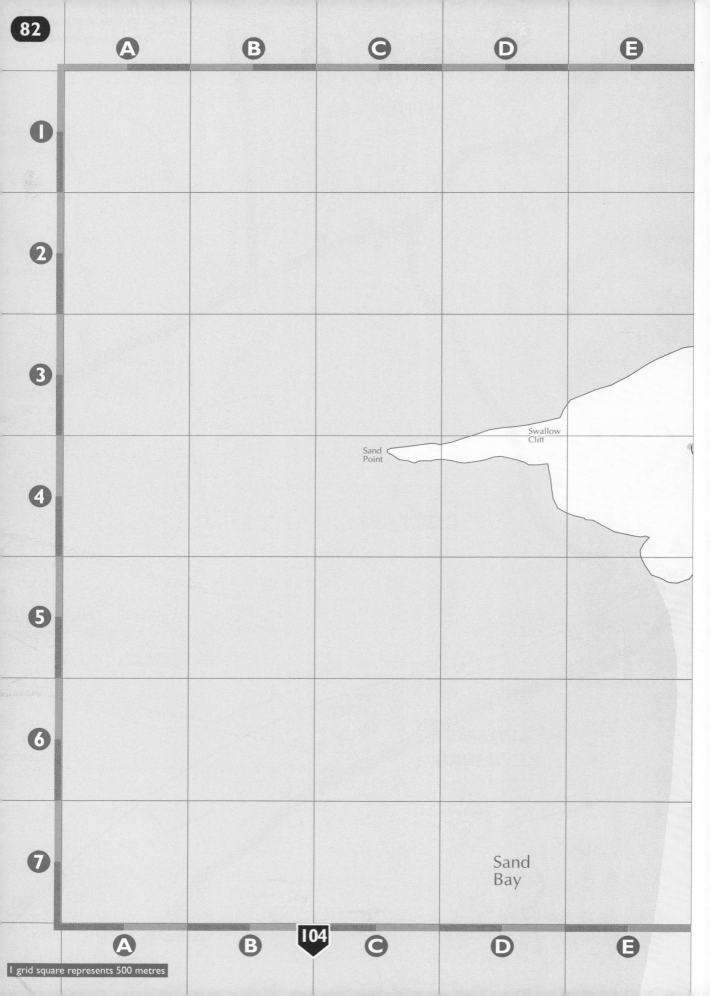

A   B   C   D   E

1

2

3

Sand
Point

Swallow
Cliff

4

5

6

7

Sand
Bay

A   B   C   D   E

1 grid square represents 500 metres

A   **B**   **C**   **D**   **E**

Woodspring
Bay

Wharf
Farm

Wick
Warth

83

River Banwell

Warth Lane

Muddy Lane

Warth Lane

Lower Wick
Farm

Icelton

✝

**Wick
St Lawrence**

Ebdon

Clover Road

Bluebell Road

Poppy Cl

Aconite Close

Lilac Way

Wheatfield Drive

Warllow Close

Warllow Close

Ebdon Road

The Cornfields

Azalea Road

Rawlins Avenue

Townshend Rd

Locksbrook Road

Priston Cl

Hobbiton Road

Castlemead Shopping Cen
Primary
School
PO

106

Manor
Farm

Cemetery

Juniper
Place

Rivendell
Way

Arnor Close

Westmr

Jocelin Dr

Barklands

Cornwallis Avenue

Dame Ct

Finmere Gdns

Roebuck

Wansbrough Road

Kelston Road

Walford

Richards
Close

Taunton

Grace Rd

Hambledon

Lane

A   **B**   **C**   **D**   **E**

BS22

I grid square represents 500 metres

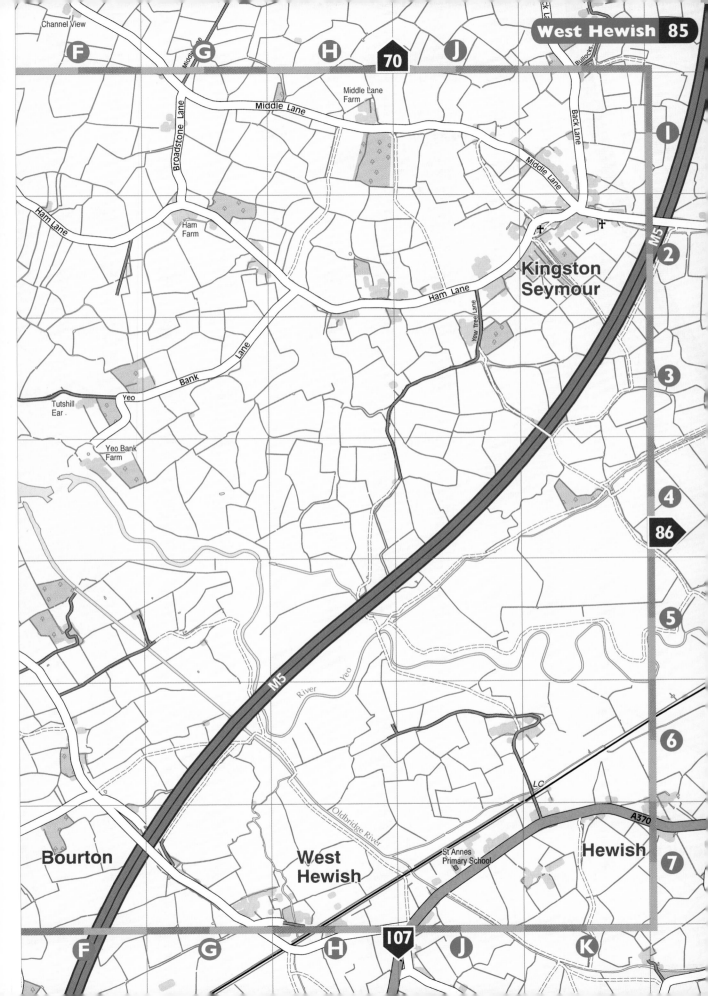

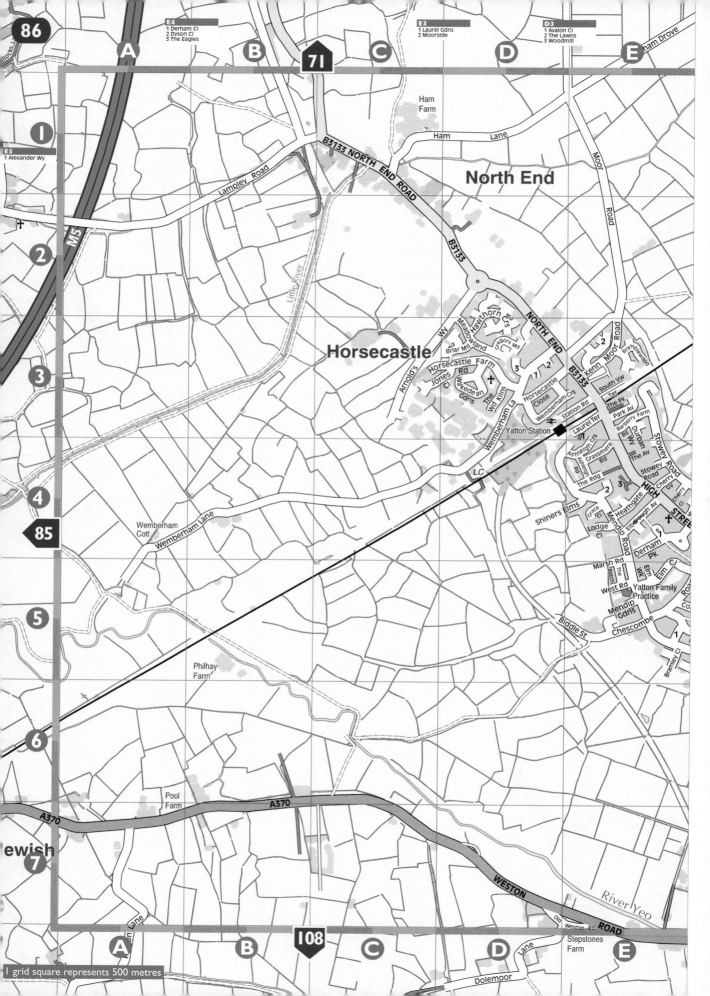

A   B   71   C   D   E

1

Ham Lane

Ham Farm

North End

B3133 NORTH END ROAD

Lampley Road

M5

2

Little River

3

Horsecastle

Moor Road

NORTH END

B3133

Hawthorn Crs
Meadowland Wy
Gregory Md
Briar Md
Arnold's Wy
Horsecastle Farm Rd
Jones Cl
Wakedean Gdns
The Wd Kilns
Horsecastle Close
Wemberham Crs
Wemberham La

Kenn
South Vw
the Pk
Park Av
Barperry Farm
Durban Wy
The Av
Stowey Road
Bramblewood

Station Rd
Station Ter
Laurel Ter
Ashleigh Crs
Ashleigh
Grassmere Rd
The Rdg
Cherry
Cherry
Stowey Road
Heathgate

Yatton Station

LC

4

85

Wemberham Cott

Wemberham Lane

Shiners Elms

Grace
Lodge Cl
Mendip Road
Derham Pk
Eldenburgh Av
HIGH STREET

Marsh Rd
The Batch
West Rd
Elm Wk
Elm Cl
Elm
Yatton Family Practice
Mendip Gdns
Chescombe
Biddle St

5

Philhay Farm

6

A370

Pool Farm

A370

ewish
7

WESTON ROAD

River Yeo

Old Weston Rd

Stepstones Farm

A   B   108   C   D   Lane   Dolemoor   E

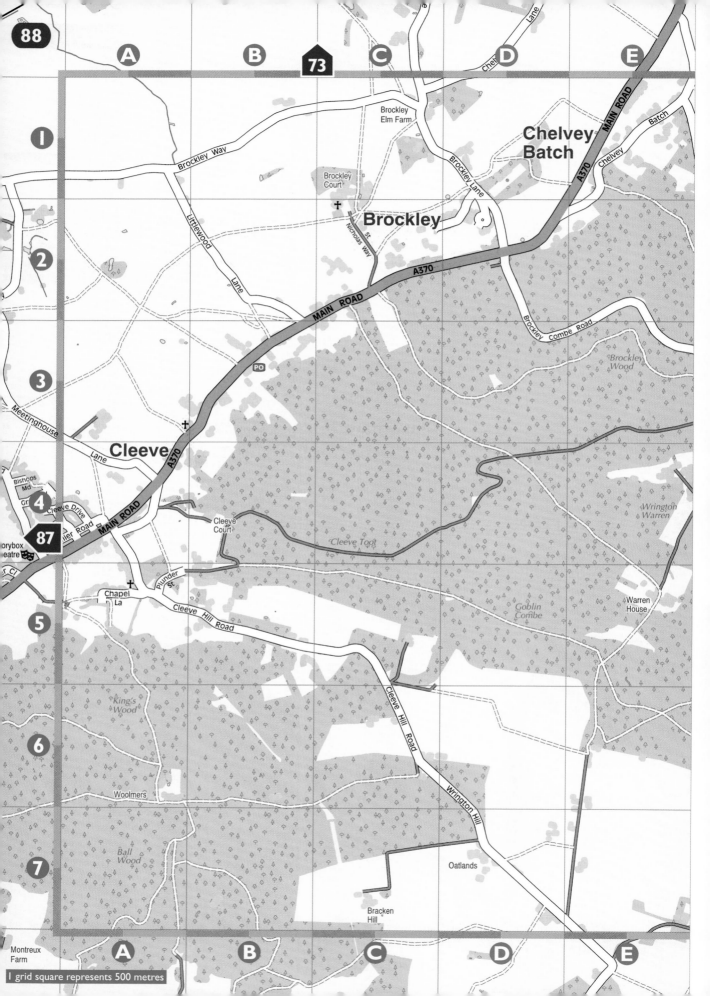

A B **73** C D E

I

Chelvey Batch

Brockley Elm Farm

Brockley Way

2 Brockley Court

Littlewood Lane

✝

Brockley

Brockley Lane

Nicholas Way

St

A370

3 Meetinghouse

MAIN ROAD

A370

PO

Brockley Combe Road

Brockley Wood

Lane

Cleeve

✝

Bishops Md

Gr

4 Cleeve Drive

lier Road

87

orybox Theatre

A370

MAIN ROAD

Cleeve Court

Plunder St

Cleeve Toot

Wrington Warren

Warren House

Chapel La

✝

Cleeve Hill Road

Goblin Combe

5

King's Wood

Cleeve Hill Road

6 Woolmers

Wrington Hill

Ball Wood

7 Oatlands

Montreux Farm

Bracken Hill

A B C D E

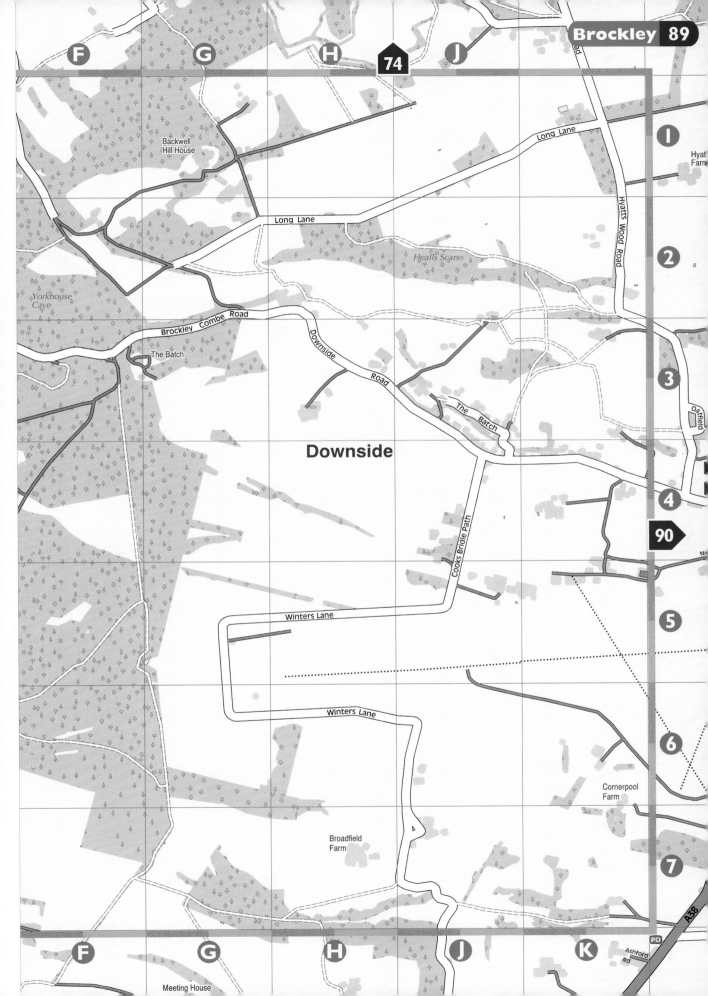

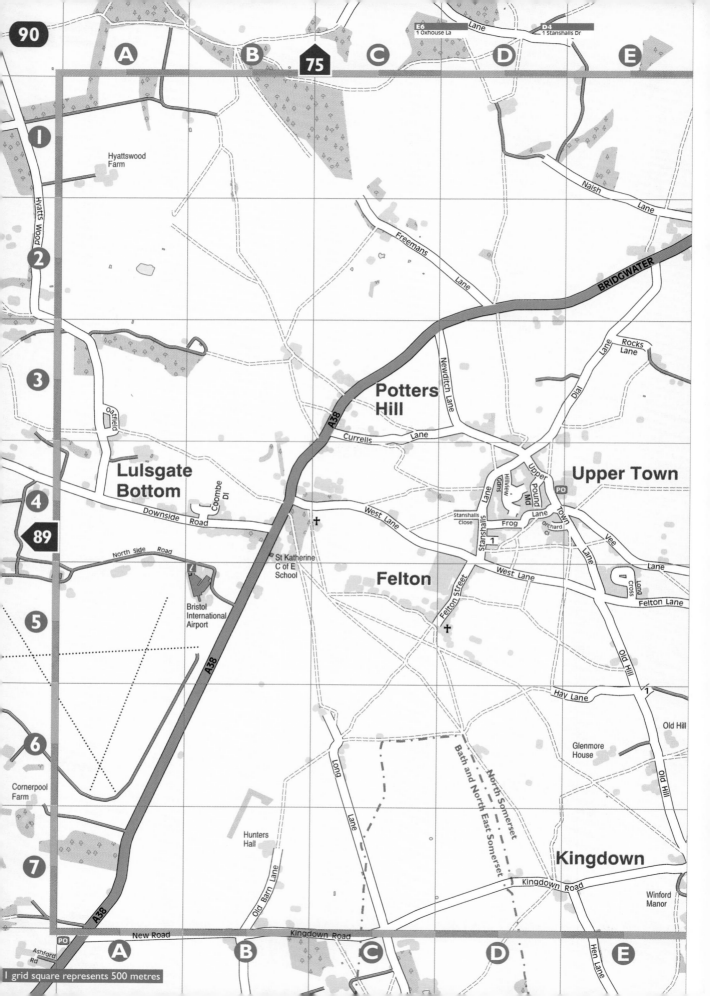

A B 75 C D E

E6
1 Oxhouse La

D4
1 Stanshalls Dr

Lane

1

Hyattswood
Farm

Hyatts Wood

2

Freemans
Lane

BRIDGWATER

Naish
Lane

Rocks
Lane

3

Potters
Hill

Newditch Lane

Lane

Oatfield

A38

Currells   Lane

Lulsgate
Bottom

Upper Town

Coombe
Dl

4

Downside   Road

West Lane

Stanshalls
Close

Hillview
Gdns

Upper
Pound
Rd

PO

Town

Frog

Orchard
Cl

Lane

Upper Town

Stanshalls Lane

1

Vee
Lane

89

St Katherine
C of E
School

North Side   Road

West Lane

Felton Lane

Long
Cross

Felton

Felton Street

5

Bristol
International
Airport

Hay Lane

1

Old Hill

6

A38

Long

Lane

Bath and North East Somerset

North Somerset

Glenmore
House

Old Hill

Cornerpool
Farm

Hunters
Hall

Kingdown

7

Kingdown   Road

Winford
Manor

A38

PO

Old Barn Lane

Kingdown Road

Hen Lane

Ashford
Rd

New Road

A B C D E

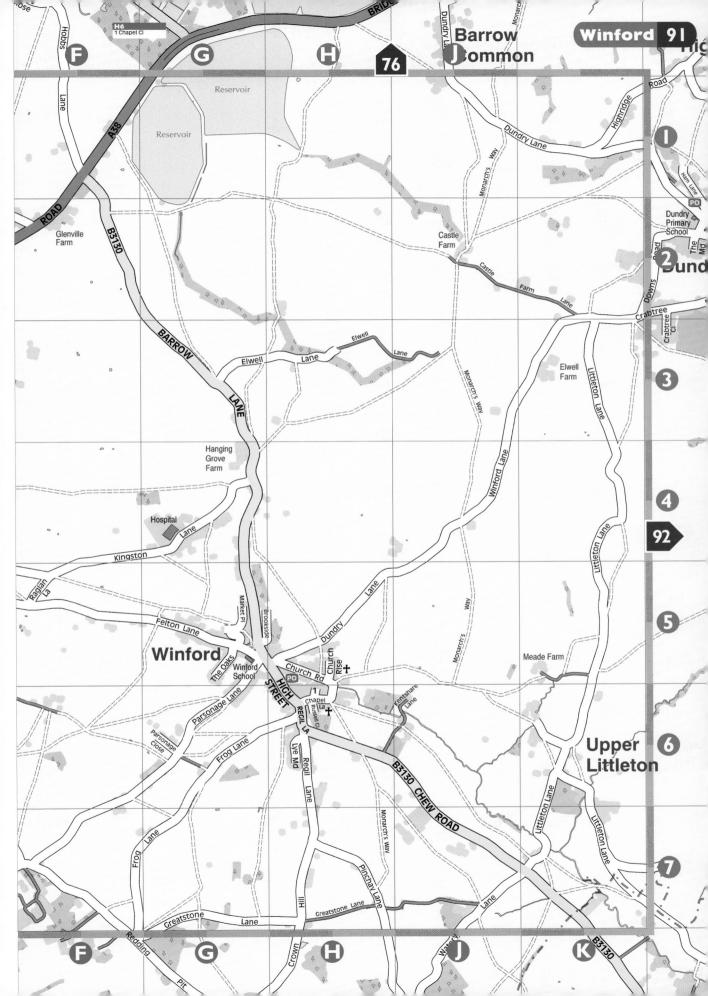

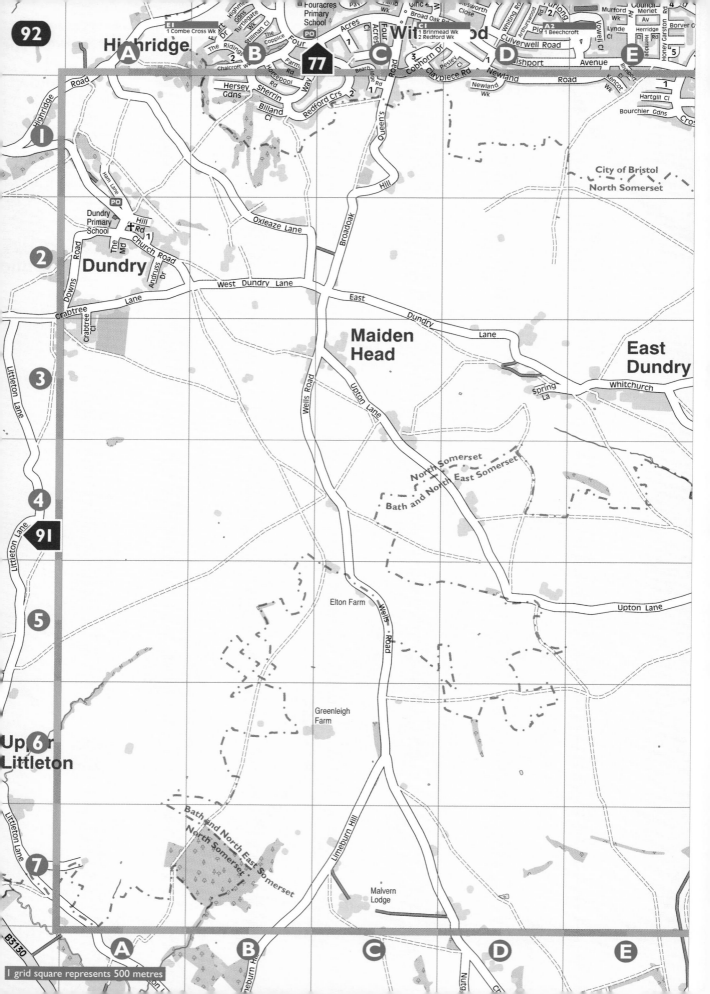

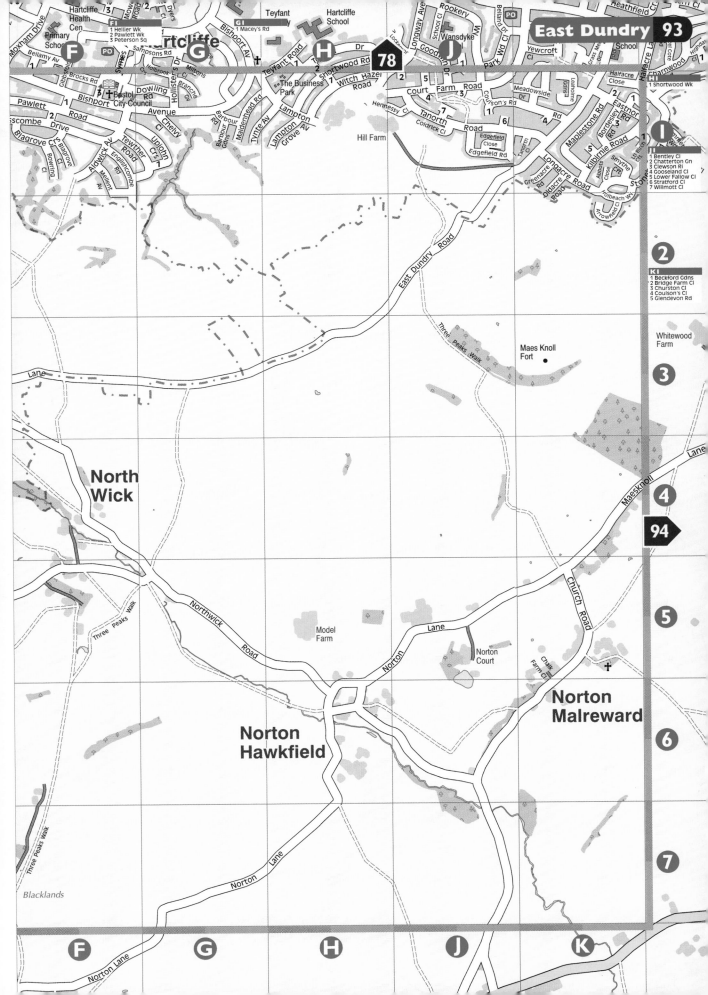

Hartcliffe
Health
Cen
Primary
School

Mow
Road
Dyer's
Cl
Hartcliffe
3
F1
1 Hellier Wk
2 Pawlett Wk
3 Peterson Sq

Teyfant
G1
1 Macey's Rd

Hartcliffe
School

F
PO
Bellamy Av
Moxham Drive

G
Bishport Av
Sampsons Rd
Syphers
Milton's
Hollister's Dr

Teyfant Road

H
Dr
Shortwood Rd
Witch Hazel
Road

78

Longway Ave
Rookery
Wk
School Cl
Goodwin Dr
Wansdyke

J

Yewcroft
Cl
Belland Dr
PO
Park

Heathfield
Heathfield
Cr

Halfacre
Close
Charnwood
Rd
Charnwood
Lane
Highdale

H1
1 Shortwood Wk

Pawlett
Road
Brocks Rd
Clibbsford Cl
Bishport
Bristol
City Council
Dowling
Rd
Holbrook
Branche
Gv

The Business
Park

Court
Farm
Road

Hennessy
Cl
Tanorth
Road

Meadowside
Dr
Edgefield
Close
Edgefield Rd

Maplestone Rd
Kilbirnie Road
Bordesley Rd
Eastnor
Rd
Smythe

I

I1
1 Bentley Cl
2 Chatterton Gn
3 Clewson Rl
4 Gooseland Cl
5 Lower Fallow Cl
6 Stratford Cl
7 Willmott Cl

Blagrove Crs
Bowring
Cl
Blagrove
Cl
Aldwick Av
Tewther
Road
Upjohn
Cr
Englishcombe
Av
Mellent
Av

Barbour Gdns
Maidenhead Rd
Tynte Av
Lampton Av
Lampton
Grove

Hill Farm

Coldrick Cl
Coulson's Rd
Tanorth
Court
Tangrth
Cl

Longacre Road
Greenacre
Rd
Oldacre
Road
Abbots
Close
Holbeach Wk
Arrowfield

Stone La

Leanome
Gdns

2

K1
1 Beckford Gdns
2 Bridge Farm Cl
3 Churston Cl
4 Coulson's Cl
5 Glendevon Rd

East Dundry Road

Three Peaks Walk

Maes Knoll
Fort

Whitewood
Farm

3

Lane

**North
Wick**

Maesknoll
Lane

4

94

Northwick
Road

Model
Farm

Norton
Lane

Lane

Norton
Court

Church Road

Chalk
Farm Cl

Norton
Malreward

5

6

**Norton
Hawkfield**

Three Peaks Walk

Norton
Lane

Blacklands

Norton Lane

7

F

G

H

J

K

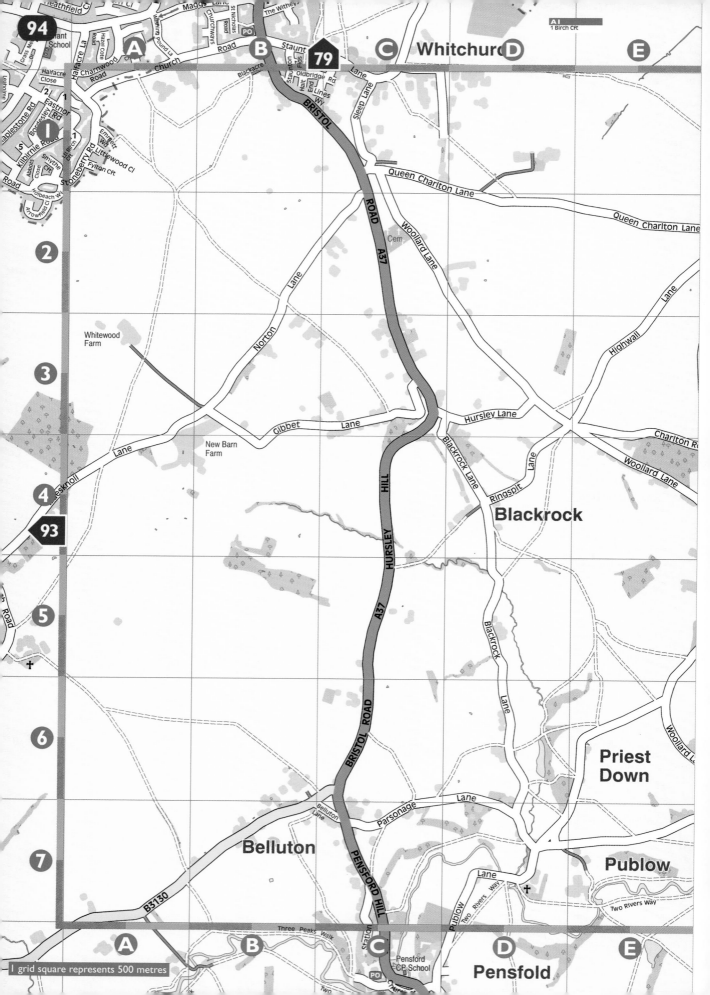

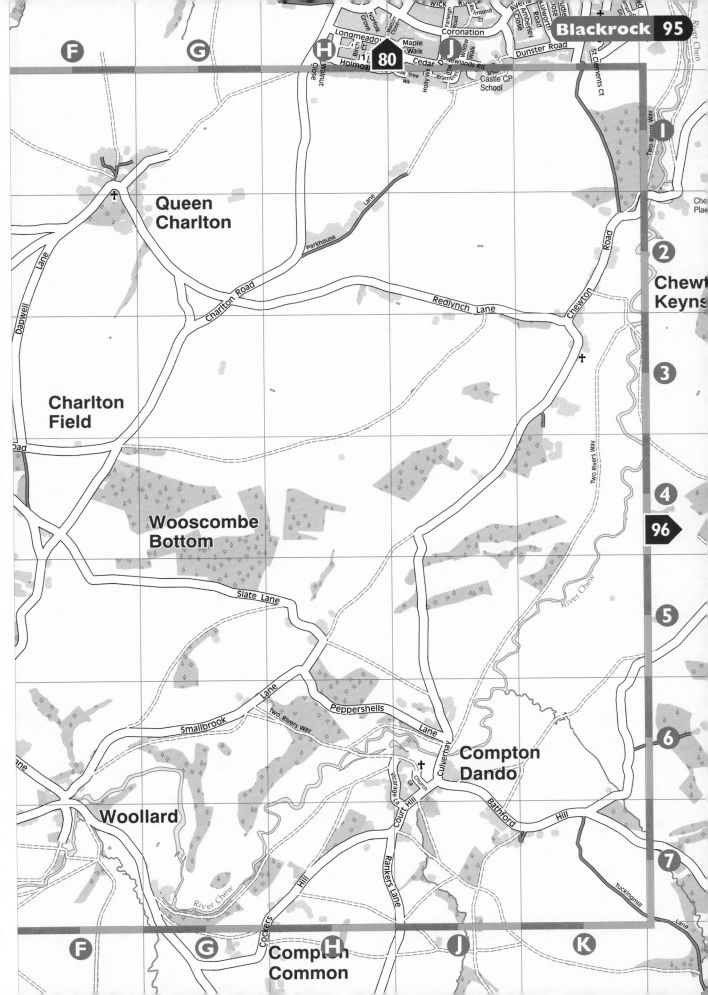

F G H J

80

Coronation

Dunster Road

Castle CP
School

Longmeadow

Maple
Walk

Cedar

Newlands Rd

Willow
Walk

Holmoa

Walnut
Close

Oak Tree
Wk

Holly Wk

St Clements Ct

Two Rivers Way

I

2

Chew
Keyns

3

Queen
Charlton

Parkhouse

Lane

Charlton Road

Redlynch Lane

Chewton

Road

Dapwell

Lane

Charlton
Field

Oad

4

96

Two Rivers Way

River Chew

5

**Wooscombe
Bottom**

Slate Lane

6

Lane

Peppershells

Lane

Two Rivers Way

Smallbrook

Culverhay

**Compton
Dando**

Bathford

Hill

7

Woollard

Vicarage La

Church

Court Hill

Hill

Rankers Lane

River Chew

Cockers Hill

Tuckingmill

Lane

F G H J K

**Compton
Common**

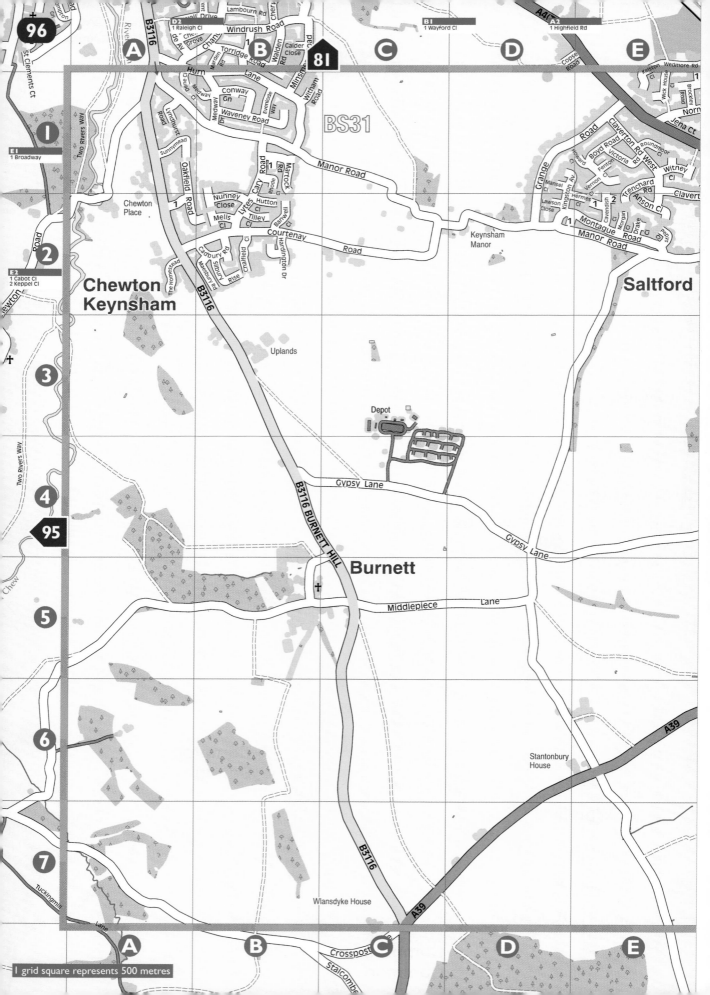

F1
1 Camerton Cl

F2
1 Golf Club La
2 Harcourt Cl
3 Somerville Cl

G1
1 Queen Sq

F   G   H   J

I

Kelston

Chelwood Rd
Stratton Rd
Hinton Road
Iford Close
Lansdowne Road
High Street
Homefield Rd
Homefield Cl
The Shallows
A4(T)
Beech Road
Chestnut Wk
PO
Doctors Surgery

Justice Av
on Road
Primary School
Manor Road
Collingwood Close
Tyning Road
Haselbury Grove
Uplands
Fairways
Rodney Road
Beresford Close
Uplands Dr
Road
The Folly
The Glen
The

Manor Farm

Kelston Park

A431

2

Golf Course

North Breach

Ashton Hill

BATH ROAD

Avon Walkway

River Avon

Avon Walkway

3

Corston

Gypsy Lane

Ashton Hill

Church Farm Business Park

Goold Cl

Corston Lane

The Barton

Mead

Land's

PO

St Teresas Private Hospital

BRISTOL ROAD A4(T)

4

98

A4(T)   **BRISTOL**

PH

5

A39

A39

Corston Field

Pennyquick

PO

Nwto **6**

Bath Spa University College

Newton Park College

7

F   G   H   J   K

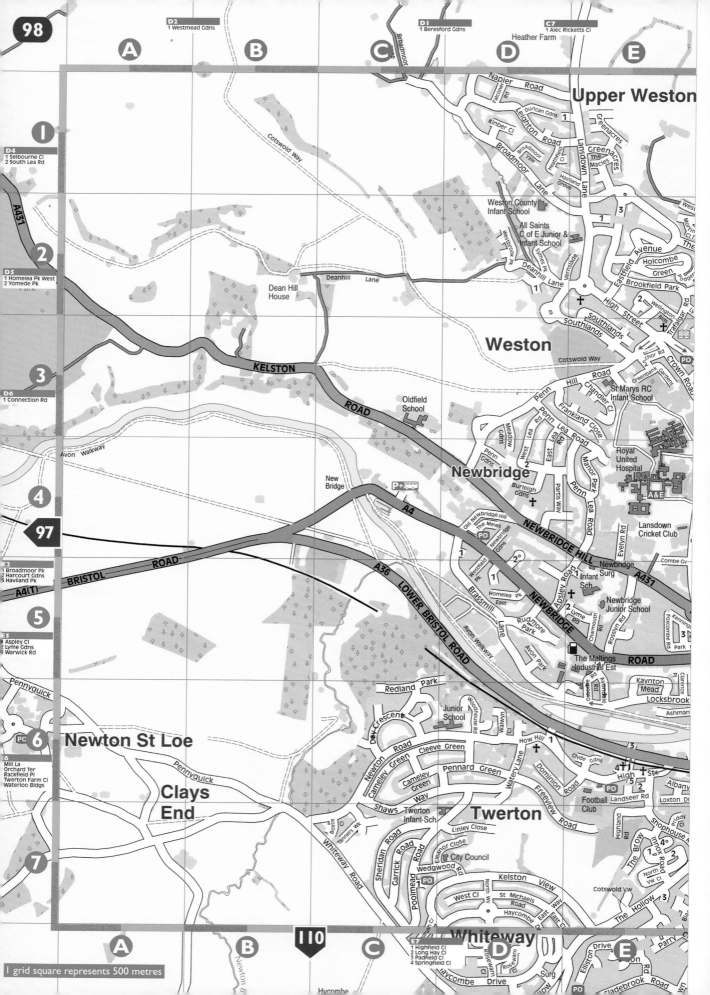

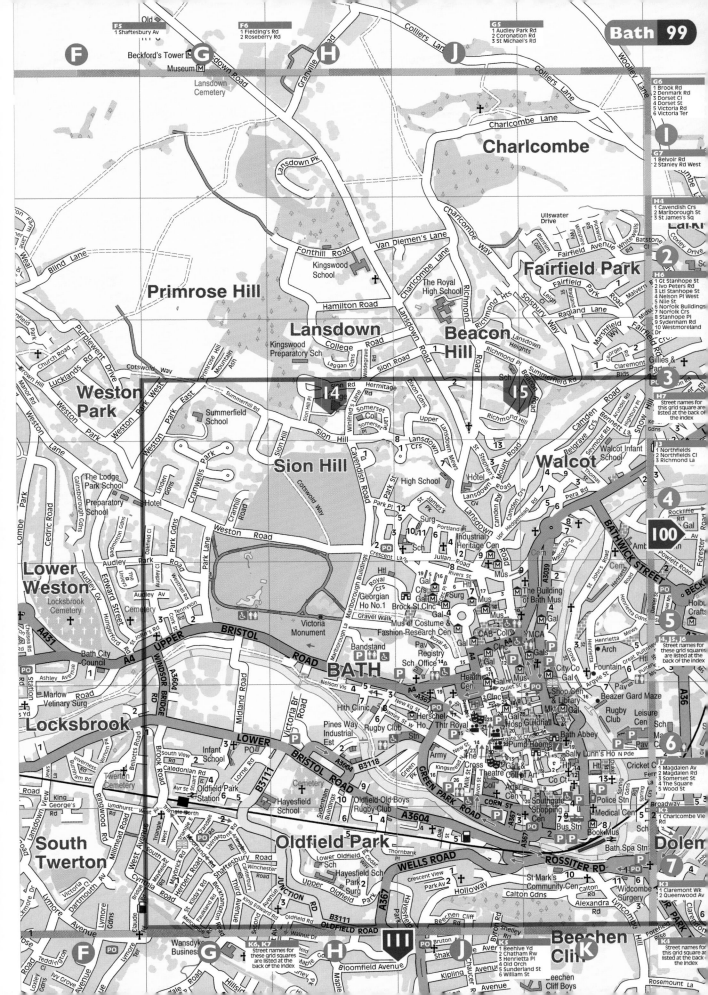

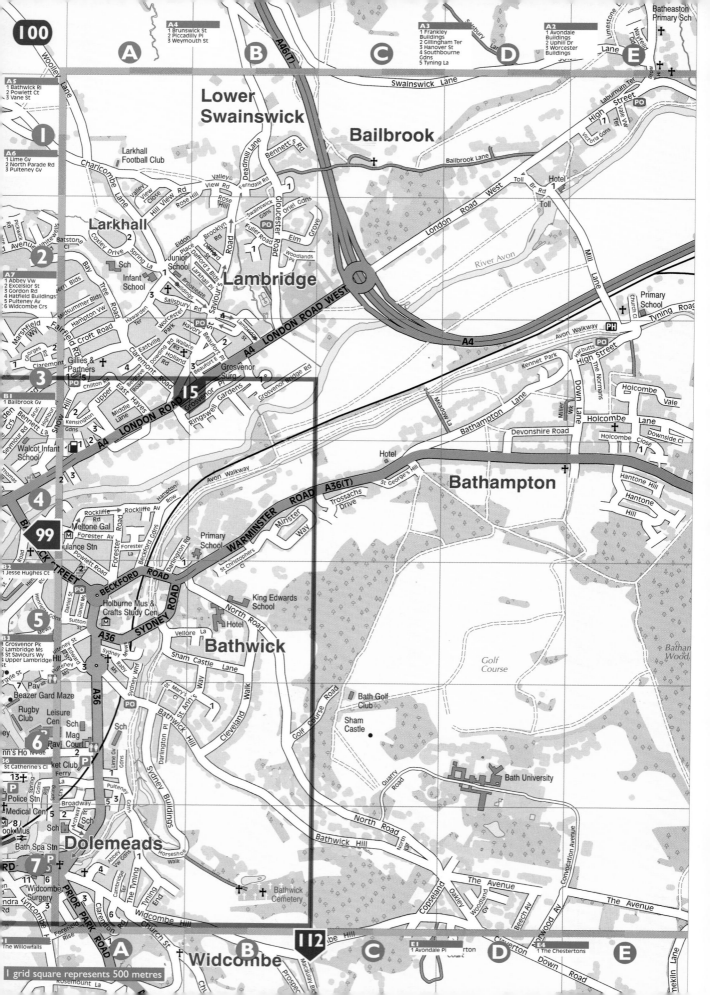

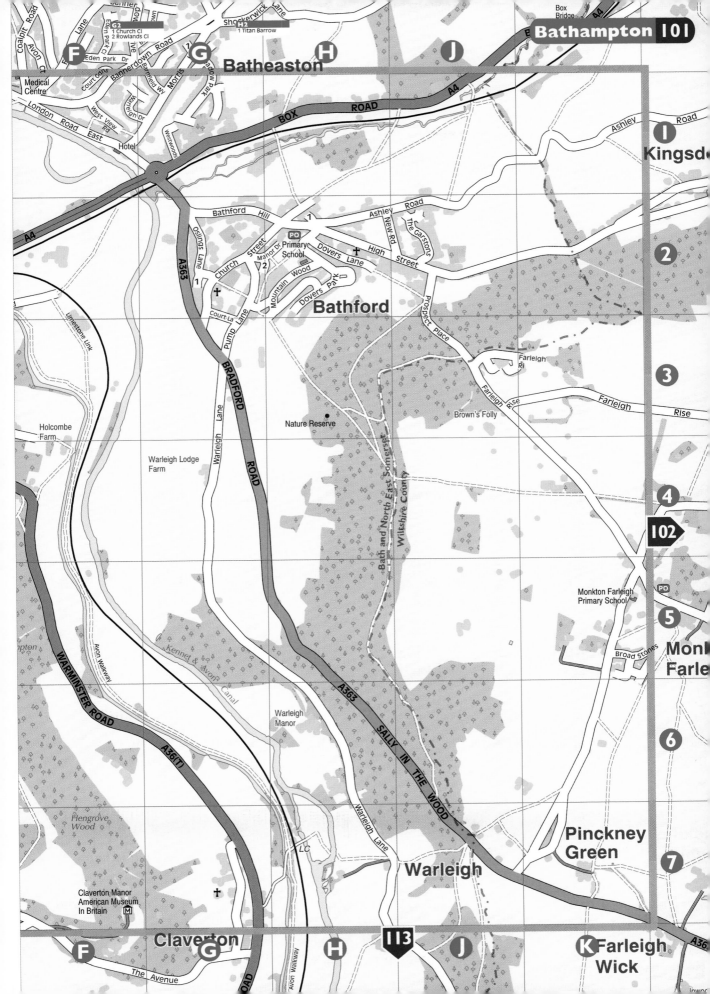

A **B** **C** **D** **E**

Henley

Prospect

BI
Ve

Kingsdown F

Longsplatt

ley Road

Henley Lane

1

Kingsdown

Lower Kingsdown Road

Kingsdown GV

Kingsdown
Golf Club

Macmillan Way

2

Link Lane

3

Farleigh Rise

Norbin Barton
Farm

Link Lane

4

onkton Farleigh
mary School

PO

5

Monkton
Farleigh

Broad stones

Rushmead
Farm

6

uckney
een

7

Duckmead
House

Farleigh
Wick

A3

A **B** **C** **D** **E**

1 grid square represents 500 metres

Chapel
Plaister

F
G
H
J
I

Wadswick
Lane

A365

Hatt
House

A365

Wormwood
Farm

B3109

2

BATH ROAD

Norbin
Farm

3

Hobb's Bottom
Farm

4

Macmillan Way

Atwo

Stonar
School

Macmillan Way

5

Coombe Lane

South
Wraxall

6

anbrook
Farm

B3109

Macmillan Wy

7

Ivy Lane

Lower
Wraxall

F
G
H
J
K

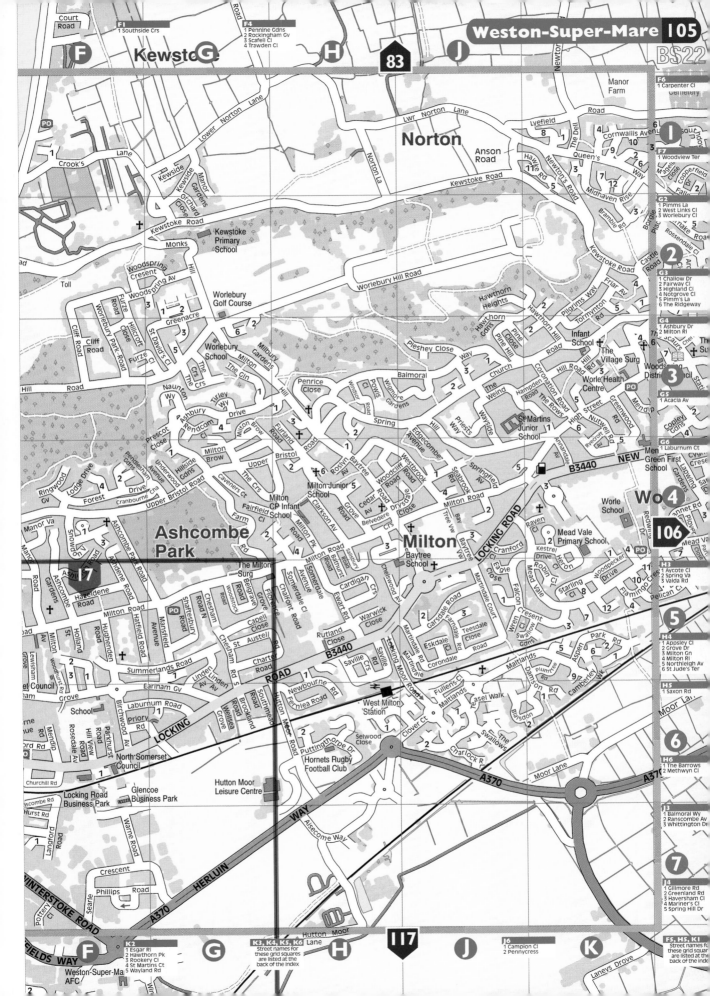

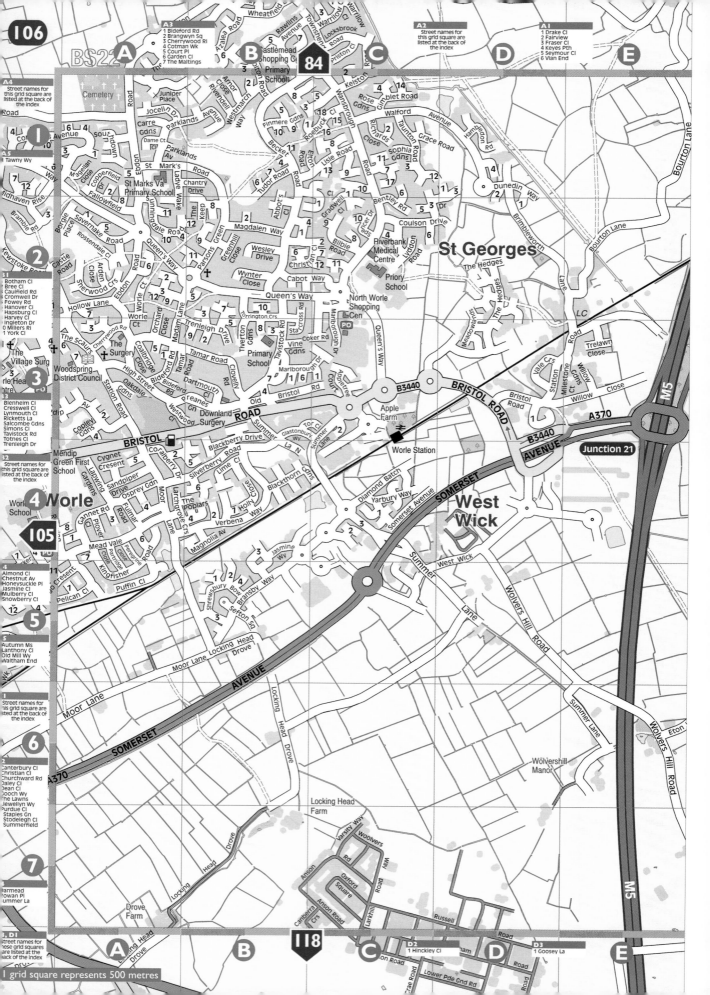

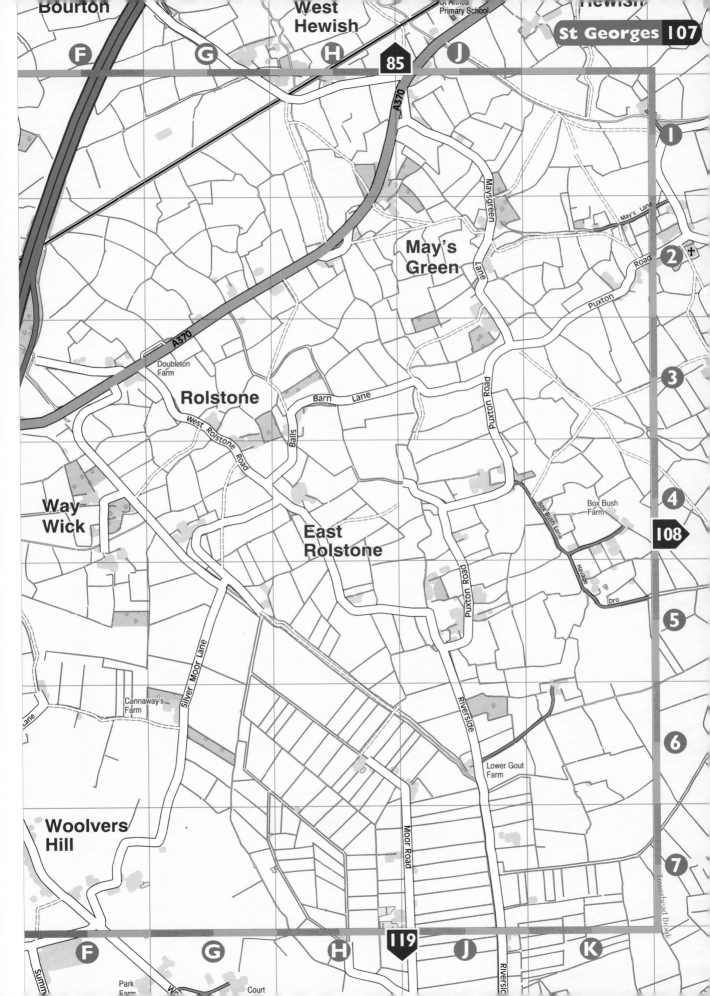

Bourton

West Hewish

Hewish

F

G

H

85

J

I

2 +

3

4

108

5

6

7

A370

A370

Maysgreen Lane

May's Lane

Road

Puxton

May's Green

Doubleton Farm

Rolstone

Barn Lane

West Rolstone Road

Balls

Puxton Road

St Anne's Primary School

Box Bush Lane

Box Bush Farm

Havage

Dro

Way Wick

East Rolstone

Puxton Road

Silver Moor Lane

Cannaway's Farm

Riverside

Lane

Lower Gout Farm

Woolvers Hill

Moor Road

Trowelhead Brook

Park Farm

Court

Summ

119

F

G

H

J

K

Riversid

86

A   B   C   D   E

1

Puxton

2

3

4

107

5

6

7

A   B   120   C   D   E

WESTON   River Yeo
Old Weston Rd   ROAD
Stepstones
Farm
Lane
Dolemoor

Oldbridge River

May's Lane

Puxton Road

Puxton Lane

Puxton Moor Lane   Puxton
Moor

South
Farm

ox Bush
Farm

Dro

Havage Drove

Nye Drove

Drove Way

Nye

Rookery
Farm

Carditch Drove

Green
Farm

Common
Lane

Towerhead Brook

Droveway
Farm

Nye
yanel
La

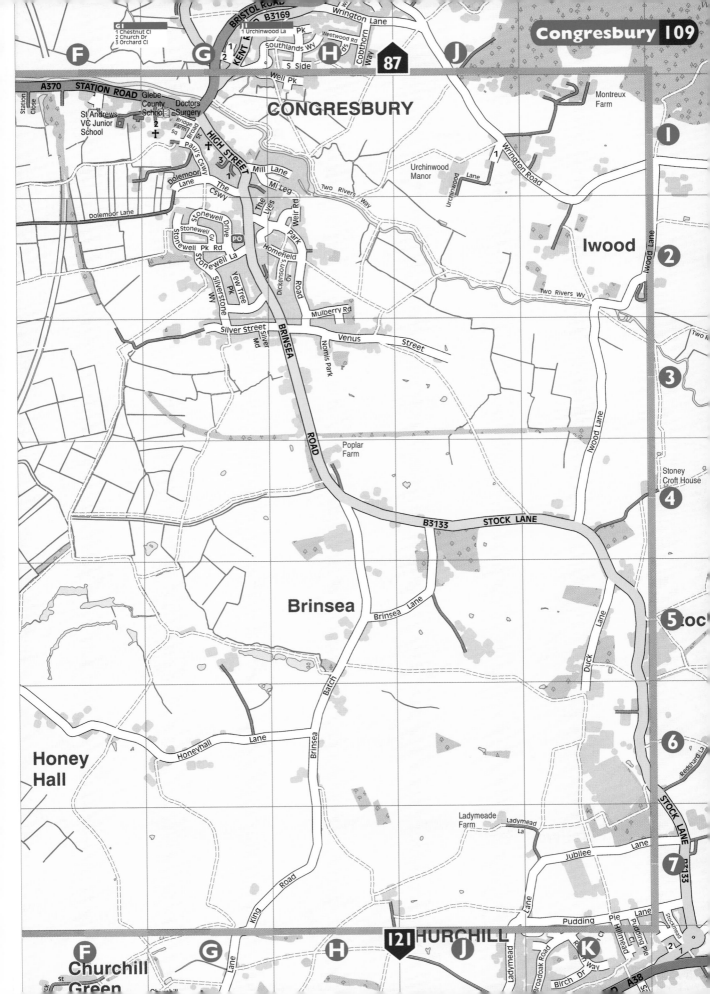

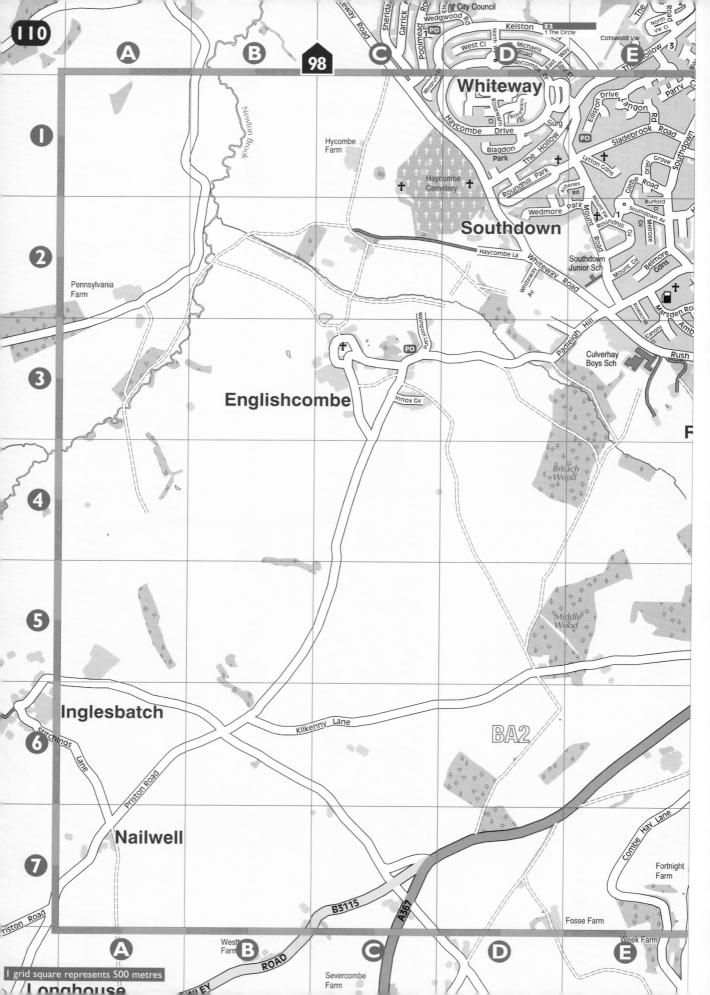

98

I

2

3

4

5

6

7

A
B
C
D
E

Whiteway

City Council

Kelston
E2
1 The Circle

West Cl

St Michaels Road

Haycombe Dr

Cotswold Vw

The Hollow

North Cl

3

Elliston Drive

Langon Rd

Parry

Hycombe Farm

Haycombe Drive

Roseware Cl

Rosewarn

Surg

PO

Sladebrook Road

Grove

Southdown

Blagdon Park

The Hollow

Roundhill Park

Anderley Rd

Lytton Gdns

Glebe Road

Melrose

Burford Cl

Southdown Av

Southdown

Wedmore

Park

Mount Vw

Mount

Roundhill

1

southdown Gv

Haycombe La

Whiteway Av

Whiteway Road

Southdown Junior Sch

Mount Gv

Belmore Gdns

Pennsylvania Farm

Rowacres

Canons

Marsden Ro

Amb

Rush

Washpool Lane

PO

Padleigh Hill

Culverhay Boys Sch

F

Englishcombe

Innox Gv

Breach Wood

Middle Wood

BA2

Inglesbatch

Kilkenny Lane

Stirchings Lane

Priston Road

Combe Hay Lane

Nailwell

Fortnight Farm

Priston Road

B3115

A367

Fosse Farm

Week Farm

A
B
C
D
E

Westb Farm

EY ROAD

Severcombe Farm

Longhouse

Newton Brook

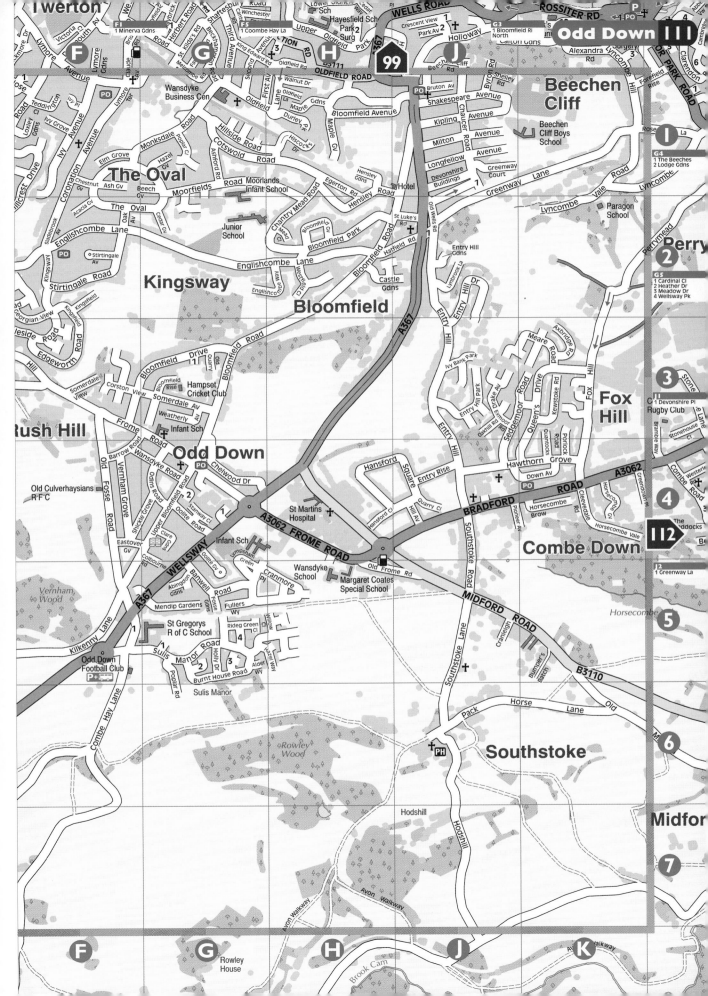

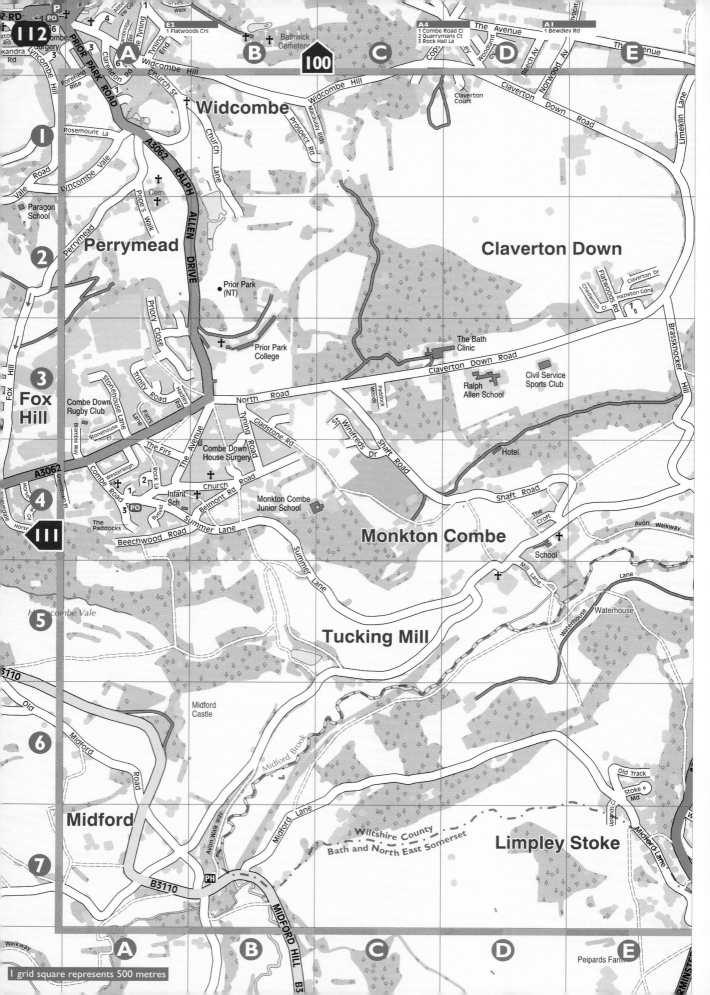

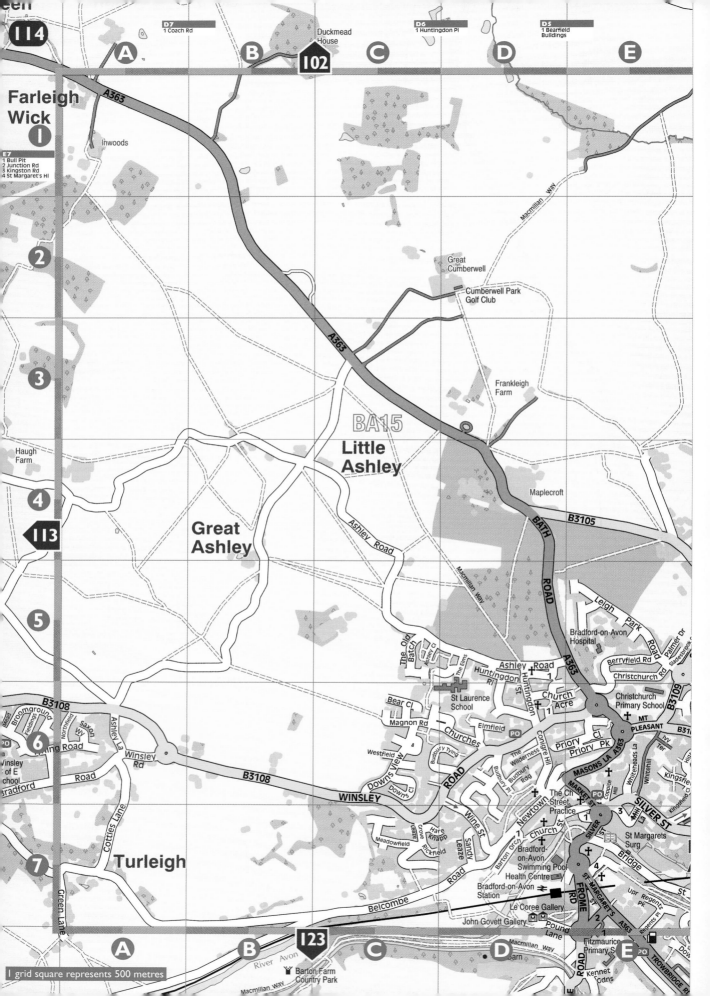

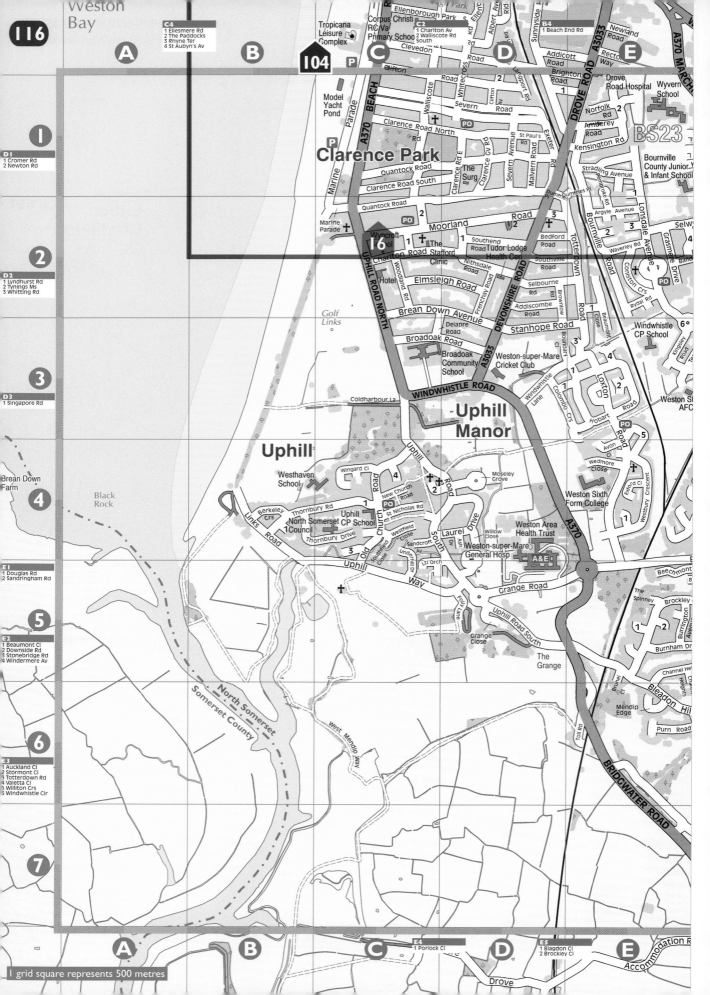

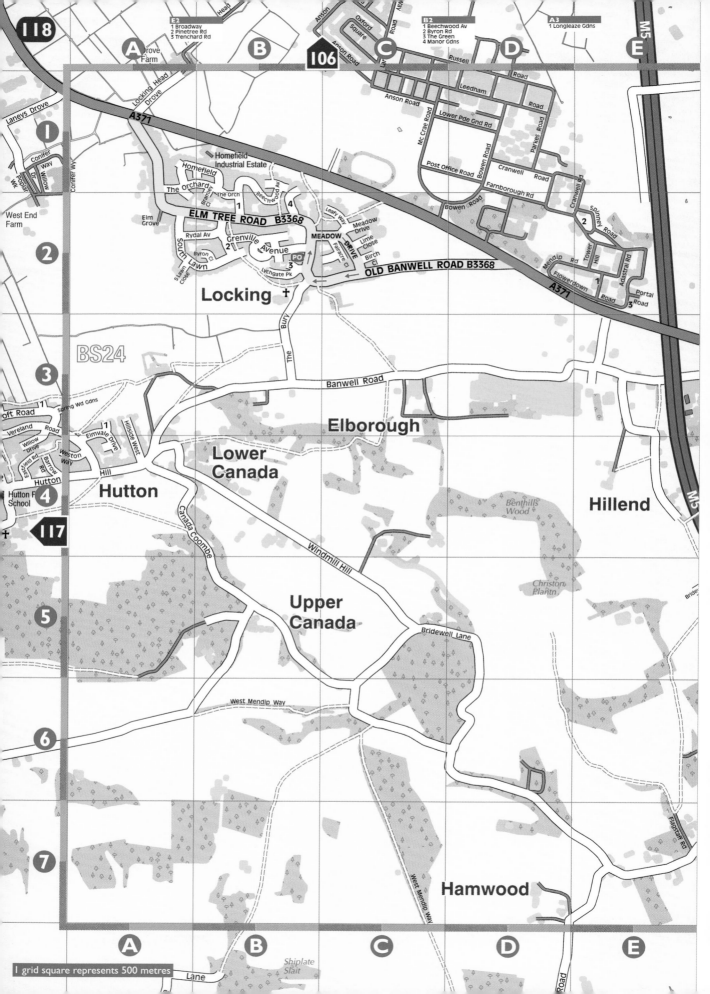

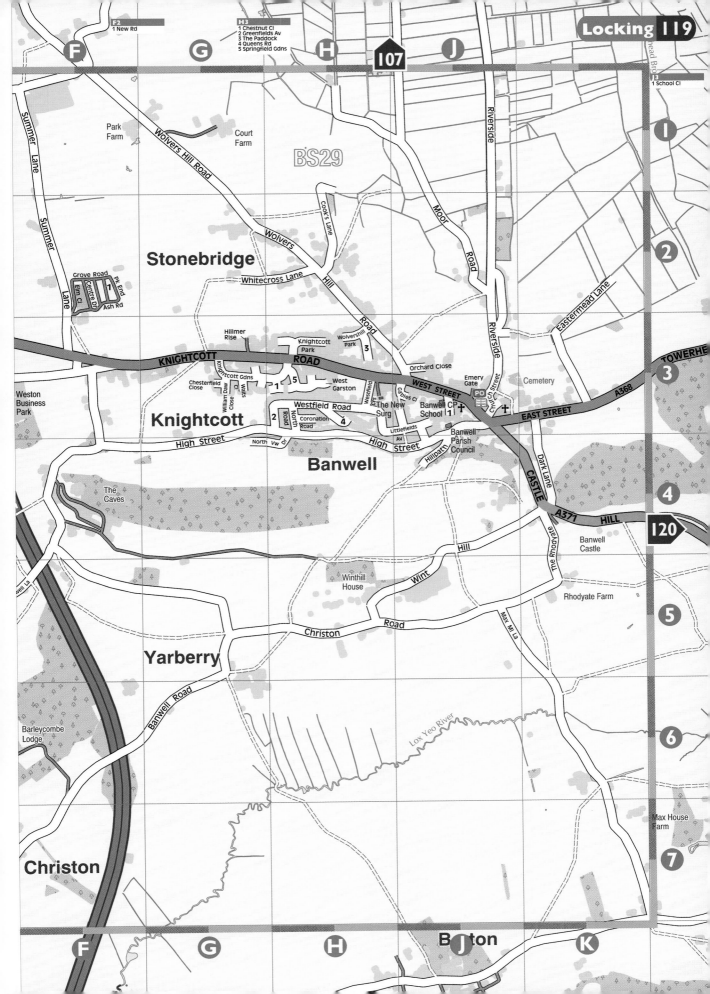

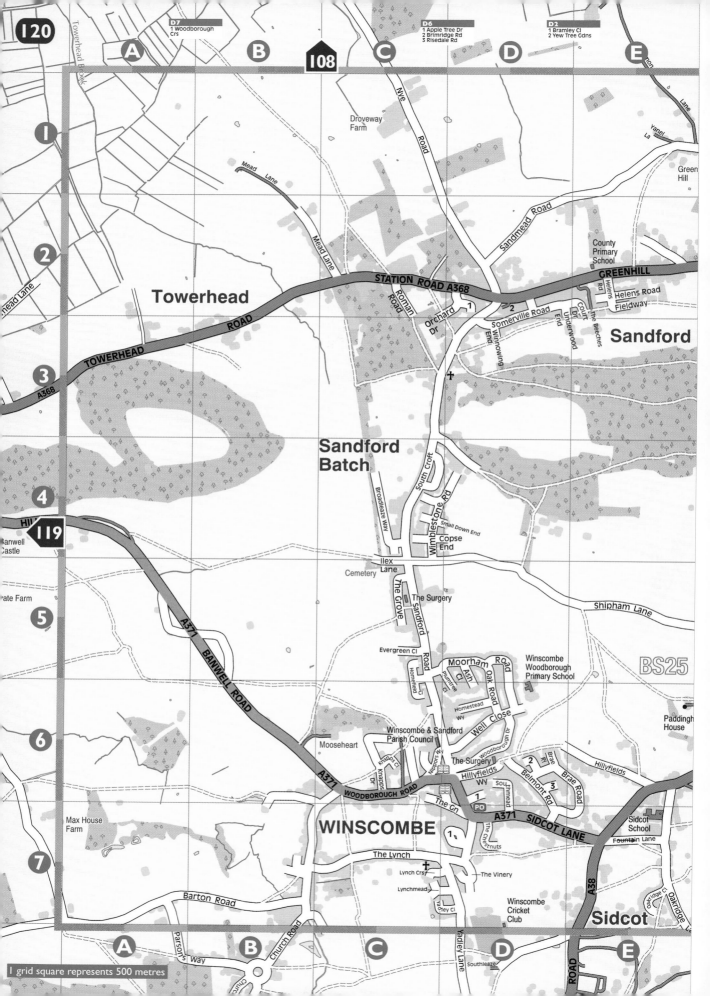

A   B   108   C   D   E

D7
1 Woodborough
Crs

D6
1 Apple Tree Dr
2 Brimridge Rd
3 Risedale Rd

D2
1 Bramley Cl
2 Yew Tree Gdns

Towerhead Brook

1

Droveway
Farm

Nye Road

Mead Lane

Yanel La

Green Hill

2

mead Lane

Towerhead

STATION ROAD A368

Sandmead Road

County Primary School

GREENHILL

Roman Road

Orchard Dr

1

2

Helens Rd

Helens Road

TOWERHEAD ROAD

Winnowing End

Underwood End

Somerville Road

The Beeches

Fieldway

Sandford

3

A368

✝

Court

Sandford Batch

South Croft

Wimblestone Rd

Small Down End

Copse End

Shipham Lane

4

Broadleaze Way

119

HILL

Banwell Castle

Ilex Lane

Cemetery

The Grove

The Surgery

Sandford Road

5

ate Farm

A371 BANWELL ROAD

Evergreen Cl

Homefield

Moorham Cl

Ash Cl

Oak Road

Plumtree Cl

Winscombe Woodborough Primary School

BS25

Paddingh House

Homestead Wy

Well Close

6

Mooseheart

Winscombe & Sandford Parish Council

Knapps Cl

The Surgery

Woodborough Dr

2 Brae Rd

Hillyfields

A371

WOODBOROUGH ROAD

Knapps Dr

Nipors Wy

The Gn

Hillyfields Wy

Sou hmead

Belmont Rd

3

Brae Road

PO

1

1

A371 SIDCOT LANE

Sidcot School

Fountain Lane

7

Max House Farm

WINSCOMBE

The Lynch

1

The Chestnuts

The Ch rnuts

A38

Oakridge Cl

Oakridge

Barton Road

✝

Lynch Crs

The Vinery

Winscombe Cricket Club

Sidcot

Parsons Way

Church Road

Lynchmead

Ya ley Cl

Yadley Lane

Southleaze

ROAD

A   B   C   D   E

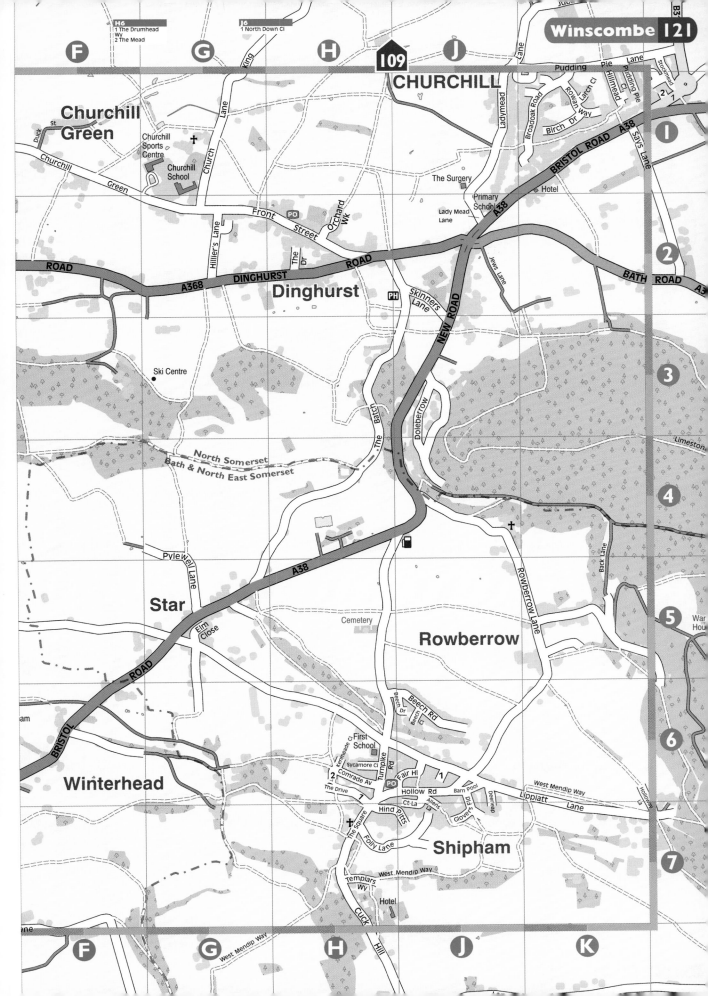

F G H J

109

CHURCHILL

Churchill
Green

Duck St

Churchill Green

Churchill
Sports
Centre

Churchill
School

Church Lane

King Lane

Pudding Pie Lane

Pudding Pie Ln

Hillmead Cl

Larch Cl

Rowan Way

Broadoak Road

Birch Dr

Stockmead

BRISTOL ROAD A38

Says Lane

B3

I

The Surgery

Hotel

2

Hiller's Lane

Front Street

PO

Orchard Wk

The Dr

DINGHURST ROAD

A368

Dinghurst

ROAD

Primary School

A38

Lady Mead Lane

Ladymead Lane

PH

Skinners Lane

Jews Lane

BATH ROAD A3

2

NEW ROAD

Doleberrow

The Batch

Ski Centre

3

North Somerset
Bath & North East Somerset

Limeston

4

†

Back Lane

Pylewell Lane

A38

Cemetery

Rowberrow Lane

Rowberrow

War
Hou

5

Star

Elm Close

BRISTOL ROAD

Beech Dr

Beech Rd

Beech Ci

6

Winterhead

Kempheade Cl

First
School

Sycamore Cl

2

Comrade Av

The Drive

7

Turnpike Rd

Fair Hl

PO

Hollow Rd

Ct La

Hind Pitts

1

Barn Pool

Allens La

Glover's Fld

Deerleap

West Mendip Way

Lippiatt Lane

Hollow La

6

†

The Square

Folly Lane

Shipham

7

Templars Wy

Hotel

West Mendip Way

CUCK Hill

F G West Mendip Way H J K

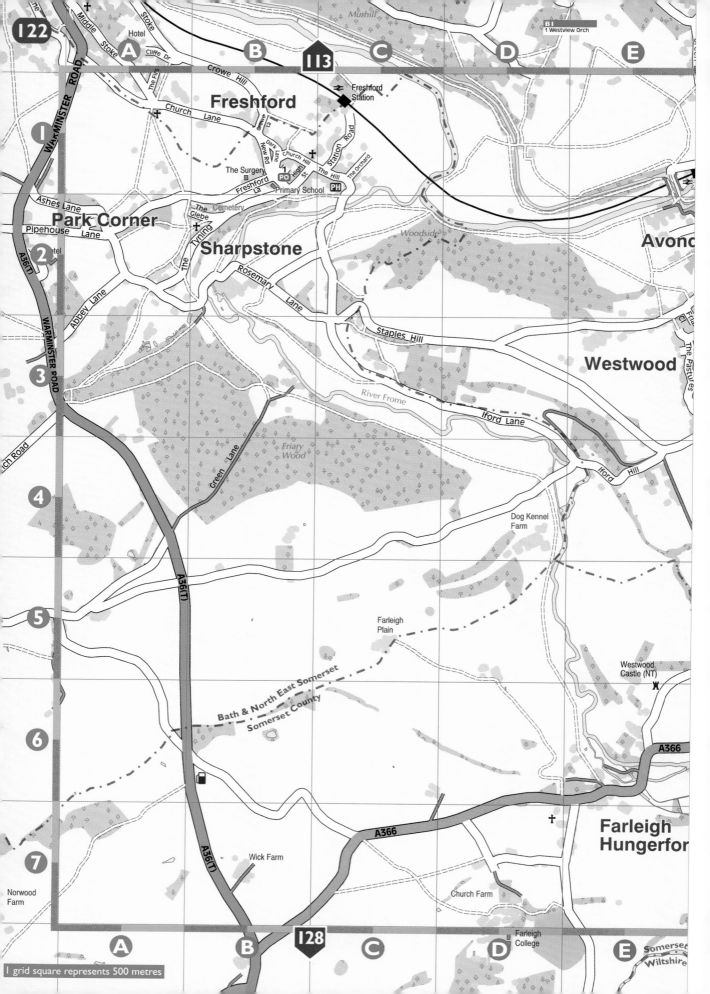

A
Hotel
Cliffe Dr

B

113

C

D

E

B 1 Westview Orch

Murhill

Stoke
Middle Stoke
WARMINSTER ROAD

The Firs
Crowe Hill

Church Lane

Freshford

Freshford Station

1

Grove La
Dark Lane
New Rd
Church Hill
Station Road

The Surgery
PO
High St
The Hill
PH
The Orchard

Freshford La
Primary School

Ashes Lane

Park Corner

Pipehouse Lane

Cemetery

The Glebe

The Tyning

Sharpstone

Woodside

2

A36(T)
WARMINSTER ROAD

Abbey Lane

Rosemary Lane

Staples Hill

Westwood

Avonc

3

ch Road
A36(T)

River Frome

Iford Lane

Iford Hill

The Pastures

4

Green Lane

Friary Wood

Dog Kennel Farm

5

Farleigh Plain

Westwood Castle (NT)

6

Bath & North East Somerset
Somerset County

A366

7

A36(T)

Wick Farm

Church Farm

Norwood Farm

Farleigh Hungerfor

A

B

128

C

D

Farleigh College

E

Somerset
Wiltshire

1 grid square represents 500 metres

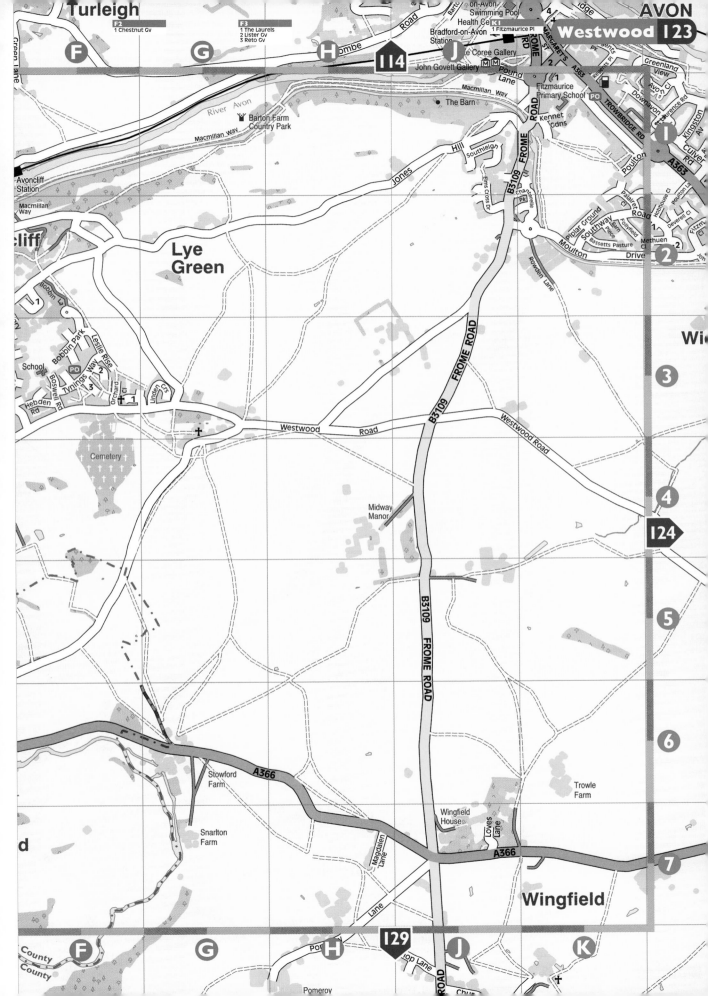

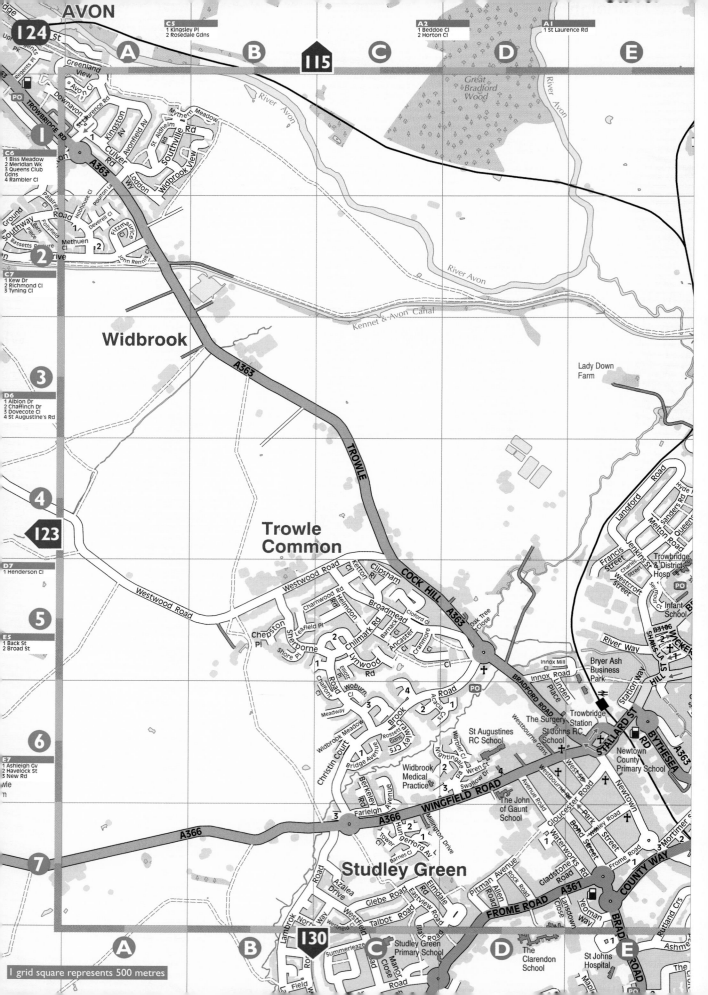

124

A   B   **115**   C   D   E

Greenland View

Great Bradford Wood

River Avon

River Avon

1

PO

TROWBRIDGE RD

Downavon

Avon

St Laurence Rd

Kingston Av

Avonfield Av

Mythern Meadow

Culver Rd

Southville Rd

Widbrook View

St Aldhelm

C6
1 Biss Meadow
2 Meridian Wk
3 Queens Club Gdns
4 Rambler Cl

A363

Loddon

Hobhouse Cl

Pouton La

Deverell Cl

Fitzmaurice Cl

Ground

Southway

Palairet Place

Follyfield

Methuen Cl

Bassetts

John Rennie Cl

2

C7
1 Kew Dr
2 Richmond Cl
3 Tyning Cl

River Avon

Widbrook

A363

Kennet & Avon Canal

3

D6
1 Albion Dr
2 Chaffinch Dr
3 Dovecote Cl
4 St Augustine's Rd

Lady Down Farm

TROWLE

4

123

D7
1 Henderson Cl

Trowle Common

Westwood Road

Westwood Road

Kerton

Clipsham Rd

Broadmead

COCK HILL A363

Oak Tree Close

Langford Road

Hyde Rd

Sanders Rd

Melton Road

Queens

Francis Street

Jenkins St

Charles Street

Trowbridge & District Hosp

Westcroft Street

Seymour

PO

Infant School

B3106

WICKER

SHAILS LA

5

E5
1 Back St
2 Broad St

Chepston Pl

Sherborne

Leafield Pl

Chilmark Rd

Charnwood Rd

Helmdon

Barnack

Ancaster

Cramm

Cranmore Cl

Cl

Innox Mill Cl

Innox Road

Linden Place

Bryer Ash Business Park

River Way

HILL

Station Way

6

E7
1 Ashleigh Gv
2 Havelock St
3 New Rd

Chaffont

Elliot

Lynwood Rd

Shore Pl

Woburn

Acacia

Road

PO

BRADFORD ROAD

The Surgery

St Johns RC School

Trowbridge Station

STALLARD ST

Newtown County Primary School

BYTHESEA

A363

Meadway

Brook

Crawl

Rossetti Gdns

St Augustines RC School

Warbler Cl

Nightingale

Wren Cl

Westbourne Gdns

West St

Newtown

7

Widbrook Meadow

Christin Court

Berkeley

Bridge Avenue

Farleigh

A366

Widbrook Medical Practice

Swallow Dr

WINGFIELD ROAD

The John of Gaunt School

Avenue Road

Gloucester Road

Bond Street

Frome Road

Park

COUNTY WAY

BRAD

A366

Tower Cl

Barnes Cl

Hungerford Av

Millington Drive

Pitman Avenue

Allen Road

Waterworks Rd

Gladstone Road

FROME ROAD A361

Lansdown Close

Yeoman Way

Mortimer

Rutland Crs

Studley Green

Lambrok

North Way

Azalea Drive

Glebe Road

Westfield

Talbot Road

Eastview Rd

Elmdale Rd

Blair Road

Summerleaze

Studley Green Primary School

The Clarendon School

St Johns Hospital

Ashm

A   B   **130**   C   D   E

1 grid square represents 500 metres

F4
1 James St
2 Kensington Cl

F5
1 Charlotte St
2 Roundstone St

F **G** **H** **J**

NEW TERRACE
MARSH ROAD
B3105

Staverton
C of E School
School Lane

Smallbrook
Gardens

Marina Dr
Swan Dr

The Slipway
Thestfield Dr

HAMMOND WAY
Towpath Road
HAMMOND WAY
B3106

Navigator Cl
Kings Gdns
Hanover Cl
Tudor Dr
Saxon Dr

Carisbrooke Crs

Princess Gdns
Queens Gardens
St Mary's Gdns
St Mary's Cl
St Mary's Road
Saxon Drive

Horse Road

Marshmead

Newleaze

Hilperton Marsh

HILL STREET
B3105

Greenhill Gdns

Hilperton
Primary
School

Dymott Sq

Whaddon Lane

Hilperton Marsh

B3106 CANAL ROAD

Brick Lane

Avon Way
Kennet Way

Wyke Road

Wyke Rd

Canal Rd

Hayes Cl

Wyke Road

Greenway Gdns

The Down

Downside Pk

Cemetery

The Knap
Cherry
Gardens

Church Lane

The Knap

PO

Hilperton

CHURCH ST

Ashton Road
Ashton Rise

Devizes Road

Devizes Road

DEVIZ

A361

CANAL ROAD

Parklands

Avonvale Road
Murray Rd
Palmer Road
Seymour Road
Downhayes Rd
Lower Cl

THE DOWN

Junior
School
Windermere Road
Coniston Road
The Mount
Delamere Road

Victoria Gardens
Ragletham Rd
Rodwell Park
Cleveland Gdns
Lowmead
Fulford Rd
Grasmere

Victoria Road
Albert Road
Middle
Fulney Cl
Albany Cl
Victoria Rd
Victoria Road

Hotel

Royce Clnc

Thomas
Springfield
Park
Stancomb Av

A361 HILPERTON ROAD

The Halfway
The Beeches
Kenton Dr
Pepperacre Lane
Ravenscroft

TROWBRIDGE RD

Castley Road
A361

Newhurst Pk

HILPERTON DRIVE

Faverole Way
Painters Mead
Gate
Leap
Gibbs Leaze

Corbin Road
Cusance Way
Walmesley Chn
Walmesley Chase
Montague Court

Paxcroft Brook

Ashton

G4
1 Springfield Cl

G6
1 Ashton St
2 Lower Alma St

G7
1 Honeysuckle Cl
2 Lavender Cl
3 Sheepcote Barton
4 Worsted Cl

F6
1 Mill St

F7
1 Ashmead Ct
2 Haden Rd
3 Harmony Pl
4 New Rd
5 Spinners Cft

G2
1 Stuart Cl

Adcroft
Surgery
York
Buildings

BRITISH ROW
PROSPECT PLACE
George Street
Cross St
Timbrell St
Union St
Church Street
Taylors
The Halve
Bellefield
Cr's
Duke Street

Yerbury Street
Clark St
Polebarn Road

Eastbourne Road
Furlong Gdns

TROWBRIDGE

Quarterway La
Larkrise School

Paxcroft
Primary School

Barn Glebe

Lark Down

Heather Shaw

Paxcroft Way

Wyneham

BA14

Green Lane

Green Lane
Farm

Castle Place
Leisure
Centre

Lovemead
Group Practice

St Stephen's Pl

Silver St
PO

Market

Alma St

Kenwood Cl
Honeymans Cl
Cadby Cl

Slowgrove Cl

Clarence Rd

Southwood Rd

Green Lane

Trowbridge
Rugby
Football Club

H6
1 Smithywell Cl

COUNTY WAY

Clarendon Road
West Ashton Road
Clarendon Av

Green Lane
Amouracre

Jasmine Way

West Ashton Road

COUNTY WAY

Longfield

LONGFIELD RD
Brown St
A361

Trowbridge Mosque
Longfield Road
South Way
Chevlot Cl
Broadcloth Lane
Quilling

Broadcloth East Lane

Magnolia Rl

Orchard Road
Bramley Lane
Cherry Gdns
Weavers Drive
Woolpack
Meadow
Ryeland WY7

Shearman Rd
Carters Cnr

Fleece Cottages
Millhand Villas

Lower Studley

Dursley Rd
Studley Rise
Wilton Drive
Dryham
White Horse

Biss Farm

Biss Wood

131

F **G** **H** **J** **K**

F5
1 Pavely Gdns
2 Proby Pl

J4
1 Fairwood Cl

J3
1 Nursery Cl
2 St Michael's Cl

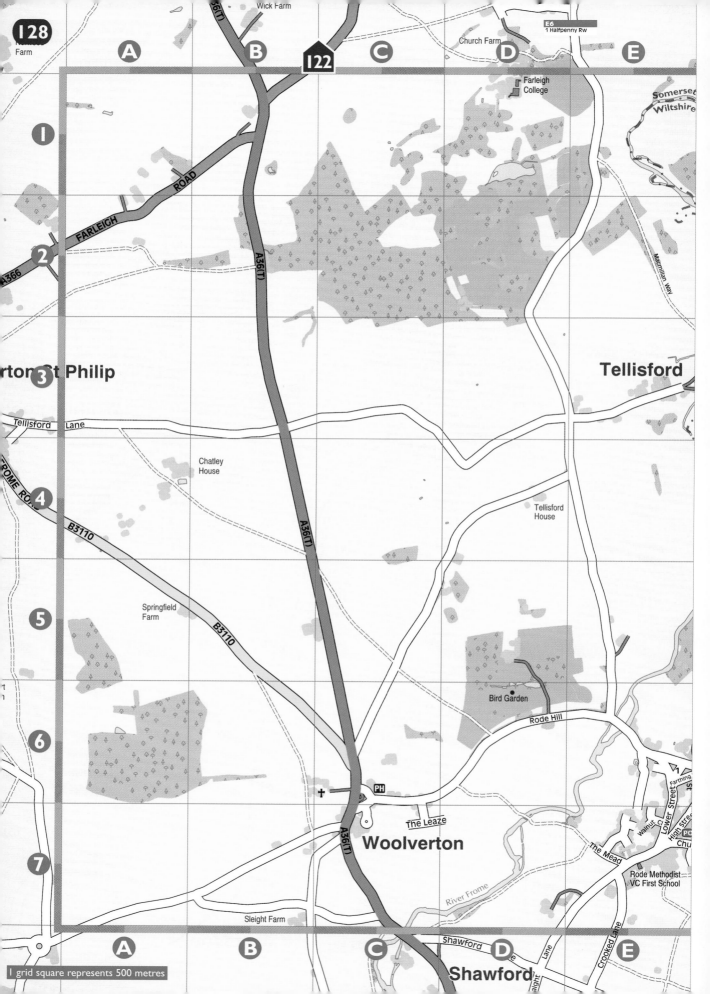

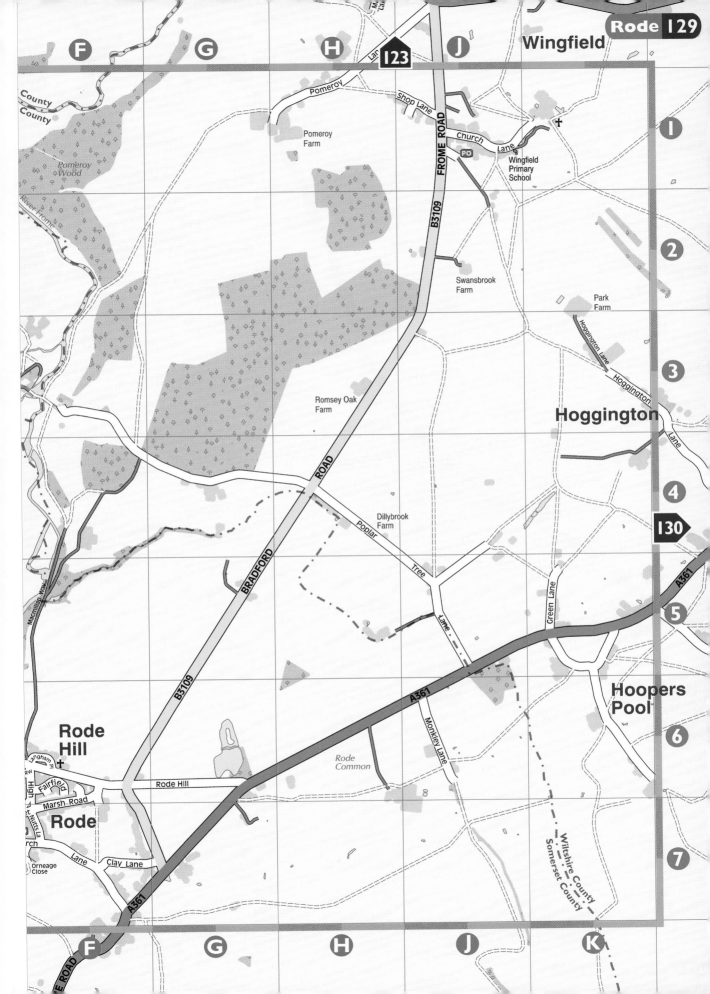

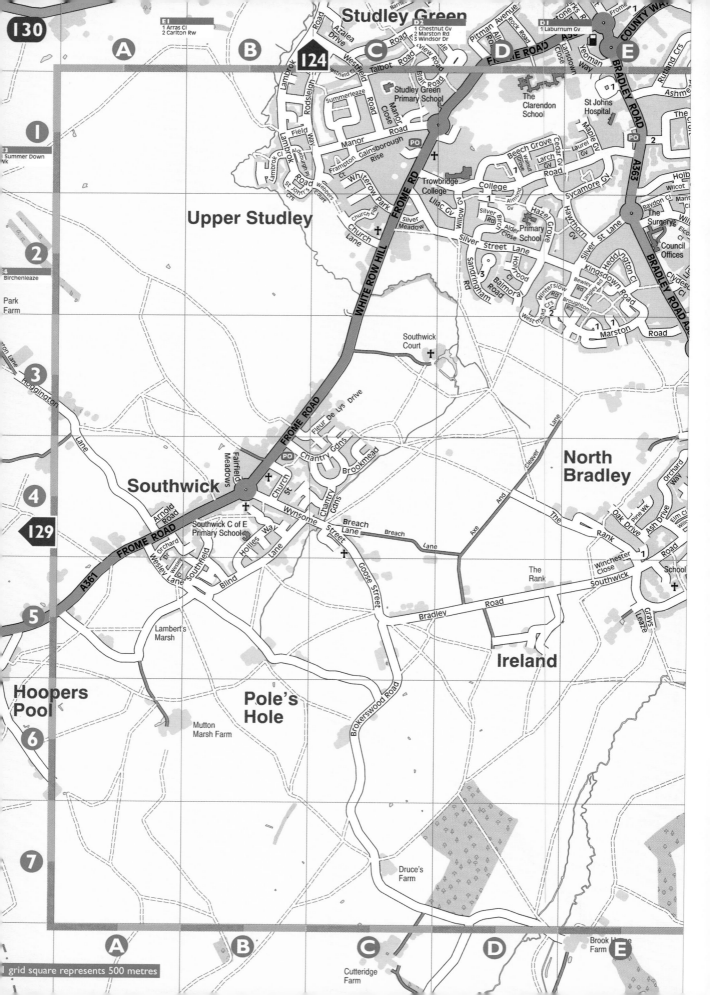

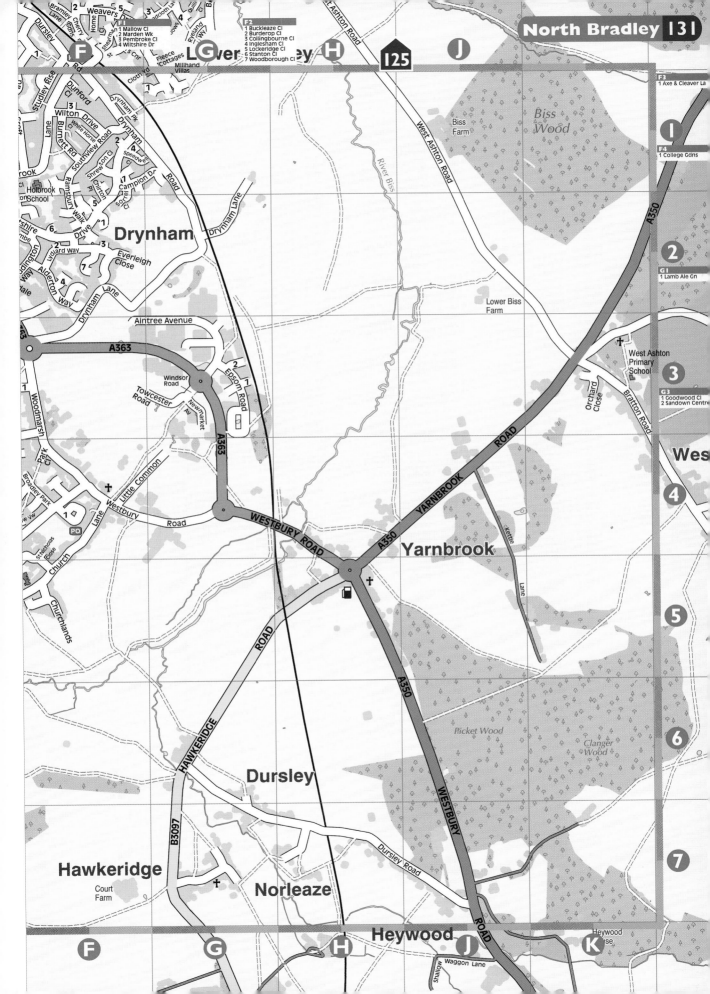

Abbots Leigh	64 C2	Conkwell	113 H4	Honey Hall
Abson	57 F7	Coombe Dingle	50 E1	Hoopers Pool
Almondsbury	30 B3	Coomb's End	45 K2	Horfield
Alveston	22 E1	Corston	97 H4	Horsecastle
Alveston Down	22 C1	Cotham	2 F8	Hotwells
Arno's Vale	12 D1	Cowhorn Hill	69 J6	Hutton
Ashcombe Park	105 G4	Crew's Hole	9 L3	Icellon
Ashley Down	3 L2	Cribbs Causeway	38 C2	Inglesbatch
Ashton Gate	65 H6	Cromhall	21 H4	Ireland
Ashton Vale	77 H1	Cromhall Common	21 H6	Iron Acton
Avoncliff	122 E2	Crossways	20 A3	Itchington
Avonmouth	36 C6	Dinghurst	121 H2	Iwood
Aztec West	29 K5	Dodington	45 H3	Kelston
Backwell	74 B5	Dolemeads	15 H8	Kendleshire
Backwell Common	74 A3	Downend	54 D2	Kenn
Backwell Green	74 D3	Downside	89 H4	Kenn Moor Gate
Bagstone	25 G2	Drynham	131 F2	Kewstoke
Bailbrook	100 C1	Dundry	92 A2	Keynsham
Banwell	119 H4	Dursley	131 G6	Kingdown
Barrow Common	76 D7	Dyer's Common	27 K4	Kingsdown
Barrow Gurney	76 A6	Earthcott Green	24 A7	Kingston Seymour
Barton Hill	8 D4	East Clevedon	59 H7	Kingsway
The Batch	69 H5	East Dundry	92 E3	Kingswood
Bath	14 D5	East End	74 B2	Kington
Bathampton	100 D4	Easter Compton	28 C6	The Knapp
Bathford	101 H2	Eastfield	51 K2	Knightcott
Bathwick	15 K5	Easton	4 D8	Knowle
Beacon Hill	99 J3	Easton-in-Gordano	49 F5	Lambridge
Bedminster	10 C2	East Rolstone	107 H4	Lansdown
Bedminster Down	10 B7	Eastville	4 F3	Larkhall
Beechen Cliff	15 G9	Ebdon	84 B6	Latteridge
Belluton	94 B7	Elborough	118 C3	Lawrence Weston
Berwick	38 A2	Emerson's Green	55 J3	Leigh Woods
Bibstone	21 J2	Engine Common	33 J2	Limpley Stoke
Bishopston	3 H2	Englishcombe	110 B3	Little Ashley
Bishopsworth	77 H6	Failand	63 J6	Little Chalfield
Blackhorse	55 F2	Fairfield Park	99 K2	Little Sodbury
Blackrock	94 D4	Farleigh	74 C4	Little Sodbury End
Blaise Hamlet	38 A6	Farleigh Hungerford	122 E7	Little Stoke
Bleadon	117 H7	Farleigh Wick	113 K1	Locking
Bloomfield	111 H2	Farley	59 K1	Lockleaze
Blue Vein	102 E1	Felton	90 C5	Locksbrook
Bourton	85 F7	Filton	40 A5	Lodway
Bower Ashton	65 F6	Filwood Park	11 L8	Long Ashton
Bradford Leigh	115 G3	Fishponds	53 K4	Longfield
Bradford-on-Avon	114 E7	Flax Bourton	75 G4	Longwell Green
Bradley Stoke	30 D7	Forewoods Common	115 J6	Lower Canada
Brentry	38 E6	Fox Hill	111 K5	Lower Failand
Brinsea	109 H5	Frampton Cotterell	42 B1	Lower Hazel
Brislington	13 K3	Frampton End	32 D7	Lower Knowle
Bristol	7 L5	Frenchay	54 B1	Lower Morton
Brockley	88 C2	Freshford	122 B1	Lower Studley
Bromley Heath	41 H6	Frogland Cross	31 H3	Lower Swainswick
Broom Hill	9 L9	Frost Hill	87 F6	Lower Weston
Broomhill	53 J3	Gaunt's Earthcott	31 G2	Lower Wraxall
Buckover	20 B3	Golden Hill	52 B3	Lulsgate Bottom
Burnett	96 C5	Goose Green	34 A4	Lyde Green
Cadbury Heath	69 G5	Goose Green	69 J1	Lye Green
Cambridge Batch	75 J3	Great Ashley	114 B4	Maiden Head
Catbrain	38 E2	Great Stoke	41 F3	Mangotsfield
Charlcombe	99 J1	Grovesend	20 A6	Marsh Common
Charlton Field	95 F3	The Hacket	20 A5	May's Green
Chelvey	73 H6	Hallen	37 K3	Mayshill
Chelvey Batch	88 D1	Hambrook	41 H6	Mead Riding
Chewton Keynsham	96 A2	Ham Green	50 A5	Middle Bridge
Chipping Sodbury	35 G6	Ham Green	115 K5	Middletown
Christon	119 F7	Hamwood	118 C7	Midford
Churchill	121 J1	Hangstone Hill	58 E7	Milbury Heath
Churchill Green	121 F1	Hanham	68 C5	Milton
Clandown	126 E1	Hanham Green	68 C7	Monkton Combe
Clapton in Gordano	61 H1	Harry Stoke	40 D6	Monkton Farleigh
Clapton Wick	60 C4	Hartcliffe	78 B7	Montpelier
Clarence Park	16 D8	Hawkeridge	131 F7	Moorend
Claverham	87 H3	Haydon	127 F5	Morton
Claverton	113 G1	Headley Park	77 J5	Mount Hill
Claverton Down	112 D2	Heath End	21 J5	Nailsea
Clay Hill	5 L6	Henbury	38 B6	Nailwell
Clays End	98 A6	Henfield	42 E5	Netham
Cleeve	88 A4	Hengrove	78 E5	Newbridge
Clevedon	58 D6	Hengrove Park	78 C5	New Cheltenham
Clifton	6 A1	Henleaze	52 A3	Newton St Loe
Coalpit Heath	42 E2	Hewish	85 K7	Nibley
Codrington	44 D6	Hicks Gate	80 B3	Norleaze
Colt's Green	35 H7	Highridge	77 F7	North Bradley
Combe Down	111 K4	Hillend	118 C4	North Common
Compton Dando	95 J6	Hillfields	54 B6	North Corner
Compton Greenfield	28 B7	Hilperton	125 J3	North End
Congresbury	109 G1	Hilperton Marsh	125 G2	North Weston
Conham	68 A5	Hoggington	129 K3	North Wick

Honey Hall	109 F6	Norton	105 J1	Totteroak	35 H2
Hoopers Pool	129 K6	Norton Hawkfield	93 G6	Towerhead	120 A2
Horfield	52 D2	Norton Hill	126 C4	Townwell	21 J4
Horsecastle	86 C3	Norton Malreward	93 K6	Trowbridge	125 G5
Hotwells	6 A6	Norton's Wood	59 K4	Trowle Common	124 B4
Hutton	118 A4	Novers Park	11 G7	Tucking Mill	112 C5
Icellon	84 E4	Nye	108 B5	Turleigh	114 A7
Inglesbatch	110 A6	Odd Down	111 G4	Twerton	98 D7
Ireland	130 D5	Old Down	22 B3	Two Mile Hill	68 B1
Iron Acton	32 E3	Oldfield Park	14 B8	Tyning	127 H2
Itchington	24 A4	Oldland	69 G7	Tyntesfield	62 E6
Iwood	109 K2	Oldland Common	69 K7	Tytherington	24 D1
Kelston	97 K1	Oldmixon	117 G5	Uphill	116 B4
Kendleshire	42 B5	The Oval	111 F1	Uphill Manor	116 D3
Kenn	71 H4	Over	29 G5	Upper Canada	118 B5
Kenn Moor Gate	72 D7	Parkfield	56 C2	Upper Littleton	91 J6
Kewstoke	83 F7	Patchway	29 K6	Upper Morton	19 K1
Keynsham	81 G6	Perrymead	112 A2	Upper Studley	130 B2
Kingdown	90 D7	Pill	49 J5	Upper Town	90 E4
Kingsdown	102 A1	Pinckney Green	101 K7	Upper Weston	98 E1
Kingston Seymour	85 K2	Pole's Hole	130 B6	Vinney Green	55 G2
Kingsway	111 G2	Portbury	48 C6	Walcot	15 H2
Kingswood	68 E2	Portishead	47 F5	Walton-in-Gordano	59 K3
Kington	18 D4	Potters Hill	90 C3	Walton St Mary	59 G4
The Knapp	20 A2	Priest Down	94 E6	Wapley	44 B4
Knightcott	119 G3	Primrose Hill	99 G2	Warleigh	101 J7
Knowle	12 A5	Publow	94 E7	Warmley	69 H3
Lambridge	100 B2	Pucklechurch	56 C4	Warmley Hill	69 F2
Lansdown	99 H3	Purn	117 F7	Warmley Tower	69 H4
Larkhall	100 A2	Puxton	108 A1	Watley's End	42 B1
Latteridge	32 C1	Pye Corner	41 J5	Way Wick	107 F4
Lawrence Weston	37 H6	Queen Charlton	95 G2	Welton	126 B3
Leigh Woods	64 E4	Radstock	127 F4	Westbury on Trym	51 G3
Limpley Stoke	112 D7	Ram Hill	42 E4	Westbury Park	2 C1
Little Ashley	114 C4	Rangeworthy	25 H5	West End	70 C1
Little Chalfield	115 K2	Redcliff Bay	46 A6	West End	72 E4
Little Sodbury	35 K4	Redland	2 E4	Westerleigh	43 H4
Little Sodbury End	35 H3	Ridgeway	5 L4	Westerleigh Hill	44 A5
Little Stoke	40 C1	The Rocks	34 C2	Westfield	126 D4
Locking	118 B2	Rode	129 F7	West Hewish	85 H7
Lockleaze	53 G2	Rode Hill	129 F6	West Hill	46 E4
Locksbrook	99 F6	Rolstone	107 G3	Weston	98 D3
Lodway	49 H4	Rowberrow	121 J5	Weston-in-Gordano	60 E1
Long Ashton	76 C2	Rudgeway	22 E5	Weston Park	14 A1
Longfield	125 F6	Rush Hill	110 E3	Weston Park	99 F3
Longwell Green	68 E7	St Anne's Park	9 J5	Weston-Super-Mare	16 A2
Lower Canada	118 B4	St George	68 A3	West Town	73 K6
Lower Failand	63 G3	St Georges	106 C2	West Wick	106 D4
Lower Hazel	22 D3	Saltford	96 E2	Westwood	122 E3
Lower Knowle	11 J5	Sandford	120 E3	Whitchurch	79 H7
Lower Morton	19 J1	Sandford Batch	120 C4	Whitehall	5 G8
Lower Studley	125 G7	Sea Mills	50 E4	Whiteshill	41 H5
Lower Swainswick	100 B1	Severn Beach	27 J1	Whiteway	110 D1
Lower Weston	99 F5	Sharpstone	122 B2	Whitfield	20 E2
Lower Wraxall	103 F7	Sheepway	48 C4	Wick St Lawrence	84 C5
Lulsgate Bottom	90 A4	Shipham	121 J7	Widbrook	124 A3
Lyde Green	56 A1	Shirehampton	50 A2	Widcombe	112 B1
Lye Green	123 G2	Shortwood	55 K5	Willsbridge	81 H1
Maiden Head	92 C3	Sidcot	120 E7	Windmill Hill	11 K1
Mangotsfield	55 F4	Siston	56 B6	Winford	91 G5
Marsh Common	28 B3	Siston Common	69 G1	Wingfield	123 K7
May's Green	107 J2	Sneyd Park	51 F5	Winscombe	120 C7
Mayshill	33 F6	Somerdale	80 E4	Winsley	113 J6
Mead Riding	35 F4	Soundwell	54 E6	Winterbourne	41 J2
Middle Bridge	47 K6	Southdown	110 D2	Winterbourne Down	42 A4
Middletown	60 C6	Southmead	38 D7	Winterhead	121 F6
Midford	112 A7	Southstoke	111 J6	Withywood	77 H7
Milbury Heath	20 C4	South Twerton	99 F7	Woodhill	47 G2
Milton	105 J4	Southwick	130 A4	Woodhouse Down	22 C7
Monkton Combe	112 C4	South Wraxall	103 F6	Woodspring Priory	83 J5
Monkton Farleigh	102 A5	Speedwell	54 A7	Woollard	95 F7
Montpelier	3 J5	Staple Hill	54 E5	Woolley	115 F6
Moorend	41 K6	Stapleton	5 G1	Woolley Green	115 G5
Morton	19 J3	Star	121 G5	Woolvers Hill	107 F7
Mount Hill	68 E4	Staverton	115 K7	Woolverton	128 C7
Nailsea	73 J2	Stockwood	79 H5	Wooscombe Bottom	95 G4
Nailwell	110 A7	Stockwood Vale	80 B5	Worle	105 K4
Netham	8 A4	Stoke Bishop	51 F3	Worlebury	104 E3
Newbridge	98 D4	Stoke Gifford	40 C3	Wraxall	62 C6
New Cheltenham	69 F1	Stonebridge	119 G2	Writhlington	127 K3
Newton St Loe	98 A6	Stone-edge Batch	61 G6	Yanley	76 E3
Nibley	33 H6	Stone Hill	68 E6	Yarberry	119 G5
Norleaze	131 G7	Stub Riding	34 E4	Yarnbrook	131 J4
North Bradley	130 E4	Studley Green	124 C7	Yate	34 A6
North Common	69 K4	Talbot's End	21 K3	Yate Rocks	34 C1
North Corner	32 A6	Tellisford	128 E3	Yatton	87 F4
North End	86 D1	Thicket Mead	126 A2		
North Weston	47 H6	Thornbury	19 G4		
North Wick	93 F4	Tickenham	60 D6		

USING THE STREET INDEX

Street names are listed alphabetically. Each street name is followed by its postal town or area locality, the Postcode District, the page number, and the reference to the square in which the name is found.

Example: **Abbeygate St** *CBATH/BATHN* BA1 .... 15 G7 ▯

Some entries are followed by a number in a blue box. This number indicates the location of the street within the referenced grid square. The full street name is listed at the side of the map page.

GENERAL ABBREVIATIONS

ACC	ACCESS	CO	COUNTY	EMBY	EMBASSY	GV	GROVE	LNDG	LANDING
ALY	ALLEY	COLL	COLLEGE	ESP	ESPLANADE	HGR	HIGHER	LTL	LITTLE
AP	APPROACH	COM	COMMON	EST	ESTATE	HL	HILL	LWR	LOWER
AR	ARCADE	COMM	COMMISSION	EX	EXCHANGE	HLS	HILLS	MAG	MAGISTRATE
ASS	ASSOCIATION	CON	CONVENT	EXPY	EXPRESSWAY	HO	HOUSE	MAN	MANSIONS
AV	AVENUE	COT	COTTAGE	EXT	EXTENSION	HOL	HOLLOW	MD	MEAD
BCH	BEACH	COTS	COTTAGES	F/O	FLYOVER	HOSP	HOSPITAL	MDW	MEADOWS
BLDS	BUILDINGS	CP	CAPE	FC	FOOTBALL CLUB	HRB	HARBOUR	MEM	MEMORIAL
BND	BEND	CPS	COPSE	FK	FORK	HTH	HEATH	MKT	MARKET
BNK	BANK	CR	CREEK	FLD	FIELD	HTS	HEIGHTS	MKTS	MARKETS
BR	BRIDGE	CREM	CREMATORIUM	FLDS	FIELDS	HVN	HAVEN	ML	MALL
BRK	BROOK	CRS	CRESCENT	FLS	FALLS	HWY	HIGHWAY	ML	MILL
BTM	BOTTOM	CSWY	CAUSEWAY	FLS	FLATS	IMP	IMPERIAL	MNR	MANOR
BUS	BUSINESS	CT	COURT	FM	FARM	IN	INLET	MS	MEWS
BVD	BOULEVARD	CTRL	CENTRAL	FT	FORT	IND EST	INDUSTRIAL ESTATE	MSN	MISSION
BY	BYPASS	CTS	COURTS	FWY	FREEWAY	INF	INFIRMARY	MT	MOUNT
CATH	CATHEDRAL	CTYD	COURTYARD	FY	FERRY	INFO	INFORMATION	MTN	MOUNTAIN
CEM	CEMETERY	CUTT	CUTTINGS	GA	GATE	INT	INTERCHANGE	MTS	MOUNTAINS
CEN	CENTRE	CV	COVE	GAL	GALLERY	IS	ISLAND	MUS	MUSEUM
CFT	CROFT	CYN	CANYON	GDN	GARDEN	JCT	JUNCTION	MWY	MOTORWAY
CH	CHURCH	DEPT	DEPARTMENT	GDNS	GARDENS	JTY	JETTY	N	NORTH
CHA	CHASE	DL	DALE	GLD	GLADE	KG	KING	NE	NORTH EAST
CHYD	CHURCHYARD	DM	DAM	GLN	GLEN	KNL	KNOLL	NW	NORTH WEST
CIR	CIRCLE	DR	DRIVE	GN	GREEN	L	LAKE	O/P	OVERPASS
CIRC	CIRCUS	DRO	DROVE	GND	GROUND	LA	LANE	OFF	OFFICE
CL	CLOSE	DRY	DRIVEWAY	GRA	GRANGE	LDG	LODGE	ORCH	ORCHARD
CLFS	CLIFFS	DWGS	DWELLINGS	GRG	GARAGE	LGT	LIGHT	OV	OVAL
CMP	CAMP	E	EAST	GT	GREAT	LK	LOCK	PAL	PALACE
CNR	CORNER	EMB	EMBANKMENT	GTWY	GATEWAY	LKS	LAKES	PAS	PASSAGE

PAV PAVILION
PDE PARADE
PH PUBLIC HOUSE
PK PARK
PKWY PARKWAY
PL PLACE
PLN PLAIN
PLNS PLAINS
PLZ PLAZA
POL POLICE STATION
PR PRINCE
PREC PRECINCT
PREP PREPARATORY
PRIM PRIMARY
PROM PROMENADE
PRS PRINCESS
PRT PORT
PT POINT
PTH PATH
PZ PIAZZA
QD QUADRANT
QU QUEEN
QY QUAY
R RIVER
RBT ROUNDABOUT
RD ROAD
RDG RIDGE
REP REPUBLIC
RES RESERVOIR
RFC RUGBY FOOTBALL CLUB
RI RISE
RP RAMP
RW ROW
S SOUTH
SCH SCHOOL
SE SOUTH EAST
SER SERVICE AREA
SH SHORE
SHOP SHOPPING
SKWY SKYWAY
SMT SUMMIT
SOC SOCIETY
SP SPUR
SPR SPRING
SQ SQUARE
ST STREET
STN STATION
STR STREAM
STRD STRAND
SW SOUTH WEST
TDG TRADING
TER TERRACE
THWY THROUGHWAY
TNL TUNNEL
TOLL TOLLWAY
TPK TURNPIKE
TR TRACK
TRL TRAIL
TWR TOWER
U/P UNDERPASS
UNI UNIVERSITY
UPR UPPER
V VALE
VA VALLEY
VIAD VIADUCT
VIL VILLA
VIS VISTA
VLG VILLAGE
VLS VILLAS
VW VIEW
W WEST
WD WOOD
WHF WHARF
WK WALK
WKS WALKS
WLS WELLS
WY WAY
YD YARD
YHA YOUTH HOSTEL

POSTCODE TOWNS AND AREA ABBREVIATIONS

ALMDB Almondsbury
AVONM Avonmouth
AXBR Axbridge
BATHSE Bath south & east
BLAG/CWMG/WR Blagdon/Chew Magna/Wrington
BMSTR Bedminster
BMSTRD/HC/WWD BedminsterDown/Hartcliffe/Withywood
BNWL Banwell
BOAV Bradford-on-Avon
BOS Burnham-on-Sea
BRSG/KWL/STAPK Brislington/Knowle/St Anne's Park
BRSTK/PCHW Bradley Stoke/Patchway
CBATH/BATHN Central Bath/Bath north
CBRIS/FH Central Bristol/Floating Harbour
CBRISNE Central Bristol north & east
CFTN/FAIL Clifton/Failand
CHPMW/MSHF Chippenham west/Marshfield
CLVDN Clevedon
COR/BOX Corsham/Box
EVILLE/WHL Eastville/Whitehall
FRCTL/WBN Frampton Cotterell/Winterbourne
HGRV/WHIT Hengrove/Whitchurch
HNBRY/STHM Henbury/Southmead
HNLZ/SM/SNYPK/WT Henleaze/Sea Mills/Sneyd Park/Westbury-on-Trym
HORF/LLZ Horfield/Lockleaze
KEYN Keynsham
KGWD/HNM Kingswood/Hanham
LGASH Long Ashton
MANG/FISH Mangotsfield/Fishponds
MELK Melksham
MTN/WRL Milton/Worle
NAIL Nailsea
OLD/WMLY/WICK Oldland/Warmley/Wick
OMX/HUT/LCK Oldmixon/Hutton/Locking
PLTN/PENS Paulton/Pensford
PTSHD/EG Portishead/Easton-in-Gordano
RDLND/MONT Redland/Montpelier
RDSTK/MIDN Radstock/Midsomer Norton
THNB/SVB Thornbury/Severn Beach
TRWBR Trowbridge
WBRY Westbury
WNSC Winscombe
WSM Weston-Super -Mare
WUE Wotton-under-Edge
YATE/CS Yate/Chipping Sodbury
YTN/CONG Yatton/Congresbury

Index - streets

A

Abbey Ct BRSG/KWL/STAPK BS4 9 M6
Abbeydale FRCTL/WBN BS36 41 K2
Abbeygate St
CBATH/BATHN BA1 15 G7 1
Abbey Gn CBATH/BATHN BA1 15 G7 2
Abbey La RDSTK/MIDN BA3 122 A3
THNB/SVB BS35 19 J7
Abbey Pk KEYN BS31 81 F5
Abbey Rd
HNLZ/SM/SNYPK/WT BS9 51 H3
Abbey St CBATH/BATHN BA1 15 G6 1
Abbey Vw BATHSE BA2 15 K8
Abbey View Gdns BATHSE BA2 15 J8
Abbeywood Dr
HNLZ/SM/SNYPK/WT BS9 50 E4 1
Abbots Av KGWD/HNM BS15 68 C6
Abbotsbury Rd NAIL BS48 73 H2 1
Abbots Cl HGRV/WHIT BS14 93 K1
MTN/WRL BS22 106 B2
Abbotsford Rd RDLND/MONT BS6 2 D8
Abbots Horn NAIL BS48 73 H1 1
Abbots Leigh Rd CFTN/FAIL BS8 64 D3
Abbots Rd KGWD/HNM BS15 80 C1
Abbots Wy
HNLZ/SM/SNYPK/WT BS9 52 B3
Abbotswood
KGWD/HNM BS15 68 D3 1
YATE/CS BS37 44 A1 1
Abbott Rd THNB/SVB BS35 27 H2
Aberdeen Rd RDLND/MONT BS6 2 D9
Abingdon Gdns BATHSE BA2 111 G5
Abingdon Rd MANG/FISH BS16 54 A6
Ableton La HNBRY/STHM BS10 27 G7
THNB/SVB BS35 27 H1
Ableton Wk
HNLZ/SM/SNYPK/WT BS9 50 E4 2
Abraham Cl EVILLE/WHL BS5 4 C9
Abson Rd MANG/FISH BS16 56 D4
Acacia Av MANG/FISH BS16 54 C5
WSM BS23 17 L2
Acacia Cl MANG/FISH BS16 54 C6 1
Acacia Ct KEYN BS31 80 C7 1
Acacia Crs TRWBR BA14 124 C6
Acacia Gv BATHSE BA2 111 F2
Acacia Rd MANG/FISH BS16 54 D6
RDSTK/MIDN BA3 127 F4
Aconite Cl MTN/WRL BS22 84 B7
Acorn Gv
BMSTRD/HC/WWD BS13 77 G5
Acraman's Rd BMSTR BS3 6 F8
Acresbush Cl
BMSTRD/HC/WWD BS13 77 J6
Acton Rd MANG/FISH BS16 54 A6 1
Adams Hay
BRSG/KWL/STAPK BS4 13 G5
Adastral Rd
OMX/HUT/LCK BS24 118 E2
Adcroft Dr TRWBR BA14 125 F5
Adcroft St TRWBR BA14 125 F5
Adderly Ga MANG/FISH BS16 55 H2
Addicott Rd WSM BS23 16 F6
Addiscombe Rd
HGRV/WHIT BS14 79 F6
WSM BS23 116 D2
Addison Rd BMSTR BS3 11 J2
Adelaide Pl EVILLE/WHL BS5 4 D9
MANG/FISH BS16 5 M1
Agate St BMSTR BS3 10 D1
Aiken St EVILLE/WHL BS5 8 D4
Aintree Av TRWBR BA14 131 F3
Aintree Dr MANG/FISH BS16 42 A7
Air Balloon Rd EVILLE/WHL BS5 68 A3
Airport Rd HGRV/WHIT BS14 11 L9
Aisecome Wy WSM BS23 105 H7
Akeman Wy AVONM BS11 49 J1
Alard Rd BRSG/KWL/STAPK BS4 11 L9
Albany Cl TRWBR BA14 125 H4
Albany Ga BRSTK/PCHW BS34 40 D3
Albany Rd BATHSE BA2 98 E6
RDLND/MONT BS6 3 L7
Albany St KGWD/HNM BS15 68 C2
Albany Wy
OLD/WMLY/WICK BS30 69 J5
Albermarle Rw CFTN/FAIL BS8 65 H4 1
Albert Av WSM BS23 16 E6
Albert Crs CBRISNE BS2 8 B7
Albert Gv EVILLE/WHL BS5 5 L9
Alberton Rd MANG/FISH BS16 53 K3
Albert Pde EVILLE/WHL BS5 8 F1
Albert Pk RDLND/MONT BS6 3 L7
Albert Park Pl RDLND/MONT BS6 3 K8
Albert Pl
HNLZ/SM/SNYPK/WT BS9 51 J2
Albert Qd WSM BS23 16 F1
Albert Rd CBRISNE BS2 8 C8
CLVDN BS21 58 E7 1
KEYN BS31 80 E6
KGWD/HNM BS15 68 D5
MANG/FISH BS16 54 E5
PTSHD/EG BS20 47 H4
THNB/SVB BS35 27 H1
TRWBR BA14 125 H3
WSM BS23 16 E6
Albert St EVILLE/WHL BS5 8 F2 1
Albert Ter MANG/FISH BS16 5 M3
Albion Cl MANG/FISH BS16 55 F4
Albion Dr TRWBR BA14 124 D6 1
Albion Rd EVILLE/WHL BS5 4 D7
Albion St EVILLE/WHL BS5 8 F1
Alcove Rd MANG/FISH BS16 5 K4
Aldeburgh Pl TRWBR BA14 130 B1
Alder Cl TRWBR BA14 130 D2
Aldercombe Rd
HNLZ/SM/SNYPK/WT BS9 50 E1
Alderdown Cl AVONM BS11 50 C1 1
Alder Dr EVILLE/WHL BS5 5 K8
Alderley Rd BATHSE BA2 110 D1
Aldermoor Wy
OLD/WMLY/WICK BS30 68 E6
Aldernay Av
BRSG/KWL/STAPK BS4 9 L9
Alder Ter RDSTK/MIDN BA3 127 F3
Alderton Rd HORF/LLZ BS7 52 C1
Alderton Wy TRWBR BA14 131 F2
Alder Wy BATHSE BA2 111 G5
Aldwick Av
BMSTRD/HC/WWD BS13 93 F1
Alec Ricketts Cl BATHSE BA2 98 C7 1
Alexander Wy
YTN/CONG BS49 86 E5 1
Alexandra Cl
MANG/FISH BS16 54 D5 1
Alexandra Gdns
MANG/FISH BS16 54 D5
Alexandra Pde WSM BS23 16 E3 1
Alexandra Pk MANG/FISH BS16 5 M2
RDLND/MONT BS6 2 E6
Alexandra Pl MANG/FISH BS16 54 D5
Alexandra Rd BATHSE BA2 15 H9
BMSTRD/HC/WWD BS13 77 H4
CFTN/FAIL BS8 2 C9
CLVDN BS21 58 E6
FRCTL/WBN BS36 42 E1
HNBRY/STHM BS10 52 A1 1
KGWD/HNM BS15 68 D5 1
Alexandra Wy THNB/SVB BS35 19 G2
Alford Rd BRSG/KWL/STAPK BS4 12 F3
Alfred Ct WSM BS23 16 E3 2
Alfred Hl CBRISNE BS2 7 G1
Alfred Pde CBRISNE BS2 7 G1
Alfred Pl CBRISNE BS2 2 F9
Alfred Rd BMSTR BS3 11 H1
RDLND/MONT BS6 2 B2
Alfred St CBATH/BATHN BA1 14 F4
CBRISNE BS2 8 A4
EVILLE/WHL BS5 8 F1
WSM BS23 16 F3
Algiers St BMSTR BS3 11 H1
Alison Gdns NAIL BS48 74 A4
Allanmead Rd HGRV/WHIT BS14 12 D8
Allen Rd TRWBR BA14 124 D7
Allens La WNSC BS25 121 J6
Allerton Crs HGRV/WHIT BS14 79 F7
Allerton Gdns HGRV/WHIT BS14 79 F6
Allerton Rd HGRV/WHIT BS14 78 E7
Allfoxton Rd HORF/LLZ BS7 4 B4
All Hallows Rd EVILLE/WHL BS5 4 D9
Allington Dr
OLD/WMLY/WICK BS30 69 F6
Allington Gdns NAIL BS48 73 G3
Allington Rd BMSTR BS3 6 E7
Allison Av BRSG/KWL/STAPK BS4 9 K9
Allison Rd BRSG/KWL/STAPK BS4 13 H1
All Saints' La CBRIS/FH BS1 7 H4 1
CLVDN BS21 59 H6
All Saints Rd CBATH/BATHN BA1 14 E2
CFTN/FAIL BS8 2 B9
WSM BS23 104 D4
All Saints' St CBRIS/FH BS1 7 H3
Alma Cl KGWD/HNM BS15 68 E2
Alma Rd CFTN/FAIL BS8 2 B9
KGWD/HNM BS15 68 E1
Alma Road Av CFTN/FAIL BS8 2 C9
Alma St CFTN/FAIL BS8 2 C8
TRWBR BA14 125 G6
WSM BS23 16 E3 3
Alma Vale Rd CFTN/FAIL BS8 2 B9
Almeda Rd EVILLE/WHL BS5 68 A4
Almond Cl MTN/WRL BS22 106 B4 1
Almond Gv TRWBR BA14 130 D2
Almond Wy MANG/FISH BS16 55 F4
Almorah Rd BMSTR BS3 11 J2
Alpha Rd BMSTR BS3 7 G8
Alpine Cl PLTN/PENS BS39 126 A1
Alpine Gdns
CBATH/BATHN BA1 15 G2 1
Alpine Rd EVILLE/WHL BS5 4 E8
PLTN/PENS BS39 126 A1
Alsop Rd KGWD/HNM BS15 68 D2
Alton Rd HORF/LLZ BS7 52 D3
Altringham Rd EVILLE/WHL BS5 5 H8
Alverstoke HGRV/WHIT BS14 78 D4
Alveston Hl THNB/SVB BS35 19 F7
Alveston Rd ALMDB BS32 22 B3
Alveston Wk
HNLZ/SM/SNYPK/WT BS9 50 D2
Alwins Ct
OLD/WMLY/WICK BS30 69 F6 1
Amberey Rd WSM BS23 17 G7 1
Amberlands Cl NAIL BS48 74 A4
Amberley Cl KEYN BS31 80 E7
MANG/FISH BS16 54 D2
Amberley Rd BRSTK/PCHW BS34 30 A7
MANG/FISH BS16 54 D2
Amble Cl KGWD/HNM BS15 69 F3
Ambleside Av
HNBRY/STHM BS10 38 E7
Ambleside Rd BATHSE BA2 110 E3
Ambra V CFTN/FAIL BS8 6 A5
Ambra V East CFTN/FAIL BS8 6 B5
Ambra V South CFTN/FAIL BS8 6 A5 1
Ambra V West CFTN/FAIL BS8 6 A5
Ambrose Rd CFTN/FAIL BS8 6 B5
Ambury BATHSE BA2 14 F8
Amercombe Wk
1HGRV/WHIT BS14 13 G9
Amery La CBATH/BATHN BA1 15 G7 3
Ames La RDSTK/MIDN BA3 127 J7
Amouracre TRWBR BA14 125 H6
Ancaster Cl TRWBR BA14 124 C5
Anchor Rd CBATH/BATHN BA1 98 E3
CBRIS/FH BS1 6 D5
KGWD/HNM BS15 69 G1
Anchor Wy PTSHD/EG BS20 49 K5
Andereach Cl HGRV/WHIT BS14 12 C8
Andover Rd
BRSG/KWL/STAPK BS4 11 M4
Andruss Dr LGASH BS41 92 A2
Angels Gnd BRSG/KWL/STAPK BS4 9 L4
Angers Rd BRSG/KWL/STAPK BS4 7 M9
Anglesea Pl CFTN/FAIL BS8 2 B6
Annandale Av MTN/WRL BS22 105 K4
Anson Cl KEYN BS31 96 E2
Anson Rd MTN/WRL BS22 105 J1
OMX/HUT/LCK BS24 106 C7
Anstey's Rd KGWD/HNM BS15 68 B5
Anstey St EVILLE/WHL BS5 4 D7
Anthea Rd EVILLE/WHL BS5 5 K6
Antona Ct AVONM BS11 49 K2 1
Antona Dr AVONM BS11 49 K2 2
Antrim Rd
HNLZ/SM/SNYPK/WT BS9 51 K3
Anvil Rd YTN/CONG BS49 87 J3 1
Anvil St CBRISNE BS2 7 M4
Apperley Cl YATE/CS BS37 34 A7
Appleby Wk
BRSG/KWL/STAPK BS4 11 G9
Appledore Cl HGRV/WHIT BS14 12 C8
Applegate HNBRY/STHM BS10 38 E5
Appletree Ct MTN/WRL BS22 106 C3
Apple Tree Dr WNSC BS25 120 D6 1
Appsley Cl MTN/WRL BS22 105 H4 1
Apseleys Md ALMDB BS32 30 B5
Apsley Rd CBATH/BATHN BA1 98 D5
CFTN/FAIL BS8 2 A7
Apsley St EVILLE/WHL BS5 4 E5
Arbutus Dr
HNLZ/SM/SNYPK/WT BS9 50 E2
Archer Ct OLD/WMLY/WICK BS30 69 F7
Archer Wk HGRV/WHIT BS14 79 J5
Archfield Rd RDLND/MONT BS6 2 F7
Archway St BATHSE BA2 15 J8
Arden Cl ALMDB BS32 40 D2
MTN/WRL BS22 106 A2
Ardenton Wk
HNBRY/STHM BS10 38 D5 1
Ardern Cl
HNLZ/SM/SNYPK/WT BS9 50 D1
Argus Rd BMSTR BS3 10 E2
Argyle Av EVILLE/WHL BS5 4 E5
WSM BS23 17 G9
Argyle Dr YATE/CS BS37 34 B3
Argyle Pl CFTN/FAIL BS8 6 B5
Argyle Rd CBRISNE BS2 3 K9
CLVDN BS21 59 F5
MANG/FISH BS16 54 B7
Argyle St BATHSE BA2 15 H6 1
BMSTR BS3 6 E9
EVILLE/WHL BS5 4 E5
Arley Cottages RDLND/MONT BS6 3 H7
Arley Hl RDLND/MONT BS6 3 H7
Arley Pk RDLND/MONT BS6 3 H7
Arley Ter EVILLE/WHL BS5 5 J8
Arlingham Wy
BRSTK/PCHW BS34 29 H7
Arlington Rd
BRSG/KWL/STAPK BS4 9 H6
Arlington Vls CFTN/FAIL BS8 6 B2
Armada Pl CBRIS/FH BS1 3 J9
Armidale Av RDLND/MONT BS6 3 J7 1
Armoury Sq EVILLE/WHL BS5 4 B9
Armstrong Cl THNB/SVB BS35 19 J6 1
Armstrong Dr
OLD/WMLY/WICK BS30 69 H5 1
Armstrong Wy YATE/CS BS37 33 K4
Arnall Dr HNBRY/STHM BS10 38 C7
Arneside Rd HNBRY/STHM BS10 39 F7
Arnold Rd TRWBR BA14 130 A4
Arnold's Wy YTN/CONG BS49 86 C3
Arnor Cl MTN/WRL BS22 106 B1
Arno's St BRSG/KWL/STAPK BS4 12 B1
Arras Cl TRWBR BA14 130 E1 1
Arrowfield Cl HGRV/WHIT BS14 93 K2
Artemesia Av
MTN/WRL BS22 105 K5 1
Arthur Skemp Cl EVILLE/WHL BS5 8 C3
Arthur St CBRISNE BS2 8 B6
EVILLE/WHL BS5 8 F1
Arthurswood Rd
BMSTRD/HC/WWD BS13 77 J7
Arundel Cl
BMSTRD/HC/WWD BS13 77 K7
Arundell Rd WSM BS23 16 F1
Arundel Rd CBATH/BATHN BA1 15 H1
HORF/LLZ BS7 3 H3
Ascot Cl MANG/FISH BS16 42 A7
Ascot Rd HNBRY/STHM BS10 39 G6
Ashbourne Cl
OLD/WMLY/WICK BS30 69 J4 1
Ashburton Rd
HNBRY/STHM BS10 39 F7
Ashbury Dr MTN/WRL BS22 105 G4 1
Ash Cl BRSTK/PCHW BS34 40 C1
WNSC BS25 120 D5
YATE/CS BS37 34 A4
Ashcombe Cl
OLD/WMLY/WICK BS30 69 J4 2
Ashcombe Crs
OLD/WMLY/WICK BS30 69 K4 1
Ashcombe Gdns WSM BS23 17 J1
Ashcombe Park Rd WSM BS23 105 F4
Ashcombe Rd WSM BS23 17 H3
Ashcott HGRV/WHIT BS14 78 D5
Ashcroft Av KEYN BS31 80 D6
Ashcroft Rd
HNLZ/SM/SNYPK/WT BS9 50 E2
Ashdene Av EVILLE/WHL BS5 5 H4
Ashdene Rd WSM BS23 17 K1
Ashdown Rd PTSHD/EG BS20 46 E3
Ash Dr TRWBR BA14 130 E4
Asher La CBRISNE BS2 7 L2
Ashfield Pl RDLND/MONT BS6 3 L7
Ashfield Rd BMSTR BS3 10 C1
Ashford Dr
OMX/HUT/LCK BS24 117 F5 1
Ashford Rd BATHSE BA2 111 G1
BRSTK/PCHW BS34 39 K1
Ashgrove THNB/SVB BS35 19 H4
Ash Gv BATHSE BA2 111 F1
CLVDN BS21 59 G6
MANG/FISH BS16 54 C6
WSM BS23 116 D4
Ashgrove Av CFTN/FAIL BS8 64 D3
HORF/LLZ BS7 3 M1
Ashgrove Rd BMSTR BS3 10 C2
HORF/LLZ BS7 3 M1
Ash Hayes Dr NAIL BS48 73 J2
Ash Hayes Rd NAIL BS48 73 J2
Ashland Rd
BMSTRD/HC/WWD BS13 77 J7
Ash La ALMDB BS32 29 G4
Ashleigh Crs YTN/CONG BS49 86 E4
Ashleigh Gv TRWBR BA14 124 E7 1
Ashleigh Rd WSM BS23 17 J1
YTN/CONG BS49 86 E4
Ashley KGWD/HNM BS15 69 F2
Ashley Av CBATH/BATHN BA1 99 F5
Ashley Cl BOAV BA15 114 C5
HORF/LLZ BS7 3 L1
Ashley Court Rd
RDLND/MONT BS6 3 L5
Ashley Down Rd HORF/LLZ BS7 3 L1
Ashley Grove Rd CBRISNE BS2 3 M6 1
CBRISNE BS2 4 A7 1
Ashley Hl RDLND/MONT BS6 3 L5
Ashley La BOAV BA15 114 A6
Ashley Pde CBRISNE BS2 3 M6
Ashley Pk RDLND/MONT BS6 3 L4
Ashley Rd BOAV BA15 114 C4
CBATH/BATHN BA1 101 H2
CLVDN BS21 70 D2
RDLND/MONT BS6 3 K8
Ashley St CBRISNE BS2 4 A7
Ashman Cl EVILLE/WHL BS5 8 B1
Ashmans Yd CBATH/BATHN BA1 98 E6
Ashmead TRWBR BA14 130 E1
Ashmead Ct TRWBR BA14 125 F7 1
Ashmead Rd KEYN BS31 81 H6
Ashmead Wy CBRIS/FH BS1 65 H5 1
Ash Ridge Rd ALMDB BS32 30 A4
Ash Rd BNWL BS29 119 F2
HORF/LLZ BS7 52 C4
Ashton Av CBRIS/FH BS1 6 A7
Ashton Cl CLVDN BS21 70 D2
Ashton Crs NAIL BS48 73 H2
Ashton Dr BMSTR BS3 77 G2
Ashton Gate Rd BMSTR BS3 6 B8
Ashton Gate Ter BMSTR BS3 6 B8
Ashton Hl BATHSE BA2 97 H5
Ashton Ri TRWBR BA14 125 J4
Ashton Rd BMSTR BS3 65 H7
LGASH BS41 64 E7
TRWBR BA14 125 J4
Ashton St TRWBR BA14 125 G6 1
Ashton Vale Rd BMSTR BS3 65 G7
Ashton Wy KEYN BS31 80 E5
Ash Tree Ct RDSTK/MIDN BA3 127 F4
Ashvale Cl NAIL BS48 74 A1
Ashville Rd BMSTR BS3 6 B9
Ash Wk HNBRY/STHM BS10 38 E5
Ashwell Cl HGRV/WHIT BS14 79 J5
Ashwicke HGRV/WHIT BS14 78 D5
Aspen Park Rd MTN/WRL BS22 105 K5
Aspley Cl CBATH/BATHN BA1 98 E5 1
Assembly Rooms La
CBRIS/FH BS1 7 G5 1
Astry Cl AVONM BS11 37 H7
Atchley St EVILLE/WHL BS5 8 C3 1
Atherston
OLD/WMLY/WICK BS30 69 J5
Athlone Wk
BRSG/KWL/STAPK BS4 11 J6
Atholl Cl MTN/WRL BS22 106 A2 1
Atkins Cl HGRV/WHIT BS14 79 J5
Atlantic Rd AVONM BS11 49 J1
WSM BS23 104 B4
Atlantic Rd South WSM BS23 104 B4
Atlas Cl EVILLE/WHL BS5 54 A7
Atlas St CBRISNE BS2 8 C6
Atwell Dr ALMDB BS32 30 A6
Atwood Dr AVONM BS11 37 J6
Aubrey Rd BMSTR BS3 10 C2
Auburn Av
OLD/WMLY/WICK BS30 69 H7
Auburn Rd RDLND/MONT BS6 2 D6
Auckland Cl WSM BS23 116 E3 1
Audley Av CBATH/BATHN BA1 99 F5
Audley Cl CBATH/BATHN BA1 14 A4
Audley Gv CBATH/BATHN BA1 99 F5
Audley Park Rd
CBATH/BATHN BA1 14 B4 1

Audrey Wk
HNLZ/SM/SNYPK/WT BS9..... 52 B3
Augustine's CI *PTSHD/EG* BS20 ... 46 C5
Austen Dr *MTN/WRL* BS22 .. 106 C1 🖾
Austen Gv *HORF/LLZ* BS7 .... 52 E1 🖾
Autumn Ms
OMX/HUT/LCK BS24 .... 106 B5
Avalon CI *YTN/CONG* BS49 ..... 86 D3 🖾
Avalon Rd *EVILLE/WHL* BS5 ..... 68 B4
Avebury Rd *BMSRG* BS3............ 77 G1
Avening CI *NAIL* BS48 .... 73 K3
Avening Rd *KGWD/HNM* BS15 ... 68 A2
Avenue Rd *TRWBR* BA14 .... 124 D6
The Avenue *BATHSE* BA2 .... 100 D7
BATHSE BA2 .... 112 A4
BRSTK/PCHW BS34 .... 30 A5
BRSTK/PCHW BS34 .... 40 B2
CLVDN BS21 .... 59 F5
EVILLE/WHL BS5 .... 9 L1
HNLZ/SM/SNYPK/WT BS9..... 51 F7
HORF/LLZ BS7 .... 3 K3
KEYN BS31 .... 80 E4
MANG/FISH BS16 .... 40 D7
NAIL BS48 .... 74 A4
YATE/CS BS37 .... 34 A6
YTN/CONG BS49 .... 86 E4
Averay Rd *MANG/FISH* BS16 ...... 4 F2
Avon CI *BOAV* BA15 .... 124 A1
.... 9 M5
KEYN BS31 .... 81 F5
WSM BS23............................ 116 E4
Avon Crs *CBRIS/FH* BS1 .... 6 A7
Avondale Buildings
CBATH/BATHN BA1 .... 100 A2
Avondale PI
CBATH/BATHN BA1 .... 100 E1 🖾
Avondale Rd
CBATH/BATHN BA1 .... 98 E5
Avondown CI
HNBRY/STHM BS10 .... 39 G6 🖾
Avonfield Av *BOAV* BA15 .... 124 A1
Avon Gv
HNLZ/SM/SNYPK/WT BS9..... 51 F7
Avonlea *KGWD/HNM* BS15 ...... 68 C5 🖾
Avonleaze
HNLZ/SM/SNYPK/WT BS9..... 50 D4
Avonleigh Rd *BMSTR* BS3 .... 10 C3
Avon Mill La *KEYN* BS31 .... 81 F5
Avonmouth Rd *AVONM* BS11 ... 36 C7
Avonmouth Wy *AVONM* BS11 ... 36 D7
Avonmouth Wy West
AVONM BS11 .... 36 C6
Avon Pk *CBATH/BATHN* BA1 ..... 98 D5
EVILLE/WHL BS5 .... 9 G3
Avon Rd
BMSTRD/HC/WWD BS13 ...... 77 J5 🖾
KEYN BS31 .... 81 F6
PTSHD/EG BS20 .... 49 J4
Avonside Rd *CBRISNE* BS2 .... 8 F5
Avonside Wy
BRSG/KWL/STAPK BS4 .... 9 L4 🖾
Avon St *BATHSE* BA2 .... 14 F8
CBATH/BATHN BA1 .... 14 F7
CBRISNE BS2 .... 7 L4
Avon V *HNLZ/SM/SNYPK/WT* BS9.. 51 F5
TRWBR BA14 .... 125 F4
Avonvale Rd *EVILLE/WHL* BS5 .... 8 E3
Avon Vw *KGWD/HNM* BS15 ..... 68 B7
Avon Walkway
CBATH/BATHN BA1 .... 14 D6
OLD/WMLY/WICK BS30 .... 81 J5
PTSHD/EG BS20 .... 49 K5
Avon Wy *HNBRY/STHM* BS10 ... 52 B1
HNLZ/SM/SNYPK/WT BS9..... 50 E4
PTSHD/EG BS20 .... 47 G4
THNB/SVB BS35 .... 19 H5
TRWBR BA14 .... 125 F3
Avonwood CI *AVONM* BS11 ..... 50 A3
Awdelett CI *AVONM* BS11 .... 37 J7
Axbridge CI *NAIL* BS48 .... 73 K3 🖾
Axbridge Rd *BATHSE* BA2 ...... 111 K3
BRSG/KWL/STAPK BS4......... 11 M4
Axe & Cleaver La *TRWBR* BA14... 130 D4
TRWBR BA14 .... 131 F4 🖾
Axe CI *WSM* BS23 .... 17 J8
Aycote CI *MTN/WRL* BS22 ..... 105 H3 🖾
Aylesbury Crs *BMSTR* BS3 .... 10 D5
Aylesbury Rd *BMSTR* BS3 .... 10 D5
Aylmer Crs *HGRV/WHIT* BS14 ... 79 F5
Aylminton Wk *AVONM* BS11 ..... 37 H6 🖾
Ayr St *BATHSE* BA2 .... 14 A7
Azalea Dr *TRWBR* BA14 .... 124 C7
Azalea Rd *MTN/WRL* BS22 .... 84 D7 🖾

B

Backfields *CBRISNE* BS2 .... 7 J1
Backfields La *CBRISNE* BS2 .... 3 J9
Back La *CLVDN* BS21 .... 70 C6
KEYN BS31 .... 80 E5
MANG/FISH BS16 .... 56 E5
PTSHD/EG BS20 .... 49 J5
WNSC BS25 .... 121 K5
Back of Kingsdown Pde
RDLND/MONT BS6 .... 3 G9
Back Rd *BMSTR* BS3 .... 6 B8
Back Stoke La
HNLZ/SM/SNYPK/WT BS9..... 51 H3
Back St *TRWBR* BA14 .... 124 C5
WSM BS23............................ 16 E3
Backwell Bow *NAIL* BS48 .... 74 B2
Backwell Common *NAIL* BS48 ... 74 A4
Backwell Hill Rd *NAIL* BS48 ...... 74 D4
Backwell Wk
BMSTRD/HC/WWD BS13 ...... 77 H3 🖾
Badenham Gv *AVONM* BS11 ..... 50 B1
Baden Hill Rd *WUE* GL12 .... 24 D1
Baden Rd *EVILLE/WHL* BS5 .... 8 F3
KGWD/HNM BS15 .... 68 A5
Bader CI *YATE/CS* BS37 .... 34 A4
Badger Ri *PTSHD/EG* BS20 .... 49 F4
Badgers CI *ALMDB* BS32 .... 30 C4 🖾
Badger's La *ALMDB* BS32 .... 29 F5
Badgers Wk
BRSG/KWL/STAPK BS4 .... 13 H3 🖾
Badgeworth *YATE/CS* BS37 ...... 44 A2

Badmington Rd
MANG/FISH BS16 .... 55 F1
Badminton Gdns
CBATH/BATHN BA1 .... 99 F4
Badminton Rd *CBRISNE* BS2........ 3 M7
FRCTL/WBN BS36 .... 42 B5
MANG/FISH BS16 .... 54 E2
YATE/CS BS37 .... 33 J5
YATE/CS BS37 .... 35 H7
Baglyn Av *KGWD/HNM* BS15 ... 55 F6
Bagnell CI *HGRV/WHIT* BS14 ... 79 J6
Bagnell Rd *HGRV/WHIT* BS14 ... 79 J6
Bagstone Rd *WUE* GL12 .... 25 H1
Bagworth Dr
OLD/WMLY/WICK BS30 .... 69 F7 🖾
Bailbrook Gv
CBATH/BATHN BA1 .... 100 B1
Bailbrook La
CBATH/BATHN BA1 .... 100 D1
Baildon Rd *WSM* BS23 .... 116 C2
Bailey CI *MTN/WRL* BS22 .... 105 K5 🖾
Baileys Court Rd *ALMDB* BS32 ... 40 D2
Baileys Mead Rd
MANG/FISH BS16 .... 53 G4 🖾
Bainton CI *BOAV* BA15 .... 115 F6
Baker CI *CLVDN* BS21 .... 70 D3 🖾
Bakersfield
OLD/WMLY/WICK BS30 .... 69 G7 🖾
Bakers Gnd
BRSTK/PCHW BS34 .... 40 E3 🖾
Baker St *WSM* BS23 .... 16 F2
Balaclava Rd *BMSTR* BS16........ 5 M4
Baldwin St *CBRIS/FH* BS1 .... 7 H4
Balfour Rd *BMSTR* BS3 .... 10 C1
Balliance St *CBATH/BATHN* BA1 ... 14 F3
Ballast La *AVONM* BS11 .... 36 E6
Balls Barn La
OMX/HUT/LCK BS24 .... 107 H4
Balmain St *BRSG/KWL/STAPK* BS4.. 8 B9
Balmoral CI
BRSTK/PCHW BS34 .... 40 C4 🖾
Balmoral Ct *MANG/FISH* BS16 ... 55 G4 🖾
Balmoral Rd *KEYN* BS31 .... 80 E7
OLD/WMLY/WICK BS30 .... 81 F1
RDLND/MONT BS6 .... 3 L5
TRWBR BA14 .... 130 D2
Balmoral Wy *MTN/WRL* BS22 ... 105 J3 🖾
Baltic PI *PTSHD/EG* BS20 .... 49 K5 🖾
Bamfield *HGRV/WHIT* BS14 .... 78 E5
Bampton CI
BMSTRD/HC/WWD BS13 ...... 10 D9
Bampton Dr *MANG/FISH* BS16 ... 41 J7 🖾
Bancroft *BOAV* BA15 .... 114 E5
Banfield CI *AVONM* BS11 .... 50 C1
Bangor Gv *BRSG/KWL/STAPK* BS4 .. 9 L6
Bangrove Wk *AVONM* BS11 ..... 50 A1 🖾
Bank PI *PTSHD/EG* BS20 .... 49 K5
Bank Rd *AVONM* BS11 .... 36 E1
KGWD/HNM BS15 .... 68 D2 🖾
Banks CI *CLVDN* BS21 .... 71 F3
Bankside *MANG/FISH* BS16 ..... 55 F5 🖾
Bankside Rd
BRSG/KWL/STAPK BS4 .... 13 H2
Bannerdown Rd
CBATH/BATHN BA1 .... 101 F1
Bannerleigh La *CFTN/FAIL* BS8.. 65 G4 🖾
Bannerleigh Rd *CFTN/FAIL* BS8 ... 65 G3
Bannerman Rd *EVILLE/WHL* BS5 ... 4 D9
Banner Rd *RDLND/MONT* BS6 .... 3 K8
Bannetts Tree Crs
THNB/SVB BS35 .... 23 F1
Bantry Rd *BRSG/KWL/STAPK* BS4.. 11 J7
Banwell CI
BMSTRD/HC/WWD BS13 ...... 10 B7
KEYN BS31 .... 96 B2
Banwell Rd *BATHSE* BA2 .... 111 G5
BMSTR BS3 .... 10 A2
OMX/HUT/LCK BS24 .... 118 C3
WNSC BS25 .... 119 G6
WNSC BS25 .... 120 B5
Baptist St *EVILLE/WHL* BS5 .... 4 B7 🖾
Barberry Farm Rd
YTN/CONG BS49 .... 86 E3
Barbour Gdns
BMSTRD/HC/WWD BS13 ...... 93 G1
Barbour Rd
BMSTRD/HC/WWD BS13 ...... 93 G1
Barcroft CI *KGWD/HNM* BS15 ... 68 C2 🖾
Barkers Md *YATE/CS* BS37 .... 34 C3 🖾
Barker Wk *EVILLE/WHL* BS5 .... 4 A9
Barkleys Hl *MANG/FISH* BS16 .... 53 G4
Barley CI *FRCTL/WBN* BS36 ...... 32 C7 🖾
MANG/FISH BS16 .... 55 G3
Barley Cft
HNLZ/SM/SNYPK/WT BS9..... 51 H4
Barley Cross *MTN/WRL* BS22 .... 84 B7 🖾
Barnabas St *CBRISNE* BS2 .... 3 K8
Barnaby CI *RDSTK/MIDN* BA3 .. 126 C5
Barnack CI *TRWBR* BA14 .... 124 C5
Barnard's La *YTN/CONG* BS49 ... 87 F5
Barnard Wk *KEYN* BS31 .... 80 E7
Barnes CI *TRWBR* BA14 .... 124 C7
Barnes St *EVILLE/WHL* BS5 .... 9 G1 🖾
Barn Glebe *TRWBR* BA14 .... 125 H5
Barnhill Rd *YATE/CS* BS37 .... 34 E6
Barn Owl Wy *BRSTK/PCHW* BS34 .. 40 E3
Barn Piece *ALMDB* BS32 .... 123 K2
Barn Pool *WNSC* BS25 .... 121 J6
Barns CI *NAIL* BS48 .... 73 J1
NAIL BS48 .... 76 A7
Barnstaple Rd
BRSG/KWL/STAPK BS4 .... 11 L8
Barnstaple Wk
BRSG/KWL/STAPK BS4 .... 11 L8
Barnwood Ct *NAIL* BS48 .... 73 F2
Barnwood Rd *YATE/CS* BS37 .... 43 K1
Barossa PI *CBRIS/FH* BS1 .... 7 H6
Barrack's La *AVONM* BS11 .... 49 K1
Barratt St *EVILLE/WHL* BS5 .... 4 D8
Barrington CI *KGWD/HNM* BS15... 55 F7
Barrington Ct *KGWD/HNM* BS15.. 68 C1
Barrow CI *CLVDN* BS21 .... 60 D6
Barrow Court La *NAIL* BS48 ..... 75 H5
Barrow Hill Crs *AVONM* BS11 .... 49 J3
Barrow Hill Rd *AVONM* BS11 ..... 49 J3
Barrow La
BLAG/CWMG/WR BS40 .... 91 G3
Barrowmead Dr *AVONM* BS11 ... 50 B1

Barrow Rd *BATHSE* BA2 .... 111 F4
EVILLE/WHL BS5....................... 8 C4
OMX/HUT/LCK BS24 .... 117 K4
Barrow St *NAIL* BS48 .... 75 J6
Barrs Court Av
OLD/WMLY/WICK BS30 .... 69 G5
Barrs Court Rd
OLD/WMLY/WICK BS30 .... 69 G5
Barry CI
OLD/WMLY/WICK BS30 .... 81 J2 🖾
OMX/HUT/LCK BS24 .... 117 F5 🖾
Barry Rd *OLD/WMLY/WICK* BS30 .. 81 J1 🖾
Bartlett's Rd *BMSTR* BS3 .... 10 E1
Bartlett St *CBATH/BATHN* BA1 ... 14 F4 🖾
Bartley St *BMSTR* BS3 .... 7 G9
Barton CI
BRSG/KWL/STAPK BS4 .... 9 L4 🖾
FRCTL/WBN BS36 .... 41 K3
THNB/SVB BS35 .... 23 F1
Barton Ct *EVILLE/WHL* BS5 .... 8 E4
Barton Hill Rd *EVILLE/WHL* BS5 ... 8 E4
Bartonia Gv
BRSG/KWL/STAPK BS4 .... 13 H5
Barton Mnr *CBRISNE* BS2 .... 8 A4
Barton Orch *BOAV* BA15 .... 114 D7
Barton Rd *CBRISNE* BS2............. 7 M4
WNSC BS25 .... 120 A7
Barton St *CBATH/BATHN* BA1 ... 14 F6
CBRIS/FH BS1 .... 7 H1 🖾
The Barton *BATHSE* BA2 .... 97 H5
KGWD/HNM BS15 .... 68 B6
Barton V *CBRISNE* BS2 .... 8 A4 🖾
Barwood CI *KGWD/HNM* BS15... 69 F2 🖾
Bassetts Pasture *BOAV* BA15 ... 123 K2
Batchfield La *YATE/CS* BS37 ...... 56 E1
The Batch *NAIL* BS48 .... 89 J3
WNSC BS25 .... 121 H4
YTN/CONG BS49 .... 86 E5
Bates CI *EVILLE/WHL* BS5 .... 4 A9
Bathampton La *BATHSE* BA2 ... 100 D3
Bath Br *BRSG/KWL/STAPK* BS4 ... 7 L7
Bath Buildings *RDLND/MONT* BS6.. 3 J7
Bathford HI *CBATH/BATHN* BA1 .. 101 G2
PLTN/PENS BS39 .... 95 J7
Bath HI *KEYN* BS31 .... 81 F6
Bath New Rd *RDSTK/MIDN* BA3 .. 127 G2
Bath Rd *BLAG/CWMG/WR* BS40 .. 121 K2
BOAV BA15 .... 114 D4
BRSG/KWL/STAPK BS4......... 7 M7
KEYN BS31 .... 80 B3
OLD/WMLY/WICK BS30 .... 69 F7
THNB/SVB BS35 .... 19 G5
Bath Road Brislington Hl
BMSTR BS3 .... 10 D4 🖾
BMSTRD/HC/WWD BS13 ...... 10 B5
Bath St *BMSTR* BS3 .... 6 A9
CBATH/BATHN BA1 .... 14 F7 🖾
CBRIS/FH BS1 .... 7 J4
MANG/FISH BS16 .... 54 E5
Bathurst Pde *CBRIS/FH* BS1 .... 7 G7
Bathurst Rd *MTN/WRL* BS22 ... 105 H4
Bathwell Rd
BRSG/KWL/STAPK BS4 .... 12 A1
Bathwick HI *BATHSE* BA2 .... 15 K6
Bathwick Ri *BATHSE* BA2 .... 15 K4
Bathwick St *BATHSE* BA2 .... 15 H3
Batley Ct
OLD/WMLY/WICK BS30 .... 69 K6 🖾
Batstone CI *CBATH/BATHN* BA1 .. 99 K2
Battenburg Rd *EVILLE/WHL* BS5 .. 68 E2
Batten Ct *YATE/CS* BS37 .... 35 F6
Batten's La *EVILLE/WHL* BS5 ...... 68 A4
Battens Rd *EVILLE/WHL* BS5 ..... 68 B3 🖾
Battersby Wy
HNBRY/STHM BS10 .... 38 B6
Battersea Rd *EVILLE/WHL* BS5 .... 4 E9
Battery La *PTSHD/EG* BS20 .... 47 H3
Battson Rd *HGRV/WHIT* BS14 ... 79 J7
Baugh Gdns *MANG/FISH* BS16 .. 41 K7
Baxter CI *KGWD/HNM* BS15 ..... 69 F2 🖾
Baydon CI *TRWBR* BA14......... 130 E2
Bay Gdns *EVILLE/WHL* BS5 .... 4 E6
Bayham Rd
BRSG/KWL/STAPK BS4 .... 11 M1
Bayleys Dr *KGWD/HNM* BS15 ... 68 C4
Baynton Rd *BMSTR* BS3 .... 6 A9
Bay Rd *CLVDN* BS21 .... 59 F4
Bayswater Av *RDLND/MONT* BS6 .. 2 C2
Bayswater Rd *HORF/LLZ* BS7 ..... 52 D2
Bay Tree CI *BRSTK/PCHW* BS34 ... 39 J1
Bay Tree Rd *CBATH/BATHN* BA1 .. 100 A2
CLVDN BS21 .... 71 G1
Baytree Rd *MTN/WRL* BS22 ..... 105 H4
Baytree Vw *MTN/WRL* BS22 ..... 105 J4
Beach Av *CLVDN* BS21 .... 70 D4
Beach End Rd *WSM* BS23 .... 116 B4 🖾
Beachgrove Gdns
MANG/FISH BS16 .... 54 C5
Beachgrove Rd
MANG/FISH BS16 .... 54 B5
Beach HI *PTSHD/EG* BS20 .... 47 G3
Beachley Wk *AVONM* BS11 .... 49 K2
Beach Rd *MTN/WRL* BS22 .... 83 F4
THNB/SVB BS35 .... 27 G1
WSM BS23............................ 16 C7
Beach Rd East *PTSHD/EG* BS20 ... 47 G3
Beach Rd West *PTSHD/EG* BS20 .. 47 G3
The Beach *CLVDN* BS21 .... 58 E6
Beacon La *MANG/FISH* BS16 ..... 41 G3
Beaconlea *KGWD/HNM* BS15 .... 68 D4
Beacon Rd *CBATH/BATHN* BA1 ... 99 K3
Beaconsfield Rd
BRSG/KWL/STAPK BS4 .... 12 B2
CFTN/FAIL BS8 .... 2 A6
CLVDN BS21 .... 71 G1
EVILLE/WHL BS5 .... 9 K1
WSM BS23............................ 16 E4
Beaconsfield St
EVILLE/WHL BS5 .... 8 D5 🖾
Beale CI *HGRV/WHIT* BS14 .... 79 J5 🖾
Beam St *EVILLE/WHL* BS5 .... 8 E3
The Bean Acre *AVONM* BS11 ..... 49 K1
Beanhill Crs *THNB/SVB* BS35 ..... 23 F1 🖾
Bean St *EVILLE/WHL* BS5 .... 4 B9
Bearbridge Rd
BMSTRD/HC/WWD BS13 ...... 77 H3 🖾
Bear CI *BOAV* BA15 .... 114 C6

Bearfield Buildings
BOAV BA15 .... 114 D5 🖾
Beauchamp Rd *HORF/LLZ* BS7 .... 3 G1
Beauford Sq
CBATH/BATHN BA1 .... 14 F6 🖾
Beaufort Av *RDSTK/MIDN* BA3 .. 126 B3
Beaufort CI *EVILLE/WHL* BS5 ...... 9 H2
Beaufort Crs *BRSTK/PCHW* BS34 .. 40 D4
Beaufort East
CBATH/BATHN BA1 .... 100 B3
Beaufort Hts *EVILLE/WHL* BS5 ..... 9 K2
Beaufort PI *CBATH/BATHN* BA1 .. 100 B3
EVILLE/WHL BS5 .... 9 H2
MANG/FISH BS16 .... 41 G7 🖾
Beaufort Rd *CFTN/FAIL* BS8 .... 2 A8
EVILLE/WHL BS5 .... 9 H2
FRCTL/WBN BS36 .... 32 B7
HORF/LLZ BS7 .... 52 D5
KGWD/HNM BS15 .... 68 B1 🖾
MANG/FISH BS16 .... 54 E5
WSM BS23............................ 17 G3
YATE/CS BS37 .... 34 A5
Beaufort St *BMSTR* BS3 .... 10 E3 🖾
EVILLE/WHL BS5 .... 8 A1 🖾
Beaufort Wy *HNBRY/STHM* BS10.. 52 B1
Beauley Rd *BMSTR* BS3 .... 6 D8
Beaumont CI
OLD/WMLY/WICK BS30 .... 69 C7 🖾
WSM BS23............................ 116 E2 🖾
Beaumont St *EVILLE/WHL* BS5 .... 4 B9
Beaumont Ter *EVILLE/WHL* BS5 ... 4 B9
Beau St *CBATH/BATHN* BA1 ...... 14 F7 🖾
Beaver CI *FRCTL/WBN* BS36 ..... 42 A1
Beazer CI *MANG/FISH* BS16 ..... 54 D6 🖾
Becket Dr *MTN/WRL* BS22 ...... 106 B2 🖾
Becket Rd *MTN/WRL* BS22 ...... 106 B1
Becket's La *NAIL* BS48 .... 73 J3
Beckford Gdns *BATHSE* BA2 ...... 15 K3
HGRV/WHIT BS14 .... 93 K1 🖾
Beckford Rd *BATHSE* BA2 .... 15 J4
Beckhampton Rd *BATHSE* BA2.... 14 B9
Beckington Rd *BMSTR* BS3 .... 11 L3
Beckington Wk *BMSTR* BS3 .... 11 L3
Beckspool Rd
MANG/FISH BS16 .... 54 C1 🖾
Beddoe CI *BOAV* BA15 .... 124 A2 🖾
Bedford Crs *HORF/LLZ* BS7 .... 52 D4
Bedford Rd *WSM* BS23 .... 16 F9
Bedford St *CBATH/BATHN* BA1 .. 15 H2
Bedminster Br *BMSTR* BS3 .... 7 J8
Bedminster Down Rd
BMSTR BS3 .... 10 D4 🖾
BMSTRD/HC/WWD BS13 ...... 10 B5
Bedminster Pde *BMSTR* BS3 ...... 7 H8
Bedminster PI *BMSTR* BS3 .... 7 H8 🖾
Bedminster Rd *BMSTR* BS3 .... 10 E4
Bedwin CI *PTSHD/EG* BS20 .... 46 D5 🖾
Beech Av *BATHSE* BA2 .... 112 D1
Beech CI *OLD/WMLY/WICK* BS30.. 69 G5
THNB/SVB BS35 .... 23 F1
WNSC BS25 .... 121 J6
Beechcroft *LGASH* BS41 .... 92 A2 🖾
Beechcroft Wk *HORF/LLZ* BS7 ... 52 E1 🖾
Beech Dr *NAIL* BS48 .... 74 A1
WNSC BS25 .... 121 H6
Beechen Cliff Rd *BATHSE* BA2 .... 14 E9
Beechen Dr *MANG/FISH* BS16 ... 54 B7
Beeches
BRSG/KWL/STAPK BS4 .... 13 G4 🖾
The Beeches *ALMDB* BS32........ 30 C7
BATHSE BA2 .... 111 G4 🖾
BOAV BA15 .... 115 H6
BRSG/KWL/STAPK BS4 .... 9 J7 🖾
OLD/WMLY/WICK BS30 .... 81 J1
TRWBR BA14 .... 125 H4
WNSC BS25 .... 120 E2
Beechfield CI *LGASH* BS41 .... 76 E1 🖾
Beech Gv *BATHSE* BA2 .... 111 F1
TRWBR BA14 .... 130 D1
Beech Leaze *THNB/SVB* BS35 ..... 23 F1
Beechmont CI
OMX/HUT/LCK BS24 .... 116 E5
Beechmont Dr
OMX/HUT/LCK BS24 .... 116 E5
Beechmount Gv
HGRV/WHIT BS14 .... 12 C7
Beech Rd *HORF/LLZ* BS7 .... 52 C4
KEYN BS31 .... 97 F1
WNSC BS25 .... 121 J6
YTN/CONG BS49 .... 87 F4
Beech Ter *RDSTK/MIDN* BA3 .... 126 E4
Beechwood Av
KGWD/HNM BS15 .... 68 D5
OMX/HUT/LCK BS24 .... 118 B2 🖾
Beechwood CI *HGRV/WHIT* BS14.. 12 F8
Beechwood Rd *BATHSE* BA2 .... 112 A4
MANG/FISH BS16 .... 54 A5
NAIL BS48 .... 73 H1
PTSHD/EG BS20 .... 49 G5
PTSHD/EG BS20 .... 49 G5
Beehive Yd
CBATH/BATHN BA1 .... 15 G5 🖾
Beesmoor Rd *FRCTL/WBN* BS36... 42 C1
Begbrook Dr *MANG/FISH* BS16 .. 53 K3
Begbrook La *MANG/FISH* BS16 .. 53 K3
Begbrook Pk *MANG/FISH* BS16 .. 54 A2
Beggar Bush La *CFTN/FAIL* BS8 .. 63 K6
Beggarswell CI *CBRISNE* BS2 .... 3 L9
Belcombe Rd *BOAV* BA15 .... 114 C7
Belfast Wk
BRSG/KWL/STAPK BS4 .... 11 K6
Belgrave Crs *CBATH/BATHN* BA1 .. 15 G2
Belgrave HI *CFTN/FAIL* BS8 .... 2 A6
Belgrave PI *CFTN/FAIL* BS8 .... 6 B2 🖾
Belgrave Rd *CBATH/BATHN* BA1 .. 15 K1
CFTN/FAIL BS8 .... 6 B2 🖾
EVILLE/WHL BS5 .... 2 D9
Bellamy Av
BMSTRD/HC/WWD BS13 ...... 78 A7
Bellamy CI *KGWD/HNM* BS15 ... 68 A5
Belland Dr *HGRV/WHIT* BS14 .... 78 D7
Bella Vista Rd
CBATH/BATHN BA1 .... 14 F2 🖾
Bell Barn Rd
HNLZ/SM/SNYPK/WT BS9..... 51 F3
Bell CI *HNBRY/STHM* BS10 .... 52 C1
Bellefield Crs *TRWBR* BA14 ..... 125 F5
Bellevue *CFTN/FAIL* BS8 .... 6 C4

Bellevue CI *KGWD/HNM* BS15 ... 68 E3 🖾
Bellevue Crs *CFTN/FAIL* BS8 .... 6 C4
Bellevue Pk
BRSG/KWL/STAPK BS4......... 13 H3
Bellevue Rd
BRSG/KWL/STAPK BS4............ 7 M8
CLVDN BS21 .... 59 F6
Belle Vue Rd *EVILLE/WHL* BS5 ..... 4 E6
Bellevue Rd *EVILLE/WHL* BS5 ..... 68 A2
KGWD/HNM BS15 .... 69 F3
Bellevue Ter *BMSTR* BS3 .... 7 M8
BRSG/KWL/STAPK BS4......... 13 H3
Bell HI *MANG/FISH* BS16 .... 4 E2
Bell Hill Rd *EVILLE/WHL* BS5 ...... 9 M1
Bellhouse Wk *AVONM* BS11 ..... 37 J7 🖾
Bell La *CBRIS/FH* BS1 .... 7 H3
Bellotts Rd *BATHSE* BA2 .... 99 F6
Bell Rd *FRCTL/WBN* BS36 .... 42 D2
Belluton La *PLTN/PENS* BS39 ..... 94 B7
Belluton Rd
BRSG/KWL/STAPK BS4......... 12 A2
Belmont Dr *BRSTK/PCHW* BS34 .. 40 D3
CFTN/FAIL BS8 .... 63 J7 🖾
Belmont HI *NAIL* BS48 .... 75 G2
Belmont Rd *BATHSE* BA2 .... 112 B4
BRSG/KWL/STAPK BS4......... 12 A2
RDLND/MONT BS6 .... 3 J5
WNSC BS25 .... 120 D6
Belmont St *EVILLE/WHL* BS5 ...... 4 C7
Belmore Gdns *BATHSE* BA2 ..... 110 E2
Beloe Rd *HORF/LLZ* BS7 .... 52 B4
Belroyal Av
BRSG/KWL/STAPK BS4......... 13 M2
Belsher Dr *KGWD/HNM* BS15 .... 69 G4
Belstone Wk
BRSG/KWL/STAPK BS4......... 11 L8
Belton Rd *EVILLE/WHL* BS5 .... 4 C8
PTSHD/EG BS20 .... 49 G5
Belvedere Crs *MTN/WRL* BS22 .. 105 H4
Belvedere Rd *RDLND/MONT* BS6 .. 2 B3
Belvoir Rd *BATHSE* BA2 .... 14 A9 🖾
RDLND/MONT BS6 .... 3 J5
Bence Ct *KGWD/HNM* BS15 ..... 68 B5 🖾
Benford CI *MANG/FISH* BS16 ..... 54 C3
Bennett La *CBATH/BATHN* BA1 .. 15 H1
Bennett Rd *EVILLE/WHL* BS5 ...... 9 K2
Bennett's Ct *YATE/CS* BS37 ...... 34 C6
Bennett's Rd
CBATH/BATHN BA1 .... 100 B1
Bennett St *CBATH/BATHN* BA1 .. 14 F4 🖾
Bennetts Wy *CLVDN* BS21 .... 59 G5
Bensaunt Gv *HNBRY/STHM* BS10.. 39 G4
Bentley CI *HGRV/WHIT* BS14 ..... 93 J1 🖾
Bentley Rd *MTN/WRL* BS22 ..... 106 C2
Benville Av
HNLZ/SM/SNYPK/WT BS9..... 50 E1
Berenda Dr
OLD/WMLY/WICK BS30 .... 69 H7
Beresford CI *KEYN* BS31 .... 97 F2
Beresford Gdns
CBATH/BATHN BA1 .... 98 D1 🖾
Berkeley Av *CFTN/FAIL* BS8 .... 6 E3
HORF/LLZ BS7 .... 3 G3
RDSTK/MIDN BA3 .... 126 B3
Berkeley CI *MANG/FISH* BS16 .... 55 F1
Berkeley Crs *WSM* BS23 .... 116 B4
Berkeley Gdns *KEYN* BS31 .... 80 D7
Berkeley Gn *EVILLE/WHL* BS5 ...... 4 F5
MANG/FISH BS16 .... 41 G7 🖾
Berkeley Gv *EVILLE/WHL* BS5 ...... 4 F5
Berkeley Md *ALMDB* BS32 .... 40 E2
Berkeley Rd *HORF/LLZ* BS7 .... 3 G3
KGWD/HNM BS15 .... 68 E3 🖾
MANG/FISH BS16 .... 54 A7
RDLND/MONT BS6 .... 2 B2
TRWBR BA14 .... 124 C6
Berkeley Sq *CFTN/FAIL* BS8 .... 6 D3
Berkeley St *EVILLE/WHL* BS5 ...... 4 F4
Berkeley Wy *MANG/FISH* BS16 ... 55 H2
Berkshire Rd *HORF/LLZ* BS7 ...... 3 G3
Berrow Wk *BMSTR* BS3 .... 11 K3
Berryfield Rd *BOAV* BA15 .... 114 C5
Berry La *HORF/LLZ* BS7 .... 52 C3
Berwick La *HNBRY/STHM* BS10 .. 37 K3
Berwick Rd *EVILLE/WHL* BS5 ...... 4 D6
Beryl Gv *HGRV/WHIT* BS14 .... 12 F8
Beryl Rd *BMSTR* BS3 .... 10 C2
Besom La *YATE/CS* BS37 .... 43 K5
Bethel Rd *EVILLE/WHL* BS5 .... 9 L1
Betjeman Ct
OLD/WMLY/WICK BS30 .... 69 G5 🖾
Bevan Ct *BRSTK/PCHW* BS34 ..... 39 J6
Beverley Av *MANG/FISH* BS16 ... 42 A7
Beverley CI *EVILLE/WHL* BS5 ..... 68 B4 🖾
Beverley Gdns
HNLZ/SM/SNYPK/WT BS9..... 51 F2
Beverstone *KGWD/HNM* BS15 ... 68 C2 🖾
Beverston Gdns *AVONM* BS11 ... 37 J6 🖾
Bevington CI
BRSTK/PCHW BS34 .... 29 H6
Bevington Wk
BRSTK/PCHW BS34 .... 29 H6
Bewdley Rd *BATHSE* BA2 .... 112 A1 🖾
Bewley Rd *TRWBR* BA14 .... 130 E2
Bexley Rd *MANG/FISH* BS16 ..... 54 B6
Bibstone *KGWD/HNM* BS15 ...... 69 G2
Bibury Av *BRSTK/PCHW* BS34 .... 30 A7
Bibury CI
HNLZ/SM/SNYPK/WT BS9..... 52 B2
NAIL BS48 .... 74 A2
Bibury Crs
HNLZ/SM/SNYPK/WT BS9..... 52 B2
KGWD/HNM BS15 .... 68 C5
Bickerton CI *HNBRY/STHM* BS10 .. 38 C5
Bickford CI
OLD/WMLY/WICK BS30 .... 69 G4
Bickley CI *KGWD/HNM* BS15 ..... 80 C1 🖾
Bickley Rd *OLD/WMLY/WICK* BS30.. 69 G4
Biddestone Rd *HORF/LLZ* BS7 .... 52 C1
Biddisham CI *NAIL* BS48 .... 73 J2 🖾
Biddle St *YTN/CONG* BS49 .... 86 D5
Bideford Crs
BRSG/KWL/STAPK BS4............ 11 L8
Bideford Rd *MTN/WRL* BS22 ... 106 A3 🖾
Bidwell CI *HNBRY/STHM* BS10 ... 38 E5
Bifield CI *HGRV/WHIT* BS14 ...... 79 K6
Bifield Gdns *HGRV/WHIT* BS14 .. 79 J6
Bifield Rd *HGRV/WHIT* BS14 ..... 79 K6
Bigwood La *CBRIS/FH* BS1 .... 6 E4

Bilberry Cl
  HNLZ/SM/SNYPK/WT BS9 .... 50 E1 🔲
Bilbie Cl *HNBRY/STHM* BS10 .... 52 B3
Bilbie Rd *MTN/WRL* BS22............ 106 C2
Bilbury La *CBATH/BATHN* BA1 ...... 14 F7 🔲
Billand Cl
  BMSTRD/HC/WWD BS13 .... 92 B1
Bince's Lodge La
  RDSTK/MIDN BA3 .... 126 C2
Bindon Dr *HNBRY/STHM* BS10 ...... 39 G4
Binhay Rd *YTN/CONG* BS49 .... 87 F5
Binley Gv *HGRV/WHIT* BS14....... 79 H6
Binmead Gdns
  BMSTRD/HC/WWD BS13 .... 77 K7 🔲
Birbeck Rd
  HNLZ/SM/SNYPK/WT BS9 .... 51 G4
Birchall Rd *RDLND/MONT* BS6 .... 2 E1
Birch Av *CLVDN* BS21 .... 59 G6
  OMX/HUT/LCK BS24 .... 118 C2
Birch Ct *KEYN* BS31 .... 80 C7
Birch Cft *HGRV/WHIT* BS14 .... 94 A1 🔲
Birchdale Rd *HGRV/WHIT* BS14 ... 12 B8
Birch Dene *NAIL* BS48 .... 74 A1 🔲
Birch Dr *MANG/FISH* BS16 .... 56 D4
  THNB/SVB BS35 .... 22 C2
  WNSC BS25 .... 121 K1
Birchenleaze *TRWBR* BA14 ...... 130 E4 🔲
The Birches *NAIL* BS48 .... 74 A1 🔲
Birch Gv *PTSHD/EG* BS20........... 47 G5
Birch Rd *BMSTR* BS3 .... 6 C8
  KGWD/HNM BS15 .... 54 E6
  RDSTK/MIDN BA3 .... 127 F4
  YATE/CS BS37 .... 34 A5
Birchwood Av *WSM* BS23 .... 17 K3
Birchwood Rd
  BRSG/KWL/STAPK BS4............ 9 K9
Birdale Cl *HNBRY/STHM* BS10...... 38 B5
Birdcombe Cl *NAIL* BS48 .... 61 J7 🔲
Birdlip Cl *NAIL* BS48 .... 73 K3
Birdwell La *LGASH* BS41 .... 76 B2 🔲
Birdwell Rd *LGASH* BS41 .... 76 B2
Birdwood *KGWD/HNM* BS15........ 68 D4
Birkbeck Ct *WSM* BS23 .... 16 D4 🔲
Birkdale *OLD/WMLY/WICK* BS30... 69 H4
  YATE/CS BS37 .... 34 B7
Birkett Rd *WSM* BS23 .... 104 A4
Birkin St *CBRISNE* BS2 .... 7 M4
Birnbeck Rd *MTN/WRL* BS22 ..... 104 A4
Bisdee Rd *OMX/HUT/LCK* BS24... 117 J3
Bishop Av *MTN/WRL* BS22 .... 106 B2 🔲
Bishop Manor Rd
  HNBRY/STHM BS10 .... 52 B2
Bishop Rd *HORF/LLZ* BS7 .... 2 E1
Bishops Cl
  HNLZ/SM/SNYPK/WT BS9 .... 51 G4
Bishops Cove
  BMSTRD/HC/WWD BS13 .... 77 H6 🔲
Bishops Knoll
  HNLZ/SM/SNYPK/WT BS9 .... 50 E6
Bishops Md *YTN/CONG* BS49....... 87 K4
Bishops Rd *YTN/CONG* BS49 .... 87 J4
Bishop St *CBRISNE* BS2 .... 3 K9
Bishop's Wd *ALMDB* BS32 .... 30 D1
Bishopthorpe Rd
  HNBRY/STHM BS10 .... 52 B2
Bishport Av
  BMSTRD/HC/WWD BS13 .... 77 J7
Bishport Cl
  BMSTRD/HC/WWD BS13 .... 77 K7
Bisley *YATE/CS* BS37 .... 43 K1
Bissex Md *MANG/FISH* BS16 ...... 55 H4
Biss Meadow *TRWBR* BA14 ...... 124 C4
Bittern Cl *MTN/WRL* BS22 .... 106 A4 🔲
Bitterwell Cl *FRCTL/WBN* BS36 ... 42 E5
Blackacre *HGRV/WHIT* BS14 ...... 94 B1
Blackberry Av
  MANG/FISH BS16 .... 53 J4 🔲
Blackberry Dr *MTN/WRL* BS22 .. 106 B4
Blackberry Hl *MANG/FISH* BS16 ... 53 J4
Blackberry La *PTSHD/EG* BS20.... 46 C7
  RDSTK/MIDN BA3 .... 113 H5
Blackbird Cl
  RDSTK/MIDN BA3 .... 126 C5 🔲
Blackdown Ct
  HGRV/WHIT BS14 .... 79 F6 🔲
Blackdown Rd
  PTSHD/EG BS20 .... 46 E4 🔲
  PTSHD/EG BS20 .... 47 F4 🔲
Blackfriars *CBRIS/FH* BS1 .... 7 H2 🔲
Blackfriars Rd *NAIL* BS48 .... 73 F3
Blackhorse Hl *THNB/SVB* BS35 ..... 28 E7
Blackhorse La *MANG/FISH* BS16... 55 G1
Blackhorse Pl
  MANG/FISH BS16 .... 55 G3 🔲
Blackhorse Rd *KGWD/HNM* BS15.. 68 D2
  MANG/FISH BS16 .... 55 G3
Blackmoor *CLVDN* BS21 .... 70 E2
Blackmoor Rd *CFTN/FAIL* BS8...... 50 A7
Blackmoors La *BMSTR* BS3 .... 65 G7
Blackmoors Dr *BATHSE* BA2 ...... 98 E2
Blackrock La *HGRV/WHIT* BS14 .... 94 C4
  PLTN/PENS BS39 .... 94 D5
Blacksworth Rd *EVILLE/WHL* BS5 .. 9 H3
Blackthorn Cl
  BMSTRD/HC/WWD BS13 .... 78 B6
Blackthorn Dr *ALMDB* BS32 .... 40 C1 🔲
Blackthorn Gdns
  MTN/WRL BS22 .... 106 B4
Blackthorn Rd
  BMSTRD/HC/WWD BS13 .... 78 B6
Blackthorn Sq *CLVDN* BS21 .... 71 F2
Blackthorn Ter
  KGWD/HNM BS15 .... 54 E7 🔲
Blackthorn Wy *NAIL* BS48 .... 73 K1
Bladen Cl *PTSHD/EG* BS20 .... 47 J5 🔲
Blagdon Cl
  OMX/HUT/LCK BS24 .... 116 E5 🔲
Blagdon Pk *BATHSE* BA2 .... 110 D1
Blagrove Cl
  BMSTRD/HC/WWD BS13 .... 93 F1
Blagrove Crs
  BMSTRD/HC/WWD BS13 .... 93 F1 🔲
Blair Rd *TRWBR* BA14 .... 124 C4
Blaisdon *MTN/WRL* BS22 .... 105 J6
  YATE/CS BS37 .... 44 B1
Blaisdon Cl *HNBRY/STHM* BS10 ... 38 C7

Blaise Wk
  HNLZ/SM/SNYPK/WT BS9 .... 50 E3
Blakeney Gv *NAIL* BS48 .... 73 G3
Blakeney Mills *YATE/CS* BS37 .... 26 B3 🔲
Blakeney Rd *BRSTK/PCHW* BS34 ... 29 H6
  HORF/LLZ BS7 .... 52 E2
Blake Rd *HORF/LLZ* BS7 .... 53 F3
Blakes Rd *THNB/SVB* BS35 .... 19 G4
Blanchards *YATE/CS* BS37 .... 35 F7
Blandford Cl
  HNLZ/SM/SNYPK/WT BS9 .... 51 K3 🔲
  NAIL BS48 .... 73 J2 🔲
Bleadon Hl *OMX/HUT/LCK* BS24.. 116 E6
Bleadon Rd
  OMX/HUT/LCK BS24 .... 117 F7
Blenham Ct *WSM* BS23 .... 17 J2
Blenheim Ct *EVILLE/WHL* BS5 ...... 4 B8
Blenheim Dr *BRSTK/PCHW* BS34 ... 40 A4
  YATE/CS BS37 .... 33 K4
Blenheim Gdns
  CBATH/BATHN BA1 .... 99 K2
Blenheim Rd *RDLND/MONT* BS6 ..... 2 C3
Blenheim St *EVILLE/WHL* BS5 ..... 4 B8
Blenheim Wy *PTSHD/EG* BS20 .... 47 J4 🔲
Blenman Cl *MANG/FISH* BS16 .... 54 B1
Blethwin Cl *HNBRY/STHM* BS10... 38 C7
Blind La *CBATH/BATHN* BA1........ 99 F2
  TRWBR BA14 .... 130 B5
  YTN/CONG BS49 .... 87 J5
Bloomfield Av *BATHSE* BA2 ...... 111 H1
Bloomfield Dr *BATHSE* BA2 ...... 111 G3
Bloomfield Gv *BATHSE* BA2 ...... 111 H2
Bloomfield Pk *BATHSE* BA2 ...... 111 H2
Bloomfield Ri *BATHSE* BA2 .... 111 G3
Bloomfield Ri North
  BATHSE BA2 .... 111 G3 🔲
Bloomfield Rd *BATHSE* BA2 ...... 111 G3
  BRSG/KWL/STAPK BS4 .... 8 E9 🔲
Bloomfield Road Link
  BRSG/KWL/STAPK BS4.............. 8 E9
Bloy St *EVILLE/WHL* BS5 .... 4 B8
Bluebell Cl *THNB/SVB* BS35 .... 19 J5
Bluebell Rd *MTN/WRL* BS22 ...... 84 B6 🔲
The Bluebells *ALMDB* BS32 .... 40 D1 🔲
  ALMDB BS32 .... 40 E1 🔲
Blueberry Wy
  MTN/WRL BS22 .... 106 A4 🔲
Blythe Gdns *MTN/WRL* BS22 .... 106 B2 🔲
Boat Stall La
  CBATH/BATHN BA1 .... 15 G6 🔲
Bobbin La *BOAV* BA15 .... 123 F2
Bobbin Pk *BOAV* BA15 .... 123 F3
Bockenem Cl *THNB/SVB* BS35 .... 19 J6 🔲
Bodey Cl *OLD/WMLY/WICK* BS30 .. 69 G5
Bodmin Wk
  BRSG/KWL/STAPK BS4............ 11 M7
Bodyce Rd *THNB/SVB* BS35 .... 23 F1 🔲
Boiling Wells La *CBRISNE* BS2 ...... 4 A4
Bolton Rd *HORF/LLZ* BS7 .... 52 E4
Bond St *CBRIS/FH* BS1 .... 7 K1
  TRWBR BA14 .... 124 E7
Bonnington Wk *HORF/LLZ* BS7 ... 53 F2
Bonville Rd
  BRSG/KWL/STAPK BS4.............. 13 K5
Booth Rd *BMSTR* BS3 .... 6 F9 🔲
Boot La *BMSTR* BS3 .... 7 H8
Bordesley Rd *HGRV/WHIT* BS14 ... 93 K1 🔲
Borgie Pl *MTN/WRL* BS22 .... 105 K2
Borleyton Wk
  BMSTRD/HC/WWD BS13 .... 77 H7 🔲
Borver Gv
  BMSTRD/HC/WWD BS13 .... 77 K7
Boscombe Crs
  MANG/FISH BS16 .... 55 F2 🔲
Boswell Rd *BOAV* BA15 .... 123 F3
Boswell St *EVILLE/WHL* BS5 .... 4 E1
Botham Cl *MTN/WRL* BS22 .... 106 B1 🔲
Bottom Cl *HGRV/WHIT* BS14 .... 78 E5
Boucher Pl *CBRISNE* BS2 .... 4 A5 🔲
Boulevard *WSM* BS23 .... 16 E2
Boulters Rd
  BMSTRD/HC/WWD BS13 .... 78 A7 🔲
Boulton's Rd *KGWD/HNM* BS15.... 68 D2
Boundary Cl *RDSTK/MIDN* BA3... 126 C6
  WSM BS23 .... 116 D3
Boundary Rd *AVONM* BS11 .... 36 E4
  FRCTL/WBN BS36 .... 42 E1
Bourchier Gdns
  BMSTRD/HC/WWD BS13 .... 92 C1 🔲
Bourne Cl *FRCTL/WBN* BS36 .... 41 K1
  KGWD/HNM BS15 .... 68 B2
Bourne La *EVILLE/WHL* BS5.......... 4 D5
Bourne Rd *KGWD/HNM* BS15 ...... 68 A2
Bourneville Rd *EVILLE/WHL* BS5 .... 5 G9
Bournmil Cl *BOAV* BA15 .... 113 J6 🔲
Bournville Rd *WSM* BS23 .... 17 G9
Boursland Cl *ALMDB* BS32 .... 30 C5 🔲
Bourton Av *BRSTK/PCHW* BS34 ... 30 B7
Bourton Cl *BRSTK/PCHW* BS34 .... 30 B7
Bourton Combe *NAIL* BS48 .... 75 F4
Bourton La *MTN/WRL* BS22 ...... 106 E2
Bourton Md *NAIL* BS48 .... 75 F3 🔲
Bourton Wk
  BMSTRD/HC/WWD BS13 .... 10 B7
Bouverie St *EVILLE/WHL* BS5 .... 4 C9
Boverton Rd *BRSTK/PCHW* BS34 .. 40 A5
Bowden Cl
  HNLZ/SM/SNYPK/WT BS9 .... 50 E1
Bowden Pl *MANG/FISH* BS16 ..... 55 F2 🔲
Bowden Rd *EVILLE/WHL* BS5 .... 5 J8
Bowden Wy *CFTN/FAIL* BS8 .... 63 H7
Bowen Rd *OMX/HUT/LCK* BS24 .. 118 C2
Bowerleaze
  HNLZ/SM/SNYPK/WT BS9 .... 50 D4
Bower Rd *BMSTR* BS3 .... 10 A2
Bower Wk *BMSTR* BS3 .... 11 K2
Bowlditch La *RDSTK/MIDN* BA3 .. 126 C1
Bowling Hl *YATE/CS* BS37 .... 34 D6
Bowling Rd *YATE/CS* BS37 .... 34 E7
Bowring Cl
  BMSTRD/HC/WWD BS13 .... 93 F1
Bowsland Wy *ALMDB* BS32 .... 30 C5
Bowstreet La *THNB/SVB* BS35 .... 28 D7
Box Bush La
  OMX/HUT/LCK BS24 .... 107 K4
Boxhedge Farm La
  FRCTL/WBN BS36 .... 43 F5

Box Rd *CBATH/BATHN* BA1 .... 101 H1
Boyce Cl *BATHSE* BA2 .... 98 C7
Boyce Dr *CBRISNE* BS2 .... 4 A5
Boyce's Av *CFTN/FAIL* BS8 .... 6 A3
Boyd Rd *KEYN* BS31 .... 96 E1
Brabazon Rd *BRSTK/PCHW* BS34 .. 40 A6
Bracewell Gdns
  HNBRY/STHM BS10 .... 39 F4
Bracey Dr *MANG/FISH* BS16 ...... 54 C3 🔲
Brackenbury Dr
  BRSTK/PCHW BS34 .... 40 D3
Brackendene *ALMDB* BS32 .... 30 B6 🔲
Brackenwood Rd *CLVDN* BS21 .... 59 G4
Bracton Dr *HGRV/WHIT* BS14 ..... 78 E7
Bradeston Gv *MANG/FISH* BS16 ... 54 A2
Bradford Cl *CLVDN* BS21 .... 70 E2 🔲
Bradford Rd *BATHSE* BA2 .... 111 J4
  BOAV BA15 .... 113 J7
  CBATH/BATHN BA1 .... 101 G3
  TRWBR BA14 .... 115 K6
  TRWBR BA14 .... 129 G5
Bradhurst St *EVILLE/WHL* BS5 ..... 8 D5
Bradley Av *AVONM* BS11 .... 50 A5
  FRCTL/WBN BS36 .... 41 K3
Bradley Crs *AVONM* BS11 .... 50 A3
Bradley Rd *BRSTK/PCHW* BS34 .... 29 J7
  PTSHD/EG BS20 .... 48 E4
  TRWBR BA14 .... 124 E7
  TRWBR BA14 .... 130 C5
Bradley Stoke Wy *ALMDB* BS32 .. 30 B5
Bradstone Rd
  FRCTL/WBN BS36 .... 41 J3 🔲
Bradville Gdns *LGASH* BS41 .... 76 B3
Bradwell Gv *HNBRY/STHM* BS10 ... 52 A1
Braemar Av *CLVDN* BS21 .... 55 F6
Braemar Crs *HORF/LLZ* BS7 .... 39 J7
Brae Hl *WNSC* BS25 .... 120 D6
Brae Rd *WNSC* BS25 .... 120 D6
Bragg's La *CBRISNE* BS2 .... 7 M2
Braikenridge Cl *CLVDN* BS21 ...... 70 E2 🔲
Braikenridge Rd
  BRSG/KWL/STAPK BS4.............. 9 H8
Brainsfield
  HNLZ/SM/SNYPK/WT BS9 .... 51 H3
Brake Cl *ALMDB* BS32 .... 40 D2
  KGWD/HNM BS15 .... 69 F3 🔲
The Brake *FRCTL/WBN* BS36 ...... 42 D3
  YATE/CS BS37 .... 34 B2
Bramble Dr
  HNLZ/SM/SNYPK/WT BS9 .... 50 E6
Bramble La
  HNLZ/SM/SNYPK/WT BS9 .... 50 E6
Bramble Rd *MTN/WRL* BS22 ..... 105 K2
The Brambles *KEYN* BS31 .... 95 J1
Bramble Wy *BATHSE* BA2 .... 112 A3
Bramblewood *YTN/CONG* BS49 ... 86 E3
Brambling Wk *MANG/FISH* BS16 .. 53 K3
Bramley Cl *OMX/HUT/LCK* BS24.. 118 B2 🔲
  PTSHD/EG BS20 .... 40 A5
  WNSC BS25 .... 120 D2 🔲
  YTN/CONG BS49 .... 86 E5
Bramley Ct
  OLD/WMLY/WICK BS30 .... 69 F6 🔲
Bramley Dr *NAIL* BS48 .... 74 A6
Bramley La *TRWBR* BA14.......... 125 F7
The Bramleys *NAIL* BS48 .... 73 F3
Brampton Wy *PTSHD/EG* BS20.... 47 J4
Branche Gv
  BMSTRD/HC/WWD BS13 .... 93 G1
Brandash Rd *YATE/CS* BS37 .... 35 F6
Brandon Steep *CBRIS/FH* BS1 ..... 6 E4 🔲
Brandon St *CBRIS/FH* BS1 .... 6 E5
Brangwyn Gv *HORF/LLZ* BS7 ...... 53 F2
Brangwyn Sq
  MTN/WRL BS22 .... 106 A3 🔲
Branksome Crs
  BRSTK/PCHW BS34 .... 40 A5
Branksome Dr
  BRSTK/PCHW BS34 .... 40 A5
  FRCTL/WBN BS36 .... 41 K2
Branksome Rd *RDLND/MONT* BS6.. 2 D3
Bransby Wy
  OMX/HUT/LCK BS24 .... 106 B5
Branscombe Rd
  HNLZ/SM/SNYPK/WT BS9 .... 50 E5
Branscombe Wk
  PTSHD/EG BS20 .... 46 D6 🔲
Branwhite Cl *HORF/LLZ* BS7 .... 53 F2 🔲
Brassknocker Hl *BATHSE* BA2 .... 112 E3
Brassmill La *CBATH/BATHN* BA1 .. 98 D5
Bratton Rd
  BRSG/KWL/STAPK BS4............. 11 H9
  TRWBR BA14 .... 131 H3
Braunton Rd *BMSTR* BS3 .... 10 E1
Braydon Av *BRSTK/PCHW* BS34 ... 30 C7
Brayne Ct
  OLD/WMLY/WICK BS30 .... 69 F7
Breaches Ga *BMSTR* BS3 .... 40 E2
The Breaches *PTSHD/EG* BS20 .... 49 H5
Breach La *NAIL* BS48 .... 72 D4
  TRWBR BA14 .... 130 C4
Breach Rd *BMSTR* BS3 .... 10 B2
Brean Down Av
  HNLZ/SM/SNYPK/WT BS9 .... 2 C1
  WSM BS23 .... 116 C2
Brecknock Rd
  BRSG/KWL/STAPK BS4............. 12 A2
Brecon Cl
  HNLZ/SM/SNYPK/WT BS9........... 51 J3
Brecon Vw *OMX/HUT/LCK* BS24.. 117 F5
Bredon *YATE/CS* BS37 .... 44 A1
Bredon Cl *KGWD/HNM* BS15 ...... 69 F3 🔲
Bredon Nook Rd
  HNBRY/STHM BS10 .... 52 A2 🔲
Bree Cl *MTN/WRL* BS22 .... 106 B1 🔲
Brendon Av *WSM* BS23 .... 17 H1
Brendon Cl
  OLD/WMLY/WICK BS30 .... 69 J6 🔲
Brendon Rd *BMSTR* BS3 .... 11 H2
  PTSHD/EG BS20 .... 46 E4
Brenner St *EVILLE/WHL* BS5 .... 8 B1
Brent Cl *OMX/HUT/LCK* BS24 .... 117 G4 🔲
Brent Rd *HORF/LLZ* BS7 .... 52 D4
Brentry Av *EVILLE/WHL* BS5 .... 8 C2
Brentry La *HNBRY/STHM* BS10.... 38 D3
Brentry Rd *MANG/FISH* BS16 .... 5 K3
Brereton Wy
  OLD/WMLY/WICK BS30 .... 69 H6

Brewerton Cl
  HNBRY/STHM BS10 .... 39 F5
Briar Cl *NAIL* BS48 .... 74 A1
  RDSTK/MIDN BA3 .... 126 E5
Briarfield Av
  KGWD/HNM BS15 .... 68 C5 🔲
Briarleaze *THNB/SVB* BS35 .... 22 E4
Briar Md *YTN/CONG* BS49 .... 86 D3
Briar Rd *OMX/HUT/LCK* BS24 .... 117 K3
Briarside Rd *HNBRY/STHM* BS10 .. 39 F5
The Briars *NAIL* BS48 .... 73 K4 🔲
Briar Wk *MANG/FISH* BS16 .... 54 C6
Briar Wy *MANG/FISH* BS16 .... 54 B5
Briarwood
  HNLZ/SM/SNYPK/WT BS9 .... 51 H3
Briary Rd *PTSHD/EG* BS20 .... 47 G4
Briavels Gv *RDLND/MONT* BS6 ..... 3 M5
Brick St *CBRISNE* BS2 .... 7 M2
Bridewell La
  CBATH/BATHN BA1 .... 14 F6 🔲
  OMX/HUT/LCK BS24 .... 118 E5
Bridewell St *CBRIS/FH* BS1 .... 7 H2 🔲
Bridge Av *TRWBR* BA14 .... 124 C6
Bridge Cl *HGRV/WHIT* BS14 .... 79 G7 🔲
Bridge Farm Cl
  HGRV/WHIT BS14 .... 93 K1 🔲
Bridge Farm Sq
  YTN/CONG BS49 .... 109 G1
Bridgeleap Rd *MANG/FISH* BS16 .. 55 F1
Bridge Rd *BATHSE* BA2 .... 99 F7
  CFTN/FAIL BS8 .... 65 F4
  EVILLE/WHL BS5 .... 4 C4
  KGWD/HNM BS15 .... 55 F6
  MANG/FISH BS16 .... 55 J5
  WSM BS23 .... 17 H5
  YATE/CS BS37 .... 33 H5
Bridges Dr *MANG/FISH* BS16 ..... 54 C3 🔲
Bridge St *BOAV* BA15 .... 114 E7
  CBRIS/FH BS1 .... 7 H3
  EVILLE/WHL BS5 .... 5 G5
Bridge Valley Rd *CFTN/FAIL* BS8... 65 G2
Bridge Wk *HORF/LLZ* BS7 .... 52 E1
Bridge Wy *FRCTL/WBN* BS36....... 32 C7
Bridgman Gv *BRSTK/PCHW* BS34.. 40 A5
Bridgwater Ct
  OMX/HUT/LCK BS24 .... 117 F3
Bridgwater Rd
  BMSTRD/HC/WWD BS13 .... 77 H3
  NAIL BS48 .... 76 C7
  OMX/HUT/LCK BS24 .... 116 D4
  OMX/HUT/LCK BS24 .... 116 D4
Bridle Wy *THNB/SVB* BS35.......... 22 E2
Briercliffe Rd
  HNLZ/SM/SNYPK/WT BS9 .... 51 F2
Brierly Furlong
  BRSTK/PCHW BS34 .... 40 C5
Briery Leaze Rd
  HGRV/WHIT BS14 .... 78 E6
Brighton Crs *BMSTR* BS3 .... 10 D8
Brighton Pk *EVILLE/WHL* BS5 .... 4 D9 🔲
Brighton Pl *KGWD/HNM* BS15 ..... 68 D1 🔲
Brighton Rd *BRSTK/PCHW* BS34 .. 29 J7
  RDLND/MONT BS6 .... 2 E7
  WSM BS23 .... 16 F6
Brighton St *CBRISNE* BS2 .... 3 K8
Brighton Ter *BMSTR* BS3 .... 10 D7
Bright St *EVILLE/WHL* BS5 .... 8 D2
  KGWD/HNM BS15 .... 68 D2
Brigstocke Rd *CBRISNE* BS2 .... 3 J8
Brimbles *HORF/LLZ* BS7 .... 40 A6
Brimbleworth La
  MTN/WRL BS22 .... 106 D1
Brimridge Rd *WNSC* BS25 .... 120 D6 🔲
Brinkmarsh La *WUE* GL12 .... 20 C2
Brinkworthy Rd
  MANG/FISH BS16 .... 53 J7
Brinmead Wk
  BMSTRD/HC/WWD BS13 .... 92 C1 🔲
Brins Cl *BRSTK/PCHW* BS34 .... 40 E4
Brinsea Batch *WNSC* BS25 .... 109 H5
Brinsea La *YTN/CONG* BS49 .... 109 H5
Brinsea Rd *YTN/CONG* BS49 .... 109 H3
Brinsham La *YATE/CS* BS37 .... 34 D1
Briscoes Av
  BMSTRD/HC/WWD BS13 .... 78 A7
Brislington Hl
  BRSG/KWL/STAPK BS4............. 13 H4
Bristol Br *CBRIS/FH* BS1 .... 7 J4
Bristol Hl *BRSG/KWL/STAPK* BS4.. 13 G4
Bristol Rd *BATHSE* BA2 .... 97 J4
  FRCTL/WBN BS36 .... 32 A7
  HGRV/WHIT BS14 .... 94 B1
  KEYN BS31 .... 80 D5
  MANG/FISH BS16 .... 41 J5
  MTN/WRL BS22 .... 106 C3
  NAIL BS48 .... 62 C6
  OMX/HUT/LCK BS24 .... 106 D3
  PLTN/PENS BS39 .... 94 C6
  PTSHD/EG BS20 .... 47 H5
  RDSTK/MIDN BA3 .... 127 G2
  THNB/SVB BS35 .... 19 G6
  WNSC BS25 .... 121 J2
  WUE GL12 .... 21 H7
  YTN/CONG BS49 .... 87 G7
Bristol Road Lower *WSM* BS23 .. 104 E4
Bristow Broadway *AVONM* BS11.. 36 D7
Britannia Crs *BRSTK/PCHW* BS34.. 40 C3
Britannia Rd *BRSTK/PCHW* BS34 .. 39 G1
  EVILLE/WHL BS5....................... 4 D8
  KGWD/HNM BS15 .... 68 C2
Britannia Wy *CLVDN* BS21 .... 70 E2 🔲
British Rd *BMSTR* BS3 .... 10 E2
British Rw *TRWBR* BA14 .... 124 E5
Brittan Pl *PTSHD/EG* BS20 .... 48 E6
Britten Ct
  OLD/WMLY/WICK BS30 .... 69 F6 🔲
Brixham Rd *BMSTR* BS3 .... 10 F4
Brixton Rd *EVILLE/WHL* BS5 .... 8 D1
Broadbury Rd
  BRSG/KWL/STAPK BS4............. 11 J7
Broadcloth East La
  TRWBR BA14 .... 125 G7
Broadcloth La *TRWBR* BA14 ...... 125 G7
Broad Cft *ALMDB* BS32 .... 30 B5 🔲
Broadcroft Av *YTN/CONG* BS49 ... 87 J3
Broadcroft Cl *YTN/CONG* BS49 .... 87 J3

Broadfield Av *KGWD/HNM* BS15 .. 68 C2
Broadfield Rd
  BRSG/KWL/STAPK BS4............. 12 B7
Broadlands *CLVDN* BS21 .... 59 H7
Broadlands Av *BMSTR* BS3 .... 80 D5
Broadlands Dr *AVONM* BS11 .... 37 H4
Broad La *FRCTL/WBN* BS36 .... 42 E3
  YATE/CS BS37 .... 33 K3
  YATE/CS BS37 .... 43 H4
Broadleas
  BMSTRD/HC/WWD BS13 .... 77 K4
Broadleaze *AVONM* BS11 .... 50 A2 🔲
Broadleaze Wy *WNSC* BS25 ...... 120 C4
Bradley Pk *TRWBR* BA14 .... 131 F4
Broadleys Av
  HNLZ/SM/SNYPK/WT BS9 .... 51 K2
Broadmead *CBRIS/FH* BS1 .... 7 J2
  TRWBR BA14 .... 124 C5
Broadmead La *KEYN* BS31 .... 81 G5
Broadmoor Pk
  CBATH/BATHN BA1 .... 98 E2 🔲
Broadmoor V
  CBATH/BATHN BA1 .... 98 D1
Broadoak Hl *LGASH* BS41 .... 92 C2
Broad Oak Rd
  BMSTRD/HC/WWD BS13 .... 77 H7
Broadoak Rd *WNSC* BS25 .... 121 K1
  WSM BS23 .... 116 C3
Broad Oaks *CFTN/FAIL* BS8 .... 65 G4 🔲
Broadoak Wk *MANG/FISH* BS16 ... 54 B5 🔲
Broad Quay *BATHSE* BA2 .... 14 F8
  CBRIS/FH BS1 .... 7 G4
Broad Rd *KGWD/HNM* BS15 .... 68 C1
Broadstone La *CLVDN* BS21 .... 85 G1
Broad Stones *BOAV* BA15 .... 101 K5
Broadstone Wk
  BMSTRD/HC/WWD BS13 .... 78 B6
Broad St *CBATH/BATHN* BA1 .... 14 F5
  CBRIS/FH BS1 .... 7 H3
  MANG/FISH BS16 .... 54 E5
  TRWBR BA14 .... 124 E5 🔲
  YATE/CS BS37 .... 34 E6
  YTN/CONG BS49 .... 109 G1
Broad Wk *BRSG/KWL/STAPK* BS4.. 12 A4
Broadway *BATHSE* BA2 .... 15 J8
  KEYN BS31 .... 96 E1 🔲
  OMX/HUT/LCK BS24 .... 116 E5
  OMX/HUT/LCK BS24 .... 118 C2 🔲
  YATE/CS BS37 .... 34 C5 🔲
Broadway Av
  HNLZ/SM/SNYPK/WT BS9 .... 52 B3
Broadway Rd
  BMSTRD/HC/WWD BS13 .... 77 H6 🔲
  HORF/LLZ BS7 .... 3 H3
Broadways Dr
  MANG/FISH BS16 .... 53 K2 🔲
Broad Weir *CBRIS/FH* BS1 .... 7 K3
Brock End *PTSHD/EG* BS20 .... 46 C6
Brockhurst Gdns
  KGWD/HNM BS15 .... 68 A2
Brockhurst Rd
  KGWD/HNM BS15 .... 68 A2
Brockley Cl
  BRSTK/PCHW BS34 .... 40 B1 🔲
  NAIL BS48 .... 73 H2 🔲
  OMX/HUT/LCK BS24 .... 116 E5 🔲
Brockley Combe Rd *NAIL* BS48.... 88 D2
Brockley Crs
  OMX/HUT/LCK BS24 .... 116 E5
Brockley La *NAIL* BS48 .... 73 H7
Brockley Rd *KEYN* BS31 .... 96 E5
Brockley Wk
  BMSTRD/HC/WWD BS13 .... 10 A7
Brockley Wy *YTN/CONG* BS49..... 87 K2
Brockridge La *FRCTL/WBN* BS36 .. 42 D1
Brocks Rd
  BMSTRD/HC/WWD BS13 .... 93 F1
Brock St *CBATH/BATHN* BA1 .... 14 E4 🔲
Brockway *NAIL* BS48 .... 73 K1
Brockworth *YATE/CS* BS37 .... 43 K2
Brockworth Crs
  MANG/FISH BS16 .... 53 K3
Brokerswood Rd *TRWBR* BA14 .. 130 C3
Bromfield Wk
  MANG/FISH BS16 .... 55 H2 🔲
Bromley Dr *MANG/FISH* BS16 ..... 54 D1
Bromley Heath Av
  MANG/FISH BS16 .... 54 D1
Bromley Heath Rd
  MANG/FISH BS16 .... 54 D1 🔲
Bromley Rd *HORF/LLZ* BS7 .... 52 D4
Brompton Cl *KGWD/HNM* BS15 ... 69 F2
Brompton Rd
  OMX/HUT/LCK BS24 .... 117 F4
Broncksea Rd *HORF/LLZ* BS7 ...... 39 J7
Brook Cl *LGASH* BS41 .... 76 D2
Brookcote Dr
  BRSTK/PCHW BS34 .... 40 C2
Brookdale Rd
  BMSTRD/HC/WWD BS13 .... 77 K5
Brookfield Av *HORF/LLZ* BS7 .... 3 H4
Brookfield Cl *YATE/CS* BS37 .... 35 F6
Brookfield La *RDLND/MONT* BS6 ... 3 H6
Brookfield Pk
  CBATH/BATHN BA1 .... 98 E2
Brookfield Rd
  BRSTK/PCHW BS34 .... 30 A7
  RDLND/MONT BS6 .... 3 H6 🔲
Brookfield Wk *CLVDN* BS21 .... 59 H7
  OLD/WMLY/WICK BS30 .... 69 J7 🔲
Brook Ga *BMSTR* BS3 .... 77 G2
Brook Hl *RDLND/MONT* BS6 .... 3 K7
Brookland Rd *MTN/WRL* BS22 .... 17 M3
  RDLND/MONT BS6 .... 52 B4
Brook La *MANG/FISH* BS16 .... 53 J3
  RDLND/MONT BS6 .... 3 L7
Brooklea *OLD/WMLY/WICK* BS30 .. 69 H6
Brookleaze
  HNLZ/SM/SNYPK/WT BS9 .... 50 E4
Brookleaze Buildings
  CBATH/BATHN BA1 .... 100 A2
Brook Lintons
  BRSG/KWL/STAPK BS4............. 13 H1
Brooklyn Rd
  BMSTRD/HC/WWD BS13 .... 10 C8
  CBATH/BATHN BA1 .... 100 B2
Brookmead *THNB/SVB* BS35 .... 19 J6 🔲
  TRWBR BA14 .... 130 C4

Brook Rd *BATHSE* BA2 .... 14 A7
BMSTR BS3 .... 7 C8 ⓑ
EVILLE/WHL BS5 .... 5 K7
KGWD/HNM BS15 .... 69 C2 ⓑ
MANG/FISH BS16 .... 55 F3
RDLND/MONT BS6 .... 3 L7
TRWBR BA14 .... 124 C6
Brookside
BLAG/CWMG/WR BS40 .... 91 G5
PTSHD/EG BS20 .... 49 K6
Brookside Dr *FRCTL/WBN* BS36 .... 32 C7
Brookside Rd
BRSG/KWL/STAPK BS4 .... 13 H3
Brook St *EVILLE/WHL* BS5 .... 8 E2
YATE/CS BS37 .... 34 D6
Brookthorpe *YATE/CS* BS37 ...... 34 A7
Brookthorpe Av *AVONM* BS11 .... 50 C1
Brookview Wk
BMSTRD/HC/WWD BS13 ...... 10 C9
Brook Wy *ALMDB* BS32 .... 30 B6
Broom Farm Cl *NAIL* BS48 ...... 73 J5 ⓑ
Broomground *BOAV* BA15 .... 113 K6
Broom Hl *MANG/FISH* BS16 ...... 53 J4
Broomhill Rd
BRSG/KWL/STAPK BS4........ 13 L1
BRSG/KWL/STAPK BS4........ 13 M5
The Brooms *MANG/FISH* BS16 .... 42 B6
Brougham Hayes *BATHSE* BA2 .... 14 B7
Broughton *TRWBR* BA14 .... 130 D2
Brow Hl *CBATH/BATHN* BA1 ...... 100 E1
Browning Ct *HORF/LLZ* BS7 ...... 53 F1 ⓑ
Brownlow Rd *WSM* BS23 .... 116 D2
Brown St *TRWBR* BA14 .... 125 F7
The Brow *BATHSE* BA2 .... 98 E7
Broxholme Wk *AVONM* BS11 ..... 50 B1 ⓑ
Bruce Av *EVILLE/WHL* BS5 .... 4 F7
Bruce Rd *EVILLE/WHL* BS5 .... 4 F8
Brue Cl *WSM* BS23 .... 17 J8
Brunel Cl *OLD/WMLY/WICK* BS30 69 J3
OMX/HUT/LCK BS24 .... 116 E6
Brunel Lock Rd *CBRIS/FH* BS1 .. 65 H5
Brunel Rd
BMSTR/HC/WWD BS13 .... 77 H3
NAIL BS48 .... 73 F2
Brunel Wy *BMSTR* BS3 .... 65 H5
THNB/SVB BS35 .... 19 G6
Brunswick Pl *CBRIS/FH* BS1 ..... 65 H5 ⓑ
Brunswick Sq *CBRISNE* BS2 ...... 7 J1
Brunswick St *CBATH/BATHN* BA1.. 3 J9
CBRISNE BS2...................... 3 J9
EVILLE/WHL BS5 .... 8 E3
Bruton Av *BATHSE* BA2 .... 111 J2
PTSHD/EG BS20 .... 46 E4 ⓑ
Bruton Cl *EVILLE/WHL* BS5 .... 5 M9
NAIL BS48 .... 73 J3 ⓑ
Bryansons Cl
MANG/FISH BS16 .... 53 H3 ⓑ
Bryant Av *RDSTK/MIDN* BA3 ...... 126 E4
Bryant Cl *CLVDN* BS21 .... 70 E2 ⓑ
Bryants Cl *MANG/FISH* BS16 ..... 41 H7 ⓑ
Bryant's Hl *EVILLE/WHL* BS5 ...... 68 B4
Brynland Av *HORF/LLZ* BS7 ...... 3 K1
Buckingham Dr
BRSTK/PCHW BS34 .... 40 C4
Buckingham Gdns
MANG/FISH BS16 .... 54 E3
Buckingham Pl
MANG/FISH BS16 .... 54 E3 ⓑ
Buckingham Rd
BRSG/KWL/STAPK BS4........ 9 H7
OMX/HUT/LCK BS24 .... 116 A6
Buckingham St *BMSTR* BS3 ...... 10 E3 ⓑ
Buckingham V *CFTN/FAIL* BS8 ... 2 B1 ⓑ
Bucklands Batch *NAIL* BS48 ..... 73 K3
Bucklands Dr *NAIL* BS48 .... 73 K3 ⓑ
Bucklands Gv *NAIL* BS48 .... 73 K3
Bucklands La *NAIL* BS48 .... 73 K3
Bucklands Vw *NAIL* BS48 .... 74 A3
Buckleaze Cl *TRWBR* BA14 ...... 131 F2
Budbury Cl *BOAV* BA15 .... 114 C6
Budbury Pl *BOAV* BA15 .... 114 C6
Budbury Rdg *BOAV* BA15 .... 114 C6
Budbury Tyning *BOAV* BA15 ..... 114 C6
Bude Av *EVILLE/WHL* BS5 .... 68 C4
Bude Cl *NAIL* BS48 .... 74 A2
Bude Rd *BRSTK/PCHW* BS34 ..... 40 A5
Buller Rd *BRSG/KWL/STAPK* BS4.. 12 C5
Bull La *EVILLE/WHL* BS5 .... 9 M5
PTSHD/EG BS20 .... 49 J5
Bullocks La *CLVDN* BS21 .... 70 E7
Bull Pit *BOAV* BA15 .... 114 E7 ⓑ
Bunting Ct *MTN/WRL* BS22 ...... 105 K4 ⓑ
Burbank Cl
OLD/WMLY/WICK BS30 ...... 69 G7
Burchells Green Cl
KGWD/HNM BS15 .... 68 B2
Burchells Green Rd
KGWD/HNM BS15 .... 68 B1
Burcombe Cl *FRCTL/WBN* BS36 .. 42 E1
Burcott Rd *AVONM* BS11 .... 36 D3
Burden Cl *ALMDB* BS32 .... 40 D2
Burderop La *TRWBR* BA14 ...... 131 F2 ⓑ
Burfoote Gdns *HGRV/WHIT* BS14 .79 J7
Burfoot Rd *HGRV/WHIT* BS14 .... 79 J7
Burford Cl *BATHSE* BA2 .... 110 E3
PTSHD/EG BS20 .... 47 J5
Burford Gv *AVONM* BS11 .... 50 B4
Burgage Cl *YATE/CS* BS37 ...... 34 E7 ⓑ
Burgess Green Cl
BRSG/KWL/STAPK BS4........ 9 K3
Burghill Rd *HNBRY/STHM* BS10 .. 38 D7
Burghley Ct *FRCTL/WBN* BS36 ... 41 K3 ⓑ
Burghley Rd *RDLND/MONT* BS6 .. 3 J5
Burgis Rd *HGRV/WHIT* BS14 ..... 79 H5 ⓑ
Burleigh Gdns
CBATH/BATHN BA1 .... 98 D4
Burley Av *MANG/FISH* BS16 ..... 55 F4
Burley Crest *MANG/FISH* BS16 .. 55 F5
Burley Gv *MANG/FISH* BS16 ..... 55 F5
Burlington Rd *RDLND/MONT* BS6 .. 2 C6
RDSTK/MIDN BA3 .... 126 D3
Burlington St *CBATH/BATHN* BA1.. 14 F3
WSM BS23 .... 16 E2 ⓑ
The Burltons *WUE* GL12 .... 21 J3
Burnbush Cl *HGRV/WHIT* BS14 ... 79 J5
Burnell Dr *CBRISNE* BS2 .... 3 L9
Burneside Cl
HNBRY/STHM BS10 .... 39 F6 ⓑ

Burnett Hl *KEYN* BS31 .... 96 B4
Burnett Rd *TRWBR* BA14 .... 131 F1
Burney Wy
OLD/WMLY/WICK BS30 ...... 69 G7
Burnham Cl *KGWD/HNM* BS15 ... 69 F1 ⓑ
Burnham Dr *KGWD/HNM* BS15... 69 F1
OMX/HUT/LCK BS24 .... 116 E5
Burnham Rd *AVONM* BS11 ...... 49 K3
BATHSE BA2 .... 99 F6
Burnt House Rd *BATHSE* BA2 ... 111 G5
Burrington Cl
OMX/HUT/LCK BS24 .... 116 E5
Burrington Cl *NAIL* BS48 .... 73 J2 ⓑ
Burrington Wk
BMSTRD/HC/WWD BS13 ...... 10 A8
Burrough Wy *FRCTL/WBN* BS36.. 41 K3
Burton Cl *CBRIS/FH* BS1 .... 7 J7
Burton Ct *CFTN/FAIL* BS8 .... 6 C3 ⓑ
Burwalls Rd *CFTN/FAIL* BS8...... 65 G4
Burycourt Cl *AVONM* BS11 ...... 37 H7 ⓑ
Bury Hl *MANG/FISH* BS16........ 41 K5
The Bury *OMX/HUT/LCK* BS24 .... 118 B2
Bush Av *BRSTK/PCHW* BS34 ..... 40 B3
Bushes La *YATE/CS* BS37 .... 35 K1
Bushy Pk *BRSG/KWL/STAPK* BS4 .. 7 M9
Butcombe Wk *HGRV/WHIT* BS14 .. 79 F6
Butlers Cl *EVILLE/WHL* BS5 ...... 9 L3
Butterfield Cl
HNBRY/STHM BS10 .... 52 C2
Butterfield Pk *CLVDN* BS21 ..... 70 E2
Butterfield Rd
HNBRY/STHM BS10 .... 52 C2
Buttermere Rd *WSM* BS23 ...... 17 K8
Butterworth Ct
BRSG/KWL/STAPK BS4 .... 78 B4 ⓑ
Butt La *THNB/SVB* BS35 .... 19 H2
Buxton Wk *HORF/LLZ* BS7 .... 52 E1
Bye Md *MANG/FISH* BS16 .... 55 C1
Byfield *BATHSE* BA2 .... 112 A4
Byfields *CLVDN* BS21 .... 70 E3
Byfield Rd *BATHSE* BA2 .... 112 A4
Byron Cl *MTN/WRL* BS22 .... 105 K6
Byron Pl *CFTN/FAIL* BS8 .... 6 D3 ⓑ
MANG/FISH BS16 .... 54 E5 ⓑ
Byron Rd *BATHSE* BA2 .... 111 J1
OMX/HUT/LCK BS24 .... 118 B2 ⓑ
WSM BS23 .... 117 F2
Byron St *CBRISNE* BS2 .... 4 A7
EVILLE/WHL BS5................. 8 F2
Bythesea Rd *TRWBR* BA14 ...... 124 E6

C

Cabot Cl *KEYN* BS31 .... 96 E2 ⓑ
YATE/CS BS37 .... 34 C6
Cabot Ri *PTSHD/EG* BS20 .... 46 E4 ⓑ
Cabot Wy *CFTN/FAIL* BS8........ 65 H4
MTN/WRL BS22 .... 106 B2
PTSHD/EG BS20 .... 49 K6
Cabstand *PTSHD/EG* BS20 .... 47 H3
Cadbury Camp La *CLVDN* BS21.... 61 F4
Cadbury Camp La West
CLVDN BS21 .... 60 A6
Cadbury Farm Rd
YTN/CONG BS49 .... 87 F5
Cadbury Heath Rd
OLD/WMLY/WICK BS30 ...... 69 H5
Cadbury La *PTSHD/EG* BS20 .... 60 D1
Cadbury Rd *KEYN* BS31 .... 96 B2
PTSHD/EG BS20 .... 47 H5
Cadby Cl *TRWBR* BA14 .... 125 H6
Caddick Cl *KGWD/HNM* BS15 ... 55 F7
Cade Cl *BRSTK/PCHW* BS34 ..... 40 D3
KGWD/HNM BS15 .... 69 H5
Cadogan Rd *HGRV/WHIT* BS14 .. 12 B7
Caen Rd *BMSTR* BS3 .... 11 H2
Caernarvon Rd *KEYN* BS31 ...... 80 C7
Caine Rd *HORF/LLZ* BS7 .... 52 D2 ⓑ
Cains Cl *KGWD/HNM* BS15 ...... 68 C4
Cairn Cl *NAIL* BS48 .... 74 A2 ⓑ
Cairn Gdns *FRCTL/WBN* BS36 .... 41 K4 ⓑ
Cairns' Crs *CBRISNE* BS2 .... 3 M7
Cairns Rd *RDLND/MONT* BS6 .... 2 C2
Calcott Rd
BRSG/KWL/STAPK BS4........ 12 A3
Caldbeck Cl
HNBRY/STHM BS10 .... 39 G6 ⓑ
Calder Cl *KEYN* BS31 .... 81 G7
Caldicot Cl *AVONM* BS11 .... 37 K6 ⓑ
OLD/WMLY/WICK BS30 ...... 81 H1
Caledonian Rd *BATHSE* BA2 .... 14 A7
Caledonia Pl *CFTN/FAIL* BS8 .... 65 H4
California Rd
OLD/WMLY/WICK BS30 ...... 69 H6 ⓑ
Callicroft Rd *BRSTK/PCHW* BS34 .. 39 K1
Callington Rd
BRSG/KWL/STAPK BS4........ 13 J5
Callowhill Ct *CBRIS/FH* BS1 ..... 7 J2
Calton Gdns *BATHSE* BA2 .... 14 F3
Calton Rd *BATHSE* BA2 .... 15 G9
Camberley Dr *FRCTL/WBN* BS36 .. 32 A7
Camberley Rd
BRSG/KWL/STAPK BS4........ 13 J5
Camberley Wk *MTN/WRL* BS22 .. 105 K6
Camborne Rd *HORF/LLZ* BS7 .... 52 E2
Cambrian Dr *YATE/CS* BS37 ..... 34 B4
Cambridge Crs
HNLZ/SM/SNYPK/WT BS9 .... 51 J2
Cambridge Gv *CLVDN* BS21 ..... 59 F5
Cambridge Pk *RDLND/MONT* BS6.. 2 C4
Cambridge Pl *WSM* BS23 .... 16 D2 ⓑ
Cambridge Rd *CLVDN* BS21 ..... 59 F5
HORF/LLZ BS7 .... 3 H1
Cambridge St *BMSTR* BS3 ...... 7 L8
EVILLE/WHL BS5................. 8 F3
Cambridge Ter *BATHSE* BA2 .... 15 J9
Camden Cl *BATHSE* BA1.......... 14 F3
Camden Rd *BMSTR* BS3 .... 6 D8
CBATH/BATHN BA1 .... 15 H1
Camden Rw *CBATH/BATHN* BA1... 14 F5
Camden Ter *CFTN/FAIL* BS8 ..... 6 A5 ⓑ
CBATH/BATHN BA1 .... 16 F3 ⓑ
Cameley Gn *BATHSE* BA2........ 98 C6
Camelford Rd *EVILLE/WHL* BS5 .. 54 D6
Cameron Wk *HORF/LLZ* BS7 .... 53 G3 ⓑ
Cameroons Cl *KEYN* BS31 .... 88 E6
Camerton Cl *KEYN* BS31 .... 97 F1 ⓑ

Camerton Rd *EVILLE/WHL* BS5 .... 5 G7
Campbell Farm Dr *AVONM* BS11 .. 37 G7
Campbell St *CBRISNE* BS2 .... 3 K8
Campion Cl *MTN/WRL* BS22 .... 105 J6 ⓑ
THNB/SVB BS35 .... 19 J3
Campion Dr *ALMDB* BS32 .... 30 C5 ⓑ
TRWBR BA14 .... 131 F1
Camp Rd *CFTN/FAIL* BS8 .... 65 H3
Camp Rd North *WSM* BS23 ..... 104 B4 ⓑ
Camp Vw *FRCTL/WBN* BS36 ..... 41 K4
NAIL BS48 .... 73 H1 ⓑ
Camwal Rd *CBRISNE* BS2 .... 8 B6
Canada Coombe
OMX/HUT/LCK BS24 .... 118 A4
Canada Wy *CBRIS/FH* BS1 ...... 6 B7
Canal Rd *TRWBR* BA14 .... 125 G2
Canberra Crs
OMX/HUT/LCK BS24 .... 106 B7
Canberra Gv *BRSTK/PCHW* BS34 .. 40 A4
Canford La
HNLZ/SM/SNYPK/WT BS9 .... 51 C2
Canford Rd
HNLZ/SM/SNYPK/WT BS9 .... 51 H2
Cannans Cl *FRCTL/WBN* BS36 ... 41 K1
Cannons Ga *CLVDN* BS21 .... 70 E3
Cannon St *BMSTR* BS3 .... 7 H2
CBRIS/FH BS1 .... 7 H2
Canons Cl *BATHSE* BA2 .... 110 E3
Canon's Rd *CBRIS/FH* BS1 ...... 6 D6
CBRIS/FH BS1 .... 6 D6
Canon St *EVILLE/WHL* BS5 ...... 8 E1
Canon's Wk *KGWD/HNM* BS15 .. 54 E7
Canons Wy *CBRIS/FH* BS1 ...... 6 E5
Canowie Rd *RDLND/MONT* BS6 .. 2 D4
Cantell Gv *HGRV/WHIT* BS14 .... 79 K6 ⓑ
Canterbury Cl
MTN/WRL BS22 .... 106 C2 ⓑ
YATE/CS BS37 .... 34 B4
Canterbury Rd *BATHSE* BA2 .... 14 B8
Canterbury St *EVILLE/WHL* BS5 .. 8 D4 ⓑ
Canvey Cl *HNBRY/STHM* BS10 .. 52 C2 ⓑ
Canynge Rd *CFTN/FAIL* BS8..... 65 H2
Canynge Sq *CFTN/FAIL* BS8 .... 65 H2
Canynge St *CBRIS/FH* BS1 ...... 7 J5
Capel Cl *KGWD/HNM* BS15...... 69 H2
Capell Cl *MTN/WRL* BS22 .... 17 M2
Capel Rd *AVONM* BS11 .... 37 J5
Capenor Cl *PTSHD/EG* BS20 .... 47 G5
Capgrave Cl
BRSG/KWL/STAPK BS4........ 68 A7
Capgrave Crs
BRSG/KWL/STAPK BS4........ 68 A7
Caraway Gdns *EVILLE/WHL* BS5 .. 4 F6
Carders Cnr *TRWBR* BA14 ...... 125 F7
Cardigan Crs *MTN/WRL* BS22 .. 105 H5
Cardigan Rd
HNLZ/SM/SNYPK/WT BS9 .... 51 K3
Cardill Cl
BMSTRD/HC/WWD BS13 ...... 10 B6
Cardinal Cl *BATHSE* BA2 .... 111 G5 ⓑ
Card) Dro *YTN/CONG* BS49 ..... 108 E5
Carey's Cl *CLVDN* BS21 .... 59 H6
Carice Gdns *CLVDN* BS21 .... 71 F3
Carisbrooke Crs *TRWBR* BA14 .. 125 G1
Carisbrooke Rd
BRSG/KWL/STAPK BS4........ 11 H8
Carlingford Terrace Rd
RDSTK/MIDN BA3 .... 127 H3
Carlow Rd
BRSG/KWL/STAPK BS4........ 11 J7
Carlton Pk *EVILLE/WHL* BS5 ..... 8 E1
Carlton Rw *TRWBR* BA14 .... 130 E1 ⓑ
Carlton St *WSM* BS23 .... 16 D4
Carlyle Rd *EVILLE/WHL* BS5 ..... 4 F7
Carmarthen Cl *YATE/CS* BS37 .. 34 C3 ⓑ
Carmarthen Gv
OLD/WMLY/WICK BS30 ...... 81 H2 ⓑ
Carmarthen Rd
HNLZ/SM/SNYPK/WT BS9 .... 51 J4 ⓑ
Carnarvon Rd *RDLND/MONT* BS6 .. 2 D7
Caroline Cl *KEYN* BS31 .... 80 C7
YATE/CS BS37 .... 34 E5 ⓑ
Carpenter Cl *WSM* BS23 .... 17 K4 ⓑ
Carpenters La *KEYN* BS31 ...... 80 E6
Carre Gdns *MTN/WRL* BS22 .... 106 A1 ⓑ
Carrington Rd *BMSTR* BS3 ...... 6 B9
Carsons Rd *MANG/FISH* BS16 ... 55 H6
Carter Wk *ALMDB* BS32 .... 30 C7 ⓑ
Cartledge Rd *EVILLE/WHL* BS5 .. 4 E7 ⓑ
Cassell Rd *MANG/FISH* BS16 .... 54 C4
Cassey Bottom La
EVILLE/WHL BS5................. 68 A3 ⓑ
Castle Cl *HNBRY/STHM* BS10.... 38 B6
NAIL BS48 .... 74 E4
Castle Coombe *THNB/SVB* BS35 .. 19 H3
Castle Ct *BRSG/KWL/STAPK* BS4 .. 8 E8
THNB/SVB BS35 .... 19 C4
Castle Farm La *LGASH* BS41 .... 91 J2
Castle Farm Rd
KGWD/HNM BS15 .... 80 B1
Castle Gdns *BATHSE* BA2 .... 111 H2
Castle Hl *BNWL* BS29 .... 119 K4
Castle Hl *CLVDN* BS21 .... 59 F4
KGWD/HNM BS15 .... 54 C7
MANG/FISH BS16 .... 56 E3
MTN/WRL BS22 .... 105 K2
OLD/WMLY/WICK BS30 ...... 69 J3
Castle St *CBRISNE* BS2 .... 7 K3
THNB/SVB BS35 .... 19 F3
TRWBR BA14 .... 125 F6
Castle View Rd *CLVDN* BS21 .... 59 F5
Castlewood Cl *CLVDN* BS21 .... 59 F6
Castley Rd *TRWBR* BA14 .... 125 J4
Caswell Hl *PTSHD/EG* BS20 .... 62 A2
Caswell La *PTSHD/EG* BS20 .... 61 K1
Catbrain Hl *HNBRY/STHM* BS10 .. 38 E2
Catbrain La *HNBRY/STHM* BS10 .. 38 E2
Catchpot La *YATE/CS* BS37 ..... 45 K2
Catemead *CLVDN* BS21 .... 70 D3
Cater Rd
BMSTRD/HC/WWD BS13 ...... 77 K5
Catharine Pl
CBATH/BATHN BA1 .... 14 E4
Catherine Mead St *BMSTR* BS3 .. 6 F9
Catherine St *AVONM* BS11 ..... 49 J2
Catley Gv *LGASH* BS41 .... 76 D2
Cato St *EVILLE/WHL* BS5 .... 4 D7 ⓑ
Cattistock Dr *EVILLE/WHL* BS5 .. 68 A4

Cattle Market Rd *CBRIS/FH* BS1 .. 7 L6
Cattybrook Rd *MANG/FISH* BS16 .. 55 K4
Cattybrook St *EVILLE/WHL* BS5 .. 8 D1 ⓑ
EVILLE/WHL BS5................. 8 D2 ⓑ
Caulfield Rd *MTN/WRL* BS22 ... 106 B1 ⓑ
Causeway *CLVDN* BS21 .... 61 F1
The Causeway *FRCTL/WBN* BS36.. 42 D1
PTSHD/EG BS20 .... 61 J2
YTN/CONG BS49 .... 109 G1
Causeway Vw *NAIL* BS48 .... 73 C1
Causley Dr
OLD/WMLY/WICK BS30 ...... 69 F5 ⓑ
Cautletts Cl *RDSTK/MIDN* BA3 .. 126 A5
Cavan Wk *BRSG/KWL/STAPK* BS4.. 11 H5
Cave Ct *MANG/FISH* BS16 ...... 54 D3
Cave Gv *MANG/FISH* BS16 ...... 55 H2
Cavell Ct *CLVDN* BS21 .... 70 E2
Cavendish Cl *KEYN* BS31 .... 96 E2
Cavendish Crs
CBATH/BATHN BA1 .... 14 D2
Cavendish Gdns
HNLZ/SM/SNYPK/WT BS9 .... 50 E5
Cavendish Rd
BRSTK/PCHW BS34 .... 29 J7
CBATH/BATHN BA1 .... 14 D2
HNLZ/SM/SNYPK/WT BS9 .... 51 J4
WSM BS23....................... 104 D3
Caveners Ct *MTN/WRL* BS22 .... 105 G4 ⓑ
Caversham Dr *NAIL* BS48 .... 74 A1
Cave St *CBRISNE* BS2 .... 3 K9
Cecil Av *EVILLE/WHL* BS5 .... 5 L8
Cecil Rd *CFTN/FAIL* BS8 .... 65 H2 ⓑ
KGWD/HNM BS15 .... 68 D2
WSM BS23........................ 104 D3
Cedar Av *MTN/WRL* BS22 ...... 105 H4 ⓑ
Cedar Cl *BRSTK/PCHW* BS34 .... 39 J1
LGASH BS41..................... 76 D2 ⓑ
OLD/WMLY/WICK BS30 ...... 69 H6 ⓑ
Cedar Dr *KEYN* BS31 .... 80 D7
Cedar Gv *BATHSE* BA2 .... 111 C2 ⓑ
HNLZ/SM/SNYPK/WT BS9 .... 51 F4
TRWBR BA14 .... 130 D1
Cedarhurst Rd *PTSHD/EG* BS20 .. 46 C6
Cedar Pk
HNLZ/SM/SNYPK/WT BS9 .... 51 F4
Cedar Ter *RDSTK/MIDN* BA3 .... 126 E4
Cedar Wy *BATHSE* BA2 .... 14 D8
FRCTL/WBN BS36 .... 41 J3
MANG/FISH BS16 .... 56 D4
NAIL BS48 .... 74 A1
PTSHD/EG BS20 .... 47 F5
Cedric Rd *CBATH/BATHN* BA1 ... 99 F4 ⓑ
Celandine Cl *THNB/SVB* BS35 ... 19 J5
Celestine Rd *YATE/CS* BS37 .... 33 F5
Celia Ter *BRSG/KWL/STAPK* BS4 .. 9 L4 ⓑ
Celtic Wy *OMX/HUT/LCK* BS24 .. 117 G6
Cemetery La
BRSG/KWL/STAPK BS4........ 12 B1
Cennick Av *KGWD/HNM* BS15 .. 68 C1
Centaurus Rd
BRSTK/PCHW BS34 .... 39 F1
Central Av *HNBRY/STHM* BS10 .. 27 H4
KGWD/HNM BS15 .... 68 C5
Central Wy *CLVDN* BS21 .... 71 F2 ⓑ
Centre Dr *BNWL* BS29 .... 119 F2
Ceres Cl *OLD/WMLY/WICK* BS30 .. 81 F1
Cerimon Ga
BRSTK/PCHW BS34 .... 40 D3 ⓑ
Cerney Gdns *NAIL* BS48 .... 74 A1 ⓑ
Cerney La *AVONM* BS11 .... 50 A4
Cesson Cl *YATE/CS* BS37 .... 35 F6
Chadleigh Gv
BRSG/KWL/STAPK BS4........ 78 A4
Chaffinch Dr
RDSTK/MIDN BA3 .... 126 C5 ⓑ
TRWBR BA14 .... 124 D6 ⓑ
The Chaffins *CLVDN* BS21 ...... 71 G1
Chaingate La *YATE/CS* BS37 .... 33 G1
Chakeshill Cl *HNBRY/STHM* BS10 .. 39 F5
Chakeshill Dr
HNBRY/STHM BS10 .... 39 F5
Chalcombe Cl
BRSTK/PCHW BS34 .... 30 B7
Chalcroft Wk
BMSTRD/HC/WWD BS13 ...... 77 G7
Chalfield Cl *KEYN* BS31 .... 96 B2
Chalfont Cl *TRWBR* BA14 ...... 124 C5
Chalfont Rd *MTN/WRL* BS22 ... 105 H5
Chalford Cl *YATE/CS* BS37 ..... 34 A7
Chalk Farm Cl *PLTN/PENS* BS39 .. 93 K5
Chalks Rd *EVILLE/WHL* BS5 ..... 5 G9
Challender Av
HNBRY/STHM BS10 .... 38 C6
Challoner Ct *CBRIS/FH* BS1 ..... 7 G7
Challow Dr *MTN/WRL* BS22 .... 105 G3 ⓑ
Champion Rd *KGWD/HNM* BS15 .. 55 G7
Champneys Av
HNBRY/STHM BS10 .... 38 C5 ⓑ
Chancel Cl
HNLZ/SM/SNYPK/WT BS9 .... 51 F6
NAIL BS48 .... 73 H2
Chancery St *EVILLE/WHL* BS5 ... 8 C3
Chandag Rd *KEYN* BS31 .... 81 G7
Chandler Cl *CBATH/BATHN* BA1 .. 98 E3
Chandos Cl *KEYN* BS31 .... 80 E4
RDLND/MONT BS6 .... 2 D7
Channel Hts
OMX/HUT/LCK BS24 .... 116 E5
Channell's Hl
HNLZ/SM/SNYPK/WT BS9 .... 51 J1
Channel Rd *CLVDN* BS21 .... 59 F4
Channel View Crs
PTSHD/EG BS20 .... 47 F4 ⓑ
Channel View Rd
PTSHD/EG BS20 .... 47 F4 ⓑ
Channon's Hl *MANG/FISH* BS16 .. 5 M1
Chanterelle Pk *BOAV* BA15 .... 123 J2
Chantry Cl *NAIL* BS48 .... 73 G2 ⓑ
Chantry Dr *MTN/WRL* BS22 .... 106 A1
Chantry Gdns *TRWBR* BA14 .... 130 C4
Chantry La *MANG/FISH* BS16 ... 42 A7
Chantry Mead Rd *BATHSE* BA2 .. 111 H2
Chantry Rd *CFTN/FAIL* BS8 ..... 2 C8
THNB/SVB BS35 .... 19 G3
Chapel Barton *NAIL* BS48 ...... 73 G2 ⓑ
Chapel Cl
BLAG/CWMG/WR BS40 ...... 91 H6 ⓑ

Chapel Gdns *HNBRY/STHM* BS10 .. 38 D7
Chapel Green La
RDLND/MONT BS6 .... 2 D5
Chapel Hl *CLVDN* BS21 .... 59 F7
NAIL BS48 .... 74 D3
Chapel La *MTN/WRL* BS22 ...... 37 J6
BLAG/CWMG/WR BS40 ...... 91 H6
EVILLE/WHL BS5................. 5 K6
KGWD/HNM BS15 .... 69 H2
MANG/FISH BS16 .... 54 C2
WUE GL12 .... 20 B4
YATE/CS BS37 .... 45 K2
YTN/CONG BS49 .... 87 J4
YTN/CONG BS49 .... 88 A5
Chapel Lawns
RDSTK/MIDN BA3 .... 127 F1
Chapel Rd
BMSTRD/HC/WWD BS13 ...... 77 J5
EVILLE/WHL BS5................. 4 D7
KGWD/HNM BS15 .... 68 C5
RDSTK/MIDN BA3 .... 127 F1
Chapel Rw *CBATH/BATHN* BA1 .. 14 E6
PTSHD/EG BS20 .... 49 J5 ⓑ
Chapel St *CBRISNE* BS2 .... 8 A6
THNB/SVB BS35 .... 19 G5
Chapel Wy *BRSG/KWL/STAPK* BS4 .. 9 J4
Chaplin Rd *EVILLE/WHL* BS5 .... 4 C8
Chapter St *CBRISNE* BS2 .... 3 K9
Charbon Ga
BRSTK/PCHW BS34 .... 40 D3 ⓑ
Charborough Rd
BRSTK/PCHW BS34 .... 39 J6
Chard Ct *NAIL* BS48 .... 73 K3
Chard Rd *CLVDN* BS21 .... 71 C2
Chardstock Av
HNLZ/SM/SNYPK/WT BS9 .... 50 E1
Charfield *KGWD/HNM* BS15 ..... 69 G2 ⓑ
Charfield Rd *HNBRY/STHM* BS10 .. 38 F7
Chargrove
OLD/WMLY/WICK BS30 ...... 69 J4 ⓑ
YATE/CS BS37 .... 44 A1
Charis Av *HNBRY/STHM* BS10 ... 52 A2
Charlcombe La
CBATH/BATHN BA1 .... 99 J2
Charlcombe View Rd
CBATH/BATHN BA1 .... 99 K2 ⓑ
Charlcombe Wy
CBATH/BATHN BA1 .... 99 J2
Charlecote Av
HNLZ/SM/SNYPK/WT BS9 .... 51 H3
Charles Av *BRSTK/PCHW* BS34 .. 40 D4 ⓑ
Charles Cl *THNB/SVB* BS35 ..... 19 H2
Charles Pl *CFTN/FAIL* BS8....... 6 A5
Charles Rd *BRSTK/PCHW* BS34 .. 40 A5
Charles St *CBATH/BATHN* BA1 .. 14 E6 ⓑ
CBRISNE BS2..................... 7 H1
TRWBR BA14 .... 124 E5
Charlock Rd *MTN/WRL* BS22 ... 105 J6
Charlotte St *CBATH/BATHN* BA1... 14 E6
CBRIS/FH BS1 .... 6 E4
CBRISNE BS2..................... 7 L1 ⓑ
TRWBR BA14 .... 125 F5 ⓑ
Charlotte St South *CBRIS/FH* BS1 .. 6 E4
Charlton Av *BRSTK/PCHW* BS34 .. 39 J6
WSM BS23 .... 16 D9
Charlton Dr *NAIL* BS48 .... 62 C3
Charlton Gdns
HNBRY/STHM BS10 .... 39 G4
Charlton La *HNBRY/STHM* BS10 .. 39 G4
RDSTK/MIDN BA3 .... 126 D6
Charlton Mead Dr
HNBRY/STHM BS10 .... 39 G4
Charlton Pk *KEYN* BS31 .... 80 D6
RDSTK/MIDN BA3 .... 126 C5
Charlton Pl
HNBRY/STHM BS10 .... 39 G4 ⓑ
Charlton Rd *HGRV/WHIT* BS14 .. 94 E3
HNBRY/STHM BS10 .... 39 G4
KGWD/HNM BS15 .... 68 B1
RDSTK/MIDN BA3 .... 126 C5
WSM BS23 .... 116 C2
Charlton St *EVILLE/WHL* BS5 .... 8 C3
Charlton Vw *PTSHD/EG* BS20 ... 47 C4 ⓑ
Charminster Rd
MANG/FISH BS16 .... 54 B6
Charmouth Rd
CBATH/BATHN BA1 .... 98 E5
Charnell Rd *MANG/FISH* BS16 .. 54 E5
Charnhill Brow *MANG/FISH* BS16 .. 55 G5
Charnhill Crs *MANG/FISH* BS16 .. 55 F5
Charnhill Dr *MANG/FISH* BS16 .. 55 F5
Charnhill Rdg *MANG/FISH* BS16 .. 55 G5
Charnhill V *MANG/FISH* BS16 ... 55 G5
Charnwood *MANG/FISH* BS16.... 55 G5
Charnwood Rd
HGRV/WHIT BS14 .... 94 A1
TRWBR BA14 .... 124 B5
Charterhouse Cl *NAIL* BS48 .... 73 K2 ⓑ
Charterhouse Rd
EVILLE/WHL BS5................. 5 H9 ⓑ
Charter Rd *MTN/WRL* BS22 ..... 17 M2
Chasefield La
MANG/FISH BS16 .... 54 E5 ⓑ
Chase Rd *KGWD/HNM* BS15 .... 54 D7
The Chase *MANG/FISH* BS16 .... 54 C6 ⓑ
Chatcombe Rw *YATE/CS* BS37 .. 44 B1 ⓑ
Chatham Rw *CBATH/BATHN* BA1 .. 15 G4
Chatsworth Pk *THNB/SVB* BS35.. 19 H3
Chatsworth Rd
BRSG/KWL/STAPK BS4........ 8 D9
MANG/FISH BS16 .... 54 B6
Chatterton Gn
HGRV/WHIT BS14 .... 93 J1 ⓑ
Chatterton Rd *YATE/CS* BS37 ... 34 A6
Chatterton Sq *CBRIS/FH* BS1 ... 7 K7
Chaucer Rd *BATHSE* BA2 .... 111 J1
RDSTK/MIDN BA3 .... 126 C5
WSM BS23 .... 117 F2
Chaundey Gv
BMSTRD/HC/WWD BS13 ...... 77 K6
Cheapside *CBRISNE* BS2 .... 3 L9
Cheapside St *BMSTR* BS3 ...... 7 M9
Cheap St *CBATH/BATHN* BA1 ... 15 G6 ⓑ
Cheddar Cl *NAIL* BS48 .... 73 K3
Cheddar Gv
BMSTRD/HC/WWD BS13 ...... 10 A8
Chedworth *KGWD/HNM* BS15 ... 54 E6

YATE/CS BS37 .... 43 J1
Chedworth Cl BATHSE BA2 .... 112 E2
Chedworth Wk HORF/LLZ BS7 .... 52 E3
Cheese La CBRISNE BS2 .... 7 K4
Chelford Gv
  BRSTK/PCHW BS34 .... 30 A7
Chelmer Rd KEYN BS31 .... 81 F7
Chelmsford Wk
  BRSG/KWL/STAPK BS4.......... 9 K6
Chelsea Cl KEYN BS31 .... 81 G6
Chelsea Pk EVILLE/WHL BS5 ...... 4 E9
Chelsea Rd CBATH/BATHN BA1 .. 99 F5
  EVILLE/WHL BS5.......... 4 D8
Chelston Rd
  BRSG/KWL/STAPK BS4.......... 78 B4
Chelswood Av MTN/WRL BS22 .. 105 H5
Cheltenham La
  RDLND/MONT BS6.......... 3 J6
Cheltenham Rd
  RDLND/MONT BS6.......... 3 J6
Cheltenham St BATHSE BA2 ...... 14 D8
Chelvey Batch NAIL BS48 .... 88 E1
Chelvey La NAIL BS48 .... 73 J7
Chelvey Ri NAIL BS48 .... 74 A3
Chelvey Rd NAIL BS48 .... 73 G5
Chelvy Cl
  BMSTRD/HC/WWD BS13.......... 93 G1
Chelwood Dr BATHSE BA2 ...... 111 G4
Chelwood Rd AVONM BS11....... 49 K2
Chepston Pl TRWBR BA14 ...... 124 B5
Chepstow Pk
  MANG/FISH BS16 .... 42 A7
Chepstow Rd
  BRSG/KWL/STAPK BS4.......... 11 H8
Chequers Cl
  OLD/WMLY/WICK BS30 ...... 69 J7
Cherington KGWD/HNM BS15 .. 68 B5
  YATE/CS BS37 .... 44 A2
Cherington Rd
  HNBRY/STHM BS10 ...... 52 A2
  NAIL BS48 .... 74 A2
Cheriton Pl
  HNLZ/SM/SNYPK/WT BS9.... 51 K2
  OLD/WMLY/WICK BS30 .... 69 J4
Cherry Av CLVDN BS21 ...... 71 G1
Cherry Cl YTN/CONG BS49 .... 86 E4
Cherry Garden La
  OLD/WMLY/WICK BS30 .... 81 H1
Cherry Garden Rd
  OLD/WMLY/WICK BS30 .... 81 J2
Cherry Gdns
  OLD/WMLY/WICK BS30 .... 81 J2
  TRWBR BA14 .... 125 F7
  TRWBR BA14 .... 125 J3
Cherry Gv MANG/FISH BS16 .... 55 G3
  YTN/CONG BS49.......... 86 E4
Cherry Hay CLVDN BS21 ...... 71 F2
Cherry La CBRIS/FH BS1 ...... 7 H1
Cherry Orchard La
  EVILLE/WHL BS5 .... 9 L1
Cherry Rd LGASH BS41 ...... 76 B1
  NAIL BS48 .... 73 H2
  YATE/CS BS37 .... 34 D6
Cherry Tree Cl KEYN BS31 .... 80 C7
  RDSTK/MIDN BA3 .... 127 F4
Cherrytree Ct
  MANG/FISH BS16 .... 56 E4
Cherrytree Crs MANG/FISH BS16.. 54 C7
Cherrytree Rd KGWD/HNM BS15 .. 54 C7
Cherry Wd
  OLD/WMLY/WICK BS30 .... 81 H1
Cherrywood Ri
  MTN/WRL BS22 .... 106 A3
Cherrywood Rd
  MTN/WRL BS22 .... 106 A3
Chertsey Rd RDLND/MONT BS6.. 2 C7
Cherwell Cl THNB/SVB BS35 .. 19 H6
Cherwell Rd KEYN BS31 ...... 81 G7
Chescombe Rd YTN/CONG BS49 .. 86 E5
Chesham Rd North
  MTN/WRL BS22 .... 17 L1
Chesham Rd South
  MTN/WRL BS22 .... 17 M2
Chesham Wy
  KGWD/HNM BS15 .... 68 D1
Cheshire Cl YATE/CS BS37 .... 34 B4
Chesle Cl PTSHD/EG BS20 .... 46 C6
Cheslefield PTSHD/EG BS20 .. 46 C6
Chesle Wy PTSHD/EG BS20 .... 46 C6
Chessel Cl ALMDB BS32 ...... 30 B5
Chessel St BMSTR BS3 ...... 10 C2
Chessington Av
  HGRV/WHIT BS14 .... 79 F6
Chesterfield Av
  RDLND/MONT BS6.......... 3 J6
Chesterfield Cl BNWL BS29 .. 119 G3
Chesterfield Rd
  MANG/FISH BS16 .... 54 E4
  RDLND/MONT BS6.......... 3 K6
Chestermaster Cl
  ALMDB BS32 .... 29 K2
Chester Pk EVILLE/WHL BS5 .. 5 J9
Chester Park Rd
  MANG/FISH BS16 .... 54 B7
Chester Rd EVILLE/WHL BS5 .... 5 J8
Chesters
  OLD/WMLY/WICK BS30 .... 69 G6
Chester St EVILLE/WHL BS5 .... 4 D6
Chesterton Dr NAIL BS48 .... 74 A1
The Chestertons
  BATHSE BA2 .... 100 E4
Chestnut Av MTN/WRL BS22 .. 106 B4
Chestnut Cha NAIL BS48 .... 74 A1
Chestnut Cl BNWL BS29 ...... 119 H3
  HGRV/WHIT BS14 .... 79 J6
  RDSTK/MIDN BA3 .... 127 F4
  YTN/CONG BS49 .... 109 G1
Chestnut Ct MANG/FISH BS16 .. 55 G4
Chestnut Dr THNB/SVB BS35 .. 19 H4
  YATE/CS BS37 .... 34 D6
  YTN/CONG BS49.......... 87 H3
Chestnut Gv BATHSE BA2 ...... 111 F1
  BOAV BA15 .... 123 F2
  CLVDN BS21 .... 59 G6
  TRWBR BA14 .... 130 D2
Chestnut La
  OMX/HUT/LCK BS24 .... 117 G7

Chestnut Rd
  KGWD/HNM BS15 .... 55 F6
  LGASH BS41 .... 76 D1
  MANG/FISH BS16 .... 54 D3
The Chestnuts WNSC BS25 .. 120 D7
Chestnut Wk
  BMSTRD/HC/WWD BS13.......... 77 J5
  KEYN BS31 .... 97 F1
Chestnut Wy KGWD/HNM BS15 .. 55 F6
Chetwode Cl HNBRY/STHM BS10.. 39 G5
Chevening Cl
  BRSTK/PCHW BS34 .... 40 C4
Cheviot Cl TRWBR BA14 ...... 125 D7
Cheviot Dr THNB/SVB BS35 .. 19 K5
Cheviot Wy
  OLD/WMLY/WICK BS30 .... 69 J5
Chewton Cl MANG/FISH BS16 .. 54 D6
Chewton Rd KEYN BS31 ...... 95 K3
Cheyne Rd
  HNLZ/SM/SNYPK/WT BS9.... 51 F3
Chichester Wy YATE/CS BS37 .. 34 A4
Chillington Ct
  BRSTK/PCHW BS34 .... 29 H6
Chillwood Cl YATE/CS BS37 .. 33 F4
Chilmark Rd TRWBR BA14 .... 124 C5
Chiltern Cl HGRV/WHIT BS14 .. 79 F7
  OLD/WMLY/WICK BS30 .... 69 J5
Chiltern Pk THNB/SVB BS35 .. 19 K5
Chilton Rd
  BRSG/KWL/STAPK BS4.......... 12 A7
  CBATH/BATHN BA1 .... 15 J1
The Chimes NAIL BS48 ...... 73 G3
The Chine MANG/FISH BS16 .. 53 H4
Chine Vw MANG/FISH BS16 .. 55 F1
Chiphouse Rd KGWD/HNM BS15 .. 54 E7
Chipperfield Dr
  KGWD/HNM BS15 .... 69 F1
Chipping Cross CLVDN BS21 .. 70 E3
The Chippings MANG/FISH BS16.. 53 H4
Chirton Pl TRWBR BA14 .... 131 F1
Chisbury St EVILLE/WHL BS5 .. 4 E4
Chittening Rd AVONM BS11 .. 37 F1
Chock La
  HNLZ/SM/SNYPK/WT BS9.... 51 J2
Christchurch Av
  MANG/FISH BS16 .... 54 D4
Christchurch Cl NAIL BS48 .. 73 J1
Christchurch La
  MANG/FISH BS16 .... 54 D4
Christchurch Pth South
  WSM BS23 .... 16 F2
Christchurch Rd BOAV BA15 .. 114 E5
  CFTN/FAIL BS8 .... 6 A2
Christian Cl MTN/WRL BS22 .. 106 C2
Christin Ct TRWBR BA14 .... 124 C6
Christmas St CBRIS/FH BS1 .. 7 G3
Christon Rd BNWL BS29 .... 119 H5
Chubb Cl OLD/WMLY/WICK BS30.. 69 F5
Church Acre BOAV BA15 .... 114 D6
Church Av EVILLE/WHL BS5.... 4 D7
  HNLZ/SM/SNYPK/WT BS9.... 51 G5
  OLD/WMLY/WICK BS30 .... 69 J4
Church Cl BATHSE BA2 ...... 100 E2
  CBATH/BATHN BA1 .... 101 G2
  CLVDN BS21 .... 70 C1
  FRCTL/WBN BS36.......... 32 C7
  PTSHD/EG BS20 .... 47 H4
  YTN/CONG BS49.......... 87 F5
Church Ct RDSTK/MIDN BA3 .. 126 B4
Church Dr EVILLE/WHL BS5.... 9 K1
  YTN/CONG BS49.......... 109 G1
Churches BOAV BA15 ...... 114 D6
Churchfarm Cl YATE/CS BS37 .. 34 C4
Church Farm Rd
  MANG/FISH BS16 .... 55 J3
Church Flds TRWBR BA14 .... 131 F5
Church Hayes Cl NAIL BS48 .. 73 J5
Church Hayes Dr NAIL BS48 .. 73 J3
Church Hl BRSG/KWL/STAPK BS4.. 13 J3
  RDSTK/MIDN BA3 .... 122 B1
  RDSTK/MIDN BA3 .... 127 K3
Churchill Av CLVDN BS21 .... 70 E1
Churchill Cl CLVDN BS21 .... 71 F1
  OLD/WMLY/WICK BS30 .... 69 G5
Churchill Dr
  HNLZ/SM/SNYPK/WT BS9.... 51 F2
Churchill Gn WNSC BS25 .... 121 F1
Churchill Rd
  BRSG/KWL/STAPK BS4.......... 8 F9
  WSM BS23.......... 17 J4
Churchlands TRWBR BA14 .... 131 F5
Church La BATHSE BA2 ...... 112 B1
  CBRIS/FH BS1 .... 7 K5
  CFTN/FAIL BS8 .... 6 C5
  CLVDN BS21 .... 61 F6
  FRCTL/WBN BS36.......... 41 M2
  FRCTL/WBN BS36.......... 42 D7
  HNBRY/STHM BS10 .... 38 B6
  LGASH BS41 .... 76 B1
  MANG/FISH BS16 .... 41 K6
  NAIL BS48 .... 73 G2
  NAIL BS48 .... 74 B6
  NAIL BS48 .... 75 F4
  OMX/HUT/LCK BS24 .... 117 J4
  PLTN/PENS BS39 .... 95 H3
  PTSHD/EG BS20 .... 48 E6
  RDSTK/MIDN BA3 .... 122 A1
  RDSTK/MIDN BA3 .... 126 B4
  RDSTK/MIDN BA3 .... 128 E7
  TRWBR BA14 .... 129 J1
  TRWBR BA14 .... 130 C2
  TRWBR BA14 .... 131 F5
  WNSC BS25 .... 121 G1
  WUE GL12 .... 21 H4
  YATE/CS BS37 .... 25 G5
  YTN/CONG BS49.......... 87 F5
Church Pde
  BRSG/KWL/STAPK BS4.......... 13 H4
Churchpath Rd PTSHD/EG BS20 .. 49 J3
Church Pl PTSHD/EG BS20 .... 49 J3
Church Ri BLAG/CWMG/WR BS40.. 91 H5
Church Rd ALMDB BS32 ...... 29 K2
  BATHSE BA2 .... 112 B4
  BLAG/CWMG/WR BS40 .... 91 H1
  BMSTR BS3 .... 6 F9

  BMSTRD/HC/WWD BS13.......... 77 J6
  BRSTK/PCHW BS34 .... 39 K5
  BRSTK/PCHW BS34 .... 40 D5
  CBATH/BATHN BA1 .... 99 F3
  CFTN/FAIL BS8 .... 64 D1
  CFTN/FAIL BS8 .... 65 F4
  EVILLE/WHL BS5 .... 8 E2
  FRCTL/WBN BS36.......... 32 B6
  FRCTL/WBN BS36.......... 41 K4
  HGRV/WHIT BS14 .... 94 A1
  HNLZ/SM/SNYPK/WT BS9.... 51 F6
  HNLZ/SM/SNYPK/WT BS9.... 51 J2
  HORF/LLZ BS7 .... 52 C5
  KGWD/HNM BS15 .... 68 B5
  KGWD/HNM BS15 .... 68 E2
  LGASH BS41 .... 92 A2
  MANG/FISH BS16 .... 54 B2
  MANG/FISH BS16 .... 54 D7
  MTN/WRL BS22 .... 105 J3
  PLTN/PENS BS39 .... 93 K5
  PTSHD/EG BS20 .... 49 G5
  THNB/SVB BS35 .... 18 A1
  THNB/SVB BS35 .... 19 G3
  THNB/SVB BS35 .... 23 F4
  THNB/SVB BS35 .... 27 H1
  THNB/SVB BS35 .... 28 D6
  YATE/CS BS37 .... 34 B4
  YTN/CONG BS49.......... 87 F5
Church Rd North
  PTSHD/EG BS20 .... 47 H4
Church Rd South
  PTSHD/EG BS20 .... 47 H5
Churchside MANG/FISH BS16 .. 54 B2
Church Sq RDSTK/MIDN BA3 .. 126 B4
Church St BATHSE BA2 ...... 15 K9
  BNWL BS29 .... 119 J3
  BOAV BA15 .... 114 D7
  CBATH/BATHN BA1 .... 15 G7
  CBATH/BATHN BA1 .... 101 C2
  CBRIS/FH BS1 .... 7 K5
  EVILLE/WHL BS5 .... 4 D7
  EVILLE/WHL BS5 .... 8 D4
  RDSTK/MIDN BA3 .... 127 G4
  TRWBR BA14 .... 125 F5
  TRWBR BA14 .... 125 J3
  TRWBR BA14 .... 130 B4
Church Town NAIL BS48 .... 74 C6
Church Vw ALMDB BS32 .... 29 J3
Church Wk PTSHD/EG BS20 .. 49 J5
Churchward Cl
  KGWD/HNM BS15 .... 68 B5
Churchward Rd
  MTN/WRL BS22 .... 106 C2
  YATE/CS BS37 .... 33 J4
Churchways HGRV/WHIT BS14 .. 79 C7
Churchways Av HORF/LLZ BS7 .. 52 C3
Churchways Crs HORF/LLZ BS7 .. 52 C3
Churclands Rd BMSTR BS3 .. 10 D3
Churston Rd HGRV/WHIT BS14 .. 93 K1
The Circle BATHSE BA2 .... 110 E2
Circular Rd
  HNLZ/SM/SNYPK/WT BS9.... 51 G7
Circus Ms CBATH/BATHN BA1 .. 14 F4
Circus Pl CBATH/BATHN BA1 .. 14 E4
City Rd CBRISNE BS2 ...... 3 K9
The Clamp
  OLD/WMLY/WICK BS30 .... 69 J7
Clanage Rd BMSTR BS3 .... 65 G6
Clandown Rd PLTN/PENS BS39 .. 94 A1
Clapton Dro PTSHD/EG BS20 .. 61 H1
Clapton La PTSHD/EG BS20.... 47 H6
Clapton Wk
  HNLZ/SM/SNYPK/WT BS9.... 50 D4
Clare Av HORF/LLZ BS7 .... 2 F3
Clare Gdns BATHSE BA2 .... 111 G4
Claremont Av HORF/LLZ BS7 .. 2 F3
Claremont Buildings
  CBATH/BATHN BA1 .... 99 K3
Claremont Gdns CLVDN BS21 .. 71 G2
Claremont Rd
  CBATH/BATHN BA1 .... 100 A3
  HORF/LLZ BS7 .... 3 G4
Claremont St EVILLE/WHL BS5 .. 4 B8
Claremont Ter EVILLE/WHL BS5 .. 9 G2
Claremont Wk
  CBATH/BATHN BA1 .... 99 K3
Clarence Av MANG/FISH BS16... 54 E4
Clarence Gdns
  MANG/FISH BS16 .... 54 E4
Clarence Grove Rd WSM BS23 .. 16 E8
Clarence Pl CBATH/BATHN BA1 .. 98 E5
  CBRISNE BS2.......... 6 F1
Clarence Rd CBRIS/FH BS1 .. 7 J8
  CBRISNE BS2.......... 8 A2
  KGWD/HNM BS15 .... 68 B1
  MANG/FISH BS16 .... 54 D4
  TRWBR BA14 .... 125 H6
Clarence Rd East WSM BS23.... 16 E8
Clarence Rd North WSM BS23 .. 16 D8
Clarence Rd South WSM BS23 .. 16 C8
Clarence St CBATH/BATHN BA1 .. 15 G2
Clarendon Av TRWBR BA14.... 125 G6
Clarendon Rd BATHSE BA2 .. 15 J9
  RDLND/MONT BS6.......... 2 E5
  TRWBR BA14 .... 125 G6
  WSM BS23.......... 17 G2
Clare Rd EVILLE/WHL BS5 .... 4 D6
  KGWD/HNM BS15 .... 54 C7
  RDLND/MONT BS6.......... 3 G8
Clare St EVILLE/WHL BS5 .... 8 F1
  CBRIS/FH BS1 .... 7 G4
Clark Cl NAIL BS48 ...... 74 A1
Clark Dr MANG/FISH BS16 .. 53 K3
Clarken Cl NAIL BS48 .... 73 J2
Clarken Coombe LGASH BS41 .. 64 C7
Clarke St BMSTR BS3 ...... 7 H9
Clarkson Av MTN/WRL BS22 .. 105 H4
Clark's Pl TRWBR BA14 .... 125 G6
Clark St EVILLE/WHL BS5 .... 4 A9
Clatworthy Dr HGRV/WHIT BS14 .. 78 E4
Claude Av BATHSE BA2 ...... 111 F1
Clavell Rd HNBRY/STHM BS10 .. 38 C6
Claverham Cl YTN/CONG BS49 .. 87 G4
Claverham Dro CLVDN BS21 .. 71 K7
Claverham Pk YTN/CONG BS49 .. 87 J3
Claverham Rd
  MANG/FISH BS16 .... 54 A4
  YTN/CONG BS49.......... 87 J4

Claverton Ct BATHSE BA2 .... 112 D1
Claverton Down Rd
  BATHSE BA2 .... 112 D1
Claverton Dr BATHSE BA2 .... 112 D1
Claverton Rd KEYN BS31 .... 96 E2
Claverton Rd West KEYN BS31.. 96 E1
Claverton St BATHSE BA2 .... 15 H9
Clay Bottom EVILLE/WHL BS5 .. 5 J5
Clayfield YATE/CS BS37 .... 34 B2
Clayfield Rd
  BRSG/KWL/STAPK BS4.......... 13 J2
Clay Hl EVILLE/WHL BS5...... 5 K5
Clay La BRSTK/PCHW BS34 .. 40 B1
  OLD/WMLY/WICK BS30 .... 81 K3
  RDSTK/MIDN BA3 .... 129 F7
  THNB/SVB BS35 .... 19 K4
Claymore Crs
  KGWD/HNM BS15 .... 68 B1
Claypiece Rd
  BMSTRD/HC/WWD BS13.......... 77 H7
Claypit Hl YATE/CS BS37 .... 44 E1
Clay Pit Rd
  HNLZ/SM/SNYPK/WT BS9.... 2 B3
Claypool Rd KGWD/HNM BS15 .. 68 D3
Clayton Cl PTSHD/EG BS20 .. 47 H3
Clayton St AVONM BS11 .... 36 B7
  EVILLE/WHL BS5.......... 8 D1
Cleave St CBRISNE BS2 .... 4 A6
Cleeve Av MANG/FISH BS16 .. 54 E2
Cleevedale Rd BATHSE BA2 .. 111 K4
Cleeve Dr YTN/CONG BS49 .. 87 K4
Cleeve Gdns MANG/FISH BS16 .. 54 D2
Cleeve Gn BATHSE BA2 .... 98 D5
Cleeve Gv KEYN BS31 ...... 80 D6
Cleeve Hl MANG/FISH BS16 .. 54 D2
Cleeve Hill Extension
  MANG/FISH BS16 .... 54 E3
Cleeve Hill Rd YTN/CONG BS49 .. 88 A5
Cleeve Lawns MANG/FISH BS16 .. 54 D2
Cleeve Lodge Rd
  MANG/FISH BS16 .... 54 E2
Cleeve Park Rd MANG/FISH BS16.. 54 E2
Cleeve Pl NAIL BS48 ...... 74 A2
Cleeve Rd BRSG/KWL/STAPK BS4.. 12 D3
  MANG/FISH BS16 .... 54 D2
  YATE/CS BS37 .... 34 B6
Cleeve Wood Rd
  MANG/FISH BS16 .... 54 D2
Clement St CBRISNE BS2 .... 7 L1
Clevedale MANG/FISH BS16 .. 54 D2
Clevedon La CLVDN BS21 .... 60 B5
Clevedon Rd CFTN/FAIL BS8 .. 63 F5
  CLVDN BS21 .... 60 B6
  HORF/LLZ BS7 .... 3 H1
  NAIL BS48 .... 61 K5
  NAIL BS48 .... 74 E1
  PTSHD/EG BS20 .... 47 G6
  RDSTK/MIDN BA3 .... 126 B3
  WSM BS23.......... 7 H7
Clevedon Ter RDLND/MONT BS6 .. 3 G9
Cleveland Cl THNB/SVB BS35 .. 19 K4
Cleveland Gdns TRWBR BA14 .. 125 J4
Cleve Rd BRSTK/PCHW BS34 .. 39 K4
Clewson Ri HGRV/WHIT BS14 .. 93 J1
Cliff Court Dr MANG/FISH BS16 .. 54 B2
Cliffe Dr RDSTK/MIDN BA3 .. 113 F7
Clifford Gdns AVONM BS11 .. 50 A3
Clifford Rd MANG/FISH BS16 .. 54 C5
Cliff Rd MTN/WRL BS22 .... 105 F3
Clift House Rd BMSTR BS3 .. 6 A9
Clifton Down CFTN/FAIL BS8 .. 65 H2
Clifton Down Rd CFTN/FAIL BS8 .. 6 A3
  CFTN/FAIL BS8 .... 65 H3
Clifton Gv
  HNLZ/SM/SNYPK/WT BS9.... 51 G4
Clifton Hl CFTN/FAIL BS8 .... 6 A5
Clifton Pk CFTN/FAIL BS8.... 6 A2
Clifton Park Rd CFTN/FAIL BS8 .. 65 H2
Clifton Pl EVILLE/WHL BS5 .. 8 B1
Clifton Rd CFTN/FAIL BS8 .... 6 A5
  WSM BS23.......... 16 D7
Clifton St BMSTR BS3 ...... 10 E2
  PTSHD/EG BS20 .... 47 G7
Clifton V CFTN/FAIL BS8...... 6 A5
Clifton Vale CFTN/FAIL BS8 .. 6 A4
Cliftonvale Crs CFTN/FAIL BS8 .. 6 C5
Clifton Wood Rd CFTN/FAIL BS8 .. 6 C4
Cliftonwood Ter CFTN/FAIL BS8 .. 6 C4
Clift Pl CBRIS/FH BS1 ...... 7 H6
Clift Rd BMSTR BS3 ...... 6 A8
Clinton Rd BMSTR BS3 .... 10 F3
Clipsham Ri TRWBR BA14 .. 124 C5
Clive Rd HGRV/WHIT BS14 .. 12 E9
Cloford Cl TRWBR BA14 .... 124 C5
Cloisters Rd FRCTL/WBN BS36 .. 41 K7
Clonmel Rd
  BRSG/KWL/STAPK BS4.......... 11 H5
Closemead CLVDN BS21 .... 71 F2
The Close BRSTK/PCHW BS34 .. 30 B6
  FRCTL/WBN BS36.......... 42 D2
  HNBRY/STHM BS10 .... 38 C7
  MANG/FISH BS16 .... 54 D6
  PTSHD/EG BS20 .... 60 D1
Clothier Leaze TRWBR BA14 .. 125 F7
Clothier Rd
  BRSG/KWL/STAPK BS4.......... 13 L4
Cloth Yd TRWBR BA14 ...... 131 F1
Clouds Hill Av EVILLE/WHL BS5 .. 5 K9
Clouds Hill Rd EVILLE/WHL BS5 .. 9 K1
Clovelly Cl EVILLE/WHL BS5 .. 9 M1
Clovelly Rd EVILLE/WHL BS5 .. 9 M1
  MTN/WRL BS22 .... 106 B3
Clover Cl CLVDN BS21 ...... 59 H7
Clover Ct MTN/WRL BS22 .. 105 J6
Cloverdale Dr
  OLD/WMLY/WICK BS30 .... 69 G7
Clover Gnd
  HNLZ/SM/SNYPK/WT BS9.... 51 K1
Cloverlea Rd
  OLD/WMLY/WICK BS30 .... 69 J5
Clover Leaze BRSTK/PCHW BS34.. 30 A6
Clover Rd MTN/WRL BS22 .. 84 B6
Clyde Av KEYN BS31 ...... 81 F7
Clyde Gdns BATHSE BA2 .... 98 E5
  EVILLE/WHL BS5.......... 68 B4
Clyde Gv BRSTK/PCHW BS34 .. 39 G4
Clyde La RDLND/MONT BS6 .. 2 D6
Clyde Rd BRSG/KWL/STAPK BS4 .. 12 B2

  FRCTL/WBN BS36.......... 32 C7
  RDLND/MONT BS6.......... 2 D6
  TRWBR BA14 .... 130 E2
Clyde Ter BMSTR BS3 ...... 10 E1
  BRSG/KWL/STAPK BS4.......... 12 B1
Clynder Gv CLVDN BS21 .... 59 G4
Coach Rd BOAV BA15 ...... 114 D7
Coalbridge Cl MTN/WRL BS22 .. 106 A3
Coaley Rd AVONM BS11 .... 49 K4
Coalsack La FRCTL/WBN BS36 .. 42 C5
Coalville Rd FRCTL/WBN BS36 .. 42 E1
Coape Rd HGRV/WHIT BS14 .. 79 K6
Coates Gv NAIL BS48 ...... 74 A1
Cobblestone Ms CFTN/FAIL BS8 .. 6 A2
Cobden St EVILLE/WHL BS5 .. 8 D2
Coberley KGWD/HNM BS15 .. 68 C4
Cobhorn Dr
  BMSTRD/HC/WWD BS13.......... 77 H7
Cobley Cft CLVDN BS21 .... 70 D3
Cobourg Rd RDLND/MONT BS6 .. 3 L7
Cobthorn Wy YTN/CONG BS49 .. 87 H7
Cock Hl TRWBR BA14 ...... 124 C5
Cock Rd KGWD/HNM BS15 .. 68 E4
Codrington Pl CFTN/FAIL BS8 .. 6 B2
Codrington Rd HORF/LLZ BS7 .. 3 H3
Cogan Rd MANG/FISH BS16 .. 54 E6
Cogsall Rd HGRV/WHIT BS14 .. 79 K5
Coker Rd MTN/WRL BS22 .. 106 C3
Colbourne Rd BATHSE BA2 .. 111 G4
Colchester Crs
  BRSG/KWL/STAPK BS4.......... 11 G9
Coldharbour La
  BRSTK/PCHW BS34 .... 40 D7
  MANG/FISH BS16 .... 53 J1
Coldharbour Rd
  RDLND/MONT BS6.......... 2 C3
Coldpark Gdns
  BMSTRD/HC/WWD BS13.......... 77 G6
Coldpark Rd
  BMSTRD/HC/WWD BS13.......... 77 G6
Coldrick Cl HGRV/WHIT BS14 .. 93 J1
Colebrook Rd KGWD/HNM BS15 .. 68 C2
Coleford Rd HNBRY/STHM BS10 .. 52 E3
Colehouse La CLVDN BS21 .. 70 E3
Colemead
  BMSTRD/HC/WWD BS13.......... 77 K6
Coleridge Rd CLVDN BS21 .. 58 E7
  EVILLE/WHL BS5.......... 4 E4
  WSM BS23.......... 117 F3
Coleridge Vale Rd East
  CLVDN BS21 .... 71 F1
Coleridge Vale Rd North
  CLVDN BS21 .... 70 E1
Coleridge Vale Rd South
  CLVDN BS21 .... 70 E1
Coleridge Vale Rd West
  CLVDN BS21 .... 70 E1
Cole Rd CBRISNE BS2 ...... 8 D5
Colesborne Cl YATE/CS BS37 .. 34 B7
Coleshill Dr
  BMSTRD/HC/WWD BS13.......... 77 K6
Colin Cl THNB/SVB BS35 .... 19 G4
College Av MANG/FISH BS16 .. 54 A4
College Ct MANG/FISH BS16 .. 54 A4
College Flds CFTN/FAIL BS8.... 65 H2
College Gdns MANG/FISH BS16.. 131 F4
College Gn CBRIS/FH BS1 .... 6 F4
College Park Dr
  HNBRY/STHM BS10 .... 38 C7
College Rd CBATH/BATHN BA1 .. 99 H3
  CFTN/FAIL BS8 .... 65 H2
  HNLZ/SM/SNYPK/WT BS9.... 51 J2
  MANG/FISH BS16 .... 54 A4
  TRWBR BA14 .... 130 C1
College Sq CBRIS/FH BS1 .... 6 E5
College St CBRIS/FH BS1 .... 6 E5
Collett Cl KGWD/HNM BS15 .. 68 B5
  MTN/WRL BS22 .... 106 D1
Collett Wy YATE/CS BS37 .... 33 K4
Colliers Break MANG/FISH BS16.. 55 H4
Collingbourne Cl
  TRWBR BA14 .... 131 F2
Collingwood Av
  KGWD/HNM BS15 .... 68 E1
Collingwood Cl KEYN BS31 .. 97 F2
  MTN/WRL BS22 .... 105 K1
Collingwood Rd
  RDLND/MONT BS6.......... 2 D7
Collin Rd BRSG/KWL/STAPK BS4 .. 9 H8
Collins Av BRSTK/PCHW BS34 .. 40 B2
Collinson Rd
  BMSTRD/HC/WWD BS13.......... 77 K6
Collins St AVONM BS11 .... 49 H1
Colliter Crs BMSTR BS3 .... 10 B3
Collum La MTN/WRL BS22 .. 83 J3
Colombo Crs WSM BS23 .... 116 D3
Coln Sq THNB/SVB BS35 .... 19 H5
Colston Av CBRIS/FH BS1 .. 7 G4
Colston Cl FRCTL/WBN BS36 .. 41 K4
  MANG/FISH BS16 .... 54 D6
Colston Dl MANG/FISH BS16 .. 5 J1
Colston Hl MANG/FISH BS16 .. 5 G1
Colston Pde CBRIS/FH BS1 .. 7 J6
Colston Rd EVILLE/WHL BS5 .. 4 E8
  MANG/FISH BS16 .... 54 D6
Colston St CBRIS/FH BS1 .. 7 G4
  FRCTL/WBN BS36.......... 41 K4
Colthurst Dr KGWD/HNM BS15.. 68 E5
Colts Gn YATE/CS BS37 .... 35 H7
Colwyn Rd EVILLE/WHL BS5 .. 4 E8
Combe Av PTSHD/EG BS20 .. 47 G3
Combe Cross Wk
  BMSTRD/HC/WWD BS13.......... 92 E1
Combe Flds PTSHD/EG BS20 .. 47 G3
Combe Gv CBATH/BATHN BA1 .. 98 E5
Combe Hay La BATHSE BA2 .. 110 E2
Combe Pk CBATH/BATHN BA1 .. 99 F4
Combermere THNB/SVB BS35 .. 19 J5
Combe Rd CBATH/BATHN BA2 .. 112 A4
  PTSHD/EG BS20 .... 47 H4
Combe Road Cl BATHSE BA2 .. 112 A4
Combe Side NAIL BS48 .... 74 A4
Combfactory La
  EVILLE/WHL BS5.......... 4 C9
Comb Paddock
  HNLZ/SM/SNYPK/WT BS9.... 51 K2
Commercial Rd CBRIS/FH BS1 .. 7 G7

The Common (East)
ALMDB BS32 .... 30 B6
Commonfield Rd *AVONM* BS11 .... 37 J7
Common La *PTSHD/EG* BS20 ...... 63 H1
WNSC BS25 .... 108 E7
Common Mead La
MANG/FISH BS16 .... 41 F7
Commonmead La *YATE/CS* BS37 ... 35 J6
Common Rd
FRCTL/WBN BS36 .... 42 A1
KCWD/HNM BS15 .... 68 B7
The Common
BRSTK/PCHW BS34 .... 30 A6
MANG/FISH BS16 .... 54 B2
Compton Gn *KEYN* BS31 .... 80 E7
Compton St *EVILLE/WHL* BS5 ...... 8 F3
Comrade Av *WNSC* BS25 .... 121 H6
Comyn Wk *MANG/FISH* BS16 ...... 54 A4
Concorde Dr *CLVDN* BS21 .... 70 D2
HNBRY/STHM BS10 .... 38 E6
Condor Cl *MTN/WRL* BS22 ...... 105 J5
Condover Rd
BRSG/KWL/STAPK BS4 .... 13 M2
Conduit Pl *CBRISNE* BS2 .... 4 A7
Conduit Rd *CBRISNE* BS2 .... 4 A7
Conference Av *PTSHD/EG* BS20 ... 47 J4
Conham Hl *KCWD/HNM* BS15 ...... 68 A5
Conham Rd *KCWD/HNM* BS15 ...... 9 M7
Conifer Cl *FRCTL/WBN* BS36 ...... 32 B6
MANG/FISH BS16 .... 54 D3
Conifer Wy *OMX/HUT/LCK* BS24 .. 117 K1
Conigre Hl *BOAV* BS15 .... 114 D6
Coniston Av
HNLZ/SM/SNYPK/WT BS9 ...... 51 J5
Coniston Cl *WICK* BS30 .... 69 K4
Coniston Crs *WSM* BS23 .... 116 E2
Coniston Rd *BRSTK/PCHW* BS34 .. 29 H7
TRWBR BA14 .... 125 C4
Connaught Pl *WSM* BS23 .... 16 E1
Connaught Rd
BRSG/KWL/STAPK BS4 .... 11 J7
Connection Rd *BATHSE* BA2 ...... 98 D6
Constable Cl *KEYN* BS31 .... 81 F5
Constable Dr *MTN/WRL* BS22 .... 106 A2
Constable Rd *HORF/LLZ* BS7 ...... 52 E3
Constantine Av
BRSTK/PCHW BS34 .... 40 D3
Constitution Hl *CFTN/FAIL* BS8 ...... 6 C4
Convent Cl *HNBRY/STHM* BS10 ... 38 A5
Conway Gn *KEYN* BS31 .... 96 B1
Conway Rd
BRSG/KWL/STAPK BS4 .... 8 F8
Conygar Cl *CLVDN* BS21 .... 59 H5
Conygre Gv
BRSTK/PCHW BS34 .... 40 B5
Conygre Rd *BRSTK/PCHW* BS34 ... 40 A4
Cook Cl *OLD/WMLY/WICK* BS30 .... 69 J6
Cooke's Dr *THNB/SVB* BS35 ...... 28 D6
Cooks Bridle Pth *NAIL* BS48 ...... 89 J5
Cooks Cl *ALMDB* BS32 .... 30 B4
Cook's Folly Rd
HNLZ/SM/SNYPK/WT BS9 ...... 51 F6
Cook's La *BNWL* BS29 .... 119 H2
CLVDN BS21 .... 71 K1
FRCTL/WBN BS36 .... 42 E5
Cooksley Rd *EVILLE/WHL* BS5 ...... 8 F1
Cook St *AVONM* BS11 .... 49 H1
Cookworthy Cl *EVILLE/WHL* BS5 .... 8 D4
Coombe Av *THNB/SVB* BS35 ...... 19 G3
Coombe Bridge Av
HNLZ/SM/SNYPK/WT BS9 ...... 51 F3
Coombe Cl
HNBRY/STHM BS10 .... 38 A5
Coombe Dl
HNLZ/SM/SNYPK/WT BS9 ...... 50 E3
NAIL BS48 .... 90 B4
Coombe Gdns
HNLZ/SM/SNYPK/WT BS9 ...... 51 G3
Coombe Hay La *BATHSE* BA2 .... 111 F5
Coombe La *CFTN/FAIL* BS8 ...... 63 F1
HNLZ/SM/SNYPK/WT BS9 ...... 51 F3
MELK SN12 .... 103 K5
Cotswold Vw *KCWD/HNM* BS15 ... 54 D7
Cotswold Wy *YATE/CS* BS37 ...... 45 K3
Cottage Pl *CBRISNE* BS2 .... 7 G1
Coombe End *RDSTK/MIDN* BA3 .. 127 F7
Coombe Rd *EVILLE/WHL* BS5 ...... 4 F4
NAIL BS48 .... 73 H4
WSM BS23 .... 16 E1
Coombes Wy
OLD/WMLY/WICK BS30 .... 69 K6
Coombe Wy *HNBRY/STHM* BS10 .. 38 C7
Cooperage La *BMSTR* BS3 .... 6 C7
Cooperage Rd *EVILLE/WHL* BS5 ...... 8 F3
Co-operation Rd *EVILLE/WHL* BS5 .... 4 F7
Cooper Rd
HNLZ/SM/SNYPK/WT BS9 ...... 51 H2
THNB/SVB BS35 .... 19 G6
Coopers Dr *YATE/CS* BS37 ...... 34 C2
The Coots *HGRV/WHIT* BS14 ...... 79 H6
Copeland Dr *HGRV/WHIT* BS14 .. 79 F6
Cope Pk *ALMDB* BS32 .... 30 B2
Copford La *LGASH* BS41 .... 76 D2
Copley Ct *KCWD/HNM* BS15 ...... 68 E5
Copley Gdns *HORF/LLZ* BS7 ...... 53 F3
MTN/WRL BS22 .... 106 A3
Copperfield Dr *MTN/WRL* BS22 .. 106 A1
Coppice Hl *BOAV* BA15 .... 114 E6
The Coppice *ALMDB* BS32 .... 40 D1
BMSTRD/HC/WWD BS13 ...... 77 G7
Copse Cl *OMX/HUT/LCK* BS24 .... 117 F5
Copse End *WNSC* BS25 .... 120 C4
Copseland *BATHSE* BA2 .... 100 C7
Copse Rd *BRSG/KWL/STAPK* BS4 .. 12 C2
CLVDN BS21 .... 58 E6
KEYN BS31 .... 81 J7
Copthorne Cl *HGRV/WHIT* BS14 ... 79 F6
Coralberry Dr *MTN/WRL* BS22 .... 106 A4
Corbet Cl *AVONM* BS11 .... 37 J6
Corbin Rd *TRWBR* BA14 .... 125 H5
Cordwell Wk
HNBRY/STHM BS10 .... 52 B2
Corey Cl *CBRISNE* BS2 .... 3 L8
Corfe Cl *NAIL* BS48 .... 73 H2
Corfe Crs *KEYN* BS31 .... 80 E6
Corfe Pl *OLD/WMLY/WICK* BS30 .. 81 H2
Corfe Rd *BRSG/KWL/STAPK* BS4 .. 11 G9
Coriander Dr *ALMDB* BS32 ...... 41 F1
Coriander Wk *EVILLE/WHL* BS5 ...... 4 E6

CLVDN BS21 .... 59 J7
WNSC BS25 .... 121 J7
Cormorant Cl
MTN/WRL BS22 .... 106 A4
Corner Cft *CLVDN* BS21 .... 71 F2
The Cornfields *MTN/WRL* BS22 .... 84 A7
Cornhill Dr *HGRV/WHIT* BS14 ...... 78 E4
Cornish Gv *HGRV/WHIT* BS14 ...... 79 J5
Cornish Rd *HGRV/WHIT* BS14 ...... 79 J5
Cornish Wk *HGRV/WHIT* BS14 ...... 79 J5
Cornleaze
BMSTRD/HC/WWD BS13 ...... 77 J6
Corn St *CBATH/BATHN* BA1 ...... 14 F7
CBRIS/FH BS1 .... 7 H4
Cornwall Crs *YATE/CS* BS37 ...... 34 C4
Cornwallis Av *CFTN/FAIL* BS8 ...... 65 H4
MTN/WRL BS22 .... 105 K1
Cornwallis Crs *CFTN/FAIL* BS8 ...... 65 H4
Cornwall Rd *HORF/LLZ* BS7 .... 3 G1
Coronation Av *BATHSE* BA2 ...... 111 F2
KEYN BS31 .... 80 D7
MANG/FISH BS16 .... 54 A5
Coronation Cl
OLD/WMLY/WICK BS30 .... 69 G5
Coronation Pl *CBRIS/FH* BS1 ...... 7 H4
Coronation Rd *BMSTR* BS3 .... 6 A8
BNWL BS29 .... 119 H3
CBATH/BATHN BA1 .... 14 A4
KCWD/HNM BS15 .... 54 D7
MANG/FISH BS16 .... 54 E4
MTN/WRL BS22 .... 105 K3
OLD/WMLY/WICK BS30 .... 69 H7
Corsdale Rd *MTN/WRL* BS22 .... 105 J5
Corsley Wk
BRSG/KWL/STAPK BS4 .... 11 L8
Corston La *BATHSE* BA2 .... 97 H4
Corston Vw *BATHSE* BA2 .... 111 F3
Corston Wk *AVONM* BS11 ...... 49 K2
Cossham Cl *THNB/SVB* BS35 ...... 19 H3
Cossham Rd *EVILLE/WHL* BS5 ...... 9 H2
MANG/FISH BS16 .... 56 E5
Cossham St *MANG/FISH* BS16 .... 55 H4
Cossham Wk *EVILLE/WHL* BS5 ...... 68 A1
Cossington Rd
BRSG/KWL/STAPK BS4 .... 11 L7
Cossins Rd *RDLND/MONT* BS6 ...... 2 E2
Costers Cl *THNB/SVB* BS35 ...... 19 F7
Costiland Dr
BMSTRD/HC/WWD BS13 ...... 77 H5
Cote Dr *HNLZ/SM/SNYPK/WT* BS9 .. 2 A1
Cote House La
HNLZ/SM/SNYPK/WT BS9 ...... 51 J4
Cote La
HNLZ/SM/SNYPK/WT BS9 ...... 51 J4
Cote Lea Pk
HNLZ/SM/SNYPK/WT BS9 ...... 51 J2
Cote Pk
HNLZ/SM/SNYPK/WT BS9 ...... 51 G3
Cote Rd *HNLZ/SM/SNYPK/WT* BS9 .. 2 A1
Cothan Brow *RDLND/MONT* BS6 .... 3 H6
Cotham Gdns
RDLND/MONT BS6 .... 2 D8
Cotham Gv *RDLND/MONT* BS6 ...... 3 G8
Cotham Hl *RDLND/MONT* BS6 ...... 2 D8
Cotham Lawn Rd
RDLND/MONT BS6 .... 2 E9
Cotham Pk *RDLND/MONT* BS6 ...... 2 F8
Cotham Pk North
RDLND/MONT BS6 .... 2 F7
Cotham Rd *RDLND/MONT* BS6 ...... 2 F9
Cotham Rd South
RDLND/MONT BS6 .... 3 G9
Cotham Side *RDLND/MONT* BS6 .... 3 G8
Cotham V *RDLND/MONT* BS6 ...... 2 E8
Cotman Wk *HORF/LLZ* BS7 ...... 53 F3
MTN/WRL BS22 .... 106 A3
Cotrith Gv *HNBRY/STHM* BS10 ... 38 B5
Cotswold Cl *PTSHD/EG* BS20 ...... 47 J5
Cotswold La *YATE/CS* BS37 ...... 35 K7
Cotswold Rd *BATHSE* BA2 ...... 111 G1
BMSTR BS3 .... 11 G2
YATE/CS BS37 .... 34 E7
Cottisford Rd *EVILLE/WHL* BS5 ...... 4 D2
Cottle Gdns *HGRV/WHIT* BS14 ...... 79 K5
Cottle Rd *HGRV/WHIT* BS14 ...... 79 K5
Cottles La *BOAV* BA15 .... 114 A7
Cottonwood Dr
OLD/WMLY/WICK BS30 .... 69 G7
Cottrell Av *KCWD/HNM* BS15 ...... 54 B7
Cottrell Rd *EVILLE/WHL* BS5 ...... 4 E1
Coulson Dr *MTN/WRL* BS22 ...... 106 C2
Coulson's Cl *HGRV/WHIT* BS14 ...... 93 K1
Coulson's Rd *HGRV/WHIT* BS14 .... 93 K1
Coulson Wk *KCWD/HNM* BS15 .... 54 C7
Counterpool Rd
KCWD/HNM BS15 .... 68 C3
Counterslip *CBRIS/FH* BS1 .... 7 J4
Counterslip Gdns
HGRV/WHIT BS14 .... 79 G5
Countess Wk
MANG/FISH BS16 .... 53 H3
County St *BRSG/KWL/STAPK* BS4 .. 7 M9
County Wy *TRWBR* BA14 .... 124 E7
Court Av *BRSTK/PCHW* BS34 ...... 40 E3
Court Av *YTN/CONG* BS49 .... 86 E5
Court Cl *HORF/LLZ* BS7 .... 74 C6
NAIL BS48 .... 74 C6
PTSHD/EG BS20 .... 47 G5
Court Dr *WNSC* BS25 .... 120 E2
Courtenay Crs
BRSG/KWL/STAPK BS4 .... 78 B4
Courteney Rd *KEYN* BS31 .... 96 B2
Court Farm Rd *HGRV/WHIT* BS14 .. 93 J1
OLD/WMLY/WICK BS30 .... 80 D2
Courtfield Gv *MANG/FISH* BS16 .... 54 A5
Court Gdns *CBATH/BATHN* BA1 .. 101 F1
Court Hl *PLTN/PENS* BS39 ...... 141 J7
Courtlands *ALMDB* BS32 .... 30 B5
KEYN BS31 .... 80 E6
Courtlands La *BMSTR* BS3 .... 65 G6
Court La *CBATH/BATHN* BA1 ...... 101 G2

TRWBR BA14 .... 130 E1
Croft Vw
HNLZ/SM/SNYPK/WT BS9 ...... 52 A3
Crokeswood Wk *AVONM* BS11 .... 37 H7
Crome Rd *HORF/LLZ* BS7 .... 53 F2
Cromer Rd *EVILLE/WHL* BS5 ...... 4 E6
WSM BS23 .... 16 F7
Cromhall La *WUE* GL12 .... 21 F4
Cromwell Ct
KCWD/HNM BS15 .... 68 E5
Cromwell Dr *MTN/WRL* BS22 .... 106 B1
Cromwell Rd *EVILLE/WHL* BS5 ...... 68 A2
RDLND/MONT BS6 .... 3 J6
Cromwells Hide
MANG/FISH BS16 .... 53 J4
Cromwell St *BMSTR* BS3 .... 10 E2
Crook's La *MTN/WRL* BS22 ...... 105 F1
Croomes Hl *MANG/FISH* BS16 .... 54 B2
Cropthorne Rd *HORF/LLZ* BS7 .... 39 K7
Cropthorne Rd South
HORF/LLZ BS7 .... 52 E1
Crosby Rw *CFTN/FAIL* BS8 ...... 6 B5
Crosscombe Dr
BMSTRD/HC/WWD BS13 ...... 92 E1
Cross Elms La
HNLZ/SM/SNYPK/WT BS9 ...... 51 G4
Crossfield Rd *MANG/FISH* BS16 ... 54 E6
Cross La *PTSHD/EG* BS20 ...... 49 H5
Crossleaze Rd *KCWD/HNM* BS15 .. 68 C7
Crossley Cl *FRCTL/WBN* BS36 ...... 24 B3
Crossman Av *AVONM* BS11 ...... 37 J7
Crossman Wk *CLVDN* BS21 ...... 71 H1
Cross St *KEYN* BS31 .... 81 F4
KCWD/HNM BS15 .... 68 C1
TRWBR BA14 .... 125 F5
WSM BS23 .... 16 E3
Cross Tree Gv *ALMDB* BS32 ...... 30 C7
Crossways Rd
BRSG/KWL/STAPK BS4 .... 12 A5
THNB/SVB BS35 .... 19 J4
Crowe Hl *RDSTK/MIDN* BA3 ...... 113 G7
Crowe La *RDSTK/MIDN* BA3 ...... 122 B1
Crow La *CBRIS/FH* BS1 .... 7 H4
HNBRY/STHM BS10 .... 38 C6
Crowley Wy *AVONM* BS11 ...... 36 C7
Crowndale Rd
BRSG/KWL/STAPK BS4 .... 12 A2
Crown Gdns
OLD/WMLY/WICK BS30 .... 69 H3
Crown Hl *CBATH/BATHN* BA1 ...... 99 F3
EVILLE/WHL BS5 .... 5 L9
Crown Hill Wk *EVILLE/WHL* BS5 ...... 5 L9
Crownleaze *MANG/FISH* BS16 .... 54 D6
Crown Rd *CBATH/BATHN* BA1 ...... 98 E3
KCWD/HNM BS15 .... 54 D7
OLD/WMLY/WICK BS30 .... 69 J4
Crows Gv *ALMDB* BS32 .... 30 C4
Crowther Pk *HORF/LLZ* BS7 ...... 4 B1
Crowther Rd *HORF/LLZ* BS7 ...... 4 B1
Crowthers Av *YATE/CS* BS37 ...... 34 B4
Crowther St *BMSTR* BS3 .... 10 D1
Croydon St *EVILLE/WHL* BS5 ...... 8 C1
The Crunnis *ALMDB* BS32 ...... 40 D2
Crusty La *PTSHD/EG* BS20 ...... 49 J4
Cuck Hl *WNSC* BS25 .... 121 H7
Cuckoo La *FRCTL/WBN* BS36 ...... 42 A5
NAIL BS48 .... 62 A4
Cuffington Av
BRSG/KWL/STAPK BS4 .... 9 G8
Culverhay *PLTN/PENS* BS39 ...... 95 J6
Culverhill Rd *YATE/CS* BS37 ...... 34 D6
Culver Rd *BOAV* BA15 .... 124 A1
Culvers Rd *KEYN* BS31 .... 80 E5
Culver St *CBRIS/FH* BS1 .... 6 F4
The Culvert *ALMDB* BS32 ...... 30 C7
Culverwell Rd
BMSTRD/HC/WWD BS13 ...... 77 J7
Cumberland Basin Rd
CFTN/FAIL BS8 .... 65 H5
Cumberland Cl *CBRIS/FH* BS1 ...... 6 B7
Cumberland Gv
RDLND/MONT BS6 .... 3 M6
Cumberland Pl *CFTN/FAIL* BS8 .... 65 H4
Cumberland Rd *CBRIS/FH* BS1 ...... 6 A7
CBRIS/FH BS1 .... 65 H5
Cumberland Rw
CBATH/BATHN BA1 .... 14 E6
Cumberland St *CBRISNE* BS2 ...... 7 J1
Cumbria Cl *THNB/SVB* BS35 ...... 19 K4
Cunningham Gdns
MANG/FISH BS16 .... 54 B4
Curland Gv *HGRV/WHIT* BS14 ...... 79 F6
Curlew Cl *MANG/FISH* BS16 ...... 53 K3
Curlew Gdns *MTN/WRL* BS22 .... 106 A4
Currells La
BLAG/CWMG/WR BS40 ...... 90 C3
Curtis La *BRSTK/PCHW* BS34 ...... 41 F5
Cusance Wy *TRWBR* BA14 ...... 125 J5
Custom Cl *HGRV/WHIT* BS14 ...... 12 A9
Cutler Rd
BMSTRD/HC/WWD BS13 ...... 77 H5
Cuttsheath Rd *WUE* GL12 ...... 20 D5
Cygnet Crs *MTN/WRL* BS22 ...... 106 A4
Cylde Pk *RDLND/MONT* BS6 ...... 2 D6
Cynder Wy *MANG/FISH* BS16 ...... 42 B7
Cynthia Rd *BATHSE* BA2 .... 99 F7
Cypress Gdns *CFTN/FAIL* BS8 ...... 65 G4
Cypress Gv
HNLZ/SM/SNYPK/WT BS9 ...... 52 A3
Cypress Ter
RDSTK/MIDN BA3 .... 126 E4
Cyrus Ct *MANG/FISH* BS16 ...... 55 H2

Dalston Rd *BMSTR* BS3 .... 6 D8
Dalton Sq *CBRISNE* BS2 .... 3 J9
Dame Court Cl *MTN/WRL* BS22 .. 106 A1
Dampier Rd *BMSTR* BS3 .... 10 B1
Damson Rd *MTN/WRL* BS22 ...... 105 K6
Danbury Crs *HNBRY/STHM* BS10 .. 39 F7
Danbury Wk
HNBRY/STHM BS10 .... 39 F7
Dancey Md
BMSTRD/HC/WWD BS13 ...... 77 G5
Dandy's Meadow
PTSHD/EG BS20 .... 47 J5
Daneacre Rd *RDSTK/MIDN* BA3 .. 127 H2
Dane Cl *BOAV* BA15 .... 113 K6
Dane Ri *BOAV* BA15 .... 113 K6
Dangerfield Av
BMSTRD/HC/WWD BS13 ...... 77 G5
Daniel Cl *CLVDN* BS21 .... 59 H7
Daniel Ms *BATHSE* BA2 .... 15 J4
Daniel St *BATHSE* BA2 .... 15 J4
Dano View Gdns
PTSHD/EG BS20 .... 47 G4
Dapps Hl *KEYN* BS31 .... 81 F6
Dapwell La *HGRV/WHIT* BS14 ...... 95 F3
Dark La *BNWL* BS29 .... 119 K4
NAIL BS48 .... 74 B6
RDSTK/MIDN BA3 .... 122 B1
Darley Cl *HNBRY/STHM* BS10 ...... 38 A5
Darlington Pl *BATHSE* BA2 ...... 15 K7
Darlington Rd *BATHSE* BA2 ...... 15 J4
Darlington St *BATHSE* BA2 .... 15 J5
Darmead
OMX/HUT/LCK BS24 .... 106 C4
Darnley Av *HORF/LLZ* BS7 ...... 52 D3
Dart Cl *THNB/SVB* BS35 ...... 19 G5
Dartmoor St *BMSTR* BS3 .... 6 D9
Dartmoor Av *BATHSE* BA2 .... 99 F3
Dartmouth Cl *MTN/WRL* BS22 .... 106 A3
Dart Rd *CLVDN* BS21 .... 71 F2
Daubeny Cl *MANG/FISH* BS16 .... 54 B4
Daventry Rd
BRSG/KWL/STAPK BS4 .... 11 L5
Davey St *CBRISNE* BS2 .... 3 M8
Davids Cl *THNB/SVB* BS35 ...... 23 F2
David's La *THNB/SVB* BS35 ...... 23 F2
David's Rd *HGRV/WHIT* BS14 ...... 79 G5
David St *CBRISNE* BS2 .... 7 L3
Davies Dr *BRSG/KWL/STAPK* BS4 .. 9 M6
Davin Crs *PTSHD/EG* BS20 ...... 49 J6
Davis Cl
OLD/WMLY/WICK BS30 .... 69 F5
Davis Ct *THNB/SVB* BS35 ...... 19 H3
Davis La *CLVDN* BS21 .... 71 J3
CLVDN BS21 .... 71 F3
Davis St *AVONM* BS11 .... 49 H1
Dawes Cl *CLVDN* BS21 .... 71 F2
Dawley Cl *FRCTL/WBN* BS36 ...... 41 K1
Dawlish Rd *BMSTR* BS3 .... 11 G4
Dawn Ri *KCWD/HNM* BS15 ...... 69 G1
Daws Ct *MANG/FISH* BS16 ...... 54 B5
Day Crs *BATHSE* BA2 .... 98 C6
Day's Rd *CBRISNE* BS2 .... 8 B4
Deacon Ct *FRCTL/WBN* BS36 ...... 41 K3
Deacons Cl *MTN/WRL* BS22 ...... 105 K3
Deadmill La *CBATH/BATHN* BA1 .. 100 B1
Dean Cl *THNB/SVB* BS35 .... 19 H3
Dean Cl *KCWD/HNM* BS15 ...... 68 A4
MTN/WRL BS22 .... 106 C2
Dean Crs *BMSTR* BS3 .... 7 G8
Deanery Rd *CBRIS/FH* BS1 ...... 6 E5
KCWD/HNM BS15 .... 69 H2
Deanhill La *CBATH/BATHN* BA1 .... 98 C2
Dean La *BMSTR* BS3 .... 6 F9
Dean Rd *AVONM* BS11 .... 36 D3
YATE/CS BS37 .... 33 K4
Dean's Dr *EVILLE/WHL* BS5 ...... 54 A7
Deans Md *AVONM* BS11 .... 50 C1
The Deans *PTSHD/EG* BS20 ...... 47 F5
Dean St *BMSTR* BS3 .... 6 F9
CBRISNE BS2 .... 3 K9
Debecca's La *PTSHD/EG* BS20 .... 49 F5
De Clifford Rd *AVONM* BS11 ...... 37 K6
Deep Coombe Rd *BMSTR* BS3 .. 10 B3
Deep Pit Rd *EVILLE/WHL* BS5 ...... 5 K7
Deerhurst *KCWD/HNM* BS15 ...... 54 E7
YATE/CS BS37 .... 33 K7
Deering Cl *AVONM* BS11 .... 37 J7
Deerleap *WNSC* BS25 .... 121 J6
Deer Md *CLVDN* BS21 .... 70 D2
Deerswood *KCWD/HNM* BS15 .... 55 G7
Delabere Av *MANG/FISH* BS16 .... 54 B4
Delamere Rd *TRWBR* BA14 ...... 125 F4
Delapre Rd *WSM* BS23 .... 116 D3
Delius Gv
BRSG/KWL/STAPK BS4 .... 78 B4
The Dell *ALMDB* BS32 .... 40 D1
HNLZ/SM/SNYPK/WT BS9 ...... 51 H4
MTN/WRL BS22 .... 105 K1
NAIL BS48 .... 73 H1
OLD/WMLY/WICK BS30 .... 69 J5
Delvin Rd *HNBRY/STHM* BS10 .... 52 A1
Denbigh St *CBRISNE* BS2 .... 3 K8
Dene Cl *KEYN* BS31 .... 96 A1
Dene Rd *HGRV/WHIT* BS14 ...... 79 G7
Denleigh Cl *HGRV/WHIT* BS14 ...... 78 E7
Denmark Pl *HORF/LLZ* BS7 .... 3 J3
Denmark Rd *BATHSE* BA2 .... 14 A7
Denmark St *CBRIS/FH* BS1 .... 6 E4
Denning Ct *MTN/WRL* BS22 ...... 106 C1
Dennisworth
MANG/FISH BS16 .... 56 D4
Dennor Pk *HGRV/WHIT* BS14 ...... 12 C9
Denny Cl *PTSHD/EG* BS20 .... 46 E4
Denny Isle Dr *THNB/SVB* BS35 ...... 27 H2
Denny Vw *PTSHD/EG* BS20 ...... 46 E4
Dennyview Rd *CFTN/FAIL* BS8 ...... 64 B2
Denston Dr *PTSHD/EG* BS20 ...... 47 J5
Denston Wk
BMSTRD/HC/WWD BS13 ...... 10 A9
Denton Patch
MANG/FISH BS16 .... 55 H2
Dentwood Gv
HNLZ/SM/SNYPK/WT BS9 ...... 50 D2
Derby Rd *HORF/LLZ* BS7 .... 3 K4
Derby St *EVILLE/WHL* BS5 .... 9 G2
Derham Cl *YTN/CONG* BS49 ...... 86 E4
Derham Pk *YTN/CONG* BS49 ...... 87 F5

Corker's Hl *EVILLE/WHL* BS5 .... 9 M4
Cork St *CBATH/BATHN* BA1 .... 14 A4
Courtney Rd *KCWD/HNM* BS15 ... 68 E3
Courtney Wy *KCWD/HNM* BS15 ... 69 G3
Court Hl *FRCTL/WBN* BS36 ...... 32 A7
HORF/LLZ BS7 .... 52 D3
KCWD/HNM BS15 .... 68 D3
MTN/WRL BS22 .... 83 F7
OLD/WMLY/WICK BS30 .... 69 H7
WUE GL12 .... 21 J1
Courtside Ms *RDLND/MONT* BS6 ... 2 F7
Court St *TRWBR* BA14 .... 124 E6
Court View Cl *ALMDB* BS32 ...... 29 K2
Courville Cl *THNB/SVB* BS35 ...... 23 F2
Cousins Cl *HNBRY/STHM* BS10 .. 38 A5
Cousins Ms
BRSG/KWL/STAPK BS4 .... 9 L5
Cousins Wy *MANG/FISH* BS16 ... 55 G1
Couzens Cl *YATE/CS* BS37 ...... 34 E5
Couzens Pl *BRSTK/PCHW* BS34 .. 40 E3
Coventry Wk
BRSG/KWL/STAPK BS4 .... 9 L5
Cowdray Rd
BRSG/KWL/STAPK BS4 .... 11 H9
Cowhorn Hl
OLD/WMLY/WICK BS30 .... 69 J6
Cowler Wk
BMSTRD/HC/WWD BS13 ...... 77 H7
Cowling Dr *HGRV/WHIT* BS14 ...... 79 G6
Cowling Rd *HGRV/WHIT* BS14 ...... 79 G6
Cowper Rd *RDLND/MONT* BS6 ...... 2 F7
Cowper St *EVILLE/WHL* BS5 ...... 8 E2
Cowship La *WUE* GL12 .... 21 J6
Cox Ct *OLD/WMLY/WICK* BS30 .... 69 F6
Coxley Dr *CBATH/BATHN* BA1 .... 100 A2
Coxway *CLVDN* BS21 .... 71 G1
Crabtree Cl *BRSG/KWL/STAPK* BS4 .. 92 A3
Crabtree La *LGASH* BS41 ...... 91 K3
Crabtree Wk *EVILLE/WHL* BS5 ...... 5 H6
Cradock Cl
OLD/WMLY/WICK BS30 .... 69 H6
Cranberry Wk
HNLZ/SM/SNYPK/WT BS9 ...... 50 E1
Cranbourne Cha *WSM* BS23 .... 105 F4
Cranbourne Rd
BRSTK/PCHW BS34 .... 39 J1
Cranbrook Rd *RDLND/MONT* BS6 ... 2 F3
Crandale Rd *BATHSE* BA2 ...... 14 A8
Crandell Cl *HNBRY/STHM* BS10 .. 38 C4
Crane Cl *KCWD/HNM* BS15 ...... 69 H2
Cranford Cl *MTN/WRL* BS22 ...... 105 J4
Cranham *YATE/CS* BS37 .... 43 K1
Cranham Cl *KCWD/HNM* BS15 ... 55 F7
Cranham Dr *BRSTK/PCHW* BS34 .. 30 B6
Cranham Rd *HNBRY/STHM* BS10 .. 52 A1
Cranhill Rd *CBATH/BATHN* BA1 .... 14 B3
Cranleigh *BATHSE* BA2 .... 111 J5
Cranleigh Court Rd
YATE/CS BS37 .... 34 A5
Cranleigh Gdns
HNLZ/SM/SNYPK/WT BS9 ...... 51 G5
Cranleigh Rd
HGRV/WHIT BS14 .... 79 F6
Cranmore Av *KEYN* BS31 ...... 80 E5
Cranmore Cl *TRWBR* BA14 ...... 124 D5
Cranmore Crs
HNBRY/STHM BS10 .... 39 G7
Cranmore Pl *BATHSE* BA2 ...... 111 G5
Cranside Av *RDLND/MONT* BS6 ...... 2 E3
Cransley Crs
HNLZ/SM/SNYPK/WT BS9 ...... 52 A2
Crantock Av
BMSTRD/HC/WWD BS13 ...... 10 D8
Crantock Dr *ALMDB* BS32 ...... 30 B2
Crantock Rd *YATE/CS* BS37 ...... 34 A6
Cranwell Gv *HGRV/WHIT* BS14 .... 78 E6
Cranwell Rd
OMX/HUT/LCK BS24 .... 118 D2
Cranwells Pk *CBATH/BATHN* BA1 .. 14 A2
Craven Cl *OLD/WMLY/WICK* BS30 .. 69 F5
Craven Wy
OLD/WMLY/WICK BS30 .... 69 F5
Crawford Cl *CLVDN* BS21 .... 70 D2
Crawley Crs *TRWBR* BA14 ...... 124 C6
Crawl La *RDSTK/MIDN* BA3 ...... 126 D1
Craydon Rd *HGRV/WHIT* BS14 ...... 79 H7
Craydon Rd *HGRV/WHIT* BS14 ...... 79 H7
Craydon Wk *HGRV/WHIT* BS14 .... 79 H6
Crediton Crs
BRSG/KWL/STAPK BS4 .... 11 L6
Crescent La *CBATH/BATHN* BA1 .... 14 D3
Crescent Rd *MANG/FISH* BS16 .... 54 C3
The Crescent
HNLZ/SM/SNYPK/WT BS9 ...... 50 E4
HNLZ/SM/SNYPK/WT BS9 ...... 52 A3
MANG/FISH BS16 .... 40 E7
MANG/FISH BS16 .... 54 D6
MTN/WRL BS22 .... 105 G3
NAIL BS48 .... 74 A5
Crescent Vw *BATHSE* BA2 ...... 14 E9
Cresswell Cl *MTN/WRL* BS22 ...... 106 B3
The Crest *BRSG/KWL/STAPK* BS4 .. 12 E3
Creswicke Av
KCWD/HNM BS15 .... 68 C5
Creswicke Rd
BRSG/KWL/STAPK BS4 .... 11 H9
Crewkerne Cl *NAIL* BS48 ...... 74 B2
Crew's Hole Rd *EVILLE/WHL* BS5 ... 9 H3
Cribbs Cswy *HNBRY/STHM* BS10 .. 38 C1
Cricklade Cl *NAIL* BS48 ...... 74 A2
Cricklade Rd *HORF/LLZ* BS7 ...... 3 J2
Cripps Rd *BMSTR* BS3 .... 10 C3
Crispin La *THNB/SVB* BS35 ...... 19 G4
Crispin Wy *KCWD/HNM* BS15 ...... 55 F7
Crockerne Dr *PTSHD/EG* BS20 ...... 49 J6
Croft Av *MANG/FISH* BS16 .... 4 F2
Croft Cl *OLD/WMLY/WICK* BS30 .... 81 K3
Crofters Wk *ALMDB* BS32 ...... 30 C7
Crofton Av *HORF/LLZ* BS7 ...... 52 D3
Croft Rd *CBATH/BATHN* BA1 .... 100 A3
Crofts End Rd *EVILLE/WHL* BS5 ...... 5 K7
The Croft *BATHSE* BA2 .... 112 D4
CLVDN BS21 .... 59 H6
MANG/FISH BS16 .... 55 F4
NAIL BS48 .... 74 A4
OMX/HUT/LCK BS24 .... 117 K3

Dafford's Buildings
CBATH/BATHN BA1 .... 100 A2
Dafford St *CBATH/BATHN* BA1 .. 100 B2
Daisy Rd *EVILLE/WHL* BS5 .... 4 E6
Dakota Dr *HGRV/WHIT* BS14 ...... 78 E7
Dalby Av *BMSTR* BS3 .... 11 G1
Dale St *CBRISNE* BS2 .... 7 L1
EVILLE/WHL BS5 .... 5 M9
Daley Cl *MTN/WRL* BS22 ...... 106 C2
Dalkeith Av *KCWD/HNM* BS15 ... 68 C1
Dalrymple Rd *RDLND/MONT* BS6 .... 3 K8

D

Derham Rd
BMSTRD/HC/WWD BS13 77 J6
Dermot St CBRISNE BS2 3 M8
Derricke Rd HGRV/WHIT BS14 79 K5
Derrick Rd KGWD/HNM BS15 68 D2
Derry Rd BMSTR BS3 10 C3
Derwent Cl BRSTK/PCHW BS34 29 K7
Derwent Gv KEYN BS31 81 G6
Derwent Rd EVILLE/WHL BS5 5 M8
WSM BS23 17 J8
Deverell Cl BOAV BA15 124 A2
De Verose Ct KGWD/HNM BS15 68 E6
Devizes Rd TRWBR BA14 125 K3
Devon Gv EVILLE/WHL BS5 4 F9
Devon Rd EVILLE/WHL BS5 4 E7
Devonshire Buildings
BATHSE BA2 111 J1
Devonshire Dr PTSHD/EG BS20 46 D4
Devonshire Pl BATHSE BA2 111 J1 1
Devonshire Rd BATHSE BA2 100 D3
RDLND/MONT BS6 2 C2
WSM BS23 116 D3
Dewfalls Dr ALMDB BS32 30 C6
Dial Hill Rd CLVDN BS21 59 F5
Dial La BLAG/CWMG/WR BS40 90 E3
MANG/FISH BS16 54 D3
Diamond Batch
OMX/HUT/LCK BS24 106 C4
Diamond Rd EVILLE/WHL BS5 9 L2
Diamond St BMSTR BS3 10 F1
Diana Gdns ALMDB BS32 30 D7
Dibden Cl MANG/FISH BS16 55 C1
Dibden La MANG/FISH BS16 55 C2
Dibden Rd MANG/FISH BS16 55 C1
Dickens Cl HORF/LLZ BS7 52 E1
Dickenson Rd WSM BS23 16 F6
Dickenson's Gv
YTN/CONG BS49 109 H2
Didsbury Cl HNBRY/STHM BS10 38 C7
Dighton Ga
BRSTK/PCHW BS34 40 D3 3
Dighton St CBRISNE BS2 7 H1
Dinghurst Rd WNSC BS25 121 G2
Dingle Cl
HNLZ/SM/SNYPK/WT BS9 50 E3
Dingle Rd
HNLZ/SM/SNYPK/WT BS9 50 E2
The Dingle FRCTL/WBN BS36 41 K5
HNLZ/SM/SNYPK/WT BS9 50 E2
YATE/CS BS37 34 C3
Dingle Vw
HNLZ/SM/SNYPK/WT BS9 50 E2
Dinglewood Cl
HNLZ/SM/SNYPK/WT BS9 51 F2 1
Dings Wk CBRISNE BS2 8 A4 2
Dixon Gdns CBATH/BATHN BA1 14 E1
Dixon Rd BRSG/KWL/STAPK BS4 13 M4
Dock Gate La CFTN/FAIL BS8 6 B6 1
Dodington La YATE/CS BS37 44 E2
Dodington Rd YATE/CS BS37 44 E1
Dodisham Wk MANG/FISH BS16 54 B3
Doleberrow WNSC BS25 121 J4
Dolemoor La YTN/CONG BS49 108 D1
Dolman Cl HNBRY/STHM BS10 38 C5 2
Dominion Rd BATHSE BA2 98 D6
MANG/FISH BS16 5 L4
Donald Rd
BMSTRD/HC/WWD BS13 77 H4
Doncaster Rd
HNBRY/STHM BS10 38 E7
Dongola Av HORF/LLZ BS7 3 K1
Dongola Rd HORF/LLZ BS7 3 K1
Doone Rd HORF/LLZ BS7 52 D1
Dorcas Av BRSTK/PCHW BS34 40 E3
Dorchester Cl NAIL BS48 73 H2 3
Dorchester Rd HORF/LLZ BS7 52 E2
Dorchester St
CBATH/BATHN BA1 15 G8
Dorester Cl HNBRY/STHM BS10 39 F4
Dorian Cl HORF/LLZ BS7 52 C2
Dorian Rd HORF/LLZ BS7 52 C2
Dorian Wy HNBRY/STHM BS10 52 C1
Dormer Cl FRCTL/WBN BS36 42 E2
Dormer Rd EVILLE/WHL BS5 4 C4
Dorset Cl BATHSE BA2 14 B7
Dorset Gv CBRISNE BS2 4 A6 1
Dorset Rd
HNLZ/SM/SNYPK/WT BS9 51 K3
KGWD/HNM BS15 68 D1
Dorset St BATHSE BA2 14 A7
BMSTR BS3 10 D1
Dorset Wy YATE/CS BS37 34 D4
Douglas Rd HORF/LLZ BS7 52 D2
KGWD/HNM BS15 68 D3
WSM BS23 17 G9 1
Doulton Wy HGRV/WHIT BS14 78 E6
Dovecote YATE/CS BS37 44 B1
Dovecote Cl TRWBR BA14 124 D6 3
Dovedale THNB/SVB BS35 19 J6
Dove La CBRISNE BS2 3 L9
Dovercourt Rd HORF/LLZ BS7 52 E4
Dovers La CBATH/BATHN BA1 101 H2
Dovers Pk CBATH/BATHN BA1 101 H2
Dove St CBRISNE BS2 3 H9
Dove St South CBRISNE BS2 7 H1
Dovey Ct OLD/WMLY/WICK BS30 69 J5
Dowdeswell Cl
HNBRY/STHM BS10 38 C5 3
Dowding Cl YATE/CS BS37 35 F5 1
Dowding Rd
CBATH/BATHN BA1 100 A3
Dowling Rd
BMSTRD/HC/WWD BS13 93 G1
Down Av BATHSE BA2 111 K4
Downavon BOAV BA15 123 K1
Down Cl PTSHD/EG BS20 46 D4 1
Downend Pk HORF/LLZ BS7 52 D4
Downend Park Rd
MANG/FISH BS16 54 D4 3
Downend Rd HORF/LLZ BS7 52 D4
KGWD/HNM BS15 68 D1
MANG/FISH BS16 54 C4
Downfield Cl THNB/SVB BS35 22 E1
Downfield Dr
FRCTL/WBN BS36 32 C7 2
Downfield Rd CFTN/FAIL BS8 2 A7
Downhayes Rd TRWBR BA14 125 F4
Down La BATHSE BA2 100 E3
Downleaze
HNLZ/SM/SNYPK/WT BS9 51 H6
MANG/FISH BS16 54 D1
PTSHD/EG BS20 46 E4
Down Leaze THNB/SVB BS35 23 F1 3
Downman Rd HORF/LLZ BS7 52 E4
Downend Rd FRCTL/WBN BS36 41 K4
PTSHD/EG BS20 46 C6
THNB/SVB BS35 23 F1
Downs Cl BOAV BA15 114 C6
MTN/WRL BS22 106 A4 5
THNB/SVB BS35 23 F1 4
Downs Cote Av
HNLZ/SM/SNYPK/WT BS9 51 H3
Downs Cote Dr
HNLZ/SM/SNYPK/WT BS9 51 H3
Downs Cote Gdns
HNLZ/SM/SNYPK/WT BS9 51 H3
Downs Cote Pk
HNLZ/SM/SNYPK/WT BS9 51 J3
Downs Cote Vw
HNLZ/SM/SNYPK/WT BS9 51 J3
Downside PTSHD/EG BS20 47 G4
Downside Close
OLD/WMLY/WICK BS30 69 F5 2
Downside Cl BATHSE BA2 100 E3
Downside Pk TRWBR BA14 125 G4
Downside Rd CFTN/FAIL BS8 2 A7
NAIL BS48 89 H3
NAIL BS48 90 A4
WSM BS23 17 G9
Downs Pk East
RDLND/MONT BS6 51 J4
Downs Pk West
HNLZ/SM/SNYPK/WT BS9 51 J4
Downs Rd
HNLZ/SM/SNYPK/WT BS9 51 J3
LGASH BS41 92 A2
The Downs PTSHD/EG BS20 46 E5
Downs Vw BOAV BA15 114 C6
The Down ALMDB BS32 22 C3
THNB/SVB BS35 22 E1
TRWBR BA14 125 G4
Downton Rd
BRSG/KWL/STAPK BS4 11 G6
Dowry Rd CFTN/FAIL BS8 6 A5 3
Dowry Sq CFTN/FAIL BS8 65 H4 4
Doynton La CHPMW/MSHF SN14 57 K6
Dragon Rd FRCTL/WBN BS36 41 J4
Dragons Hill Cl KEYN BS31 81 F6
Dragons Hill Ct KEYN BS31 81 F6
Dragons Hill Gdns KEYN BS31 81 F6 1
Dragonswell Rd
HNBRY/STHM BS10 38 D6
Dragon Wk EVILLE/WHL BS5 5 M8 1
Drake Av BATHSE BA2 111 J3
Drake Cl KEYN BS31 96 E2
MTN/WRL BS22 106 A1 1
Drake Rd BMSTR BS3 10 B1
Drakes Wy PTSHD/EG BS20 46 E4
Draycot Pl CBRIS/FH BS1 7 G7
Draycott Rd HORF/LLZ BS7 52 D4 1
Draydon Rd
BRSG/KWL/STAPK BS4 10 F9
Drayton Cl HGRV/WHIT BS14 12 C8
Drayton Rd
HNLZ/SM/SNYPK/WT BS9 50 E1 3
The Dring RDSTK/MIDN BA3 127 F3 1
The Drive HGRV/WHIT BS14 79 G6
HNLZ/SM/SNYPK/WT BS9 51 K4
WNSC BS25 121 H6
WNSC BS25 121 H2
WSM BS23 17 H1
Drove Rd WSM BS23 17 G4
Drove Wy OMX/HUT/LCK BS24 108 B5
Druetts Cl HNBRY/STHM BS10 52 C3 1
Druid Cl
HNLZ/SM/SNYPK/WT BS9 51 G4
Druid Hl
HNLZ/SM/SNYPK/WT BS9 51 G4
Druid Rd
HNLZ/SM/SNYPK/WT BS9 51 F5
Druid Stoke Av
HNLZ/SM/SNYPK/WT BS9 50 E4
Druid Woods
HNLZ/SM/SNYPK/WT BS9 50 E4 3
The Drumhead Wy
WNSC BS25 121 H6 1
Drummond Ct
OLD/WMLY/WICK BS30 69 F6 4
Drummond Rd MANG/FISH BS16 5 L3
RDLND/MONT BS6 3 K8
Dryleaze KEYN BS31 80 E4
YATE/CS BS37 34 B2 1
Dryleaze Rd MANG/FISH BS16 53 K3
Drynham La TRWBR BA14 131 F3
Drynham Pk TRWBR BA14 131 F1
Drynham Rd TRWBR BA14 131 F1
Drysdale Cl MTN/WRL BS22 105 H4
Dubbers La EVILLE/WHL BS5 5 J5
Dublin Crs
HNLZ/SM/SNYPK/WT BS9 51 K3
Duchess Rd CFTN/FAIL BS8 2 B8
Duchess Wy MANG/FISH BS16 53 H4
Ducie Rd EVILLE/WHL BS5 8 D2
MANG/FISH BS16 54 E5
Duck La BLAG/CWMG/WR BS40 109 K5
CLVDN BS21 71 J5
Duckmoor Rd BMSTR BS3 10 A1
Duck St WNSC BS25 121 F1
WUE GL12 24 C1
Dudley Cl KEYN BS31 80 E7
Dudley Ct
OLD/WMLY/WICK BS30 69 F6 3
Dudley Gv HORF/LLZ BS7 52 D1
Dugar Wk RDLND/MONT BS6 2 E3
Duke St BATHSE BA2 15 H7
TRWBR BA14 125 F5
Dulverton Rd HORF/LLZ BS7 3 G2
Dumaine Av BRSTK/PCHW BS34 40 D3
Dumfries Pl WSM BS23 16 F9 1
Duncan Gdns CBATH/BATHN BA1 98 D1
Duncombe La KGWD/HNM BS15 54 A7
Duncombe Rd
KGWD/HNM BS15 68 B1 3
Dundas Cl HNBRY/STHM BS10 38 B6 1
Dundonald Rd RDLND/MONT BS6 2 D3
Dundridge Gdns
EVILLE/WHL BS5 68 A4 1
Dundridge La EVILLE/WHL BS5 68 A4
Dundry Cl KGWD/HNM BS15 68 D4 1
Dundry La
BLAG/CWMG/WR BS40 91 H5
LGASH BS41 76 D7
Dundry Vw
BRSG/KWL/STAPK BS4 12 A6
Dunedin Wy MTN/WRL BS22 106 D1
Dunford Cl TRWBR BA14 131 F1
Dunford Rd BMSTR BS3 11 H2
Dunkeld Av BRSTK/PCHW BS34 39 J6
Dunkerry Rd BMSTR BS3 11 G2
Dunkery Cl NAIL BS48 73 J2 4
Dunkery Rd WSM BS23 104 E4
Dunkirk Rd MANG/FISH BS16 5 L3
Dunmail Rd HNBRY/STHM BS10 39 F6
Dunmore St BMSTR BS3 7 M8 1
Dunster Crs
OMX/HUT/LCK BS24 117 F4
Dunster Gdns
OLD/WMLY/WICK BS30 81 H1 1
Dunster Rd
BRSG/KWL/STAPK BS4 11 M7
KEYN BS31 80 E7
Dunsters Rd YTN/CONG BS49 87 J3
Durban Rd BRSTK/PCHW BS34 29 J7
Durban Wy YTN/CONG BS49 86 E3
Durbin Park Rd CLVDN BS21 58 E5
Durbin Wk EVILLE/WHL BS5 8 B1 1
Durdham Pk RDLND/MONT BS6 2 B5
Durham Gv KEYN BS31 80 D7
Durham Rd CBRISNE BS2 4 A6 2
Durleigh Cl
BMSTRD/HC/WWD BS13 77 J5
Durley Hl KEYN BS31 80 B3
Durley La KEYN BS31 80 D4
Durley Pk BATHSE BA2 111 H1
Durnford Av BMSTR BS3 6 B9
Durnford St BMSTR BS3 6 A9
Dursley Cl YATE/CS BS37 34 B6
Dursley Rd AVONM BS11 50 A4
TRWBR BA14 125 F7
WBRY BA13 131 H7
Durville Rd
BMSTRD/HC/WWD BS13 77 K5
Durweston Wk
HGRV/WHIT BS14 12 F8
Dutton Cl HGRV/WHIT BS14 79 H5 2
Dutton Rd HGRV/WHIT BS14 79 H6
Dutton Wk HGRV/WHIT BS14 79 H5 3
Dyers Cl BMSTRD/HC/WWD BS13 78 B7
Dyer's La YATE/CS BS37 33 H4
Dylan Thomas Ct
OLD/WMLY/WICK BS30 69 G5 4
Dymboro Av RDSTK/MIDN BA3 126 A4
Dymboro Cl RDSTK/MIDN BA3 126 A4
Dymboro Gdns
RDSTK/MIDN BA3 126 A4 1
The Dymboro
RDSTK/MIDN BA3 126 A4
Dymott Sq TRWBR BA14 125 J3
Dyrham Cl
HNLZ/SM/SNYPK/WT BS9 52 B3
KGWD/HNM BS15 69 F2 3
THNB/SVB BS35 19 H2
Dyrham Pde BRSTK/PCHW BS34 30 B7
Dyrham Rd KGWD/HNM BS15 69 F2
Dyson Cl YTN/CONG BS49 86 E4 2

E

Eagle Cl MTN/WRL BS22 105 J5
Eagle Crs MANG/FISH BS16 56 E5
Eagle Dr BRSTK/PCHW BS34 29 H7
Eagle Rd BRSG/KWL/STAPK BS4 13 G3
The Eagles YTN/CONG BS49 86 E4 3
Earlesfield NAIL BS48 73 G2
Earlham Gv WSM BS23 17 L3
Earl Russell Wy EVILLE/WHL BS5 8 C2
Earlsmead MANG/FISH BS16 5 H1
Earlstone Cl
OLD/WMLY/WICK BS30 69 G6
Earlstone Crs
OLD/WMLY/WICK BS30 69 G5 5
Earl St CBRIS/FH BS1 7 H1
Early Wy HNBRY/STHM BS10 52 C1
Earthcott Rd THNB/SVB BS35 23 K6
Easedale Cl
HNBRY/STHM BS10 39 G6 3
Eastbourne Rd EVILLE/WHL BS5 4 D9
TRWBR BA14 125 G5
Eastbury Cl THNB/SVB BS35 19 H4
Eastbury Rd MANG/FISH BS16 54 A5
East Cl BATHSE BA2 98 D7
Eastcombe Gdns WSM BS23 104 E4
Eastcombe Rd WSM BS23 104 E4
Eastcote Pk HGRV/WHIT BS14 79 F6
East Cft
HNLZ/SM/SNYPK/WT BS9 52 A2
East Dundry La LGASH BS41 92 C2
East Dundry Rd
HGRV/WHIT BS14 93 J2
Eastermeed La BNWL BS29 119 K3
Eastfield
HNLZ/SM/SNYPK/WT BS9 51 K2
Eastfield Av CBATH/BATHN BA1 98 E2
Eastfield Dr YATE/CS BS37 34 B3
Eastfield Gdns WSM BS23 104 E4 1
Eastfield Pk WSM BS23 104 D4
Eastfield Rd
HNLZ/SM/SNYPK/WT BS9 51 J2
OMX/HUT/LCK BS24 117 K4
RDLND/MONT BS6 3 H6
East Gv RDLND/MONT BS6 3 L7
East Hill Eastfield Rd
HNLZ/SM/SNYPK/WT BS9 51 J2 2
Eastlake Cl HORF/LLZ BS7 53 F2
Eastland Av THNB/SVB BS35 19 H3
Eastland Rd THNB/SVB BS35 19 H3
Eastlea CLVDN BS21 70 D2
East Lea Rd CBATH/BATHN BA1 98 D4
Eastleigh Cl MANG/FISH BS16 54 E5 2
Eastleigh Rd HNBRY/STHM BS10 39 G7
MANG/FISH BS16 54 E5
Eastlyn Rd
BMSTRD/HC/WWD BS13 10 C8
East Md RDSTK/MIDN BA3 126 C3
Eastmead La
HNLZ/SM/SNYPK/WT BS9 51 G5
Eastnor Rd HGRV/WHIT BS14 93 K1
Easton Hill Rd THNB/SVB BS35 19 J3
Easton Rd CBRISNE BS2 8 A2
EVILLE/WHL BS5 4 D9
PTSHD/EG BS20 49 J5
Easton Wy EVILLE/WHL BS5 4 B8
Eastover Cl
HNLZ/SM/SNYPK/WT BS9 51 J1
Eastover Gv BATHSE BA2 111 F4
East Pde
HNLZ/SM/SNYPK/WT BS9 50 E3
East Pk EVILLE/WHL BS5 4 E6
East Park Dr EVILLE/WHL BS5 4 F5
East Priory Cl
HNLZ/SM/SNYPK/WT BS9 51 J2
East Ridge Dr
BMSTRD/HC/WWD BS13 77 H6
East Shrubbery
RDLND/MONT BS6 2 C5 1
East St AVONM BS11 36 B7 1
BMSTR BS3 10 F1
BNWL BS29 119 K3
CBRISNE BS2 7 L1
East Vw MANG/FISH BS16 55 F3
Eastview Rd TRWBR BA14 124 C7
Eastville CBATH/BATHN BA1 100 A3
East Wy BATHSE BA2 98 D7
Eastway NAIL BS48 61 H7
Eastway Cl NAIL BS48 73 H1 3
Eastway Sq NAIL BS48 61 J7
Eastwood Crs
BRSG/KWL/STAPK BS4 9 M9
East Wood Pl PTSHD/EG BS20 47 H2
Eastwood Rd
BRSG/KWL/STAPK BS4 9 L8
Eaton Cl HGRV/WHIT BS14 79 J6
MANG/FISH BS16 54 B5
Eaton Crs CFTN/FAIL BS8 6 B1
Eaton St BMSTR BS3 10 F1 1
Ebdon Rd MTN/WRL BS22 106 A1
Ebenezer La
HNLZ/SM/SNYPK/WT BS9 51 G4 2
HNLZ/SM/SNYPK/WT BS9 51 F3 1
Ebenezer St EVILLE/WHL BS5 9 H2
Eden Gv HORF/LLZ BS7 39 K7
Edgecombe Av MTN/WRL BS22 105 J3
Edgecumbe Rd
RDLND/MONT BS6 3 G6
Edgefield Cl HGRV/WHIT BS14 93 J1
Edgefield Rd HGRV/WHIT BS14 93 J1
Edgehill Rd CLVDN BS21 59 F4
Edgeware Rd BMSTR BS3 6 E8
MANG/FISH BS16 54 C5 1
Edgewood Cl HGRV/WHIT BS14 12 D8
OLD/WMLY/WICK BS30 69 G7
Edgeworth YATE/CS BS37 43 K2
Edgeworth Rd BATHSE BA2 111 F3
Edinburgh Pl WSM BS23 16 D1
Edinburgh Rd KEYN BS31 80 E7
Edington Gv HNBRY/STHM BS10 38 D6
Edmund Cl MANG/FISH BS16 54 D3 3
Edmund Ct MANG/FISH BS16 56 D3
Edna Av BRSG/KWL/STAPK BS4 13 J2
Edward Rd BRSG/KWL/STAPK BS4 8 D9
CLVDN BS21 59 G5
KGWD/HNM BS15 68 E2
Edward Rd South CLVDN BS21 59 G5
Edward Rd West CLVDN BS21 59 G4
Edward St BATHSE BA2 15 J5
CBATH/BATHN BA1 99 F5
EVILLE/WHL BS5 5 G5
Effingham Rd RDLND/MONT BS6 3 J5
Egerton Brow HORF/LLZ BS7 3 H2 1
Egerton Rd BATHSE BA2 111 H1
HORF/LLZ BS7 3 G2
Eggshill La YATE/CS BS37 34 A6
Eighth Av HORF/LLZ BS7 53 F1
Eirene Ter PTSHD/EG BS20 49 K5
Elberton KGWD/HNM BS15 69 G2 3
Elberton Rd
HNLZ/SM/SNYPK/WT BS9 50 D2
Elborough Av YTN/CONG BS49 86 E4
Elbury Av KGWD/HNM BS15 54 C7
Elcombe Cl TRWBR BA14 130 E2
Elderberry Wk
HNBRY/STHM BS10 39 F6
Elderwood Dr
OLD/WMLY/WICK BS30 69 G7
Elderwood Rd HGRV/WHIT BS14 12 D9
Eldon Pl CBATH/BATHN BA1 100 A2
Eldon Ter BMSTR BS3 11 G2
Eldon Wy BRSG/KWL/STAPK BS4 8 F7
Eldred Cl
HNLZ/SM/SNYPK/WT BS9 50 E4
Eleanor Cl BATHSE BA2 98 D7
Eleventh Av HORF/LLZ BS7 40 A7 1
Elfin Rd MANG/FISH BS16 54 A4
Elgar Cl BRSG/KWL/STAPK BS4 78 B5 1
CLVDN BS21 71 G2
Elgin Av HORF/LLZ BS7 39 J7
Elgin Pk RDLND/MONT BS6 2 C5
Elgin Rd MANG/FISH BS16 54 B7
Eliot Cl HORF/LLZ BS7 52 E1
WSM BS23 117 F3 1
Elizabeth Cl
OMX/HUT/LCK BS24 117 J3
THNB/SVB BS35 19 J5
Elizabeth Crs BRSTK/PCHW BS34 40 D4
Elizabeths Ms
BRSG/KWL/STAPK BS4 9 L5 2
Ellacombe Rd
OLD/WMLY/WICK BS30 80 E1
Ellan Hay Rd ALMDB BS32 41 F2
Ellbridge Cl
HNLZ/SM/SNYPK/WT BS9 51 F4 1
Ellenborough Crs WSM BS23 16 E6
Ellenborough Pk North
WSM BS23 16 D5
Ellenborough Park Rd
WSM BS23 16 E5
Ellenborough Pk South
WSM BS23 16 D5
Ellesmere THNB/SVB BS35 19 H5
Ellesmere Rd
BRSG/KWL/STAPK BS4 13 G6
KGWD/HNM BS15 68 D2 2
WSM BS23 116 C4 1
Elfield Cl
BMSTRD/HC/WWD BS13 77 H5
Ellicks Cl ALMDB BS32 30 D5
Ellicott Rd HORF/LLZ BS7 52 D3
Ellinghurst Cl
HNBRY/STHM BS10 38 D6 1
Elliott Av MANG/FISH BS16 41 H7
Elliott Pl TRWBR BA14 124 C5
Ellis Av BMSTRD/HC/WWD BS13 10 B8
Ellis Pk MTN/WRL BS22 106 D1 2
Elliston Dr BATHSE BA2 110 E1
Elliston La RDLND/MONT BS6 2 E6
Elliston Rd RDLND/MONT BS6 2 E6
Ellsbridge Cl KEYN BS31 81 H6
Ellsworth Rd HNBRY/STHM BS10 38 C6
Elm Cl BNWL BS29 119 F2
BRSTK/PCHW BS34 40 C1
NAIL BS48 73 G2 3
TRWBR BA14 130 E4
WNSC BS25 121 G5
YATE/CS BS37 34 D6
YTN/CONG BS49 86 E5
Elmcroft Crs HORF/LLZ BS7 4 B2
Elmdale Crs THNB/SVB BS35 19 H4
Elmdale Rd BMSTR BS3 10 C3
CFTN/FAIL BS8 6 D1
TRWBR BA14 124 C7
Elmfield BOAV BA15 114 D6
KGWD/HNM BS15 68 E4
Elmfield Cl KGWD/HNM BS15 68 E4 1
Elmfield Rd
HNLZ/SM/SNYPK/WT BS9 51 J1 1
Elm Gv BATHSE BA2 111 F1
CBATH/BATHN BA1 100 B2
OMX/HUT/LCK BS24 118 A2
Elmgrove Av EVILLE/WHL BS5 4 D9 2
Elmgrove Dr YATE/CS BS37 34 C5 2
Elmgrove Pk RDLND/MONT BS6 3 G7
Elmgrove Rd MANG/FISH BS16 5 K3
RDLND/MONT BS6 3 G7
Elm Hayes
BMSTRD/HC/WWD BS13 77 H5
Elmhirst Gdns YATE/CS BS37 34 D5 1
Elmhurst Av EVILLE/WHL BS5 5 H4
Elmhurst Rd
OMX/HUT/LCK BS24 117 K4 1
Elmhyrst Rd WSM BS23 17 H2 1
Elming Down Cl ALMDB BS32 40 C2 1
Elm La RDLND/MONT BS6 2 C5
Elmlea Av
HNLZ/SM/SNYPK/WT BS9 51 H4
Elmleigh Av MANG/FISH BS16 55 H4
Elmleigh Cl MANG/FISH BS16 55 G4 2
Elmleigh Rd MANG/FISH BS16 55 G4
Elm Lodge Rd NAIL BS48 62 A7
Elmore KGWD/HNM BS15 55 F7 2
YATE/CS BS37 34 A7 1
Elmore Rd BRSTK/PCHW BS34 29 J6
HORF/LLZ BS7 52 E3
Elm Pk BRSTK/PCHW BS34 39 K6
Elm Rd HORF/LLZ BS7 52 C4
KGWD/HNM BS15 68 E4
Elms Cross Dr BOAV BA15 123 J1
Elms Gv BRSTK/PCHW BS34 30 A6
Elmsleigh Rd WSM BS23 116 C2
Elmsley La MTN/WRL BS22 83 H7
The Elms BOAV BA15 114 D5
Elm Tree Av MANG/FISH BS16 55 G2
RDSTK/MIDN BA3 126 E4
Elmtree Cl KGWD/HNM BS15 68 D1
Elmtree Dr
BMSTRD/HC/WWD BS13 77 H6
Elm Tree Rd CLVDN BS21 71 F1 3
OMX/HUT/LCK BS24 118 A2
Elmvale Dr OMX/HUT/LCK BS24 118 A4
Elm Vw RDSTK/MIDN BA3 126 C3
Elm Wk PTSHD/EG BS20 47 G5
YTN/CONG BS49 86 E5
Elm Wd YATE/CS BS37 34 B7
Elsbert Dr
BMSTRD/HC/WWD BS13 77 G5
Elstree Rd EVILLE/WHL BS5 5 J7
Elton La HORF/LLZ BS7 3 H5
Elton Rd CFTN/FAIL BS8 6 D2
CLVDN BS21 58 E7
HORF/LLZ BS7 3 G4
KGWD/HNM BS15 68 B1
MTN/WRL BS22 106 B1
Elton St CBRISNE BS2 7 M1
Elvard Cl
BMSTRD/HC/WWD BS13 77 J7
Elvard Rd
BMSTRD/HC/WWD BS13 77 J6
Elvaston Rd BMSTR BS3 11 J2
Elwell La LGASH BS41 91 G3
Ely Gv HNLZ/SM/SNYPK/WT BS9 50 D2
Embassy Rd EVILLE/WHL BS5 5 J8
Embassy Wk EVILLE/WHL BS5 5 J8
Embercourt Dr NAIL BS48 74 A5
Embleton Rd
HNBRY/STHM BS10 38 E6
Emersons Green La
MANG/FISH BS16 55 H3
Emerson Sq HORF/LLZ BS7 52 E1
Emersons Wy
MANG/FISH BS16 55 J2 1
Emery Ga BNWL BS29 119 J3
Emery Rd BRSG/KWL/STAPK BS4 13 L4
Emet Gv MANG/FISH BS16 55 H3
Emet La MANG/FISH BS16 55 H3
Emlyn Rd EVILLE/WHL BS5 4 E6
Emma-chris Wy
BRSTK/PCHW BS34 40 B6
Emmett Wd HGRV/WHIT BS14 94 A1
Emra Cl EVILLE/WHL BS5 5 M8
Enfield Rd MANG/FISH BS16 54 A6
Engine Common La
YATE/CS BS37 33 K1
Engine La NAIL BS48 73 F3
England's Crs FRCTL/WBN BS36 41 K1
Englishcombe La BATHSE BA2 111 F2
Englishcombe Rd
BMSTRD/HC/WWD BS13 93 F1
Englishcombe Wy BATHSE BA2 111 G2

Ennerdale Cl WSM BS23 17 K8 1
Ennerdale Rd
HNBRY/STHM BS10 39 G6
Entry Hl BATHSE BA2 111 J2
Entry Hill Dr BATHSE BA2 111 J3
Entry Hill Gdns BATHSE BA2 111 J2
Entry Hill Pk BATHSE BA2 111 J3
Entry Ri BATHSE BA2 111 J4
Epney Cl BRSTK/PCHW BS34 29 J6
Epsom Cl MANG/FISH BS16 42 A7
Epsom Rd TRWBR BA14 131 G3
Epworth Rd HNBRY/STHM BS10 38 D6
Erin Wk BRSG/KWL/STAPK BS4 11 H7
Ermine Wy AVONM BS11 49 J2
Ermleet Rd RDLND/MONT BS6 2 E5
Ernest Barker Cl
EVILLE/WHL BS5 8 C3 2
Ernestville Rd MANG/FISH BS16 5 M3
Ervine Ter CBRISNE BS2 3 L9
Esgar Ri MTN/WRL BS22 105 K2 1
Eskdale THNB/SVB BS35 19 J6
Eskdale Cl MTN/WRL BS22 105 J5
Esmond Gv CLVDN BS21 59 F6
Esplanade Rd PTSHD/EG BS20 47 G2
Essery Rd EVILLE/WHL BS5 4 F6
Esson Rd KGWD/HNM BS15 68 B1
Estoril YATE/CS BS37 34 C6
Estune Wk LGASH BS41 76 C2
Etloe Rd RDLND/MONT BS6 2 B2
Eton La BNWL BS29 106 E6
Eton Rd BRSG/KWL/STAPK BS4 13 G2
Ettlingen Wy CLVDN BS21 71 G1
Ettricke Dr MANG/FISH BS16 54 B3
Eugene St CBRISNE BS2 7 G1
EVILLE/WHL BS5 7 M1
Evans Cl BRSG/KWL/STAPK BS4 9 M6
Evans Rd RDLND/MONT BS6 2 C6
Evelyn Rd CBATH/BATHN BA1 98 E4
HNBRY/STHM BS10 52 A2 2
Evenlode Gdns AVONM BS11 50 B4
Evenlode Wy KEYN BS31 96 B1
Evercreech Rd HGRV/WHIT BS14 78 E7
Everest Av MANG/FISH BS16 5 K2
Everest Rd MANG/FISH BS16 5 K2
Evergreen Cl WNSC BS25 120 C5
Everleigh Cl TRWBR BA14 131 F2
Eve Rd EVILLE/WHL BS5 4 C8
Ewart Rd MTN/WRL BS22 105 H5
Excelsior St BATHSE BA2 15 H8
Excelsior Ter RDSTK/MIDN BA3 126 C4
Exeter Buildings
RDLND/MONT BS6 2 C6
Exeter Rd BMSTR BS3 6 C9
PTSHD/EG BS20 47 J5
WSM BS23 16 F7
Exford Cl WSM BS23 116 E4
Exley Cl OLD/WMLY/WICK BS30 69 J5
Exmoor Rd BATHSE BA2 111 J3
Exmoor St BMSTR BS3 6 D9
Exmouth Rd
BRSG/KWL/STAPK BS4 11 M6
Eyer's La CBRISNE BS2 7 L2

F

Faber Gv
BMSTRD/HC/WWD BS13 78 A7 2
Fabian Dr BRSTK/PCHW BS34 40 D3
Factory Rd FRCTL/WBN BS36 42 A1
Failand Cresent
HNLZ/SM/SNYPK/WT BS9 50 E4
Failand La CFTN/FAIL BS8 63 F1
Failand Wk
HNLZ/SM/SNYPK/WT BS9 50 E3 1
Fairacre Cl HORF/LLZ BS7 53 F4
OMX/HUT/LCK BS24 118 C2
Fairacres Cl KEYN BS31 80 E7
Fairfax St CBRIS/FH BS1 7 J3
Fairfield RDSTK/MIDN BA3 129 F6
Fairfield Av CBATH/BATHN BA1 99 K2
Fairfield Cl MTN/WRL BS22 105 G4
NAIL BS48 74 D4 1
Fairfield Md NAIL BS48 74 C4
Fairfield Mdw TRWBR BA14 130 B4
Fairfield Park Rd
CBATH/BATHN BA1 99 K2
Fairfield Pl BMSTR BS3 6 D9
Fairfield Rd BMSTR BS3 6 D9
CBATH/BATHN BA1 99 K3
RDLND/MONT BS6 3 L6
Fairfield Wy NAIL BS48 74 C5
Fairfoot Rd
BRSG/KWL/STAPK BS4 12 A1
Fairford Cl KGWD/HNM BS15 55 F7 1
Fairford Crs BRSTK/PCHW BS34 30 A7
Fairford Rd AVONM BS11 49 J2
Fair Furlong
BMSTRD/HC/WWD BS13 77 J7
Fairhaven YATE/CS BS37 34 C6 1
Fairhaven Rd RDLND/MONT BS6 2 E1
Fair Hl WNSC BS25 121 J6
Fair Lawn
OLD/WMLY/WICK BS30 69 G6
Fairlawn Rd RDLND/MONT BS6 3 L6
Fairlyn Dr KGWD/HNM BS15 55 F6
Fairoaks
OLD/WMLY/WICK BS30 69 G7 1
Fairview MTN/WRL BS22 106 A1 2
Fair View Dr RDLND/MONT BS6 2 E6
Fairview Rd KGWD/HNM BS15 69 F2
Fairway BRSG/KWL/STAPK BS4 13 H6
Fairway Cl MTN/WRL BS22 105 G3 1
OLD/WMLY/WICK BS30 69 H6
Fairways KEYN BS31 97 F2
Fairwood Cl TRWBR BA14 125 J4 1
Falcon Cl BRSTK/PCHW BS34 29 H7
HNLZ/SM/SNYPK/WT BS9 51 H1
PTSHD/EG BS20 47 H5
Falcon Crs MTN/WRL BS22 105 K5 1
Falcondale Rd
HNLZ/SM/SNYPK/WT BS9 51 H1
Falcondale Wk
HNLZ/SM/SNYPK/WT BS9 51 J1
Falcon Dr BRSTK/PCHW BS34 29 H7
Falconer Rd CBATH/BATHN BA1 98 D1
Falcon Wk BRSTK/PCHW BS34 29 H7
Falcon Wy THNB/SVB BS35 19 J3
Falfield Rd
BRSG/KWL/STAPK BS4 12 E2
Falfield Wk
HNBRY/STHM BS10 52 A1 2
Falkland Rd RDLND/MONT BS6 3 L6
Fallodon Ct
HNLZ/SM/SNYPK/WT BS9 51 K4 1
Fallodon Wy
HNLZ/SM/SNYPK/WT BS9 51 K4
Fallowfield MTN/WRL BS22 106 A1
OLD/WMLY/WICK BS30 69 J6
Falmouth Cl NAIL BS48 74 A2 1
Falmouth Rd HORF/LLZ BS7 3 H2
Fane Cl HNBRY/STHM BS10 38 D5 2
Fanshawe Rd HGRV/WHIT BS14 12 B9
Far Handstones
OLD/WMLY/WICK BS30 69 G6
Farington Rd
HNLZ/SM/SNYPK/WT BS9 52 B2
Farleigh Av TRWBR BA14 124 C7
Farleigh La WUE GL12 21 K3
Farleigh Ri CBATH/BATHN BA1 101 J3
Farleigh Rd CLVDN BS21 70 C2
KEYN BS31 80 D7
NAIL BS48 74 C5
RDSTK/MIDN BA3 128 A2
Farleigh Wk
BMSTRD/HC/WWD BS13 10 A8
Farler's End NAIL BS48 73 K3
Farley Cl BRSTK/PCHW BS34 40 B1
Farm Cl MANG/FISH BS16 55 H3 1
Farm Ct MANG/FISH BS16 54 E2
Farmer Rd
BMSTRD/HC/WWD BS13 77 G7
Farmhouse Cl NAIL BS48 73 J2 2
Farmhouse Ct NAIL BS48 73 J2 2
Farm La THNB/SVB BS35 28 A4
Farm Rd MANG/FISH BS16 54 E2
MTN/WRL BS22 105 G4
OMX/HUT/LCK BS24 117 K4
Farmwell Cl
BMSTRD/HC/WWD BS13 77 K6 1
Farnborough Rd
OMX/HUT/LCK BS24 118 D1
Farndale EVILLE/WHL BS5 68 A4
Farndale Rd MTN/WRL BS22 105 J5
Farne Cl
HNLZ/SM/SNYPK/WT BS9 51 K4
Farrant Cl BRSG/KWL/STAPK BS4 78 B5
Farr's La CBRIS/FH BS1 7 G5
Farr St AVONM BS11 49 H1
Farthing Rw RDSTK/MIDN BA3 128 E6
Faulkland Rd BATHSE BA2 14 A9
Faverole Wy TRWBR BA14 125 H5
Faversham Dr
OMX/HUT/LCK BS24 117 F5
Fawkes Cl KGWD/HNM BS15 69 H2
Fearnville Est CLVDN BS21 70 E1 2
Featherstone Rd
MANG/FISH BS16 5 K2
Feeder Rd CBRISNE BS2 8 A6
CBRISNE BS2 8 E5
Felix Rd EVILLE/WHL BS5 4 B9
Felstead Rd HNBRY/STHM BS10 39 H7
Feltham Rd MANG/FISH BS16 56 E4
Felton Gv
BMSTRD/HC/WWD BS13 77 H3
Felton La BLAG/CWMG/WR BS40 90 E5
Felton St BLAG/CWMG/WR BS40 90 D5
Fennel Dr ALMDB BS32 41 F1
Fennell Gv
HNBRY/STHM BS10 38 D6 2
Fenners MTN/WRL BS22 106 C1 3
Fenshurst Gdns LGASH BS41 76 B3
Fenswood Md LGASH BS41 76 A2
Fenswood Rd LGASH BS41 76 A2
Fenton Cl KEYN BS31 96 E1
Fenton Rd HORF/LLZ BS7 3 G1
Fermaine Av
BRSG/KWL/STAPK BS4 13 L1
Fernbank Rd RDLND/MONT BS6 2 E6
Fernbrook Cl MANG/FISH BS16 41 G7
Fern Cl HNBRY/STHM BS10 38 E5
RDSTK/MIDN BA3 126 C5
Ferndale Av
OLD/WMLY/WICK BS30 69 F7
Ferndale Rd CBATH/BATHN BA1 100 B1
HORF/LLZ BS7 39 K6
PTSHD/EG BS20 47 H3
Ferndene ALMDB BS32 30 B5
Ferndown YATE/CS BS37 34 B6
Ferndown Cl AVONM BS11 50 C2 1
Fern Gv BRSTK/PCHW BS34 40 C1
NAIL BS48 73 G3
Fernhill ALMDB BS32 22 A6
Fernhill La AVONM BS11 37 J7
Fernhurst Rd EVILLE/WHL BS5 5 L7
Fernlea Gdns PTSHD/EG BS20 49 H5 1
Fernlea Rd MTN/WRL BS22 105 H6
Fernleaze FRCTL/WBN BS36 42 D2
Fern Rd MANG/FISH BS16 54 D4
Fernsteed Rd
BMSTRD/HC/WWD BS13 77 H5
Fern St CBRISNE BS2 3 M8
Ferry La BATHSE BA2 15 H7
Ferry Rd KGWD/HNM BS15 80 D2
Ferry St CBRIS/FH BS1 7 J5 1
Fiddes Rd RDLND/MONT BS6 2 E2
The Fielders MTN/WRL BS22 106 C1 2
Field Farm Cl BRSTK/PCHW BS34 40 E4
Fieldings BOAV BA15 113 K6
Fielding's Rd BATHSE BA2 99 F6 1
Field La OLD/WMLY/WICK BS30 68 E7
THNB/SVB BS35 23 K3
Field Rd KGWD/HNM BS15 68 C1
Field View Dr MANG/FISH BS16 54 C3
Field Wy TRWBR BA14 130 B1
Fieldway WNSC BS25 120 E2
Fiennes Cl MANG/FISH BS16 54 E5 1
Fifth Av HORF/LLZ BS7 39 K7
Filby Dr BRSTK/PCHW BS34 30 B7 1
Filton Av BRSTK/PCHW BS34 40 A5
HORF/LLZ BS7 52 C3
Filton Gv HORF/LLZ BS7 52 D3
Filton La BRSTK/PCHW BS34 40 C6
Filton Rd BRSTK/PCHW BS34 40 C6
HORF/LLZ BS7 52 D2
MANG/FISH BS16 40 E7
Filwood Broadway
BRSG/KWL/STAPK BS4 11 K8
Filwood Ct MANG/FISH BS16 54 B6 1
Filwood Dr KGWD/HNM BS15 69 F2
Filwood Rd MANG/FISH BS16 54 A6
Finch Cl MTN/WRL BS22 105 K5 4
THNB/SVB BS35 19 H3
Finch Rd YATE/CS BS37 34 C7
Finmere Gdns MTN/WRL BS22 106 B1
Fircliff Pk PTSHD/EG BS20 47 H2
Fire Engine La
FRCTL/WBN BS36 42 E1 1
Firework Cl KGWD/HNM BS15 69 H2
Firfield St BRSG/KWL/STAPK BS4 8 A9
Firgrove Crs YATE/CS BS37 34 D5
Fir Leaze NAIL BS48 73 F2 1
First Av BATHSE BA2 111 H1
BRSG/KWL/STAPK BS4 9 K7
RDSTK/MIDN BA3 126 D6
The Firs BATHSE BA2 112 A4
RDSTK/MIDN BA3 122 A1
First Wy AVONM BS11 36 D7
Firtree Av PLTN/PENS BS39 126 A1
Fir Tree Cl BRSTK/PCHW BS34 39 J6
Fir Tree La EVILLE/WHL BS5 68 A4
Fisher Av KGWD/HNM BS15 69 G1
Fisher Rd KGWD/HNM BS15 69 G1
Fishponds Rd EVILLE/WHL BS5 4 E5
Fishpool Hl HNBRY/STHM BS10 38 E4
Fitchett Wk HNBRY/STHM BS10 38 C5
Fitzgerald Rd BMSTR BS3 11 L2
Fitzmaurice Cl BOAV BA15 124 A2
Fitzmaurice Pl BOAV BA15 123 K1 1
Fitzroy Rd MANG/FISH BS16 54 B7
Fitzroy St BRSG/KWL/STAPK BS4 8 B9
Five Acre Dr MANG/FISH BS16 53 K2
Five Arches Cl
RDSTK/MIDN BA3 126 E3
Flagstaff Rd AXBR BS26 118 E7
Flamingo Crs MTN/WRL BS22 105 K5
Flatwoods Crs BATHSE BA2 112 E2 1
Flatwoods Rd BATHSE BA2 112 E2
Flax Bourton Rd
CFTN/FAIL BS8 63 H7 1
Flaxman Cl HORF/LLZ BS7 53 F3
Flaxpits La FRCTL/WBN BS36 41 J2
Fleece Cottages TRWBR BA14 125 G7
Fleur De Lys Dr TRWBR BA14 130 C3
Florence Gv MTN/WRL BS22 17 M1
Florence Pk ALMDB BS32 30 A2
RDLND/MONT BS6 2 C2
Florence Rd MANG/FISH BS16 54 E6
Flowerdown Rd
OMX/HUT/LCK BS24 118 D2
Flowers Hl
BRSG/KWL/STAPK BS4 13 K7
Flowerwell Rd
BMSTRD/HC/WWD BS13 77 K6 2
Folleigh Cl LGASH BS41 76 D1
Folleigh Dr LGASH BS41 76 D1
Folleigh La LGASH BS41 76 D1
Folliot Cl MANG/FISH BS16 54 A1
Folly Bridge Cl YATE/CS BS37 34 A5 2
Folly Brook Rd MANG/FISH BS16 42 B6
Follyfield BOAV BA15 123 K2
Folly La CBRISNE BS2 8 B3
WNSC BS25 121 H7
WSM BS23 116 D5
Folly Rd YATE/CS BS37 32 A3
The Folly KEYN BS31 97 G2
MANG/FISH BS16 55 F2
Fontana Cl
OLD/WMLY/WICK BS30 69 H7
Fonthill Rd CBATH/BATHN BA1 99 H2
HNBRY/STHM BS10 39 G6
Fontmell Ct HGRV/WHIT BS14 79 H4 1
Fontwell Dr MANG/FISH BS16 42 A7
Footes La FRCTL/WBN BS36 42 C1
Footshill Cl KGWD/HNM BS15 68 C4
Footshill Dr KGWD/HNM BS15 68 C3
Footshill Rd KGWD/HNM BS15 68 C4
Forde Cl
OLD/WMLY/WICK BS30 69 F5 3
Fordell Pl
BRSG/KWL/STAPK BS4 12 B1 1
Ford La MANG/FISH BS16 55 H3
Ford St EVILLE/WHL BS5 8 E4
Forefield Pl BATHSE BA2 15 H9
Forefield Ri BATHSE BA2 111 K1
Forest Av MANG/FISH BS16 54 B6
Forest Dr HNBRY/STHM BS10 39 F5
WSM BS23 105 F4
Forest Edge KGWD/HNM BS15 68 C6
Forester Av BATHSE BA2 15 H3
Forester La BATHSE BA2 15 J3
Forester Rd BATHSE BA2 15 J4
PTSHD/EG BS20 47 H5
Forest Hills ALMDB BS32 30 A2
Fore St TRWBR BA14 125 F5
Forest Rd KGWD/HNM BS15 68 D3
MANG/FISH BS16 54 B6
WUE GL12 21 J1
Forest Wk KGWD/HNM BS15 68 C3
MANG/FISH BS16 54 B7 1
Forge End PTSHD/EG BS20 48 E6
Fortescue Rd
RDSTK/MIDN BA3 127 G3 1
Fortfield Rd HGRV/WHIT BS14 79 F6
Forty Acre La THNB/SVB BS35 23 F3
Fosse Barton NAIL BS48 73 H1 1
Fosse Cl NAIL BS48 73 G1 1
Fossedale Av HGRV/WHIT BS14 79 F5
Fossefield Rd
RDSTK/MIDN BA3 126 C7
Fosse Gdns BATHSE BA2 111 G5
Fosse La NAIL BS48 73 G1
RDSTK/MIDN BA3 126 E2
Fosse Wy NAIL BS48 73 G1
Fosseway CLVDN BS21 71 F2
RDSTK/MIDN BA3 126 D6
Fosseway Gdns
RDSTK/MIDN BA3 126 D4
The Fosseway CFTN/FAIL BS8 6 B3
Foster St EVILLE/WHL BS5 4 D6
Foundry La EVILLE/WHL BS5 5 L6
Fountaine Ct EVILLE/WHL BS5 4 E5
Fountain La WNSC BS25 120 E7
Fountains Dr
OLD/WMLY/WICK BS30 69 F4
Four Acre Av MANG/FISH BS16 54 E1
Four Acre Crs MANG/FISH BS16 41 K7
Four Acre Rd MANG/FISH BS16 41 K7
Four Acres
BMSTRD/HC/WWD BS13 77 G7
Four Acres Cl
BMSTRD/HC/WWD BS13 77 H7
NAIL BS48 73 J3
Fourth Av HORF/LLZ BS7 39 K6
Fowey Cl NAIL BS48 74 A3
Fowey Rd MTN/WRL BS22 106 B1 2
Fox & Hounds La KEYN BS31 81 F6 2
Fox Av YATE/CS BS37 34 A5
Foxborough Gdns
ALMDB BS32 30 C5 3
Foxcombe Rd
CBATH/BATHN BA1 98 E5
HGRV/WHIT BS14 79 F7 1
Foxcote KGWD/HNM BS15 69 F3
Foxcote Rd BMSTR BS3 10 B2
Fox Ct OLD/WMLY/WICK BS30 69 F7
Foxcroft Cl ALMDB BS32 40 E2
Foxcroft Rd EVILLE/WHL BS5 5 G9
Fox Den Rd BRSTK/PCHW BS34 40 C5
Foxe Rd FRCTL/WBN BS36 32 B7
Foxfield Av ALMDB BS32 30 C4
Foxglove Cl THNB/SVB BS35 19 J3 2
Fox Hl BATHSE BA2 111 K3
Foxholes La ALMDB BS32 22 B3
Fox Rd EVILLE/WHL BS5 4 C7
Fraley Rd
HNLZ/SM/SNYPK/WT BS9 51 J2
Frampton Ct
OLD/WMLY/WICK BS30 69 F6 3
TRWBR BA14 130 C1
Frampton Crs MANG/FISH BS16 54 C5
Frampton End Rd
FRCTL/WBN BS36 32 D6
Francis Fox Rd WSM BS23 16 F4 1
Francis Pl
OLD/WMLY/WICK BS30 69 F6
Francis Rd BMSTR BS3 10 F3
HNBRY/STHM BS10 52 A1 1
Francis St TRWBR BA14 124 E5
Francis Wy
OLD/WMLY/WICK BS30 69 K4
Francombe Gv
HNBRY/STHM BS10 52 C3
Frankland Cl CBATH/BATHN BA1 98 D3
Franklin's Wy YTN/CONG BS49 87 J3
Franklyn La CBRISNE BS2 3 M8 1
Franklyn St CBRISNE BS2 3 L8
Fraser Cl MTN/WRL BS22 106 A1 1
Fraser St BMSTR BS3 11 H1
Frayne Rd BMSTR BS3 6 A8
Frederick Pl CFTN/FAIL BS8 6 C2
Fredrick St
BRSG/KWL/STAPK BS4 8 A9 1
Freeland Buildings
EVILLE/WHL BS5 4 F5 1
Freeland Pl CFTN/FAIL BS8 65 H4 1
Freelands CLVDN BS21 70 E3
Freemans La NAIL BS48 90 C2
Freemantle Gdns
EVILLE/WHL BS5 4 F4 1
Freemantle Rd EVILLE/WHL BS5 4 E4
Freestone Rd CBRISNE BS2 8 A5
Free Tank CBRISNE BS2 7 M5
Freeview Rd BATHSE BA2 98 D6
Fremantle La RDLND/MONT BS6 3 G8
Fremantle Rd
RDLND/MONT BS6 3 G7 1
Frenchay Hl MANG/FISH BS16 54 B2
Frenchay Rd MANG/FISH BS16 54 C2
WSM BS23 116 D2
French Cl NAIL BS48 61 K7
Freshford La RDSTK/MIDN BA3 122 B1
Freshland Wy KGWD/HNM BS15 68 B2
Freshmoor CLVDN BS21 59 H7
Friar Av MTN/WRL BS22 105 K2
Friary Cl BOAV BA15 122 E2
CLVDN BS21 58 E5
Friary Grange Pk
FRCTL/WBN BS36 41 K2
Friary Rd HORF/LLZ BS7 3 G3
PTSHD/EG BS20 47 F4
Friendly Rw PTSHD/EG BS20 49 J4
Friendship Gv NAIL BS48 73 K1 1
Friendship Rd
BRSG/KWL/STAPK BS4 11 M4
NAIL BS48 61 K7
Friezewood Rd BMSTR BS3 6 B9
Fripp Cl EVILLE/WHL BS5 8 C4
Frobisher Av PTSHD/EG BS20 46 E4
Frobisher Cl MTN/WRL BS22 105 K1 3
PTSHD/EG BS20 46 E4 3
Frobisher Rd BMSTR BS3 10 B1
Frog La BLAG/CWMG/WR BS40 90 D4
CBRIS/FH BS1 6 E4
FRCTL/WBN BS36 33 F7
Frogmore St CBRIS/FH BS1 6 F4 1
Frome Ct THNB/SVB BS35 19 H5
Frome Gln FRCTL/WBN BS36 41 K4
Frome Old Rd
RDSTK/MIDN BA3 127 H3
Frome Pl MANG/FISH BS16 53 J4 3
Frome Rd BATHSE BA2 111 H4
BOAV BA15 114 E7
RDSTK/MIDN BA3 127 H3
TRWBR BA14 129 J1
YATE/CS BS37 35 F6
Frome St CBRISNE BS2 7 L1 2
Frome Valley Rd
MANG/FISH BS16 53 K3
Frome Valley Walkway
FRCTL/WBN BS36 33 F5
FRCTL/WBN BS36 41 K5
MANG/FISH BS16 54 C2
YATE/CS BS37 33 K4
Frome Valley Wy YATE/CS BS37 35 H7
Frome Vw FRCTL/WBN BS36 42 C1
Frome Wy FRCTL/WBN BS36 41 K3
Front St WNSC BS25 121 G2
Froomshaw Rd
MANG/FISH BS16 54 A2
Frost Hl YTN/CONG BS49 87 G5
Fry's Cl MANG/FISH BS16 5 G1 1
Frys Hl KGWD/HNM BS15 54 E7 2
KGWD/HNM BS15 68 E1 2
Fryth Wy NAIL BS48 73 G1
Fulford Rd
BMSTRD/HC/WWD BS13 77 K6 3
TRWBR BA14 125 G4
Fulford Wk
BMSTRD/HC/WWD BS13 77 K6 4
Fullens Cl MTN/WRL BS22 105 J6
Fuller Rd CBATH/BATHN BA1 100 B2
Fullers Wy BATHSE BA2 111 G5
Fulmar Cl THNB/SVB BS35 19 J3 3
Fulmar Rd MTN/WRL BS22 106 A4
Fulney Cl TRWBR BA14 125 H4
Furber Ct EVILLE/WHL BS5 68 B4
Furber Rdg EVILLE/WHL BS5 68 B4
Furber Rd EVILLE/WHL BS5 68 B4
Furber V EVILLE/WHL BS5 68 B4
Furland Rd MTN/WRL BS22 105 H3
Furlong Cl RDSTK/MIDN BA3 126 A6
Furlong Gdns TRWBR BA14 125 G5
The Furlong
HNLZ/SM/SNYPK/WT BS9 52 A4
Furnwood EVILLE/WHL BS5 68 A4
Furze Cl MTN/WRL BS22 105 F3
Furze Rd MANG/FISH BS16 54 C6
MTN/WRL BS22 105 F2
Furzewood Rd
KGWD/HNM BS15 69 F2
Fylton Cft HGRV/WHIT BS14 94 A1

G

Gable Cl THNB/SVB BS35 28 D5
Gable Rd EVILLE/WHL BS5 4 B7 2
Gables Cl BNWL BS29 119 J3
Gadshill Dr BRSTK/PCHW BS34 40 D3
Gadshill Rd EVILLE/WHL BS5 4 F4
Gages Cl KGWD/HNM BS15 69 F3
Gages Rd KGWD/HNM BS15 69 F3
Gainsborough Dr
MTN/WRL BS22 106 A2 2
Gainsborough Gdns
CBATH/BATHN BA1 99 F4
Gainsborough Ri TRWBR BA14 130 C1
Gainsborough Rd KEYN BS31 81 F6
Galingale Wy PTSHD/EG BS20 47 K4
Gallivan Cl BRSTK/PCHW BS34 40 A1
Gander Cl
BMSTRD/HC/WWD BS13 77 K6 2
Gannet Rd MTN/WRL BS22 106 A4
Garden Cl
HNLZ/SM/SNYPK/WT BS9 50 E4
MTN/WRL BS22 106 A3 3
Gardeners Wk LGASH BS41 76 D2 1
Gardens Rd CLVDN BS21 58 E6
The Gardens MANG/FISH BS16 40 E7
Gardner Av
BMSTRD/HC/WWD BS13 77 H4
Gardner Rd PTSHD/EG BS20 47 H3
Garfield Rd EVILLE/WHL BS5 68 A2
Garnet St BMSTR BS3 10 C2
Garnett Pl MANG/FISH BS16 55 F2
Garrett Dr ALMDB BS32 40 C1 2
Garrick Rd BATHSE BA2 98 C7
Garsdale Rd MTN/WRL BS22 105 J5 2
Garstons CLVDN BS21 70 D3
The Garstons
CBATH/BATHN BA1 101 J2
PTSHD/EG BS20 47 G5
Garth Rd
BMSTRD/HC/WWD BS13 10 B8
Gasferry Rd CBRIS/FH BS1 6 D7
The Gaskins HORF/LLZ BS7 52 E4
Gas La CBRISNE BS2 8 A5
Gaston Av KEYN BS31 81 F6
The Gastons AVONM BS11 50 C1
Gatcombe Dr
BRSTK/PCHW BS34 40 D4
Gatcombe Rd
BMSTRD/HC/WWD BS13 77 K6
Gatehouse Av
BMSTRD/HC/WWD BS13 77 J6
Gatehouse Cl
BMSTRD/HC/WWD BS13 77 J6 2
Gatehouse Ct
BMSTRD/HC/WWD BS13 77 K6 3
Gatehouse Wy
BMSTRD/HC/WWD BS13 77 J6
Gatesby Md BRSTK/PCHW BS34 40 D3
Gathorne Rd BMSTR BS3 6 C9
Gatton Rd CBRISNE BS2 4 B7
Gaunts Cl PTSHD/EG BS20 46 D5 2
Gaunt's Earthcott La
ALMDB BS32 31 G2
Gaunt's La CBRIS/FH BS1 6 F4 2
Gaunts Rd YATE/CS BS37 34 E7
Gay Elms Rd
BMSTRD/HC/WWD BS13 77 J7
Gayner Rd HORF/LLZ BS7 39 K7
Gay's Hl CBATH/BATHN BA1 15 G2
Gays Rd KGWD/HNM BS15 68 B6
Gay St CBATH/BATHN BA1 14 F5 2
Gaythorne Crs YATE/CS BS37 34 A5
Gazelle Rd OMX/HUT/LCK BS24 117 G3
Gazzard Cl FRCTL/WBN BS36 41 K1
Gee Moors KGWD/HNM BS15 69 F3 3
Gefle Cl CBRIS/FH BS1 6 C7
Geldof Dr RDSTK/MIDN BA3 126 B3 1
Geoffrey Cl
BMSTRD/HC/WWD BS13 77 G5
George Cl NAIL BS48 74 D4
George's Rd CBATH/BATHN BA1 99 K3
George St CBATH/BATHN BA1 14 F5
EVILLE/WHL BS5 8 F1
PTSHD/EG BS20 47 G7
TRWBR BA14 125 F5
WSM BS23 16 F3
George Whitefield Ct
CBRIS/FH BS1 7 K2 1
Georgian Vw BATHSE BA2 110 E2
Gerald Rd BMSTR BS3 10 A1
Gerard Rd WSM BS23 16 F2
Gerrard Cl BRSG/KWL/STAPK BS4 78 B4
Gerrish Av EVILLE/WHL BS5 8 E1

MANG/FISH BS16 .... 55 F4
Gibbet La *HGRV/WHIT* BS14 .... 94 B3
Gibbsfold Rd
  BMSTRD/HC/WWD BS13 .... 93 J7
Gibbs Leaze *TRWBR* BA14 .... 125 J3
Gibson Rd *RDLND/MONT* BS6 ...... 3 H7
Gifford Cl *YATE/CS* BS37 .... 25 H6
Gifford Rd *HNBRY/STHM* BS10 .... 38 C4
Giffords Pl
  BMSTRD/HC/WWD BS13 .... 77 J4
Gilbeck Rd *NAIL* BS48 .... 73 C1 ⁴
Gilbern Rd *EVILLE/WHL* BS5 .... 4 F9
  KGWD/HNM BS15 .... 68 D1
Gilberyn Dr *MTN/WRL* BS22 .... 106 B2 ⁶
Gilda Cl *HGRV/WHIT* BS14 .... 79 F6
Gilda Crs *HGRV/WHIT* BS14 ...... 79 F5
Gilda Sq West *HGRV/WHIT* BS14 .. 79 F6
Gillard Cl *KGWD/HNM* BS15 ...... 68 B2
Gillard Rd *KGWD/HNM* BS15 ...... 68 B2
Gill Av *MANG/FISH* BS16 .... 54 B2 ¹
Gillebank Cl *HGRV/WHIT* BS14 ... 79 H6 ²
Gillingham Hl *EVILLE/WHL* BS5 .. 68 B5 ¹
Gillingham Ter
  CBATH/BATHN BA1 .... 15 J1
Gillingstool *THNB/SVB* BS35 ...... 19 H5
Gill Ms *MTN/WRL* BS22 .... 106 C1 ⁸
Gillmore Rd *MTN/WRL* BS22 ..... 105 J4 ³
Gillray Cl *HORF/LLZ* BS7 .... 53 F3
Gillson Rd *OMX/HUT/LCK* BS24 .. 117 J4 ¹
Gilpin Cl *KGWD/HNM* BS15 .... 69 F1 ³
Gilroy Cl *OLD/WMLY/WICK* BS30 . 69 H7 ¹
Gilslake Av *HNBRY/STHM* BS10 ... 38 C5 ¹
Gimblet Rd *MTN/WRL* BS22 ...... 106 C1 ²
Gipsy Patch La
  BRSTK/PCHW BS34 .... 40 A2
The Glades *EVILLE/WHL* BS5 .... 5 J5
Gladstone Dr
  MANG/FISH BS16 .... 54 E6 ⁵
Gladstone La
  FRCTL/WBN BS36 .... 42 D1 ¹
Gladstone Rd *BATHSE* BA2 ...... 112 B3
  HGRV/WHIT BS14 .... 79 F5
  KGWD/HNM BS15 .... 68 D1 ⁶
  TRWBR BA14 .... 124 D7
Gladstone St *BMSTR* BS3 .... 10 D1
  EVILLE/WHL BS5 .... 9 G2 ²
  MANG/FISH BS16 .... 54 D6
  RDSTK/MIDN BA3 .... 126 C2
Glaisdale Rd *MANG/FISH* BS16 ... 54 A4
Glanville Gdns *KGWD/HNM* BS15 . 68 E3
Glass House La *CBRISNE* BS2 ..... 8 C6
Glastonbury Cl *NAIL* BS48 .... 74 C2 ⁷
  OLD/WMLY/WICK BS30 .... 69 F5 ⁵
Glastonbury Wy
  MTN/WRL BS22 .... 106 B2
Glebe Av *PTSHD/EG* BS20 .... 47 J5
Glebe Cl *LGASH* BS41 .... 76 D1
Glebe Fld *ALMDB* BS32 .... 29 K2
Glebelands *RDSTK/MIDN* BA3 .. 126 E4
Glebelands Rd
  BRSTK/PCHW BS34 .... 39 K5 ⁸
Glebe Rd *BATHSE* BA2 .... 110 E1
  CLVDN BS21 .... 70 E1
  EVILLE/WHL BS5 .... 9 K1
  LGASH BS41 .... 76 E2
  PTSHD/EG BS20 .... 47 J5
  TRWBR BA14 .... 124 E7
  WSM BS23 .... 16 F2 ²
The Glebe *RDSTK/MIDN* BA3 ..... 122 B2
Gledemoor Dr *FRCTL/WBN* BS36 . 42 E1
Glena Av *BRSG/KWL/STAPK* BS4 . 12 D3
Glenarm Rd
  BRSG/KWL/STAPK BS4 .... 13 J4
Glenarm Wk
  BRSG/KWL/STAPK BS4 .... 13 J4
Glen Av *CFTN/FAIL* BS8 .... 64 B2
Glenavon Pk
  HNLZ/SM/SNYPK/WT BS9 .... 50 E5 ⁶
Glen Brook
  HNLZ/SM/SNYPK/WT BS9 .... 51 F5
Glenburn Rd *KGWD/HNM* BS15 ... 68 B1
Glencoyne Sq
  HNBRY/STHM BS10 .... 39 F6
Glendale *CFTN/FAIL* BS8 .... 65 H4 ⁸
  MANG/FISH BS16 .... 54 C6 ⁸
  MANG/FISH BS16 .... 54 E1
Glendare St *EVILLE/WHL* BS5 ...... 8 E4
Glendevon Rd
  HGRV/WHIT BS14 .... 93 K1 ¹
Glen Dr
  HNLZ/SM/SNYPK/WT BS9 .... 51 F4
Gleneagles *YATE/CS* BS37 .... 34 B6
Gleneagles Cl
  MTN/WRL BS22 .... 106 A2 ¹
  NAIL BS48 .... 74 A2 ³
Gleneagles Dr
  HNBRY/STHM BS10 .... 38 A5 ⁴
Gleneagles Rd
  OLD/WMLY/WICK BS30 .... 69 H4 ⁶
Glenfall *YATE/CS* BS37 .... 44 A1
Glenfrome Rd *CBRISNE* BS2 .... 4 C4
  EVILLE/WHL BS5 .... 4 D5
Glen La *BRSG/KWL/STAPK* BS4 ... 13 C4
Glen Pk *EVILLE/WHL* BS5 .... 68 A2
Glen Park Gdns *EVILLE/WHL* BS5 . 68 A2
Glenside Cl *MANG/FISH* BS16 ..... 54 C2 ⁸
Glenside Pk *MANG/FISH* BS16 .... 53 J4 ⁸
The Glen *KEYN* BS31 .... 97 G3 ²
  KGWD/HNM BS15 .... 68 B6
  MTN/WRL BS22 .... 105 J3
  RDLND/MONT BS6 .... 2 C3
  YATE/CS BS37 .... 25 H6
Glentworth Rd *CFTN/FAIL* BS8 .... 6 C4 ¹
  RDLND/MONT BS6 .... 2 F5
Glenview Rd
  BRSG/KWL/STAPK BS4 .... 13 C4
Glenwood *MANG/FISH* BS16 ..... 54 C6 ⁴
Glenwood Dr
  OLD/WMLY/WICK BS30 .... 69 H6
Glenwood Ri *PTSHD/EG* BS20 .... 46 D4
Glenwood Rd
  OLD/WMLY/WICK BS30 .... 52 A2
Gloster Av *EVILLE/WHL* BS5 .... 5 G4
Gloucester La *CBRISNE* BS2 .... 7 M2 ⁴
Gloucester Rd *BRSTK/PCHW* BS34 . 40 A3
  AVONM BS11 .... 36 B7

Gloucester Rd North
  BRSTK/PCHW BS34 .... 39 K3
  HORF/LLZ BS7 .... 39 J7
Gloucester St
  CBATH/BATHN BA1 .... 14 E4 ⁴
  CBRISNE BS2 .... 7 K1 ¹
  CFTN/FAIL BS8 .... 65 H3 ²
  EVILLE/WHL BS5 .... 4 D2 ²
  WSM BS23 .... 16 D3
Glovers Fld *WNSC* BS25 .... 121 J7
Glyn V *BMSTR* BS3 .... 11 H5
Goddard Dr *NAIL* BS48 .... 73 G1
Godfrey Ct
  OLD/WMLY/WICK BS30 .... 69 F6 ⁷
Godwin Dr *NAIL* BS48 .... 73 C1
Goffenton Dr *MANG/FISH* BS16 .. 54 B3
Goldcrest Rd *YATE/CS* BS37 ...... 34 D7
Goldfinch Wy
  MANG/FISH BS16 .... 56 E5 ⁸
Goldney Av *CFTN/FAIL* BS8 .... 6 A4
  OLD/WMLY/WICK BS30 .... 69 J3
Goldney Rd *CFTN/FAIL* BS8 .... 6 B5
Goldsbury Wk *AVONM* BS11 ...... 37 H7
Golf Club La *KEYN* BS31 .... 97 F2 ¹
Golf Course La
  BRSTK/PCHW BS34 .... 39 J5
Golf Course Rd *BATHSE* BA2 ..... 15 M6
Gooch Ct *OLD/WMLY/WICK* BS30 . 69 J7
Goodeve Rd
  HNLZ/SM/SNYPK/WT BS9 .... 51 F7
Goodhind St *EVILLE/WHL* BS5 ..... 4 A9
Goodneston Rd
  MANG/FISH BS16 .... 54 A6
Goodring Hl *AVONM* BS11 .... 37 H7
Good Shepherd Cl *HORF/LLZ* BS7 . 2 F1
Goodwin Dr *HGRV/WHIT* BS14 .... 78 D7
Goodwood Cl *TRWBR* BA14 .... 131 G3 ⁸
Goodwood Gdns
  MANG/FISH BS16 .... 42 A7 ⁵
Goold Cl *BATHSE* BA2 .... 97 H4
Goolden St
  BRSG/KWL/STAPK BS4 .... 12 A1
Goose Acre *ALMDB* BS32 .... 40 E2 ¹
  ALMDB BS32 .... 41 F2 ²
Goosegreen *FRCTL/WBN* BS36 ... 32 C7
Goose Gn *OLD/WMLY/WICK* BS30 . 69 J1
  YATE/CS BS37 .... 33 K3
Goose Green Wy *YATE/CS* BS37 .. 33 K3
Gooseland Cl *BRSTK* BS14 .... 93 J1 ¹
Goosey La *MTN/WRL* BS22 ..... 106 D3 ¹
Gordano Gdns *AVONM* BS11 ..... 49 H5
Gordano Rd *PTSHD/EG* BS20 .... 48 D2
Gordano Wy *PTSHD/EG* BS20 .... 49 F4
Gordon Av *EVILLE/WHL* BS5 .... 5 H7
Gordon Cl *EVILLE/WHL* BS5 .... 5 K7
Gordon Rd *BATHSE* BA2 .... 15 J9
  CBRISNE BS2 .... 3 M7
  CFTN/FAIL BS8 .... 64 B2 ¹
  EVILLE/WHL BS5 .... 5 H6
  WSM BS23 .... 17 G3
Gore Rd *BMSTR* BS3 .... 10 B2
Gore's Marsh Rd *BMSTR* BS3 .... 10 B3
Gorham Cl *AVONM* BS11 .... 37 K6 ³
Gorlands Rd *YATE/CS* BS37 ...... 35 F6
Gorlangton Cl *HGRV/WHIT* BS14 . 12 A9
Gorse Hl *MANG/FISH* BS16 .... 54 C6
Gorse La *CFTN/FAIL* BS8 .... 6 C4
Gosforth Rd *HNBRY/STHM* BS10 . 38 E7
Goslet Rd *HGRV/WHIT* BS14 ...... 79 H6
Goss Barton *NAIL* BS48 .... 73 H2 ⁶
Goss Cl *NAIL* BS48 .... 73 C2 ⁴
Goss La *NAIL* BS48 .... 73 C2 ³
Goss Vw *NAIL* BS48 .... 73 C2 ⁸
Gotley Rd *BRSG/KWL/STAPK* BS4 . 13 C4
Gott Dr *BRSG/KWL/STAPK* BS4 ..... 9 G6
Goulston Rd
  BMSTRD/HC/WWD BS13 ..... 77 J6
Goulston Wk
  BMSTRD/HC/WWD BS13 ..... 77 J6 ⁸
Goulter St *EVILLE/WHL* BS5 .... 8 D4
Gourney Cl *AVONM* BS11 .... 37 J6
Gover Rd *KGWD/HNM* BS15 ...... 68 C7
Grace Cl *YATE/CS* BS37 .... 35 F6
  YTN/CONG BS49 .... 86 E4
Grace Ct *MANG/FISH* BS16 .... 54 D3
Grace Dr *KGWD/HNM* BS15 ...... 69 C1
  RDSTK/MIDN BA3 .... 126 B3 ⁸
Grace Park Rd
  BRSG/KWL/STAPK BS4 .... 13 H6
Grace Rd *MANG/FISH* BS16 ...... 54 C4
  MTN/WRL BS22 .... 106 C2
Gradwell Cl *MTN/WRL* BS22 .... 106 C2
Graeme Cl *MANG/FISH* BS16 .... 54 A5
Graham Rd *BMSTR* BS3 .... 10 E1 ¹
  EVILLE/WHL BS5 .... 4 D8
  MANG/FISH BS16 .... 55 F3
  WSM BS23 .... 16 E5
Grainger Ct *AVONM* BS11 .... 50 A2 ³
Graitney Cl *YTN/CONG* BS49 ..... 87 K4 ¹
Grampian Cl
  OLD/WMLY/WICK BS30 .... 69 J3
Granby Hl *CFTN/FAIL* BS8 .... 65 H4
Grand Pde *CBATH/BATHN* BA1 .. 15 G6 ¹
Grange Av *BRSTK/PCHW* BS34 ... 40 B2
  KGWD/HNM BS15 .... 68 D5
Grange Cl *ALMDB* BS32 .... 30 B5
  ALMDB BS32 .... 116 D5
Grange Cl North
  HNLZ/SM/SNYPK/WT BS9 .... 51 K3 ⁸
Grange Ct *KGWD/HNM* BS15 .... 68 D5 ⁵
Grange Court Rd
  HNLZ/SM/SNYPK/WT BS9 .... 51 J3
Grange Dr *MANG/FISH* BS16 ..... 54 C3
Grange End *RDSTK/MIDN* BA3 .. 126 B6
Grange Pk
  HNLZ/SM/SNYPK/WT BS9 .... 51 K3
  MANG/FISH BS16 .... 54 C1
Grange Rd
  BMSTRD/HC/WWD BS13 ...... 77 J6 ¹
  CFTN/FAIL BS8 .... 6 A2

KEYN BS31 .... 96 D1
  WSM BS23 .... 116 D5
The Grange
  HNLZ/SM/SNYPK/WT BS9 .... 51 F2
Grange Vw *BOAV* BA15 .... 115 F6
Grangeville Cl
  OLD/WMLY/WICK BS30 .... 69 H7
Grangewood Cl
  MANG/FISH BS16 .... 54 C3 ⁸
Granny's La *KGWD/HNM* BS15 .... 69 H3
Grantham La
  KGWD/HNM BS15 .... 68 C2 ³
Grantham Rd *KGWD/HNM* BS15 .. 68 C1
Grantson Cl
  BRSG/KWL/STAPK BS4 .... 13 J3
Granville Cl *KGWD/HNM* BS15 .... 68 B7
Granville Rd *CBATH/BATHN* BA1 .. 99 H1
Granville St *EVILLE/WHL* BS5 ...... 8 E4
Grasington Dr *YATE/CS* BS37 .... 34 D6
Grasmere *TRWBR* BA14 .... 125 G4
Grasmere Cl *HNBRY/STHM* BS10 . 51 J1
Grasmere Dr *WSM* BS23 .... 17 H9
Grass Meers Dr
  HGRV/WHIT BS14 .... 78 E7
Grassmere Gdns
  OLD/WMLY/WICK BS30 .... 69 K4
Grassmere Rd *YTN/CONG* BS49 .. 86 E4
Gratitude Rd *EVILLE/WHL* BS5 ..... 4 F7
Gravel Hill Rd *YATE/CS* BS37 ..... 34 C3
Gravel Wk *CBATH/BATHN* BA1 ... 14 E4
Grayle Rd *HNBRY/STHM* BS10 ... 38 C5
Gray's Cl *HNBRY/STHM* BS10 .... 38 B6 ¹
Grays Leaze *TRWBR* BA14 ...... 130 E5
Great Ann St *CBRISNE* BS2 .... 7 M2
Great Bedford St
  CBATH/BATHN BA1 .... 14 E3 ⁴
Great Brockeridge
  HNLZ/SM/SNYPK/WT BS9 .... 51 H3
Great Dowles
  OLD/WMLY/WICK BS30 .... 69 G6
Great George St *CBRIS/FH* BS1 ... 6 D4
  CBRISNE BS2 .... 7 L2
Great Hayles Rd
  HGRV/WHIT BS14 .... 78 E4
Great Leaze
  OLD/WMLY/WICK BS30 .... 69 G6
Great Meadow Rd *ALMDB* BS32 . 40 E1 ⁴
Great Park Rd *ALMDB* BS32 ...... 30 B4
Great Pulteney St *BATHSE* BA2 .. 15 H5
Great Stanhope St
  CBATH/BATHN BA1 .... 14 D6
Great Stoke Wy
  BRSTK/PCHW BS34 .... 40 C5
Greatstone La
  BLAG/CWMG/WR BS40 ...... 91 G7
Great Western Br *WSM* BS23 .... 17 G4
Great Western La
  EVILLE/WHL BS5 .... 8 E4
Great Western Rd *CLVDN* BS21... 59 F7
Greenacre *MTN/WRL* BS22 .... 105 G3
Greenacre *HGRV/WHIT* BS14.... 93 K1
Greenacres *CBATH/BATHN* BA1 .. 98 C1
Greenbank Av *EVILLE/WHL* BS5 ... 4 E7
Greenbank Av West
  EVILLE/WHL BS5 .... 4 D7
Greenbank Gdns
  CBATH/BATHN BA1 .... 98 C3
Greenbank Rd *BMSTR* BS3 .... 6 B8
  EVILLE/WHL BS5 .... 4 E7
  KGWD/HNM BS15 .... 68 D5
Greenbank Vw *EVILLE/WHL* BS5 .. 4 F5
Green Cft *EVILLE/WHL* BS5 .... 68 A1
Greendale *BMSTR* BS3 .... 11 K2
  RDLND/MONT BS6 .... 2 D2
Greendale Rd *BMSTR* BS3 .... 11 K2 ²
  RDLND/MONT BS6 .... 2 D2
Green Dell Cl
  HNBRY/STHM BS10 .... 38 A5 ⁴
Greenditch Av
  BMSTRD/HC/WWD BS13 ...... 78 A6
Greendown *EVILLE/WHL* BS5 ..... 68 A3
Greendown Pl *BATHSE* BA2 .... 111 K4
Green Dragon Rd
  FRCTL/WBN BS36 .... 41 J3
Greenfield Av
  HNBRY/STHM BS10 .... 52 B1 ⁸
Greenfield Crs *NAIL* BS48 .... 61 J7
Greenfield Pk *PTSHD/EG* BS20 ... 47 G6
Greenfield Pl *WSM* BS23 .... 16 B1 ⁸
Greenfield Rd
  HNBRY/STHM BS10 .... 39 G7 ¹
Greenfields Av *BNWL* BS29 ..... 119 H3 ⁸
Greengage Cl
  MTN/WRL BS22 .... 105 K5 ⁸
Green Hayes *YATE/CS* BS37 ...... 35 F7
Greenhill *THNB/SVB* BS35 .... 23 F2
Greenhill Cl *MTN/WRL* BS22 .... 106 B2
  NAIL BS48 .... 73 H1 ⁸
Greenhill Down *THNB/SVB* BS35 . 23 F2 ¹
Greenhill Gdns *THNB/SVB* BS35 .. 23 F2 ¹
  TRWBR BA14 .... 125 J2
Greenhill Gv *BMSTR* BS3 .... 10 A3
Greenhill La *AVONM* BS11 ...... 37 K7 ¹
  THNB/SVB BS35 .... 22 E3
Greenhill Pl *RDSTK/MIDN* BA3 . 126 B3 ¹
Greenhill Rd *RDSTK/MIDN* BA3 .. 126 B3
  THNB/SVB BS35 .... 23 F2
  WNSC BS25 .... 120 E2
Greenland Rd
  MTN/WRL BS22 .... 105 J4 ²
Greenlands Wy
  HNBRY/STHM BS10 .... 38 A4
Greenland Vw *BOAV* BA15 ..... 115 F6
Green La *AVONM* BS11 .... 49 H1
  BOAV BA15 .... 113 K7
  CFTN/FAIL BS8 .... 63 J6
  FRCTL/WBN BS36 .... 41 H1
  HNBRY/STHM BS10 .... 27 K6
  RDSTK/MIDN BA3 .... 122 B4
  TRWBR BA14 .... 125 G6
  TRWBR BA14 .... 129 K5
  WUE GL12 .... 20 C4
Greenleaze
  BRSG/KWL/STAPK BS4 .... 12 C5
Greenleaze Av *MANG/FISH* BS16 . 41 J7
Greenmore Rd
  BRSG/KWL/STAPK BS4 .... 12 C5
Greenore *KGWD/HNM* BS15 ..... 68 C3
Green Pk *BATHSE* BA2 .... 14 D7
Green Park Rd *BATHSE* BA2 ..... 14 E7

Greenpark Rd
  HNBRY/STHM BS10 .... 39 H7 ⁸
Green Pastures Rd *NAIL* BS48 ... 74 B1
Greenridge Cl
  BMSTRD/HC/WWD BS13 ..... 77 C1 ⁸
Green Side *MANG/FISH* BS16 .... 55 C5
Greenside Cl
  HNBRY/STHM BS10 .... 38 A5 ⁴
Greenslade Gdns *NAIL* BS48 .... 61 H7
Greensplott Rd *AVONM* BS11 ... 36 E1
Green St *BMSTR* BS3 .... 11 H5
  CBATH/BATHN BA1 .... 15 G6 ⁸
The Green *BRSTK/PCHW* BS34 ... 40 C4
  KGWD/HNM BS15 .... 54 E7
  NAIL BS48 .... 73 K6
  OMX/HUT/LCK BS24 .... 118 B2 ⁸
  WNSC BS25 .... 120 C6
  WUE GL12 .... 21 J5
Green Tree Rd
  RDSTK/MIDN BA3 .... 126 C2
Greenview
  OLD/WMLY/WICK BS30 .... 81 C1 ⁸
Green Wk *BRSG/KWL/STAPK* BS4 . 12 B5
Greenway Bush La *BMSTR* BS3 ... 6 B8
Greenway Ct *BATHSE* BA2 ...... 111 J1
Greenway Dr
  HNBRY/STHM BS10 .... 52 B1 ⁸
Greenway Gdns *TRWBR* BA14 .. 125 C3
Greenway La *BATHSE* BA2 ...... 111 J2 ³
Greenway Pk *CLVDN* BS21 ...... 59 H7 ²
  HNBRY/STHM BS10 .... 52 B1 ⁸
Greenway Rd *RDLND/MONT* BS6 . 2 C6
Greenways *KGWD/HNM* BS15 .... 69 C1 ⁸
  YATE/CS BS37 .... 34 A4
The Greenway
  MANG/FISH BS16 .... 54 C6 ⁸
Greenwood Cl *HORF/LLZ* BS7 .... 52 C2 ⁸
Greenwood Dr *THNB/SVB* BS35 .. 22 E2
Greenwood Rd
  BRSG/KWL/STAPK BS4 .... 12 B4
  MTN/WRL BS22 .... 105 K3
Gregory Ct
  OLD/WMLY/WICK BS30 .... 69 G4 ⁸
Gregory Md *YTN/CONG* BS49 .... 86 D3
Grenville Av
  OMX/HUT/LCK BS24 .... 118 B2
Grenville Cl *EVILLE/WHL* BS5 ...... 9 M1
Grenville Pl *CBRIS/FH* BS1 .... 65 H5 ⁸
Grenville Rd *RDLND/MONT* BS6 ... 3 J4
Greve Ct
  OLD/WMLY/WICK BS30 .... 69 F6 ⁸
Greville Rd *BMSTR* BS3 .... 6 C9
Greville St *BMSTR* BS3 .... 6 E9
Greylands Rd
  BMSTRD/HC/WWD BS13 ..... 77 H4
Greystoke Av
  HNBRY/STHM BS10 .... 51 J1
Greystoke Gdns
  HNLZ/SM/SNYPK/WT BS9 .... 51 J1 ⁸
Greystones *MANG/FISH* BS16 .... 41 K7 ⁸
Griffin Cl *MTN/WRL* BS22 ...... 106 C3 ⁸
Griffin Rd *CLVDN* BS21 .... 59 F7
Griggfield Wk *HGRV/WHIT* BS14 . 11 M9
Grimsbury Rd *KGWD/HNM* BS15 . 69 C2
Grindell Rd *EVILLE/WHL* BS5 .... 9 G3
Grinfield Av
  BMSTRD/HC/WWD BS13 ..... 78 A7
Grinfield Cl
  BMSTRD/HC/WWD BS13 ..... 78 A7 ⁸
Grinfield Ct
  BMSTRD/HC/WWD BS13 ..... 78 A7 ⁸
Grittleton Rd *HORF/LLZ* BS7 ..... 52 C1
Grosvenor Pl *CBATH/BATHN* BA1 . 15 L1 ¹
Grosvenor Rd *CBRISNE* BS2 .... 3 L9
Grove Av *CBRIS/FH* BS1 .... 7 H6
  HNLZ/SM/SNYPK/WT BS9 .... 50 E2
  MANG/FISH BS16 .... 5 L2
Grove Bank *MANG/FISH* BS16 ... 41 H7
Grove Dr *MTN/WRL* BS22 ...... 105 H4 ⁴
Grove La *WSM* BS23 .... 16 D1
Grove Leaze *AVONM* BS11 ...... 49 K3
  BOAV BA15 .... 114 C7
Grove Pk
  BRSG/KWL/STAPK BS4 .... 13 H3
  RDLND/MONT BS6 .... 2 F6
Grove Park Av
  BRSG/KWL/STAPK BS4 .... 13 H3
Grove Park Rd
  BRSG/KWL/STAPK BS4 .... 13 H3
  WSM BS23 .... 104 C4 ⁴
Grove Rd *BNWL* BS29 .... 119 F2
  HNLZ/SM/SNYPK/WT BS9 .... 51 F1
  MANG/FISH BS16 .... 5 L2
  MTN/WRL BS22 .... 105 H4
  RDLND/MONT BS6 .... 2 B5
  WSM BS23 .... 16 D1
Grovesend Rd *THNB/SVB* BS35 .. 19 H5
Grove St *CBATH/BATHN* BA1 .... 15 G5
The Grove *CBRIS/FH* BS1 .... 7 G6
  NAIL BS48 .... 62 C7
  OLD/WMLY/WICK BS30 .... 69 G6
  WNSC BS25 .... 120 C5
  YATE/CS BS37 .... 25 H6
Grove Vw *MANG/FISH* BS16 ..... 53 J3 ⁸
Grove Wood Rd
  RDSTK/MIDN BA3 .... 127 F5
Guernsey Av
  BRSG/KWL/STAPK BS4 .... 9 L9
Guest Av *MANG/FISH* BS16 ...... 55 H3
Guildford Rd
  BRSG/KWL/STAPK BS4 .... 9 K6
Guinea La *CBATH/BATHN* BA1 ... 14 F4 ⁸
  MANG/FISH BS16 .... 54 A4 ⁸
Guinea St *CBRIS/FH* BS1 .... 7 H7
Gulliford's Bank *CLVDN* BS21 .... 71 C1
Gullimores Gdns
  BMSTRD/HC/WWD BS13 ..... 77 K7 ²
Gullivers Pl *YATE/CS* BS37 ...... 34 D7
Gullock Tyning
  RDSTK/MIDN BA3 .... 126 C4
Gullons Cl
  BMSTRD/HC/WWD BS13 ..... 77 J5 ²
Gullon Wk
  BMSTRD/HC/WWD BS13 ..... 77 H6
The Gully *FRCTL/WBN* BS36 ..... 42 A1
Gunning Cl *KGWD/HNM* BS15 ... 68 D4
Gunter's Hl *EVILLE/WHL* BS5 .... 68 A4 ²
Gwilliam St *BMSTR* BS3 .... 11 H1

Gwyn St *CBRISNE* BS2 .... 3 K8
Gypsy La *KEYN* BS31 .... 96 C4

H

Haberfield Hl *PTSHD/EG* BS20 ... 49 K7
Hacket Hl *THNB/SVB* BS35 ...... 20 A5
Hacket La *THNB/SVB* BS35 ...... 19 K5
Haden Rd *TRWBR* BA14 .... 125 F7 ⁸
Hadley Ct
  OLD/WMLY/WICK BS30 .... 69 H4 ⁸
Hadley Rd *BATHSE* BA2 .... 112 A3
Hadrian Cl
  HNLZ/SM/SNYPK/WT BS9 .... 50 E5 ⁸
Halbrow Crs *MANG/FISH* BS16 ... 54 E4
Haldon Cl *BMSTR* BS3 .... 11 C5
Hale Cl *KGWD/HNM* BS15 .... 68 D6 ⁸
Hales Horn Cl *ALMDB* BS32 ..... 40 C3
Halfacre Cl *HGRV/WHIT* BS14 .... 93 K1
Halfacre La *HGRV/WHIT* BS14 .... 94 A1
Halfpenny Rw
  RDSTK/MIDN BA3 .... 128 E6 ⁸
Halfway Cl *TRWBR* BA14 .... 125 H4
Halifax Rd *YATE/CS* BS37 .... 34 A3
Hallam Rd *CLVDN* BS21 .... 58 E7
Hallards Cl *AVONM* BS11 .... 36 B5 ¹
Hallen Cl *HNBRY/STHM* BS10 .... 38 A5
Hall End La *YATE/CS* BS37 .... 25 K4
Hallen Dr
  HNLZ/SM/SNYPK/WT BS9 .... 50 E2
Hallen Rd *HNBRY/STHM* BS10 ... 37 K4
Halletts Wy *PTSHD/EG* BS20 .... 47 H4 ⁸
Halliwell Rd *PTSHD/EG* BS20 .... 46 B5
Halls Rd *KGWD/HNM* BS15 ...... 68 D2 ⁸
Halsbury Rd *RDLND/MONT* BS6 ... 2 F5
Halstock Av *MANG/FISH* BS16 .... 5 L4
Halston Dr *CBRISNE* BS2 .... 3 L9
Halswell Gdns
  BMSTRD/HC/WWD BS13 ..... 77 K7
Halswell Rd *CLVDN* BS21 .... 71 F2
Halt End *HGRV/WHIT* BS14 ...... 94 B1
The Halve *TRWBR* BA14 .... 125 F5
Halwyn Cl
  HNLZ/SM/SNYPK/WT BS9 .... 51 F4 ²
Hamble Cl *THNB/SVB* BS35 ..... 19 H5
Hambledon Rd *MTN/WRL* BS22 . 106 D1
Hambrook La
  BRSTK/PCHW BS34 .... 40 E4
Ham Farm La *MANG/FISH* BS16 . 55 H3
Ham Gn *PTSHD/EG* BS20 .... 49 K5
Hamilton Rd *BMSTR* BS3 .... 6 D8
  CBATH/BATHN BA1 .... 99 H2
  EVILLE/WHL BS5 .... 4 B9
  WSM BS23 .... 104 B4 ⁸
Ham La *CLVDN* BS21 .... 85 F2
  LGASH BS41 .... 92 A1
  MANG/FISH BS16 .... 53 J3
  NAIL BS48 .... 62 A6
  YTN/CONG BS49 .... 86 C1
The Hamlet *NAIL* BS48 .... 62 A7
Hammersmith Rd
  BRSG/KWL/STAPK BS4 .... 5 G9
Hammond Gdns
  HNLZ/SM/SNYPK/WT BS9 .... 51 G2 ⁸
Hammond Wy *TRWBR* BA14 .... 125 F2
Hampden Cl *YATE/CS* BS37 ...... 34 A3
Hampden Rd
  BRSG/KWL/STAPK BS4 .... 12 C2
  MTN/WRL BS22 .... 105 J3
Hampshire Wy *YATE/CS* BS37 ... 34 C3 ⁸
Hampstead Rd
  BRSG/KWL/STAPK BS4 .... 12 E2
Hampton Cl
  OLD/WMLY/WICK BS30 .... 69 G5
Hampton Pk *RDLND/MONT* BS6 ... 2 D7
Hampton Rd *RDLND/MONT* BS6 ... 2 D6
Hampton Rw *BATHSE* BA2 ...... 15 K3
Hampton St
  KGWD/HNM BS15 .... 68 D1 ⁸
Hampton Vw
  CBATH/BATHN BA1 .... 100 A3
Hams Rd *KEYN* BS31 .... 81 F4
Ham Wood Cl
  OMX/HUT/LCK BS24 .... 117 G4 ⁸
Hanbury Cl *KGWD/HNM* BS15 ... 68 D5
Hanbury Rd *CFTN/FAIL* BS8 .... 6 B1
Handel Av *EVILLE/WHL* BS5 .... 9 H2
Handel Rd *KEYN* BS31 .... 80 D6
Handford Wy
  OLD/WMLY/WICK BS30 .... 69 H7 ⁸
Hanford Ct *HGRV/WHIT* BS14 .... 13 L9
Hanham Rd *KGWD/HNM* BS15 ... 68 D3
Hanham Wy *NAIL* BS48 .... 73 F1
Hannah More Rd *NAIL* BS48 .... 73 G2
Hanover Ct *MTN/WRL* BS22 ... 106 B1 ⁸
  TRWBR BA14 .... 125 G2
Hanover Pl *CBRIS/FH* BS1 .... 7 K2 ²
Hanover Pl *CBRIS/FH* BS1 .... 6 D7
Hanover St *EVILLE/WHL* BS5 ...... 8 E3
Hansford Cl *BATHSE* BA2 ...... 111 H4
Hansford Sq *BATHSE* BA2 ..... 111 H4
Hanson's Wy *CLVDN* BS21 ...... 70 E1 ⁸
Hans Price Cl *WSM* BS23 .... 16 F2 ³
Hantone Hl *BATHSE* BA2 .... 100 E4
Happerton La *PTSHD/EG* BS20 ... 49 J7
Hapsburg Cl *MTN/WRL* BS22 ... 106 B1 ³
Harbour Rd *PTSHD/EG* BS20 .... 47 J3
Harbour Wall
  HNLZ/SM/SNYPK/WT BS9 .... 50 E5 ³
Harbour Wy *CBRIS/FH* BS1 .... 6 E6
Harbury Rd
  HNLZ/SM/SNYPK/WT BS9 .... 52 A2
Harbutts *BATHSE* BA2 .... 100 E3
Harcombe Hl *FRCTL/WBN* BS36 . 41 K4
Harcombe Rd *FRCTL/WBN* BS36 . 41 J4
Harcourt Av *EVILLE/WHL* BS5 .... 68 A4 ⁸
Harcourt Cl *KEYN* BS31 .... 97 F2 ²
Harcourt Gdns
  CBATH/BATHN BA1 .... 98 E2 ²
Harcourt Hl *RDLND/MONT* BS6 ... 2 E5
Harcourt Rd *RDLND/MONT* BS6 . 2 D2
Hardenhuish Rd
  BRSG/KWL/STAPK BS4 .... 9 G7
Harden Rd *HGRV/WHIT* BS14 .... 79 J6
Hardington Dr *KEYN* BS31 ...... 96 B2

Hardwick Cl
 BRSG/KWL/STAPK BS4.............. 13 J1
 OLD/WMLY/WICK BS30 .... 69 K5 🈁
Hardwicke *YATE/CS* BS37............. 43 K1
Hardwick Rd *PTSHD/EG* BS20.... 49 J5
Hardy Av *BMSTR* BS3.................. 10 A1
Hardy Ct *OLD/WMLY/WICK* BS30 .. 69 F5
Hardy Rd *BMSTR* BS3.................. 10 B4
Hareclive Rd
 BMSTRD/HC/WWD BS13.......... 77 K6
Harefield Cl *KGWD/HNM* BS15 .. 80 C1 🈁
Hare Knapp *BOAV* BA15........... 114 C7
Harescombe *YATE/CS* BS37......... 44 B1
Harewood Rd *EVILLE/WHL* BS5.. 68 A1
Harford Cl
 HNLZ/SM/SNYPK/WT BS9....... 50 E2 🈁
Harford Dr *MANG/FISH* BS16 ..... 41 H7
Harford St *TRWBR* BA14.......... 125 D4
Harington Pl
 CBATH/BATHN BA1 .... 14 F6 🈁
Harlech Wy
 OLD/WMLY/WICK BS30 .... 81 H1
Harleston St *EVILLE/WHL* BS5....... 7 M1
Harley La *CLVDN* BS21............... 60 A4
Harley St *CBATH/BATHN* BA1 ..... 14 E3
Harmer Cl *HNBRY/STHM* BS10 .... 38 C5
Harmony Dr *PTSHD/EG* BS20...... 46 D5
Harmony Pl *TRWBR* BA14........ 125 F7 🈁
Harnhill Cl
 BMSTRD/HC/WWD BS13.......... 77 K7 🈁
Harolds Wy *KGWD/HNM* BS15 .... 68 C4
Harptree Cl *NAIL* BS48............... 73 H3
Harptree
 OLD/WMLY/WICK BS30 .... 69 C6 🈁
Harptree Gv *BMSTR* BS3............. 10 D3 🈁
Harrington Av *HGRV/WHIT* BS14 .. 79 J5
Harrington Gv
 HGRV/WHIT BS14 .... 79 J5
Harrington Rd
 HGRV/WHIT BS14 .... 79 J5
Harrington Wk
 HGRV/WHIT BS14 .... 79 J5 🈁
Harris Barton *FRCTL/WBN* BS36.. 42 B1
Harris Ct
 OLD/WMLY/WICK BS30 .... 69 F6 🈁
Harris La *CFTN/FAIL* BS8............ 64 B2
Harrison Cl *MANG/FISH* BS16 ..... 55 H3 🈁
Harrowdene Rd
 BRSG/KWL/STAPK BS4............. 12 C2
Harrow Rd
 BRSG/KWL/STAPK BS4............. 13 G1
Harry Stoke Rd
 BRSTK/PCHW BS34................... 40 A4
Hartcliffe Rd
 BRSG/KWL/STAPK BS4............. 11 J8
Hartcliffe Wk
 BRSG/KWL/STAPK BS4............. 11 L8
Hartfield Av *RDLND/MONT* BS6 ... 2 F9
Hartgill Cl
 BMSTRD/HC/WWD BS13.......... 92 E1
Hartington Pk *RDLND/MONT* BS6 .. 2 D5
Hartley Cl *YATE/CS* BS37.......... 35 F6
Harts Cft *YATE/CS* BS37............ 34 C3 🈁
Harts Paddock
 RDSTK/MIDN BA3 .... 126 A2
Harvest Cl *ALMDB* BS32.............. 30 C6
Harvest Wy *MTN/WRL* BS22 ..... 105 K1 🈁
Harvey Rd *MTN/WRL* BS22 ..... 106 B1 🈁
Harwood Gdns
 MTN/WRL BS22 .... 105 K1 🈁
Haselbury Gv *KEYN* BS31........... 97 F2
Haskins Ct *OLD/WMLY/WICK* BS30 .. 69 G6 🈁
Hassell Dr *CBRISNE* BS2............... 8 A2
Hastings Cl *BMSTR* BS3............. 10 E5
Hastings Rd *BMSTR* BS3............ 10 E5
Hatchet La *BRSTK/PCHW* BS34..... 40 D4
Hatchet Rd *BRSTK/PCHW* BS34..... 40 C3
Hatchmere *THNB/SVB* BS35........ 19 J5
Hatfield Buildings *BATHSE* BA2 ... 15 J3
Hatfield Rd *BATHSE* BA2.......... 111 H2
 WSM BS23.............................. 17 K2
Hatherley *YATE/CS* BS37............ 44 B1
Hatherley Rd *HORF/LLZ* BS7 .... 3 H2
Hathway Wk *EVILLE/WHL* BS5 ..... 4 A9
Hatters' La *YATE/CS* BS37........... 35 F6
Havage Dro
 OMX/HUT/LCK BS24.............. 107 K5
Havelock St *TRWBR* BA14........ 124 E7 🈁
The Haven *KGWD/HNM* BS15 .... 68 E1
Haversham Cl
 MTN/WRL BS22 .... 105 J4 🈁
Haverstock Rd
 BRSG/KWL/STAPK BS4............. 12 A1
Haviland Gv *CBATH/BATHN* BA1 .. 98 D1
Haviland Pk
 CBATH/BATHN BA1 .... 98 E2 🈁
Havory *CBATH/BATHN* BA1........ 100 A3
Hawarden Ter
 CBATH/BATHN BA1 .... 100 A3
Hawburn Cl
 BRSG/KWL/STAPK BS4............. 13 G4
Haweswater Cl
 OLD/WMLY/WICK BS30 .... 69 K4 🈁
Hawke Rd *MTN/WRL* BS22 ...... 105 H1
Hawkesbury Rd *MANG/FISH* BS16.. 5 K3
Hawkesley Dr
 BRSTK/PCHW BS34................... 40 C2
Hawkfield Cl
 BMSTRD/HC/WWD BS13.......... 78 B6
Hawkfield Rd
 BMSTRD/HC/WWD BS13.......... 78 B6
Hawkfield Wy
 BMSTRD/HC/WWD BS13.......... 78 B6 🈁
Hawkins Cl
 OLD/WMLY/WICK BS30 .... 69 J6 🈁
Hawkins Cls *ALMDB* BS32........... 30 C7
Hawkins St *CBRISNE* BS2............. 7 L3
Hawkley Dr *ALMDB* BS32............ 30 C4
Hawkridge Dr *MANG/FISH* BS16.. 56 E4
Hawksmoor Cl *HGRV/WHIT* BS14.. 78 E5
Hawksworth Dr
 KGWD/HNM BS15 .... 68 B6
 MTN/WRL BS22 .... 106 D1 🈁
Hawthorn Av
 KGWD/HNM BS15 .... 68 B6
Hawthorn Cl *BRSTK/PCHW* BS34.. 39 H1

 PTSHD/EG BS20...................... 46 D4
Hawthorn Crs
 THNB/SVB BS35...................... 19 H3 🈁
 YTN/CONG BS49..................... 86 D3
The Hawthornes
 MANG/FISH BS16.................... 55 F5
Hawthorne St
 BRSG/KWL/STAPK BS4............. 12 B1
Hawthorn Gdns
 MTN/WRL BS22 .... 105 J3
Hawthorn Gv *BATHSE* BA2....... 111 J4
 TRWBR BA14.......................... 130 D2
Hawthorn Hts *MTN/WRL* BS22... 105 J2
Hawthorn Hl *MTN/WRL* BS22.... 105 K3 🈁
Hawthorn Pk
 MTN/WRL BS22 .... 105 K2 🈁
Hawthorn Rd
 RDSTK/MIDN BA3 .... 127 J3
Hawthorns La *KEYN* BS31.......... 80 E6
Hawthorn Wy
 BRSTK/PCHW BS34................... 40 D3
 NAIL BS48.............................. 73 K1
Haycombe *HGRV/WHIT* BS14 ..... 78 D5 🈁
Haycombe Dr *BATHSE* BA2......... 98 D7
Haycombe La *BATHSE* BA2......... 110 D2
Hay Ct *PTSHD/EG* BS20.............. 49 C5
Hayden Cl *BATHSE* BA2.............. 14 D9
Haydock Cl *MANG/FISH* BS16 ..... 42 A7 🈁
Haydon Gdns *HORF/LLZ* BS7 ...... 53 F4 🈁
Haydon Ga *RDSTK/MIDN* BA3 ... 127 C5
Haydon Hl *RDSTK/MIDN* BA3 .... 127 C5
Hayeley Dr *BRSTK/PCHW* BS34.... 40 D2
Hayes Cl *CBRISNE* BS2.................. 8 A2
 TRWBR BA14.......................... 125 G4
Hayesfield Pk *BATHSE* BA2......... 14 E9
Hayes Park Rd
 RDSTK/MIDN BA3 .... 126 A3
Hayes Rd *RDSTK/MIDN* BA3 ..... 126 A3
Hay Hl *CBATH/BATHN* BA1 .... 14 F5
Hay La *BLAG/CWMG/WR* BS40.... 90 D6
Hay Leaze *YATE/CS* BS37............. 34 A3 🈁
The Haymarket *CBRIS/FH* BS1 ...... 7 H2
Haynes La *MANG/FISH* BS16 ...... 54 D4
Haythorn Ct *MANG/FISH* BS16 .... 55 F4
Haytor Pk
 HNLZ/SM/SNYPK/WT BS9....... 51 F3
Hayward Cl *CLVDN* BS21............. 70 E2
Hayward Rd *EVILLE/WHL* BS5 .... 8 E3
 MANG/FISH BS16.................... 54 D6
Haywood Cl
 OMX/HUT/LCK BS24.............. 117 F5 🈁
Haywood Gdns
 OMX/HUT/LCK BS24.............. 117 F5
Hazel Av *RDLND/MONT* BS6 .... 2 C5
Hazelbury Dr
 OLD/WMLY/WICK BS30 .... 69 J4
Hazelbury Rd *HGRV/WHIT* BS14 ... 12 E8
 NAIL BS48.............................. 73 H2
Hazel Cote Rd *HGRV/WHIT* BS14 .. 79 F7
Hazel Crescent *THNB/SVB* BS35.... 19 J4
Hazeldene Rd
 BRSTK/PCHW BS34................... 39 K1
 WSM BS23.............................. 17 J1
Hazel Gdns *THNB/SVB* BS35 ...... 22 E2 🈁
Hazel Gv *BATHSE* BA2.............. 111 G1
Hazelgrove *FRCTL/WBN* BS36 ..... 41 J5 🈁
Hazel Gv *HORF/LLZ* BS7 .... 52 E1
 RDSTK/MIDN BA3 .... 126 C5
 TRWBR BA14.......................... 130 D2
Hazel La *ALMDB* BS32................. 22 D3
Hazell Cl *CLVDN* BS21................. 71 G2
Hazel Ter *RDSTK/MIDN* BA3 ...... 126 C5
Hazelton Rd *HORF/LLZ* BS7 .... 3 G4
Hazel Wy *BATHSE* BA2.............. 111 G5
Hazelwood Rd
 HNLZ/SM/SNYPK/WT BS9....... 51 F6
Hazleton Gdns *BATHSE* BA2....... 112 E2
Head Cft *NAIL* BS48.................... 75 H1
Headford Av *EVILLE/WHL* BS5 .... 68 B3
Headford Rd
 BRSG/KWL/STAPK BS4............. 11 H6
Headington Cl
 KGWD/HNM BS15 .... 68 D6 🈁
Headley Ct
 BMSTRD/HC/WWD BS13.......... 77 K5
Headley La
 BMSTRD/HC/WWD BS13.......... 77 K5
Headley Park Av
 BMSTRD/HC/WWD BS13.......... 77 K4
Headley Park Rd
 BMSTRD/HC/WWD BS13.......... 77 J4
Headley Rd
 BMSTRD/HC/WWD BS13.......... 77 J5
Headley Wk
 BMSTRD/HC/WWD BS13.......... 77 K4
Heart Meers *HGRV/WHIT* BS14 ... 79 F6 🈁
Heath Cl *FRCTL/WBN* BS36......... 41 K2
Heathcote Dr *FRCTL/WBN* BS36... 41 K2
Heathcote Rd
 MANG/FISH BS16.................... 54 E4 🈁
Heathcote Wk *KGWD/HNM* BS15.. 54 C7
Heath Ct *MANG/FISH* BS16 .... 54 D2 🈁
Heather Av *FRCTL/WBN* BS36..... 42 C2
Heather Cl *KGWD/HNM* BS15 ..... 68 B2
Heatherdene *HGRV/WHIT* BS14 ... 78 D4
Heather Dr *BATHSE* BA2........... 111 G5 🈁
Heather Shaw *BATHSE* BA14..... 125 G6
Heathfield Cl *CBATH/BATHN* BA1.. 98 D1
 KEYN BS31.............................. 80 C6
Heathfield Crs *HGRV/WHIT* BS14.. 78 E7
Heathfield Rd *NAIL* BS48............. 73 J1
Heathfields *MANG/FISH* BS16 ..... 54 D1
Heathfield Wy *NAIL* BS48........... 73 J1 🈁
Heath Gdns *FRCTL/WBN* BS36..... 42 D2
Heathgate *YTN/CONG* BS49........ 86 D4
Heath House La *EVILLE/WHL* BS5... 4 F1
 MANG/FISH BS16.................... 53 G4 🈁
Heath Rdg *LGASH* BS41.............. 76 C1
Heath Ri
 OLD/WMLY/WICK BS30 .... 69 H5 🈁
Heath Rd *EVILLE/WHL* BS5 .... 4 D3
 KGWD/HNM BS15 .... 68 B6
 MANG/FISH BS16.................... 54 D2
 NAIL BS48.............................. 73 K1 🈁
Heath St *EVILLE/WHL* BS5 .... 4 E4

Heath Wk *MANG/FISH* BS16 .... 54 D2
Hebden Rd *BOAV* BA15............ 123 F3
Heber St *EVILLE/WHL* BS5 .... 8 E1
Hebron Rd *BMSTR* BS3.............. 10 E1
Heddington Ct *TRWBR* BA14..... 130 E1
Hedgemead Vw
 MANG/FISH BS16.................... 53 H4
Hedges Cl *CLVDN* BS21............... 70 D3
The Hedges *MTN/WRL* BS22..... 106 D2
Hedwick Av *EVILLE/WHL* BS5 .... 9 J2 🈁
Hedwick St *EVILLE/WHL* BS5 .... 9 J2
Heggard Cl
 BMSTRD/HC/WWD BS13.......... 77 K6 🈁
Helens Rd *WNSC* BS25.............. 120 E2
Hellier Wk
 BMSTRD/HC/WWD BS13.......... 93 F1 🈁
Helmdon Rd *TRWBR* BA14....... 124 C5
Helston Rd *NAIL* BS48................ 74 A2
Helting Ct *CBATH/BATHN* BA1 ..... 14 F7 🈁
Hemming Wy
 OMX/HUT/LCK BS24.............. 117 K3 🈁
Hemplow Cl *HGRV/WHIT* BS14 ... 13 G9
Hempton La *ALMDB* BS32........... 29 K5
Henacre Rd *AVONM* BS11.......... 50 B1
Henbury Rd
 HNBRY/STHM BS10 .... 38 B6 🈁
 HNLZ/SM/SNYPK/WT BS9....... 51 J1
 KGWD/HNM BS15 .... 68 B5 🈁
Henbury Road Henbury Hl
 HNLZ/SM/SNYPK/WT BS9....... 51 H1
Hencliffe Rd *HGRV/WHIT* BS14 ... 79 H5
Hencliffe Wy *KGWD/HNM* BS15 ... 68 E7 🈁
Henderson Cl *TRWBR* BA14....... 124 D7 🈁
Henderson Rd *KGWD/HNM* BS15.. 68 B5 🈁
Hendre Rd *BMSTR* BS3............... 10 A3
Henfield Crs
 OLD/WMLY/WICK BS30 .... 69 H6
Henfield Rd *FRCTL/WBN* BS36..... 42 D4
Hengaston St *BMSTR* BS3........... 10 D4
Hengrove Av *HGRV/WHIT* BS14 ... 12 C7
Hengrove La *HGRV/WHIT* BS14 ... 12 C8
Hengrove Rd
 BRSG/KWL/STAPK BS4............. 12 B3
Hengrove Wy
 BMSTRD/HC/WWD BS13.......... 77 K6
 BRSG/KWL/STAPK BS4............. 78 C5
Henleaze Av
 HNLZ/SM/SNYPK/WT BS9....... 51 J4
Henleaze Gdns
 HNLZ/SM/SNYPK/WT BS9....... 51 J4
Henleaze Pk
 HNLZ/SM/SNYPK/WT BS9....... 52 A4
Henleaze Park Dr
 HNLZ/SM/SNYPK/WT BS9....... 52 A3
Henleaze Rd
 HNLZ/SM/SNYPK/WT BS9....... 51 J4
Henleaze Ter
 HNLZ/SM/SNYPK/WT BS9....... 51 J4
Henley Gv
 HNLZ/SM/SNYPK/WT BS9....... 51 K4
Henley La *COR/BOX* SN13........ 102 C1
 YTN/CONG BS49..................... 87 G5
Henley Ldg *YTN/CONG* BS49 ...... 87 G5 🈁
Henley Pk *YTN/CONG* BS49 .... 87 F5
Hennessy Cl *HGRV/WHIT* BS14 .... 93 H1
Henrietta Gdns *BATHSE* BA2....... 15 H4
Henrietta Ms *BATHSE* BA2.......... 15 H5
Henrietta Pl *BATHSE* BA2............ 15 G5 🈁
Henrietta Rd *BATHSE* BA2........... 15 H4
Henrietta St *BATHSE* BA2............ 15 H5
 CBRISNE BS2............................ 2 F9
 EVILLE/WHL BS5 .... 4 D7 🈁
Henry St *BMSTR* BS3................... 7 M9
 CBATH/BATHN BA1 .... 15 G7 🈁
Henry Williamson Ct
 OLD/WMLY/WICK BS30 .... 69 G5 🈁
Henshaw Cl *KGWD/HNM* BS15 ... 54 C7 🈁
Henshaw Rd *KGWD/HNM* BS15... 54 C7
Henshaw Wk *KGWD/HNM* BS15... 54 C7
Hensley Gdns *BATHSE* BA2....... 111 H1
Hensley Rd *BATHSE* BA2........... 111 H2
Hensman's Hl *CFTN/FAIL* BS8........ 6 A4
Hepburn Rd *CBRISNE* BS2............ 3 J9
Herald Cl
 HNLZ/SM/SNYPK/WT BS9....... 51 F4
Herapath St *EVILLE/WHL* BS5 .... 8 E5
Herbert Crs *EVILLE/WHL* BS5 .... 5 G4
Herbert Rd *BATHSE* BA2............. 14 A9
 CLVDN BS21............................ 59 F6
Herbert St *BMSTR* BS3................. 6 F9
 EVILLE/WHL BS5 .... 6 F9
Hercules Cl *BRSTK/PCHW* BS34.... 40 C2
Hereford Cl *CBRISNE* BS2............. 4 B6
Hereford Rd
 CBATH/BATHN BA1 .... 14 D1
 MANG/FISH BS16.................... 54 D4
Hereford St *BMSTR* BS3.............. 11 G1
Herkomer Cl *HORF/LLZ* BS7 .... 53 F2
Herluin Wy *WSM* BS23............... 17 L6
Hermes Cl *KEYN* BS31................ 96 D2
Hermitage Cl *AVONM* BS11......... 50 A2
Hermitage Rd
 CBATH/BATHN BA1 .... 14 D1
 EVILLE/WHL BS5 .... 5 K7
Hern La *NAIL* BS48..................... 76 A6
Heron Rd *MTN/WRL* BS22 .... 105 K4
Heron Gdns *PTSHD/EG* BS20....... 47 J5
Heron Rd *EVILLE/WHL* BS5 .... 4 D8
Heron Wy *YATE/CS* BS37............ 44 C1
Herridge Cl
 BMSTRD/HC/WWD BS13.......... 77 K7
Herridge Rd
 BMSTRD/HC/WWD BS13.......... 77 K7
Hersey Gdns
 BMSTRD/HC/WWD BS13.......... 92 B1 🈁
Hesding Cl *KGWD/HNM* BS15 .... 68 C7 🈁
Hestercombe Rd
 BMSTRD/HC/WWD BS13.......... 77 K5 🈁
Hewland Ct *AVONM* BS11........... 37 K6 🈁
Heyford Av *EVILLE/WHL* BS5 .... 4 C3
Heyron Wk
 BMSTRD/HC/WWD BS13.......... 77 K7
Heywood Rd *PTSHD/EG* BS20...... 49 J5 🈁
Heywood Ter *PTSHD/EG* BS20..... 49 J5 🈁
Hicks Av *MANG/FISH* BS16......... 55 H1
Hicks Common Rd
 FRCTL/WBN BS36.................... 41 K2
Hicks Ct
 OLD/WMLY/WICK BS30 .... 69 F6 🔟
High Acre *PLTN/PENS* BS39...... 126 A1

Higham St
 BRSG/KWL/STAPK BS4 .... 7 M8 🈁
Highbury Pl *CBATH/BATHN* BA1 ... 15 H1
Highbury Rd *BMSTR* BS3............. 10 E5
 HORF/LLZ BS7 .... 52 D2
 WSM BS23............................ 104 D3
Highbury Vls *CBRISNE* BS2............ 6 E1
Highcroft
 OLD/WMLY/WICK BS30 .... 69 J4 🈁
Highdale Av *CLVDN* BS21............ 59 F7
Highdale Cl *HGRV/WHIT* BS14 ..... 79 F7
Highdale Rd *CLVDN* BS21............ 59 F7
High Elm *KGWD/HNM* BS15 .... 68 E4 🈁
Highett Dr *EVILLE/WHL* BS5 .... 4 E1
Highfield Av *KGWD/HNM* BS15.... 68 D5
Highfield Cl *BATHSE* BA2............. 98 E7 🈁
Highfield Dr *PTSHD/EG* BS20....... 46 C6
Highfield Gdns
 OLD/WMLY/WICK BS30 .... 81 J1
Highfield Gv *HORF/LLZ* BS7 .... 52 B9
Highfield Rd *BOAV* BA15........... 114 E6
 KEYN BS31.............................. 96 A2 🈁
 OMX/HUT/LCK BS24.............. 117 F5
 YATE/CS BS37......................... 34 D6
Highfields *RDSTK/MIDN* BA3..... 126 E3
Highfields Cl *BRSTK/PCHW* BS34.. 40 E5
High Gv
 HNLZ/SM/SNYPK/WT BS9....... 50 D2
Highgrove St
 BRSG/KWL/STAPK BS4............. 8 A9
Highland Cl *MTN/WRL* BS22...... 105 G3 🈁
Highland Crs *CFTN/FAIL* BS8 .... 2 B6 🈁
Highland Rd *BATHSE* BA2........... 98 E2
Highlands *LGASH* BS41............... 76 C1
Highleaze Rd
 OLD/WMLY/WICK BS30 .... 69 J6
Highmead Gdns
 BMSTRD/HC/WWD BS13.......... 77 H6
High Mdw *RDSTK/MIDN* BA3 .... 126 A4
Highmore Gdns *HORF/LLZ* BS7.... 53 G2
Highnam Cl *BRSTK/PCHW* BS34 ... 30 A6
Hignave Rd
 BRSG/KWL/STAPK BS4............. 12 B5
Hignave Wy
 BMSTRD/HC/WWD BS13.......... 77 H6
Highridge Cres
 BMSTRD/HC/WWD BS13.......... 77 H6
Highridge Gn
 BMSTRD/HC/WWD BS13.......... 77 H6 🈁
Highridge Pk
 BMSTRD/HC/WWD BS13.......... 77 H6 🈁
Highridge Rd *BMSTR* BS3........... 10 C4
 LGASH BS41............................ 91 K1
Highridge Wk
 BMSTRD/HC/WWD BS13.......... 77 G4
High St *AVONM* BS11................. 49 K2
 BATHSE BA2........................... 100 E3
 BATHSE BA2........................... 100 E3
 BLAG/CWMG/WR BS40............ 91 H5
 BNWL BS29............................ 119 G4
 CBATH/BATHN BA1 .... 15 G5 🈁
 CBATH/BATHN BA1 .... 98 E2
 CBATH/BATHN BA1 .... 100 E1
 CBATH/BATHN BA1 .... 101 H2 🈁
 CBRIS/FH BS1 .... 7 H3
 CFTN/FAIL BS8......................... 2 B6
 EVILLE/WHL BS5 .... 4 D7
 FRCTL/WBN BS36.................... 41 J2
 HNLZ/SM/SNYPK/WT BS9....... 51 J1
 KEYN BS31.............................. 80 E5
 KEYN BS31.............................. 97 F1
 KGWD/HNM BS15 .... 68 E2
 KGWD/HNM BS15 .... 68 C5
 KGWD/HNM BS15 .... 69 H2
 MANG/FISH BS16.................... 54 C5
 MTN/WRL BS22 .... 105 K3
 NAIL BS48.............................. 73 J1
 OLD/WMLY/WICK BS30 .... 69 K6
 OLD/WMLY/WICK BS30 .... 69 K3
 PTSHD/EG BS20...................... 47 H4
 PTSHD/EG BS20...................... 48 D6
 RDSTK/MIDN BA3 .... 122 B1
 RDSTK/MIDN BA3 .... 126 C4
 RDSTK/MIDN BA3 .... 128 E7
 RDSTK/MIDN BA3 .... 129 F6
 THNB/SVB BS35...................... 19 G4
 WSM BS23.............................. 16 D3 🈁
 YATE/CS BS37......................... 32 E3
 YATE/CS BS37......................... 34 E6
 YTN/CONG BS49..................... 86 E4
 YTN/CONG BS49..................... 87 J3
 YTN/CONG BS49..................... 109 G1
High Vw *PTSHD/EG* BS20............ 46 E5
Highview Rd *KGWD/HNM* BS15... 54 E7
Highwall La *HGRV/WHIT* BS14 .... 94 E3
Highway *YATE/CS* BS37.............. 34 C5
Highwood La
 BRSTK/PCHW BS34................... 39 H1
 HNBRY/STHM BS10 .... 39 G1
Highwood Rd
 BRSTK/PCHW BS34................... 39 G1
Highworth Crs *YATE/CS* BS37...... 34 A7
Highworth Rd
 BRSG/KWL/STAPK BS4 .... 9 H5
Hildesheim Cl *WSM* BS23........... 17 H5 🈁
Hill Av *BATHSE* BA2.................. 111 J4
 BMSTR BS3............................. 11 K2
Hillbrook Rd *THNB/SVB* BS35....... 19 J5 🈁
Hill Burn
 HNLZ/SM/SNYPK/WT BS9....... 52 A3
Hillburn Rd *EVILLE/WHL* BS5 .... 68 A2
Hillcote Est
 OMX/HUT/LCK BS24.............. 117 G6
Hill Crest *BRSG/KWL/STAPK* BS4.. 12 C6
Hillcrest *THNB/SVB* BS35............ 19 G4
Hillcrest Cl *NAIL* BS48................ 73 J4
Hillcrest Dr *BATHSE* BA2........... 110 E2
Hillcrest Rd *NAIL* BS48............... 73 J4
 PTSHD/EG BS20...................... 46 C5
Hillcroft Cl *MTN/WRL* BS22 ...... 105 F3
Hilldale Rd *NAIL* BS48................ 74 B6
Hill Dr *CFTN/FAIL* BS8................. 63 J7
Hill End Dr *HNBRY/STHM* BS10.... 38 A5
Hillfields Av *MANG/FISH* BS16 .... 54 C6
Hill Frost *YTN/CONG* BS49 .... 87 F6
Hill Gay Cl *PTSHD/EG* BS20........ 46 D5 🈁
Hill Gv *HNLZ/SM/SNYPK/WT* BS9 .. 52 A3
Hillgrove St *CBRISNE* BS2............. 3 J9 🈁
Hill House Rd *MANG/FISH* BS16 .. 55 F4
Hillier's La *WNSC* BS25............. 121 G2
Hill La *PTSHD/EG* BS20............... 60 D1

Hill Lawn *BRSG/KWL/STAPK* BS4.. 13 H1
Hillmead
 BLAG/CWMG/WR BS40............ 109 K7
Hillmer Ri *BNWL* BS29.............. 119 G3
Hill Moor *CLVDN* BS21................ 71 G1
Hill Pk *YTN/CONG* BS49............. 87 H7
Hillpath *BNWL* BS29.................. 119 J4
Hill Rd *CLVDN* BS21.................... 58 E6
 LGASH BS41............................ 92 A2
 MTN/WRL BS22 .... 105 K3
 WSM BS23.............................. 17 J5
Hill Rd East *MTN/WRL* BS22...... 105 K3 🈁
Hillsborough
 BRSG/KWL/STAPK BS4.............. 8 F8
Hills Cl *KEYN* BS31..................... 81 G6
Hillsdon Rd
 HNLZ/SM/SNYPK/WT BS9....... 51 H1
Hillside *MANG/FISH* BS16........... 55 F4
 PTSHD/EG BS20...................... 48 D6
 RDLND/MONT BS6.................... 2 E9
Hillside Av *BRSTK/PCHW* BS34..... 68 C2
Hillside Cl *FRCTL/WBN* BS36........ 42 D1
Hillside Gdns *MTN/WRL* BS22 .... 105 G4
Hillside La *FRCTL/WBN* BS36....... 42 D1 🈁
Hillside Rd *BATHSE* BA2............ 111 G1
 CLVDN BS21............................ 59 F7
 EVILLE/WHL BS5 .... 68 A3
 LGASH BS41............................ 76 D1
 NAIL BS48.............................. 74 A6
 OMX/HUT/LCK BS24.............. 117 G6
 PTSHD/EG BS20...................... 46 B5
 RDSTK/MIDN BA3 .... 122 C1
Hillside St *BRSG/KWL/STAPK* BS4.. 8 A9
Hillside West
 OMX/HUT/LCK BS24.............. 118 A3
Hill St *BMTR* BS3......................... 7 L9
 CBRIS/FH BS1 .... 6 E4
 EVILLE/WHL BS5 .... 5 M9
 TRWBR BA14.......................... 124 E6
 TRWBR BA14.......................... 125 J2
The Hill *ALMDB* BS32................. 30 A3
 RDSTK/MIDN BA3 .... 122 C1
Hilltop Gdns *EVILLE/WHL* BS5 .... 68 A3
Hilltop Rd *MANG/FISH* BS16 ...... 54 D7
Hilltop Vw *EVILLE/WHL* BS5 .... 68 A3
Hill Vw *CFTN/FAIL* BS8................. 6 C4
 HNLZ/SM/SNYPK/WT BS9....... 52 A3
 MANG/FISH BS16.................... 54 D7
Hillview Av *CLVDN* BS21............ 71 F1 🈁
Hill View Cl
 OLD/WMLY/WICK BS30 .... 69 J6
Hillview Gdns
 BLAG/CWMG/WR BS40............ 90 D4
Hill View Rd
 BMSTRD/HC/WWD BS13.......... 10 B8
 CBATH/BATHN BA1 .... 100 A2
 MANG/FISH BS16.................... 56 E4
 WSM BS23.............................. 17 K3
Hillyfield Rd
 BMSTRD/HC/WWD BS13.......... 77 J5
Hillyfields *WNSC* BS25.............. 120 E6
Hillyfields Wy *WNSC* BS25........ 120 D6
Hilperton Dr *TRWBR* BA14........ 125 J4
Hilperton Rd *TRWBR* BA14....... 125 H5
Hinckley Cl *MTN/WRL* BS22 ...... 106 D2 🈁
Hind Pitts *WNSC* BS25.............. 121 H7
Hinton Cl *KEYN* BS31................. 97 F1
Hinton Dr
 OLD/WMLY/WICK BS30 .... 69 J4
Hinton Rd *EVILLE/WHL* BS5 .... 4 F7
 MANG/FISH BS16.................... 54 A5 🈁
Hiscocks Dr *BATHSE* BA2.......... 111 H4
Hither Gn *CLVDN* BS21.............. 71 H1
Hobart Rd *WSM* BS23............... 116 E3
Hobbiton Rd *MTN/WRL* BS22..... 84 B7
Hobb's La *CBRIS/FH* BS1 .... 6 F4 🈁
 KGWD/HNM BS15 .... 69 K1
 NAIL BS48.............................. 76 A1
Hobhouse Cl *BOAV* BA15.......... 124 A2
Hobwell La *LGASH* BS41............ 76 E1 🈁
Hockey's La *MANG/FISH* BS16 .... 54 A1
Hoddon La *MANG/FISH* BS16 ..... 56 E4
Hodshill *BATHSE* BA2............... 111 J7
Hogarth Ms *MTN/WRL* BS22 .... 106 B2 🈁
Hogarth Wk *HORF/LLZ* BS7 .... 53 F2
Hoggington La *TRWBR* BA14..... 129 K3
Hogues Wk
 BMSTRD/HC/WWD BS13.......... 77 K7 🈁
Holbeach Wy *HGRV/WHIT* BS14... 93 K1
Holbrook Crs
 BMSTRD/HC/WWD BS13.......... 78 D7
Holbrook La *TRWBR* BA14......... 130 E1
Holcombe *HGRV/WHIT* BS14 ...... 78 D5 🈁
Holcombe Cl *BATHSE* BA2.......... 100 E3
Holcombe Gn
 CBATH/BATHN BA1 .... 98 E2
Holcombe Gv *KEYN* BS31.......... 80 D6
Holcombe La *BATHSE* BA2......... 100 E3
Holcombe V *BATHSE* BA2.......... 100 E3
Holdenhurst Rd
 KGWD/HNM BS15 .... 68 C1
Holders Wk *LGASH* BS41........... 76 B2
Holford Cl *NAIL* BS48................. 73 J4
Holford Ct *HGRV/WHIT* BS14...... 79 F6
Holland Rd *CBATH/BATHN* BA1.... 100 A3
 CLVDN BS21............................ 17 J2
Holland St *WSM* BS23................ 17 J2
Hollies Wy *TRWBR* BA14........... 130 B4
Hollis Av *PTSHD/EG* BS20........... 47 G6
Hollis Cl *LGASH* BS41................. 76 B3
Hollis Crs *PTSHD/EG* BS20.......... 47 G6 🈁
Hollister's Dr
 BMSTRD/HC/WWD BS13.......... 93 G1
Holloway *BATHSE* BA2................ 14 F9
Holloway La *WNSC* BS25........... 121 K6
Hollow La *MTN/WRL* BS22......... 84 B3
Hollowmead Cl *YTN/CONG* BS49... 87 J4
Hollow Rd *ALMDB* BS32............. 29 K3
 KGWD/HNM BS15 .... 68 C2
 WNSC BS25........................... 121 J6
The Hollows *FRCTL/WBN* BS36... 42 D6
The Hollow *BATHSE* BA2........... 110 D1
Hollway Cl *HGRV/WHIT* BS14...... 79 J6
Hollway Rd *HGRV/WHIT* BS14..... 79 J6
Hollybush La *BOAV* BA15.......... 113 K6
Hollybush La
 HNLZ/SM/SNYPK/WT BS9....... 51 G4
Holly Cl *EVILLE/WHL* BS5 .... 54 A7

MANG/FISH BS16 .... 56 E4
MTN/WRL BS22 .... 106 B4
NAIL BS48 .... 62 A7 🔢
THNB/SVB BS35 .... 22 E1
Holly Crs *KGWD/HNM* BS15 ...... 68 E1 🔢
Holly Dr *BATHSE* BA2 .... 111 G5
Holly Gn *KGWD/HNM* BS15 .... 69 G1
Holly Gv *MANG/FISH* BS16 .... 54 C6
Hollyguest Rd *KGWD/HNM* BS15.. 68 E4
Holly Hl *YATE/CS* BS37 .... 33 H4
Holly Hill Rd *KGWD/HNM* BS15 ... 69 F2
Holly La *CLVDN* BS21 .... 59 H4
Hollyleigh Av *BRSTK/PCHW* BS34 .. 39 J6
Holly Lodge Rd *EVILLE/WHL* BS5 ... 5 M6
Hollyman Wk *CLVDN* BS21 .... 59 H7 🔢
Hollymead La
   HNLZ/SM/SNYPK/WT BS9 .... 51 G5
Hollyridge *HGRV/WHIT* BS14 ..... 79 C5
Holly Rdg *PTSHD/EG* BS20 .... 46 E4
Holly Wk *KEYN* BS31 .... 95 J1
   RDSTK/MIDN BA3 .... 127 F4 🔢
Hollywood La *THNB/SVB* BS35 .. 38 D1
Hollywood Rd
   BRSG/KWL/STAPK BS4 .... 13 H2
Holmdale Rd *BRSTK/PCHW* BS34.. 40 A5
Holmesdale Rd *BMSTR* BS3 .... 11 J2
Holmes Gv
   HNLZ/SM/SNYPK/WT BS9 .... 51 K4
Holmes Hill Rd *EVILLE/WHL* BS5 ... 5 L9
Holmes St *EVILLE/WHL* BS5 .... 8 D4
Holmoak Rd *KEYN* BS31 .... 80 C7
Holm Rd *OMX/HUT/LCK* BS24 .. 117 K4
Holms Rd *WSM* BS23 .... 17 K8
Holmwood *KGWD/HNM* BS15 .... 68 C5
Holmwood Gdns
   HNLZ/SM/SNYPK/WT BS9 .... 51 J1
Holsom Cl *HGRV/WHIT* BS14 ...... 79 J5
Holsom Rd *HGRV/WHIT* BS14 .. 79 K5 🔢
Holst Gdns
   BRSG/KWL/STAPK BS4 .... 78 A4
Holton Rd *HORF/LLZ* BS7 .... 52 E3
Holt Rd *BOAV* BA15 .... 115 F7
Holyrood Cl
   BRSTK/PCHW BS34 .... 40 C4 🔢
   TRWBR BA14 .... 130 D2
Holy Well Cl
   BRSG/KWL/STAPK BS4 .... 9 K4 🔢
Home Cl *HNBRY/STHM* BS10 ...... 39 H6
   TRWBR BA14 .... 125 F7
Home Farm Rd *CFTN/FAIL* BS8 .. 64 C3
Home Farm Wy *THNB/SVB* BS35 .. 28 D6
Homefield *OMX/HUT/LCK* BS24 .. 118 A1
   THNB/SVB BS35 .... 19 J5 🔢
   YATE/CS BS37 .... 34 B4
   YTN/CONG BS49 .... 109 G2
Homefield Cl *KEYN* BS31 .... 97 F1
Home Field Cl *MANG/FISH* BS16 .. 55 H3
Homefield Cl *WNSC* BS25 .... 120 C5
Homefield Rd *KEYN* BS31 .... 97 F1
   MANG/FISH BS16 .... 56 D4
Home Gnd *AVONM* BS11 .... 49 K2
Home Gnd
   HNLZ/SM/SNYPK/WT BS9 .... 51 K2
Homelea Pk East
   CBATH/BATHN BA1 .... 98 D5
Homelea Pk West
   CBATH/BATHN BA1 .... 98 D5 🔢
Homeleaze Rd
   HNBRY/STHM BS10 .... 39 C5
Home Md
   OLD/WMLY/WICK BS30 .... 69 C6
Homemead Dr
   BRSG/KWL/STAPK BS4 .... 13 C5
Home Orch *YATE/CS* BS37 .... 34 A5
Homestead *PTSHD/EG* BS20 .... 46 C6 🔢
Homestead Gdns
   MANG/FISH BS16 .... 41 C7
Homestead Rd
   BRSTK/PCHW BS34 .... 39 J5
The Homestead *CLVDN* BS21 ..... 58 E7
   KEYN BS31 .... 96 A2
Homestead Wy *WNSC* BS25 .... 120 D6
Honey Garston Cl
   BMSTRD/HC/WWD BS13 .... 77 K7 🔢
Honey Garston Rd
   BMSTRD/HC/WWD BS13 .... 77 K7
Honeyhall La *YTN/CONG* BS49 .. 109 G6
Honey Hill Rd *KGWD/HNM* BS15.. 69 F2
Honeylands *PTSHD/EG* BS20 ..... 47 C6
Honeymead *HGRV/WHIT* BS14 .. 79 G5 🔢
Honeysuckle Cl *ALMDB* BS32 ..... 30 D5 🔢
   TRWBR BA14 .... 125 G7 🔢
Honey Suckle La
   MANG/FISH BS16 .... 5 J1
Honeysuckle Pl
   OMX/HUT/LCK BS24 .... 106 B4 🔢
Honiton Rd *CLVDN* BS21 .... 71 G2 🔢
   MANG/FISH BS16 .... 54 A6
Hooper Rd *HGRV/WHIT* BS14 ..... 79 H6
Hopechapel Hl *CFTN/FAIL* BS8 .. 65 H4 🔢
   YATE/CS BS37 .... 33 H5
Hope Rd *BMSTR* BS3 .... 10 E1
Hope Sq *CFTN/FAIL* BS8 .... 65 H4 🔢
Hopetoun Rd *CBRISNE* BS2 .... 3 M4
Hopewell Gdns *AVONM* BS11 ..... 50 B2
Hopkin Cl *THNB/SVB* BS35 .... 19 J6
Hopkins St *WSM* BS23 .... 16 E2 🔢
Hopland Cl
   OLD/WMLY/WICK BS30 .... 69 H7
Hopp's Rd *KGWD/HNM* BS15 ..... 68 D3
Horesham Gv
   BMSTRD/HC/WWD BS13 .... 78 A6 🔢
Horfield Rd *CBRISNE* BS2 .... 7 G2
Horley Rd *CBRISNE* BS2 .... 4 A7
Horsecastle Cl *YTN/CONG* BS49 .. 86 D3
Horsecastle Farm Rd
   YTN/CONG BS49 .... 86 C3
Horsecombe Brow
   BATHSE BA2 .... 111 K4
Horsecombe Gv *BATHSE* BA2 ... 111 K4
Horsecombe V *BATHSE* BA2 ..... 111 K4
Horsecroft Gdns
   OLD/WMLY/WICK BS30 .... 69 G4 🔢
The Horsefair *CBRIS/FH* BS1 .... 7 J2

Horsepool Rd
   BMSTRD/HC/WWD BS13 .... 77 G7
Horse Race La *CFTN/FAIL* BS8 ..... 63 G3
Horse Rd *TRWBR* BA14 .... 125 G2
Horseshoe Dr
   HNLZ/SM/SNYPK/WT BS9 .... 50 E5
Horseshoe La *YATE/CS* BS37 ...... 34 E6
Horseshoe Wk *BATHSE* BA2 .... 15 K8
Horse St *YATE/CS* BS37 .... 35 F7
Hortham La *ALMDB* BS32 .... 30 B1
Horton Cl *BOAV* BA15 .... 124 A2 🔢
Horton Rd *YATE/CS* BS37 .... 35 F5
Horton St *CBRISNE* BS2 .... 7 M4
Horwood Ct
   OLD/WMLY/WICK BS30 .... 69 C6 🔢
Horwood Rd *NAIL* BS48 .... 73 K2
Hosey Wk
   BMSTRD/HC/WWD BS13 .... 77 J6
Host St *CBRIS/FH* BS1 .... 7 G3
Hottom Gdns *HORF/LLZ* BS7 ...... 52 E2
Hot Water La *KGWD/HNM* BS15 .. 55 F6
Hotwell Rd *CFTN/FAIL* BS8 .... 65 H4 🔢
Houlton St *CBRISNE* BS2 .... 7 L1
Hounds Rd *YATE/CS* BS37 .... 34 E7
Howard Av *EVILLE/WHL* BS5 .... 5 J9
Howard Cl *KEYN* BS31 .... 96 D1
Howard Rd *BMSTR* BS3 .... 6 E8
   MANG/FISH BS16 .... 54 D5
   RDLND/MONT BS6 .... 2 D1
   THNB/SVB BS35 .... 19 H3 🔢
Howard St *EVILLE/WHL* BS5 .... 5 J8
Howecroft Gdns
   HNLZ/SM/SNYPK/WT BS9 .... 51 C5 🔢
Howells Md *MANG/FISH* BS16 .... 55 H2 🔢
Howes Cl *OLD/WMLY/WICK* BS30 .. 69 G4
Howett Rd *EVILLE/WHL* BS5 .... 8 F2 🔢
How Hl *BATHSE* BA2 .... 98 D6
Howsmoor La *MANG/FISH* BS16... 55 H1
Hoylake Dr
   OLD/WMLY/WICK BS30 .... 69 H4
Huckford La *FRCTL/WBN* BS36 .... 42 B4
Huckford Rd *FRCTL/WBN* BS36 ... 41 K3
Huckley Wy *ALMDB* BS32 .... 40 E2
Hudd's Hill Gdns
   EVILLE/WHL BS5 .... 5 M9 🔢
Hudd's Hill Rd *EVILLE/WHL* BS5 .. 5 M9
Hudd's Vale Rd *EVILLE/WHL* BS5 .. 5 L9
Hudson Cl *YATE/CS* BS37 .... 34 C7
Hughenden Rd *CFTN/FAIL* BS8 ..... 2 A6
   HORF/LLZ BS7 .... 52 C4
   WSM BS23 .... 17 K2
Huish Ct *RDSTK/MIDN* BA3 .... 127 J4
Hulbert Cl
   BRSG/KWL/STAPK BS4 .... 80 A1 🔢
Hulse Rd *BRSG/KWL/STAPK* BS4.. 13 C5
Humberstan Wk *AVONM* BS11 ... 50 A1 🔢
Humber Wy *AVONM* BS11 .... 36 E3
Humphrys Barton
   BRSG/KWL/STAPK BS4 .... 9 M6 🔢
Hungerford Av *TRWBR* BA14 .... 124 C7
Hungerford Cl
   BRSG/KWL/STAPK BS4 .... 13 J7
Hungerford Crs
   BRSG/KWL/STAPK BS4 .... 13 J6
Hungerford Gdns
   BRSG/KWL/STAPK BS4 .... 13 J7
Hungerford Rd
   BRSG/KWL/STAPK BS4 .... 13 J7
   CBATH/BATHN BA1 .... 99 F5
Hungerford Wk
   BRSG/KWL/STAPK BS4 .... 13 J6
Hung Rd *AVONM* BS11 .... 50 A3
Hunters Cl *KGWD/HNM* BS15 ..... 68 E5
Hunters Dr *KGWD/HNM* BS15 .... 69 F1
Hunters Rd *KGWD/HNM* BS15 .... 68 C5
Hunters Rd East
   KGWD/HNM BS15 .... 68 C5
Hunter's Wy *BRSTK/PCHW* BS34.. 40 A5
Huntingdon Pl *BOAV* BA15 ...... 114 D6 🔢
Huntingdon Ri *BOAV* BA15 ...... 114 D5
Huntingdon St *BOAV* BA15 ...... 114 D5
Huntingham Rd
   BMSTRD/HC/WWD BS13 .... 77 G7
Huntley Gv *NAIL* BS48 .... 74 A2
Hunt's La *YTN/CONG* BS49 .... 87 H4
Hurle Crs *CFTN/FAIL* BS8 .... 2 B7
Hurle Rd *CFTN/FAIL* BS8 .... 2 C7
Hurlingham Rd
   RDLND/MONT BS6 .... 3 L5
Hurn La *KEYN* BS31 .... 81 F7
Hurn Rd *CLVDN* BS21 .... 71 G1
Hursey Hl *PLTN/PENS* BS39 .... 94 C5
Hursley La *HGRV/WHIT* BS14 ..... 94 D3
Hurston Rd
   BRSG/KWL/STAPK BS4 .... 11 G8
Hurst Rd *BRSG/KWL/STAPK* BS4 .. 11 K8
   WSM BS23 .... 17 J5
Hurst Wk *BRSG/KWL/STAPK* BS4 .. 11 K8
Hurstwood Rd *MANG/FISH* BS16.. 54 D4
Hutton Cl
   HNLZ/SM/SNYPK/WT BS9 .... 51 G2
   KEYN BS31 .... 96 D1
Hutton Hl *OMX/HUT/LCK* BS24 . 117 K4
Hutton Moor La
   OMX/HUT/LCK BS24 .... 117 H1
Huyton Rd *EVILLE/WHL* BS5 .... 5 J4
Hyatts Wood Rd *NAIL* BS48 ...... 89 K1
Hyde Av *THNB/SVB* BS35 .... 19 G2
Hyde Rd *TRWBR* BA14 .... 124 E4
The Hyde *CLVDN* BS21 .... 70 E3
Hyland Gv
   HNLZ/SM/SNYPK/WT BS9 .... 51 H1

I

Ida Rd *EVILLE/WHL* BS5 .... 4 F9
Iddesleigh Rd *RDLND/MONT* BS6.... 2 C4
Idstone Rd *MANG/FISH* BS16 ...... 54 B5
Iford Cl *KEYN* BS31 .... 97 F1
Iford Hl *BOAV* BA15 .... 122 E4
Iford La *RDSTK/MIDN* BA3 .... 122 D3
Ilchester Crs
   BMSTRD/HC/WWD BS13 .... 10 C5
Ilchester Rd
   BMSTRD/HC/WWD BS13 .... 10 B7
Iles Cl *KGWD/HNM* BS15 .... 68 D6
Ilex Av *CLVDN* BS21 .... 71 G1 🔢
Ilex Cl *BMSTRD/HC/WWD* BS13 .. 77 H5
Ilex La *WNSC* BS25 .... 120 C5
Ilminster Av
   BRSG/KWL/STAPK BS4 .... 11 L7
Ilminster Cl *CLVDN* BS21 .... 71 G1 🔢
Ilsyn Gv *HGRV/WHIT* BS14 .... 13 G9
Imber Court Cl *HGRV/WHIT* BS14... 12 C8
Imperial Rd *CFTN/FAIL* BS8 .... 2 C8
   HGRV/WHIT BS14 .... 12 E8
Imperial Wk *HGRV/WHIT* BS14 ... 12 E8
Inglesham Cl *TRWBR* BA14 ...... 131 F2 🔢
Ingleside Rd *KGWD/HNM* BS15 ... 68 C1
Ingleton Dr *MTN/WRL* BS22 .... 106 B1 🔢
Ingmire Rd *EVILLE/WHL* BS5 .... 4 C4
Inkerman Cl *HORF/LLZ* BS7 .... 52 C2
The Inner Down *ALMDB* BS32 ..... 22 C3
Innox Gdns
   BMSTRD/HC/WWD BS13 .... 77 J6 🔢
Innox Gv *BATHSE* BA2 .... 110 C3
Innox Mill Cl *TRWBR* BA14 .... 124 D5
Innox Rd *BATHSE* BA2 .... 98 E7
   TRWBR BA14 .... 124 D5
Inns Court Av
   BRSG/KWL/STAPK BS4 .... 11 G9
Inns Court Dr
   BRSG/KWL/STAPK BS4 .... 78 B5 🔢
Instow Rd *BRSG/KWL/STAPK* BS4.. 11 K7
Instow Wk
   BRSG/KWL/STAPK BS4 .... 11 K7
Inverness Rd *BATHSE* BA2 .... 99 F6
Ipswich Dr *BRSG/KWL/STAPK* BS4... 9 K5
Irby Rd *BMSTR* BS3 .... 10 C2
Ireland Rd *BMSTR* BS3 .... 10 D2 🔢
Iron Acton Wy *YATE/CS* BS37 ..... 33 H4
Ironchurch Rd *AVONM* BS11 ...... 36 C3
Iron Hogg La *WUE* GL12 .... 20 D2
Ironmould La
   BRSG/KWL/STAPK BS4 .... 80 A1 🔢
Irving Cl *CLVDN* BS21 .... 59 H7
   MANG/FISH BS16 .... 54 E5 🔢
Island Gdns *MANG/FISH* BS16 ..... 4 E1 🔢
The Island *RDSTK/MIDN* BA3 ... 126 B4
Isleys Ct
   OLD/WMLY/WICK BS30 .... 69 F7 🔢
Islington *TRWBR* BA14 .... 125 F1 🔢
Islington Rd *BMSTR* BS3 .... 6 D8
Ison Hill Rd
   HNBRY/STHM BS10 .... 38 A5 🔢
Itchington Rd *THNB/SVB* BS35 .... 19 K7
Ivo Peters Rd *BATHSE* BA2 .... 14 D7
Ivor Rd *EVILLE/WHL* BS5 .... 4 F9
Ivy Av *BATHSE* BA2 .... 111 F1
Ivy Bank Pk *BATHSE* BA2 .... 111 J3
Ivy Ct *PTSHD/EG* BS20 .... 46 D4 🔢
Ivy Gv *BATHSE* BA2 .... 111 F1
Ivy La *BOAV* BA15 .... 103 F7
   MANG/FISH BS16 .... 54 A6 🔢
Ivy Pl *BATHSE* BA2 .... 111 F1
Ivy Ter *BOAV* BA15 .... 114 E6
Ivy Wk *RDSTK/MIDN* BA3 .... 126 C5
Ivywell Rd
   HNLZ/SM/SNYPK/WT BS9 .... 51 G6
Iwood La
   BLAG/CWMG/WR BS40 .... 109 K4

J

Jacob St *CBRISNE* BS2 .... 7 K3
Jacob's Wells Rd *CFTN/FAIL* BS8..... 6 C4
Jamaica St *CBRISNE* BS2 .... 3 H9
James Cl *MANG/FISH* BS16 .... 54 E5 🔢
James Rd *MANG/FISH* BS16 .... 54 E5
James St *CBRISNE* BS2 .... 4 A5
   EVILLE/WHL BS5 .... 7 M1
   TRWBR BA14 .... 125 F4 🔢
James St West
   CBATH/BATHN BA1 .... 14 D6
Jane St *EVILLE/WHL* BS5 .... 8 D2
Jarvis St *EVILLE/WHL* BS5 .... 8 C4
Jasmine Cl *MTN/WRL* BS22 ...... 106 B4 🔢
Jasmine Gv *AVONM* BS11 .... 37 K6 🔢
Jasmine La *YTN/CONG* BS49 ...... 87 J2
Jasmine Wy
   OMX/HUT/LCK BS24 .... 106 B4
   TRWBR BA14 .... 125 G2
Jasper St *BMSTR* BS3 .... 10 D7
Jean Rd *BRSG/KWL/STAPK* BS4 ... 13 J3
Jefferies Hill Bottom
   KGWD/HNM BS15 .... 68 B5
Jeffery Ct
   OLD/WMLY/WICK BS30 .... 69 H4
Jellicoe Ct *MTN/WRL* BS22 ...... 105 K1 🔢
Jena Ct *KEYN* BS31 .... 96 E1
Jenkins St *TRWBR* BA14 .... 124 E4
Jenner Cl *YATE/CS* BS37 .... 35 G7
Jersey Av *BRSG/KWL/STAPK* BS4... 9 L9
Jesmond Rd *CLVDN* BS21 .... 58 E7 🔢
   MTN/WRL BS22 .... 106 D1 🔢
Jesse Hughes Ct
   CBATH/BATHN BA1 .... 100 B2 🔢
Jessop Under/pass *BMSTR* BS3 ... 65 H6
Jews La *BATHSE* BA2 .... 99 F6
   WNSC BS25 .... 121 J2
Jocelin Dr *MTN/WRL* BS22 .... 106 A1
Jocelyn Rd *HORF/LLZ* BS7 .... 52 D2
Jockey La *EVILLE/WHL* BS5 .... 68 A8
John Carr's Ter *CFTN/FAIL* BS8 ..... 6 C4
John Rennie Cl *BOAV* BA15 ..... 124 A2
Johnson Dr
   OLD/WMLY/WICK BS30 .... 69 F5
Johnsons La *EVILLE/WHL* BS5 ...... 5 G8
Johnsons Rd *EVILLE/WHL* BS5 ..... 5 G9
Johnstone St *BATHSE* BA2 .... 15 H6
John St *CBATH/BATHN* BA1 .... 14 F5
   CBRIS/FH BS1 .... 7 H3 🔢
   CBRISNE BS2 .... 4 A6
   KGWD/HNM BS15 .... 68 C2
John Wesley Rd *EVILLE/WHL* BS5.. 68 A4
Jones Cl *YTN/CONG* BS49 .... 86 C3
Jones Hl *BOAV* BA15 .... 123 J1
Jordan Wk *ALMDB* BS32 .... 30 C7
Joy Hl *CFTN/FAIL* BS8 .... 65 H4 🔟
Jubilee Crs *MANG/FISH* BS16 ..... 55 G3
Jubilee Dr *CFTN/FAIL* BS8 .... 63 H6

   THNB/SVB BS35 .... 19 J5
Jubilee Gdns *YATE/CS* BS37 ...... 34 D5 🔢
Jubilee La
   BLAG/CWMG/WR BS40 .... 109 K7
   WUE GL12 .... 21 H6
Jubilee Pl *CBRIS/FH* BS1 .... 7 H6 🔢
   CLVDN BS21 .... 71 F2
Jubilee Rd
   BRSG/KWL/STAPK BS4 .... 12 E4
   CBRISNE BS2 .... 4 A7
   EVILLE/WHL BS5 .... 9 M2
   KGWD/HNM BS15 .... 54 E6
   RDSTK/MIDN BA3 .... 127 J4
   WSM BS23 .... 16 F3
Jubilee St *CBRISNE* BS2 .... 7 M4
Jubilee Wy *YATE/CS* BS37 .... 25 K4
   YATE/CS BS37 .... 34 C2
Julian Cl
   HNLZ/SM/SNYPK/WT BS9 .... 51 F6
Julian Rd *CBATH/BATHN* BA1 ..... 14 E3
   HNLZ/SM/SNYPK/WT BS9 .... 51 C6
Julius Rd *HORF/LLZ* BS7 .... 3 C3
Junction Av *BATHSE* BA2 .... 14 C9 🔢
Junction Rd *BATHSE* BA2 .... 14 C9
   BOAV BA15 .... 114 E7 🔢
   BRSG/KWL/STAPK BS4 .... 8 E5
Juniper Ct *EVILLE/WHL* BS5 .... 4 E5
Juniper Pl *MTN/WRL* BS22 .... 106 A1
Juniper Wy *ALMDB* BS32 .... 30 E1
Jupiter Rd *BRSTK/PCHW* BS34 ... 39 C1
Justice Av *KEYN* BS31 .... 97 F1
Justice Rd *MANG/FISH* BS16 ...... 54 B7
   MANG/FISH BS16 .... 54 A6 🔢
Jutland Rd *AVONM* BS11 .... 36 C7

K

Karen Cl *NAIL* BS48 .... 74 A7
Karen Dr *NAIL* BS48 .... 74 A6
Kathdene Gdns *HORF/LLZ* BS7 ..... 3 M3
Kaynton Md *CBATH/BATHN* BA1... 98 E5
Keates Cl *TRWBR* BA14 .... 125 F5
Keats Rd *RDSTK/MIDN* BA3 ...... 126 C5
Keble Av
   BMSTRD/HC/WWD BS13 .... 77 H6
Keeds La *LGASH* BS41 .... 76 B2
Keedwell Hl *LGASH* BS41 .... 76 B2
Keene's Wy *CLVDN* BS21 .... 70 D1
Keinton Wk *HNBRY/STHM* BS10 .. 38 D6
Kelbra Crs *FRCTL/WBN* BS36 ...... 42 C2
Kellaway Av
   HNBRY/STHM BS10 .... 52 C3 🔢
   RDLND/MONT BS6 .... 52 B4
Kellaway Crs *HORF/LLZ* BS7 .... 52 B3
Kellways *NAIL* BS48 .... 73 K7
Kelston Cl *KEYN* BS31 .... 96 E1
Kelston Gdns
   HNBRY/STHM BS10 .... 52 B1 🔢
   KGWD/HNM BS15 .... 68 E4
Kelston Rd *CBATH/BATHN* BA1 ... 98 B3
   HNBRY/STHM BS10 .... 52 A1
   KEYN BS31 .... 80 D7
   MTN/WRL BS22 .... 106 C1
Kelston Vw *BATHSE* BA2 .... 98 D7
Kelston Wk *MANG/FISH* BS16 .... 54 C5
Kelting Gv *CLVDN* BS21 .... 71 H1
Kemble Cl *KGWD/HNM* BS15 ..... 68 E6
   NAIL BS48 .... 74 A2 🔢
Kemperleye Wy *ALMDB* BS32 .... 40 C1 🔢
Kempe's Cl *LGASH* BS41 .... 76 C1
Kempton Cl *THNB/SVB* BS35 ...... 19 G2 🔢
Kencot Wk
   BMSTRD/HC/WWD BS13 .... 92 C1 🔢
Kendall Gdns *MANG/FISH* BS16 .. 54 D5
Kendall Rd *MANG/FISH* BS16 ..... 54 D5
Kendal Rd *HORF/LLZ* BS7 .... 52 C2
Kendon Dr *HNBRY/STHM* BS10 ... 52 B2
Kendon Wy *HNBRY/STHM* BS10... 52 B1
Kenilworth *YATE/CS* BS37 .... 34 C7
Kenilworth Cl *KEYN* BS31 .... 80 D7
Kenilworth Dr
   OLD/WMLY/WICK BS30 .... 81 H2 🔢
Kenilworth Rd
   RDLND/MONT BS6 .... 2 E8
Kenmare Rd
   BRSG/KWL/STAPK BS4 .... 11 J6
Kenmeade Cl *WNSC* BS25 .... 121 H6
Kenmore Crs *HORF/LLZ* BS7 .... 39 H7
Kenmore Dr *HORF/LLZ* BS7 .... 39 H7
Kenmore Gv *HORF/LLZ* BS7 ..... 39 H7 🔢
Kennard Ri *KGWD/HNM* BS15 ... 68 C3
Kennard Rd *KGWD/HNM* BS15 ... 68 C2
Kennaway Rd *CLVDN* BS21 .... 71 F1
Kenn Cl *WSM* BS23 .... 17 J8
Kennedy Wy *YATE/CS* BS37 .... 34 B6
Kennel Lodge Rd *BMSTR* BS3 ..... 65 C6
Kennet Gdns *BOAV* BA15 .... 123 K1
Kenneth Rd
   BRSG/KWL/STAPK BS4 .... 13 H4
Kennet Pk *BATHSE* BA2 .... 100 D3
Kennet Rd *KEYN* BS31 .... 81 F7
Kennet Wy *THNB/SVB* BS35 .... 19 J5
   TRWBR BA14 .... 125 F3
Kennington Av *HORF/LLZ* BS7 ...... 3 J2
   KGWD/HNM BS15 .... 68 D1 🔢
Kennington Rd
   CBATH/BATHN BA1 .... 98 E5
Kennion Rd *EVILLE/WHL* BS5 .... 68 A3 🔢
Kenn Moor Dr *CLVDN* BS21 .... 71 G2
Kennmoor Rd *CLVDN* BS21 .... 71 K4
Kenn Moor Rd *YTN/CONG* BS49.. 86 D3
Kenn Rd *CLVDN* BS21 .... 59 F7
   EVILLE/WHL BS5 .... 68 A5
Kenn St *CLVDN* BS21 .... 71 H4
Kensal Av *BMSTR* BS3 .... 11 J2
Kensal Rd *BMSTR* BS3 .... 11 J2
Kensington Cl
   THNB/SVB BS35 .... 19 G3 🔢
   TRWBR BA14 .... 125 F4 🔢
Kensington Gdns
   CBATH/BATHN BA1 .... 15 H1
Kensington Pk *EVILLE/WHL* BS5 ... 4 B8

Kensington Park Rd
   BRSG/KWL/STAPK BS4 .... 12 E3
Kensington Pl *CFTN/FAIL* BS8 .... 6 B3
Kensington Rd
   EVILLE/WHL BS5 .... 4 B8
   MANG/FISH BS16 .... 54 D5 🔢
   RDLND/MONT BS6 .... 2 E7
   WSM BS23 .... 17 G8
Kent Av *YATE/CS* BS37 .... 34 C4
Kent Cl *BRSTK/PCHW* BS34 .... 40 C4
Kenton Dr *TRWBR* BA14 .... 125 H5
Kenton Ms
   HNLZ/SM/SNYPK/WT BS9 .... 52 A4
Kent Rd *HORF/LLZ* BS7 .... 3 K3
   YTN/CONG BS49 .... 87 G7
Kents Gn *KGWD/HNM* BS15 ...... 54 E7
Kentshare La
   BLAG/CWMG/WR BS40 .... 91 J6
Kent St *BMSTR* BS3 .... 10 F1 🔢
Kent Wy *MTN/WRL* BS22 .... 106 C1 🔢
Kenwood Cl *TRWBR* BA14 .... 125 H6
Keppel Cl *KEYN* BS31 .... 96 E2 🔢
Kersteman Rd
   RDLND/MONT BS6 .... 3 G4 🔢
Kestrel Cl *BRSTK/PCHW* BS34 .... 29 H7
   THNB/SVB BS35 .... 19 J3 🔢
   YATE/CS BS37 .... 34 C7
Kestrel Dr *MTN/WRL* BS16 .... 56 E5
   MTN/WRL BS22 .... 105 K4
Keswick Wk
   HNBRY/STHM BS10 .... 39 F6 🔢
Ketch Rd *BMSTR* BS3 .... 11 M2
Kettle La *TRWBR* BA14 .... 131 J4
Ketton Cl *TRWBR* BA14 .... 124 C5
Kew Dr *TRWBR* BA14 .... 124 C7 🔢
Kew Rd *WSM* BS23 .... 104 D4
Kewside *MTN/WRL* BS22 .... 105 G1
Kewstoke Rd *BATHSE* BA2 .... 111 K3
   HNLZ/SM/SNYPK/WT BS9 .... 51 C5
   WSM BS23 .... 104 D2
Kew Wk *BRSG/KWL/STAPK* BS4 .. 12 F7
Keyes Pth *MTN/WRL* BS22 ...... 106 A1 🔢
Kielder Dr *MTN/WRL* BS22 ...... 106 A2 🔢
Kilbirnie Rd *HGRV/WHIT* BS14 ... 93 K1
Kilburn St *EVILLE/WHL* BS5 .... 4 D9 🔢
Kildare Rd
   BRSG/KWL/STAPK BS4 .... 11 H6
Kilkenny La *BATHSE* BA2 .... 110 B6
Kilkenny St *CBRISNE* BS2 .... 7 M4
Kilmersdon Rd
   BMSTRD/HC/WWD BS13 .... 77 K7
   RDSTK/MIDN BA3 .... 127 F5
Kilminster Rd *AVONM* BS11 ..... 49 K2 🔢
Kiln Cl *KGWD/HNM* BS15 .... 68 B1
Kilnhurst Cl
   OLD/WMLY/WICK BS30 .... 81 F1
Kilvert Cl *BRSG/KWL/STAPK* BS4... 9 G7
Kimberley Av *MANG/FISH* BS16 .. 55 F2 🔢
Kimberley Cl *MANG/FISH* BS16.... 55 F2 🔢
Kimberley Crs *MANG/FISH* BS16... 54 A2
Kimberley Rd *CLVDN* BS21 .... 70 E1
   KGWD/HNM BS15 .... 68 D1 🔢
   MANG/FISH BS16 .... 54 C4
Kinber Cl *CBATH/BATHN* BA1 ..... 98 D1
King Alfred Wy *BOAV* BA15 ...... 113 F6
King Dick's La *EVILLE/WHL* BS5 ... 9 L1 🔢
King Edward Rd *BATHSE* BA2 ..... 14 B9
Kingfisher Cl *ALMDB* BS32 .... 30 D5 🔢
   THNB/SVB BS35 .... 19 J3 🔢
Kingfisher Dr
   MANG/FISH BS16 .... 53 J3 🔢
   RDSTK/MIDN BA3 .... 126 C5
Kingfisher Rd *MTN/WRL* BS22 .. 106 A5
   YATE/CS BS37 .... 34 D7
King George's Rd *BATHSE* BA2 ... 99 F6
   BMSTRD/HC/WWD BS13 .... 77 H6
King John's Rd
   KGWD/HNM BS15 .... 54 B7
King Rd *BRSG/KWL/STAPK* BS4 .. 12 D7
   WNSC BS25 .... 109 G7
King Road Av *AVONM* BS11 .... 36 B6
Kingrove Crs *YATE/CS* BS37 .... 35 F7
Kingrove La *YATE/CS* BS37 .... 45 F1
Kings Av *KGWD/HNM* BS15 .... 68 B6
   RDLND/MONT BS6 .... 2 E1
Kingscote *YATE/CS* BS37 .... 44 A2
Kingscote Pk *EVILLE/WHL* BS5 ... 68 B4
Kingscourt Cl *HGRV/WHIT* BS14 .. 78 E6
Kingsdown Gv
   CBATH/BATHN BA1 .... 102 A2
Kingsdown Pde
   RDLND/MONT BS6 .... 7 G1
Kingsdown Rd *TRWBR* BA14 .... 130 E2
King's Dr *HORF/LLZ* BS7 .... 52 A4
   KGWD/HNM BS15 .... 68 B6
Kingsfield *BATHSE* BA2 .... 111 F2
   BOAV BA15 .... 114 E6
Kingsfield Cl *BOAV* BA15 .... 114 E7
Kingsfield Grange Rd
   BOAV BA15 .... 115 F7
Kingsfield La *KGWD/HNM* BS15 .. 68 E5
   OLD/WMLY/WICK BS30 .... 68 E6
Kings Gdns *TRWBR* BA14 .... 125 G2
King's Head La
   BMSTRD/HC/WWD BS13 .... 77 G4
Kingshill *NAIL* BS48 .... 73 G1
Kingshill Rd
   BRSG/KWL/STAPK BS4 .... 12 C4
Kingsholme Rd
   KGWD/HNM BS15 .... 68 D1
Kingsholm Rd
   HNBRY/STHM BS10 .... 52 B1
Kingsland Cl *CBRISNE* BS2 .... 8 A4
Kingsland Rd *CBRISNE* BS2 .... 8 A4
Kingsland Road Br *CBRISNE* BS2... 8 A4
King's La *WSM* BS23 .... 16 E2 🔢
Kingsleigh Ct
   KGWD/HNM BS15 .... 69 F3 🔢
Kingsleigh Gdns
   KGWD/HNM BS15 .... 69 F3 🔢
Kingsley Pl *TRWBR* BA14 .... 124 C5 🔢
Kingsley Rd *CLVDN* BS21 .... 71 F1 🔢
   EVILLE/WHL BS5 .... 4 F7
   RDLND/MONT BS6 .... 3 J3

RDSTK/MIDN BA3 .... 126 C4
WSM BS23 .... 116 E3
Kingsmead NAIL BS48 .... 73 G1
Kingsmead North
  CBATH/BATHN BA1 ...... 14 E7
Kingsmead Rd EVILLE/WHL BS5... 68 A1
Kingsmead Sq
  CBATH/BATHN BA1 ..... 14 F6
Kingsmead St
  CBATH/BATHN BA1 ...... 14 F6
Kingsmead Wk
  EVILLE/WHL BS5.......... 68 A1
Kingsmead West
  CBATH/BATHN BA1 ..... 14 E7
Kingsmill
  HNLZ/SM/SNYPK/WT BS9...... 51 F4
King's Parade Av CFTN/FAIL BS8 ... 2 C7
King's Parade Ms CFTN/FAIL BS8 ... 2 C7
Kings Park Av CBRISNE BS2 ...... 8 E5
King Sq CBRISNE BS2 .... 3 H9
King's Sq BRSG/KWL/STAPK BS4 ... 12 E1
  CFTN/FAIL BS8 .... 6 A3
  CLVDN BS21 .... 59 F5
  PTSHD/EG BS20 ...... 46 D5
Kings Sq OLD/WMLY/WICK BS30 .... 81 K3
Kingston Av BOAV BA15 ..... 124 A1
  CLVDN BS21 ...... 59 C7
  KEYN BS31 .... 96 D2
Kingston Cl MANG/FISH BS16 ... 55 C2
Kingston Dr MANG/FISH BS16 ... 55 G2
Kingston La
  BLAG/CWMG/WR BS40 ..... 91 F4
Kingston Rd BMSTR BS3 .... 6 E8
  BOAV BA15 .... 114 E7
  CBATH/BATHN BA1 ..... 15 G7
Kingstree St
  BRSG/KWL/STAPK BS4 .... 8 A9
King St AVONM BS11 ...... 36 B7
  CBRIS/FH BS1 .... 7 G5
  EVILLE/WHL BS5 ...... 4 E8
  KGWD/HNM BS15 .... 68 B2
Kings Wk
  BMSTRD/HC/WWD BS13....... 77 K7
Kingsway BATHSE BA2....... 111 F2
  BRSTK/PCHW BS34 ...... 40 B2
  EVILLE/WHL BS5......... 68 A1
  PTSHD/EG BS20 .... 46 D5
Kingsway Av KGWD/HNM BS15... 68 B2
Kingsway Crs KGWD/HNM BS15 ... 68 B2
Kingswear Rd BMSTR BS3 ...... 11 H5
Kings Weston Av AVONM BS11...... 37 J5
Kings Weston La AVONM BS11...... 36 D4
Kings Weston Rd
  AVONM BS11 .... 38 A6
Kington La THNB/SVB BS35 ...... 18 E4
King William Av CBRIS/FH BS1 ... 7 H5
King William St BMSTR BS3 .... 6 D9
Kinsale Rd HGRV/WHIT BS14...... 12 E9
Kinvara Rd
  BRSG/KWL/STAPK BS4........ 11 K7
Kipling Av BATHSE BA2 .... 111 J1
Kipling Rd HORF/LLZ BS7 .... 40 A7
  RDSTK/MIDN BA3 ...... 126 D5
  WSM BS23 .... 117 F3
Kirkby Rd AVONM BS11 ...... 37 H7
Kirtlington Rd EVILLE/WHL BS5... 4 D3
Kite Hay Cl MANG/FISH BS16 ..... 53 J4
Kites Cl ALMDB BS32 .... 30 B5
Kitley Hl RDSTK/MIDN BA3 ..... 126 D1
Knap La WUE GL12 .... 21 J2
Knapp Rd THNB/SVB BS35 ...... 20 A3
Knapps Cl WNSC BS25 .... 120 C6
Knapps Dr WNSC BS25 .... 120 C6
Knapps La EVILLE/WHL BS5 ...... 5 K6
The Knapp YATE/CS BS37 ...... 34 C2
The Knap TRWBR BA14 .... 125 J3
Knightcott Gdns BNWL BS29 ... 119 G3
Knightcott Pk BNWL BS29 ...... 119 H3
Knightcott Rd BNWL BS29 ...... 119 G3
  CFTN/FAIL BS8 .... 64 B2
Knighton Rd HNBRY/STHM BS10... 38 D7
Knights Cl MTN/WRL BS22 ..... 84 B7
Knightstone Cswy WSM BS23 ... 16 A1
Knightstone Rd WSM BS23 ...... 16 B1
Knightwood Rd
  BRSTK/PCHW BS34 .... 40 E3
Knobsbury La
  RDSTK/MIDN BA3 .... 127 K5
Knole Cl ALMDB BS32 .... 29 J3
Knole La HNBRY/STHM BS10 ..... 38 D5
Knole Pk ALMDB BS32 .... 29 J4
Knoll Hl
  HNLZ/SM/SNYPK/WT BS9...... 51 F6
The Knoll PTSHD/EG BS20 ...... 47 H2
Knovill Cl AVONM BS11 .... 37 J7
Knowle Rd
  BRSG/KWL/STAPK BS4........ 11 M1
Knowles Rd CLVDN BS21 ...... 70 E1
Knowsley Rd MANG/FISH BS16 ... 5 J3
Kyght Cl KGWD/HNM BS15 ...... 69 G2
Kylross Av HGRV/WHIT BS14...... 79 F6
Kynges Mill Cl MANG/FISH BS16 ... 54 A2

L

The Labbott KEYN BS31........ 80 E6
Laburnum Cl
  RDSTK/MIDN BA3 .... 126 A5
Laburnum Ct WSM BS23 ...... 17 L3
Laburnum Gv MANG/FISH BS16 ... 54 B5
  RDSTK/MIDN BA3 ...... 126 A5
  TRWBR BA14 .... 130 D1
Laburnum Rd
  KGWD/HNM BS15 .... 68 C5
  WSM BS23 .... 17 K3
Lacey Rd HGRV/WHIT BS14 ..... 79 J1
Lacock Dr
  OLD/WMLY/WICK BS30 ..... 69 F5
Ladd Cl KGWD/HNM BS15 ...... 69 F3
Ladden Ct THNB/SVB BS35 ...... 19 H5
Ladies Mile
  HNLZ/SM/SNYPK/WT BS9...... 65 H1
Ladman Gv HGRV/WHIT BS14...... 79 J5
Ladman Rd HGRV/WHIT BS14...... 79 J6

Ladycroft CLVDN BS21 ...... 70 D2
Ladye Bay CLVDN BS21 ...... 59 F4
Ladye Wake MTN/WRL BS22 ..... 106 A1
Ladymead La
  BLAG/CWMG/WR BS40 ..... 109 J7
  WNSC BS25 .... 121 J2
Ladysmith Rd
  RDLND/MONT BS6 .... 2 C2
Laggan Gdns CBATH/BATHN BA1 ... 99 H3
Lakemead Gv
  BMSTRD/HC/WWD BS13....... 77 H5
Lake Rd HNBRY/STHM BS10 ..... 52 A2
  PTSHD/EG BS20 .... 47 G3
Lakeside MANG/FISH BS16 ...... 5 K4
Lake View Rd EVILLE/WHL BS5... 5 H9
Lakewood Crs
  HNBRY/STHM BS10 ...... 51 K1
Lakewood Rd
  HNBRY/STHM BS10 ...... 51 K1
Lamb Ale Gn TRWBR BA14 ..... 131 G1
Lambert Cl
  BRSG/KWL/STAPK BS4 .... 78 B5
Lambley Rd EVILLE/WHL BS5 ...... 9 K1
Lambourne Wy PTSHD/EG BS20 ... 47 K5
Lambourn Rd KEYN BS31 .... 81 G7
Lambridge Ms
  CBATH/BATHN BA1 .... 100 B3
Lambridge St
  CBATH/BATHN BA1 .... 100 B3
Lambrok Cl TRWBR BA14 .... 130 B1
Lambrok Rd TRWBR BA14 ...... 130 B1
Lamb St CBRISNE BS2 .... 7 M2
Lamord Ga BRSTK/PCHW BS34..... 40 D3
Lampeter Rd
  HNLZ/SM/SNYPK/WT BS9...... 51 H2
Lampley Rd CLVDN BS21 ...... 86 B2
Lampton Av
  BMSTRD/HC/WWD BS13....... 93 H1
Lampton Gv
  BMSTRD/HC/WWD BS13....... 93 H1
Lampton Rd LGASH BS41 ...... 76 B2
Lanaway Rd MANG/FISH BS16 ... 54 B3
Lancashire Rd HORF/LLZ BS7 ... 3 K3
Lancaster Cl
  BRSTK/PCHW BS34 .... 40 C4
Lancaster Rd CBRISNE BS2 ...... 4 B6
  YATE/CS BS37 .... 34 B4
Lancaster St EVILLE/WHL BS5..... 8 F3
Landemann Circ WSM BS23 ..... 104 D4
Landemann Pth WSM BS23 ..... 16 F1
Landseer Av HORF/LLZ BS7 ...... 53 F2
Landseer Cl MTN/WRL BS22 ... 106 A2
Landseer Rd BATHSE BA2 ...... 98 E6
The Land FRCTL/WBN BS36 ..... 42 D1
Lanercost Rd
  HNBRY/STHM BS10 ...... 39 F6
Lanesborough Ri
  HGRV/WHIT BS14 .... 79 H4
The Lane THNB/SVB BS35 ...... 28 C5
Laneys Dro OMX/HUT/LCK BS24 ... 117 K1
Langdale Rd MANG/FISH BS16 ... 5 L2
Langdon Rd BATHSE BA2 ...... 110 E1
Langfield Cl
  HNBRY/STHM BS10 ...... 38 C5
Langford Rd
  BMSTRD/HC/WWD BS13....... 77 H3
  TRWBR BA14 .... 124 E4
  WSM BS23 .... 17 J4
Langford Wy KGWD/HNM BS15... 68 E3
Langham Pl RDSTK/MIDN BA3 ... 129 F6
Langham Rd
  BRSG/KWL/STAPK BS4........ 12 D3
Langhill Av
  BRSG/KWL/STAPK BS4........ 78 B4
Langley Crs BMSTR BS3 .... 77 G2
Langley Mow
  MANG/FISH BS16 .... 55 H2
Langley Rd TRWBR BA14 ...... 130 E2
Langport Gdns NAIL BS48 ...... 73 J3
Langport Rd WSM BS23 .... 16 F6
Langthorn Cl FRCTL/WBN BS36 ... 42 C1
Langton Court Rd
  BRSG/KWL/STAPK BS4........ 9 H6
Langton Pk BMSTR BS3 .... 6 E9
Langton Rd
  BRSG/KWL/STAPK BS4........ 9 H7
Langton Wy
  BRSG/KWL/STAPK BS4........ 9 K4
Lansdown CI CBATH/BATHN BA1 ... 14 F2
Lansdown Cl KGWD/HNM BS15 ... 54 D7
  TRWBR BA14 .... 124 D7
Lansdown Gv
  CBATH/BATHN BA1 .... 14 F2
Lansdown Hts
  CBATH/BATHN BA1 .... 99 J3
Lansdown La CBATH/BATHN BA1... 98 E1
Lansdown Pk
  CBATH/BATHN BA1 .... 99 H1
Lansdown Pl East
  CBATH/BATHN BA1 .... 14 E2
Lansdown Rd
  CBATH/BATHN BA1 .... 14 F3
  CFTN/FAIL BS8 .... 6 A2
  EVILLE/WHL BS5......... 4 B8
  KEYN BS31 .... 97 F1
  KGWD/HNM BS15 .... 54 D7
  MANG/FISH BS16 .... 56 B3
  RDLND/MONT BS6 .... 2 E7
Lansdown Ter
  RDLND/MONT BS6 .... 52 B4
Lansdown Vw BATHSE BA2 ..... 99 F7
  KGWD/HNM BS15 .... 68 E2
Lanthony Cl
  OMX/HUT/LCK BS24 ...... 106 B5
Lapahams Ct
  OLD/WMLY/WICK BS30 ..... 69 F6
Lapwing Cl ALMDB BS32 ...... 30 C5
Lapwing Gdns
  MANG/FISH BS16 .... 53 K3
  MTN/WRL BS22 .... 106 A4
Larch Cl BLAG/CWMG/WR BS40 ... 121 K1
  NAIL BS48 .... 74 A1
Larch Ct RDSTK/MIDN BA3 ..... 126 B5
Larch Gv TRWBR BA14 ...... 130 D1
Larchgrove Crs MTN/WRL BS22... 106 A4

Larch Wy BRSTK/PCHW BS34 ..... 39 H1
Lark Cl RDSTK/MIDN BA3 ...... 126 C5
Lark Down TRWBR BA14 ...... 125 C5
Larkfield FRCTL/WBN BS36 ...... 42 E1
Larkhall Pl CBATH/BATHN BA1 ... 100 B2
Larkhill Rd OMX/HUT/LCK BS24 ... 106 C7
Lark Rd MTN/WRL BS22 .... 106 A4
Lark's Fld MANG/FISH BS16 ..... 53 J4
Lark's La YATE/CS BS37 ...... 24 C7
Larksleaze Rd
  OLD/WMLY/WICK BS30 ..... 80 E1
Larkspur Cl THNB/SVB BS35 ...... 19 J3
Lasbury Gv
  BMSTRD/HC/WWD BS13....... 78 A6
Late Broads BOAV BA15 .... 113 J6
Latimer Cl BRSG/KWL/STAPK BS4... 9 K9
Latteridge La THNB/SVB BS35 ..... 24 B5
Latteridge Rd YATE/CS BS37 ..... 32 E3
Latton Rd HORF/LLZ BS7 .... 52 D1
Launceston Av
  KGWD/HNM BS15 .... 68 B5
Launceston Rd
  KGWD/HNM BS15 .... 68 B1
Laurel Dr NAIL BS48 .... 73 K1
  WSM BS23 .... 116 D4
Laurel Gdns YTN/CONG BS49 ..... 86 E3
Laurel Gv TRWBR BA14 .... 130 E1
The Laurels BOAV BA15 ...... 123 F3
  HNBRY/STHM BS10 ...... 38 D2
  MANG/FISH BS16 .... 55 C3
Laurel St KGWD/HNM BS15 ...... 68 D2
Laurel Ter YTN/CONG BS49 ..... 86 E3
Laurie Crs
  HNLZ/SM/SNYPK/WT BS9...... 52 B3
Laurie Lee Ct
  OLD/WMLY/WICK BS30 ..... 69 G5
  TRWBR BA14 .... 125 G2
Lavender Cl THNB/SVB BS35 ..... 19 J4
Lavender Wy ALMDB BS32 ..... 40 E1
Lavenham Rd YATE/CS BS37 ..... 33 J5
Lavers Cl KGWD/HNM BS15 ..... 68 E4
Lavington Cl CLVDN BS21 ...... 70 C2
Lavington Rd EVILLE/WHL BS5... 68 B4
Lawford Av BRSTK/PCHW BS34 ... 40 B2
Lawfords Ga CBRISNE BS2 ...... 7 M2
Lawn Av MANG/FISH BS16 ...... 54 B4
Lawn Rd MANG/FISH BS16 ...... 54 B4
Lawns Rd YATE/CS BS37 ...... 34 B4
The Lawns MTN/WRL BS22 ..... 106 C2
  YTN/CONG BS49 .... 86 D3
Lawnwood Rd
  EVILLE/WHL BS5......... 4 D9
Lawrence Av EVILLE/WHL BS5 ..... 4 D7
Lawrence Cl KGWD/HNM BS15... 55 C7
Lawrence Close Ms
  MTN/WRL BS22 .... 105 K3
Lawrence Dr YATE/CS BS37...... 33 J5
Lawrence Gv
  HNLZ/SM/SNYPK/WT BS9...... 51 K4
Lawrence Hl CBRISNE BS2 ...... 8 A2
Lawrence Weston Rd
  AVONM BS11 .... 37 K7
Lawson Cl KEYN BS31 .... 96 D3
Laxey Rd HORF/LLZ BS7 .... 52 D2
Lays Dr KEYN BS31 .... 80 C7
Leach Cl CLVDN BS21 .... 71 F2
Leafield Pl TRWBR BA14 ...... 124 B5
Leafy Wy OMX/HUT/LCK BS24 ... 118 D1
Lea Grove Rd CLVDN BS21 ..... 58 E6
Leaholme Gdns
  HGRV/WHIT BS14 .... 93 K1
Leaman Cl YATE/CS BS37 ...... 34 E6
Leap Ga TRWBR BA14....... 125 J5
Leap V MANG/FISH BS16....... 55 F1
Leap Valley Crs MANG/FISH BS16... 55 F1
The Leaze RDSTK/MIDN BA3..... 126 E5
  RDSTK/MIDN BA3 .... 128 C7
  YATE/CS BS37 .... 34 A5
Leda Av HGRV/WHIT BS14 ..... 12 B9
Ledbury Rd MANG/FISH BS16..... 54 C5
Leechpool Wy YATE/CS BS37 ... 34 B2
Lee Cl BRSTK/PCHW BS34 ...... 29 J7
Leedham Rd
  OMX/HUT/LCK BS24 ...... 118 D1
Leeming Wy AVONM BS11...... 49 J1
Lees Hl KGWD/HNM BS15 ...... 54 E7
Leeside PTSHD/EG BS20 ...... 47 G4
Lees La OLD/WMLY/WICK BS30... 69 K5
Leewood Rd WSM BS23 ...... 104 D4
Leicester Sq MANG/FISH BS16 .. 54 D6
Leicester St BMSTR BS3 ...... 7 G9
Leicester Wk
  BRSG/KWL/STAPK BS4........ 9 L6
Leigh Cl CBATH/BATHN BA1...... 99 K2
Leigh La YATE/CS BS37 ...... 43 J7
Leigh Park Rd BOAV BA15 ...... 114 E5
Leigh Rd BOAV BA15......... 115 F4
  CFTN/FAIL BS8 .... 2 B9
  TRWBR BA14 .... 115 K3
Leigh St BMSTR BS3 .... 6 B8
Leighton Crs
  OMX/HUT/LCK BS24 ...... 117 F6
Leighton Rd BMSTR BS3 ...... 6 D8
  BRSG/KWL/STAPK BS4........ 12 D3
  CBATH/BATHN BA1 .... 98 D1
Leigh View Rd PTSHD/EG BS20... 47 H2
Leighwood Dr NAIL BS48 ...... 73 F2
Leinster Av
  BRSG/KWL/STAPK BS4........ 11 G9
Lemon La CBRISNE BS2 .... 3 K9
Lena Av EVILLE/WHL BS5...... 4 F8
Lena St EVILLE/WHL BS5 ...... 4 D8
Lenover Gdns
  BMSTRD/HC/WWD BS13....... 77 K7
Leonard La CBRIS/FH BS1 ...... 7 C3
Leonard Rd EVILLE/WHL BS5..... 8 D1
Leonards Av EVILLE/WHL BS5..... 4 F8
Leopold Rd RDLND/MONT BS6 ..... 3 K1
Leslie Ri BOAV BA15 .... 123 F3
Lester Dr MTN/WRL BS22 ..... 106 B2
Lewington Rd MANG/FISH BS16... 54 C5
Lewins Md CBRIS/FH BS1 ...... 7 G2
Lewin St EVILLE/WHL BS5 ...... 9 H1
Lewis Cl OLD/WMLY/WICK BS30 ... 69 K6
Lewisham Gv WSM BS23 ...... 17 J3
Lewis Rd
  BMSTRD/HC/WWD BS13....... 10 B8

Lewis St CBRISNE BS2 .... 8 B6
Lewton La FRCTL/WBN BS36 ..... 41 K1
Leyland Wk
  BMSTRD/HC/WWD BS13....... 77 H7
The Leys CLVDN BS21 .... 70 D2
Leyton Vls RDLND/MONT BS6..... 2 D6
Lichfield Rd
  BRSG/KWL/STAPK BS4........ 9 K5
Liddington Wy TRWBR BA14 ... 130 E2
Lilac Cl HNBRY/STHM BS10 ...... 39 F7
Lilac Gv TRWBR BA14 ...... 130 C2
Lilac Ter RDSTK/MIDN BA3 ..... 126 D3
Lilac Wy MTN/WRL BS22 ...... 84 B7
Lillian St EVILLE/WHL BS5 ...... 8 F1
Lillington Cl RDSTK/MIDN BA3 ... 127 J3
Lillington Rd RDSTK/MIDN BA3 ... 127 J4
Lilliput Av YATE/CS BS37 ...... 34 C7
Lilliput Ct YATE/CS BS37 ...... 34 D7
Lilstock Rd HORF/LLZ BS7 ...... 3 M2
Lilymead Av
  BRSG/KWL/STAPK BS4........ 11 M1
Lime Cl HNBRY/STHM BS10 ...... 38 E5
  MTN/WRL BS22 .... 106 B4
  OMX/HUT/LCK BS24 ...... 118 C2
Lime Cft YATE/CS BS37 ...... 34 D3
Lime Gv BATHSE BA2 .... 15 J7
  THNB/SVB BS35 .... 22 E1
Lime Grove Gdns BATHSE BA2 ... 15 K7
Lime Kiln Cl BRSTK/PCHW BS34 ... 40 C6
Lime Kiln Gdns ALMDB BS32 .... 30 C4
Limekiln La BATHSE BA2 ...... 112 E1
Lime Kiln La CLVDN BS21 ...... 59 F7
Limekiln Rd WUE GL12 ...... 25 K4
Limerick Rd RDLND/MONT BS6 .... 2 F5
Lime Rd BMSTR BS3 .... 6 C9
  KGWD/HNM BS15 .... 68 A5
Limestone Link BATHSE BA2 ..... 101 F2
Lime Ter RDSTK/MIDN BA3 ..... 126 E4
Lime Tree Gv PTSHD/EG BS20... 49 K6
Limpley Stoke Rd BOAV BA15 ... 113 J7
Lincoln Cl KEYN BS31 .... 80 C7
Lincoln St EVILLE/WHL BS5 ...... 8 D3
Lincombe Av MANG/FISH BS16 ... 54 C4
Lincombe Rd MANG/FISH BS16 ... 54 B2
  RDSTK/MIDN BA3 .... 126 D5
Linden Av WSM BS23 .... 17 L2
Linden Cl FRCTL/WBN BS36 ..... 41 K2
  KGWD/HNM BS15 .... 68 C1
  RDSTK/MIDN BA3 .... 127 F5
Linden Dr ALMDB BS32 ...... 30 C7
Linden Gdns CBATH/BATHN BA1 ... 14 A2
Linden Pl TRWBR BA14 .... 124 D5
Linden Rd CLVDN BS21 ...... 59 F6
  RDLND/MONT BS6 .... 2 D3
The Lindens MTN/WRL BS22 ... 105 K1
Lindrea St BMSTR BS3 .... 10 D1
Lindsay Rd HORF/LLZ BS7...... 4 B1
Lindsey Cl PTSHD/EG BS20 ..... 46 D5
Linemere Cl NAIL BS48 ...... 74 D5
Lines Wy HGRV/WHIT BS14...... 94 B1
Lingfield Pk FRCTL/WBN BS36 ... 42 A1
Link La BOAV BA15 .... 102 A4
Link Rd BRSTK/PCHW BS34 ...... 39 J5
  NAIL BS48 .... 73 K1
  PTSHD/EG BS20 .... 47 F3
  YATE/CS BS37 .... 34 C6
Linkside CLVDN BS21 ...... 59 G4
Links Rd WSM BS23 .... 116 B4
Linley Cl BATHSE BA2 ...... 98 D7
The Linleys CBATH/BATHN BA1 ... 99 F3
Linnell Cl BRSTK/PCHW BS34 ..... 29 H7
  MTN/WRL BS22 .... 105 K4
Linnet Wy RDSTK/MIDN BA3 ..... 126 C5
Lintern Crs
  OLD/WMLY/WICK BS30 ..... 69 G4
Lintham Dr KGWD/HNM BS15..... 69 F4
Lion Cl NAIL BS48 .... 73 G1
Lippiatt La WNSC BS25 ...... 121 J6
Lisburn Rd
  BRSG/KWL/STAPK BS4........ 11 J4
Lisle Rd MTN/WRL BS22 .... 106 C1
Lister Gv BOAV BA15 .... 123 F3
Litfield Rd CFTN/FAIL BS8 ..... 65 H2
Little Ann St CBRISNE BS2 ...... 7 M4
Little Birch Cft HGRV/WHIT BS14 ... 93 K1
Little Bishop St CBRISNE BS2 ..... 3 K9
Little Caroline Pl
  CFTN/FAIL BS8 .... 65 H5
Little Common TRWBR BA14 ... 131 F4
Littledean YATE/CS BS37 ...... 34 A2
Little Dowles
  OLD/WMLY/WICK BS30 ..... 69 G6
Littlefields Av BNWL BS29 ..... 119 H3
Little George St CBRISNE BS2 ..... 7 M1
  WSM BS23 .... 16 F3
Little Halt PTSHD/EG BS20 ..... 46 C5
Little Ham CLVDN BS21 ...... 70 D2
Little Hayes MANG/FISH BS16 ... 54 B3
Little Headley Cl
  BMSTRD/HC/WWD BS13....... 77 K4
Little King St CBRIS/FH BS1 ...... 7 H5
Little Md AVONM BS11 .... 37 J7
Little Mead
  OMX/HUT/LCK BS24 ...... 117 K3
Little Meadow ALMDB BS32 ..... 40 E1
Little Meadow End NAIL BS48 ... 73 J3
Little Orch WSM BS23 .... 116 C5
Little Paradise BMSTR BS3 ...... 7 G9
Little Parr Cl MANG/FISH BS16 ... 53 G4
Little Paul St CBRISNE BS2 ...... 2 F9
Little Stanhope St
  CBATH/BATHN BA1 .... 14 D6
Little Stoke La
  BRSTK/PCHW BS34 .... 40 B1
Little Stoke Rd
  HNLZ/SM/SNYPK/WT BS9...... 51 G5
Little Withey Md
  HNLZ/SM/SNYPK/WT BS9...... 51 H3
Littleton La YTN/CONG BS49..... 94 A1
Littlewood La YTN/CONG BS49... 88 A2
Livingstone Rd BATHSE BA2 ..... 14 A8

Llewellyn Wy
  MTN/WRL BS22 .... 106 C2
Lockemor Rd
  BMSTRD/HC/WWD BS13....... 78 D7
Lockeridge Cl TRWBR BA14 .... 131 F2
Lock Gdns
  BMSTRD/HC/WWD BS13....... 77 G4
Locking Head Dro
  OMX/HUT/LCK BS24 ...... 106 A7
Locking Moor Rd
  MTN/WRL BS22 .... 105 H5
Locking Rd MTN/WRL BS22 ..... 105 J5
  WSM BS23 .... 16 F3
Lockingwell Rd KEYN BS31 ..... 80 D6
Lockleaze Rd HORF/LLZ BS7 ..... 52 E3
Locksbrook Rd
  CBATH/BATHN BA1 .... 98 E6
  MTN/WRL BS22 .... 84 C7
Loddon Wy BOAV BA15 ...... 124 A1
Lodge Cl YTN/CONG BS49 ...... 86 E4
Lodge Dr LGASH BS41 .... 76 D1
  OLD/WMLY/WICK BS30 ..... 81 J1
  WSM BS23 .... 105 H4
Lodge Gdns BATHSE BA2 ...... 111 G4
Lodge Hl KGWD/HNM BS15...... 54 A7
Lodge La NAIL BS48 .... 62 A7
Lodore Rd KGWD/HNM BS15 ..... 5 L3
Lodway PTSHD/EG BS20 ...... 49 H5
Lodway Cl PTSHD/EG BS20 ..... 49 J5
Lodway Gdns PTSHD/EG BS20 ... 49 J5
Lodway Rd
  BRSG/KWL/STAPK BS4........ 12 E3
Logan Rd HORF/LLZ BS7 ...... 3 G3
Logus Ct
  OLD/WMLY/WICK BS30 ..... 69 F6
Lombard St BMSTR BS3 ...... 7 G9
Lombardy Cl MTN/WRL BS22 ... 105 K5
Lomond Rd HORF/LLZ BS7 ...... 39 J7
London Rd CBATH/BATHN BA1 ... 15 G3
  CBRISNE BS2 .... 3 M8
  OLD/WMLY/WICK BS30 ..... 69 J3
London Rd East
  CBATH/BATHN BA1 .... 101 F1
London Rd West
  CBATH/BATHN BA1 .... 100 C2
London St KGWD/HNM BS15 ..... 68 D2
Longacre CLVDN BS21 .... 70 D3
Longacre Rd HGRV/WHIT BS14...... 93 K1
Long Acres Cl
  HNLZ/SM/SNYPK/WT BS9...... 51 F2
Long Ashton Rd LGASH BS41..... 76 C2
Long Av CLVDN BS21 .... 70 D1
Long Barnaby
  RDSTK/MIDN BA3 .... 126 B3
Long Beach Rd
  OLD/WMLY/WICK BS30 ..... 81 G1
Long Cl ALMDB BS32 .... 40 D2
  MANG/FISH BS16 .... 54 B5
Long Cft YATE/CS BS37 ...... 34 A2
Long Cross AVONM BS11 ...... 50 E1
  BLAG/CWMG/WR BS40 ..... 90 B5
Longden Rd MANG/FISH BS16 ... 55 G1
Longdown Dr
  MTN/WRL BS22 .... 106 C1
Long Eaton Dr HGRV/WHIT BS14 ... 12 D8
Longfellow Av BATHSE BA2 ..... 111 J1
Longfellow Rd
  BATHSE BA2 .... 126 D4
Longfield Rd HORF/LLZ BS7 ..... 3 J3
  TRWBR BA14 .... 125 F7
Longford YATE/CS BS37 ...... 33 K7
Longford Av HNBRY/STHM BS10... 52 B1
Long Handstones
  OLD/WMLY/WICK BS30 ..... 69 G6
Long Hay Cl BATHSE BA2 ...... 98 E7
Long La BLAG/CWMG/WR BS40 ... 90 C6
  NAIL BS48 .... 89 H2
Longleat Cl
  HNLZ/SM/SNYPK/WT BS9...... 52 A4
Longleaze Gdns
  OMX/HUT/LCK BS24 ...... 118 A3
Long Md YATE/CS BS37 ...... 34 B2
Longmead Av HORF/LLZ BS7 ..... 52 B4
Long Meadow MANG/FISH BS16... 53 H4
Longmeadow Rd KEYN BS31 ..... 80 C7
Longmoor Rd BMSTR BS3 ...... 10 B3
Longney Pl BRSTK/PCHW BS34 ... 29 J6
Longreach Gv HGRV/WHIT BS14 ... 79 H4
Long Rd MANG/FISH BS16 ...... 55 G4
Long Rw CBRIS/FH BS1 ...... 7 J5
Longs Dr YATE/CS BS37 ...... 33 K4
  YATE/CS BS37 .... 34 A5
Longsplatt COR/BOX SN13 ..... 102 D1
Longton Grove Rd WSM BS23 ... 16 E1
Longway Av HGRV/WHIT BS14...... 78 D7
Longwood
  BRSG/KWL/STAPK BS4........ 80 A1
Longwood La CFTN/FAIL BS8 ..... 64 A6
Lonsdale Av WSM BS23 ...... 17 H8
Lorain Wk HNBRY/STHM BS10 ... 38 C6
Lorton Rd HNBRY/STHM BS10 ... 38 C6
Lotts' Av NAIL BS48 .... 74 B6
Louisa St CBRISNE BS2 ...... 7 M4
Louise Av MANG/FISH BS16 ..... 55 G4
Love La YATE/CS BS37 ...... 34 D7
  YATE/CS BS37 .... 34 D3
Lovelinch Gdns LGASH BS41 ..... 76 B2
Lovell Av
  OLD/WMLY/WICK BS30 ..... 69 K6
Lovell's Hl KGWD/HNM BS15 ..... 68 B5
Loveringe Cl HNBRY/STHM BS10 ... 38 C4
Loves La TRWBR BA14 .... 123 J7
Lowbourne HGRV/WHIT BS14...... 78 D5
Lower Alma St TRWBR BA14 ... 125 G6
Lower Ashley Rd CBRISNE BS2...... 3 M7
  EVILLE/WHL BS5......... 4 A7
Lower Borough Walls
  CBATH/BATHN BA1 .... 14 F7
Lower Bristol Rd BATHSE BA2 ..... 14 D7

BATHSE BA2 .... 98 C5
Lower Castle St *CBRIS/FH* BS1 ..... 7 K2
Lower Chapel La
FRCTL/WBN BS36 .... 42 D1
Lower Chapel Rd
KGWD/HNM BS15 .... 68 C5 ②
Lower Cheltenham Pl
RDLND/MONT BS6 .... 3 L7
Lower Church La *CBRISNE* BS2 .... 6 F3
Lower Church Rd *WSM* BS23 .... 16 D1
Lower Claverham
YTN/CONG BS49 .... 87 J1
Lower Clifton Hl *CFTN/FAIL* BS8 .... 6 C4
Lower Cock Rd
KGWD/HNM BS15 .... 69 F3
Lower College St *CBRIS/FH* BS1 .. 6 E5 ⑤
Lower Ct *TRWBR* BA14............ 125 F4
Lower Court Rd *ALMDB* BS32 ..... 29 K2
Lower Down Rd *PTSHD/EG* BS20... 47 F4
Lower Fallow Cl
HGRV/WHIT BS14 .... 93 J1 ①
Lower Gay St *CBRISNE* BS2 .... 3 H9 ②
Lower Grove Rd *MANG/FISH* BS16.. 5 K2
Lower Guinea St *CBRIS/FH* BS1 ... 7 H7
Lower Hanham Rd
KGWD/HNM BS15 .... 68 C5
Lower Hedgemead Rd
CBATH/BATHN BA1 .... 15 G3
Lower High St *AVONM* BS11 .... 49 K1
Lower House Crs
BRSTK/PCHW BS34 .... 40 A4
Lower Kingsdown Rd
CBATH/BATHN BA1 .... 102 A1
Lower Knole La
HNBRY/STHM BS10 .... 38 C5
Lower Knowles Rd
CLVDN BS21 .... 70 E1 ⑤
Lower Lamb St *CBRIS/FH* BS1 ...... 6 A6
Lower Linden Rd *CLVDN* BS21 ..... 59 F7
Lower Maudlin St
CBRIS BS1 .... 7 H2 ⑧
Lower Moor Rd *YATE/CS* BS37 .... 34 B3
Lower Norton La
MTN/WRL BS22 .... 105 G1
Lower Oldfield Pk *BATHSE* BA2 .... 14 C8
Lower Parade Ground Rd
OMX/HUT/LCK BS24 .... 118 C1
Lower Park Rw *CBRIS/FH* BS1 ... 7 G3 ②
Lower Queen's *CLVDN* BS21 .... 59 F7 ①
Lower Redland Rd
RDLND/MONT BS6 .... 2 C6
Lower Sidney St *BMSTR* BS3 .... 6 B8
Lower Station Approach Rd
CBRIS/FH BS1 .... 7 L6 ④
Lower Stoke *BATHSE* BA2 .... 113 F6
RDSTK/MIDN BA3 .... 113 F7
Lower Stone Cl
FRCTL/WBN BS36 .... 32 D7
Lower St *RDSTK/MIDN* BA3........ 128 E7
Lower Strode Rd *CLVDN* BS21 ..... 70 C4
Lower Tockington Rd *ALMDB* BS32 22 A6
Lowlis Cl *HNBRY/STHM* BS10 ..... 38 C5
Lowmead *TRWBR* BA14.......... 125 F1
Lowther Rd *HNBRY/STHM* BS10 .. 39 F6 ③
Loxley Gdns *BATHSE* BA2 .... 111 F1
Loxton Dr *BATHSE* BA2 .... 98 E6
Loxton Rd *WSM* BS23 .... 116 E3
Loxton Sq *HGRV/WHIT* BS14 ...... 78 E5
Lucas Cl *BRSG/KWL/STAPK* BS4... 13 H7
Luccombe Hl *RDLND/MONT* BS6 .... 2 D5
Luckington Rd *HORF/LLZ* BS7 ..... 52 C1
Lucklands Rd *CBATH/BATHN* BA1... 99 F3
Luckley Av
BMSTRD/HC/WWD BS13 ..... 78 A3 ①
Luckwell Rd *BMSTR* BS3 .... 10 C2
Lucky La *BMSTR* BS3 .... 7 G8
Ludlow Cl *CBRISNE* BS2 .... 3 L8
KEYN BS31 .... 80 D6
OLD/WMLY/WICK BS30 .... 81 H1
Ludlow Rd *HORF/LLZ* BS7 .... 52 E2
Ludwell Cl *FRCTL/WBN* BS36 ..... 41 J3 ①
Lullington Rd
BRSG/KWL/STAPK BS4... 12 D3
Lulsgate Rd
BMSTRD/HC/WWD BS13 ..... 10 B7
Lulworth Crs *MANG/FISH* BS16..... 55 F1
Lulworth Rd *KEYN* BS31 .... 80 E7
Lurgan Wk
BRSG/KWL/STAPK BS4... 11 H5
Lux Furlong
HNLZ/SM/SNYPK/WT BS9 ..... 50 D2
Luxton St *EVILLE/WHL* BS5 .... 4 D9
Lychgate Pk
OMX/HUT/LCK BS24 .... 118 B2
Lydbrook Cl *YATE/CS* BS37 ..... 34 A7 ②
Lyddington Rd *HORF/LLZ* BS7 .... 39 H7
Lyddon Rd *MTN/WRL* BS22 ...... 106 C2
Lydford Wk *BMSTR* BS3 .... 10 F4
Lydiard Cft *KGWD/HNM* BS15 ..... 68 C6
Lydiard Wy *TRWBR* BA14......... 131 F2
Lydney Rd *HNBRY/STHM* BS10.... 52 B2
MANG/FISH BS16 .... 54 E5
Lydstep Ter *BMSTR* BS3 .... 6 E9
Lyefield Rd *MTN/WRL* BS22.... 105 K1
Lye Md *BLAG/CWMG/WR* BS40 ... 91 H6
The Lyes *YTN/CONG* BS49 .... 109 G2
Lyme Gdns *CBATH/BATHN* BA1.. 98 E5 ③
Lyme Rd *CBATH/BATHN* BA1....... 98 E5
Lymore Av *BATHSE* BA2 .... 99 F7
Lymore Gdns *BATHSE* BA2 .... 99 F7
Lymore Ter *BATHSE* BA2 .... 111 F1
Lympsham Gn *BATHSE* BA2 ...... 111 C4
Lynbrook *LGASH* BS41 .... 76 B2
Lynbrook La *BATHSE* BA2 .... 99 F7
Lynch Cl *MTN/WRL* BS22 .... 106 A2 ⑦
Lynch Ct
OLD/WMLY/WICK BS30 ... 69 F6 ⑬
Lynch Crs *WNSC* BS25........... 120 C7
Lynchmead *WNSC* BS25 .... 120 C7
The Lynch *WNSC* BS25 .... 120 C7
Lyncombe Hl *BATHSE* BA2 .... 15 H9
Lyncombe Vale Rd *BATHSE* BA2 .. 111 K2
Lyncombe Wk
MANG/FISH BS16 .... 54 B7 ②
Lyndale Av
HNLZ/SM/SNYPK/WT BS9........ 50 E4

Lyndale Rd *EVILLE/WHL* BS5 .... 9 G1
YATE/CS BS37 .... 34 A6
Lynde Cl
BMSTRD/HC/WWD BS13 ..... 77 K7
Lyndhurst Rd *BATHSE* BA2 .... 99 F6
HNLZ/SM/SNYPK/WT BS9 ..... 51 H2
KEYN BS31 .... 96 A1
RDSTK/MIDN BA3 .... 126 C5 ③
WSM BS23 .... 18 F8
Lyneham Wy *TRWBR* BA14....... 125 H6
Lynfield Pk *CBATH/BATHN* BA1... 98 B3 ①
Lynmouth Rd *MTN/WRL* BS22 ... 106 B3 ③
Lynmouth Rd *CBRISNE* BS2 .... 3 M5
Lynn Rd *MANG/FISH* BS16 .... 53 H4 ①
Lynton Cl *PTSHD/EG* BS20 .... 47 J5 ②
Lynton Pl *EVILLE/WHL* BS5 .... 8 F1
Lynton Rd *BMSTR* BS3 .... 10 F5
RDSTK/MIDN BA3 .... 126 C5
Lynton Wy *MANG/FISH* BS16 ..... 41 G7
Lynwood Cl *RDSTK/MIDN* BA3 ... 126 B6
Lynwood Rd *TRWBR* BA14 ...... 124 C5
Lynx Crs *OMX/HUT/LCK* BS24 .... 117 G4
Lyons Ct *WSM* BS23 .... 17 G3
Lyons Court Rd
HGRV/WHIT BS14 .... 13 G9
Lyppiatt Rd *EVILLE/WHL* BS5 .... 9 G1
Lyppincourt Rd
HNBRY/STHM BS10 .... 38 D5
Lysander Rd *BRSTK/PCHW* BS34 .. 39 F2
Lysander Wk
BRSTK/PCHW BS34 .... 40 D3 ④
Lytchet Dr *MANG/FISH* BS16 ..... 55 F1 ⑥
Lytes Cary Rd *KEYN* BS31 .... 96 B2
Lytton Gdns *BATHSE* BA2 .... 110 E1
Lytton Gv *HORF/LLZ* BS7 .... 52 E1
KEYN BS31 .... 81 G6
Lyveden Gdns
BMSTRD/HC/WWD BS13 ..... 77 K6 ②
Lyvedon Wy *LGASH* BS41.......... 76 D2

M

Macaulay Buildings
BATHSE BA2 .... 112 B1
Macauley Rd *HORF/LLZ* BS7 .... 52 E1
Macey's Rd
BMSTRD/HC/WWD BS13 ..... 93 G1 ①
Machin Cl *HNBRY/STHM* BS10 .... 38 C5
Machin Gdns
HNBRY/STHM BS10 .... 38 D5 ⑤
Machin Rd *HNBRY/STHM* BS10 .... 38 C5
The Macies *CBATH/BATHN* BA1... 98 E1
Mackie Av *BRSTK/PCHW* BS34 .... 40 A6
Mackie Gv *BRSTK/PCHW* BS34 .... 40 A6
Mackie Rd *BRSTK/PCHW* BS34 .... 40 A6
Macleod Cl *CLVDN* BS21 .... 70 C1 ⑥
RDSTK/MIDN BA3 .... 128 E2
Macmillan Wy *BOAV* BA15....... 114 D5
Macrae Ct *KGWD/HNM* BS15 ..... 68 E2 ①
Madam La *MTN/WRL* BS22 ...... 106 A3 ①
Madeira Rd *CLVDN* BS21 .... 59 F7 ②
WSM BS23........... 104 B4
Madeline Rd *MANG/FISH* BS16 .... 5 M5 ①
Madison Cl *YATE/CS* BS37 .... 34 A5
Maesbury *KGWD/HNM* BS15 ...... 68 E4
Maesbury Rd *KEYN* BS31 .... 96 B2
Maesknoll La *PLTN/PENS* BS39 ... 93 K4
Maesknoll Rd
RDSTK/MIDN BA3 .... 127 K3
Magdalen Av *BATHSE* BA2........ 14 E9
Magdalene Pl *CBRISNE* BS2 .... 3 M6
Magdalene Rd
RDSTK/MIDN BA3 .... 127 K3
Magdalen La *TRWBR* BA14....... 123 H7
Magdalen Rd *BATHSE* BA2 .... 14 E9
Magdalen Wy *MTN/WRL* BS22 .... 106 B2
Magellan Cl *MTN/WRL* BS22 ..... 106 A1
Maggs Cl *HNBRY/STHM* BS10 .... 39 F5
Maggs La *EVILLE/WHL* BS5 .... 5 K5
HGRV/WHIT BS14 .... 79 F7
Magnolia Av *MTN/WRL* BS22 .... 106 B4
Magnolia Cl *MTN/WRL* BS22 ..... 105 K6 ③
Magnolia Ri *TRWBR* BA14....... 125 G2
Magnolia Rd *RDSTK/MIDN* BA3 .. 126 E4
Magnon Rd *BOAV* BA15........... 114 C6
Magpie Bottom La
EVILLE/WHL BS5 .... 68 B4
KGWD/HNM BS15 .... 68 C4 ①
Magpie Cl *MTN/WRL* BS22 .... 105 K5 ②
Maidenhead Rd
BMSTRD/HC/WWD BS13 ..... 93 G1
Maiden Wy *AVONM* BS11 .... 49 J2 ①
Maidstone Gv
OMX/HUT/LCK BS24 .... 117 F5 ④
Maidstone St *BMSTR* BS3 .... 11 L1
Main Rd *MANG/FISH* BS16 .... 55 J5
NAIL BS48 .... 75 F4
OMX/HUT/LCK BS24 .... 117 J4
YTN/CONG BS49 .... 88 A4
Main Vw *FRCTL/WBN* BS36 ...... 42 E1
Maisemore *YATE/CS* BS37 .... 44 B2
Maisemore Av
BRSTK/PCHW BS34 .... 30 A6
Makin Cl
OLD/WMLY/WICK BS30 ...... 69 J5 ③
Malago Rd *BMSTR* BS3 .... 11 G1
Malago Wk
BMSTRD/HC/WWD BS13 ..... 77 G7 ③
Maldowers La *EVILLE/WHL* BS5 ... 68 A1
Mallard Cl *ALMDB* BS32........... 30 C5
EVILLE/WHL BS5 .... 5 L7
YATE/CS BS37 .... 34 D7
Mallow Cl *CLVDN* BS21 .... 71 G1 ⑤
THNB/SVB BS35 .... 19 J3
TRWBR BA14 .... 131 F1 ①
The Mall *CFTN/FAIL* BS8........... 65 H3
Malmains Dr *MANG/FISH* BS16.... 41 G7
Malmesbury Cl
OLD/WMLY/WICK BS30 ...... 69 F5 ①
RDLND/MONT BS6 .... 2 F2
The Maltings *MTN/WRL* BS22 .... 106 A3 ③
Maltlands *MTN/WRL* BS22 .... 105 J5
Malvern Buildings
CBATH/BATHN BA1 .... 99 K2
Malvern Ct *EVILLE/WHL* BS5 .... 9 L2

Malvern Dr
OLD/WMLY/WICK BS30 ...... 69 J5
THNB/SVB BS35 .... 19 J5
Malvern Rd
BRSG/KWL/STAPK BS4....... 13 G2
EVILLE/WHL BS5 .... 9 L2
WSM BS23 .... 18 F8
Mancroft Av *AVONM* BS11 .... 50 B2
Mandy Mdw *RDSTK/MIDN* BA3 .. 126 A4
Mangotsfield Rd
MANG/FISH BS16 .... 55 F5
Manilla Pl *WSM* BS23........... 104 B4 ②
Manilla Rd *CFTN/FAIL* BS8 .... 6 A2
Manmoor La *CLVDN* BS21 .... 71 J2
Manor Cl *ALMDB* BS32........... 22 A5
FRCTL/WBN BS36 .... 42 D2
PTSHD/EG BS20 .... 49 G5
TRWBR BA14 .... 130 C1
The Manor Cl *CFTN/FAIL* BS8 ...... 64 C2
Manor Copse Rd
RDSTK/MIDN BA3 .... 127 K3
Manor Ct *NAIL* BS48 .... 74 A4
Manor Court Dr *HORF/LLZ* BS7 .... 52 C2
Manor Dr *CBATH/BATHN* BA1 .... 101 G2
Manor Farm Crs *ALMDB* BS32 .... 30 C6
OMX/HUT/LCK BS24 .... 117 G4
Manor Gdns *MTN/WRL* BS22 ..... 105 G1
OMX/HUT/LCK BS24 .... 118 B2 ⑥
Manor Gra *OMX/HUT/LCK* BS24 .. 117 G7
Manor Gv *ALMDB* BS32 .... 30 A5 ①
MANG/FISH BS16 .... 55 G5
Manor La *CFTN/FAIL* BS8 .... 64 B2
FRCTL/WBN BS36 .... 42 A1
Manor Pk *ALMDB* BS32 .... 22 B4
CBATH/BATHN BA1 .... 98 E4
RDLND/MONT BS6 .... 2 C4
RDSTK/MIDN BA3 .... 127 K3
Manor Pl *MANG/FISH* BS16 .... 41 H7
Manor Rd
BMSTRD/HC/WWD BS13 ..... 77 H5
CBATH/BATHN BA1 .... 99 F3
CFTN/FAIL BS8 .... 64 B4
HORF/LLZ BS7 .... 3 J2
KEYN BS31 .... 96 B1
MANG/FISH BS16 .... 53 K4
MANG/FISH BS16 .... 55 C5
RDSTK/MIDN BA3 .... 127 K3
TRWBR BA14 .... 130 C1
WSM BS23........... 104 E4
YATE/CS BS37 .... 25 H7
Manor Va *WSM* BS23........... 105 F4
Manor Wk *THNB/SVB* BS35 .... 19 G2
Manor Wy *CFTN/FAIL* BS8 .... 63 J6
YATE/CS BS37 .... 25 H7
Mansel Cl *KEYN* BS31 .... 96 D1
Mansfield Av *WSM* BS23 .... 17 L1
Mansfield St *BMSTR* BS3 .... 10 D4
Manston Cl *HGRV/WHIT* BS14 .... 12 F9
Manton Cl *TRWBR* BA14 .... 130 E2
Manvers St
CBATH/BATHN BA1 .... 15 G7 ⑧
Manworthy Rd
BRSG/KWL/STAPK BS4....... 13 H2
Manx Rd *HORF/LLZ* BS7 .... 52 D2
Maple Av *MANG/FISH* BS16 .... 54 C6
THNB/SVB BS35 .... 19 H4
Maple Cl *BRSTK/PCHW* BS34 ..... 40 B1
HGRV/WHIT BS14 .... 79 H6
OLD/WMLY/WICK BS30 ...... 69 H6
WSM BS23 .... 17 K2
Maple Dr *RDSTK/MIDN* BA3 ..... 127 F3
Maple Gdns *BATHSE* BA2 .... 111 H1
Maple Rd *BRSG/KWL/STAPK* BS4... 9 H6
HORF/LLZ BS7 .... 52 B4
The Maples *NAIL* BS48 .... 73 G2
Maplestone Rd
HGRV/WHIT BS14 .... 93 K1
Maple Wk *KEYN* BS31 .... 80 D7
MANG/FISH BS16 .... 54 A7
Marbeck Rd *HNBRY/STHM* BS10 .. 38 E7
Marchfields Wy *WSM* BS23 .... 17 H6
Marconi Rd *PTSHD/EG* BS20 ...... 46 D5
Mardale Cl *HNBRY/STHM* BS10 .. 39 F6 ①
Marden Rd *KEYN* BS31........... 81 G7
Marden Wk *TRWBR* BA14 ...... 131 F1 ②
Mardon Rd *BRSG/KWL/STAPK* BS4.. 9 G5
Mardyke Ferry Rd *CBRIS/FH* BS1... 6 C6
Margaret's Hl
CBATH/BATHN BA1 .... 15 G2 ③
Margate St *BMSTR* BS3 .... 11 K1
Marguerite Rd
BMSTRD/HC/WWD BS13 ..... 77 H3
Marigold Wk *BMSTR* BS3 .... 10 B3
Marina Dr *TRWBR* BA14 .... 125 F1
Marina Gdns *MANG/FISH* BS16 ..... 5 K4
Marindrin Dr *MTN/WRL* BS22 .... 106 C1 ⑤
Marine Hl *CLVDN* BS21 .... 58 E6
Marine Pde *CLVDN* BS21 .... 58 E6
PTSHD/EG BS20 .... 49 J4
WSM BS23........... 16 C8
Mariner's Cl *MTN/WRL* BS22 .... 105 J4 ④
NAIL BS48 .... 74 A5
Mariners Dr
HNLZ/SM/SNYPK/WT BS9 ..... 51 F5
NAIL BS48 .... 74 A5
Mariners' Pth
HNLZ/SM/SNYPK/WT BS9 ..... 51 F5
Mariner's Wy *PTSHD/EG* BS20 .... 49 J4
Marion Rd *KGWD/HNM* BS15 .... 68 B7
Marion Wk *EVILLE/WHL* BS5 ...... 68 A3
Marissal Cl *HNBRY/STHM* BS10 ... 38 B5
Marissal Rd *HNBRY/STHM* BS10 .. 38 B5
Mariston Wy
OLD/WMLY/WICK BS30 ...... 69 J4
Marjoram Pl *ALMDB* BS32........ 30 C6 ③
Market La *WSM* BS23 .... 16 D1 ⑩
Market Pl *BLAG/CWMG/WR* BS40.. 91 G5
Market Sq *MANG/FISH* BS16 ...... 54 C6 ⑧
Market St *BOAV* BA15........... 114 E6
TRWBR BA14 .... 125 F6
Mc Crae Rd
OMX/HUT/LCK BS24 .... 118 C1
Mead Cl *AVONM* BS11........... 50 A3 ①
Mark La *CBRIS/FH* BS1 .... 6 F4

Marksbury Rd *BMSTR* BS3 .... 10 F4
Marlborough Av
EVILLE/WHL BS5 .... 5 J4 ①
Marlborough Buildings
CBATH/BATHN BA1 .... 14 D4
Marlborough Dr
MANG/FISH BS16 .... 41 G7
MTN/WRL BS22 .... 106 B3
Marlborough Hl
RDLND/MONT BS6 .... 7 G1
Marlborough Hill Pl
CBRISNE BS2 .... 7 G1 ①
Marlborough La
CBATH/BATHN BA1 .... 14 C5
Marlborough St
CBATH/BATHN BA1 .... 14 D3 ①
CBRIS/FH BS1 .... 7 H1
CBRISNE BS2 .... 7 G2
TRWBR BA14 .... 5 J4
Marlepit Gv
BMSTRD/HC/WWD BS13 ..... 77 H5 ②
Marlfield Wk
BMSTRD/HC/WWD BS13 ..... 77 C4
Marling Rd *EVILLE/WHL* BS5 .... 9 M1
EVILLE/WHL BS5 .... 68 A3 ③
Marlwood Dr
HNBRY/STHM BS10 .... 38 D5
Marmaduke St *BMSTR* BS3 .... 11 L1
Marmion Crs *HNBRY/STHM* BS10.. 38 C5
Marne Cl *HGRV/WHIT* BS14 ...... 79 H6
Marsden Rd *BATHSE* BA2......... 110 E2
Marsham Wy
OLD/WMLY/WICK BS30 ...... 68 E5
Marsh Cl *FRCTL/WBN* BS36 ...... 41 K4
Marsh Common Rd *THNB/SVB* BS35.. 28 A1
Marshfield Rd *MANG/FISH* BS16.... 54 B5
Marshfield Wy
CBATH/BATHN BA1 .... 99 K3
Marsh La *EVILLE/WHL* BS5 .... 8 E4
PTSHD/EG BS20 .... 48 E3
Marshmead *TRWBR* BA14........ 125 F1
Marsh Rd *BMSTR* BS3 .... 65 H7
RDSTK/MIDN BA3 .... 129 F7
TRWBR BA14 .... 125 C1
YTN/CONG BS49 .... 86 E5
Marsh St *AVONM* BS11 .... 49 J1
CBRIS/FH BS1 .... 7 G4
Marshwall La *ALMDB* BS32 .... 29 J1
Marson Rd *CLVDN* BS21 .... 59 F7
Marston Rd
BRSG/KWL/STAPK BS4....... 12 C3
TRWBR BA14 .... 130 D2
Martcombe Rd *PTSHD/EG* BS20.... 49 H6
Martin Cl *BRSTK/PCHW* BS34 ..... 29 H7
Martindale Rd *MTN/WRL* BS22 ... 105 J5
Martindale Rd *MTN/WRL* BS22 ... 105 J5
Martingale Rd
BRSG/KWL/STAPK BS4....... 9 G8
Martins Cl *KGWD/HNM* BS15 ..... 68 C5 ②
Martins Gv *MTN/WRL* BS22 ...... 105 K3 ②
Martin's Rd *KGWD/HNM* BS15 .... 68 C5
Martin St *BMSTR* BS3 .... 10 C1
Martlock Crs *BMSTR* BS3 .... 10 E5
Martock Rd *BMSTR* BS3 .... 10 E5
KEYN BS31 .... 96 B1
Marwood Rd
BRSG/KWL/STAPK BS4....... 11 K7
Marybush La *CBRISNE* BS2 .... 7 K3 ③
Marygold Leaze
OLD/WMLY/WICK BS30 ...... 69 G6 ③
Mary St *EVILLE/WHL* BS5 .... 9 G1
Mascot Rd *BMSTR* BS3 .... 11 H2
Masefield Wy *HORF/LLZ* BS7 ..... 52 E2 ①
Maskelyne Av
HNBRY/STHM BS10 .... 52 B2
Masons La *BOAV* BA15........... 114 E6
Masons Vw *FRCTL/WBN* BS36 .... 41 K1
Materman Rd *HGRV/WHIT* BS14... 79 H6
Matford Cl *FRCTL/WBN* BS36 ..... 41 K3
HNBRY/STHM BS10 .... 39 G4
Matthews Cl *HGRV/WHIT* BS14.... 79 K5
Matthew's Rd *EVILLE/WHL* BS5 .... 8 E2 ①
Maules La *MANG/FISH* BS16 ...... 40 E6
Maunsell Rd *AVONM* BS11 .... 37 J4
Maurice Rd *RDLND/MONT* BS6 ..... 3 K5
Mautravers Cl *ALMDB* BS32 .... 40 C1
Max Mill La *BNWL* BS29 .... 119 J5
Maxse Rd *BRSG/KWL/STAPK* BS4... 12 C2
Maybec Gdns
EVILLE/WHL BS5 .... 68 A4 ①
Maybourne
BRSG/KWL/STAPK BS4....... 80 A1 ②
Maybrick Rd *BATHSE* BA2......... 14 A9
Maycliffe Pk *RDLND/MONT* BS6..... 3 M6
Mayfair Av *NAIL* BS48........... 73 J2
Mayfield Av *MANG/FISH* BS16..... 54 A7
MTN/WRL BS22 .... 105 K4 ③
Mayfield Pk *MANG/FISH* BS16 .... 54 A7
Mayfield Pk North
MANG/FISH BS16 .... 54 A7
Mayfield Pk South
MANG/FISH BS16 .... 54 A7
Mayfield Rd *BATHSE* BA2......... 14 A9
Mayfields *KEYN* BS31 .... 80 E6
Mayflower Gdns *NAIL* BS48 .... 74 A1
Maynard Cl
BMSTRD/HC/WWD BS13 ..... 78 A6
CLVDN BS21 .... 59 H7 ②
Maynard Rd
BMSTRD/HC/WWD BS13 ..... 78 A6
Maysfield Cl *PTSHD/EG* BS20 ..... 47 H6
Maysgreen La
OMX/HUT/LCK BS24 .... 107 J1
May's La *OMX/HUT/LCK* BS24 .... 107 K2
May St *KGWD/HNM* BS15 .... 68 C1
Maytree Av
BMSTRD/HC/WWD BS13 ..... 10 D9
Maytree Cl
BMSTRD/HC/WWD BS13 ..... 10 D9
May Tree Cl *NAIL* BS48 .... 73 G2 ⑤
May Tree Rd *RDSTK/MIDN* BA3 .. 127 F4
Mayville Av *BRSTK/PCHW* BS34 ... 39 K5
Maywood Crs *MANG/FISH* BS16 ... 54 E5
Maywood Rd *MANG/FISH* BS16 ... 54 C5
Mc Crae Rd
OMX/HUT/LCK BS24 .... 118 C1
Mead Cl *AVONM* BS11........... 50 A3 ①

BATHSE BA2 .... 111 H2
Meadgate *MANG/FISH* BS16 .... 55 H1
Mead Lands *BATHSE* BA2 .... 97 H5
Mead La *WNSC* BS25........... 120 B2
Meadowbank
MTN/WRL BS22 .... 106 A2 ③
Meadow Cl *MANG/FISH* BS16 ..... 55 F2 ③
NAIL BS48 .... 61 J7
NAIL BS48 .... 74 B5
PTSHD/EG BS20 .... 46 D4 ③
Meadow Court Dr
OLD/WMLY/WICK BS30 ...... 69 J7
Meadowcroft
MANG/FISH BS16 .... 55 G1 ③
Meadow Cft
OMX/HUT/LCK BS24 .... 117 G4
Meadow Dr *BATHSE* BA2......... 111 G5 ③
OMX/HUT/LCK BS24 .... 118 B2
PTSHD/EG BS20 .... 60 D1
Meadowfield *BOAV* BA15....... 114 C7
Meadow Gdns
CBATH/BATHN BA1 .... 98 D3
Meadow Gv *AVONM* BS11 .... 49 K2
Meadowland *YTN/CONG* BS49 .... 86 D3
Meadowland Rd
HNBRY/STHM BS10 .... 38 B4
Meadowlands *MTN/WRL* BS22 .... 106 D3
Meadow La *BATHSE* BA2......... 100 C3
Meadow Md *FRCTL/WBN* BS36.... 32 C7
YATE/CS BS37 .... 34 B2
Meadow Rd *CLVDN* BS21 .... 59 G7 ③
PLTN/PENS BS39 .... 126 A1
WUE GL12 .... 21 J1
Meadowside *THNB/SVB* BS35 ..... 19 J5 ③
Meadowside Dr
HGRV/WHIT BS14 .... 93 K1
The Meadows *KGWD/HNM* BS15 .. 68 D5
Meadow St *AVONM* BS11......... 36 B7
CBRISNE BS2 .... 7 K2 ③
WSM BS23........... 16 E2
Meadowsweet Av
BRSTK/PCHW BS34 .... 40 A5
Meadow V *EVILLE/WHL* BS5 .... 68 A1
Meadow Vw *FRCTL/WBN* BS36.... 42 D1
RDSTK/MIDN BA3 .... 127 H4
Meadow Wy *ALMDB* BS32........ 40 D1
Mead Ri *BMSTR* BS3 .... 7 L8
Mead Rd *BRSTK/PCHW* BS34 ..... 40 A2
PTSHD/EG BS20 .... 47 G6
YATE/CS BS37 .... 35 F7
The Meads *MANG/FISH* BS16 ..... 55 F2 ③
Mead St *BMSTR* BS3 .... 7 L8
The Mead *BOAV* BA15........... 113 K6
BRSTK/PCHW BS34 .... 40 A4
LGASH BS41 .... 92 A2
RDSTK/MIDN BA3 .... 128 E3
THNB/SVB BS35 .... 23 F1
WNSC BS25........... 121 H6 ②
Mead V *MTN/WRL* BS22 .... 105 K5
Mead Wy *THNB/SVB* BS35 .... 19 G6
Meadway
HNLZ/SM/SNYPK/WT BS9 ..... 50 E3
TRWBR BA14 .... 124 C6
Meadway Av *NAIL* BS48 .... 73 H1
Meardon Rd *HGRV/WHIT* BS14 ... 79 J5 ③
Meare Rd *BATHSE* BA2 .... 111 K3
Mede Cl *CBRIS/FH* BS1 .... 7 J7 ③
Medical Av *CFTN/FAIL* BS8 .... 6 B3
Medina Cl *THNB/SVB* BS35 .... 19 H6 ②
Medway Cl *KEYN* BS31........... 96 B1
Medway Dr *THNB/SVB* BS35 ...... 19 J5
Medway Dr *FRCTL/WBN* BS36 .... 42 C1
KEYN BS31 .... 96 B1
Meere Bank *AVONM* BS11 .... 37 J7
Meetinghouse La
YTN/CONG BS49 .... 87 K3
Meg Thatchers Cl
EVILLE/WHL BS5 .... 68 B3 ①
Melbourne Dr *YATE/CS* BS37...... 34 E6
Melbourne Rd *HORF/LLZ* BS7 ...... 3 H2
Melbourne Ter *CLVDN* BS21 .... 71 F1 ⑦
Melbury Rd
BRSG/KWL/STAPK BS4....... 11 M4
Melcombe Rd *BATHSE* BA2........ 14 A9
Melita Rd *RDLND/MONT* BS6 ...... 3 K4
Mellent Av
BMSTRD/HC/WWD BS13 ..... 93 F1
Mells Cl *KEYN* BS31........... 96 B2
Mells La *RDSTK/MIDN* BA3........ 127 J4
Melrose Av *CFTN/FAIL* BS8 .... 2 C9
YATE/CS BS37 .... 34 C5
Melrose Cl *YATE/CS* BS37 .... 34 D5
Melrose Gv *BATHSE* BA2......... 110 E2
Melrose Pl *CFTN/FAIL* BS8 .... 2 C9 ⑧
Melton Crs *HORF/LLZ* BS7 .... 52 E2
Melton Rd *TRWBR* BA14 .... 124 E4
Melville *RDLND/MONT* BS6 .... 2 D7
Melville Ter *BMSTR* BS3 .... 10 E1
Memorial Cl *KGWD/HNM* BS15 ... 68 B6
Memorial Rd *KGWD/HNM* BS15 .. 68 B5
Mendip Av *MTN/WRL* BS22 ..... 105 K3
Mendip Cl *KEYN* BS31 .... 80 D6
NAIL BS48 .... 73 J2 ⑦
Mendip Crs *MANG/FISH* BS16 ..... 55 G2
Mendip Edge
OMX/HUT/LCK BS24 .... 116 E6
Mendip Gdns *BATHSE* BA2........ 111 C5
YTN/CONG BS49 .... 86 E5
Mendip Rd *BMSTR* BS3 .... 11 G2
OMX/HUT/LCK BS24 .... 118 D2
PTSHD/EG BS20 .... 46 E4
WSM BS23 .... 17 J3
YTN/CONG BS49 .... 86 E4
Mendip View Av
MANG/FISH BS16 .... 54 A6
Mendip Wy *RDSTK/MIDN* BA3.... 127 G2
Merchants Rd *CBRIS/FH* BS1 .... 6 A6
CFTN/FAIL BS8 .... 6 A3
Merchant St *CBRIS/FH* BS1 .... 7 J2
Mercia Dr *CBRISNE* BS2 .... 4 A5
Mercier Cl *YATE/CS* BS37......... 34 C7
Merfield Rd
BRSG/KWL/STAPK BS4....... 12 D3
Meridian Pl *CFTN/FAIL* BS8......... 6 C3
Meridian Rd *RDLND/MONT* BS6 .... 2 F7
Meridian Vale *CFTN/FAIL* BS8 ...... 6 C3
Meridian Wk *TRWBR* BA14 ...... 124 C6 ③

Meriet Av
BMSTRD/HC/WWD BS13........... 77 K7
Merioneth St *BMSTR* BS3........ 11 L1
Meriton St *CBRISNE* BS2............ 8 C7
Merlin Cl
HNLZ/SM/SNYPK/WT BS9...... 51 H1
MTN/WRL BS22......................... 105 K5 🔟
Merlin Pk *PTSHD/EG* BS20....... 46 D5
Merlin Rd *BRSTK/PCHW* BS34... 39 F2
Merlin Wy *YATE/CS* BS37........... 44 C1
Merrimans Rd *AVONM* BS11....... 49 K1
Merryweather Cl *ALVMDB* BA32... 30 B7
Merrywood Rd *BMSTR* BS3.......... 6 E8
Merstham Rd *CBRISNE* BS2.......... 4 B6
Merton Rd *HORF/LLZ* BS7.......... 52 C4
Mervyn Rd *HORF/LLZ* BS7........... 3 J2
Metford Gv *RDLND/MONT* BS6.... 2 D3
Metford Pl *RDLND/MONT* BS6..... 2 D3
Metford Rd *RDLND/MONT* BS6.... 2 D3
Methuen Cl *BOAV* BA15............. 123 K2
The Mews *CBATH/BATHN* BA1..... 99 K3
Middle Av *CBRIS/FH* BS1............ 7 G5 🔟
Middle La *CBATH/BATHN* BA1..... 15 J1
CLVDN BS21............................... 70 B7
TRWBR BA14............................. 125 H4
Middlepiece La *KEYN* BS31......... 96 C5
Middle Rd *KGWD/HNM* BS15...... 54 E6
Middle Stoke *RDSTK/MIDN* BA3.. 113 F7
Middleton Rd *AVONM* BS11......... 50 B1
Midford Hl *BATHSE* BA2............. 112 B7
Midford La *BATHSE* BA2............. 112 B7
Midford Rd *BATHSE* BA2............. 111 J3
Midhaven Ri *MTN/WRL* BS22..... 105 K1
Midland Bridge Rd *BATHSE* BA2.. 14 D7
Midland Rd *BATHSE* BA2............. 14 B6
CBRISNE BS2............................... 7 M3
MANG/FISH BS16........................ 54 D5
Midland St *CBRISNE* BS2............ 7 M4
Midland Ter *MANG/FISH* BS16.... 5 L3
Midland Wy *THNB/SVB* BS35...... 19 C5
Midsummer Buildings
CBATH/BATHN BA1..................... 99 K3
Milburn Rd *WSM* BS23.............. 17 G3
Milbury Gdns *MTN/WRL* BS22.... 105 C5
Mildred St *EVILLE/WHL* BS5........ 8 E3
Miles Ct
OLD/WMLY/WICK BS30........... 69 F6 🔟
Miles Rd *CFTN/FAIL* BS8............. 2 A8
Miles St *BATHSE* BA2................. 15 H8
Milestone Ct *MTN/WRL* BS22..... 106 E3
Milford St *BMSTR* BS3................. 6 E9
Milk St *CBATH/BATHN* BA1......... 14 F7
Millard Cl *HNBRY/STHM* BS10..... 39 F6 🔟
Millard's Hl *RDSTK/MIDN* BA3.... 126 C2
Mill Av *CBRIS/FH* BS1................. 7 H5
Millbank Cl
BRSG/KWL/STAPK BS4.............. 13 J1
Millbrook Av
BRSG/KWL/STAPK BS4 .... 13 M1 🔟
Millbrook Cl
OLD/WMLY/WICK BS30........... 69 J4
Millbrook Pl *BATHSE* BA2............ 15 H9
Millbrook Rd *YATE/CS* BS37........ 33 J5
Mill Cl *FRCTL/WBN* BS36............ 42 D1
PTSHD/EG BS20.......................... 48 D7
Mill Crs *YATE/CS* BS37................ 43 J4
Millcross *CLVDN* BS21................ 70 C4
Miller Ct *WSM* BS23................... 17 G2
Millers Cl *PTSHD/EG* BS20........... 49 J3 🔟
Millers Dr *OLD/WMLY/WICK* BS30.. 69 J4
Millers Ri *MTN/WRL* BS22.......... 106 B1 🔟
Miller Wk *BATHSE* BA2.............. 100 D3
Millfield *RDSTK/MIDN* BA3......... 126 A5
THNB/SVB BS35........................ 19 H3
Millfield Dr
OLD/WMLY/WICK BS30........... 69 J4
Millground Rd
BMSTRD/HC/WWD BS13........... 77 G7
Millhand Vls *TRWBR* BA14.......... 125 G7
Millier Rd *YTN/CONG* BS49......... 87 K4
Milliman Cl
BMSTRD/HC/WWD BS13........... 78 A6
Millington Dr *TRWBR* BA14......... 124 C7
Mill La *BATHSE* BA2.................... 98 E6 🔟
BATHSE BA2.............................. 100 E2
BATHSE BA2.............................. 112 D5
BMSTR BS3................................. 7 C9
BOAV BA15............................... 114 E7
FRCTL/WBN BS36....................... 32 C7
OLD/WMLY/WICK BS30........... 69 J5
PTSHD/EG BS20......................... 48 E7
YATE/CS BS37............................ 45 J2
YTN/CONG BS49........................ 109 C1
Mill Leg *YTN/CONG* BS49........... 109 H1
Millmead Rd *BATHSE* BA2........... 99 F7
Millpond St *EVILLE/WHL* BS5....... 4 A7
Mill Rd *FRCTL/WBN* BS36............ 41 J4
RDSTK/MIDN BA3....................... 127 H3
Mill St *TRWBR* BA14................. 125 F6
Millward Gv *MANG/FISH* BS16.... 54 C5
Milner Gn *OLD/WMLY/WICK* BS30.. 69 J5
Milner Rd *HORF/LLZ* BS7............ 52 C4
Milsom St *CBATH/BATHN* BA1..... 14 F5 🔟
EVILLE/WHL BS5.......................... 8 A1
WSM BS23................................. 17 J2
Milton Av *BATHSE* BA2.............. 111 J1
WSM BS23................................. 17 J2
Milton Brow *MTN/WRL* BS22..... 105 C3
YATE/CS BS37............................ 34 A5
Milton Cl *NAIL* BS48................... 61 J7
YATE/CS BS37............................ 34 A5
Milton Gn *MTN/WRL* BS22......... 105 H4 🔟
Milton Hl *MTN/WRL* BS22.......... 105 C3
Milton Pk *EVILLE/WHL* BS5.......... 8 E2
Milton Park Rd *MTN/WRL* BS22.. 105 H4 🔟
Milton Ri *MTN/WRL* BS22.......... 105 H4 🔟
MTN/WRL BS22.......................... 105 C4 🔟
Milton Rd *HORF/LLZ* BS7............ 52 C3
RDSTK/MIDN BA3....................... 126 D4
WSM BS23................................. 17 G2
YATE/CS BS37............................ 34 A5
Miltons Cl
BMSTRD/HC/WWD BS13........... 78 B7
Milverton Gdns
RDLND/MONT BS6...................... 3 M6 🔟
Milward Rd *KEYN* BS31.............. 80 E5
Mina Rd *CBRISNE* BS2................. 3 M4
Minehead Rd
BRSG/KWL/STAPK BS4.............. 11 M5

Minerva Gdns *BATHSE* BA2........ 111 F1 🔟
Minor's La *HNBRY/STHM* BS10.... 27 H7
Minsmere Rd *KEYN* BS31............. 96 B1
Minster Wy *BATHSE* BA2............ 15 M3
Minton Cl *HGRV/WHIT* BS14....... 79 F6
Minto Rd *CBRISNE* BS2................ 4 A6
Mission Rd *YATE/CS* BS37........... 33 H3
Mitchell La *CBRIS/FH* BS1............ 7 J5
Mitchell Wk
OLD/WMLY/WICK BS30........... 69 K4 🔟
Mivart St *EVILLE/WHL* BS5........... 8 D1
Mizzymead Cl *NAIL* BS48............. 73 H2 🔟
Mizzymead Ri *NAIL* BS48............ 73 H2 🔟
Mizzymead Rd *NAIL* BS48............ 73 J1 🔟
Modecombe Gv
HNBRY/STHM BS10.................... 38 C5 🔟
Mogg St *CBRISNE* BS2................. 4 A6
Molesworth Cl
BMSTRD/HC/WWD BS13........... 77 J7
Molesworth Dr
BMSTRD/HC/WWD BS13........... 77 J7
Monarch's Wy
BLAG/CWMG/WR BS40.............. 91 J5
EVILLE/WHL BS5.......................... 9 C4
LGASH BS41............................... 76 A1
OLD/WMLY/WICK BS30........... 80 E2
YATE/CS BS37............................ 45 F1
Monger La *RDSTK/MIDN* BA3..... 126 A1
Monkley La *TRWBR* BA14.......... 129 J6
Monk Rd *HORF/LLZ* BS7.............. 3 H2
Monks Av *KGWD/HNM* BS15...... 68 B2 🔟
Monksdale Rd *BATHSE* BA2........ 111 G1
Monks Hl *MTN/WRL* BS22.......... 105 G2
Monk's Park Av *HORF/LLZ* BS7... 39 H7
Monks Park Wy
MTN/WRL BS22........................... 52 C1
Monkton Av
OMX/HUT/LCK BS24................... 117 F4
Monmouth Cl *KGWD/HNM* BS15.. 68 B6
Monmouth Hl *ALMDB* BS32......... 29 C3
Monmouth Pl
CBATH/BATHN BA1..................... 14 E6
Monmouth Rd *HORF/LLZ* BS7...... 3 H2
KEYN BS31................................. 80 D6
PTSHD/EG BS20......................... 49 J4
Monmouth St *BMSTR* BS3........... 11 L1
CBATH/BATHN BA1..................... 14 E6
Monsdale Cl *HNBRY/STHM* BS10.. 38 D6
Monsdale Dr *HNBRY/STHM* BS10.. 38 D6
Montague Cl
BRSTK/PCHW BS34.................... 40 D3 🔟
Montague Ct *TRWBR* BA14........ 125 J5
Montague Hl *RDLND/MONT* BS6.. 3 C9
Montague Hl South
CBRISNE BS2............................... 7 H1 🔟
Montague Rd *KEYN* BS31............ 96 E2
Montepelier *WSM* BS23.............. 16 F1 🔟
Montgomery St *BMSTR* BS3......... 7 L9
Montpelier East *WSM* BS23....... 104 E4 🔟
Montreal Av *HORF/LLZ* BS7......... 52 D1
Montrose Av *RDLND/MONT* BS6.. 2 E7
Montrose Dr
OLD/WMLY/WICK BS30........... 69 H4
Montrose Pk
BRSG/KWL/STAPK BS4.............. 13 G3
Montroy Cl
HNLZ/SM/SNYPK/WT BS9........ 52 A3
Moon St *CBRISNE* BS2................. 7 J1
Moor Croft Dr
OLD/WMLY/WICK BS30........... 69 F6
Moor Croft Rd
OMX/HUT/LCK BS24................... 117 K3
Moordell Cl *YATE/CS* BS37.......... 34 A6
Moorend Gdns *AVONM* BS11...... 50 B2
Moorend Rd *MANG/FISH* BS16.... 41 J5
Moor End Spout *NAIL* BS48......... 73 H1 🔟
Moorfield Rd *NAIL* BS48.............. 73 K4
Moorfields Rd *BATHSE* BA2........ 111 G1
NAIL BS48................................. 73 H1
Moor Gv *AVONM* BS11................ 50 B1
Moorham Rd *WNSC* BS25.......... 120 D5
Moorhill St *EVILLE/WHL* BS5......... 4 C8 🔟
Moorhouse La *AVONM* BS11........ 37 C3
HNBRY/STHM BS10.................... 26 E1
The Moorings *PTSHD/EG* BS20.... 49 J5
Moorland Rd *BATHSE* BA2........... 14 A8
WSM BS23................................. 16 E9
YATE/CS BS37............................ 34 A6
Moorlands Cl *NAIL* BS48............. 73 H1
Moorlands Rd *MANG/FISH* BS16.. 5 M4
Moor La *CLVDN* BS21.................. 60 D6
CLVDN BS21............................... 71 H1
MTN/WRL BS22........................ 106 A4
NAIL BS48................................. 73 K4
OMX/HUT/LCK BS24................... 105 K6
PTSHD/EG BS20......................... 61 J1
Moor Pk *CLVDN* BS21................ 71 C1
Moorpark Av *YATE/CS* BS37........ 33 K6
Moor Rd *BNWL* BS29................. 107 J7
YTN/CONG BS49........................ 86 E1
Moorside *YTN/CONG* BS49........ 86 E3 🔟
Moravian Rd *KGWD/HNM* BS15.. 68 D2
Morden Wk *HGRV/WHIT* BS14.... 13 C9
Moreton St *CBATH/BATHN* BA1... 14 F4
Morford St *CBATH/BATHN* BA1... 14 E4
Morgan Cl *KEYN* BS31................. 96 E2
Morgans Hill Cl *NAIL* BS48........... 73 H3
Morgan St *CBRISNE* BS2.............. 3 M8
Morley Av *MANG/FISH* BS16........ 55 C5
Morley Cl *BRSTK/PCHW* BS34..... 40 A1
MANG/FISH BS16........................ 54 D6
Morley Rd *BMSTR* BS3................. 6 E8
EVILLE/WHL BS5.......................... 9 H1
Morley Sq *HORF/LLZ* BS7............ 3 J2
Morley St *CBRISNE* BS2............... 3 M7
EVILLE/WHL BS5.......................... 8 D3
Morley Ter *KGWD/HNM* BS15..... 68 D1 🔟
RDSTK/MIDN BA3....................... 127 H2
Mornington Rd *CFTN/FAIL* BS8.... 2 B6
Morpeth Rd
BRSG/KWL/STAPK BS4.............. 11 H8
Morris La *CBATH/BATHN* BA1..... 101 G1
Morris Rd *HORF/LLZ* BS7............. 52 E4
Morse Rd *EVILLE/WHL* BS5........... 8 F2
Mortimer Cl *CBATH/BATHN* BA1.. 98 E2
Mortimer Rd *BRSTK/PCHW* BS34.. 40 A7
CFTN/FAIL BS8............................ 6 A3

Mortimer St *TRWBR* BA14........ 124 E7
Morton St *EVILLE/WHL* BS5.......... 8 D2
THNB/SVB BS35......................... 19 H1
Morton Wy *THNB/SVB* BS35....... 19 K5
Moseley Gv *WSM* BS23.............. 116 D4
Moulton Dr *BOAV* BA15............ 123 K2
Mountain Ash
CBATH/BATHN BA1..................... 99 C3
Mountain Wd
CBATH/BATHN BA1.................... 101 H2
Mountbatten Cl
MTN/WRL BS22.......................... 105 K1 🔟
YATE/CS BS37............................ 34 A4
Mount Cl *FRCTL/WBN* BS36......... 32 A7
Mount Crs *FRCTL/WBN* BS36....... 41 K3
Mount Gdns *KGWD/HNM* BS15... 68 D4
Mount Gv *BATHSE* BA2............. 110 E2
Mount Hill Rd *KGWD/HNM* BS15.. 68 C4
Mount Pleasant *BOAV* BA15...... 114 E6
PTSHD/EG BS20......................... 49 K5
RDSTK/MIDN BA3..................... 127 J3 🔟
Mount Pleasant Ter *BMSTR* BS3.. 6 D9
Mount Rd *BATHSE* BA2............. 110 E2
CBATH/BATHN BA1..................... 14 F2
The Mount *TRWBR* BA14........... 125 F4
Mount Vw *BATHSE* BA2............ 110 E1
Mow Barton
BMSTRD/HC/WWD BS13........... 77 G5
YATE/CS BS37............................ 34 A5 🔟
Mowbray Rd *HGRV/WHIT* BS14... 12 E9
Mowcroft Rd
BMSTRD/HC/WWD BS13........... 78 A7
Moxham Dr
BMSTRD/HC/WWD BS13........... 78 A7
Muddy La *MTN/WRL* BS22.......... 84 B4
Mud La *YTN/CONG* BS49............. 87 H2
Muirfield *OLD/WMLY/WICK* BS30.. 69 C4
Mulberry Av *PTSHD/EG* BS20...... 47 J4 🔟
Mulberry Cl *KGWD/HNM* BS15.... 68 C2
MTN/WRL BS22......................... 106 A4 🔟
NAIL BS48................................. 74 A5
Mulberry Dr *KGWD/HNM* BS15... 69 F1
Mulberry Rd *YTN/CONG* BS49.... 109 H2
Mulberry Wk
HNLZ/SM/SNYPK/WT BS9........ 50 E1 🔟
Muller Av *HORF/LLZ* BS7.............. 3 L1
Muller Rd *EVILLE/WHL* BS5........... 4 F4
HORF/LLZ BS7............................ 52 D3
Mulready Cl *HORF/LLZ* BS7......... 53 C3
Mumbleys La *THNB/SVB* BS35.... 18 D6
Murford Av
BMSTRD/HC/WWD BS13........... 77 K7
Murford Wk
BMSTRD/HC/WWD BS13........... 77 K7
Murray Rd *TRWBR* BA14........... 125 F4
Murray St *BMSTR* BS3................. 6 E9
Musgrove Cl *AVONM* BS11.......... 37 K6
Myrtleberry *MTN/WRL* BS22...... 84 B7 🔟
Myrtle Dr *AVONM* BS11.............. 50 A4
Myrtle Gdns *YTN/CONG* BS49..... 86 E4
Myrtle Hl *PTSHD/EG* BS20........... 49 K4 🔟
PTSHD/EG BS20......................... 49 J5 🔟
Myrtle Rd *CBRISNE* BS2................ 6 F1
Myrtle St *BMSTR* BS3................... 6 D9
Mythern Meadow *BOAV* BA15.... 124 A1

N

Nags Head Hl *EVILLE/WHL* BS5..... 68 A4
Nailsea Cl
BMSTRD/HC/WWD BS13........... 10 A3
Nailsea Moor La *NAIL* BS48......... 72 D4
Nailsea Pk *NAIL* BS48................ 73 K1 🔟
Nailsea Park Cl *NAIL* BS48.......... 73 K1 🔟
Nailsea Wall *CLVDN* BS21........... 71 K3
Nailsea Wall La *NAIL* BS48.......... 72 C4
Nailsworth Av *YATE/CS* BS37...... 34 B6
Naish Hl *PTSHD/EG* BS20............. 61 K1
Naish La *NAIL* BS48.................... 90 E1
Napier Miles Rd *AVONM* BS11..... 50 C1
Napier Rd *AVONM* BS11.............. 36 C7
CBATH/BATHN BA1..................... 98 D1
EVILLE/WHL BS5.......................... 5 D5
RDLND/MONT BS6...................... 2 D5
Napier Sq *AVONM* BS11............. 36 B7
Napier St *EVILLE/WHL* BS5........... 8 D4
Narroways Rd *CBRISNE* BS2......... 4 B4
Narrow La *MANG/FISH* BS16....... 54 E5
Narrow Pln *CBRISNE* BS2............. 7 K4
Narrow Quay *CBRIS/FH* BS1........ 7 C5
Naseby Wk *EVILLE/WHL* BS5........ 5 L8
Nash Cl *KEYN* BS31................... 81 C6 🔟
Nash Dr *HORF/LLZ* BS7................ 53 C2
Naunton Wy *MTN/WRL* BS22..... 105 C3
Navigator Cl *TRWBR* BA14......... 125 C2
Neads Dr
OLD/WMLY/WICK BS30........... 69 J5 🔟
Neale Wy *AVONM* BS11............. 36 D7 🔟
Neath Rd *EVILLE/WHL* BS5............ 5 C9
Nelson Cl *MTN/WRL* BS22.......... 105 K1 🔟
Nelson Pl West
CBATH/BATHN BA1..................... 14 D6
Nelson Rd *MANG/FISH* BS16........ 54 D4 🔟
MANG/FISH BS16........................ 54 D5 🔟
Nelson St *BMSTR* BS3................. 10 B4
CBRIS/FH BS1............................. 7 H3
Nelson Ter *CBATH/BATHN* BA1.... 15 G3
Nelson Vls *CBATH/BATHN* BA1.... 14 C6
Neston Wk
BRSG/KWL/STAPK BS4.............. 11 L8
Netham Rd *EVILLE/WHL* BS5......... 9 C4
Netherton Wood La *NAIL* BS48.... 72 D5
Netherways *CLVDN* BS21............ 70 D2
Nettlestone Cl
HNBRY/STHM BS10.................... 38 B4 🔟
Nevalan Dr *EVILLE/WHL* BS5........ 68 A4
Neva Rd *WSM* BS23.................... 16 E5
Neville Rd *KGWD/HNM* BS15....... 54 E7
Nevil Rd *HORF/LLZ* BS7................ 3 K1
Newark St *CBATH/BATHN* BA1.... 15 G8
Newbolt Cl *WSM* BS23.............. 116 D4
New Bond St
CBATH/BATHN BA1..................... 15 G6 🔟
Newbourne Rd *MTN/WRL* BS22.. 105 H6
Newbrick Rd *BRSTK/PCHW* BS34.. 41 F3
New Br *BATHSE* BA2.................... 98 C4

Newbridge Cl
BRSG/KWL/STAPK BS4.............. 9 G6
Newbridge Gdns
CBATH/BATHN BA1..................... 98 D4
Newbridge Hl
CBATH/BATHN BA1..................... 98 D4
Newbridge Rd
BRSG/KWL/STAPK BS4.............. 9 J5
CBATH/BATHN BA1..................... 98 D5
New Bristol Rd *MTN/WRL* BS22.. 105 K4
New Brunswick Av
EVILLE/WHL BS5.......................... 68 B3
New Buildings *MANG/FISH* BS16.. 5 L1
Newbury Rd *HORF/LLZ* BS7......... 52 E2
New Charlotte St *BMSTR* BS3...... 7 H8
New Cheltenham Rd
KGWD/HNM BS15....................... 68 D1
New Church Rd *WSM* BS23....... 116 C4
Newcombe Dr
HNLZ/SM/SNYPK/WT BS9........ 50 E5 🔟
Newcombe Rd
HNLZ/SM/SNYPK/WT BS9........ 51 H1
New Cut Bow *CLVDN* BS21.......... 70 C5
Newditch La
BLAG/CWMG/WR BS40.............. 90 D3
Newent Av *KGWD/HNM* BS15..... 68 B3
New Fosseway Rd
HGRV/WHIT BS14....................... 79 F5
Newfoundland Rd *CBRISNE* BS2... 7 L1
Newfoundland St *CBRISNE* BS2.... 7 K1
Newfoundland Wy *CBRISNE* BS2.. 7 M1
Newgate *CBRIS/FH* BS1................ 7 J3
Newhaven Pl *PTSHD/EG* BS20...... 46 C5
Newhaven Rd *PTSHD/EG* BS20.... 46 B6
Newhurst Pk *TRWBR* BA14........ 125 J4
New John St *BMSTR* BS3.............. 10 E1
New Kingsley Rd *CBRISNE* BS2..... 7 L4 🔟
New King St *CBATH/BATHN* BA1... 14 E6
Newland Dr
BMSTRD/HC/WWD BS13........... 77 J7 🔟
Newland Rd
BMSTRD/HC/WWD BS13........... 77 J7
WSM BS23................................. 17 C6
Newlands Av *FRCTL/WBN* BS36... 24 C1
Newlands Gn *CLVDN* BS21.......... 71 F2 🔟
Newlands Hl *PTSHD/EG* BS20....... 47 C5
Newlands Rd *KEYN* BS31............. 80 D7
The Newlands *MANG/FISH* BS16.. 54 B2
Newland Wk
BMSTRD/HC/WWD BS13........... 92 D1
New La *THNB/SVB* BS35.............. 23 H1
New Leaze *ALMDB* BS32.............. 30 B4
Newleaze *TRWBR* BA14............ 125 H2
Newlyn Av
HNLZ/SM/SNYPK/WT BS9........ 51 F4
Newlyn Wk
BRSG/KWL/STAPK BS4.............. 12 C5
Newlyn Wy *YATE/CS* BS37........... 34 C5
Newman Cl *YATE/CS* BS37.......... 43 J4
Newmarket Av *TRWBR* BA14..... 131 G3
Newnham Cl *HGRV/WHIT* BS14.... 13 L9
Newnham Pl
BRSTK/PCHW BS34.................... 29 J6 🔟
New Orchard St
CBATH/BATHN BA1..................... 15 G7 🔟
Newport Cl *CLVDN* BS21............. 70 E1 🔟
PTSHD/EG BS20......................... 46 D5 🔟
Newport Rd *PTSHD/EG* BS20...... 49 J4 🔟
Newport St *BMSTR* BS3............... 11 K2
Newquay Rd
BRSG/KWL/STAPK BS4.............. 11 M7
New Queen St *BMSTR* BS3........... 7 J9
KGWD/HNM BS15....................... 68 B1
New Rd *BNWL* BS29.................. 119 F2 🔟
BOAV BA15............................... 115 F6
BRSTK/PCHW BS34.................... 39 J5
BRSTK/PCHW BS34.................... 40 C4
CBATH/BATHN BA1.................... 101 H2
CLVDN BS21............................... 71 F7
PTSHD/EG BS20......................... 49 J5
RDSTK/MIDN BA3..................... 122 B1
TRWBR BA14............................ 124 E3 🔟
TRWBR BA14............................ 125 F7 🔟
WNSC BS25.............................. 121 J3
WUE GL12................................. 20 D7
YATE/CS BS37............................ 25 H6
Newry
BRSG/KWL/STAPK BS4.............. 11 K6
Newsome Av *PTSHD/EG* BS20..... 49 J5
New Stadium Rd *EVILLE/WHL* BS5.. 4 C5
New Station Rd
MANG/FISH BS16........................ 54 C7
New St *CBATH/BATHN* BA1......... 14 F7 🔟
CBRISNE BS2............................... 7 L2
New Ter *TRWBR* BA14.............. 125 F1
New Thomas St *CBRISNE* BS2....... 7 L3
Newton Cl *KGWD/HNM* BS15...... 69 C1
Newton Gn *NAIL* BS48................. 73 C1
Newton Rd *BATHSE* BA2............. 98 C6
OLD/WMLY/WICK BS30........... 69 H2
WSM BS23................................. 16 E7
Newton's Rd *MTN/WRL* BS22..... 83 K7
Newton St *EVILLE/WHL* BS5.......... 8 A1
Newtown *BOAV* BA15............... 114 D7
TRWBR BA14............................ 124 E6
New Wk *KGWD/HNM* BS15......... 68 E6
New Walls *BRSG/KWL/STAPK* BS4.. 7 M8
Niblett Cl *KGWD/HNM* BS15........ 69 F4 🔟
Niblett's Hl *EVILLE/WHL* BS5......... 9 H1
Nibley La *YATE/CS* BS37............... 33 C4
Nibley Rd *AVONM* BS11.............. 50 A4
Nicholas La *EVILLE/WHL* BS5......... 68 A4
Nicholas Rd *EVILLE/WHL* BS5........ 4 C8
Nicholls La *FRCTL/WBN* BS36........ 41 K1
Nichol's Rd *PTSHD/EG* BS20......... 46 D3
Nigel Pk *AVONM* BS11................. 50 A2
Nicholettes
OLD/WMLY/WICK BS30........... 69 K5
Nightingale Cl *FRCTL/WBN* BS36.. 42 B2
MTN/WRL BS22......................... 105 K4 🔟
THNB/SVB BS35......................... 19 J3 🔟
Nightingale Gdns *NAIL* BS48....... 73 C1
Nightingale La
FRCTL/WBN BS36........................ 42 B1 🔟
Nightingale Ri *PTSHD/EG* BS20.... 46 D6
Nightingale Rd *TRWBR* BA14..... 124 C6

Nightingale Wy
RDSTK/MIDN BA3..................... 126 C5
Nile St *CBATH/BATHN* BA1.......... 14 D6
Nine Tree Hl *CBRIS/FH* BS1........... 3 H8
Ninth Av *HORF/LLZ* BS7............... 40 A7
Nippors Wy *WNSC* BS25........... 120 C6
Nithsdale Rd *WSM* BS23............ 116 D2
Noble Av *OLD/WMLY/WICK* BS30.. 69 J6
Nomis Pk *YTN/CONG* BS49......... 109 H3
Nore Gdns *PTSHD/EG* BS20.......... 47 C3 🔟
Nore Park Dr *PTSHD/EG* BS20...... 46 C5
Nore Rd *PTSHD/EG* BS20............. 46 C5
Norfolk Av *CBRISNE* BS2............... 7 K1
RDLND/MONT BS6...................... 3 K5
Norfolk Buildings
CBATH/BATHN BA1..................... 14 D6 🔟
Norfolk Crs *CBATH/BATHN* BA1... 14 D6
Norfolk Gv *KEYN* BS31................ 80 C7
Norfolk Pl *BMSTR* BS3................. 10 F1 🔟
Norfolk Rd *PTSHD/EG* BS20......... 47 J5
WSM BS23................................. 17 C7
Norland Rd *CFTN/FAIL* BS8.......... 65 H2 🔟
Norley Rd *HORF/LLZ* BS7............. 52 D2
Normanby Rd *EVILLE/WHL* BS5..... 4 C8
Norman Gv *KGWD/HNM* BS15..... 54 D7 🔟
Norman Rd *CBRISNE* BS2.............. 4 B6
KEYN BS31................................. 96 E1
OLD/WMLY/WICK BS30........... 69 H2
The Normans *BATHSE* BA2........ 100 E3
Normanton Rd *CFTN/FAIL* BS8..... 2 A6
Norrisville Rd
RDLND/MONT BS6...................... 3 K8 🔟
Northampton St
CBATH/BATHN BA1..................... 14 E3
Northcote Rd *CFTN/FAIL* BS8....... 65 H1
EVILLE/WHL BS5.......................... 9 J1
MANG/FISH BS16........................ 55 F3
Northcote St *EVILLE/WHL* BS5...... 4 C8 🔟
North Cft
OLD/WMLY/WICK BS30........... 69 K6 🔟
North Devon Rd
MANG/FISH BS16........................ 54 A4
North Down Cl *WNSC* BS25....... 121 J6 🔟
North Dro *CLVDN* BS21................ 72 C1
North East Rd
THNB/SVB BS35......................... 19 H3 🔟
North End *YTN/CONG* BS49......... 86 D2
Northend Av *KGWD/HNM* BS15... 54 D7
Northend Gdns *KGWD/HNM* BS15.. 54 E4
North End Rd *YTN/CONG* BS49.... 86 E1
Northern Wy *CLVDN* BS21........... 59 H7
Northfield *BOAV* BA15............... 114 A6
YATE/CS BS37............................ 34 A7
Northfield Av *KGWD/HNM* BS15.. 68 D5
Northfield Rd *EVILLE/WHL* BS5...... 68 B3
PTSHD/EG BS20......................... 46 B6
Northfields
CBATH/BATHN BA1..................... 99 J3 🔟
Northfields Cl
CBATH/BATHN BA1..................... 14 E1
Northgate St
CBATH/BATHN BA1..................... 15 G6 🔟
North Green St
CFTN/FAIL BS8............................ 65 H4 🔟🔟
North Gv *PTSHD/EG* BS20............ 49 J5
North Hills Cl
OMX/HUT/LCK BS24................... 117 C4
North La *BATHSE* BA2................. 100 C7
NAIL BS48................................. 73 F2
Northleach Wk *AVONM* BS11...... 50 B4 🔟
North Leaze *LGASH* BS41............ 76 C1 🔟
Northleigh Av *MTN/WRL* BS22... 115 F4
Northleigh *BOAV* BA15.............. 115 F4
Northleigh Av
MTN/WRL BS22......................... 105 H4 🔟
Northmead Av
RDSTK/MIDN BA3..................... 126 A3 🔟
Northmead Cl
RDSTK/MIDN BA3..................... 126 A3 🔟
Northmead La *YATE/CS* BS37....... 32 E1
Northmead Rd
RDSTK/MIDN BA3..................... 126 A3
Northover Rd
HNLZ/SM/SNYPK/WT BS9........ 38 C7
North Parade Rd
CBATH/BATHN BA1..................... 15 H7
North Pk *KGWD/HNM* BS15......... 68 C5
North Rd *BATHSE* BA2................. 15 L4
BATHSE BA2.............................. 112 B3
BMSTR BS3................................. 6 A9 🔟
BNWL BS29.............................. 119 H3
BRSTK/PCHW BS34.................... 40 D4
CFTN/FAIL BS8............................ 65 F4
FRCTL/WBN BS36....................... 42 A1
RDLND/MONT BS6...................... 3 H6
RDSTK/MIDN BA3..................... 126 A4
THNB/SVB BS35......................... 19 H3
YATE/CS BS37............................ 33 J1
YATE/CS BS37............................ 33 K5
North Side Rd *NAIL* BS48............. 90 C4
North St *BMSTR* BS3.................... 6 C9
CBRIS/FH BS1............................. 7 J1
MANG/FISH BS16........................ 54 D4
NAIL BS48................................. 73 C1
OLD/WMLY/WICK BS30........... 69 K5
WSM BS23................................. 16 D2 🔟
Northumberland Pl
CBATH/BATHN BA1..................... 15 G6 🔟
Northumberland Rd
RDLND/MONT BS6...................... 2 F5
Northumbria Dr
HNLZ/SM/SNYPK/WT BS9........ 51 K4
RDLND/MONT BS6...................... 2 C1 🔟
North Vw *MANG/FISH* BS16........ 54 D5 🔟
RDLND/MONT BS6...................... 2 F5
North View Cl *BATHSE* BA2......... 98 E7
North View Dr *BNWL* BS29........ 119 C4
Northville Rd *HORF/LLZ* BS7........ 39 K7
North Wy *BATHSE* BA2................. 98 D7
RDSTK/MIDN BA3..................... 126 B4
TRWBR BA14............................ 124 B7
Northway *BRSTK/PCHW* BS34..... 40 A4
Northwick Rd *HORF/LLZ* BS7....... 52 D1
LGASH BS41............................... 93 C5
Northwoods Wk
HNBRY/STHM BS10.................... 39 G5 🔟
Norton Cl *KGWD/HNM* BS15....... 69 F3 🔟
Norton La *HGRV/WHIT* BS14....... 94 B3
MTN/WRL BS22......................... 105 H1

PLTN/PENS BS39 .... **93** H5
Norton Rd
BRSG/KWL/STAPK BS4............ **12** B3
Nortons Wood La *CLVDN* BS21 ... **59** K5
Norwich Dr
BRSG/KWL/STAPK BS4............ **9** K5
Norwood Av *BATHSE* BA2 .... **112** D1
Norwood Gv *PTSHD/EG* BS20 .... **46** D4
Notgrove Cl *MTN/WRL* BS22 .... **105** G3
Nottingham Rd *HORF/LLZ* BS7 ... **3** K3
Nottingham St *BMSTR* BS3 ...... **11** K2
Nova Scotia Pl *CBRIS/FH* BS1 ..... **6** A7
Novers Crs
BRSG/KWL/STAPK BS4............ **10** F8
Novers Hl *BRSG/KWL/STAPK* BS4.. **10** F8
Novers La *BRSG/KWL/STAPK* BS4.. **10** F8
Novers Park Dr
BRSG/KWL/STAPK BS4............ **11** G7
Novers Park Rd
BRSG/KWL/STAPK BS4............ **11** G7
Novers Rd *BRSG/KWL/STAPK* BS4.. **10** F7
Nugent Hl *RDLND/MONT* BS6 ..... **3** H8
Nunney Cl *KEYN* BS31 .... **96** B2
The Nurseries *WUE* GL12 ...... **24** C1
Nursery Cl *TRWBR* BA14 ..... **125** J3
Nursery Gdns
HNBRY/STHM BS10 .... **38** D5
The Nursery *BMSTR* BS3 .... **10** C1
Nutfield Gv *BRSTK/PCHW* BS34 ... **40** A6
Nutgrove Av *BMSTR* BS3 .... **11** J1
Nuthatch Dr *MANG/FISH* BS16 ... **53** K3
Nuthatch Gdns *MANG/FISH* BS16.. **54** A3
Nutts La *RDSTK/MIDN* BA3 ..... **129** F7
Nutwell Rd *MTN/WRL* BS22 .... **105** K4
Nutwell Sq *MTN/WRL* BS22 .... **105** K3
Nye Dro *OMX/HUT/LCK* BS24 .... **108** B5
Nye Rd *WNSC* BS25 .... **120** C1
Nympsfield *KGWD/HNM* BS15 .... **54** E7

O

Oak Av *BATHSE* BA2 .... **111** F2
Oak Cl *BRSTK/PCHW* BS34 .... **40** C1
YATE/CS BS37 .... **34** A4
Oakdale Av *MANG/FISH* BS16 ..... **54** D1
Oakdale Cl *MANG/FISH* BS16 ..... **54** D1
Oakdale Ct *MANG/FISH* BS16 ... **54** E2
Oakdale Gdns *MTN/WRL* BS22 ... **106** A3
MANG/FISH BS16 .... **54** E1
Oakdene Av *EVILLE/WHL* BS5 ..... **5** H3
Oak Dr *PTSHD/EG* BS20 .... **47** F5
TRWBR BA14 .... **130** E4
Oakenhill Rd
BRSG/KWL/STAPK BS4............ **13** J4
Oakenhill Wk
BRSG/KWL/STAPK BS4............ **13** J4
Oakfield Cl *CBATH/BATHN* BA1 ... **14** A3
Oakfield Gv *CFTN/FAIL* BS8 ...... **6** C1
Oakfield Pl *CFTN/FAIL* BS8........ **6** C1
Oakfield Rd *CFTN/FAIL* BS8 ...... **2** C9
KEYN BS31 .... **96** A1
KGWD/HNM BS15 .... **68** D3
Oakford Av *WSM* BS23 .... **17** H2
Oak Gv *PTSHD/EG* BS20 .... **49** J5
Oakhanger Dr *AVONM* BS11 ...... **37** J7
Oakhill *HNBRY/STHM* BS10 ...... **37** K4
Oakhill Av
OLD/WMLY/WICK BS30 .... **81** J1
Oakhill Cl *NAIL* BS48 .... **74** B2
Oakhill Rd *BATHSE* BA2 .... **111** J3
Oakhurst Rd
HNLZ/SM/SNYPK/WT BS9 .... **51** H4
Oakland Dr
OMX/HUT/LCK BS24 .... **117** K3
Oakland Rd *CFTN/FAIL* BS8 ...... **2** C7
EVILLE/WHL BS5................. **5** K9
Oaklands Cl *MANG/FISH* BS16 ... **55** H4
Oaklands Dr *ALMDB* BS32 .... **29** K3
MANG/FISH BS16 .... **54** A1
OLD/WMLY/WICK BS30 .... **81** J1
Oaklands Rd *MANG/FISH* BS16 .. **55** G4
Oak La *EVILLE/WHL* BS5 .... **5** L6
Oakleaze *FRCTL/WBN* BS36 ...... **42** E1
Oakleaze Rd *THNB/SVB* BS35 ..... **19** H4
Oakleigh Av *EVILLE/WHL* BS5 ..... **5** J9
Oakleigh Cl *NAIL* BS48 .... **74** B6
Oakleigh Gdns
OLD/WMLY/WICK BS30 .... **81** J1
Oakley *BATHSE* BA2 .... **100** D1
CLVDN BS21 .... **70** D3
Oakley Rd *HORF/LLZ* BS7 .... **52** D2
Oakmeade Pk
BRSG/KWL/STAPK BS4............ **12** C3
Oakridge Cl *KGWD/HNM* BS15 ... **69** G3
WNSC BS25 .... **120** E7
Oakridge La *WNSC* BS25 .... **120** E7
Oak Rd *HORF/LLZ* BS7 .... **52** C4
WNSC BS25 .... **120** D5
Oaksey Gv *NAIL* BS48 .... **74** A1
The Oaks *BLAG/CWMG/WR* BS40 .. **91** G5
NAIL BS48 .... **74** A1
Oak St *BATHSE* BA2............. **14** E8
Oak Ter *RDSTK/MIDN* BA3 ...... **126** E4
Oak Tree Av *MANG/FISH* BS16... **56** D5
Oak Tree Cl *KGWD/HNM* BS15 ... **68** C7
TRWBR BA14 .... **124** D5
Oaktree Ct *AVONM* BS11 .... **50** A2
Oaktree Crs *ALMDB* BS32 .... **30** C5
Oaktree Gdns
BMSTRD/HC/WWD BS13 .... **77** G6
Oak Tree Wy *KEYN* BS31 .... **95** J1
Oakwood Av
HNLZ/SM/SNYPK/WT BS9 .... **51** K3
Oakwood Rd
HNLZ/SM/SNYPK/WT BS9 .... **51** K3
Oatfield *NAIL* BS48 .... **90** A3
Oatlands Av *HGRV/WHIT* BS14 .... **78** E5
Oberon Av *EVILLE/WHL* BS5 ...... **5** J6
Odins Rd *BATHSE* BA2 .... **111** G4
Okebourne Cl
HNBRY/STHM BS10 .... **38** E4
Okebourne Rd
HNBRY/STHM BS10 .... **38** E5
Oldacre Rd *HGRV/WHIT* BS14 .... **93** K2

Old Ashley Hl *RDLND/MONT* BS6 ... **3** L6
Old Aust Rd *ALMDB* BS32 .... **30** B1
Old Banwell Rd
OMX/HUT/LCK BS24 .... **118** C2
Old Barn La
BLAG/CWMG/WR BS40 .... **90** B7
Old Barrow Hl *AVONM* BS11 ..... **49** K2
The Old Batch *BOAV* BA15...... **114** C5
Old Bond St
CBATH/BATHN BA1 .... **14** F6
Old Bread St *CBRISNE* BS2....... **7** L4
Oldbridge Rd *HGRV/WHIT* BS14 ... **94** B1
Old Bristol Rd *MTN/WRL* BS22 .. **106** B3
Oldbury Cha
OLD/WMLY/WICK BS30 .... **81** G1
Oldbury Court Dr
MANG/FISH BS16 .... **54** B3
Oldbury Court Rd
MANG/FISH BS16 .... **54** A4
Oldbury La *THNB/SVB* BS35 ...... **19** G1
Old Church Rd *CLVDN* BS21 ...... **70** D1
NAIL BS48 .... **73** H3
WSM BS23 .... **116** C4
Old Down Rd *ALMDB* BS32 .... **22** B4
Old Farm La *EVILLE/WHL* BS5 ..... **68** B3
Oldfield La *BATHSE* BA2 .... **111** G1
Old Fosse Rd *BATHSE* BA2 ...... **111** F4
Old Frome Rd *BATHSE* BA2 ...... **111** H5
Old Gloucester Rd
FRCTL/WBN BS36 .... **41** G1
MANG/FISH BS16 .... **41** G1
THNB/SVB BS35 .... **23** G1
WUE GL12 .... **24** C1
Old Hl *BLAG/CWMG/WR* BS40 .... **90** E5
Old King St *CBATH/BATHN* BA1 ... **14** F5
Old King Street Ct
CBRIS/FH BS1 .... **7** J2
Oldlands Av *FRCTL/WBN* BS36 .... **42** D2
Old La *CLVDN* BS21 .... **61** G6
Old Market St *CBRISNE* BS2 ...... **7** L3
Oldmead Wk
BMSTRD/HC/WWD BS13 .... **77** G4
Old Midford Rd *BATHSE* BA2 .... **111** K6
Old Millard's Hl
RDSTK/MIDN BA3 .... **126** C2
Old Mill Cl *YATE/CS* BS37 .... **43** J4
Old Mill Rd *PTSHD/EG* BS20 ..... **47** H4
Old Mill Wy
OMX/HUT/LCK BS24 .... **106** B5
Oldmixon Crs
OMX/HUT/LCK BS24 .... **117** F3
Oldmixon Rd
OMX/HUT/LCK BS24 .... **117** F5
Old Mixon Rd
OMX/HUT/LCK BS24 .... **117** H4
Old Newbridge Hl
CBATH/BATHN BA1 .... **98** D4
Old Orch *CBATH/BATHN* BA1 ..... **15** G4
Old Pk *CBRISNE* BS2 .... **6** F2
Old Park Hl *CBRISNE* BS2 .... **6** F3
Old Park Rd *AVONM* BS11 .... **49** K2
CLVDN BS21 .... **59** F5
Old Pit Rd *RDSTK/MIDN* BA3 .... **126** C5
Old Post Office La *WSM* BS23 ... **16** D1
Old Priory Rd *PTSHD/EG* BS20 .. **49** H5
Old Quarry *BATHSE* BA2 .... **111** G3
Old Quarry Ri *AVONM* BS11 ...... **50** A2
Old Quarry Rd *AVONM* BS11 ..... **49** K2
Old Rd *RDSTK/MIDN* BA3 .... **127** K4
Old Sneed Av
HNLZ/SM/SNYPK/WT BS9 .... **51** F5
Old Sneed Pk
HNLZ/SM/SNYPK/WT BS9 .... **51** F5
Old Sneed Rd
HNLZ/SM/SNYPK/WT BS9 .... **51** F5
Old St *CLVDN* BS21 .... **59** G7
Old Tr *RDSTK/MIDN* BA3 .... **112** E6
Oldville Av *CLVDN* BS21 .... **71** F1
Old Wells Rd *BATHSE* BA2 ...... **111** J2
Old Weston Rd *NAIL* BS48 .... **75** H4
YTN/CONG BS49 .... **86** D7
Oldwood La *YATE/CS* BS37 ...... **25** J6
Olive Gdns *THNB/SVB* BS35 ...... **22** E2
Olveston Rd *HORF/LLZ* BS7 ...... **52** C4
Olympus Cl
BRSTK/PCHW BS34 .... **40** C2
Olympus Rd *BRSTK/PCHW* BS34... **39** G1
Oolite Gv *BATHSE* BA2 .... **111** G4
Oolite Rd *BATHSE* BA2 .... **111** G4
Oram Ct *OLD/WMLY/WICK* BS30 .. **69** F6
Orange Gv
CBATH/BATHN BA1 .... **15** G6
Orange St *CBRISNE* BS2 .... **7** L1
Orchard Av *CBRIS/FH* BS1 .... **6** F4
CLVDN BS21 .... **60** C5
RDSTK/MIDN BA3 .... **126** A4
THNB/SVB BS35 .... **19** H4
Orchard Bvd
OLD/WMLY/WICK BS30 .... **69** H6
Orchard Cl
BLAG/CWMG/WR BS40 .... **91** G6
BNWL BS29 .... **119** J3
BOAV BA15 .... **114** E5
FRCTL/WBN BS36 .... **41** K2
HNLZ/SM/SNYPK/WT BS9 .... **51** H4
KEYN BS31 .... **80** D5
KGWD/HNM BS15 .... **68** C2
MTN/WRL BS22 .... **105** G2
NAIL BS48 .... **75** G3
PTSHD/EG BS20 .... **47** H4
TRWBR BA14 .... **131** K3
YATE/CS BS37 .... **34** C5
YTN/CONG BS49 .... **109** G1
Orchard Crs *AVONM* BS11 .... **49** K2
Orchard Dr *TRWBR* BA14 .... **130** A4
WNSC BS25 .... **120** C3
Orchard Gdns *KGWD/HNM* BS15 .. **69** F2
Orchard Gra *THNB/SVB* BS35 .... **19** G3
Orchard La *CBRIS/FH* BS1 .... **6** F4
Orchard Lea *PTSHD/EG* BS20 ..... **49** K5
THNB/SVB BS35 .... **23** F1
Orchard Pl *WSM* BS23 .... **16** E3

Orchard Rd *CLVDN* BS21 .... **71** F2
EVILLE/WHL BS5................. **5** L9
FRCTL/WBN BS36 .... **42** E1
HORF/LLZ BS7 .... **3** K1
KGWD/HNM BS15 .... **68** E2
LGASH BS41 .... **76** B1
MANG/FISH BS16 .... **56** D4
NAIL BS48 .... **73** G2
NAIL BS48 .... **74** A5
OMX/HUT/LCK BS24 .... **117** J4
TRWBR BA14 .... **125** F7
Orchard Sq *EVILLE/WHL* BS5 ...... **9** G3
The Orchards *KGWD/HNM* BS15... **69** F2
Orchard St *CBRIS/FH* BS1 .... **6** F4
WSM BS23 .... **16** E3
Orchard Ter *BRSTK/PCHW* BS34 ... **40** E3
The Orchard *BRSTK/PCHW* BS34 .. **40** E3
OMX/HUT/LCK BS24 .... **118** A1
PTSHD/EG BS20 .... **49** J5
RDSTK/MIDN BA3 .... **122** C1
WUE GL12 .... **24** C1
Orchard V *KGWD/HNM* BS15...... **69** F3
RDSTK/MIDN BA3 .... **126** A4
Orchard Wk *WNSC* BS25 .... **121** H2
Orchard Wy *TRWBR* BA14 ...... **130** E4
Oriel Gdns *CBATH/BATHN* BA1 ... **100** B2
Oriel Gv *BATHSE* BA2 .... **110** E1
Orion Dr *BRSTK/PCHW* BS34 ..... **40** C2
Orland Wy
OLD/WMLY/WICK BS30 .... **69** G7
Orlebar Gdns *AVONM* BS11 ...... **37** J6
Orme Dr *CLVDN* BS21 .... **59** F5
Ormerod Rd
HNLZ/SM/SNYPK/WT BS9 .... **51** G5
Ormonds Cl *ALMDB* BS32 .... **30** D5
Ormsley Cl *BRSTK/PCHW* BS34 ... **30** D7
Orneage Cl *RDSTK/MIDN* BA3 ... **129** F7
Orpen Gdns *HORF/LLZ* BS7 ...... **53** F4
Orpheus Av *BRSTK/PCHW* BS34 ... **40** C2
Orwell Dr *KEYN* BS31 .... **81** F7
Orwell St *BMSTR* BS3 .... **11** H1
Osborne Av *HORF/LLZ* BS7 .... **3** L3
WSM BS23 .... **17** H3
Osborne Cl
BRSTK/PCHW BS34 .... **40** C4
Osborne Rd *BMSTR* BS3 .... **6** E8
CBATH/BATHN BA1 .... **98** E6
CFTN/FAIL BS8 .... **2** B8
TRWBR BA14 .... **125** G3
WSM BS23 .... **17** H3
Osborne St *BMSTR* BS3 .... **10** D3
Osborne Vls *CBRISNE* BS2 .... **6** F1
Oslings La *CBATH/BATHN* BA1 .... **101** G2
Osprey Gdns *MTN/WRL* BS22 .... **106** A4
Osprey Pk *THNB/SVB* BS35 .... **19** J2
Osprey Rd *EVILLE/WHL* BS5 .... **8** E3
Otterford Cl *HGRV/WHIT* BS14 ... **79** F6
Otter Rd *CLVDN* BS21 .... **71** G2
Ottery Cl *AVONM* BS11 .... **37** H7
Ottrells Md *BRSTK/PCHW* BS34 ... **30** B4
The Oval *BATHSE* BA2 .... **111** F2
Overhill *PTSHD/EG* BS20 .... **49** J6
Over La *ALMDB* BS32 .... **29** F6
ALMDB BS32 .... **29** K3
Overndale Rd *MANG/FISH* BS16 ... **54** C4
Overnhill Ct *MANG/FISH* BS16..... **54** C4
Overnhill Rd *MANG/FISH* BS16 ... **54** C4
Overton Rd *RDLND/MONT* BS6 .... **3** J5
Owen Dr *CFTN/FAIL* BS8 .... **63** H6
Owen Gv
HNLZ/SM/SNYPK/WT BS9 .... **51** K4
Owen St *EVILLE/WHL* BS5 .... **4** D9
Owls Head Rd *KGWD/HNM* BS15 .. **68** E4
Oxbarton *BRSTK/PCHW* BS34 ..... **40** E3
Oxen Leaze *ALMDB* BS32 .... **30** D5
Oxford Pl *CFTN/FAIL* BS8 .... **65** H4
EVILLE/WHL BS5................. **4** B7
WSM BS23 .... **16** D3
Oxford Sq *OMX/HUT/LCK* BS24 .. **106** C7
Oxford St *BMSTR* BS3 .... **7** M9
CBRISNE BS2 .... **8** A5
EVILLE/WHL BS5................. **8** F3
RDLND/MONT BS6 .... **2** F9
WSM BS23 .... **16** D4
Oxhouse La
BLAG/CWMG/WR BS40 .... **90** E6
CFTN/FAIL BS8 .... **63** H5
Oxleaze *BMSTRD/HC/WWD* BS13 .. **78** B7
Oxleaze La *LGASH* BS41 .... **92** B2
Ozleworth *KGWD/HNM* BS15 .... **69** G2

P

Pack Horse La *BATHSE* BA2 ..... **111** J6
Paddock Cl *ALMDB* BS32 .... **30** C5
MANG/FISH BS16 .... **55** J3
Paddock Gdns *BRSTK/PCHW* BS14 .. **78** E7
THNB/SVB BS35 .... **23** F1
The Paddocks *BATHSE* BA2 ..... **112** A4
THNB/SVB BS35 .... **19** J4
WSM BS23 .... **116** C4
The Paddock *BNWL* BS29 ...... **119** H3
CLVDN BS21 .... **71** F2
PTSHD/EG BS20 .... **47** H5
Paddock Woods *BATHSE* BA2 ... **112** C3
Padfield Cl *BATHSE* BA2 .... **98** E7
Padleigh Hl *BATHSE* BA2 .... **110** D3
Padstow Rd
BRSG/KWL/STAPK BS4............ **11** L7
Page Rd *MANG/FISH* BS16 .... **54** D5
Pages Md *AVONM* BS11 .... **49** J1
Painswick Av *BRSTK/PCHW* BS34... **30** A7
Painswick Dr *YATE/CS* BS37 ...... **34** B6
Painters Md *TRWBR* BA14 ...... **125** J4
Palace Yard Ms
CBATH/BATHN BA1 .... **14** E6
Palairet Cl *BOAV* BA15 .... **123** K1
Palmdale Cl
OLD/WMLY/WICK BS30 .... **81** G1
Palmer Dr *BOAV* BA15 .... **114** E5
Palmer Rd *TRWBR* BA14 .... **125** F4
Palmer Rw *WSM* BS23 .... **16** E2
Palmers Cl
OLD/WMLY/WICK BS30 .... **69** G4
Palmers Leaze *ALMDB* BS32 ..... **41** F1

Palmerston Rd
RDLND/MONT BS6 .... **2** D2
Palmerston St *BMSTR* BS3 .... **10** D1
Palmer St *CBRIS/FH* BS1 .... **16** E2
Palmyra Rd *BMSTR* BS3 .... **10** C3
Parade South
CBATH/BATHN BA1 .... **15** H7
The Parade *AVONM* BS11 .... **50** A3
YATE/CS BS37 .... **34** D6
Paragon Rd *WSM* BS23 .... **104** B4
The Paragon *CFTN/FAIL* BS8 .... **65** H4
Parish Brook Rd *NAIL* BS48 ..... **73** F1
Park Av *ALMDB* BS32 .... **29** J5
BATHSE BA2 .... **14** E9
BMSTR BS3 .... **11** K2
EVILLE/WHL BS5................. **5** K9
FRCTL/WBN BS36 .... **41** K2
FRCTL/WBN BS36 .... **42** C1
YTN/CONG BS49 .... **86** E3
Park Cl *KEYN* BS31 .... **80** D6
KGWD/HNM BS15 .... **69** H5
OLD/WMLY/WICK BS30 .... **69** H5
TRWBR BA14 .... **131** F4
Park Crs *EVILLE/WHL* BS5 .... **5** H9
MANG/FISH BS16 .... **41** H7
OLD/WMLY/WICK BS30 .... **69** H5
Park End *BNWL* BS29 .... **119** F2
Parkers Barton *EVILLE/WHL* BS5 ... **8** D5
Parkers Cl *HNBRY/STHM* BS10 .... **39** H4
Parker St *BMSTR* BS3 .... **10** D1
Parkes Rd *OMX/HUT/LCK* BS24 .. **118** D1
Park Farm Ct
OLD/WMLY/WICK BS30 .... **69** F6
Parkfield Av *EVILLE/WHL* BS5 ...... **9** H2
Parkfield Rd *MANG/FISH* BS16 .... **56** C2
Park Gdns *CBATH/BATHN* BA1 .... **14** A3
Park Gv *RDLND/MONT* BS6 .... **52** A4
Parkhouse La *KEYN* BS31 .... **95** H2
Parkhurst Av
MANG/FISH BS16 .... **54** B5
Parkhurst Rd *WSM* BS23 .... **17** J5
Parklands *KGWD/HNM* BS15 ..... **68** D2
TRWBR BA14 .... **125** F4
Parklands Av *MTN/WRL* BS22 ... **106** A1
Parklands Rd *BMSTR* BS3 .... **65** G6
Parkland Wy *THNB/SVB* BS35..... **19** G2
Park La *CBATH/BATHN* BA1 .... **14** B4
FRCTL/WBN BS36 .... **42** B4
Park Pl *CBATH/BATHN* BA1 .... **14** D3
CBRISNE BS2 .... **6** F2
CFTN/FAIL BS8 .... **6** D2
EVILLE/WHL BS5................. **5** J4
WSM BS23 .... **16** C1
Park Rd *AVONM* BS11 .... **50** A3
BMSTR BS3 .... **6** D7
CBATH/BATHN BA1 .... **98** E5
CLVDN BS21 .... **59** F6
HORF/LLZ BS7 .... **39** J7
KEYN BS31 .... **80** E6
KGWD/HNM BS15 .... **68** D1
MANG/FISH BS16 .... **53** H4
MANG/FISH BS16 .... **54** E4
OLD/WMLY/WICK BS30 .... **69** H5
THNB/SVB BS35 .... **19** G3
WUE GL12 .... **21** J1
YTN/CONG BS49 .... **109** H2
Park Rw *CBRIS/FH* BS1 .... **6** E3
FRCTL/WBN BS36 .... **32** B7
Parkside Av *FRCTL/WBN* BS36 .... **41** K2
Parkside Gdns *EVILLE/WHL* BS5 .... **4** D9
Parkstone Av *HORF/LLZ* BS7...... **52** D5
Park St *BRSG/KWL/STAPK* BS4 .... **8** B9
CBATH/BATHN BA1 .... **14** D2
CBRIS/FH BS1 .... **6** E3
EVILLE/WHL BS5................. **5** M9
TRWBR BA14 .... **124** E7
YATE/CS BS37 .... **32** E3
Park Street Av *CBRIS/FH* BS1 ..... **6** E3
Park Street Ms
CBATH/BATHN BA1 .... **14** D3
The Park *ALMDB* BS32 .... **30** B4
KEYN BS31 .... **80** E5
KGWD/HNM BS15 .... **68** E2
MANG/FISH BS16 .... **41** G7
OLD/WMLY/WICK BS30 .... **81** H2
YTN/CONG BS49 .... **86** E3
Park Vw *KGWD/HNM* BS15 ...... **68** E3
Park View Av *THNB/SVB* BS35 .... **19** H3
Park View Ter *EVILLE/WHL* BS5 .... **9** K1
Parkwall Crs
OLD/WMLY/WICK BS30 .... **69** F6
Parkwall Rd
OLD/WMLY/WICK BS30 .... **69** G6
Parkway *BRSTK/PCHW* BS34 ..... **41** F4
Park Wy *OLD/WMLY/WICK* BS30... **69** H5
RDSTK/MIDN BA3 .... **126** B5
Park Wood Cl *HGRV/WHIT* BS14 .. **78** D7
Parliament St
BRSG/KWL/STAPK BS4............ **8** A9
Parnall Crs *YATE/CS* BS37 .... **33** K5
Parnall Rd *MANG/FISH* BS16 ..... **54** A6
Parnell Rd *CLVDN* BS21 .... **59** G7
Parry Cl *BATHSE* BA2 .... **110** E1
Parry's Cl
HNLZ/SM/SNYPK/WT BS9 .... **51** G4
Parrys Gv
HNLZ/SM/SNYPK/WT BS9 .... **51** G4
Parry's La
HNLZ/SM/SNYPK/WT BS9 .... **51** H4
Parslow Barton
EVILLE/WHL BS5................. **68** A3
Parsonage Cl
BLAG/CWMG/WR BS40 .... **91** G6
Parsonage La
BLAG/CWMG/WR BS40 .... **14** F6
CBATH/BATHN BA1 .... **94** C7
PLTN/PENS BS39 .... **76** B1
Parsonage Rd *LGASH* BS41 ...... **76** B1
Parsons Av *BRSTK/PCHW* BS34 ... **40** E3
Parsons Gn *CLVDN* BS21 .... **70** D3
MTN/WRL BS22 .... **106** B2
Parsons Md *NAIL* BS48 .... **75** F4
Parsons Paddock
HGRV/WHIT BS14 .... **12** A9
Parson St *BMSTR* BS3 .... **10** E5

Parsons Wk
OLD/WMLY/WICK BS30 .... **69** K3
Partis Wy *CBATH/BATHN* BA1 .... **98** D4
Partition St *CBRIS/FH* BS1 .... **6** E5
Partridge Cl *MTN/WRL* BS22 .... **106** A4
Partridge Rd *MANG/FISH* BS16.... **56** E5
Passage Leaze *AVONM* BS11...... **49** K3
Passage Rd
HNBRY/STHM BS10 .... **38** D5
HNLZ/SM/SNYPK/WT BS9 .... **51** J1
Passage Road Brentry Hl
HNBRY/STHM BS10 .... **38** D5
Passage St *CBRIS/FH* BS1 .... **7** K4
The Pastures *BOAV* BA15 .... **122** E3
Patch Cft *CLVDN* BS21 .... **70** E3
Patch Elm La *YATE/CS* BS37 ..... **25** F7
Patch La *YATE/CS* BS37 .... **25** H6
Paulman Gdns *LGASH* BS41 ..... **76** B3
Paul's Cswy *YTN/CONG* BS49 ... **109** G1
Paul St *CBRISNE* BS2 .... **7** H1
Paulton Dr *HORF/LLZ* BS7 .... **2** F2
Paulton Rd *RDSTK/MIDN* BA3 ... **126** A5
Paultow Av *BMSTR* BS3 .... **11** J2
Paultow Rd *BMSTR* BS3 .... **11** J2
Pavely Gdns *TRWBR* BA14 ...... **125** J5
Pavey Cl
BMSTRD/HC/WWD BS13 .... **78** A7
Pavey Rd
BMSTRD/HC/WWD BS13 .... **78** A7
Pawlett Rd
BMSTRD/HC/WWD BS13 .... **93** F1
Pawlett Wk
BMSTRD/HC/WWD BS13 .... **93** F1
Paxcroft Wy *TRWBR* BA14 ...... **125** H6
Paybridge Rd
BMSTRD/HC/WWD BS13 .... **77** H7
Payne Dr *EVILLE/WHL* BS5 .... **8** C2
Payne Rd *OMX/HUT/LCK* BS24 .. **117** J4
Peache Rd *MANG/FISH* BS16 ..... **54** E3
Peacocks La *KGWD/HNM* BS15 ... **68** C2
Pearces Hl *MANG/FISH* BS16 ..... **54** C4
Pearl St *BMSTR* BS3 .... **10** C2
Pearsall Rd
OLD/WMLY/WICK BS30 .... **80** E1
Pearse Cl *MTN/WRL* BS22 .... **84** C7
Peart Cl *BMSTRD/HC/WWD* BS13 .. **77** G6
Peart Dr
BMSTRD/HC/WWD BS13 .... **77** G7
Pear Tree Hey *YATE/CS* BS37 .... **34** B2
Peartree La *EVILLE/WHL* BS5 ..... **68** B4
KGWD/HNM BS15 .... **55** F7
Pear Tree Rd *ALMDB* BS32 ...... **30** D5
Pedder Rd *CLVDN* BS21 .... **71** F2
Peel St *EVILLE/WHL* BS5........... **3** M9
Pegasus Rd *BRSTK/PCHW* BS34 ... **39** G1
Pelican Cl *MTN/WRL* BS22 ...... **105** K5
Pemberton Ct
MANG/FISH BS16 .... **54** C4
Pembery Rd *BMSTR* BS3 .... **10** D2
Pembroke Av *AVONM* BS11 ...... **50** A3
Pembroke Gv *CFTN/FAIL* BS8 ..... **6** B2
Pembroke Pl *CFTN/FAIL* BS8 ...... **6** B6
Pembroke Rd *AVONM* BS11 ...... **50** A3
BMSTR BS3 .... **6** E8
CFTN/FAIL BS8 .... **2** A9
KGWD/HNM BS15 .... **54** E7
PTSHD/EG BS20 .... **46** B6
WSM BS23 .... **17** G8
Pembroke St *CBRISNE* BS2 .... **7** K1
Pembroke V *CFTN/FAIL* BS8 ...... **6** A1
Penard Wy *KGWD/HNM* BS15 .... **69** F3
Penarth Dr
OMX/HUT/LCK BS24 .... **117** F5
Pendennis Av
MANG/FISH BS16 .... **54** D5
Pendennis Pk
BRSG/KWL/STAPK BS4............ **13** H3
Pendennis Rd *MANG/FISH* BS16... **54** D4
Pendlesham Gdns *WSM* BS23 ... **105** F4
Pendock Cl
OLD/WMLY/WICK BS30 .... **81** J2
Pendock Ct *MANG/FISH* BS16 .... **55** H2
Pendock Rd *FRCTL/WBN* BS36 ... **41** K3
MANG/FISH BS16 .... **54** B3
Penfield Rd *CBRISNE* BS2 .... **4** A3
Penlea Ct *AVONM* BS11 .... **49** K2
Pennard Ct *HGRV/WHIT* BS14 .... **78** D6
Pennard Gn *BATHSE* BA2 .... **98** D6
Pen Dr *MANG/FISH* BS16 .... **54** B5
Penn Gdns *CBATH/BATHN* BA1 ... **98** D4
Penngrove
OLD/WMLY/WICK BS30 .... **69** G7
Penn Hill Rd *CBATH/BATHN* BA1 .. **98** D3
Pennine Gdns *WSM* BS23 .... **105** F4
Pennine Rd
OLD/WMLY/WICK BS30 .... **69** J6
Pennlea *BMSTRD/HC/WWD* BS13.. **77** K4
Penn Lea Rd *CBATH/BATHN* BA1 .. **98** D3
The Penns *CLVDN* BS21 .... **71** G1
Penn St *CBRIS/FH* BS1 .... **7** K2
Pennycress *MTN/WRL* BS22 ..... **105** J6
Pennyquick *BATHSE* BA2 .... **97** K6
Pennyroyal Gv
MANG/FISH BS16 .... **53** J4
Pennywell Rd *EVILLE/WHL* BS5 .... **4** A8
Pen Park Rd *HNBRY/STHM* BS10 .. **39** F5
Penpole Av *AVONM* BS11 .... **50** A3
Penpole Cl *AVONM* BS11 .... **49** K2
Penpole La *AVONM* BS11 .... **50** A2
Penpole Pk *AVONM* BS11 .... **50** A2
Penpole Pl *AVONM* BS11 .... **50** A3
Penrice Cl *MTN/WRL* BS22 ...... **105** H3
Penrose *HGRV/WHIT* BS14 .... **78** D5
Penrose Dr
BRSTK/PCHW BS34 .... **40** C1
Pensfield Pk *HNBRY/STHM* BS10 .. **38** D3
Pensford Ct *HGRV/WHIT* BS14 ... **79** H6
Pensford Hl *PLTN/PENS* BS39 .... **94** C7
Pentire Av
BMSTRD/HC/WWD BS13 .... **77** G4
Pentland Av *THNB/SVB* BS35 ..... **19** K5
Pepperacre La *TRWBR* BA14 .... **125** H5
Peppershells La
PLTN/PENS BS39 .... **95** H6
Pepys Cl *KEYN* BS31 .... **96** B2
Pera Pl *CBATH/BATHN* BA1 .... **15** G2
Pera Rd *CBATH/BATHN* BA1....... **15** G3

Percival Rd *CFTN/FAIL* BS8 .... 65 H3
Peregrine Cl *MTN/WRL* BS22 .. 106 A4
The Perrings *NAIL* BS48 .... 73 J2 ⓫
Perrinpit Rd *FRCTL/WBN* BS36 .. 31 J4
Perrott Rd *KGWD/HNM* BS15 .. 69 G1 ⓫
Perry Cl *FRCTL/WBN* BS36 .... 41 J4
Perrycroft Av
BMSTRD/HC/WWD BS13 .... 77 J5
Perrycroft Rd
BMSTRD/HC/WWD BS13 .... 77 J5
Perrymans Cl *MANG/FISH* BS16 .. 54 A3
Perrymead *BATHSE* BA2 .... 112 A2
MTN/WRL BS22 .... 84 C7 ⓫
Perry Rd *CBRIS/FH* BS1 .... 6 F3
Perrys Lea *ALMDB* BS32 .... 30 C5 ⓫
Perry St *EVILLE/WHL* BS5 .... 4 A9
Pesley Cl
BMSTRD/HC/WWD BS13 .... 77 H7
Petercole Dr
BMSTRD/HC/WWD BS13 .... 77 J5
Peterside Rd
BMSTRD/HC/WWD BS13 .... 93 F1 ⓫
Peterson Sq
BMSTRD/HC/WWD BS13 .... 93 F1 ⓫
Petersway Gdns
EVILLE/WHL BS5 .... 68 A4 ⓫
Petherton Cl *KGWD/HNM* BS15 .. 68 E3
Petherton Gdns
HGRV/WHIT BS14 .... 79 F4
Petherton Rd *HGRV/WHIT* BS14 .. 12 C8
Pettigrove Gdns
KGWD/HNM BS15 .... 68 E3
Pettigrove Rd *KGWD/HNM* BS15 .. 68 E4
Pevensey Wk
BRSG/KWL/STAPK BS4 .... 11 H9
Peverell Cl *HNBRY/STHM* BS10 .. 38 C5
Peverell Dr *HNBRY/STHM* BS10 .. 38 C5
Philadelphia Ct *CBRIS/FH* BS1 .... 7 K2 ⓫
Philippa Cl *HGRV/WHIT* BS14 .... 78 E4
Philip St *BMSTR* BS3 .... 7 H9
CBRISNE BS2 .... 8 C6
Phillips Rd *WSM* BS23 .... 17 K6
Phillis Hl *PLTN/PENS* BS39 .... 126 A1
Phippen St *CBRIS/FH* BS1 .... 7 J6 ⓫
Phipps St *BMSTR* BS3 .... 6 C8
Phoenix Gv *RDLND/MONT* BS6 .. 52 A4
Pickwick Rd *CBATH/BATHN* BA1 .. 99 K2 ⓫
Picton La *RDLND/MONT* BS6 .... 3 J8
Picton St *RDLND/MONT* BS6 .... 3 J8
Pierrepont Pl
CBATH/BATHN BA1 .... 15 G7 ⓫
Pierrepont St
CBATH/BATHN BA1 .. 15 G7 ⓫ ⓰
Pier Rd *PTSHD/EG* BS20 .... 47 H2
Pigeon House Dr
BMSTRD/HC/WWD BS13 ...... 78 B7 ⓫
Pigott Av
BMSTRD/HC/WWD BS13 .... 77 J7
Pile Marsh *EVILLE/WHL* BS5 .... 9 G2
Pilgrims Wy *AVONM* BS11 ...... 49 J2 ⓫
MANG/FISH BS16 .... 54 D1 ⓫
MTN/WRL BS22 .... 105 K3
Pilgrims Whf
BRSG/KWL/STAPK BS4 .... 9 L4
Pilkington Cl *BRSTK/PCHW* BS34 .. 40 B6
Pillingers Rd *KGWD/HNM* BS15 .. 68 C3
Pill Rd *CFTN/FAIL* BS8 .... 64 B1
PTSHD/EG BS20 .... 49 K6
Pill Wy *CLVDN* BS21 .... 70 D1
Pimms La *MTN/WRL* BS22 ...... 105 G2 ⓫
MTN/WRL BS22 .... 105 G3 ⓫
Pimpernel Md *ALMDB* BS32 ...... 40 D1
Pinchay La
BLAG/CWMG/WR BS40 .... 91 H4
Pine Rd *MTN/WRL* BS22 .... 105 J3
THNB/SVB BS35 .... 19 H4
Pine Ct *RDSTK/MIDN* BA3 .... 126 C3
Pinecroft *HGRV/WHIT* BS14 .... 78 D4 ⓫
Pine Gv *HORF/LLZ* BS7 .... 39 J7
Pine Grove Pl *HORF/LLZ* BS7 .... 3 H5
Pine Hl *MTN/WRL* BS22 .... 105 J3
Pine Lea *OMX/HUT/LCK* BS24 .. 117 G7
Pine Ridge Cl
HNLZ/SM/SNYPK/WT BS9 .... 50 E5 ⓫
Pine Rd *HNBRY/STHM* BS10 ...... 38 A6
Pines Rd *OLD/WMLY/WICK* BS30 .. 81 J1
Pines Wy *BATHSE* BA2 .... 14 C7
RDSTK/MIDN BA3 .... 127 H3
Pinetree Rd
OMX/HUT/LCK BS24 ...... 118 E2 ⓫
Pine Wk *RDSTK/MIDN* BA3 ...... 127 F1 ⓫
TRWBR BA14 .... 130 E4
Pinewood Av *RDSTK/MIDN* BA3 .. 126 A4
Pinewood Cl
HNLZ/SM/SNYPK/WT BS9 .... 51 K2
RDSTK/MIDN BA3 .. 126 A4
Pinewood Gv *RDSTK/MIDN* BA3 .. 126 A4
Pinewood Rd
RDSTK/MIDN BA3 .... 126 A4
Pinhay Rd
BMSTRD/HC/WWD BS13 ...... 77 K5 ⓫
Pinkers Md *MANG/FISH* BS16 .... 55 J3
Pioneer Av *BATHSE* BA2........... 111 J4
Pioneer Pk *BRSG/KWL/STAPK* BS4 .. 8 F7
Pipe La *CBRIS/FH* BS1 .... 6 F4
CBRIS/FH BS1 .... 6 E4
Piper Rd *YATE/CS* BS37 .... 34 B4 ⓫
Piplar Gnd *BOAV* BA15 .... 123 K2
Pippin Ct
OLD/WMLY/WICK BS30 .. 69 F6 ⓫⓰
Pitch & Pay La
HNLZ/SM/SNYPK/WT BS9 .... 51 K2
Pitchcombe *YATE/CS* BS37 ...... 43 K1 ⓫
Pitchcombe Gdns
HNLZ/SM/SNYPK/WT BS9 .... 51 F2
Pitch La *RDLND/MONT* BS6 .... 2 C6
Pithay Ct *CBRIS/FH* BS1 .... 7 H3 ⓫
Pitman Av *TRWBR* BA14 ...... 124 D7 ⓫
Pitman Rd *WSM* BS23 .... 16 E6 ⓫
Pit Rd *RDSTK/MIDN* BA3 ...... 126 C4
Pitt Rd *HORF/LLZ* BS7 .... 52 C4
Pixash La *KEYN* BS31 .... 81 H6
Pizey Av *CLVDN* BS21 .... 70 D1
Pizey Cl *CLVDN* BS21 .... 70 D1
Players Cl *MANG/FISH* BS16 ...... 41 G4
Playford Gdns *AVONM* BS11 .... 50 A1
Pleasant Rd *MANG/FISH* BS16 .... 54 D4
Pleshey Cl *MTN/WRL* BS22 ...... 105 J3

Ploughed Paddock *NAIL* BS48 .. 73 H2 ⓫
Plover Cl *MTN/WRL* BS22 ...... 106 A4
YATE/CS BS37 .... 33 K5
Plovers Ri *RDSTK/MIDN* BA3 .... 127 H2
Plumers Cl *CLVDN* BS21 .... 71 G2 ⓫
Plummer's Hl *EVILLE/WHL* BS5 .... 5 K9
Plumpton Ct
MANG/FISH BS16 .... 42 A7 ⓫
Plumtree Cl *WNSC* BS25 .... 120 C5
Plumtree Rd *MANG/FISH* BS16 .... 48 A5
Plunder St *YTN/CONG* BS49 .... 88 A5
Podgers Dr *CBATH/BATHN* BA1 .. 98 E2
Poets' Cl *EVILLE/WHL* BS5 .... 5 G9
Polden Cl *NAIL* BS48 .... 73 J2
Polden Rd *PTSHD/EG* BS20 .... 46 E4 ⓫
WSM BS23 .... 17 H1 ⓫
Polebarn Rd *TRWBR* BA14 .... 125 F5
Polly Barnes Cl
KGWD/HNM BS15 .... 68 B5 ⓫
Polly Barnes Hl
KGWD/HNM BS15 .... 68 B5
Polygon Rd *CFTN/FAIL* BS8 .... 6 A5
Pomeroy La *TRWBR* BA14 ...... 129 H1
Pomfrett Gdns
HGRV/WHIT BS14 .... 79 J6 ⓫
Pomphrey Hl *MANG/FISH* BS16 .. 55 J5
Ponsford Rd
BRSG/KWL/STAPK BS4........ 12 C7
Ponting Cl *EVILLE/WHL* BS5 .... 68 A1 ⓫
Pool Cnr *ALMDB* BS32 .... 22 A4
Poole Court Dr *YATE/CS* BS37.... 34 B5
Poole St *AVONM* BS11 .... 49 H1
Pooles Whf *CFTN/FAIL* BS8 .... 6 B6
Pooles Wharf Ct *CFTN/FAIL* BS8.. 6 B6
Poolmead Rd *BATHSE* BA2 .... 98 C7
Pool Rd *KGWD/HNM* BS15 .... 54 E6
Pope's Wk *BATHSE* BA2 .... 112 A1
The Poplars *MTN/WRL* BS22 .... 106 A4
PTSHD/EG BS20 .... 49 H5 ⓫
Poplar Cl *BATHSE* BA2 .... 111 G1
OLD/WMLY/WICK BS30 .... 69 J4 ⓫
Poplar Dr *MANG/FISH* BS16...... 56 D4
Poplar Pl *MANG/FISH* BS16 ...... 54 A6 ⓫
Poplar Rd *BATHSE* BA2 .... 111 G5
BMSTRD/HC/WWD BS13 ...... 77 H4
EVILLE/WHL BS5 .... 5 M7
KGWD/HNM BS15 .... 68 A5
OLD/WMLY/WICK BS30 .... 69 K4
Poplar Ter *KGWD/HNM* BS15 .. 69 F2 ⓫
Poplar Tree La *TRWBR* BA14 .... 129 H4
Poplar Wk *OMX/HUT/LCK* BS24 .. 117 H1
Poppy Cl *MTN/WRL* BS22 .... 84 B7
Poppy Md *ALMDB* BS32 .... 40 D1
Porlock Cl *CLVDN* BS21 .... 71 G2 ⓫
WSM BS23 .... 116 E4 ⓫
Porlock Gdns *NAIL* BS48 .... 73 J2
Porlock Rd *BATHSE* BA2 .... 111 K3
BMSTR BS3 .... 11 G2 ⓫
Portal Rd *OMX/HUT/LCK* BS24 .. 118 E2
Portbury Common
PTSHD/EG BS20 .... 47 J5
Portbury Gv *AVONM* BS11 ...... 49 K3
The Portbury Hundred
PTSHD/EG BS20 .... 48 A6
Portbury La *PTSHD/EG* BS20 .... 48 E7
Portbury Wk *AVONM* BS11 ...... 49 K3 ⓫
Portbury Wy *PTSHD/EG* BS20 .... 48 D4
Portishead Rd
MTN/WRL BS22 ...... 106 C1 ⓫⓰
Portland Cl *NAIL* BS48 .... 73 H2
Portland Dr *PTSHD/EG* BS20 .... 47 J5
Portland Pl *CBATH/BATHN* BA1 .. 14 E3
MANG/FISH BS16 .... 54 D6 ⓫
Portland Sq *CBRISNE* BS2 .... 7 K1
Portland St *CBRISNE* BS2 .... 2 F9
CFTN/FAIL BS8 .... 65 H3
MANG/FISH BS16 .... 54 D6
Portmeirion Cl
HGRV/WHIT BS14 .... 78 E6 ⓫
Port Vw *PTSHD/EG* BS20 ...... 49 J4 ⓫
Portview Rd *AVONM* BS11 ...... 49 H1
Portwall La *CFTN/FAIL* BS8 .... 7 K6
Portwall La East *CBRIS/FH* BS1 .. 7 K6 ⓫
Portway *AVONM* BS11 .... 49 J7
HNLZ/SM/SNYPK/WT BS9 .... 50 E6
Portway La *YATE/CS* BS37 .... 27 J8
Post Office La *NAIL* BS48 .... 75 F4
Post Office Rd
OMX/HUT/LCK BS24 .... 118 C1
Poston Wy *BOAV* BA15 .... 113 J6
Pottery Rd *WSM* BS23 .... 17 J6
Poulton *BOAV* BA15 .... 123 K1
Poulton La *BOAV* BA15............ 124 A2
Pound Dr *MANG/FISH* BS16...... 53 K4
Pound La *BOAV* BA15 .... 114 D7
MANG/FISH BS16 .... 5 M1
NAIL BS48 .... 61 H7
Pound Md
BLAG/CWMG/WR BS40 .... 90 D4
Pound Rd *KGWD/HNM* BS15 .... 55 F7
The Pound *ALMDB* BS32 .... 29 K2
Pountney Dr *EVILLE/WHL* BS5 .. 8 C1 ⓫
Powis Cl *MTN/WRL* BS22 .... 105 H3
Powlett Ct *BATHSE* BA2 .... 15 J4
Powlett Rd *BATHSE* BA2 .... 15 J3
Pow's Hl *RDSTK/MIDN* BA3 ...... 126 E1
Pow's Orch
RDSTK/MIDN BA3 .... 126 B4 ⓫
Pow's Rd *KGWD/HNM* BS15 .... 68 D3
Poyntz Ct
OLD/WMLY/WICK BS30 .. 69 F7 ⓫
Poyntz Rd
BRSG/KWL/STAPK BS4........ 11 L8
Preanes Gn *MTN/WRL* BS22 .... 106 A3
Preddy's La *EVILLE/WHL* BS5 ...... 68 A4
Prescott Cl *MTN/WRL* BS22 .... 105 G4
Prescott *YATE/CS* BS37 .... 34 A7 ⓫
Press Moor Dr
OLD/WMLY/WICK BS30 .. 69 F6 ⓫⓰
Prestbury *YATE/CS* BS37 .... 34 A7
Preston Wk
BRSG/KWL/STAPK BS4........ 12 B6
Prestwick Cl
BRSG/KWL/STAPK BS4........ 13 G6
Pretoria Rd *BRSTK/PCHW* BS34 .. 29 J7
Prewett St *CBRIS/FH* BS1 .... 7 J7

Priddy Cl *BATHSE* BA2 .... 98 E7
Priddy Ct *HGRV/WHIT* BS14 ...... 79 F6
Priddy Dr *HGRV/WHIT* BS14 ...... 79 F6
Priests Wy *MTN/WRL* BS22 ...... 105 J3
Priestwood Cl
HNBRY/STHM BS10 .... 38 D5 ⓫
Primrose Cl *ALMDB* BS32 .... 30 C5 ⓫
KGWD/HNM BS15 .... 68 B1
Primrose Dr *THNB/SVB* BS35 .... 19 J3
Primrose Hl *CBATH/BATHN* BA1 .. 99 G3
Primrose La *KGWD/HNM* BS15 .. 68 C2
RDSTK/MIDN BA3 .... 126 C4 ⓫
Princes Ct
OLD/WMLY/WICK BS30 .... 69 F6
Princes' La *CFTN/FAIL* BS8 .... 65 H4
Princes' Pl *HORF/LLZ* BS7 .... 3 J3
Prince's Rd *CLVDN* BS21 .... 59 F7
Princess Cl *KEYN* BS31 .... 80 E6
Princess Gdns
MANG/FISH BS16 .... 53 H3 ⓫
TRWBR BA14 .... 125 G2
Princess Rw *CBRISNE* BS2 .... 7 H1
CBRISNE BS2 .... 8 A4
Princess St *CBATH/BATHN* BA1 .. 14 F6 ⓫
CBRISNE BS2 .... 3 K9
Princess Victoria St
CFTN/FAIL BS8 .... 65 H4
Prince St *CBRIS/FH* BS1 .... 7 G6
CBRIS/FH BS1 .... 8 D3
Prior Park Rd *BATHSE* BA2 ...... 15 J9
Priors Lea *YATE/CS* BS37 .... 34 B6
Priory Av
HNLZ/SM/SNYPK/WT BS9 .... 51 J2
Priory Cl *BATHSE* BA2 .... 112 A2
BOAV BA15 .... 114 D6
RDSTK/MIDN BA3 .... 126 B4
Priory Court Rd
HNLZ/SM/SNYPK/WT BS9 .... 51 J2
Priory Dene
HNLZ/SM/SNYPK/WT BS9 .... 51 J2 ⓫
Priory Gdns *AVONM* BS11 ...... 49 K3 ⓫
HORF/LLZ BS7 .... 52 D1
PTSHD/EG BS20 .... 49 H5
Priory Ms *WSM* BS23 .... 17 K3
Priory Pk *BATHSE* BA2 .... 114 C6
Priory Rd *AVONM* BS11 .... 49 K3
BRSG/KWL/STAPK BS4........ 12 D4
CFTN/FAIL BS8 .... 6 D1
KEYN BS31 .... 80 E4
PTSHD/EG BS20 .... 48 D6
PTSHD/EG BS20 .... 49 H5
WSM BS23 .... 17 K3
Priston La *MTN/WRL* BS22 ...... 84 C7
Pritchard St *CBRISNE* BS2 .... 7 K1
Probyn Cl *MANG/FISH* BS16 .... 54 A2 ⓫
Proby Pl *TRWBR* BA14 .... 125 F5 ⓫
Prospect Av *KGWD/HNM* BS15 .. 68 B1 ⓫
Prospect Crs *KGWD/HNM* BS15 .. 55 F7 ⓫
Prospect La *FRCTL/WBN* BS36 .... 32 A7 ⓫
Prospect Pl *CBATH/BATHN* BA1 .. 101 J2
EVILLE/WHL BS5 .... 4 F9
TRWBR BA14 .... 125 F5
WSM BS23 .... 16 E2
Prospect Rd *BATHSE* BA2 .... 112 B1
THNB/SVB BS35 .... 27 H1
Providence La *LGASH* BS41 ...... 76 B1
Providence Pl *CBRISNE* BS2 ...... 7 L4 ⓫
Providence Vw *LGASH* BS41 ...... 76 C2 ⓫
Prudham St *EVILLE/WHL* BS5 .... 4 E7 ⓫
Pudding Pie Cl
BLAG/CWMG/WR BS40 ...... 109 K7
Pudding Pie La
BLAG/CWMG/WR BS40 ...... 109 K7
Puffin Cl *MTN/WRL* BS22 ...... 106 A5
Pullin Ct *OLD/WMLY/WICK* BS30.. 69 K6
Pulteney Av *BATHSE* BA2 .... 15 J7 ⓫
Pulteney Gdns *BATHSE* BA2 ...... 15 J7
Pulteney Ms *BATHSE* BA2 .... 15 H5
Pulteney Rd *BATHSE* BA2 .... 15 J6
Pump La *ALMDB* BS32 .... 22 C2
CBATH/BATHN BA1 .... 101 G3
CBRIS/FH BS1 .... 7 J7
PTSHD/EG BS20 .... 49 K4 ⓫
Purcell Wk
BRSG/KWL/STAPK BS4........ 78 B4 ⓫⓰
Purdown Rd *HORF/LLZ* BS7 ...... 52 D4
Purdue Cl *MTN/WRL* BS22 ...... 106 C2 ⓫
Purlewent Dr
CBATH/BATHN BA1 .... 99 F3
Purn La *OMX/HUT/LCK* BS24...... 117 F6
Purn Rd *OMX/HUT/LCK* BS24 .... 116 E6
Purn Wy *OMX/HUT/LCK* BS24 .... 117 G7
Pursey Dr *ALMDB* BS32 .... 40 D2
Purton Cl *KGWD/HNM* BS15 .... 68 E4
Purton Rd *HORF/LLZ* BS7 .... 3 H5
Puttingthorpe Dr *WSM* BS23 .... 105 H6
Puxley Cl *HGRV/WHIT* BS14 ...... 79 J5 ⓫
Puxton La *MANG/FISH* BS16 .... 108 A1
Puxton Moor La
OMX/HUT/LCK BS24 .... 108 B3
Puxton Rd *OMX/HUT/LCK* BS24 .. 107 J5
Pye Cft *ALMDB* BS32 .... 30 D4
Pyecroft Av
HNLZ/SM/SNYPK/WT BS9 .... 51 K2
Pylewell La *WNSC* BS25 .... 121 G4
Pylle Hill Crs *BMSTR* BS3 .... 7 L9
Pyne Point *CLVDN* BS21 .... 58 E7
Pynne Cl *HGRV/WHIT* BS14 ...... 79 K6
Pynne Rd *HGRV/WHIT* BS14 ...... 79 K6

Q

The Quadrangle *YATE/CS* BS37.... 43 K4
Quadrant East
MANG/FISH BS16 .... 54 C6 ⓫
The Quadrant *RDLND/MONT* BS6 .. 2 C3
Quadrant West
MANG/FISH BS16 .... 54 C6 ⓫
Quaker La *THNB/SVB* BS35 ...... 19 G4 ⓫
Quaker's Cl *MANG/FISH* BS16 .... 54 D1 ⓫
Quakers' Friars *CBRIS/FH* BS1 .... 7 J2 ⓫
Quaker's Rd *MANG/FISH* BS16 .... 54 D1

Quantock Cl
OLD/WMLY/WICK BS30 ...... 69 J5
Quantock Rd *BMSTR* BS3 ...... 11 G2
PTSHD/EG BS20 .... 47 F4
WSM BS23 .... 16 D8
Quantocks *BATHSE* BA2 .... 111 K3
The Quarries *ALMDB* BS32 ...... 30 A2
Quarrington Rd *HORF/LLZ* BS7 .. 52 C4
Quarry Barton *MANG/FISH* BS16 .. 41 H4
Quarry Cl *BATHSE* BA2 .... 111 J4
RDSTK/MIDN BA3 .... 113 J7
Quarry La *AVONM* BS11 .... 37 K7
FRCTL/WBN BS36 .... 41 K4
Quarry Md *THNB/SVB* BS35 ...... 22 E1
Quarry Rd *KGWD/HNM* BS15 .... 68 D4
MANG/FISH BS16 .... 54 C2 ⓫
THNB/SVB BS35 .... 22 E1
YATE/CS BS37 .... 34 D6
Quarry Steps *CFTN/FAIL* BS8 .... 2 A6
Quarry Wy *MANG/FISH* BS16.... 42 B7
NAIL BS48 .... 73 H1
Quarterway La *TRWBR* BA14 .... 125 C5
Quays Av *PTSHD/EG* BS20 ...... 47 J4
Quayside La *EVILLE/WHL* BS5 .... 9 M4
Quay St *CBRIS/FH* BS1 .... 7 H3
Quedgeley *YATE/CS* BS37 ...... 33 K7 ⓫
Queen Ann Rd *CBRISNE* BS2 ...... 8 C5
EVILLE/WHL BS5 .... 8 D3
Queen Charlotte St
CBRIS/FH BS1 .... 7 H4 ⓫
Queen Charlton La
HGRV/WHIT BS14 .... 94 C1
Queen's Av *CFTN/FAIL* BS8 ...... 6 D2
PTSHD/EG BS20 .... 47 G4
Queens Club Gdns
TRWBR BA14 .... 124 C6 ⓫
Queenscote *PTSHD/EG* BS20 .... 47 K4
Queensdale Crs
BRSG/KWL/STAPK BS4........ 12 B5
Queensdown Gdns
BRSG/KWL/STAPK BS4........ 12 B5
Queens Down Gdns
BRSG/KWL/STAPK BS4........ 12 C2
Queen's Dr *BATHSE* BA2 .... 111 K3
HORF/LLZ BS7 .... 2 F1
KGWD/HNM BS15 .... 68 B6
Queens Gdns *BATHSE* BA2 ...... 125 C2
Queens Ga
HNLZ/SM/SNYPK/WT BS9 .... 51 F4
Queenshill Rd
BRSG/KWL/STAPK BS4........ 12 B6
Queensholm Av
MANG/FISH BS16 .... 41 K7 ⓫
Queensholm Cl *MANG/FISH* BS16 .. 41 J7
Queensholm Crs
MANG/FISH BS16 .... 41 J7
Queensholm Dr
MANG/FISH BS16 .... 54 E1
Queen's Pde
CBATH/BATHN BA1 .... 14 E5 ⓫
CBRIS/FH BS1 .... 6 D5
Queen's Parade Pl
CBATH/BATHN BA1 .... 14 F5 ⓫
Queen's Rd
BMSTRD/HC/WWD BS13 ...... 77 H7
BNWL BS29 .... 119 H3 ⓫
BRSG/KWL/STAPK BS4........ 12 E4
CFTN/FAIL BS8 .... 6 B2
CLVDN BS21 .... 59 F7
EVILLE/WHL BS5 .... 9 L2
HORF/LLZ BS7 .... 3 L1
KEYN BS31 .... 80 E5
LGASH BS41 .... 92 C1 ⓫
MANG/FISH BS16 .... 56 D4
NAIL BS48 .... 73 J3
NAIL BS48 .... 73 G2
OLD/WMLY/WICK BS30 .... 69 G6
RDSTK/MIDN BA3 .... 127 J5 ⓫
TRWBR BA14 .... 124 E4
WSM BS23 .... 104 C4 ⓫
Queen Sq *CBRIS/FH* BS1 .... 7 G5
KEYN BS31 .... 97 G1 ⓫
Queen Square Av
CBRIS/FH BS1 .... 7 H5 ⓫
Queen's Rd
BMSTRD/HC/WWD BS13 ...... 77 H7
Queen St *AVONM* BS11 .... 36 B7
CBATH/BATHN BA1 .... 14 F6 ⓫⓰
CBRISNE BS2 .... 7 K3
EVILLE/WHL BS5 .... 5 J8
KGWD/HNM BS15 .... 68 B3
THNB/SVB BS35 .... 19 G2
Queensway *BRSTK/PCHW* BS34 .. 40 B2
Queen's Wy *MTN/WRL* BS22 .... 106 A2
PTSHD/EG BS20 .... 46 C5
Queen Victoria Rd
RDLND/MONT BS6 .... 2 B1
Queen Victoria St *CBRISNE* BS2 .. 8 B4
Queenwood Av
CBATH/BATHN BA1 .... 99 K3 ⓫
Quickthorn Cl *HGRV/WHIT* BS14.. 78 E5
Quiet St *CBATH/BATHN* BA1 .... 14 F6 ⓫⓰
Quilling Cl *TRWBR* BA14 .... 125 G7

R

Raby Ms *BATHSE* BA2 .... 15 J5
Rackfield Pl *BATHSE* BA2 .... 98 E6 ⓫
Rackham Cl *HORF/LLZ* BS7 ...... 53 F3
Rackhay *CBRIS/FH* BS1 .... 7 H4 ⓫
Rackvernal Rd
RDSTK/MIDN BA3 .... 126 C4
Radley Rd *MANG/FISH* BS16 .... 54 B5
Radnor Rd
HNLZ/SM/SNYPK/WT BS9 .... 51 K4
HORF/LLZ BS7 .... 52 B4
Radstock Rd
RDSTK/MIDN BA3 .... 126 D3 ⓫
Raeburn Rd *EVILLE/WHL* BS5 .... 68 B3
Ragland La *CBATH/BATHN* BA1.... 99 J3
Ragland Rd *CBATH/BATHN* BA1 .. 99 J3
Ragland La *BLAG/CWMG/WR* BS40.. 91 F5
Raglan Pl *HORF/LLZ* BS7 .... 3 H5
THNB/SVB BS35 .... 19 G5
Raglan Rd *HORF/LLZ* BS7 .... 3 H4
Ragleth Gv *TRWBR* BA14 ...... 125 G4

Railton Jones Cl
BRSTK/PCHW BS34 .... 40 D5
Railway Pl *CBATH/BATHN* BA1 .... 15 H8
Railway St *CBATH/BATHN* BA1 .... 15 G8
Railway Ter *MANG/FISH* BS16 .... 54 C5
Railway View Pl
RDSTK/MIDN BA3 .... 126 C3
Raleigh Cl *KEYN* BS31 .... 96 D2 ⓫
Raleigh Ri *PTSHD/EG* BS20 ...... 47 F3
Raleigh Rd *BMSTR* BS3 .... 6 C9
Ralph Allen Dr *BATHSE* BA2 ...... 112 A1
Ralph Rd *HORF/LLZ* BS7 .... 3 L1
Rambler Cl *TRWBR* BA14 ...... 124 C6 ⓫
Ram Hl *FRCTL/WBN* BS36 .... 42 E4
Ramsay Cl *MTN/WRL* BS22 ...... 105 K1 ⓫⓰
Ramsbury Wk *TRWBR* BA14 .... 131 F1
Ramsey Rd *HORF/LLZ* BS7 .... 52 D2
Ranchways *PTSHD/EG* BS20 ...... 46 D5 ⓫
Randall Cl *KGWD/HNM* BS15 .... 55 F7
Randall Rd *CFTN/FAIL* BS8 .... 6 B5
Randolph Av
BMSTRD/HC/WWD BS13 ...... 77 K6
YATE/CS BS37 .... 34 A3
Randolph Cl
BMSTRD/HC/WWD BS13 ...... 77 K6
Rangers Wk *KGWD/HNM* BS15 .. 69 F1 ⓫
Rankers La *PLTN/PENS* BS39 ...... 95 H7
The Rank *TRWBR* BA14 .... 130 D4
Rannoch Rd *BRSTK/PCHW* BS34 .. 39 J6
Ranscombe Av
MTN/WRL BS22 .... 105 J3 ⓫
Ransford *PTSHD/EG* BS20 .... 70 D2
Ratcliffe Dr *BRSTK/PCHW* BS34 .. 40 D3
Rathbone Cl *FRCTL/WBN* BS36 .... 42 D7
Raven Cl *MTN/WRL* BS22 .... 105 K4
Ravendale Dr
OLD/WMLY/WICK BS30 ...... 69 H7
Ravenglass Crs
HNBRY/STHM BS10 .... 39 F6
Ravenhead Dr *HGRV/WHIT* BS14.. 12 D8
Ravenhill Av *BMSTR* BS3 .... 11 M3
Ravenhill Rd *BMSTR* BS3 .... 11 L1
Ravenscroft Gdns
TRWBR BA14 .... 125 H5
Ravenswood Rd
RDLND/MONT BS6 .... 2 E8
Rawens Wd
OLD/WMLY/WICK BS30 .. 69 H7 ⓫
Rawlins Av *MTN/WRL* BS22 ...... 84 B7
Rayens Cross Rd *LGASH* BS41 .... 76 B2
Rayleigh Rd
HNLZ/SM/SNYPK/WT BS9 .... 51 F2
Raymend Rd *BMSTR* BS3 .... 11 J2
Raymend Wk *BMSTR* BS3 .... 11 K3
Raymill *BRSG/KWL/STAPK* BS4 .... 80 A1 ⓫
Raymore Ri *LGASH* BS41 .... 76 B3
Raynes Rd *BMSTR* BS3 .... 10 A1
Rector's Wy *WSM* BS23 .... 17 G6
Rectory Cl *NAIL* BS48 .... 74 A1
YATE/CS BS37 .... 34 C4 ⓫
Rectory Dr *YTN/CONG* BS49 ...... 87 F5
Rectory La *BRSTK/PCHW* BS34 .... 39 K5
WUE GL12 .... 21 H4
Rectory Rd *FRCTL/WBN* BS36 .... 32 C7
PTSHD/EG BS20 .... 49 H6
Rectory Wy *YTN/CONG* BS49 ...... 87 F5
Redcar Ct *FRCTL/WBN* BS36 ...... 42 A7 ⓫
Redcatch Rd
BRSG/KWL/STAPK BS4........ 11 M4
Redcliffe Cl *PTSHD/EG* BS20 ...... 46 C6 ⓫
Redcliffe Pde East *CBRIS/FH* BS1 .. 7 H6
Redcliffe Pde West *CBRIS/FH* BS1 .. 7 H6
Redcliffe Wy *CBRIS/FH* BS1 ...... 7 H6
Redcliff Hl *CBRIS/FH* BS1.......... 7 J7
Redcliff Mead La *CBRIS/FH* BS1 .. 7 J7
Redcliff St *CBRIS/FH* BS1.......... 7 J4
Redcross St *CBRISNE* BS2 .... 7 L3
The Reddings *KGWD/HNM* BS15 .. 55 F7
Redfield Gv *RDSTK/MIDN* BA3 .... 126 B4
Redfield Hl
OLD/WMLY/WICK BS30 ...... 69 K6
Redfield Rd *BRSTK/PCHW* BS34 .. 40 A1
RDSTK/MIDN BA3 .... 126 A5
Redford Crs
BMSTRD/HC/WWD BS13 ...... 92 B1
Redford La *MANG/FISH* BS16 .... 57 F5
Redford Wk
BMSTRD/HC/WWD BS13 ...... 92 C1 ⓫
Redhill Cl *MANG/FISH* BS16 ...... 5 J3
Redhill Dr *MANG/FISH* BS16 ...... 5 J3
Red House La *ALMDB* BS32 .... 30 A3
HNLZ/SM/SNYPK/WT BS9 .... 51 G3
Redland Court Rd
RDLND/MONT BS6 .... 2 E4
Redland Green Rd
RDLND/MONT BS6 .... 2 E4
Redland Gv *RDLND/MONT* BS6 .. 2 F6
Redland Hl *RDLND/MONT* BS6 .. 2 B5
Redland Pk *BATHSE* BA2 .... 98 C6
RDLND/MONT BS6 .... 2 C6
Redland Rd *PTSHD/EG* BS20 ...... 49 F3
RDLND/MONT BS6 .... 2 B3
Redland Ter *RDLND/MONT* BS6 .. 2 B6 ⓫
Redlynch La *KEYN* BS31 .... 95 J2
Redshelf Wk *HNBRY/STHM* BS10.. 39 F5
Redwick Cl *AVONM* BS11 .... 37 K6
Redwing Dr *MTN/WRL* BS22 .... 105 K4
Redwing Gdns
MANG/FISH BS16 .... 53 J3 ⓫
Redwood Cl *NAIL* BS48 .... 74 A1 ⓫
OLD/WMLY/WICK BS30 .... 69 G7 ⓫
RDSTK/MIDN BA3 .... 127 F5 ⓫
Redwood La *NAIL* BS48 .... 75 J4
Reed Cl *HNBRY/STHM* BS10 ...... 52 B2 ⓫
Reed Ct
OLD/WMLY/WICK BS30 .. 69 F7 ⓫
Reedley Rd
HNLZ/SM/SNYPK/WT BS9 .... 51 H4
Reedling Cl *MANG/FISH* BS16 .... 53 J3 ⓫
Regency Dr
BRSG/KWL/STAPK BS4........ 80 A1 ⓫
Regent St *BMSTR* BS3 .... 7 H8 ⓫
Regents Cl *THNB/SVB* BS35 ...... 19 G2
Regents Pl *BOAV* BA15 .... 123 K1
Regent St *CFTN/FAIL* BS8 .... 6 A3 ⓫
KGWD/HNM BS15 .... 68 C2
WSM BS23 .... 16 D3 ⓫

Regil La BLAG/CWMG/WR BS40 .... 91 H6
Remenham Dr HNLZ/SM/SNYPK/WT BS9 ...... 51 K4 2
Remenham Pk HNLZ/SM/SNYPK/WT BS9 ...... 51 K4
Rendcomb Cl MTN/WRL BS22 ... 105 G3
Rene Rd EVILLE/WHL BS5 .... 4 C8
Repton Rd BRSG/KWL/STAPK BS4........ 12 F1
Reto Gv BOAV BA15 .... 123 F3 2
Reubens Ct MTN/WRL BS22 ... 106 A2 2
Reynolds Cl KEYN BS31 .... 81 G6
Reynold's Wk HORF/LLZ BS7 .... 52 E2
Rhode Cl KEYN BS31 .... 96 B2
The Rhodeyate BNWL BS29 ... 119 K5
Rhodyate Hl YTN/CONG BS49 .. 87 J6
Rhodyate La YTN/CONG BS49 .. 87 K5
Rhyne Ter WSM BS23 .... 116 C4 2
Rhyne Vw NAIL BS48 .... 73 F2
Ribblesdale THNB/SVB BS35 ... 19 H5
Richards Cl MTN/WRL BS22 ... 106 C1
Richeson Cl HNBRY/STHM BS10.. 38 C6
Richeson Wk HNBRY/STHM BS10 .... 38 C6
Richmond Av BRSTK/PCHW BS34 .... 40 D3
  RDLND/MONT BS6 .... 3 L6
Richmond Cl KEYN BS31 .... 80 D7
  PTSHD/EG BS20 .... 47 J4 2
  TRWBR BA14 .... 124 C7 2
Richmond Dl CFTN/FAIL BS8 .... 2 A6
Richmond Gn NAIL BS48 .... 73 K2
Richmond Hts CBATH/BATHN BA1 .... 99 J3
Richmond Hl CBATH/BATHN BA1.. 14 F1
  CFTN/FAIL BS8 .... 6 C2
Richmond Hill Av CFTN/FAIL BS8.. 6 C3
Richmond La CBATH/BATHN BA1.. 14 F1
  CFTN/FAIL BS8 .... 6 B3
Richmond Park Rd CFTN/FAIL BS8 .... 6 B3
Richmond Pl CBATH/BATHN BA1.. 99 J3
Richmond Rd CBATH/BATHN BA1 .... 99 J2
  EVILLE/WHL BS5 .... 9 J1
  MANG/FISH BS16 .... 55 G4
  RDLND/MONT BS6 .... 3 K6
Richmond St BMSTR BS3 .... 7 L9
  WSM BS23 .... 16 D3 3
Richmond Ter AVONM BS11 ... 36 B7
  CFTN/FAIL BS8 .... 6 B3
Ricketts La MTN/WRL BS22 ... 106 B3 1
Rickfield BOAV BA15 .... 114 C7
Rickford Rd NAIL BS48 .... 73 K2
The Ride BRSG/KWL/STAPK BS15 .. 55 G7
Ridge Cl PTSHD/EG BS20 ...... 46 E5
Ridge Green Cl BATHSE BA2 ... 111 G5
Ridgehill HNLZ/SM/SNYPK/WT BS9....... 52 A3
The Ridge AVONM BS11 .... 50 A2
  FRCTL/WBN BS36 .... 42 D1
  YTN/CONG BS49 .... 86 E4
Ridgeview LGASH BS41 .... 76 D1 1
Ridgeway FRCTL/WBN BS36 .... 42 D1
  NAIL BS48 .... 73 G2
  YATE/CS BS37 .... 34 D5
Ridgeway Av WSM BS23 .... 16 F6
Ridgeway Cl HNBRY/STHM BS10.. 38 C7
Ridgeway Gdns HGRV/WHIT BS14 .... 79 G6
Ridgeway La HGRV/WHIT BS14 .. 79 F7
Ridgeway Pde EVILLE/WHL BS5 .. 5 J4
Ridgeway Rd LGASH BS41 ..... 76 C2
  MANG/FISH BS16 .... 5 K4
The Ridgeway HNBRY/STHM BS10 .... 38 D7
  MTN/WRL BS22 .... 105 G3 3
Ridingleaze AVONM BS11 ..... 37 H7
Ridings Cl YATE/CS BS37 ...... 35 F6
Ridings Rd FRCTL/WBN BS36 ... 42 D2
The Ridings BMSTRD/HC/WWD BS13 ..... 77 G7
  FRCTL/WBN BS36 .... 42 D2
Ringspit La PLTN/PENS BS39 ... 94 D4
Ringswell Gdns CBATH/BATHN BA1 .... 15 L1
Ringwood Crs HNBRY/STHM BS10 .... 39 G7
Ringwood Gv WSM BS23 ..... 105 H4
Ringwood Rd BATHSE BA2 .... 99 F6
Ripley Rd EVILLE/WHL BS5 .... 68 A1
Ripon Ct MANG/FISH BS16 .... 42 A7
Ripon Rd BRSG/KWL/STAPK BS4.. 9 K5
Rippleside PTSHD/EG BS20 .... 47 G4
Rippleside Rd CLVDN BS21 .... 59 G5
The Ripple CLVDN BS21 .... 61 H6
Risdale Rd BMSTR BS3 .... 77 G2
Risedale Rd WNSC BS25 ..... 120 D6 3
Rivendell MTN/WRL BS22 ... 106 B1
Riverland Dr BMSTRD/HC/WWD BS13 ..... 77 H7
Riverleaze HNLZ/SM/SNYPK/WT BS9....... 50 D4
  PTSHD/EG BS20 .... 46 D3
River Md HNLZ/SM/SNYPK/WT BS9.. 71 F3
River Rd PTSHD/EG BS20...... 48 E1
  YATE/CS BS37 .... 34 D6 3
Riverside BNWL BS29 .... 119 J3
  OMX/HUT/LCK BS24 ...... 107 J6
Riverside Av AVONM BS11 .... 50 B4
  CLVDN BS21 .... 70 D2 3
  RDSTK/MIDN BA3 .... 126 A6
Riverside Ct BRSG/KWL/STAPK BS4 ..... 9 L4 3
Riverside Pk THNB/SVB BS35 ... 27 G1
Riverside Rd BATHSE BA2 .... 14 E7
  RDSTK/MIDN BA3 .... 126 A6
Riverside Wk EVILLE/WHL BS5 .. 9M4
  RDSTK/MIDN BA3 .... 126 A6
Riverside Wy KGWD/HNM BS15.. 68 C3 2
Rivers St CBATH/BATHN BA1.... 14 E4
Rivers Street Ms CBATH/BATHN BA1......... 14 E4 2
River St CBRISNE BS2 .... 7 L2
River Vw MANG/FISH BS16 .... 53 J4
Riverway NAIL BS48 .... 61 K7
River Wy TRWBR BA14........ 124 E5
Riverwood Rd MANG/FISH BS16.. 41 H7

Riviera Crs MANG/FISH BS16...... 54 E5
Roath Rd PTSHD/EG BS20...... 47 H4
Robbins Cl MANG/FISH BS16..... 55 H3
Robbins Ct MANG/FISH BS16.... 55 H3
Robel Av FRCTL/WBN BS36...... 32 A7
Robert Ct MANG/FISH BS16..... 55 H2
Robertson Dr BRSG/KWL/STAPK BS4........ 9 L4
Robertson Rd EVILLE/WHL BS5... 4 E6
Robert St EVILLE/WHL BS5 ..... 5 J2
Robin Cl HNBRY/STHM BS10 .... 38 E6
  MTN/WRL BS22 .... 105 K5
  RDSTK/MIDN BA3 .... 126 C5
Robin Dr OMX/HUT/LCK BS24... 117 K4
Robin La CLVDN BS21 .... 59 F5
Robinson Cl NAIL BS48........ 74 A6
Robinson Dr EVILLE/WHL BS5.... 4 A9
Robin Wy YATE/CS BS37 .... 44 C1
Rochester Cl OMX/HUT/LCK BS24 ...... 117 F5 2
Rochester Rd BRSG/KWL/STAPK BS4........ 9 K6
Rock Av NAIL BS48 .... 73 G1
Rock Cl BRSG/KWL/STAPK BS4 .. 13 J3
Rock Hall La BATHSE BA2 .... 112 A4 3
Rockingham Gdns AVONM BS11 .... 50 C1 2
Rockingham Gv WSM BS23 ... 105 H4 2
Rockland Gv MANG/FISH BS16.. 53 H4 2
Rockland Rd MANG/FISH BS16.. 54 C2
Rock La BATHSE BA2 .... 112 A4
  BRSTK/PCHW BS34 .... 40 E4
Rockleaze HNLZ/SM/SNYPK/WT BS9....... 51 G7
Rockleaze Av HNLZ/SM/SNYPK/WT BS9....... 51 G6
Rockleaze Rd HNLZ/SM/SNYPK/WT BS9....... 51 G7
Rockliffe Av BATHSE BA2 ...... 15 K3
Rockliffe Rd BATHSE BA2 ...... 15 J3
Rock Rd KEYN BS31 .... 80 E6
  RDSTK/MIDN BA3 .... 126 C3
  TRWBR BA14 .... 124 D7
  YTN/CONG BS49 .... 87 F5
Rockside Av MANG/FISH BS16.. 55 F1
Rockside Dr HNLZ/SM/SNYPK/WT BS9....... 51 K3
Rockside Gdns FRCTL/WBN BS36.. 32 D7
  MANG/FISH BS16 .... 55 F1 2
Rocks La BLAG/CWMG/WR BS40.. 90 E3
Rockstowes Wy HNBRY/STHM BS10 .... 39 G5
Rock St THNB/SVB BS35 .... 19 G5
The Rock BRSG/KWL/STAPK BS4.. 13 J2
Rockwell Av AVONM BS11 ..... 37 J7
Rodborough YATE/CS BS37 .... 45 K1
Rode Hl RDSTK/MIDN BA3...... 128 D6
Rodfords Md HGRV/WHIT BS14.. 12 B8
Rodford Wy YATE/CS BS37 .... 45 K1
Rodmead Wk BMSTRD/HC/WWD BS13...... 77 J7 2
Rodmoor Rd PTSHD/EG BS20.. 47 F5
Rodney Av KGWD/HNM BS15.... 68 A2
Rodney Crs BRSTK/PCHW BS34.. 39 K4
Rodney Rd KEYN BS31 .... 97 F2
  KGWD/HNM BS15 .... 68 A1
  NAIL BS48 .... 74 A5
Rodney Wk KGWD/HNM BS15... 68 A1
Rodsleigh TRWBR BA14 ...... 130 B1
Rodway Hl MANG/FISH BS16 ... 55 F5
Rodway Rd BRSTK/PCHW BS34.. 29 K7
  MANG/FISH BS16 .... 55 F5
Rodway Vw KGWD/HNM BS15.. 55 F6
Roebuck Cl MTN/WRL BS22 ... 106 B1
Roegate Dr BRSG/KWL/STAPK BS4........ 9 K4
Rogers Cl OLD/WMLY/WICK BS30.. 69 H5
Rokeby Av RDLND/MONT BS6... 4 A1
Roman Farm Ct AVONM BS11.. 37 K6 2
Roman Rd CBATH/BATHN BA1.. 15 G4
  EVILLE/WHL BS5............ 4 D7
  OMX/HUT/LCK BS24 ...... 117 H6
  WNSC BS25 .... 120 C2
Roman Wk BRSG/KWL/STAPK BS4........ 12 F1
  BRSTK/PCHW BS34 .... 40 D3 3
Roman Wy HNLZ/SM/SNYPK/WT BS9....... 50 E5
Romney Av HORF/LLZ BS7 .... 53 K3 3
Ronald Rd MANG/FISH BS16.... 53 K3 3
Ronayne Wk MANG/FISH BS16.. 54 C3
Rookery Cl MTN/WRL BS22 ... 105 K2 3
Rookery La OLD/WMLY/WICK BS30 ..... 57 H6
  THNB/SVB BS35 .... 28 D1
Rookery Rd BRSG/KWL/STAPK BS4........ 12 A2
Rookery Wy HGRV/WHIT BS14.. 78 D7
Rose Acre HNBRY/STHM BS10 .. 38 D5
Roseberry Pk EVILLE/WHL BS5.... 9 K2
Roseberry Rd BATHSE BA2 .... 99 F6 2
  EVILLE/WHL BS5............ 8 F3
Rosebery Av CBRISNE BS2 ..... 4 A7
Rosedale Av WSM BS23 ...... 17 J4 2
Rosedale Gdns TRWBR BA14 .. 124 C5 2
Rosedale Rd MANG/FISH BS16.. 54 B6
Rose Gdns MTN/WRL BS22 ... 106 C1
Rose Green Cl EVILLE/WHL BS5... 5 J6
Rose Green Rd EVILLE/WHL BS5.. 5 J6
Rose Hl CBATH/BATHN BA1.... 100 A2
Rose La FRCTL/WBN BS36 ..... 42 E1
Roselarge Gdns HNBRY/STHM BS10 .... 38 D6 3
Rosemary Cl ALMDB BS32 ..... 40 E1
Rosemary La EVILLE/WHL BS5 .. 4 E6
  RDSTK/MIDN BA3 .... 122 B2
Rose Md HORF/LLZ BS7 ...... 52 E2 2
Rosemont Ter CFTN/FAIL BS8.... 6 B4
Rosemount La BATHSE BA2 ... 111 K1
Rosemount Rd NAIL BS48 ..... 75 H3
Rose Oak Dr FRCTL/WBN BS36.. 42 E1 3
Rose Oak Gdns FRCTL/WBN BS36 .... 42 E1
Rose Oak La FRCTL/WBN BS36.. 42 E1
Rose Rd EVILLE/WHL BS5 ...... 9 K2

Rosery Cl HNLZ/SM/SNYPK/WT BS9...... 51 J1
The Rosery MANG/FISH BS16 ... 54 C6 3
Rose St CBRIS/FH BS1 .... 7 K6
Roseville Av OLD/WMLY/WICK BS30 ..... 81 G1
Rose Wk MANG/FISH BS16 .... 54 C6
Rosewarn Cl BATHSE BA2 .... 110 D1
Rosewood Av THNB/SVB BS35.. 22 E1
Rosling Rd HORF/LLZ BS7 ..... 52 C3
Roslyn Av MTN/WRL BS22 ... 105 H4
Roslyn Rd RDLND/MONT BS6 ... 2 E6
Rossall Av BRSTK/PCHW BS34 .. 40 B2
Rossall Rd BRSG/KWL/STAPK BS4.. 13 G2
Ross Cl YATE/CS BS37 .... 34 E5
Rossendale Cl MTN/WRL BS22.. 106 A2
Rosett Gdns TRWBR BA14 .... 124 C5
Rossiter Rd BATHSE BA2 ...... 15 G8
Rossiter's La EVILLE/WHL BS5 .. 68 A4
Rosslyn Rd CBATH/BATHN BA1.. 98 E5
Rosslyn Wy THNB/SVB BS35 ... 19 H2
Roundhill Pk BATHSE BA2 .... 110 E2
Roundhill Pk BATHSE BA2 .... 110 E2
Roundmoor Cl KEYN BS31 .... 96 E1
Roundmoor Gdns HGRV/WHIT BS14 .... 79 H4 3
Roundstone St TRWBR BA14 .. 125 F5 3
Roundways EVILLE/WHL BS5 ... 36 D2
Rousham Rd EVILLE/WHL BS5 ... 4 B4
Rowacres BATHSE BA2 ...... 110 E2
  HGRV/WHIT BS14 .... 78 D5
Rowan Cl MANG/FISH BS16 .... 54 A1
  NAIL BS48 .... 74 A1 3
Rowan Ct RDSTK/MIDN BA3 .. 126 E4
Rowan Pl OMX/HUT/LCK BS24 ...... 106 C4 3
The Rowans PTSHD/EG BS20... 47 F5
Rowan Wy BLAC/CWMG/WR BS40 .... 121 K1
  KGWD/HNM BS15 .... 68 B7 1
Rowberrow HGRV/WHIT BS14 .. 78 D4
Rowberrow La WNSC BS25 ... 121 J5
Rowberrow Wy NAIL BS48 .... 73 J2 3
Rowden La BOAV BA15 ...... 123 K2
Rowland Av MANG/FISH BS16 ... 5 G2
Rowlands Cl CBATH/BATHN BA1 .... 101 G2 3
Rowlandson Gdns HORF/LLZ BS7 .... 53 F3 3
Rowley St BMSTR BS3 .... 10 E2 1
Rownham Cl BMSTR BS3 ...... 65 G6 1
Rownham Hl CFTN/FAIL BS8 ... 65 G4 1
Rownham Md CFTN/FAIL BS8 ... 6 A6 1
The Rows MTN/WRL BS22 ... 105 K3
Royal Albert Rd RDLND/MONT BS6 .... 2 B2
Royal Av CBATH/BATHN BA1 ... 14 D5
Royal Cl HNBRY/STHM BS10 ... 38 A5
Royal Crs CBATH/BATHN BA1 .. 14 D4
  WSM BS23 .... 16 C1
Royal Fort Rd CFTN/FAIL BS8 ... 6 F2
Royal Pde WSM BS23 .... 16 C2
Royal Pk CFTN/FAIL BS8 .... 6 A2
Royal Portbury Dock Rd PTSHD/EG BS20 .... 48 E3
Royal Rd MANG/FISH BS16 .... 55 G3
Royal York Crs CFTN/FAIL BS8 .... 65 H4 14
Royal York Vls CFTN/FAIL BS8 ... 6 A4
Royate Hl EVILLE/WHL BS5 ..... 5 M9
Roycroft Rd BRSTK/PCHW BS34.. 40 A6
Roy King Gdns OLD/WMLY/WICK BS30 ..... 69 J5
Royston Wk HNBRY/STHM BS10.. 39 G6
Rozel Rd HORF/LLZ BS7 .... 52 C3
Rubens Cl KEYN BS31 .... 81 G6 3
Ruby St BMSTR BS3 .... 10 C2
Ruddymead CLVDN BS21 ..... 71 F1
Rudford Cl BRSTK/PCHW BS34.. 30 A6
Rudge Cl KGWD/HNM BS15 .... 55 F7
Rudgeway Pk THNB/SVB BS35... 22 D5
Rudgewood Cl BMSTRD/HC/WWD BS13...... 78 B7 2
Rudgleigh Av PTSHD/EG BS20.. 49 J5 3
Rudgleigh Rd PTSHD/EG BS20.. 49 J5 1
Rudhall Gv HNBRY/STHM BS10.. 54 C2
Rudmore Pk CBATH/BATHN BA1.. 98 D5 3
Rudthorpe Rd HORF/LLZ BS7 .. 52 C4
Ruffet Rd FRCTL/WBN BS36 ... 42 C4
Rugby Rd BRSG/KWL/STAPK BS4.. 13 G1
Runnymead Av BRSG/KWL/STAPK BS4........ 9 J7
Runnymede KGWD/HNM BS15.. 68 E1 3
Runswick Rd BRSG/KWL/STAPK BS4........ 12 E2
Rupert St CBRIS/FH BS1 .... 7 H3
  EVILLE/WHL BS5 .... 8 E3
Rush Cl ALMDB BS32 .... 30 C5
Rushey La BOAV BA15 ...... 115 G2
Rush Hl BATHSE BA2 .... 110 E3
Rushmoor CLVDN BS21 ...... 70 C2
Rushmoor Gv NAIL BS48 ..... 73 K6
Rushmoor La NAIL BS48 ..... 74 A6
Rushton Dr FRCTL/WBN BS36.. 42 E1
Rushy OLD/WMLY/WICK BS30.. 69 G6
Rushy Wy MANG/FISH BS16 ... 42 B7
Ruskin Gv HORF/LLZ BS7 ..... 52 E1
Ruskin Rd RDSTK/MIDN BA3.. 126 D4
Russell Av KGWD/HNM BS15... 68 D3
Russell Gv RDLND/MONT BS6 .. 52 A4
Russell Rd CLVDN BS21 ...... 58 E7 3
  MANG/FISH BS16 .... 54 B7
  OMX/HUT/LCK BS24 ...... 106 D7
  RDLND/MONT BS6......... 52 A4
Russell St CBATH/BATHN BA1 .. 14 F4
Russell Town Av EVILLE/WHL BS5.. 8 B7
Russett Cl NAIL BS48 .... 74 B5
Russett Gv NAIL BS48 .... 73 G3 3
Russ St CLVDN BS21 .... 71 G6
Russ St CBRISNE BS2 .... 7 L4
Rutherford Cl OLD/WMLY/WICK BS30 ..... 69 G7 3
Ruthven Rd BRSG/KWL/STAPK BS4........ 11 J8
Rutland Av OLD/WMLY/WICK BS30 ..... 81 G1
Rutland Cl MTN/WRL BS22 ... 105 H5

Rutland Crs TRWBR BA14 .... 130 E1
Rutland Rd HORF/LLZ BS7 ..... 3 K3 3
Rydal Av OMX/HUT/LCK BS24 .. 118 A2
Rydal Rd WSM BS23 .... 116 E2
Ryde Rd BRSG/KWL/STAPK BS4...... 12 C3 3
Rye Cl BMSTRD/HC/WWD BS13.. 77 G5
Ryecroft Av MTN/WRL BS22 .. 105 K4
Ryecroft Ri LGASH BS41 ...... 76 D2
Ryecroft Rd FRCTL/WBN BS36.. 32 D7
Ryedown La OLD/WMLY/WICK BS30 ..... 81 J2
Ryeland Wy TRWBR BA14 .... 125 G7
Ryland Pl CBRISNE BS2 .... 4 A5 3
Rylestone Cl FRCTL/WBN BS36.. 32 A7
Rylestone Gv HNLZ/SM/SNYPK/WT BS9...... 51 H4
Rysdale Rd HNLZ/SM/SNYPK/WT BS9...... 51 H3

S

Sabrina Wy HNLZ/SM/SNYPK/WT BS9..... 50 E5
  PTSHD/EG BS20 .... 49 K5 3
Sadbury Cl MTN/WRL BS22 ... 106 C1 13
Sadlier Cl AVONM BS11 ...... 50 B1
The Saffrons MTN/WRL BS22 .... 106 C1 12
Sage Cl PTSHD/EG BS20...... 46 C5
Sages Md ALMDB BS32 ...... 30 D7 3
St Agnes Av BRSG/KWL/STAPK BS4...... 11 M3
St Agnes Cl BRSG/KWL/STAPK BS4...... 11 M3 1
  NAIL BS48 .... 74 A2 3
St Agnes Wk BRSG/KWL/STAPK BS4...... 11 M3
St Aidan's Cl EVILLE/WHL BS5... 68 A4 1
St Aidan's Rd EVILLE/WHL BS5... 68 A4
St Alban's Rd RDLND/MONT BS6.. 2 C2
St Aldams Dr MANG/FISH BS16.. 56 D4
St Aldhelm Rd BOAV BA15 ... 123 J5
St Aldwyn's Cl HORF/LLZ BS7 .. 52 D1 3
St Andrews OLD/WMLY/WICK BS30 ..... 69 H4
  YATE/CS BS37 .... 34 C6
St Andrews Cl MTN/WRL BS22 .... 106 A2 10
  NAIL BS48 .... 74 A2 3
St Andrew's Dr CLVDN BS21 .. 70 C1
St Andrew's Rd AVONM BS11 .. 36 C7
  NAIL BS48 .... 74 B6
  RDLND/MONT BS6 .... 3 K6 1
St Anne's Av KEYN BS31 ...... 80 D5
St Anne's Cl OLD/WMLY/WICK BS30 ..... 69 H6
St Anne's Dr FRCTL/WBN BS36.. 42 D3
  OLD/WMLY/WICK BS30 ..... 81 J1
St Anne's Park Rd BRSG/KWL/STAPK BS4...... 9 J7
St Anne's Rd BRSG/KWL/STAPK BS4...... 9 H4
  EVILLE/WHL BS5........... 68 B4
St Anne's Ter BRSG/KWL/STAPK BS4...... 9 J7
St Ann's Wy BATHSE BA2 ..... 15 K6
St Anthony's Cl RDSTK/MIDN BA3 .... 126 B3 3
St Aubin's Av BRSG/KWL/STAPK BS4...... 13 L1
St Aubyn's Av WSM BS23 .... 116 C4 3
St Augustine's Pde CBRIS/FH BS1.. 7 G4
St Augustine's Pl CBRIS/FH BS1 .. 7 G4 3
St Augustine's Rd TRWBR BA14 .... 124 D6 3
St Austell Cl NAIL BS48 .... 74 A3
St Austell Rd MTN/WRL BS22 .. 17 M2
St Barnabas Cl OLD/WMLY/WICK BS30 ..... 69 J5 3
  RDSTK/MIDN BA3 .... 126 C2 1
St Bartholomew's Rd HORF/LLZ BS7 .... 3 L4 3
St Bede's Rd KGWD/HNM BS15.. 54 C7
St Bernard's Rd AVONM BS11... 50 A3
St Brelades Gv BRSG/KWL/STAPK BS4...... 9 K7
St Brendan's Wy AVONM BS11.. 36 C7
St Briavels Dr YATE/CS BS37 ... 34 A7
St Bridges Cl MTN/WRL BS22 .. 83 F6
St Catherine's Cl BATHSE BA2.. 15 L6
St Catherine's Md PTSHD/EG BS20 .... 49 K6 3
St Chad's Av RDSTK/MIDN BA3.. 126 B4
St Chad's Gn RDSTK/MIDN BA3.. 126 B5
St Charles Cl RDSTK/MIDN BA3 .... 126 B3 3
St Christophers Cl BATHSE BA2.. 15 L4
St Clements Ct KEYN BS31 .... 80 E7
St Clements Rd KEYN BS31 ... 80 E6
St David's Av OLD/WMLY/WICK BS30 ..... 69 H5
St David's Cl MTN/WRL BS22 . 105 G3
St David's Crs BRSG/KWL/STAPK BS4...... 9 K6
St David's Rd THNB/SVB BS35.. 19 H4
St Dunstan's Rd BMSTR BS3 ... 10 F3
St Edward's Rd CFTN/FAIL BS8 .. 6 C5 3
St Edyth's Rd HNLZ/SM/SNYPK/WT BS9..... 50 D3
St Fagans Ct OLD/WMLY/WICK BS30 ..... 81 H1 3
St Francis Dr FRCTL/WBN BS36.. 42 A2
St Francis Rd BMSTR BS3 ..... 6 B9 1
  KEYN BS31 .... 80 C5
St Gabriel's Rd EVILLE/WHL BS5.. 4 C9
St Georges Av EVILLE/WHL BS5.. 9M5
St George's Hl BATHSE BA2 .. 100 C4 3
  PTSHD/EG BS20 .... 49 G6
St Georges Rd CBRIS/FH BS1 ... 6 E5
  KEYN BS31 .... 80 D6
  PTSHD/EG BS20 .... 48 E2
St Gregory's Rd HORF/LLZ BS7.. 52 D1
St Gregory's Wk HORF/LLZ BS7 .... 52 E1 3
St Helena Rd RDLND/MONT BS6.. 2 C2

St Helens Dr OLD/WMLY/WICK BS30 ..... 81 J1
St Helen's Wk EVILLE/WHL BS5.. 68 A1
St Helier Av BRSG/KWL/STAPK BS4...... 13 L1
St Hilary Cl HNLZ/SM/SNYPK/WT BS9..... 51 F4
St Ivel Wy OLD/WMLY/WICK BS30 ..... 69 J4
St Ives Cl NAIL BS48 .... 74 A2 3
St Ives Rd WSM BS23 .... 17 J9
St James's Pde CBATH/BATHN BA1 .... 14 F7 7
St James's Pk CBATH/BATHN BA1 .... 14 E2
St James's Sq CBATH/BATHN BA1 .... 14 D3 3
St James's St CBATH/BATHN BA1 .... 14 E3 2
  MANG/FISH BS16 .... 55 G4
St James St WSM BS23 ...... 16 D3 3
St John's Av CLVDN BS21 ..... 59 F7 3
St John's Br CBRIS/FH BS1 ..... 7 G2 1
St John's Cl WSM BS23 ...... 104 C4
St Johns Ct KEYN BS31 .... 80 E5
  RDSTK/MIDN BA3 .... 126 B3
  TRWBR BA14 .... 130 B1
St John's La BMSTR BS3 ...... 10 F2
  BRSG/KWL/STAPK BS4...... 11M1
St John's Pl CBATH/BATHN BA1 .... 14 F6 12
St John's Rd BATHSE BA2 ..... 15 G4
  BMSTR BS3 .... 7 G8
  CBATH/BATHN BA1 .... 99 F5
  CFTN/FAIL BS8 .... 2 B7
  CLVDN BS21 .... 58 E7
  NAIL BS48 .... 74 B6
St John's St BMSTR BS3 ...... 10 F1
St John St THNB/SVB BS35 .... 19 G5
St Johns Wy YATE/CS BS37 ... 35 F5
St Joseph's Rd HNBRY/STHM BS10 .... 38 E5
  WSM BS23 .... 104 D1 3
St Jude's Ter MTN/WRL BS22 . 105 H4 3
St Keyna Rd KEYN BS31 ...... 80 E6
St Kilda's Rd BMSTR BS3 ..... 14 A9
St Ladoc Rd KEYN BS31 ...... 80 D5
St Laud Cl HNLZ/SM/SNYPK/WT BS9..... 50 D3
St Laurence Rd BOAV BA15 .. 124 A1 1
St Leonard's Rd EVILLE/WHL BS5 .... 4 F6
  HORF/LLZ BS7 .... 52 C3
St Lucia Cl HORF/LLZ BS7..... 52 C1
St Lucia Crs HORF/LLZ BS7 .... 52 C2
St Luke's Crs BMSTR BS3 ...... 7 L8
St Luke's Gdns BRSG/KWL/STAPK BS4...... 13 J3
St Luke's Rd BATHSE BA2 .... 111 J2
  BMSTR BS3 .... 7 J8
  RDSTK/MIDN BA3 .... 126 A3 3
  NAIL BS48 .... 74 A6 3
St Margaret's Cl KEYN BS31 ... 80 D5 3
St Margaret's Dr HNLZ/SM/SNYPK/WT BS9 .... 52 A3 3
St Margaret's Hl BOAV BA15 . 114 F7 3
St Margaret's La NAIL BS48.... 74 A6
St Margaret's Ter WSM BS23 ... 16 D2 3
St Marks Cl KEYN BS31 .... 80 E5 3
St Mark's Gv EVILLE/WHL BS5... 4 C7
St Mark's Rd BATHSE BA2 .... 15 G9
  EVILLE/WHL BS5............ 4 C7
  MTN/WRL BS22 .... 106 A1
  RDSTK/MIDN BA3 .... 126 B3
St Mark's Ter EVILLE/WHL BS5 .. 4 C7
St Martins Cl MTN/WRL BS22 . 105 K2 3
St Martin's Gdns BRSG/KWL/STAPK BS4...... 12 D5
St Martin's Rd BRSG/KWL/STAPK BS4...... 12 D4
St Martin's Wk BRSG/KWL/STAPK BS4...... 12 C4
St Mary's Cl BATHSE BA2 ..... 15 K6
  TRWBR BA14 .... 125 G2
St Mary's Ct OMX/HUT/LCK BS24 ...... 117 F5 3
St Mary's Gdns TRWBR BA14 . 125 G2
St Mary's Gv NAIL BS48 ...... 73 G3
St Mary's Pk NAIL BS48 ...... 73 G3
St Marys Ri RDSTK/MIDN BA3.. 127 K3
St Mary's Rd AVONM BS11 .... 49 G2
  CFTN/FAIL BS8 .... 65 F4 3
  OMX/HUT/LCK BS24 ...... 117 J4
  PTSHD/EG BS20 .... 47 G5
St Mary St THNB/SVB BS35 ... 19 G5 3
St Mary's Wk AVONM BS11 .... 49 A3
St Mary's Wy YATE/CS BS37 ... 34 C5
St Matthew's Av RDLND/MONT BS6............ 3 H8
St Matthew's Cl WSM BS23 .. 104 C4 1
St Matthew's Rd RDLND/MONT BS6........... 3 H9
St Matthias Pk CBRISNE BS2 ... 7 L2
St Michael's Av CLVDN BS21 .. 71 F2
  MTN/WRL BS22 .... 106 B2 3
St Michael's Cl FRCTL/WBN BS36.. 41 K1
  TRWBR BA14 .... 125 J3 3
St Michaels Ct KGWD/HNM BS15 .... 68 B2 3
St Michael's Hl RDLND/MONT BS6.. 2 E9
St Michael's Pk CFTN/FAIL BS8 .. 6 E1 3
St Michael's Pl CBATH/BATHN BA1 .... 14 F7 6
St Michaels Rd BATHSE BA2 .. 98 D7
  CBATH/BATHN BA1 .... 14 A4
St Nicholas Cl BOAV BA15 ... 113 J6
  TRWBR BA14 .... 131 F4
St Nicholas Pk EVILLE/WHL BS5.. 4 C7
St Nicholas' Rd CBRISNE BS2 ... 3 L8
  HGRV/WHIT BS14 .... 79 G7
  WSM BS23 .... 116 C4
St Nicholas St CBRIS/FH BS1 ... 7 H4 3
St Oswald's Rd RDLND/MONT BS6.. 2 C4
St Pauls Pl RDSTK/MIDN BA3 .. 126 B3 3
St Paul's Rd BMSTR BS3 ...... 7 G8

CFTN/FAIL BS8 .... 6 C2
WSM BS23 .... 16 E7
St Paul St CBRISNE BS2 .... 7 K1
St Peter's Av WSM BS23 .... 104 C4
St Peter's Crs FRCTL/WBN BS36 .... 42 C1
St Peter's Ri
　BMSTRD/HC/WWD BS13 .... 77 J4
St Peters Rd PTSHD/EG BS20 .... 47 H5
　RDSTK/MIDN BA3 .... 126 D5
St Peter's Wk
　HNLZ/SM/SNYPK/WT BS9 .... 51 K4
St Philips Cswy
　BRSG/KWL/STAPK BS4 .... 8 E8
　CBRISNE BS2 .... 8 C5
St Philips Rd CBRISNE BS2 .... 7 M3
St Phillips Rd CBRISNE BS2 .... 8 B6
St Pierre Dr
　OLD/WMLY/WICK BS30 .... 69 H4
St Ronan's Av RDLND/MONT BS6... 2 E7
St Saviours Rd FRCTL/WBN BS36 .... 42 C2
St Saviour's Rd
　CBATH/BATHN BA1 .... 100 B3
St Saviours Wy
　CBATH/BATHN BA1 .... 100 B3
St Silas St CBRISNE BS2 .... 8 B6
St Stephen's Av CBRIS/FH BS1 ... 7 G4
St Stephen's Cl
　CBATH/BATHN BA1 .... 14 F2
　KGWD/HNM BS15 .... 54 E6
St Stephen's Pl TRWBR BA14 ... 125 F6
St Stephen's Rd
　CBATH/BATHN BA1 .... 14 F2
　MANG/FISH BS16 .... 54 D6
St Stephen's St CBRIS/FH BS1 ... 7 G3
St Thomas Rd
　RDSTK/MIDN BA3 .... 126 C3
　TRWBR BA14 .... 125 G5
St Thomas St CBRIS/FH BS1 ... 7 J5
St Vincent's HI CFTN/FAIL BS8 ...... 2 B5
St Vincent's Rd CFTN/FAIL BS8... 6 A5
St Werburgh's Pk CBRISNE BS2 ...... 4 A5
St Werburgh's Rd CBRISNE BS2 ... 3 M5
St Whytes Rd
　BRSG/KWL/STAPK BS4 .... 11 H8
St Winifreds Dr BATHSE BA2 .... 112 C3
Salcombe Gdns
　MTN/WRL BS22 .... 106 A3
Salcombe Rd
　BRSG/KWL/STAPK BS4 .... 12 A7
Salem Rd FRCTL/WBN BS36 .... 42 A1
Salisbury Av KGWD/HNM BS15 ... 68 D2
Salisbury Gdns MANG/FISH BS16 ... 54 E4
Salisbury Rd
　BRSG/KWL/STAPK BS4 .... 9 H7
　CBATH/BATHN BA1 .... 100 A2
　MANG/FISH BS16 .... 54 E3
　MTN/WRL BS22 .... 105 H4
　PLTN/PENS BS39 .... 126 A1
　RDLND/MONT BS6 .... 3 G5
Salisbury St EVILLE/WHL BS5 .... 8 D5
　EVILLE/WHL BS5 ....
Salisbury Ter WSM BS23 .... 16 D3
Sallybarn Cl
　BMSTRD/HC/WWD BS13 .... 77 K7
Sallys Wy FRCTL/WBN BS36 .... 42 A1
Salmons Wy MANG/FISH BS16 ... 55 C1
Salthouse Rd CLVDN BS21 .... 58 D7
Salthrop Rd HORF/LLZ BS7 .... 3 J3
Saltings Cl CLVDN BS21 .... 70 D1
Saltmarsh Dr AVONM BS11 .... 37 H7
Saltwell Av HGRV/WHIT BS14 ... 79 G6
Sambourne La
　PTSHD/EG BS20 .... 49 J4
Samian Wy BRSTK/PCHW BS34 ... 40 D3
Sampsons Rd
　BMSTRD/HC/WWD BS13 .... 78 A7
Samuel St EVILLE/WHL BS5 .... 8 E1
Samuel White Rd
　KGWD/HNM BS15 .... 68 C7
Samuel Wright Cl
　OLD/WMLY/WICK BS30 .... 69 K5
Sandbach Rd
　BRSG/KWL/STAPK BS4 .... 9 G9
Sandbed Rd CBRISNE BS2 .... 4 A6
Sandburrows Rd
　BMSTRD/HC/WWD BS13 .... 77 G5
Sandburrows Wk
　BMSTRD/HC/WWD BS13 .... 77 H5
Sandcroft HGRV/WHIT BS14 .... 78 D5
Sandcroft Av WSM BS23 .... 116 C4
Sanders Rd TRWBR BA14 .... 124 E4
Sand Farm La MTN/WRL BS22 ... 88 K6
Sandford Cl CLVDN BS21 .... 70 D2
Sandford Rd CFTN/FAIL BS8 .... 6 A6
　WNSC BS25 .... 120 C5
　WSM BS23 .... 17 H3
Sandgate Rd
　BRSG/KWL/STAPK BS4 .... 13 C1
Sand HI BRSG/KWL/STAPK BS4 ... 8 F9
Sandholme Cl
　MANG/FISH BS16 .... 54 E1
Sandholme Rd
　BRSG/KWL/STAPK BS4 .... 9 G9
Sandhurst YATE/CS BS37 .... 34 A7
Sandhurst Cl BRSTK/PCHW BS34 ... 30 A6
Sandhurst Rd
　BRSG/KWL/STAPK BS4 .... 12 F1
Sandling Av HORF/LLZ BS7 .... 52 E2
Sandmead Rd WNSC BS25 .... 120 D2
Sandown Centre
　TRWBR BA14 .... 131 C3
Sandown Cl MANG/FISH BS16 ... 42 A7
Sandown Rd
　BRSG/KWL/STAPK BS4 .... 9 G9
　BRSTK/PCHW BS34 .... 40 B5
Sandpiper Dr MTN/WRL BS22... 106 A4
Sandringham Av
　MANG/FISH BS16 .... 54 E1
Sandringham Pk
　MANG/FISH BS16 .... 54 E1
Sandringham Rd
　BRSG/KWL/STAPK BS4 .... 13 C1
　BRSTK/PCHW BS34 .... 40 C4
　TRWBR BA14 .... 130 D2

WSM BS23 .... 17 G7
Sand Rd MTN/WRL BS22 .... 83 G7
Sandstone Ri FRCTL/WBN BS36 ... 41 J4
Sandwich Rd
　BRSG/KWL/STAPK BS4 .... 9 G9
Sandy Cl ALMDB BS32 .... 40 D2
Sandy La CFTN/FAIL BS8 .... 63 G2
　EVILLE/WHL BS5 .... 4 E4
Sandy Leaze BOAV BA15 .... 114 D7
Sandyleaze
　HNLZ/SM/SNYPK/WT BS9 .... 51 G2
Sandy Ldg YATE/CS BS37 .... 34 B7
Sandy Park Rd
　BRSG/KWL/STAPK BS4 .... 8 F9
Saracen St CBATH/BATHN BA1 .. 15 G5
Sarah St EVILLE/WHL BS5 .... 8 E1
Sargent St BMSTR BS3 .... 7 J8
Sarum Crs HNBRY/STHM BS10 ... 39 F7
Sassoon Ct
　OLD/WMLY/WICK BS30 .... 69 F5
Satchfield Cl HNBRY/STHM BS10 .. 38 C6
Satchfield Crs
　HNBRY/STHM BS10 .... 38 C6
Sates Wy
　HNLZ/SM/SNYPK/WT BS9 .... 52 A3
Saunders Rd MANG/FISH BS16 ... 54 E5
Saunton Wk
　BRSG/KWL/STAPK BS4 .... 11 J8
Savages Wood Rd ALMDB BS32 ... 30 C7
Savernake Rd MTN/WRL BS22 ... 106 A2
Saville Crs MTN/WRL BS22 .... 105 H5
Saville Gate Cl
　HNLZ/SM/SNYPK/WT BS9 .... 51 H5
Saville Pl CFTN/FAIL BS8 .... 6 A4
Saville Rd
　HNLZ/SM/SNYPK/WT BS9 .... 51 H5
　MTN/WRL BS22 .... 105 H5
Saville Rw CBATH/BATHN BA1 ... 14 F4
Savoy Rd BRSG/KWL/STAPK BS4 ... 9 G8
Saw Cl CBATH/BATHN BA1 .... 14 F6
Saw Mill La THNB/SVB BS35 .... 19 C4
Sawyers Cl NAIL BS48 .... 74 A1
Sawyers Ct CLVDN BS21 .... 59 G7
Saxby Cl CLVDN BS21 .... 70 D2
　MTN/WRL BS22 .... 106 C1
Saxon Dr TRWBR BA14 .... 125 C2
Saxon Rd CBRISNE BS2 .... 4 B6
　MTN/WRL BS22 .... 105 H5
Saxon Wy ALMDB BS32 .... 30 B6
　BOAV BA15 .... 114 A6
Says La BLAG/CWMG/WR BS40... 121 K1
Say Wk OLD/WMLY/WICK BS30... 69 K3
Scafell Cl WSM BS23 .... 105 F4
Scandrett Cl
　HNBRY/STHM BS10 .... 38 B5
Scantleberry Cl
　MANG/FISH BS16 .... 54 D1
The Scaurs MTN/WRL BS22 .... 106 A3
School Cl BNWL BS29 .... 119 J3
　BRSTK/PCHW BS34 .... 30 B7
　EVILLE/WHL BS5 .... 5 H5
　HGRV/WHIT BS14 .... 78 D7
School La NAIL BS48 .... 75 K6
　TRWBR BA14 .... 125 F1
School Rd BRSG/KWL/STAPK BS4.. 12 A1
　FRCTL/WBN BS36 .... 32 A7
　KGWD/HNM BS15 .... 68 C2
　OLD/WMLY/WICK BS30 .... 69 C6
School Wk EVILLE/WHL BS5 .... 5 H8
　YATE/CS BS37 .... 34 B5
School Wy THNB/SVB BS35 .... 27 H1
The Scop ALMDB BS32 .... 29 K2
Scotch Horn Cl NAIL BS48 .... 73 K1
Scotch Horn Wy NAIL BS48 .... 73 K1
Scots Pine Av NAIL BS48 .... 73 K1
Scott Ct
　OLD/WMLY/WICK BS30 .... 69 F5
Scott Lawrence Cl
　MANG/FISH BS16 .... 54 A2
Scott Rd WSM BS23 .... 17 K9
Scott Wk OLD/WMLY/WICK BS30... 69 K3
Scott Wy YATE/CS BS37 .... 34 C7
Sea Bank Rd PTSHD/EG BS20 ... 48 E1
Seabrook Rd MTN/WRL BS22 ... 105 J4
Seagry Cl HNBRY/STHM BS10 ... 39 H7
Sea Mills La
　HNLZ/SM/SNYPK/WT BS9 .... 50 E5
Searle Court Av
　BRSG/KWL/STAPK BS4 .... 9 H9
Searle Crs WSM BS23 .... 17 K6
Seaton Rd EVILLE/WHL BS5 .... 4 E8
Seavale Rd CLVDN BS21 .... 58 E6
Seawalls Rd
　HNLZ/SM/SNYPK/WT BS9 .... 51 F7
Second Av BATHSE BA2 .... 111 G1
　RDSTK/MIDN BA3 .... 126 D6
Seddon Rd CBRISNE BS2 .... 3 M5
Sedgefield Gdns
　MANG/FISH BS16 .... 42 A7
Sedgemoor Cl NAIL BS48 .... 73 J3
Sedgemoor Rd BATHSE BA2 ... 111 J4
　WSM BS23 .... 104 E4
Sefton Park Rd HORF/LLZ BS7 ...... 3 K4
Sefton Sq OMX/HUT/LCK BS24... 106 B5
Selborne Rd HORF/LLZ BS7 .... 52 D4
Selbourne Cl
　CBATH/BATHN BA1 .... 98 D4
Selbourne Rd WSM BS23 .... 116 D2
Selbrooke Crs MANG/FISH BS16... 54 C3
Selby Rd EVILLE/WHL BS5 .... 5 M8
Selden Rd HGRV/WHIT BS14 ... 79 J6
Selkirk Rd KGWD/HNM BS15 ... 54 C7
Selley Wk
　BMSTRD/HC/WWD BS13 .... 77 J6
Selwood Cl WSM BS23 .... 105 H6
Selworthy KGWD/HNM BS15 ... 68 E3
Selworthy Cl KEYN BS31 .... 80 D6
Selworthy Rd
　BRSG/KWL/STAPK BS4 .... 12 J9
　WSM BS23 .... 17 J9
Seneca Pl EVILLE/WHL BS5 .... 9 H2
Seneca St EVILLE/WHL BS5 .... 9 H2
Serbert Rd PTSHD/EG BS20 .... 47 J4
Sercombe Pk CLVDN BS21 .... 71 G2
Seventh Av HORF/LLZ BS7 .... 40 A7
Seven View Rd THNB/SVB BS35... 19 H3

Severn Av WSM BS23 .... 16 F8
Severn Dr THNB/SVB BS35 .... 19 G3
Severnmeade
　PTSHD/EG BS20 .... 46 D4
Severn Rd AVONM BS11 .... 27 C7
　AVONM BS11 .... 49 K3
　HNBRY/STHM BS10 .... 27 C5
　PTSHD/EG BS20 .... 47 G4
　PTSHD/EG BS20 .... 49 J4
　WSM BS23 .... 16 D7
Severn Wy BRSTK/PCHW BS34 ... 29 J6
　KEYN BS31 .... 81 F7
　THNB/SVB BS35 .... 27 C1
Severnwood Gdns
　THNB/SVB BS35 .... 27 H2
Sevier St CBRISNE BS2 .... 3 M6
Seville Rd PTSHD/EG BS20 .... 47 J2
Seymour Cl CLVDN BS21 .... 59 C7
　MTN/WRL BS22 .... 106 A1
Seymour Ct TRWBR BA14 .... 124 E5
Seymour Rd CBATH/BATHN BA1... 15 J1
　EVILLE/WHL BS5 .... 4 B7
　HORF/LLZ BS7 .... 3 K1
　KGWD/HNM BS15 .... 68 C1
　MANG/FISH BS16 .... 54 D5
　TRWBR BA14 .... 125 F4
Seyton Wk BRSTK/PCHW BS34... 40 D3
Shackel Hendy Ms
　MANG/FISH BS16 .... 55 H4
Shackleton Av YATE/CS BS37 ... 34 C7
Shadwell Rd HORF/LLZ BS7 .... 3 H4
Shaftesbury Av
　CBATH/BATHN BA1 .... 99 F5
　RDLND/MONT BS6 .... 3 K7
Shaftesbury Rd BATHSE BA2 ... 14 B9
　WSM BS23 .... 17 L1
Shaftesbury Ter EVILLE/WHL BS5... 9 C2
Shaft Rd BATHSE BA2 .... 112 C4
Shails La TRWBR BA14 .... 124 E5
Shakespeare Av BATHSE BA2 ... 111 J1
　HORF/LLZ BS7 .... 52 E1
Shakespeare Rd
　RDSTK/MIDN BA3 .... 126 D4
Shaldon Rd HORF/LLZ BS7 .... 4 A1
The Shallows KEYN BS31 .... 97 C1
Sham Castle La BATHSE BA2 ... 15 K5
Shamrock Rd EVILLE/WHL BS5 ... 5 H4
Shanklin Dr
　BRSTK/PCHW BS34 .... 40 A5
Shannon Ct THNB/SVB BS35 ... 19 J5
Shaplands
　HNLZ/SM/SNYPK/WT BS9 .... 51 H5
Shaws Wy BATHSE BA2 .... 98 C7
Shaymoor La THNB/SVB BS35 ... 28 C3
Shearman St TRWBR BA14 .... 125 F7
Shearmore Cl HORF/LLZ BS7 ... 52 E2
Sheene La BMSTR BS3 .... 10 F2
Sheepcote Barton
　TRWBR BA14 .... 125 G7
Sheeps Cft
　BMSTRD/HC/WWD BS13 .... 77 J7
Sheepway PTSHD/EG BS20 .... 48 A5
Sheepwood Cl
　HNBRY/STHM BS10 .... 38 D7
Sheepwood Rd
　HNBRY/STHM BS10 .... 38 D6
Sheldare Barton
　EVILLE/WHL BS5 .... 68 B3
Sheldon Cl CLVDN BS21 .... 71 H1
Shellard Rd BRSTK/PCHW BS34 ... 39 K5
Shellards La THNB/SVB BS35 ... 23 H2
Shellards Rd
　OLD/WMLY/WICK BS30 .... 69 F7
Shelley Av CLVDN BS21 .... 71 F1
Shelley Cl EVILLE/WHL BS5 .... 5 M9
Shelley Rd BATHSE BA2 .... 14 F9
　RDSTK/MIDN BA3 .... 126 D4
Shelley Wy HORF/LLZ BS7 .... 52 E1
Shellmor Av BRSTK/PCHW BS34... 30 A6
Shellmor Cl ALMDB BS32 .... 30 C6
　BRSTK/PCHW BS34 .... 30 B6
Shepherds Cl MANG/FISH BS16... 54 C3
Sheppard Rd MANG/FISH BS16 ... 54 C3
Sheppy's Ml YTN/CONG BS49 ... 87 G7
Shepton Wk BMSTR BS3 .... 10 E3
Sherborne Rd BATHSE BA2 .... 124 B5
Sherbourne Av ALMDB BS32 ... 40 D1
Sherbourne Cl KGWD/HNM BS15... 55 F7
Sherbourne St EVILLE/WHL BS5 ... 5 L1
Sheridan Rd BATHSE BA2 .... 98 C7
　HORF/LLZ BS7 .... 39 K7
Sheridan Wy
　OLD/WMLY/WICK BS30 .... 81 G1
Sherrin Wy
　BMSTRD/HC/WWD BS13 .... 92 B1
Sherston Cl MANG/FISH BS16 ... 54 B4
　NAIL BS48 .... 74 A1
Sherston Rd HORF/LLZ BS7 .... 52 C1
Sherwell Rd
　BRSG/KWL/STAPK BS4 .... 13 J2
Sherwood Cl KEYN BS31 .... 80 E6
Sherwood Crs MTN/WRL BS22... 106 A2
Sherwood Rd KEYN BS31 .... 80 E6
　KGWD/HNM BS15 .... 68 A1
Shetland Rd HNBRY/STHM BS10... 39 G7
Shetland Wy NAIL BS48 .... 74 A2
Shickle Gv BATHSE BA2 .... 111 F4
Shields Av HORF/LLZ BS7 .... 39 K6
Shiels Dr ALMDB BS32 .... 40 C1
Shilton Cl KGWD/HNM BS15 ... 69 F3
Shimsey Cl MANG/FISH BS16 ... 54 C3
Shiners Elms YTN/CONG BS49 ... 86 D4
Shipham Cl HGRV/WHIT BS14 ... 79 F6
　NAIL BS48 .... 73 K3
Shipham La YTN/CONG BS49 ... 120 E5
Ship La CBRIS/FH BS1 .... 7 J7
Shipley Mow MANG/FISH BS16 ... 55 H3
Shipley Rd
　HNLZ/SM/SNYPK/WT BS9 .... 51 J1
Shipnran Cl MANG/FISH BS16 ... 54 E5
Shire Gdns AVONM BS11 .... 49 J1
Shirehampton Rd AVONM BS11... 50 B2
　HNLZ/SM/SNYPK/WT BS9 .... 50 E3
Shire Wy YATE/CS BS37 .... 43 K2
Shophouse Rd BATHSE BA2 ... 98 E7
Shop La TRWBR BA14 .... 129 J1

Shore Pl TRWBR BA14 .... 124 B5
Shorthill Rd YATE/CS BS37 .... 43 K4
Shortlands Rd AVONM BS11 ... 37 H7
Short La LGASH BS41 .... 76 B1
Short St CBRISNE BS2 .... 8 B6
Short Wy CFTN/FAIL BS8 .... 63 H7
　THNB/SVB BS35 .... 19 G6
Shortwood HI MANG/FISH BS16... 55 K4
Shortwood Rd
　BMSTRD/HC/WWD BS13 .... 93 H1
　MANG/FISH BS16 .... 55 C5
Shortwood Vw
　KGWD/HNM BS15 .... 69 F2
Shortwood Wk
　BMSTRD/HC/WWD BS13 .... 93 H1
Showering Cl
　HGRV/WHIT BS14 .... 79 H6
Showering Rd HGRV/WHIT BS14... 79 H6
Shrewsbury Bow
　OMX/HUT/LCK BS24 .... 123 K2
Shrewton Cl TRWBR BA14 .... 131 F1
Shrubbery Av WSM BS23 .... 104 B4
Shrubbery Cottages
　RDLND/MONT BS6 .... 2 C5
Shrubbery Rd MANG/FISH BS16... 54 D4
　WSM BS23 .... 104 C4
Shrubbery Ter WSM BS23 .... 104 B4
Shrubbery Wk West
　WSM BS23 .... 104 C4
Shuter Rd
　BMSTRD/HC/WWD BS13 .... 77 H6
Sibland THNB/SVB BS35 .... 19 J5
Sibland Cl THNB/SVB BS35 .... 19 J4
Sibland Rd THNB/SVB BS35 .... 19 J4
Sibland Wy THNB/SVB BS35 .... 19 H5
Sidcot BRSG/KWL/STAPK BS4 ... 80 A1
Sidcot La WNSC BS25 .... 120 D7
Sideland Cl HGRV/WHIT BS14 ... 79 J5
Sidelands Rd MANG/FISH BS16... 54 C3
Sidmouth Gdns BMSTR BS3 ... 11 H3
Sidmouth Rd BMSTR BS3 .... 11 H3
Signal Rd MANG/FISH BS16 .... 54 E5
Silbury Ri KEYN BS31 .... 96 B2
Silbury Rd BMSTR BS3 .... 77 C1
Silcox Rd
　BMSTRD/HC/WWD BS13 .... 78 A7
Silklands Gv
　HNLZ/SM/SNYPK/WT BS9 .... 50 E3
Silverberry Rd MTN/WRL BS22... 106 B4
Silverbirch Cl BRSTK/PCHW BS34... 40 C1
Silver Birch Rd TRWBR BA14 ... 130 D2
Silverhill Rd HNBRY/STHM BS10... 38 B5
Silverlow Rd NAIL BS48 .... 73 H1
Silver Md YTN/CONG BS49 .... 109 G3
Silver Mdw TRWBR BA14 .... 130 C2
Silver Moor La BNWL BS29 ... 107 C6
Silverstone Wy
　YTN/CONG BS49 .... 109 G2
Silver St BOAV BA15 .... 114 E7
　CBRIS/FH BS1 .... 7 H2
　NAIL BS48 .... 73 H1
　PTSHD/EG BS20 .... 60 C1
　RDSTK/MIDN BA3 .... 126 B7
　TRWBR BA14 .... 125 F6
　YTN/CONG BS49 .... 109 G3
Silver Street La TRWBR BA14 ... 130 D2
Silverthorne La CBRISNE BS2 ... 8 C5
Silverton Ct
　BRSG/KWL/STAPK BS4 .... 11 M7
Simmonds Vw
　BRSTK/PCHW BS34 .... 40 E4
Simons Cl MTN/WRL BS22 .... 106 B3
Singapore Rd WSM BS23 .... 116 D3
Sion HI CBATH/BATHN BA1 .... 14 C2
　CFTN/FAIL BS8 .... 65 H4
Sion Hill Pl CBATH/BATHN BA1 ... 14 C1
Sion La CFTN/FAIL BS8 .... 65 H3
Sion Pl CFTN/FAIL BS8 .... 65 H3
　CBATH/BATHN BA1 .... 14 C1
Sion Rd BMSTR BS3 .... 10 E1
　CBATH/BATHN BA1 .... 14 C1
Sir John's La EVILLE/WHL BS5 ... 4 D2
　HORF/LLZ BS7 .... 4 C1
Siston Cl KGWD/HNM BS15 ... 55 C7
Siston Pk KGWD/HNM BS15 ... 55 C7
Sixth Av HORF/LLZ BS7 .... 39 K7
Sixty Acres Cl CFTN/FAIL BS8 ... 63 H7
Skinners La WNSC BS25 .... 121 J7
Skippon Ct KGWD/HNM BS15... 68 E5
Sladacre La BLAG/CWMG/WR BS40 ... 5 K9
Sladebrook Av BATHSE BA2 ... 111 F2
Sladebrook Rd BATHSE BA2 ... 110 E1
Slade La NAIL BS48 .... 75 H7
Slade Rd PTSHD/EG BS20 .... 47 H4
Sladesbrook BOAV BA15 .... 115 F5
Sladesbrook Cl BOAV BA15 .... 114 E5
Slate La KEYN BS31 .... 95 G5
Sleep La HGRV/WHIT BS14 .... 94 C1
Slimbridge Cl YATE/CS BS37 ... 44 C1
The Slipway TRWBR BA14 .... 125 F2
Sloan St EVILLE/WHL BS5 .... 9 H1
Slowgrove Cl TRWBR BA14 .... 125 H6
Slymbridge Av
　HNBRY/STHM BS10 .... 38 D4
Smallbrook Gdns TRWBR BA14... 125 F1
Smallbrook La PLTN/PENS BS39... 95 G6
Small Down End WNSC BS25 ... 120 C4
Small La MANG/FISH BS16 .... 53 J4
Small St CBRIS/FH BS1 .... 7 H3
　CBRISNE BS2 .... 8 B6
Smallway YTN/CONG BS49 .... 87 C7
Smarts Gn YATE/CS BS37 .... 35 F7
Smeaton Rd CBRIS/FH BS1 .... 65 H5
Smithmead
　BMSTRD/HC/WWD BS13 .... 77 K6
Smithywell Cl TRWBR BA14 .... 125 H6
Smoke La AVONM BS11 .... 36 E1
Smythe Cft HGRV/WHIT BS14 ... 93 K1
Smyth Rd BMSTR BS3 .... 10 A2
Smyths Cl AVONM BS11 .... 36 C7
Snowberry Cl MTN/WRL
　BS22 .... 106 B4
Snowberry Wk EVILLE/WHL BS5 ... 5 K9
Snowdon Cl MANG/FISH BS16 ... 5 M1
Snowdon Rd MANG/FISH BS16... 54 A1
Snowdon V WSM BS23 .... 105 F4
Snow HI CBATH/BATHN BA1 .... 3 F9
Solent Wy THNB/SVB BS35 .... 19 J6
Solsbury Wy CBATH/BATHN BA1... 99 G2
Somer Av RDSTK/MIDN BA3 ... 126 A3

Somerby Cl ALMDB BS32 .... 40 C1
Somerdale Av BATHSE BA2 ... 111 G3
　BRSG/KWL/STAPK BS4 .... 11 M1
　MTN/WRL BS22 .... 105 H5
Somerdale Cl MTN/WRL BS22 ... 105 H5
Somerdale Rd KEYN BS31 .... 81 F4
Somerdale Rd North KEYN BS31... 81 F4
Somerdale Vw BATHSE BA2 ... 111 F3
Somermead BMSTR BS3 .... 10 F5
Somer Rd RDSTK/MIDN BA3 ... 126 A3
Somerset Av
　OMX/HUT/LCK BS24 .... 106 A6
　YATE/CS BS37 .... 34 C4
Somerset Crs
　BRSTK/PCHW BS34 .... 40 E3
Somerset Rd
　BRSG/KWL/STAPK BS4 .... 12 C2
　CLVDN BS21 .... 59 G7
　PTSHD/EG BS20 .... 46 D4
Somerset Sq CBRIS/FH BS1 .... 7 J7
Somerset St BATHSE BA2 .... 14 F8
　CBRIS/FH BS1 .... 7 K7
　CBRISNE BS2 .... 3 H9
Somerset Ter BMSTR BS3 .... 11 H2
Somerton Cl KGWD/HNM BS15... 68 E3
Somerton Rd CLVDN BS21 .... 71 G2
　HORF/LLZ BS7 .... 52 C3
Somervale Rd
　RDSTK/MIDN BA3 .... 127 F3
Somerville Cl KEYN BS31 .... 97 F2
Somerville Rd WNSC BS25 .... 120 D3
Sommerville Rd
　RDLND/MONT BS6 .... 3 J3
Sommerville Rd South
　RDLND/MONT BS6 .... 3 L5
Sophia Gdns MTN/WRL BS22 ... 106 C1
Sorrel Cl THNB/SVB BS35 .... 19 J3
　TRWBR BA14 .... 131 F2
Soundwell Rd
　KGWD/HNM BS15 .... 68 C1
South Av BATHSE BA2 .... 14 A8
　BATHSE BA2 .... 99 F7
　PTSHD/EG BS20 .... 47 H3
　YATE/CS BS37 .... 33 J6
Southbourne Gdns
　CBATH/BATHN BA1 .... 100 A3
Southcot Pl BATHSE BA2 .... 15 H9
South Cft
　HNLZ/SM/SNYPK/WT BS9 .... 52 A2
　WNSC BS25 .... 120 C4
South Dene
　HNLZ/SM/SNYPK/WT BS9 .... 51 G3
Southdown Av BATHSE BA2 ... 110 E1
Southdown Rd BATHSE BA2 ... 110 E1
　HNLZ/SM/SNYPK/WT BS9 .... 51 H1
Southend Rd WSM BS23 .... 16 E9
Southernhay CFTN/FAIL BS8 ... 6 C5
　MANG/FISH BS16 .... 54 C5
Southernhay Av CFTN/FAIL BS8... 6 C5
Southern Wy CLVDN BS21 .... 70 D1
Southey Av KGWD/HNM BS15... 68 D1
Southey Rd CLVDN BS21 .... 71 F1
Southey St CBRISNE BS2 .... 3 M6
Southfield TRWBR BA14 .... 130 B5
Southfield Av KGWD/HNM BS15... 68 E1
Southfield Cl NAIL BS48 .... 61 J7
　WSM BS23 .... 116 C5
Southfield Ct
　HNLZ/SM/SNYPK/WT BS9 .... 51 J2
Southfield Rd
　HNLZ/SM/SNYPK/WT BS9 .... 51 J2
　NAIL BS48 .... 61 J7
　RDLND/MONT BS6 .... 3 G7
Southgate
　CBATH/BATHN BA1 .... 15 G7
South Green St
　CFTN/FAIL BS8 .... 65 H4
South Gv PTSHD/EG BS20 .... 49 J5
　RDLND/MONT BS6 .... 2 F6
South Hayes EVILLE/WHL BS5 ... 4 D2
Southlands CBATH/BATHN BA1 ... 98 E2
Southlands Wy YTN/CONG BS49... 87 G7
South Lawn
　OMX/HUT/LCK BS24 .... 118 A2
South Lawn Cl
　OMX/HUT/LCK BS24 .... 118 A2
South Lea Rd
　CBATH/BATHN BA1 .... 98 D4
Southleigh BOAV BA15 .... 123 J1
Southleigh Rd CFTN/FAIL BS8 ... 6 C1
South Liberty La BMSTR BS3 ... 10 C4
Southmead WNSC BS25 .... 120 D6
Southmead Rd
　BRSTK/PCHW BS34 .... 39 H7
　HNBRY/STHM BS10 .... 52 A1
　HNLZ/SM/SNYPK/WT BS9 .... 51 K2
　MTN/WRL BS22 .... 17 M3
Southmead Wy
　HNBRY/STHM BS10 .... 52 B1
Southover Cl
　HNLZ/SM/SNYPK/WT BS9 .... 51 J1
South Pde WSM BS23 .... 16 D2
Southridge Hts
　OMX/HUT/LCK BS24 .... 117 F6
South Rd ALMDB BS32 .... 30 C1
　BMSTR BS3 .... 10 E2
　KGWD/HNM BS15 .... 68 D2
　PTSHD/EG BS20 .... 47 H3
　RDLND/MONT BS6 .... 2 F6
　RDSTK/MIDN BA3 .... 126 C4
　WSM BS23 .... 104 B4
Southsea Rd BRSTK/PCHW BS34... 39 K1
Southside WSM BS23 .... 16 E1
South Side YTN/CONG BS49 ... 87 H7
Southside Cl AVONM BS11 .... 50 D2
Southside Crs
　MTN/WRL BS22 .... 105 F1
Southstoke La BATHSE BA2 ... 111 J6
Southstoke Rd BATHSE BA2 ... 111 J4
South St BMSTR BS3 .... 10 D1
South Ter WSM BS23 .... 16 C1
South Vw FRCTL/WBN BS36 ... 54 E4
　MANG/FISH BS16 .... 54 E4
　PTSHD/EG BS20 .... 47 H2
Southview Cl
　OMX/HUT/LCK BS24 .... 117 K4

South View Crs
FRCTL/WBN BS36 .... 42 E2
South View Pl
RDSTK/MIDN BA3 .... 126 C3 ▣
South View Ri *FRCTL/WBN* BS36 .. 42 E2
South View Rd *BATHSE* BA2 .. 14 A7
Southview Rd *TRWBR* BA14 .. 131 F1
Southville Pl *BMSTR* BS3 .... 7 G8
Southville Rd *BMSTR* BS3 .... 6 F8
BOAV BA15 .... 124 A1
WSM BS23 .... 116 D2
South Wy *TRWBR* BA14 .... 125 F7
Southway Dr
OLD/WMLY/WICK BS30 .... 69 K5
Southway Rd *BOAV* BA15 .... 123 K2
Southwell St *CBRISNE* BS2 .... 6 F1
Southwick Rd *TRWBR* BA14 .... 130 E3
Southwood Av
HNLZ/SM/SNYPK/WT BS9 .... 50 E1
Southwood Dr
HNLZ/SM/SNYPK/WT BS9 .... 50 D1
Southwood Dr East
HNLZ/SM/SNYPK/WT BS9 .... 50 E1
Southwood Rd *BATHSE* BA2 .. 125 H6
Spalding Cl *HORF/LLZ* BS7 .... 4 A4
Spaniorum Vw *THNB/SVB* BS35 .. 28 C5
Spar Rd *YATE/CS* BS37 .... 34 A5
Spartley Dr
BMSTRD/HC/WWD BS13 .... 77 H5
Spartley Wk
BMSTRD/HC/WWD BS13 .... 77 H5 ▣
Speedwell Av *EVILLE/WHL* BS5 .... 9 H2
Speedwell Cl *THNB/SVB* BS35 .. 19 J3
TRWBR BA14 .... 131 F1
Speedwell Rd *EVILLE/WHL* BS5 .... 5 L8
KGWD/HNM BS15 .... 68 B1
Spencer Dr *MTN/WRL* BS22 .. 106 C2
RDSTK/MIDN BA3 .... 126 B3
Spencer's Ct *THNB/SVB* BS35 .. 19 G7
Sperring Ct
RDSTK/MIDN BA3 .... 126 A5 ▣
Spey Cl *THNB/SVB* BS35 .... 19 H5
Spindleberry Gv *NAIL* BS48 .... 74 A1
Spinners Cft *TRWBR* BA14 .. 125 F7 ▣
Spinners End
MTN/WRL BS22 .... 106 C1 ▣
Spinney Rd
OMX/HUT/LCK BS24 .... 118 E2
The Spinney *ALMDB* BS32 .... 40 D1
FRCTL/WBN BS36 .... 42 C1 ▣
WSM BS23 .... 116 E5
Spires Vw *MANG/FISH* BS16 .. 53 J4 ▣
Spring Crs *BATHSE* BA2 .... 15 H8
Springfield *BOAV* BA15 .... 115 F7
THNB/SVB BS35 .... 19 H3
Springfield Av *AVONM* BS11 .. 49 K3 ▣
HORF/LLZ BS7 .... 52 D4
MANG/FISH BS16 .... 55 C3
MTN/WRL BS22 .... 105 J4
Springfield Buildings
RDSTK/MIDN BA3 .... 127 H1
Springfield Cl *BATHSE* BA2 .. 98 E7 ▣
MANG/FISH BS16 .... 55 C3
TRWBR BA14 .... 125 G4 ▣
Springfield Crs
RDSTK/MIDN BA3 .... 127 H1
Springfield Gdns *BNWL* BS29 .. 119 H3 ▣
Springfield Gv
HNLZ/SM/SNYPK/WT BS9 .... 51 K4
Springfield Pk *TRWBR* BA14 .. 125 G5
Springfield Pl
RDSTK/MIDN BA3 .... 127 F1
Springfield Rd
MANG/FISH BS16 .... 55 G3 ▣
PTSHD/EG BS20 .... 49 J5 ▣
PTSHD/EG BS20 .... 49 J5 ▣
RDLND/MONT BS6 .... 3 H8
Springfields *BRSTK/PCHW* BS34 .. 39 K6
Spring Gardens Rd
CBATH/BATHN BA1 .... 15 G6 ▣
Spring Hi *KGWD/HNM* BS15 .. 54 E7
MTN/WRL BS22 .... 105 H3
RDLND/MONT BS6 .... 3 H9
Spring Hill Dr *MTN/WRL* BS22 .. 105 J4 ▣
Spring La *CBATH/BATHN* BA1 .. 100 A2
LGASH BS41 .... 92 D3
Springleaze
BRSG/KWL/STAPK BS4 .... 12 B6
MANG/FISH BS16 .... 55 C2
Spring Ri *PTSHD/EG* BS20 .. 47 C6
Spring St *BMSTR* BS3 .... 7 K8
Spring Street Pl *BMSTR* BS3 .... 7 K8
Spring Va *MTN/WRL* BS22 .. 105 H3 ▣
Springville Cl
OLD/WMLY/WICK BS30 .. 69 G7 ▣
Springwood Dr
HNBRY/STHM BS10 .... 38 A5
Spring Wood Gdns
OMX/HUT/LCK BS24 .... 117 H3
Spruce Wy *BRSTK/PCHW* BS34 .. 39 H1 ▣
The Square
BRSG/KWL/STAPK BS4 .... 12 B5
WNSC BS25 .... 121 H7
Squires Ct
OLD/WMLY/WICK BS30 .. 69 F7 ▣
Squires Leaze *THNB/SVB* BS35 .. 19 J3
Stabbins Cl *MTN/WRL* BS22 .. 84 C7 ▣
Stackpool Rd *BMSTR* BS3 .... 6 E8
Staddlestones
RDSTK/MIDN BA3 .... 126 A6
Stadium Rd *RDLND/MONT* BS6 .. 52 A4
Stafford Crs *THNB/SVB* BS35 .. 19 G4
Stafford Pl *WSM* BS23 .... 16 F1 ▣
Stafford Rd *CBRISNE* BS2 .... 4 A4
PTSHD/EG BS20 .... 47 J3 ▣
WSM BS23 .... 17 C2
Staffords Ct
OLD/WMLY/WICK BS30 .. 69 G4 ▣
Stafford St *BMSTR* BS3 .... 7 C9
Stainer Cl
BRSG/KWL/STAPK BS4 .... 78 B5 ▣
Stallard St *TRWBR* BA14 .... 124 E6
Stall St *CBATH/BATHN* BA1 .. 15 G7 ▣
Stanbridge Cl
MANG/FISH BS16 .... 55 F3 ▣
Stanbridge Rd *MANG/FISH* BS16 .. 55 F3
Stanbury Av *MANG/FISH* BS16 .. 54 B4
Stanbury Rd *BMSTR* BS3 .... 11 J2

Stancomb Av *TRWBR* BA14 .. 125 G5
Stancombe La *NAIL* BS48 .... 74 E4
Standfast Rd
HNBRY/STHM BS10 .... 38 C5
Standish Cl *BRSTK/PCHW* BS34 .. 30 A6
Standish Cl
HNBRY/STHM BS10 .... 38 C7 ▣
Standon Wy
HNBRY/STHM BS10 .... 39 F6 ▣
Stane Wy *AVONM* BS11 .... 49 J2 ▣
Stanfield Cl *HORF/LLZ* BS7 .. 53 F3 ▣
Stanford Cl *FRCTL/WBN* BS36 .. 32 A7
Stanhope Pl
CBATH/BATHN BA1 .... 14 D6 ▣
Stanhope Rd
OLD/WMLY/WICK BS30 .. 81 F1 ▣
WSM BS23 .... 116 D3
Stanhope St *CBRISNE* BS2 .... 8 D2
Stanley Av *BRSTK/PCHW* BS34 .. 40 A6
HORF/LLZ BS7 .... 3 K3
Stanley Cha *EVILLE/WHL* BS5 .... 5 H6
Stanley Ct *RDSTK/MIDN* BA3 .. 126 C3 ▣
Stanley Crs *BRSTK/PCHW* BS34 .. 40 A6
Stanley Gdns
OLD/WMLY/WICK BS30 .. 69 H6
Stanley Gv *WSM* BS23 .... 17 G3
Stanley Hi *BRSG/KWL/STAPK* BS4 .. 8 A9
Stanley Md *ALMDB* BS32 .... 30 D5 ▣
Stanley Park Rd
MANG/FISH BS16 .... 54 E6
Stanley Rd *KGWD/HNM* BS15 .. 69 H1
RDLND/MONT BS6 .... 2 E6
WSM BS23 .... 17 G3
Stanley Rd West *BATHSE* BA2 .. 14 B8
Stanley St *BMSTR* BS3 .... 10 E1 ▣
Stanley St North *BMSTR* BS3 .. 10 E2 ▣
Stanley St South *BMSTR* BS3 .. 10 E2
Stanley Ter *BMSTR* BS3 .... 10 E3
Stanshalls Cl
BLAG/CWMG/WR BS40 .... 90 D4
Stanshalls Dr
BLAG/CWMG/WR BS40 .. 90 D4 ▣
Stanshalls La
BLAG/CWMG/WR BS40 .... 90 D4
Stanshawe Crs *YATE/CS* BS37 .. 34 B6
Stanshawes Dr *YATE/CS* BS37 .. 34 C7
Stanshaw Rd *MANG/FISH* BS16 .. 54 A2
Stanshaws Cl
BRSTK/PCHW BS34 .... 30 A5
Stanton Cl *KGWD/HNM* BS15 .. 69 F1
TRWBR BA14 .... 131 F2 ▣
Stanton Rd *HNBRY/STHM* BS10 .. 39 H7
Stanway *OLD/WMLY/WICK* BS30 .. 81 H2
Stanway Cl *BATHSE* BA2 .... 111 G4
Staple Gv *KEYN* BS31 .... 80 D6
Staple Grove Crs
EVILLE/WHL BS5 .... 68 A3 ▣
Staplehill Rd *MANG/FISH* BS16 .. 54 E5
Staples Cl *CLVDN* BS21 .... 71 G2 ▣
Staples Gn *MTN/WRL* BS22 .. 106 C2 ▣
Staples Hl *RDSTK/MIDN* BA3.. 122 C1 ▣
Staples Rd *YATE/CS* BS37 .... 34 A5 ▣
Stapleton Cl *MANG/FISH* BS16 .. 53 H4 ▣
Stapleton Rd *EVILLE/WHL* BS5 .... 4 E5
Star Barn Rd *FRCTL/WBN* BS36 .. 41 K1
Starcross Rd *MTN/WRL* BS22 .. 106 B3
Star La *MANG/FISH* BS16 .... 5 L3
PTSHD/EG BS20 .... 49 K5 ▣
Starling Cl *MTN/WRL* BS22 .. 105 K5
Station Ap *WSM* BS23 .... 16 F4 ▣
Station Av *MANG/FISH* BS16 .. 54 A5
Station Cl *NAIL* BS48 .... 73 K4
OLD/WMLY/WICK BS30 .. 69 J2
YATE/CS BS37 .... 35 G7
YTN/CONG BS49 .... 109 F1
Station La *HORF/LLZ* BS7 .... 4 A2
Station Rd *AVONM* BS11 .... 49 K4
BRSG/KWL/STAPK BS4 .... 13 G4
BRSTK/PCHW BS34 .... 39 K5
BRSTK/PCHW BS34 .... 40 B6
BRSTK/PCHW BS34 .... 40 B2
CBATH/BATHN BA1 .... 99 F5
CLVDN BS21 .... 59 F7 ▣
FRCTL/WBN BS36 .... 41 K4
FRCTL/WBN BS36 .... 42 C1
HNBRY/STHM BS10 .... 38 B5
HORF/LLZ BS7 .... 3 M2
KEYN BS31 .... 80 E5
KGWD/HNM BS15 .... 55 F6
MANG/FISH BS16 .... 54 A5
MTN/WRL BS22 .... 106 A3
MTN/WRL BS22 .... 106 D3
NAIL BS48 .... 73 K2
NAIL BS48 .... 75 J5
OLD/WMLY/WICK BS30 .. 69 J3
PTSHD/EG BS20 .... 47 H3
PTSHD/EG BS20 .... 48 C5
PTSHD/EG BS20 .... 49 J5
RDLND/MONT BS6 .... 3 H6
RDSTK/MIDN BA3 .... 122 C1
RDSTK/MIDN BA3 .... 126 C3
THNB/SVB BS35 .... 27 G1
THNB/SVB BS35 .... 28 C3
WNSC BS25 .... 120 C2
WSM BS23 .... 16 F4
YATE/CS BS37 .... 32 E4
YATE/CS BS37 .... 33 K5
YATE/CS BS37 .... 34 B5
YTN/CONG BS49 .... 86 D3
YTN/CONG BS49 .... 109 F1
Station Wy *MANG/FISH* BS16 .. 54 A5
TRWBR BA14 .... 124 E6
Staunton Flds *HGRV/WHIT* BS14 .. 94 B1
Staunton La *HGRV/WHIT* BS14 .. 79 G7
Staunton Wy
HGRV/WHIT BS14 .... 79 H7 ▣
Staveley Crs *HNBRY/STHM* BS10 .. 39 F6
Stavordale Gv *HGRV/WHIT* BS14 .. 79 F5
Staynes Crs *KGWD/HNM* BS15 .. 68 E2 ▣
Steam Mills *RDSTK/MIDN* BA3 .. 126 A5
Stean Bridge Rd *ALMDB* BS32 .. 40 D2
Steel Cl *OLD/WMLY/WICK* BS30 .. 69 F4
Steel Mills *KEYN* BS31 .... 81 F7
Stella Gv *BMSTR* BS3 .... 10 A3
Stephens Dr
OLD/WMLY/WICK BS30 .. 69 F5
Stephen St *EVILLE/WHL* BS5 .... 4 F9

Stepney Rd *EVILLE/WHL* BS5 .... 4 F8
Stepney Wk *EVILLE/WHL* BS5 .... 4 F8
The Stepping Stones
BRSG/KWL/STAPK BS4 .... 9 K4
Sterncourt Rd *MANG/FISH* BS16 .. 54 A2
Stevens Cl *BMSTR* BS3 .... 7 L9
Stevens Wk *ALMDB* BS32 .... 30 C7
Stibbs Ct
OLD/WMLY/WICK BS30 .. 69 F6 ▣
Stibbs Hi *EVILLE/WHL* BS5 .... 68 A3
Stickland *CLVDN* BS21 .... 70 E2 ▣
Stidcote La *WUE* GL12 .... 25 C1
Stidcot La *WUE* GL12 .... 24 D1
Stile Acres *AVONM* BS11 .... 37 H7
Stillhouse La *BMSTR* BS3 .... 7 H8
Stillingfleet Rd
BMSTRD/HC/WWD BS13 .... 78 A6
Stillman Cl
BMSTRD/HC/WWD BS13 .... 77 G7
Stinchcombe *YATE/CS* BS37 .. 34 B6 ▣
Stirling Cl *YATE/CS* BS37 .... 34 A3 ▣
Stirling Rd *BRSG/KWL/STAPK* BS4 .. 12 B1
Stirling Wy *KEYN* BS31 .... 80 E7 ▣
Stirtingale Av *BATHSE* BA2 .. 111 F2
Stirtingale Rd *BATHSE* BA2 .. 111 F2 ▣
Stock Hi *BRSG/KWL/STAPK* BS4 .. 18 A4
Stock La *YTN/CONG* BS49 .... 109 J4
Stockton Cl *HGRV/WHIT* BS14 .. 78 D7 ▣
OLD/WMLY/WICK BS30 .. 69 H7 ▣
Stock Wy North *NAIL* BS48 .... 73 J1
Stock Wy South *NAIL* BS48 .... 73 J1 ▣
Stockwell Av *MANG/FISH* BS16.. 55 G5 ▣
Stockwell Cl *MANG/FISH* BS16 .. 55 F2
Stockwell Dr *MANG/FISH* BS16 .. 55 G3
Stockwood Crs
BRSG/KWL/STAPK BS4 .... 11 L4
Stockwood Hi *KEYN* BS31 .... 80 C4
Stockwood La *HGRV/WHIT* BS14 .. 79 J6
Stockwood Ms
BRSG/KWL/STAPK BS4 .... 9 M6 ▣
Stockwood Rd
BRSG/KWL/STAPK BS4 .... 13 L7
HGRV/WHIT BS14 .... 79 J6
Stodelegh Cl
MTN/WRL BS22 .... 106 C2 ▣
Stoke Bridge Av
BRSTK/PCHW BS34 .... 40 C2
Stokefield Cl *THNB/SVB* BS35 .. 19 G4
Stoke Gv
HNLZ/SM/SNYPK/WT BS9 .... 51 G3
Stoke Hamlet
HNLZ/SM/SNYPK/WT BS9 .. 51 H3 ▣
Stoke Hl
HNLZ/SM/SNYPK/WT BS9 .... 51 G5
Stoke La *BRSTK/PCHW* BS34 .... 30 B7
HNLZ/SM/SNYPK/WT BS9 .. 51 H3 ▣
MANG/FISH BS16 .... 53 J2
Stokeleigh Wk
HNLZ/SM/SNYPK/WT BS9 .. 50 E4 ▣
Stokemead
BRSTK/PCHW BS34 .... 30 B7 ▣
Stoke Md *RDSTK/MIDN* BA3 .. 112 E6
Stoke Mdw *ALMDB* BS32 .... 30 C6
Stoke Paddock Rd
HNLZ/SM/SNYPK/WT BS9 .... 51 F3
Stoke Park Rd
HNLZ/SM/SNYPK/WT BS9 .... 51 G5
Stoke Park Rd South
HNLZ/SM/SNYPK/WT BS9 .... 51 F5
Stoke Rd *CFTN/FAIL* BS8 .... 2 B5
HNLZ/SM/SNYPK/WT BS9 .... 51 H6
PTSHD/EG BS20 .... 47 H4
Stokes Ct
OLD/WMLY/WICK BS30 .. 69 G6 ▣
Stokes Cft *CBRIS/FH* BS1 .... 3 J9
Stoke View Rd *MANG/FISH* BS16 .. 5 L3
Stoneable Rd *RDSTK/MIDN* BA3.. 127 H2
Stoneberry Rd *HGRV/WHIT* BS14.. 93 K1
Stonebridge *CLVDN* BS21 .... 71 F2 ▣
Stonebridge Pk *EVILLE/WHL* BS5 .. 5 H5
Stonebridge Rd *WSM* BS23 .. 17 C9 ▣
Stonechat Gdns
MANG/FISH BS16 .... 53 J3
Stonehenge La *CLVDN* BS21 .. 61 J6
Stonehill *OLD/WMLY/WICK* BS30 .. 68 E6
Stonehouse Cl *BATHSE* BA2 .. 112 A4
Stonehouse La *BATHSE* BA2 .. 112 A3
Stone La *FRCTL/WBN* BS36 .... 41 K4
Stoneleigh Crs
BRSG/KWL/STAPK BS4 .... 12 A3
Stoneleigh Dr
OLD/WMLY/WICK BS30 .. 69 F5
Stoneleigh Rd
BRSG/KWL/STAPK BS4 .... 12 A3
Stoneleigh Wk
BRSG/KWL/STAPK BS4 .... 11 M4
Stonewell Dr *YTN/CONG* BS49 .. 109 F2
Stonewell Gv *YTN/CONG* BS49 .. 109 F2
Stonewell La *YTN/CONG* BS49 .. 109 G2
Stonewell Park Rd
YTN/CONG BS49 .... 109 G2
Stoneyfield Cl *PTSHD/EG* BS20.. 49 H5
Stoneyfields *PTSHD/EG* BS20 .. 49 H5
Stoney Steep *NAIL* BS48 .... 62 A5
Stoney Stile Rd *THNB/SVB* BS35 .. 23 F1
Stormont Cl *WSM* BS23 .... 116 E3 ▣
Stothard Rd *HORF/LLZ* BS7 .. 53 F2
Stottbury Rd *HORF/LLZ* BS7 .... 4 B3
Stoulton Gv
HNBRY/STHM BS10 .... 38 D5 ▣
Stourden Cl *MANG/FISH* BS16 .. 54 A2 ▣
Stourton Dr
OLD/WMLY/WICK BS30 .. 69 F6
Stover Rd *YATE/CS* BS37 .... 33 H5
Stowell Hill Rd *WUE* GL12 .... 20 C7
Stowey Pk *YTN/CONG* BS49 .. 87 C5 ▣
Stowey Rd *YTN/CONG* BS49 .... 86 E4
Stow Hill Rd *WUE* GL12 .... 20 B7
Stowick Crs *AVONM* BS11 .... 37 K7
Stradbrook Av *EVILLE/WHL* BS5 .. 68 B3
Stradling Av *WSM* BS23 .... 17 G5
Stradling Rd *AVONM* BS11 .... 37 K6
Straight St *CBRISNE* BS2 .... 7 L4
Stratford Cl *HGRV/WHIT* BS14 .. 93 J1 ▣
Strathmore Rd *HORF/LLZ* BS7 .. 52 C3
Stratton Rd *KEYN* BS31 .... 97 F1
Stratton St *CBRISNE* BS2 .... 7 K1
Strawberry Cl *NAIL* BS48 .... 73 H2 ▣

Strawberry Hi *CLVDN* BS21 .... 59 G6
Strawbridge Rd *EVILLE/WHL* BS5 .. 8 D3
Stream Cl *HNBRY/STHM* BS10 .. 39 C5
Streamcross *YTN/CONG* BS49 .. 87 H2
Streamleaze *THNB/SVB* BS35 .. 19 H5
Streamside *CLVDN* BS21 .... 59 H7 ▣
Streamside Rd *YATE/CS* BS37 .. 34 D6 ▣
The Stream *MANG/FISH* BS16 .. 41 C6
The Street *RDSTK/MIDN* BA3 .. 127 C3
THNB/SVB BS35 .... 23 C1
Stretford Av *EVILLE/WHL* BS5 .. 5 H7 ▣
Stretford Rd *EVILLE/WHL* BS5 .. 5 H9
Stride Cl *THNB/SVB* BS35 .... 27 H1 ▣
Strode Common
THNB/SVB BS35 .... 22 E1
Strode Gdns *THNB/SVB* BS35 .. 22 E1
Strode Rd *CLVDN* BS21 .... 70 D3
Strode Wy *CLVDN* BS21 .... 70 D2
Stroud Rd *AVONM* BS11 .... 50 A4
BRSTK/PCHW BS34 .... 29 H7
Stuart Cl *TRWBR* BA14 .... 125 C2 ▣
Stuart Pl *BATHSE* BA2 .... 14 A7
Stuart Rd *WSM* BS23 .... 17 K8
Stuart St *EVILLE/WHL* BS5 .... 8 E3
Studley Ri *TRWBR* BA14 .... 131 F1
Sturden La *MANG/FISH* BS16 .. 41 H5
Sturdon Rd *BMSTR* BS3 .... 10 B2
Sturmer Cl *YATE/CS* BS37 .... 34 B3
Sturminster Cl *HGRV/WHIT* BS14 .. 79 H5
Sturminster Rd
HGRV/WHIT BS14 .... 12 F8
Sulis Manor Rd *BATHSE* BA2 .. 111 C5
Sumerlin Dr *CLVDN* BS21 .... 59 H7
Summer Down Wk
TRWBR BA14 .... 130 E3 ▣
Summerfield
MTN/WRL BS22 .... 106 C2 ▣
Summerfield Rd
CBATH/BATHN BA1 .... 99 J3
Summerhayes
OLD/WMLY/WICK BS30 .. 69 K5 ▣
Summer Hl
BRSG/KWL/STAPK BS4 .... 8 A3
Summerhill Rd
CBATH/BATHN BA1 .... 14 B1
EVILLE/WHL BS5 .... 9 L1
Summerhill Ter *EVILLE/WHL* BS5 .. 9 M2
Summerhouse *CLVDN* BS21 .. 61 H6
Summerlands *NAIL* BS48 .... 74 B6
Summerlands Rd *WSM* BS23 .. 17 K2
Summer La *BATHSE* BA2 .... 112 A4
BNWL BS29 .... 106 E6
MTN/WRL BS22 .... 106 C4
OMX/HUT/LCK BS24 .... 106 C4 ▣
Summer La North
MTN/WRL BS22 .... 106 B3
Summerleaze *KEYN* BS31 .... 80 E4 ▣
MANG/FISH BS16 .... 54 C6
TRWBR BA14 .... 130 C1
Summers Md *YATE/CS* BS37 .. 34 B2
Summers Rd *CBRISNE* BS2 .... 4 A7
Summer St *BMSTR* BS3 .... 6 E9
Sundays Hi *ALMDB* BS32 .... 29 K3
Sunderland Pl *CFTN/FAIL* BS8 .. 6 C1
Sunderland St *BATHSE* BA2 .. 15 H5 ▣
Sundridge Pk *YATE/CS* BS37 .. 34 B7
Sunfield Rd
OMX/HUT/LCK BS24 .... 117 K3 ▣
Sunningdale *YATE/CS* BS37 .. 34 B7
Sunningdale Cl *NAIL* BS48 .... 74 A2 ▣
Sunningdale Dr
OLD/WMLY/WICK BS30 .. 69 H4
Sunningdale Rd
MTN/WRL BS22 .... 106 A2
Sunny Bank *KGWD/HNM* BS15 .. 68 B1
Sunnydene *BRSG/KWL/STAPK* BS4.. 9 G9
Sunny Hl
HNLZ/SM/SNYPK/WT BS9 .... 50 D2
Sunnyhill Dr *AVONM* BS11 .... 50 A3 ▣
Sunnymead *KEYN* BS31 .... 96 A1
RDSTK/MIDN BA3 .... 126 A3
Sunnymede Rd *NAIL* BS48 .... 73 H1
Sunnyside *FRCTL/WBN* BS36 .. 42 C1
HNLZ/SM/SNYPK/WT BS9 .. 51 G4 ▣
YATE/CS BS37 .... 33 K6
Sunnyside La *MANG/FISH* BS16 .. 41 C6
YATE/CS BS37 .... 33 K6
Sunnyside Rd *CLVDN* BS21 .... 59 F7
WSM BS23 .... 16 F6
Sunnyside Rd North *WSM* BS23.. 16 F6
Sunnyvale *CLVDN* BS21 .... 70 C2
Sunnyvale Dr
OLD/WMLY/WICK BS30 .. 69 H7
Sunridge *MANG/FISH* BS16 .... 54 D3
Sunridge Cl *RDSTK/MIDN* BA3 .. 126 A5
Sunridge Pk *RDSTK/MIDN* BA3 .. 126 A5
Sunrise Gv *BRSG/KWL/STAPK* BS4 .. 9 G8
Surrey Rd *HORF/LLZ* BS7 .... 3 K3
Surrey St *CBRISNE* BS2 .... 7 K1
Suspension Br *CFTN/FAIL* BS8.. 65 C3
Sussex Pl *CBRISNE* BS2 .... 3 M7
Sussex St *CBRISNE* BS2 .... 8 A4
Sutherland Av *MANG/FISH* BS16 .. 54 E2
YATE/CS BS37 .... 34 A3 ▣
Sutherland Pl *CFTN/FAIL* BS8 .... 2 A6
Sutton Av *BRSG/KWL/STAPK* BS4 .. 9 H9
Sutton Cl *MTN/WRL* BS22 .... 105 K5 ▣
Sutton St *BATHSE* BA2 .... 15 J5
Swainswick *HGRV/WHIT* BS14.. 78 D5
Swainswick Gdns
CBATH/BATHN BA1 .... 100 B2
Swainswick La
CBATH/BATHN BA1 .... 100 C1
Swaish Dr
OLD/WMLY/WICK BS30 .. 69 F6
Swallow Cl *RDSTK/MIDN* BA3.. 126 C5 ▣
Swallow Dr *BRSTK/PCHW* BS34 .. 29 F7
TRWBR BA14 .... 124 D6
Swallow Gdns *MTN/WRL* BS22 .. 105 J5
Swallow Pk *THNB/SVB* BS35 .. 19 H2
Swallows Ct *BRSTK/PCHW* BS34 .. 40 D4
The Swallows *MTN/WRL* BS22 .. 105 J6
Swallow St
CBATH/BATHN BA1 .... 15 G7 ▣

Swan Cl *MTN/WRL* BS22 .... 105 K5 ▣
Swan Dr *TRWBR* BA14 .... 125 F1
Swane Rd *HGRV/WHIT* BS14 .. 79 K5 ▣
Swan La *FRCTL/WBN* BS36 .... 31 H7
Swanmoor Crs
HNBRY/STHM BS10 .... 38 D4
Sweets Cl *KGWD/HNM* BS15 .. 54 E7
Sweets Rd *KGWD/HNM* BS15 .. 54 E7
Swift Cl *MTN/WRL* BS22 .... 106 A4 ▣
Swiss Rd *BMSTR* BS3 .... 77 H1
WSM BS23 .... 17 G3
Sycamore Cl *EVILLE/WHL* BS5 .. 5 K8
KGWD/HNM BS15 .... 68 B7 ▣
NAIL BS48 .... 73 J1 ▣
WNSC BS25 .... 121 H6
WSM BS23 .... 17 K2
Sycamore Dr *BRSTK/PCHW* BS34.. 39 H1
THNB/SVB BS35 .... 19 H4 ▣
Sycamore Gv *TRWBR* BA14 .. 130 E2
Sycamore Rd *RDSTK/MIDN* BA3.. 127 J3
Sydenham Buildings
BATHSE BA2 .... 14 C8
Sydenham Hl *RDLND/MONT* BS6 .. 3 H7
Sydenham La *RDLND/MONT* BS6 .. 3 H7
Sydenham Rd *BATHSE* BA2 .. 14 D7
BRSG/KWL/STAPK BS4 .... 12 B1
RDLND/MONT BS6 .... 3 H8
Sydenham Wy *KGWD/HNM* BS15.. 68 C4
Sydney Buildings *BATHSE* BA2 .. 15 K7
Sydney Ms *BATHSE* BA2 .... 15 J5
Sydney Pl *BATHSE* BA2 .... 15 J5
Sydney Rd *BATHSE* BA2 .... 15 J5
Sydney Rw *CBRIS/FH* BS1 .... 6 C7
Sydney Whf *BATHSE* BA2 .... 15 K6
Sylvan Wy
HNLZ/SM/SNYPK/WT BS9 .... 50 D3
Sylvia Av *BMSTR* BS3 .... 11 L2
Symes Av
BMSTRD/HC/WWD BS13 .... 93 F1
Symes Pk *CBATH/BATHN* BA1 .. 98 D2
Symington Rd *MANG/FISH* BS16 .. 54 B4
Syston Wy *KGWD/HNM* BS15 .. 68 D1

T

Tabernacle Rd *KGWD/HNM* BS15.. 68 C4
Tackley Rd *EVILLE/WHL* BS5 .... 4 C3
Talbot Av *KGWD/HNM* BS15 .. 68 B1
Talbot Rd *BRSG/KWL/STAPK* BS4.. 12 C2
TRWBR BA14 .... 130 C1
Talgarth Rd *HORF/LLZ* BS7 .... 3 L1
Tallis Gv *BRSG/KWL/STAPK* BS4.. 78 B5
Tamar Cl *THNB/SVB* BS35 .... 19 J6 ▣
Tamar Dr *KEYN* BS31 .... 81 C7
Tamar Rd *CBRISNE* BS2 .... 8 E5
MTN/WRL BS22 .... 106 B3
Tamblyn Cl *RDSTK/MIDN* BA3 .. 127 H2
Tamworth Rd *KEYN* BS31 .... 80 E7 ▣
Tanhouse La *YATE/CS* BS37 .... 25 K7
Tankard's Cl *CFTN/FAIL* BS8 .... 6 F2
Tanner Cl *OLD/WMLY/WICK* BS30 .. 69 F5
Tanners Wk *BATHSE* BA2 .... 98 C2
Tanorth Cl *HGRV/WHIT* BS14 .. 93 K1
Tanorth Rd *HGRV/WHIT* BS14 .. 93 J1
The Tanyard
OLD/WMLY/WICK BS30 .. 81 H1 ▣
Tapsters
OLD/WMLY/WICK BS30 .. 69 G6 ▣
Tarnock Av *HGRV/WHIT* BS14 .. 11 M9
Tarragon Pl *ALMDB* BS32 .... 40 E1
Taunton Rd *MTN/WRL* BS22 .. 106 C1
Taunton Wk *HORF/LLZ* BS7 .. 52 E2 ▣
Taverner Cl
BRSG/KWL/STAPK BS4 .... 78 B4 ▣
Tavistock Rd
BRSG/KWL/STAPK BS4 .... 11 K6
MTN/WRL BS22 .... 106 B3 ▣
Tavistock Wk
BRSG/KWL/STAPK BS4 .... 11 K6
Tawny Wy *MTN/WRL* BS22 .. 106 A5 ▣
Taylor Cl *KGWD/HNM* BS15 .. 69 F2 ▣
Taylor Ct *MTN/WRL* BS22 .. 106 C1 ▣
Taylor Gdns
BMSTRD/HC/WWD BS13 .... 77 H7 ▣
Taylors Vw *TRWBR* BA14 .... 125 F3
Tayman Cl *HNBRY/STHM* BS10 .. 52 C3 ▣
Tayman Rdg
OLD/WMLY/WICK BS30 .. 81 K3
Taynton Cl
OLD/WMLY/WICK BS30 .. 81 H1
Teal Cl *ALMDB* BS32 .... 30 C5 ▣
MTN/WRL BS22 .... 106 A4 ▣
Teasel Md *ALMDB* BS32 .... 40 D1 ▣
Teasel Wk *MTN/WRL* BS22 .. 105 J6
Teddington Cl *BATHSE* BA2.. 111 F1
Teesdale Cl *MTN/WRL* BS22 .. 105 J5
Teewell Av *MANG/FISH* BS16.. 54 E5
Teewell Cl *MANG/FISH* BS16 .. 54 E5
Teewell Hl *MANG/FISH* BS16 .. 54 E5
Teignmouth Rd
BRSG/KWL/STAPK BS4 .... 11 M5
CLVDN BS21 .... 59 C7
Telephone Av *CBRIS/FH* BS1 .... 7 G4
Telford Wk *EVILLE/WHL* BS5 .. 68 A1
Templar Rd *YATE/CS* BS37 .... 34 B4
Templars Wy *WNSC* BS25 .. 121 H7
Temple Back *CBRIS/FH* BS1 .... 7 K4
Temple Ga *CBRIS/FH* BS1 .... 7 K6
Templeland Rd
BMSTRD/HC/WWD BS13 .... 77 H6 ▣
Temple Rose St *CBRIS/FH* BS1 .... 7 K5
Temple St *BMSTR* BS3 .... 10 D4
CBRIS/FH BS1 .... 7 K5
KEYN BS31 .... 80 E6
Temple Wy *CBRIS/FH* BS1 .... 7 K4
Temple Way U/P *CBRISNE* BS2 .. 7 L3 ▣
Tenby Rd *KEYN* BS31 .... 80 D7
Tenby St *EVILLE/WHL* BS5 .... 8 C2
Tennessee Gv
RDLND/MONT BS6 .... 52 A4 ▣
Tenniscourt Rd
KGWD/HNM BS15 .... 69 G1
Tennis Rd *BRSG/KWL/STAPK* BS4 .. 12 A3
Tennyson Av *CLVDN* BS21 .... 70 D1
Tennyson Cl *KEYN* BS31 .... 81 F5
Tennyson Rd *CBATH/BATHN* BA1 .. 14 A4

HORF/LLZ BS7 .... 52 C4 ⒈
WSM BS23 .... 116 E3
Tenth Av HORF/LLZ BS7 .... 40 A7
Tereslake Gn HNBRY/STHM BS10.. 39 C4
Terrace Wk
  CBATH/BATHN BA1 .... 15 G7 ⒈
Terrell Gdns EVILLE/WHL BS5 ...... 9 C2
Terrell St CBRISNE BS2 .... 7 G2
Tetbury Cl BRSTK/PCHW BS34 .... 30 B7
Tetbury Gdns NAIL BS48 .... 74 A2
Tetbury Rd KGWD/HNM BS15 .... 68 B2
Teviot Rd KEYN BS31 .... 81 C7
Tewkesbury Rd CBRISNE BS2 ...... 4 B6
Tewther Rd
  BMSTRD/HC/WWD BS13 ...... 93 F1
Teyfant Rd
  BMSTRD/HC/WWD BS13 ...... 93 H1
Teyfant Wk
  BMSTRD/HC/WWD BS13 ...... 78 C7 ⒈
Thackeray Av CLVDN BS21 .... 59 F6
Thackeray Rd CLVDN BS21 .... 59 G6
Thackeray Wk HORF/LLZ BS7 .... 52 C1 ⒈
Thanet Rd BMSTR BS3 .... 10 C4
Thatcher Cl PTSHD/EG BS20 ...... 47 H5 ⒈
Thatchers Cl EVILLE/WHL BS5 .... 68 B3 ⒈
There-and-back-again La
  CFTN/FAIL BS8 .... 6 E3 ⒈
Theresa Av HORF/LLZ BS7 .... 3 K2
Thestfield Dr TRWBR BA14 ...... 125 F2
Theynes Cft LGASH BS41 .... 76 D2
Thicket Av MANG/FISH BS16 ...... 54 C6
Thicket Rd MANG/FISH BS16 ...... 54 C5
Thicket Wk THNB/SVB BS35 ...... 19 H4 ⒈
Thiery Rd BRSG/KWL/STAPK BS4 .. 12 F3
Thingwall Pk MANG/FISH BS16 .... 5 J3
Third Av BATHSE BA2 .... 14 B9
  HORF/LLZ BS7 .... 39 K7
Third Wy AVONM BS11 .... 36 D6
Thirlmere Ct
  OLD/WMLY/WICK BS30 .... 69 K4
Thirlmere Rd
  BRSTK/PCHW BS34 .... 29 K7 ⒈
  WSM BS23 .... 117 F2
Thistle St BMSTR BS3 .... 10 C1 ⒈
Thomas Av MANG/FISH BS16 .... 55 H1
Thomas Pring Wk
  EVILLE/WHL BS5 .... 68 A1 ⒈
Thomas St CBATH/BATHN BA1 .... 15 H2
  CBRIS/FH BS1 .... 3 J9
  CBRISNE BS2 .... 3 M8
  EVILLE/WHL BS5 .... 8 D2 ⒉
Thomas St North CBRISNE BS2 .... 3 H8 ⒈
Thompson Rd
  HGRV/WHIT BS14 .... 79 J5 ⒉
Thomson Rd EVILLE/WHL BS5 .... 4 C9
Thornbank Pl BATHSE BA2 .... 14 D8
Thornbury Dr WSM BS23 .... 116 B4
Thornbury Rd THNB/SVB BS35.... 23 F1
  WSM BS23 .... 116 B4
Thorn Cl MTN/WRL BS22 .... 106 C3
  YATE/CS BS37 .... 34 A6
Thorndale CFTN/FAIL BS8 .... 2 B9 ⒈
Thorndale Cl MTN/WRL BS22 .... 105 J5 ⒊
Thornhayes Cl
  FRCTL/WBN BS36 .... 32 B7 ⒈
The Thornhills MANG/FISH BS16 .. 54 B3
Thornleigh Rd HORF/LLZ BS7 .... 52 C4
Thornmead Gv
  HNBRY/STHM BS10 .... 38 D6 ⒈
Thorns Farm YATE/CS BS37 ...... 34 B6 ⒊
Thornycroft Cl HORF/LLZ BS7 .... 53 F2 ⒈
Three Peaks Wk
  BLAG/CWMG/WR BS40 .... 93 F7
Three Queens' La CBRIS/FH BS1 .. 7 J5
Three Wells Rd
  BMSTRD/HC/WWD BS13 ...... 77 H7
Thrissell St EVILLE/WHL BS5 ...... 8 A1
Throgmorton Rd
  BRSG/KWL/STAPK BS4.......... 11 L6
Thrush Cl MTN/WRL BS22 ...... 105 K5 ⒒
Thurlestone HGRV/WHIT BS14 .... 78 D6
Thurlow Rd EVILLE/WHL BS5 ...... 4 F6
Thurston's Barton
  EVILLE/WHL BS5 .... 5 H8 ⒈
Tibberton KGWD/HNM BS15 ...... 69 G2
Tibbott Rd HGRV/WHIT BS14 .... 79 G6
Tibbott Wk HGRV/WHIT BS14 .... 79 G6
Tichborne Rd EVILLE/WHL BS5 .... 8 E3 ⒈
  WSM BS23 .... 104 D1
Tickenham Hl CLVDN BS21 .... 61 H6
Tickenham Rd CLVDN BS21 .... 59 K5
Tide Gv AVONM BS11 .... 50 C1
Tidenham Wy
  BRSTK/PCHW BS34 .... 29 J6
Tilley Cl KEYN BS31 .... 96 B2
Tilling Rd HNBRY/STHM BS10 .... 52 C2
Tilling Wk HNBRY/STHM BS10 .... 52 C2
Tilting Rd THNB/SVB BS35........ 19 G3
Timber Dene MANG/FISH BS16 .... 5 H1
Timberscombe Wk
  HGRV/WHIT BS14 .... 79 G6 ⒋
The Timbers RDSTK/MIDN BA3.... 126 C6
Timbrell St TRWBR BA14 .... 125 F5
Timsbury Rd BMSTR BS3 .... 11 J4
Tindell Ct
  OLD/WMLY/WICK BS30 .... 69 F6 ⒚
Tintern Av EVILLE/WHL BS5 .... 5 H2
Tintern Cl
  OLD/WMLY/WICK BS30 .... 69 F4 ⒉
Tippetts Rd KGWD/HNM BS15 .... 68 D4
Tirley Wy MTN/WRL BS22 ...... 105 G3
Titan Barrow
  CBATH/BATHN BA1 .... 101 H2 ⒈
Tiverton Gdns MTN/WRL BS22 .. 106 B3
Tiverton Rd CLVDN BS21 .... 71 C2 ⒎
Tiverton Wk MANG/FISH BS16 .... 54 A7
Tivoli La WSM BS23 .... 16 E2 ⒉
Tockington La ALMDB BS32 ...... 29 K1
Tockington Park La
  THNB/SVB BS35 .... 22 D6
Toll Bridge Rd
  CBATH/BATHN BA1 .... 100 D1
Toll Rd WSM BS23 .... 118 E6
Tone Rd CLVDN BS21 .... 71 F2 ⒑
  MTN/WRL BS22 .... 88 D4
Tormarton Crs
  HNBRY/STHM BS10 .... 38 C4
Tormynton Rd MTN/WRL BS22 .. 105 K3

Toronto Rd HORF/LLZ BS7........ 52 E1
Torpoint Rd BMSTR BS3 .... 11 G5
Torrance Cl
  OLD/WMLY/WICK BS30 .... 69 K4
Torridge Rd KEYN BS31 .... 81 G7
Torrington Av
  BRSG/KWL/STAPK BS4.......... 11 L7
Torrington Crs
  MTN/WRL BS22 .... 106 B2 �10
Tortworth Rd HORF/LLZ BS7 .... 52 C4
Totnes Cl MTN/WRL BS22 ...... 106 B3 ⒋
Totshill Dr
  BMSTRD/HC/WWD BS13 ...... 78 C7
Totshill Gv
  BMSTRD/HC/WWD BS13 ...... 78 C7 ⒉
Totterdown La
  OMX/HUT/LCK BS24 .... 117 F5
Totterdown Rd WSM BS23 ...... 116 E3 ⒊
Touchstone Av
  BRSTK/PCHW BS34 .... 40 D3
Tovey Cl MTN/WRL BS22 .... 105 K1 ⒒
Towcester Rd TRWBR BA14 ...... 131 F3 ⒊
Tower Hl CBRISNE BS2 .... 7 K4
  OMX/HUT/LCK BS24 .... 118 C2
Tower House La NAIL BS48 ...... 62 A6 ⒈
Tower La CBRIS/FH BS1 .... 7 H3
  OLD/WMLY/WICK BS30 .... 69 G4
Tower Rd KGWD/HNM BS15 ...... 69 G4
  PTSHD/EG BS20 .... 46 E5
Tower Rd North
  KGWD/HNM BS15 .... 69 H2
Tower Rd South
  KGWD/HNM BS15 .... 69 H4
Tower St CBRIS/FH BS1 .... 7 K5
Tower Wk WSM BS23 .... 104 C4 ⒏
Townsend ALMDB BS32 .... 29 J3
Townsend Cl HGRV/WHIT BS14.... 79 K6
Townsend Rd BNWL BS29 ...... 120 A3
Townshend Rd MTN/WRL BS22 .. 84 B7
Towpath Rd TRWBR BA14 ...... 125 F2
Tozers Hl
  BRSG/KWL/STAPK BS4.......... 12 E4 ⒈
Trafalgar Rd CBATH/BATHN BA1 .. 98 E3 ⒈
Trafalgar Ter BMSTR BS3.......... 10 B5
Tramway Rd
  BRSG/KWL/STAPK BS4.......... 12 F2 ⒈
Tranmere Av HNBRY/STHM BS10.. 38 D4
Tranmere Gv HNBRY/STHM BS10.. 38 D5
Tratman Wk
  HNBRY/STHM BS10 .... 38 C5 ⒎
Travers Cl
  BRSG/KWL/STAPK BS4.......... 78 B5 ⒈
Travers Wk BRSTK/PCHW BS34 .... 40 D3
Trawden Cl WSM BS23 .... 105 H4 ⒉
Tredegar Rd MANG/FISH BS16 .... 54 B6
Treefield Pl CBRISNE BS2 .... 4 B5 ⒈
Treefield Rd CLVDN BS21 .... 71 F1
Tree Leaze YATE/CS BS37 .... 34 C5
Tregarth Rd BMSTR BS3 .... 77 H2
Trelawn Cl MTN/WRL BS22 ...... 106 E3
Trelawney Av EVILLE/WHL BS5 .... 9 G1 ⒉
Trelawney Pk
  BRSG/KWL/STAPK BS4.......... 13 H2
Trelawney Rd RDLND/MONT BS6.... 2 E8
Tremlett Ms
  MTN/WRL BS22 .... 106 C1 ⒗
Trenchard St KEYN BS31 .... 96 E2
  OMX/HUT/LCK BS24 .... 118 C2 ⒏
Trenchard St CBRIS/FH BS1 .... 6 F4
Trench La ALMDB BS32 .... 30 C4
  FRCTL/WBN BS36................ 30 E5
Trendlewood Pk
  MANG/FISH BS16 .... 5 J1
Trendlewood Wy NAIL BS48 ...... 73 K3
Trenleigh Dr MTN/WRL BS22 .... 106 B3 ⒊
Trent Dr THNB/SVB BS35 .... 19 J6
Trent Gv KEYN BS31 .... 81 G7
Trentham Cl CBRISNE BS2 .... 4 A5 ⒏
Tresham Cl ALMDB BS32 .... 30 C5
Trevanna Rd BMSTR BS3 .... 77 H2
Trevelyan Rd WSM BS23 .... 17 G4
Trevelyan Wk
  HNBRY/STHM BS10 .... 38 C5 ⒏
Treverdowe Wk
  HNBRY/STHM BS10 .... 38 A5
Trevethin Cl KGWD/HNM BS15 .... 58 E5 ⒈
Trevisa Gv HNBRY/STHM BS10 .... 39 F4
Trewartha Pk WSM BS23 .... 17 G1
Triangle East BATHSE BA2 .... 14 A8
Triangle North BATHSE BA2 ...... 14 A8
Triangle South CFTN/FAIL BS8 .... 6 D3
Triangle West BATHSE BA2 ...... 14 A8
  CFTN/FAIL BS8 .... 6 D3
Trident Cl MANG/FISH BS16........ 42 B7
Trim Br CBATH/BATHN BA1 ...... 14 F6 ⒕
Trim St CBATH/BATHN BA1 ...... 14 F6 ⒖
Trinder Rd PTSHD/EG BS20 ...... 49 H5
Trinity Cl CBATH/BATHN BA1 .... 14 E7
Trinity Rd BATHSE BA2 .... 112 A3
  CBRISNE BS2 .... 3 M2
  NAIL BS48 .... 73 H2
  WSM BS23 .... 104 B4
Trinity St CBATH/BATHN BA1 .... 14 F7 ⒑
  CBRISNE BS2 .... 8 A2
Trinity Wk CBRISNE BS2 .... 7 M2
Tripps Cnr YTN/CONG BS49 ...... 87 G5 ⒊
Troon YATE/CS BS37 .... 34 B4
Troon Dr
  OLD/WMLY/WICK BS30 .... 69 H4 ⒉
Trossachs Dr BATHSE BA2 .... 100 C4
Trowbridge Rd BOAV BS15 ...... 124 B3
  HNBRY/STHM BS10 .... 39 F7
  TRWBR BA14 .... 125 J4
Trowbridge Wk
  HNBRY/STHM BS10 .... 39 F7 ⒉
Trowle TRWBR BA14.............. 124 C4
Truro Rd BMSTR BS3 .... 10 C1
  NAIL BS48 .... 74 A2 ⒓
Trym Cross Rd
  HNLZ/SM/SNYPK/WT BS9...... 50 E4
Trymleaze
  HNLZ/SM/SNYPK/WT BS9...... 50 E4 ⒊
Trym Rd
  HNLZ/SM/SNYPK/WT BS9...... 51 J2
Trym Side
  HNLZ/SM/SNYPK/WT BS9...... 50 E4

Trymwood Cl
  HNBRY/STHM BS10 .... 38 C6
Tucker St CBRISNE BS2 .... 7 L1
Tuckett La MANG/FISH BS16 ...... 54 C2 ⒉
Tuckingmill La PLTN/PENS BS39 .. 95 K7
Tuckmill CLVDN BS21 .... 70 D2
Tudor Cl OLD/WMLY/WICK BS30 .. 69 J7
Tudor Dr TRWBR BA14 .... 125 G2
Tudor Rd CBRISNE BS2 .... 3 M8
  EVILLE/WHL BS5.................. 4 E7
  KGWD/HNM BS15 .... 68 C5
  MTN/WRL BS22 .... 106 B1
  PTSHD/EG BS20 .... 47 J5 ⒎
Tuffley Rd HNBRY/STHM BS10 .... 52 A1
Tufton Av AVONM BS11 .... 50 C1
Tugela Rd
  BMSTRD/HC/WWD BS13 ...... 77 H4
Tunstall Cl
  HNLZ/SM/SNYPK/WT BS9...... 51 G5
Turley Rd EVILLE/WHL BS5 .... 5 G7
Turnberry
  OLD/WMLY/WICK BS30 .... 69 H4 ⒉
Turnbridge Rd
  HNBRY/STHM BS10 .... 39 F4
Turnbury Av NAIL BS48 .... 74 A2
Turnbury Cl MTN/WRL BS22 .... 106 A1 ⒒
Turner Cl KEYN BS31 .... 81 G6
Turner Ct MTN/WRL BS22 ...... 106 A2 ⒓
Turner Gdns HORF/LLZ BS7 ...... 53 F3 ⒏
Turners Ct
  OLD/WMLY/WICK BS30 .... 69 F6 ⒛
Turner Wy CLVDN BS21 .... 70 D2
Turnpike Cl YATE/CS BS37 ...... 34 B5 ⒈
Turnpike Rd WNSC BS25 .... 121 H6
Turtlegate Av
  BMSTRD/HC/WWD BS13 ...... 77 G7
Turtlegate Wk
  BMSTRD/HC/WWD BS13 ...... 77 G7
Turville Dr HORF/LLZ BS7 .... 52 E3
Tutton Wy CLVDN BS21 .... 71 F3
Tweed Cl THNB/SVB BS35 .... 19 H5
Tweed Rd CLVDN BS21 .... 70 E2
Tweeny La
  OLD/WMLY/WICK BS30 .... 69 K4
Twenty Acres Rd
  HNBRY/STHM BS10 .... 39 F6 ⒎
Twerton Farm Cl BATHSE BA2 .... 98 E6 ⒈
Twickenham Rd
  RDLND/MONT BS6 .... 52 A4 ⒋
Two Acres Rd HGRV/WHIT BS14.... 12 A9
Two Mile Ct KGWD/HNM BS15 .. 68 B2 ⒊
Twomile Hill Rd
  KGWD/HNM BS15 .... 68 B5
Two Rivers Wy PLTN/PENS BS39 .. 94 D7
  YTN/CONG BS49 .... 109 H1
The Twynings KGWD/HNM BS15 .. 54 E7
Tybalt Wy BRSTK/PCHW BS34.... 40 D3
Tydeman Rd PTSHD/EG BS20 .... 47 K4
Tyler Cl KGWD/HNM BS15 .... 68 E4
Tyler's La MANG/FISH BS16 ...... 54 D4 ⒊
Tyler St CBRISNE BS2 .... 8 A5
Tylers Wy YATE/CS BS37 .... 34 C2 ⒉
Tyndale Av MANG/FISH BS16 .... 54 A5
  YATE/CS BS37 .... 34 A4
Tyndale Rd KGWD/HNM BS15 .... 54 E7 ⒊
Tyndale Vw THNB/SVB BS35 .... 19 G5 ⒊
Tyndall Av CFTN/FAIL BS8 .... 6 E1
Tyndall Rd EVILLE/WHL BS5 ...... 8 D1
Tyndalls Park Ms CFTN/FAIL BS8 .. 6 E1
Tyndall's Park Rd CFTN/FAIL BS8 .. 6 D1
Tyndalls Wy HNBRY/STHM BS10 .. 52 C1
Tyne Rd HORF/LLZ BS7............ 3 H4
Tyne St CBRISNE BS2 .... 4 A6
Tyning Cl HGRV/WHIT BS14 ...... 78 E4
  TRWBR BA14 .... 124 C7 ⒊
  YATE/CS BS37 .... 34 B5
Tyning End BATHSE BA2 .... 15 K9
Tyning Hl RDSTK/MIDN BA3 .... 127 J2
Tyning La CBATH/BATHN BA1 .... 15 J1
Tyning Rd BATHSE BA2 .... 100 E3
  BATHSE BA2 .... 112 B3
  BMSTR BS3 .... 11 L2
  BOAV BA15 .... 113 K6
  KEYN BS31 .... 97 F2
Tynings Ms WSM BS23 .... 16 F9 ⒉
Tynings Wy BOAV BA15 .... 123 F5
The Tyning BATHSE BA2 .... 15 K9
  RDSTK/MIDN BA3 .... 122 A2
Tynte Av
  BMSTRD/HC/WWD BS13...... 93 G1
Tyntesfield Rd
  BMSTRD/HC/WWD BS13...... 10 A9
Tyrone Wk
  BRSG/KWL/STAPK BS4.......... 11 J7
Tyrrel Wy BRSTK/PCHW BS34.... 40 D2
Tytherington Rd
  THNB/SVB BS35 .... 20 A7

U

Ullswater Cl
  OLD/WMLY/WICK BS30 .... 69 K4 ⒊
  WSM BS23 .... 17 J9 ⒈
  YATE/CS BS37 .... 34 B4
Ullswater Dr CBATH/BATHN BA1 .. 99 K2
Ullswater Rd HNBRY/STHM BS10.. 38 E2
Uncombe Cl NAIL BS48 .... 74 D5
Underbanks PTSHD/EG BS20 ...... 49 K5
Underhill Av RDSTK/MIDN BA3.... 126 A3
Underhill Dr WSM BS23 .... 116 C4
Underwood Av MTN/WRL BS22 .. 105 G4
Underwood Cl THNB/SVB BS35 .. 23 F2
Underwood End WNSC BS25 .... 120 D2
Underwood Rd PTSHD/EG BS20 .. 47 G6
Union Pl WSM BS23 .... 16 D3 ⒉
Union Rd CBRISNE BS2 .... 7 M4
Union St CBATH/BATHN BA1 .... 15 G6 ⒖
  CBRIS/FH BS1 .... 7 H2
  NAIL BS48 .... 73 G2
  TRWBR BA14 .... 125 F5
  WSM BS23 .... 16 D3 ⒉
Unity Rd KEYN BS31 .... 81 G6
Unity St CBRIS/FH BS1 .... 6 F4 ⒑
  CBRISNE BS2 .... 7 L3

KGWD/HNM BS15 .... 68 C2
University Rd CFTN/FAIL BS8 ...... 6 D3
University Wk CFTN/FAIL BS8 ...... 6 D3
Uphill Dr CBATH/BATHN BA1 .... 100 A2 ⒉
Uphill Rd HORF/LLZ BS7 .... 52 D4 ⒉
Uphill Rd North WSM BS23 ...... 16 C9
Uphill Rd South WSM BS23 ...... 116 C4
Uphill Wy WSM BS23 .... 116 C5
Upjohn Crs
  BMSTRD/HC/WWD BS13...... 93 G1
Uplands Cl RDSTK/MIDN BA3 .... 112 E7
Uplands Dr KEYN BS31 .... 97 G2
Uplands Rd KEYN BS31 .... 97 F2
  MANG/FISH BS16 .... 54 C6
The Uplands NAIL BS48 .... 73 G4
Upper Bath Rd
  THNB/SVB BS35 .... 19 G5 ⒉
Upper Belgrave Rd
  CFTN/FAIL BS8 .... 2 B5 ⒈
Upper Belmont Rd
  RDLND/MONT BS6 .... 3 J3
Upper Bloomfield Rd
  BATHSE BA2 .... 111 G4
Upper Borough Walls
  CBATH/BATHN BA1 .... 15 G6 ⒔
Upper Bristol Rd
  CBATH/BATHN BA1 .... 14 C5
  WSM BS23 .... 105 C4
Upper Broad St TRWBR BA14.... 124 E5
Upper Byron Pl CFTN/FAIL BS8.... 6 D3
Upper Chapel La
  FRCTL/WBN BS36................ 42 D1
Upper Cheltenham Pl
  RDLND/MONT BS6 .... 3 K7
Upper Church Rd WSM BS23 .... 104 B4
Upper Church St
  CBATH/BATHN BA1 .... 14 E4
Upper Cranbrook Rd
  RDLND/MONT BS6 .... 2 D1
Upper Hedgemead Rd
  CBATH/BATHN BA1 .... 14 F3
Upper Lambridge St
  CBATH/BATHN BA1 .... 100 B3 ⒈
Upper Lansdown Ms
  CBATH/BATHN BA1 .... 14 E1
Upper Maudlin St CBRISNE BS2 .. 7 G2
Upper Oldfield Pk BATHSE BA2 .. 14 C8
Upper Perry Hl BMSTR BS3 .... 6 E8
Upper Regents Pk BOAV BA15 .. 114 E7
Upper Sandhurst Rd
  BRSG/KWL/STAPK BS4.......... 9 G9
Upper Station Rd
  MANG/FISH BS16 .... 54 C5
Upper Stone Cl
  FRCTL/WBN BS36................ 42 D1
Upper St BRSG/KWL/STAPK BS4.. 8 B9
Upper Sydney St BMSTR BS3 .... 10 C1
Upper Town La
  BLAG/CWMG/WR BS40 .... 90 D4
Upper Wells St CBRIS/FH BS1 .... 6 F4 ⒈
Upper York St CBRISNE BS2 ...... 3 J9
Upton Cl LGASH BS41 .... 92 C3
Upton Rd BMSTR BS3 .... 6 A9
Urchinwood La
  YTN/CONG BS49 .... 109 J1 ⒊
Urfords Dr MANG/FISH BS16 .... 54 C3 ⒊

V

Valda Rd MTN/WRL BS22 ...... 105 H3 ⒊
Vale Crs MTN/WRL BS22 .... 106 D3
Vale End NAIL BS48................ 73 H2
Vale La BMSTRD/HC/WWD BS13.... 10 E7
Valentine Cl HGRV/WHIT BS14 .... 79 F6
Valerian Cl AVONM BS11 .... 50 B3
Vale St BRSG/KWL/STAPK BS4.... 12 B1
The Vale MANG/FISH BS16........ 56 B2
Valetta Cl WSM BS23 .... 116 B3 ⒊
Vale Vw RDSTK/MIDN BA3 ...... 127 H3
Vale View Ter
  CBATH/BATHN BA1 .... 100 E1 ⒈
Valley Cl NAIL BS48 .... 73 G4
Valley Gdns MANG/FISH BS16 .... 55 F1
Valley Rd
  BMSTRD/HC/WWD BS13...... 10 B8
  CFTN/FAIL BS8 .... 64 E3
  CLVDN BS21 .... 59 H5
  MANG/FISH BS16 .... 55 G4
  OLD/WMLY/WICK BS30 .... 69 K4
  PTSHD/EG BS20 .... 46 E6
Valley View Cl
  CBATH/BATHN BA1 .... 100 A2
Valley View Rd
  CBATH/BATHN BA1 .... 100 B1
Valley Wk RDSTK/MIDN BA3 .... 126 C3
Valley Way Rd NAIL BS48 .... 61 J7
The Valls AVONM BS11 .... 38 A5
Valma Rocks EVILLE/WHL BS5 .. 68 A4 ⒈
Van Diemen's La
  CBATH/BATHN BA1 .... 99 H2
Vandyck Av KEYN BS31 .... 81 F5
Vane St BATHSE BA2.............. 15 J5
Varsity Wy OMX/HUT/LCK BS24.. 106 C7
Vassall Ct MANG/FISH BS16 ...... 54 D4
Vassall Rd MANG/FISH BS16 ...... 54 B4
Vattingstone La THNB/SVB BS35.. 22 D1
Vaughan Cl HNBRY/STHM BS10 .. 38 C5
Vayre Cl YATE/CS BS37 .... 35 F6
Vellore La BATHSE BA2............ 15 K5
Ventnor Av EVILLE/WHL BS5 ...... 5 M8
Ventnor Rd BRSTK/PCHW BS34 .. 40 A5
  EVILLE/WHL BS5.................. 5 M8
Venus St YTN/CONG BS49 ...... 109 H3
Vera Rd MANG/FISH BS16 .... 5 M5
Verbena Wy MTN/WRL BS22 .... 106 B4
Vereland Rd
  OMX/HUT/LCK BS24 .... 117 K4
Verlands YTN/CONG BS49 .... 87 H7
Vernham Gv BATHSE BA2 ...... 111 F4
Vernal Ct KEYN BS31 .... 96 E1
Vernham Pk BATHSE BA2 .... 99 F6
Vernon Pk
  BRSG/KWL/STAPK BS4.......... 7 M8 ⒏
Vernslade CBATH/BATHN BA1 .... 98 D2

Verrier Rd EVILLE/WHL BS5........ 8 F2
Verwood Dr
  OLD/WMLY/WICK BS30 .... 81 J2
Vian End MTN/WRL BS22 ...... 106 A1 ⒍
Vicarage Cl MTN/WRL BS22 .... 106 B1 ⒒
Vicarage Ct KGWD/HNM BS15 .... 68 B5 ⒊
Vicarage La NAIL BS48 .... 75 J5
  PLTN/PENS BS39 .... 95 H6
Vicarage Rd BMSTR BS3 .... 6 D9
  BMSTRD/HC/WWD BS13...... 77 H5
  CFTN/FAIL BS8 .... 65 F4
  EVILLE/WHL BS5.................. 4 E9
  FRCTL/WBN BS36................ 42 D3
  KGWD/HNM BS15 .... 68 B5
Vicars Cl MANG/FISH BS16 ...... 54 B5 ⒊
Victoria Av EVILLE/WHL BS5 ...... 8 E2
Victoria Bridge Rd BATHSE BA2 .. 14 C6
Victoria Cl BATHSE BA2 .... 99 F7
  PTSHD/EG BS20 .... 47 H4 ⒏
  THNB/SVB BS35 .... 19 G2
Victoria Crs THNB/SVB BS35 ...... 27 H1
Victoria Gdns
  CBATH/BATHN BA1 .... 100 E1
  RDLND/MONT BS6 .... 3 C8
  TRWBR BA14 .... 125 G4
Victoria Gv BMSTR BS3 .... 7 J8
Victoria Pde EVILLE/WHL BS5 .... 8 F1
Victoria Pk KGWD/HNM BS15 .... 68 D2
  MANG/FISH BS16 .... 54 A4
  WSM BS23 .... 104 C4
Victoria Pl BMSTR BS3 .... 6 E9
  WSM BS23 .... 16 C1 ⒈
Victoria Qd WSM BS23 .... 16 E1
Victoria Rd AVONM BS11 .... 49 H1
  CBRISNE BS2 .... 8 A7
  CLVDN BS21 .... 58 E7
  KEYN BS31 .... 96 E1
  KGWD/HNM BS15 .... 68 C5
  OLD/WMLY/WICK BS30 .... 69 K5
  TRWBR BA14 .... 125 H4
Victoria Sq CFTN/FAIL BS8........ 7 J4
  MANG/FISH BS16 .... 54 D5
Victoria St CBRIS/FH BS1.......... 7 J4
Victoria Ter BATHSE BA2 .... 14 B7
  CBRISNE BS2 .... 8 B6
  CFTN/FAIL BS8 .... 65 H4 ⒒
Victoria Wk RDLND/MONT BS6.... 3 H8
Victor Rd BMSTR BS3 .... 10 E2
Victor St CBRISNE BS2 .... 7 M8
  EVILLE/WHL BS5.................. 8 D4
Vigor Rd
  BMSTRD/HC/WWD BS13...... 77 K6 ⒊
Village Cl YATE/CS BS37 .... 34 B6 ⒊
Villiers Rd EVILLE/WHL BS5 .... 4 C8
Vilner La THNB/SVB BS35 .... 19 G6
Vimpany Cl HNBRY/STHM BS10 .. 38 C5
Vimpennys La THNB/SVB BS35 .... 28 A6
Vincent Cl AVONM BS11 .... 37 K6
Vine Gdns MTN/WRL BS22 ...... 106 B3
The Vinery WNSC BS25 .... 120 D7
Vining Wk EVILLE/WHL BS5 .... 4 C9
Vinny Av MANG/FISH BS16 ...... 55 G2
Vintery Leys
  HNLZ/SM/SNYPK/WT BS9...... 51 K2
Virginia Cl YATE/CS BS37 .... 34 D6
Vivian St BMSTR BS3 .... 11 H1
Vivien Av RDSTK/MIDN BA3 .... 126 B3
Vowell Cl
  BMSTRD/HC/WWD BS13...... 77 K7
Vowles Cl NAIL BS48 .... 62 A7
Vynes Cl NAIL BS48 .... 74 A2 ⒔
Vynes Wy NAIL BS48 .... 74 B2
Vyvyan Rd CFTN/FAIL BS8 .... 6 A2
Vyvyan Ter CFTN/FAIL BS8 .... 6 A2

W

Wade Rd YATE/CS BS37 .... 33 H4
Wades Rd BRSTK/PCHW BS34.... 40 A5
Wade St CBRISNE BS2 .... 7 L1
Wadham Dr MANG/FISH BS16 .... 41 G7
Wadham Gv MANG/FISH BS16 .... 55 H4
Wadswick La COR/BOX SN13 .... 103 J1
Wagtail Gdns
  MTN/WRL BS22 .... 105 K5 ⒔
Wainbrook Dr EVILLE/WHL BS5 .... 5 H5
Wains Cl CLVDN BS21 .... 70 E1 ⒊
Wainwright Cl
  MTN/WRL BS22 .... 106 C1 ⒘
Waits Cl BNWL BS29 .... 119 G3
Wakedean Gdns
  YTN/CONG BS49 .... 86 D3
Wakeford Rd
  MANG/FISH BS16 .... 55 G2 ⒊
Walcot Ga CBATH/BATHN BA1 .. 15 G3
Walcot St CBATH/BATHN BA1 .. 15 G4
Waldegrave Rd
  CBATH/BATHN BA1 .... 99 H3
Waldegrave Ter
  RDSTK/MIDN BA3 .... 127 H3
Walden Rd KEYN BS31 .... 81 G7
Walford Av MTN/WRL BS22 .... 106 C1
Walker Cl EVILLE/WHL BS5 .... 55 G2
Walker St CBRISNE BS2 .... 6 F1
Walker Wy THNB/SVB BS35 ...... 19 G6
Wallace Rd CBATH/BATHN BA1.... 100 A3
Wallingford Rd
  BRSG/KWL/STAPK BS4.......... 11 H9
Walliscote Av
  HNLZ/SM/SNYPK/WT BS9...... 52 A3
Walliscote Rd
  HNLZ/SM/SNYPK/WT BS9...... 52 A3
  WSM BS23 .... 16 E4 ⒈
Walliscote Rd South WSM BS23.. 16 D9
Wallscourt Rd
  BRSTK/PCHW BS34 .... 40 A6
Wallscourt Rd South
  BRSTK/PCHW BS34 .... 40 A7
Walmesley Cha TRWBR BA14 .. 125 J5
Walnut Av YATE/CS BS37 .... 34 D5
Walnut Cl KEYN BS31 .... 80 C7
  NAIL BS48 .... 73 J3
  OMX/HUT/LCK BS24 .... 117 F4

PTSHD/EG BS20 .... **49** G6
RDSTK/MIDN BA3 .... **128** E7
THNB/SVB BS35 .... **19** J4
Walnut Crs *KGWD/HNM* BS15 .. **69** F2
Walnut Dr *BATHSE* BA2 .... **111** H1
Walnut Gv *TRWBR* BA14 .... **130** D1
Walnut La *KGWD/HNM* BS15 ... **69** G2
Walnut Tree Cl *ALMDB* BS32 ... **29** K2 ▣
Walnut Wk
  BMSTR/HC/WWD BS13 .... **77** J5
Walsh Av *EVILLE/WHL* BS5 .... **4** C8
Walsh Cl *OMX/HUT/LCK* BS24 ... **117** H1
Walshe Av *YATE/CS* BS37 .... **35** F6
Walsingham Rd
  RDLND/MONT BS6 .... **3** K5
Walter St *BMSTR* BS3 .... **6** B8
Waltham End
  OMX/HUT/LCK BS24 .... **106** B5 ▣
Walton Av *BRSG/KWL/STAPK* BS4 .. **9** H7
Walton Cl *KEYN* BS31 .... **80** D7
  OLD/WMLY/WICK BS30 ...... **81** J2 ▣
Walton Dr *CLVDN* BS21 .... **59** K3
Walton Heath *YATE/CS* BS37 ... **34** C6
Walton Ri
  HNLZ/SM/SNYPK/WT BS9 ..... **51** J1
Walton Rd *AVONM* BS11 .... **49** K3
  CLVDN BS21 .... **59** H5
  CLVDN BS21 .... **60** A2
Walton St *EVILLE/WHL* BS5 .... **4** C8
Walwyn Cl *BATHSE* BA2 .... **98** D6
Wansbeck Rd *KEYN* BS31 ...... **81** G7 ▣
Wansbrough Rd
  MTN/WRL BS22 .... **106** C1
Wanscow Wk
  HNLZ/SM/SNYPK/WT BS9 ..... **51** K3
Wansdyke Rd *BATHSE* BA2 ..... **111** F4
Wapley Hl *YATE/CS* BS37 .... **44** B3
Wapley Rd *YATE/CS* BS37 .... **44** D5
Wapping Rd *CBRIS/FH* BS1 .... **7** G6
Warbler Cl *TRWBR* BA14 .... **124** D6
Warden Rd *BMSTR* BS3 .... **6** F9
Wardour Rd
  BRSG/KWL/STAPK BS4 .... **11** G8
Wareham Cl *NAIL* BS48 .... **73** H2
Warleigh Dr *CBATH/BATHN* BA1 .. **101** F1
Warleigh La *CBATH/BATHN* BA1 .. **101** G4
Warman Cl *HGRV/WHIT* BS14 ... **79** K5
Warman Rd *HGRV/WHIT* BS14 ... **79** K5
Warmington Rd
  HGRV/WHIT BS14 .... **12** E8
Warminster Rd *BATHSE* BA2 ... **15** L3
  CBRISNE BS2 .... **4** B6
Warner Cl *KGWD/HNM* BS15 ... **69** E4 ▣
  YTN/CONG BS49 .... **87** K5
Warne Rd *WSM* BS23 .... **17** K5
The Warns
  OLD/WMLY/WICK BS30 .... **69** G6 ▣
Warren Cl *ALMDB* BS32 .... **30** C4 ▣
  OMX/HUT/LCK BS24 .... **117** J4 ▣
Warren Gdns
  HGRV/WHIT BS14 .... **79** K6 ▣
Warren La *LGASH* BS41 .... **76** A3
Warren Rd *BRSTK/PCHW* BS34 .. **40** A5
Warren Wy *YATE/CS* BS37 .... **34** B4 ▣
Warrilow Cl *MTN/WRL* BS22 ..... **84** C7
Warrington Rd
  BRSG/KWL/STAPK BS4 .... **13** H4
Warry Cl *NAIL* BS48 .... **74** B1
Warth La *MTN/WRL* BS22 .... **84** A3
Warwick Av *EVILLE/WHL* BS5 ..... **4** C7
Warwick Cl *EVILLE/WHL* BS5 ... **105** H5
  OLD/WMLY/WICK BS30 .... **81** H1 ▣
  THNB/SVB BS35 .... **19** F4
Warwick Rd
  CBATH/BATHN BA1 .... **98** E5 ▣
  EVILLE/WHL BS5 .... **4** C7
  KEYN BS31 .... **80** D7
  RDLND/MONT BS6 .... **2** D8
Washingpool Hill Rd
  ALMDB BS32 .... **22** B4
Washing Pound La *CLVDN* BS21 .. **61** F6
  HGRV/WHIT BS14 .... **79** F3
Washington Av *EVILLE/WHL* BS5 .... **4** E7
Washpool La *BATHSE* BA2 ..... **110** C2
Watch Elm Cl *ALMDB* BS32 ..... **40** D3
Watchhouse Rd *PTSHD/EG* BS20 .. **49** K5
Watchill Av
  BMSTRD/HC/WWD BS13 .... **77** H5
Watchill Cl
  BMSTRD/HC/WWD BS13 .... **77** H5
Waterbridge Rd
  BMSTRD/HC/WWD BS13 .... **77** H6
Watercress Rd *CBRISNE* BS2 ...... **3** M4
Waterdale Cl *HNBRY/STHM* BS10 .. **52** A2
Waterdale Gdns
  HNLZ/SM/SNYPK/WT BS9 ..... **52** A2
Waterford Pk
  RDSTK/MIDN BA3 .... **127** F5
Waterford Rd
  HNLZ/SM/SNYPK/WT BS9 ..... **51** K3 ▣
Waterhouse La *BATHSE* BA2 ... **112** D5
Water La *BMSTR* BS3 .... **11** L1
  BRSG/KWL/STAPK BS4 .... **13** G4
  CBRIS/FH BS1 .... **7** K4
  KGWD/HNM BS15 .... **80** B1
  PTSHD/EG BS20 .... **49** J5
  RDSTK/MIDN BA3 .... **126** B1
Waterloo Bldgs *BATHSE* BA2 ... **98** E6 ▣
Waterloo Pl *CBRISNE* BS2 .... **7** M3
Waterloo Rd *CBRISNE* BS2 .... **7** M3
  RDSTK/MIDN BA3 .... **127** H3
Waterloo St *CBRISNE* BS2 .... **7** M2
  CFTN/FAIL BS8 .... **65** H3
  .... **16** D2
Watermore Cl *FRCTL/WBN* BS36 .. **42** E4
Waterside Crs *RDSTK/MIDN* BA3 .. **126** E4
Waterside Dr *ALMDB* BS32 ...... **29** K6
Waterside La *RDSTK/MIDN* BA3 .. **126** D4
Waterside Pk *PTSHD/EG* BS20 ... **46** B5 ▣
Waterside Rd *RDSTK/MIDN* BA3 .. **126** D4
Waterside Wy
  RDSTK/MIDN BA3 .... **126** E4
Water's La
  HNLZ/SM/SNYPK/WT BS9 ..... **51** J2
Waters Rd *KGWD/HNM* BS15 ... **68** C2
Waterworks Rd *TRWBR* BA14 ... **124** D7
Watery La *BATHSE* BA2 .... **98** D6

Watkins Yd
  HNLZ/SM/SNYPK/WT BS9 ..... **51** J1 ▣
Watley's End Rd
  FRCTL/WBN BS36 .... **41** K1
Watling Wy *AVONM* BS11 .... **49** K2
Watson Av *BRSG/KWL/STAPK* BS4 .. **9** H9
Watson's Rd
  OLD/WMLY/WICK BS30 .... **69** F7
Watters Cl *FRCTL/WBN* BS36 ... **42** E2
Wavell Cl *YATE/CS* BS37 .... **34** A3
Waveney Rd *KEYN* BS31 .... **96** B1
Waverley Rd *AVONM* BS11 ...... **49** K3 ▣
  NAIL BS48 .... **74** A4
  RDLND/MONT BS6 .... **2** E7
  WSM BS23 .... **17** G9
  YATE/CS BS37 .... **33** J5
Waverley St *EVILLE/WHL* BS5 ...... **4** B7
Wayford Cl *KEYN* BS31 .... **96** B1 ▣
Wayland Rd *MTN/WRL* BS22 ... **105** K2 ▣
Wayleaze *FRCTL/WBN* BS36 .... **42** E1
Wayside *MTN/WRL* BS22 .... **105** J3
Wayside Cl *FRCTL/WBN* BS36 ... **42** C1
Wayside Dr *CLVDN* BS21 .... **59** G5
The Weal *CBATH/BATHN* BA1 ... **98** E2
Weatherley Av *BATHSE* BA2 ... **111** G3
Weatherly Dr *PTSHD/EG* BS20 .. **46** D6
Weavers Dr *TRWBR* BA14 .... **125** F7
Webbers Ct *TRWBR* BA14 ...... **130** C1
Webbs Heath
  OLD/WMLY/WICK BS30 .... **69** K3
Webb St *EVILLE/WHL* BS5 .... **4** A9
Webbs Wood Rd *ALMDB* BS32 ... **40** E1
Wedgewood Rd
  MANG/FISH BS16 .... **41** J7
Wedgwood Cl
  HGRV/WHIT BS14 .... **79** F6 ▣
Wedgwood Rd *BATHSE* BA2 ..... **98** C7
  WSM BS23 .... **116** E4
Wedmore Pk *BATHSE* BA2 ..... **110** D2
Wedmore Rd *CLVDN* BS21 ...... **70** D2
  KEYN BS31 .... **81** K7
  NAIL BS48 .... **73** J3 ▣
Wedmore V *BMSTR* BS3 .... **11** J3
Weedon Cl *CBRISNE* BS2 .... **4** A5 ▣
Weetwood Rd *YTN/CONG* BS49 .. **87** H7
Weight Rd *EVILLE/WHL* BS5 .... **8** F2
The Weind *MTN/WRL* BS22 ..... **105** J3
Weir La *CFTN/FAIL* BS8 .... **64** A5
Weir Rd *YTN/CONG* BS49 .... **109** H2
Welland Rd *KEYN* BS31 .... **81** F7
Wellard Cl *MTN/WRL* BS22 .... **106** C1 ▣
Well Cl *LGASH* BS41 .... **76** D2
  OMX/HUT/LCK BS24 .... **117** C4
  WNSC BS23 .... **120** D6
Wellgarth Rd
  BRSG/KWL/STAPK BS4 .... **12** B4
Wellgarth Wk
  BRSG/KWL/STAPK BS4 .... **12** B5
Well House Cl
  HNLZ/SM/SNYPK/WT BS9 ..... **51** G7
Wellington Av *RDLND/MONT* BS6 .. **3** K7
Wellington Buildings
  CBATH/BATHN BA1 .... **98** E2
Wellington Crs *HORF/LLZ* BS7 ... **52** C5
Wellington Dr
  HNLZ/SM/SNYPK/WT BS9 ..... **52** B3
  YATE/CS BS37 .... **33** J5
Wellington Hl *HORF/LLZ* BS7 ... **52** C5
Wellington Hl West
  HNLZ/SM/SNYPK/WT BS9 ..... **52** A2
Wellington Ms *AVONM* BS11 ... **49** K4 ▣
Wellington La *RDLND/MONT* BS6 ... **3** J8
Wellington Pk *CFTN/FAIL* BS8 .. **64** F9
Wellington Pl *WSM* BS23 .... **16** D3 ▣
Wellington Rd *CBRISNE* BS2 ...... **7** K2 ▣
  KGWD/HNM BS15 .... **54** D7 ▣
  YATE/CS BS37 .... **34** B3
Wellington Ter *CLVDN* BS21 ..... **58** E5
Wellington Wk
  HNBRY/STHM BS10 .... **52** A2
Well La *YTN/CONG* BS49 .... **87** F4
Wellow Brook Meadow
  RDSTK/MIDN BA3 .... **126** C3
Well Pk *YTN/CONG* BS49 .... **109** H1
Wells Cl *HGRV/WHIT* BS14 ...... **79** G6
  NAIL BS48 .... **74** B2
Wellsea Gv *WSM* BS23 .... **17** M3
Wells Rd *BATHSE* BA2 .... **14** E9
  BRSG/KWL/STAPK BS4 .... **7** M8
  HGRV/WHIT BS14 .... **12** D8
  LGASH BS41 .... **92** B3
  RDSTK/MIDN BA3 .... **126** E4
Wells St *BMSTR* BS3 .... **6** A9
Wellstead Av *YATE/CS* BS37 ... **34** A6
Wellsway *BATHSE* BA2 .... **111** G5
  KEYN BS31 .... **81** F7
Wellsway Pk *BATHSE* BA2 ..... **111** G5 ▣
Welsford Av *MANG/FISH* BS16 .... **5** G2
Welsford Rd *MANG/FISH* BS16 .... **4** F2
Welsh Back *CBRIS/FH* BS1 .... **7** H6
Welton Gv *RDSTK/MIDN* BA3 .. **126** B2
Welton Rd *RDSTK/MIDN* BA3 .. **127** F3
Welton V *RDSTK/MIDN* BA3 .... **126** C3
Welton Wk *KGWD/HNM* BS15 ... **54** C7 ▣
Wemberham Crs
  YTN/CONG BS49 .... **86** D3
Wemberham La
  OMX/HUT/LCK BS24 .... **86** A4
Wenmore Cl *MANG/FISH* BS16 .. **41** J7
Wentforth Dr
  KGWD/HNM BS15 .... **54** C7 ▣
Wentwood Dr
  OMX/HUT/LCK BS24 .... **117** F5
Wentworth
  OLD/WMLY/WICK BS30 .... **69** G4 ▣
  YATE/CS BS37 .... **34** B6
Wentworth Cl
  MTN/WRL BS22 .... **106** B2 ▣
Wentworth Rd *HORF/LLZ* BS7 .... **3** H3
Wesley Av *KGWD/HNM* BS15 ... **68** D5
  RDSTK/MIDN BA3 .... **126** D4
Wesley Cl *MANG/FISH* BS16 .... **54** D6 ▣
  TRWBR BA14 .... **130** A5
Wesley Dr *MTN/WRL* BS22 ..... **106** B2
Wesley Hl *KGWD/HNM* BS15 ... **68** D1 ▣

Wesley La
  OLD/WMLY/WICK BS30 .... **69** H5
  TRWBR BA14 .... **130** A4
Wesley Pl *CFTN/FAIL* BS8 .... **2** B5
Wesley Rd *HORF/LLZ* BS7 .... **3** J2
  RDSTK/MIDN BA3 .... **126** D4
  TRWBR BA14 .... **124** E7
Wesley St *BMSTR* BS3 .... **10** F1
Wessex Av *HORF/LLZ* BS7 .... **52** D2
Wessex Rd *OMX/HUT/LCK* BS24 .. **117** C4
Westacre Cl *HNBRY/STHM* BS10 .. **38** D6
West Ashton Rd *TRWBR* BA14 .. **125** H7
West Av *BATHSE* BA2 .... **99** F7
Westaway Cl *YTN/CONG* BS49 .. **87** F5 ▣
Westaway Pk *YTN/CONG* BS49 .. **87** G5
Westbourne Av *CLVDN* BS21 ... **70** E1 ▣
  KEYN BS31 .... **80** E6 ▣
Westbourne Cl
  MANG/FISH BS16 .... **55** F2 ▣
Westbourne Crs *CLVDN* BS21 ... **70** E1 ▣
Westbourne Gdns
  TRWBR BA14 .... **124** D6
Westbourne Gv *BMSTR* BS3 .... **10** E1 ▣
Westbourne Pl *CFTN/FAIL* BS8 .... **6** C1
Westbourne Rd *EVILLE/WHL* BS5 .. **4** D9
  MANG/FISH BS16 .... **55** F1
  TRWBR BA14 .... **124** D6
West Broadway
  HNLZ/SM/SNYPK/WT BS9 ..... **52** B3
Westbrook Pk
  CBATH/BATHN BA1 .... **98** D2
Westbrook Rd
  BRSG/KWL/STAPK BS4 .... **13** G7
  MTN/WRL BS22 .... **105** J4
Westbury Court Rd
  HNLZ/SM/SNYPK/WT BS9 ..... **51** H2
Westbury Crs *WSM* BS23 ...... **116** E4
Westbury Hl
  HNLZ/SM/SNYPK/WT BS9 ..... **51** J2
Westbury La
  HNLZ/SM/SNYPK/WT BS9 ..... **50** D2
Westbury Pk *RDLND/MONT* BS6 ... **2** B2
Westbury Rd
  HNLZ/SM/SNYPK/WT BS9 ...... **2** B3
  TRWBR BA14 .... **131** F4
  WBRY BA13 .... **131** J6
West Cl *BATHSE* BA2 .... **98** D7
West Coombe
  HNLZ/SM/SNYPK/WT BS9 ..... **51** F3
Westcourt Dr
  OLD/WMLY/WICK BS30 .... **69** H6
West Cft *CLVDN* BS21 .... **70** D1
  HNLZ/SM/SNYPK/WT BS9 ..... **52** A1
Westcroft St *TRWBR* BA14 .... **124** E5
West Dene
  HNLZ/SM/SNYPK/WT BS9 ..... **51** G3
West Dundry La *LGASH* BS41 ... **92** B2
West End *BMSTR* BS3 .... **6** F8
  CBRISNE BS2 .... **7** G1
West End La *NAIL* BS48 .... **72** C4
Westering Cl *MANG/FISH* BS16 .. **55** G4 ▣
Westerleigh Cl
  MANG/FISH BS16 .... **55** F2 ▣
Westerleigh Rd *BATHSE* BA2 ... **112** A4
  CLVDN BS21 .... **70** D1
  MANG/FISH BS16 .... **54** E3 ▣
  YATE/CS BS37 .... **33** K7
Western Av *FRCTL/WBN* BS36 .... **27** G4
Western Dr *HGRV/WHIT* BS14 .. **78** C4
Western Rd *HORF/LLZ* BS7 ...... **52** C3
Westfield *BOAV* BA15 .... **114** C6
  CLVDN BS21 .... **71** F3
Westfield Cl *BATHSE* BA2 .... **111** H2
  KEYN BS31 .... **80** C6
  KGWD/HNM BS15 .... **68** D5
  NAIL BS48 .... **74** A5
  TRWBR BA14 .... **124** C7
  WSM BS23 .... **116** C4
Westfield Crs *BNWL* BS29 ...... **119** H3
Westfield Dr *NAIL* BS48 .... **74** A5 ▣
Westfield La *BRSTK/PCHW* BS34 .. **40** D5
Westfield Pk *CBATH/BATHN* BA1 .. **98** D5
  RDLND/MONT BS6 .... **2** C6
Westfield Pl *CFTN/FAIL* BS8 .... **65** H3 ▣
Westfield Rd *BNWL* BS29 .... **119** H3
  HNLZ/SM/SNYPK/WT BS9 ..... **51** J1
  NAIL BS48 .... **74** A5
  TRWBR BA14 .... **124** C7
Westfield Wy *ALMDB* BS32 ..... **30** C5
West Gdns *PTSHD/EG* BS20 .... **47** G4
West Garston *BNWL* BS29 ..... **119** H3
Westgate Buildings
  CBATH/BATHN BA1 .... **14** F6 ▣
Westgate St
  CBATH/BATHN BA1 .... **14** F6 ▣
West Gv *RDLND/MONT* BS6 .... **3** L7
Westhall Rd *CBATH/BATHN* BA1 .. **14** A4
West Hl *PTSHD/EG* BS20 .... **47** G4
West Hill Rd *RDSTK/MIDN* BA3 .. **126** E4
Westland Av
  OLD/WMLY/WICK BS30 .... **69** J6
West La *BLAG/CWMG/WR* BS40 .. **90** C4
West Lea Rd *CBATH/BATHN* BA1 .. **98** D4
West Leaze Pl *ALMDB* BS32 .... **40** D2
Westleigh Cl
  HNBRY/STHM BS10 .... **39** G7 ▣
  YATE/CS BS37 .... **33** K6
Westleigh Pk *HGRV/WHIT* BS14 .. **12** B8
Westleigh Rd
  HNBRY/STHM BS10 .... **39** F7
West Links Cl
  MTN/WRL BS22 .... **105** C2 ▣
West Mall *CFTN/FAIL* BS8 .... **65** H3
Westmarch Wy *MTN/WRL* BS22 .. **106** B1
Westmead Crs *TRWBR* BA14 ... **130** D2
Westmead Gdns
  CBATH/BATHN BA1 .... **98** D2 ▣
West Mead Rd *EVILLE/WHL* BS5 .. **68** B3
West Mendip Wy *WSM* BS23 .. **116** C6
Westminster Cl
  HNLZ/SM/SNYPK/WT BS9 ..... **51** J2 ▣
Westminster Rd *EVILLE/WHL* BS5 .. **5** G9
Westmoreland Dr
  BATHSE BA2 .... **14** D7 ▣
Westmoreland Rd
  BATHSE BA2 .... **14** D8 ▣
  RDLND/MONT BS6 .... **2** B4

Westmoreland Station Rd
  BATHSE BA2 .... **14** C8
Westmoreland St *BATHSE* BA2 .. **14** D8
Weston Av *EVILLE/WHL* BS5 .... **9** H2
Weston Cl
  HNLZ/SM/SNYPK/WT BS9 ..... **50** E2
Weston Crs *HORF/LLZ* BS7 ...... **52** C3
Weston Dro *PTSHD/EG* BS20 ... **60** D2
Weston Farm La
  CBATH/BATHN BA1 .... **98** E2
Weston La *CBATH/BATHN* BA1 .. **99** F3
Weston Pk *CBATH/BATHN* BA1 .. **99** F3
Weston Pk West
  CBATH/BATHN BA1 .... **99** F3
Weston Rd *CBATH/BATHN* BA1 .. **14** C3
  CFTN/FAIL BS8 .... **63** J7
  LGASH BS41 .... **76** B2
  NAIL BS48 .... **75** K3
  YTN/CONG BS49 .... **86** D7
Westons Brake *MANG/FISH* BS16 .. **42** B7
Westons Hill Dr
  MANG/FISH BS16 .... **55** G1
Westons Wy *KGWD/HNM* BS15 .. **69** F3
Weston Wy
  OMX/HUT/LCK BS24 .... **117** K4
Weston Wood Rd
  PTSHD/EG BS20 .... **47** G6
Westover Cl
  HNLZ/SM/SNYPK/WT BS9 ..... **38** C7
Westover Dr
  HNLZ/SM/SNYPK/WT BS9 ..... **51** J1
Westover Gdns
  HNLZ/SM/SNYPK/WT BS9 ..... **51** H1 ▣
Westover Ri
  HNLZ/SM/SNYPK/WT BS9 ..... **38** D7
Westover Rd
  HNLZ/SM/SNYPK/WT BS9 ..... **51** J1
West Pde
  HNLZ/SM/SNYPK/WT BS9 ..... **50** E2
West Pk *CFTN/FAIL* BS8 .... **2** D9
West Park Rd *MANG/FISH* BS16 .. **54** E4
West Priory Cl
  HNLZ/SM/SNYPK/WT BS9 ..... **51** J2 ▣
West Rdg *FRCTL/WBN* BS36 .... **42** C1
West Rd *RDSTK/MIDN* BA3 .... **126** D3
  YTN/CONG BS49 .... **86** E5
West Rocke Av
  HNLZ/SM/SNYPK/WT BS9 ..... **51** F2
West Rolstone Rd
  OMX/HUT/LCK BS24 .... **107** G3
West Shrubbery
  RDLND/MONT BS6 .... **2** C5
West St *BMSTR* BS3 .... **10** E2
  BNWL BS29 .... **119** J3
  CBRISNE BS2 .... **7** M3
  KGWD/HNM BS15 .... **68** C2 ▣
  OLD/WMLY/WICK BS30 .... **69** J6
  TRWBR BA14 .... **124** D6
  WSM BS23 .... **16** D2 ▣
  WUE GL12 .... **24** B1
West Town Dr
  BRSG/KWL/STAPK BS4 .... **13** G6
West Town Gv
  BRSG/KWL/STAPK BS4 .... **13** G7
West Town La
  BRSG/KWL/STAPK BS4 .... **13** H5
  HGRV/WHIT BS14 .... **12** D7
West Town Pk
  BRSG/KWL/STAPK BS4 .... **13** G6
West Town Rd *AVONM* BS11 ... **49** J2 ▣
  NAIL BS48 .... **74** A6
West Vw *THNB/SVB* BS35 ...... **22** E2
Westview Orch
  RDSTK/MIDN BA3 .... **122** B1 ▣
West View Rd *BMSTR* BS3 ...... **10** C2
  CBATH/BATHN BA1 .... **101** F1
  KEYN BS31 .... **80** E6
Westward Dr *PTSHD/EG* BS20 .. **49** J5
Westward Gdns *LGASH* BS41 ... **76** D1 ▣
Westward Rd
  BMSTRD/HC/WWD BS13 .... **77** H4
West Wy *CLVDN* BS21 .... **58** E7
Westway *NAIL* BS48 .... **73** H1
West Wick *OMX/HUT/LCK* BS24 .. **106** D5
Westwood Cl *MTN/WRL* BS22 .. **106** A3
Westwood Crs
  BRSG/KWL/STAPK BS4 .... **9** H6
Westwood Rd *BOAV* BA15 .... **123** H3
  BRSG/KWL/STAPK BS4 .... **13** G7
Westwoods *CBATH/BATHN* BA1 .. **101** G1
Wetherby Cl
  FRCTL/WBN BS36 .... **42** A7 ▣
Wetherell Pl *CFTN/FAIL* BS8 ...... **6** C3
Wetlands La *PTSHD/EG* BS20 ... **47** C6
Wexford Rd
  BRSG/KWL/STAPK BS4 .... **11** H7
Weymouth Rd *BMSTR* BS3 ...... **11** H3
Weymouth St
  CBATH/BATHN BA1 .... **15** J2
Whaddon La *TRWBR* BA14 .... **125** J3
Wharfedale *THNB/SVB* BS35 ... **19** J5
Wharf Rd *PTSHD/EG* BS20 ...... **48** B4
Wharf Rd *MANG/FISH* BS16 ...... **5** M2
Wharnecliffe Cl
  HGRV/WHIT BS14 .... **79** F6 ▣
Wharnecliffe Gdns
  HGRV/WHIT BS14 .... **79** F6
Whatley Rd *CFTN/FAIL* BS8 .... **2** C8
Wheatfield Dr *ALMDB* BS32 .... **30** C6
Wheathill Cl *KEYN* BS31 .... **80** C6
Wheelers Cl
  RDSTK/MIDN BA3 .... **126** E3 ▣
Wheelers Dr
  RDSTK/MIDN BA3 .... **126** D3 ▣
Wheelers Rd *RDSTK/MIDN* BA3 .. **126** D3 ▣
Whinchat Gdns
  MANG/FISH BS16 .... **55** K3 ▣
Whippington Ct *CBRIS/FH* BS1 ... **7** J2 ▣
Whitby Rd *BRSG/KWL/STAPK* BS4 .. **8** F7
Whitchurch La
  BMSTRD/HC/WWD BS13 .... **77** J6
  HGRV/WHIT BS14 .... **78** C4
  LGASH BS41 .... **92** E2
Whitecross Av
  HGRV/WHIT BS14 .... **79** G3 ▣
Whitecross La *BNWL* BS29 .... **119** G2
Whitecross Rd *WSM* BS23 ...... **16** E7

Whitefield Av *EVILLE/WHL* BS5 ... **68** A1
  KGWD/HNM BS15 .... **68** D5 ▣
Whitefield Rd *EVILLE/WHL* BS5 ... **5** L7
Whitefields *YATE/CS* BS37 ...... **35** F6 ▣
Whitehall Av *EVILLE/WHL* BS5 ... **5** K8
Whitehall Gdns
  EVILLE/WHL BS5 .... **5** G9 ▣
Whitehall Rd *EVILLE/WHL* BS5 .... **8** D1
Whiteheads La *BOAV* BA15 .... **114** E6
Whitehill *BOAV* BA15 .... **114** E6
White Horse Cl *TRWBR* BA14 .. **131** F1
White Horse Rd *BOAV* BA15 ... **113** K6
Whitehouse La *BMSTR* BS3 .... **7** H9
  PTSHD/EG BS20 .... **62** A3
Whitehouse Pl *BMSTR* BS3 .... **7** J8
White House Rd
  YTN/CONG BS49 .... **87** J4 ▣
Whitehouse St *BMSTR* BS3 .... **7** J9
Whiteladies Rd *CFTN/FAIL* BS8 .... **2** B7
  CFTN/FAIL BS8 .... **6** D2
Whitelands Hl
  RDSTK/MIDN BA3 .... **127** J2
Whiteleaze
  HNBRY/STHM BS10 .... **52** A2 ▣
White Lodge Rd
  MANG/FISH BS16 .... **55** F5
Whiteoak Wy *NAIL* BS48 .... **73** H3
White Park Ldg *PTSHD/EG* BS20 .. **47** H3
White Row Hl *TRWBR* BA14 ... **130** C3
Whiterow Pk *TRWBR* BA14 .... **130** C1
Whitesfield Rd *NAIL* BS48 ...... **73** H2
Whites Hl *EVILLE/WHL* BS5 ..... **68** A4
Whiteshill *MANG/FISH* BS16 ... **41** J5
White St *EVILLE/WHL* BS5 .... **7** M1
White Tree Rd
  HNLZ/SM/SNYPK/WT BS9 ...... **2** C1
Whitewall La *THNB/SVB* BS35 .. **20** A3
Whiteway Av *BATHSE* BA2 .... **110** D2
Whiteway Rd
  BRSG/KWL/STAPK BS4 .... **9** K4 ▣
  EVILLE/WHL BS5 .... **68** A2
Whiteway Ms *EVILLE/WHL* BS5 .. **68** A2
Whiteway Rd *BATHSE* BA2 ..... **98** C3
  EVILLE/WHL BS5 .... **68** A1
Whitewells Rd
  CBATH/BATHN BA1 .... **99** K2
Whitewood Rd
  EVILLE/WHL BS5 .... **5** L7 ▣
Whiting Rd
  BMSTRD/HC/WWD BS13 .... **77** J7
Whitland Av
  BMSTRD/HC/WWD BS13 .... **77** K6 ▣
Whitland Rd
  BMSTRD/HC/WWD BS13 .... **77** K6
Whitley Cl *YATE/CS* BS37 .... **33** K4
Whitley Md *BRSTK/PCHW* BS34 .. **40** D5
Whitmead Gdns
  BMSTRD/HC/WWD BS13 .... **78** A7 ▣
Whitmore Av
  BRSG/KWL/STAPK BS4 .... **68** A7
Whitson St *CBRIS/FH* BS1 .... **7** H1
Whitting Rd *WSM* BS23 .... **16** F9
Whittington Dr
  MTN/WRL BS22 .... **105** J3 ▣
Whittington Rd
  MANG/FISH BS16 .... **54** C3
Whittock Rd *HGRV/WHIT* BS14 .. **79** H6
Whittock Sq *HGRV/WHIT* BS14 .. **79** H4
Whittucks Rd
  KGWD/HNM BS15 .... **68** D5 ▣
Whitwell Rd *HGRV/WHIT* BS14 .. **12** D7
Whytes Cl
  HNLZ/SM/SNYPK/WT BS9 ..... **51** J1
Wick Crs *BRSG/KWL/STAPK* BS4 .. **13** H1
Wicker Hl *TRWBR* BA14 .... **124** E5
The Wickets *HORF/LLZ* BS7 ..... **39** J7
  KGWD/HNM BS15 .... **54** D7 ▣
Wickfield *CLVDN* BS21 .... **70** E2 ▣
Wickham Cl *YATE/CS* BS37 ..... **35** G7
Wickham Gln *MANG/FISH* BS16 .. **53** H4
Wickham Hl *MANG/FISH* BS16 .. **53** H4
Wickham Vw *MANG/FISH* BS16 .. **5** H1
Wick House Cl *KEYN* BS31 ...... **96** E1
Wicklow Rd
  BRSG/KWL/STAPK BS4 .... **11** J7
Wick Rd *BRSG/KWL/STAPK* BS4 .. **13** G3
Wickwar Rd *YATE/CS* BS37 ..... **25** H6
Widbrook Meadow
  TRWBR BA14 .... **124** C6
Widbrook Vw *BOAV* BA15 .... **124** A1
Widcombe *HGRV/WHIT* BS14 ... **78** E6
Widcombe Cl *EVILLE/WHL* BS5 .. **68** A3 ▣
Widcombe Crs *BATHSE* BA2 .... **15** J3
Widcombe Hl *BATHSE* BA2 ..... **15** J3
Wigmore Gdns *MTN/WRL* BS22 .. **105** H3
Wigton Cl *HNBRY/STHM* BS10 .. **39** F7 ▣
Wilbye Gv
  BRSG/KWL/STAPK BS4 .... **78** B5 ▣
Wilcot Cl *TRWBR* BA14 .... **130** E1
Wilcox Cl *KGWD/HNM* BS15 .... **68** C3
Wildcountry La *LGASH* BS41 .... **76** A4
  NAIL BS48 .... **76** A6
Wildcroft Rd
  HNLZ/SM/SNYPK/WT BS9 ..... **51** K4
The Wilderness *BOAV* BA15 ... **114** D6
Wilder St *CBRISNE* BS2 .... **3** J9
Willada Cl *BMSTR* BS3 .... **10** D4
William Daw Cl *BNWL* BS29 ... **119** G3
William Mason Cl
  EVILLE/WHL BS5 .... **8** C3 ▣
Williams Cl
  OLD/WMLY/WICK BS30 .... **81** F1
Williamson Rd *HORF/LLZ* BS7 .... **3** L4
William St *BATHSE* BA2 .... **15** H5
  BMSTR BS3 .... **7** J8
  CBRISNE BS2 .... **3** L8
  CBRISNE BS2 .... **8** A4
  EVILLE/WHL BS5 .... **8** B1
  MANG/FISH BS16 .... **54** B6 ▣
Willinton Rd
  BRSG/KWL/STAPK BS4 .... **11** M5
  KGWD/HNM BS15 .... **68** B3 ▣
Williton Crs *WSM* BS23 .... **116** E3 ▣
Willmott Cl *HGRV/WHIT* BS14 .. **93** J1 ▣
Willoughby Cl
  BMSTRD/HC/WWD BS13 .... **77** J4

THNB/SVB BS35 .... 23 F2
Willoughby Rd *HORF/LLZ* BS7 .... 52 C4 ⬛
Willow Bed Cl *MANG/FISH* BS16 .... 54 B3
Willow Cl *BATHSE* BA2 .... 111 G5
  BRSTK/PCHW BS34 .... 39 H1
  CLVDN BS21 .... 59 G7
  LGASH BS41 .... 76 B2
  MTN/WRL BS22 .... 106 E3
  OLD/WMLY/WICK BS30 .... 69 G5 ⬛
  PTSHD/EG BS20 .... 47 G5 ⬛
  RDSTK/MIDN BA3 .... 127 F5 ⬛
  WSM BS23 .... 116 D4
Willowdown
  MTN/WRL BS22 .... 105 K1 ⬛
Willow Dr *OMX/HUT/LCK* BS24 .... 117 K4
  OMX/HUT/LCK BS24 .... 117 K1
The Willowfalls
  CBATH/BATHN BA1 .... 100 D1 ⬛
Willow Gdns *MTN/WRL* BS22 .... 106 E3
  TRWBR BA14 .... 130 D2
Willow Gv *MANG/FISH* BS16 .... 54 C7 ⬛
The Willows *ALMDB* BS32 .... 30 C7
  NAIL BS48 .... 61 K7
  YATE/CS BS37 .... 34 A5 ⬛
Willow Rd *KGWD/HNM* BS15 .... 68 C7 ⬛
Willow Vw *TRWBR* BA14 .... 130 E4
Willow Wk *HNBRY/STHM* BS10.... 38 E5
  KEYN BS31 .... 80 D7
Willow Wy *FRCTL/WBN* BS36 .... 42 D2 ⬛
Willsbridge HI
  OLD/WMLY/WICK BS30 .... 81 G1
Wills Dr *EVILLE/WHL* BS5 .... 4 B9
  CBRISNE BS2 .... 7 M3
Willway St *BMSTR* BS3 .... 7 J9
Wilmot Ct
  OLD/WMLY/WICK BS30 .... 69 G4 ⬛
Wilmots Wy *PTSHD/EG* BS20 .... 49 K5 ⬛
Wilshire Av *KGWD/HNM* BS15.... 68 D5
Wilson Pl *CBRISNE* BS2 .... 3 L9
Wilson St *CBRISNE* BS2 .... 7 K1
Wilton Cl *HNBRY/STHM* BS10 .... 52 A1
Wilton Dr *TRWBR* BA14 .... 131 F1 ⬛
Wilton Gdns *WSM* BS23 .... 16 E4 ⬛
Wiltshire Av *YATE/CS* BS37 .... 34 D4
Wiltshire Dr *TRWBR* BA14 .... 131 E1 ⬛
Wiltshire PI *MANG/FISH* BS15 .... 54 E6 ⬛
Wiltshire Wy *CBATH/BATHN* BA1 .. 99 K2
Wimbledon Rd
  RDLND/MONT BS6 .... 52 A4
Wimblestone Rd *WNSC* BS25 .... 120 C4
Winash Cl *HGRV/WHIT* BS14 .... 13 C9
Wincanton Cl
  FRCTL/WBN BS36 .... 42 A7 ⬛
  NAIL BS48 .... 74 B2 ⬛
Winchcombe Cl *NAIL* BS48 .... 74 A3
Winchcombe Rd
  FRCTL/WBN BS36 .... 32 C7 ⬛
Winchester Av
  BRSG/KWL/STAPK BS4............ 13 G2
Winchester Cl *TRWBR* BA14 .... 130 E5
Winchester Rd *BATHSE* BA2 .... 14 B8
  BRSG/KWL/STAPK BS4............ 13 G2
Wincroft *OLD/WMLY/WICK* BS30 .. 69 J6
Windcliff Crs *AVONM* BS11 .... 50 A1
Windermere Av *WSM* BS23 .... 17 H3 ⬛
Windermere Rd
  BRSTK/PCHW BS34 .... 29 K7
  TRWBR BA14 .... 125 G4
Windermere Wy
  OLD/WMLY/WICK BS30 .... 69 K4
Windmill HI *BMSTR* BS3 .... 11 H1
  OMX/HUT/LCK BS24 .... 118 B4
Windmill La *HNBRY/STHM* BS10.. 38 A5
Windrush CI *BATHSE* BA2 .... 110 C1
Windrush Ct *THNB/SVB* BS35 .... 19 H5
Windrush Rd *KEYN* BS31 .... 81 G7
Windsor Av *EVILLE/WHL* BS5 .... 68 B4
  KEYN BS31 .... 80 E7 ⬛
Windsor Bridge Rd
  CBATH/BATHN BA1 .... 14 A5
Windsor Cl *BRSTK/PCHW* BS34 .. 40 D4 ⬛
  CLVDN BS21 .... 70 E1
Windsor Ct *MANG/FISH* BS16 .... 54 E2
Windsor Crs *HNBRY/STHM* BS10 .. 37 K4
  YATE/CS BS37 .... 34 A2
Windsor Dr *TRWBR* BA14 .... 130 D2 ⬛
  YATE/CS BS37 .... 34 A2
Windsor Gv *EVILLE/WHL* BS5 .... 8 D1 ⬛
Windsor PI *CFTN/FAIL* BS8.... 65 H4 ⬛
  MANG/FISH BS16 .... 55 C4
Windsor Rd *MTN/WRL* BS22 .... 105 H3
  OLD/WMLY/WICK BS30 .... 81 F1 ⬛
  RDLND/MONT BS6 .... 3 J1
  TRWBR BA14 .... 131 G3
Windsor Ter *BMSTR* BS3 .... 7 L9

CFTN/FAIL BS8 .... 65 H4 ⬛
Windwhistle Cir *WSM* BS23 .... 116 E3 ⬛
Windwhistle La *WSM* BS23 .... 116 D3
Windwhistle Rd *WSM* BS23.... 116 C3
Wineberry Cl *EVILLE/WHL* BS5 .... 5 H8
Wine St *BOAV* BA15 .... 114 D7
  CBRIS/FH BS1 .... 7 H3
Winfield Rd
  OLD/WMLY/WICK BS30 .... 69 J3
Winford Cl *PTSHD/EG* BS20........ 47 J5
Winford Gv
  BMSTRD/HC/WWD BS13............ 10 A7
Winford La
  BLAG/CWMG/WR BS40 .... 91 J4
Wingard Cl *WSM* BS23 .... 116 C4
Wingfield Rd *BMSTR* BS3 .... 11 K4
  TRWBR BA14 .... 124 C7
Winifred's La *CBATH/BATHN* BA1 .. 14 D1
Winkworth PI *CBRISNE* BS2 .... 3 L8
Winnowing End *WNSC* BS25.... 120 D3
Winsbury Wy *ALMDB* BS32 .... 30 B7
Winscombe Cl *KEYN* BS31 .... 80 D5
Winsford St *EVILLE/WHL* BS5........ 8 A1 ⬛
Winsham Cl *HGRV/WHIT* BS14 .... 79 F6 ⬛
Winsley HI *RDSTK/MIDN* BA3 .... 113 F6
Winsley Rd *BOAV* BA15 .... 114 A6
  RDLND/MONT BS6 .... 3 H7
Winterbourne HI
  FRCTL/WBN BS36............ 41 J3
Winterbourne Rd
  BRSTK/PCHW BS34 .... 40 D2
Winters La *NAIL* BS48............ 89 H5
Winterslow Rd *TRWBR* BA14 .... 130 D2
Winterstoke Rd
  OMX/HUT/LCK BS24 .... 117 G5 ⬛
  WSM BS23 .... 17 L8
Wint HI *BNWL* BS29 .... 119 J5
Winton St *BRSG/KWL/STAPK* BS4.... 7 M9
Wistaria Av *YATE/CS* BS37.... 34 D6 ⬛
Wisteria Av
  OMX/HUT/LCK BS24 .... 117 J4
Witchell Rd *EVILLE/WHL* BS5............ 8 F2
Witch Hazel Rd
  BMSTRD/HC/WWD BS13............ 93 H1
Witcombe Gv *YATE/CS* BS37............ 43 K1
Witcombe Cl *KGWD/HNM* BS15 .... 68 C1
Witham Rd *KEYN* BS31............ 96 B1
Witherlies Rd
  MANG/FISH BS16 .... 53 K3 ⬛
Withey Cl West
  HNLZ/SM/SNYPK/WT BS9............ 51 G4
The Witheys *HGRV/WHIT* BS14 .... 79 G7
Withies La *RDSTK/MIDN* BA3 .... 126 A6
Withies Pk *RDSTK/MIDN* BA3 .... 126 A5
Withington Cl
  OLD/WMLY/WICK BS30 .... 81 J1 ⬛
Withleigh Rd
  BRSG/KWL/STAPK BS4............ 12 D3
Withy Cl *NAIL* BS48............ 61 K7 ⬛
  TRWBR BA14 .... 125 G3
Withy Cl East
  HNLZ/SM/SNYPK/WT BS9............ 51 H4
Withypool Gdns
  HGRV/WHIT BS14 .... 79 F6 ⬛
Withywood Rd
  BMSTRD/HC/WWD BS13............ 77 H7
Witney Cl *KEYN* BS31............ 96 E1
Woburn Cl
  OLD/WMLY/WICK BS30 .... 69 F5 ⬛
  TRWBR BA14 .... 124 C6
Woburn Rd *EVILLE/WHL* BS5............ 4 D3
Wolferton Rd *RDLND/MONT* BS6.... 3 L5
Wolfridge Gdns
  HNBRY/STHM BS10............ 38 D4
Wolfridge La *THNB/SVB* BS35.... 22 E2
Wolfridge Ride *THNB/SVB* BS35.... 22 E2
Wolseley La *HORF/LLZ* BS7............ 3 H4
Wolvershill Pk *BNWL* BS29 .... 119 H3
Wolvers Hill Rd *BNWL* BS29 .... 119 G2
  OMX/HUT/LCK BS24 .... 106 D5
Woodbine Rd *EVILLE/WHL* BS5.... 4 F9
Woodborough Cl
  TRWBR BA14 .... 131 F2 ⬛
Woodborough Crs
  WNSC BS25 .... 120 D7 ⬛
Woodborough Dr *WNSC* BS25.... 120 D6
Woodborough La
  RDSTK/MIDN BA3 .... 127 H2
Woodborough Rd
  RDSTK/MIDN BA3 .... 127 H2
  WNSC BS25 .... 120 C6
Woodborough St
  EVILLE/WHL BS5............ 4 C8

Woodbridge Rd
  BRSG/KWL/STAPK BS4............ 12 B3
Woodbury La *CFTN/FAIL* BS8 .... 2 B6 ⬛
Woodchester
  KGWD/HNM BS15 .... 54 E6 ⬛
  YATE/CS BS37 .... 44 B2
Woodchester Rd
  HNBRY/STHM BS10............ 52 A2 ⬛
Woodcliff Rd *MTN/WRL* BS22.... 105 H4
Woodcote *KGWD/HNM* BS15 .... 68 D4 ⬛
Woodcote Rd *MANG/FISH* BS16 .. 54 B7
Woodcote Wk *MANG/FISH* BS16 .. 54 B7
Woodcroft Av *EVILLE/WHL* BS5 .... 5 G9
Woodcroft Cl
  BRSG/KWL/STAPK BS4............ 9 K8
Woodcroft Rd
  BRSG/KWL/STAPK BS4............ 9 K8
Woodend *KGWD/HNM* BS15 .... 68 D4 ⬛
Woodend Rd *FRCTL/WBN* BS36.... 42 C1
Wood End Wk
  HNLZ/SM/SNYPK/WT BS9............ 50 E3
Woodfield Rd *RDLND/MONT* BS6.... 2 D7
Woodford Cl *NAIL* BS48............ 74 A2 ⬛
Woodgrove Rd
  HNBRY/STHM BS10............ 38 A6
Woodhall Cl *MANG/FISH* BS16 .... 55 F3 ⬛
Wood HI *YTN/CONG* BS49 .... 87 G6
Woodhill Av *PTSHD/EG* BS20 .... 47 H3
Wood Hill Pk *PTSHD/EG* BS20 .. 47 H2 ⬛
Woodhill Rd *PTSHD/EG* BS20 .... 47 H3
Woodhill Views *NAIL* BS48 .... 61 K7
Woodhouse Av *ALMDB* BS32.... 22 C7
Woodhouse Cl *ALMDB* BS32.... 22 C7
Woodhouse Gv *HORF/LLZ* BS7.... 52 C3
Woodhouse Rd *BATHSE* BA2.... 98 D6
Woodhurst Rd *WSM* BS23 .... 17 J2 ⬛
Woodington Ct
  OLD/WMLY/WICK BS30 .... 69 F6 ⬛
Woodington Rd *CLVDN* BS21.... 70 E2 ⬛
The Wood Kilns *YTN/CONG* BS49 .. 86 D3
Woodland Av
  KGWD/HNM BS15 .... 54 D7 ⬛
Woodland Cl *CFTN/FAIL* BS8.... 63 H6
  MANG/FISH BS16 .... 54 C7 ⬛
Woodland Gdn *CLVDN* BS21.... 59 G5
Woodland Gv *BATHSE* BA2.... 100 D7
  HNLZ/SM/SNYPK/WT BS9............ 51 F3
Woodland Rd *CFTN/FAIL* BS8 .... 6 E2
  NAIL BS48 .... 61 J7
  WSM BS23 .... 116 C2
  WUE GL12 .... 21 J1
Woodlands *ALMDB* BS32 .... 30 C4
  CLVDN BS21 .... 58 E6 ⬛
  MANG/FISH BS16 .... 54 E3 ⬛
Woodlands La *ALMDB* BS32 .... 30 A5
  ALMDB BS32 .... 30 D2
Woodlands Pk
  CBATH/BATHN BA1 .... 100 B2
Woodlands Ri *MANG/FISH* BS16.... 54 D3
Woodlands Rd *PTSHD/EG* BS20 .... 47 H1
Woodland Ter *KGWD/HNM* BS15 .. 68 D3
  RDLND/MONT BS6............ 2 C6
Woodland Wy *CFTN/FAIL* BS8 .... 63 H6
  KGWD/HNM BS15 .... 54 C7
Wood La *PTSHD/EG* BS20 .... 61 J3
  WSM BS23 .... 104 E4
Woodleaze
  HNLZ/SM/SNYPK/WT BS9............ 50 D3
Woodleigh *THNB/SVB* BS35 .... 19 H4
Woodleigh Gdns
  HGRV/WHIT BS14 .... 79 G5
Woodmancote *YATE/CS* BS37.... 34 A7
Woodmancote Rd
  RDLND/MONT BS6............ 3 K7 ⬛
Woodmans Cl *YATE/CS* BS37.... 34 E7
Woodmans Rd *YATE/CS* BS37.... 34 E7
Woodmans V *YATE/CS* BS37 .... 35 F7 ⬛
Woodmarsh *TRWBR* BA14 .... 131 F3 ⬛
Woodmarsh Cl *HGRV/WHIT* BS14.. 78 E7
Woodmead Gdns
  BMSTRD/HC/WWD BS13............ 78 A7
Woodmill *YTN/CONG* BS49 .... 86 D3 ⬛
Woodpecker Av
  RDSTK/MIDN BA3 .... 126 C5
Woodpecker Crs
  MANG/FISH BS16 .... 56 E5 ⬛
Woodpecker Dr
  MTN/WRL BS22 .... 105 K5
Wood Rd *KGWD/HNM* BS15 .... 68 D2 ⬛
Woods HI *RDSTK/MIDN* BA3 .... 112 E7
Woodside Av
  OMX/HUT/LCK BS24 .... 117 G4
Woodside Gdns *PTSHD/EG* BS20 .. 46 C4
Woodside Gv
  HNBRY/STHM BS10............ 38 A5

Woodside Rd
  BRSG/KWL/STAPK BS4............ 9 J5
  CLVDN BS21 .... 59 G5
  FRCTL/WBN BS36............ 42 E1
  KGWD/HNM BS15 .... 68 C2
  MANG/FISH BS16 .... 54 C2
Woodspring Av *MTN/WRL* BS22.. 105 F2
Woodspring Crs
  MTN/WRL BS22 .... 105 F2
Woodstock Av *RDLND/MONT* BS6 .. 2 E7
Woodstock Cl
  KGWD/HNM BS15 .... 69 F2 ⬛
Woodstock Rd
  KGWD/HNM BS15 .... 69 F3 ⬛
  MTN/WRL BS22 .... 17 M1
  RDLND/MONT BS6 .... 2 E5
Wood St *BATHSE* BA2 .... 14 F6
  CBATH/BATHN BA1 .... 14 F6
  EVILLE/WHL BS5 .... 4 D7 ⬛
Woodview *CLVDN* BS21 .... 59 F7 ⬛
Woodview Cl *AVONM* BS11 .... 50 A2
Woodview Dr *YTN/CONG* BS49 .. 87 K4 ⬛
Woodview Ter *NAIL* BS48 .... 73 K1
  WSM BS23 .... 17 J5 ⬛
Woodward Dr
  OLD/WMLY/WICK BS30 .... 69 F6
Woodwell Rd *AVONM* BS11........ 50 A3
Woodyleaze Dr
  KGWD/HNM BS15 .... 68 C4
Wookey Cl *NAIL* BS48 .... 73 K3
Woolcot St *RDLND/MONT* BS6 .... 2 D5
Wooler Rd *WSM* BS23 .... 16 F2
Woollard La *HGRV/WHIT* BS14 .... 94 C2
Woolley Cl *BOAV* BA15 .... 115 F6
Woolley Dr *BOAV* BA15 .... 115 F6
Woolley Rd *HGRV/WHIT* BS14 .... 79 J6 ⬛
Woolley St *BOAV* BA15 .... 115 F7
Woolley Ter *BOAV* BA15 .... 115 F6
Woolpack Mdw *TRWBR* BA14.... 125 G7
Woolvers Wy
  OMX/HUT/LCK BS24 .... 106 C7
Wootton Crs
  BRSG/KWL/STAPK BS4............ 9 J4
Wootton Pk *HGRV/WHIT* BS14 .... 12 D7
Wootton Rd
  BRSG/KWL/STAPK BS4............ 9 K4
Worcester Buildings
  CBATH/BATHN BA1 .... 100 A2 ⬛
Worcester Cl *MANG/FISH* BS16.... 54 B7
Worcester Crs *CFTN/FAIL* BS8 .... 6 A1 ⬛
Worcester Gdns *NAIL* BS48 .... 73 F3
Worcester Pk
  CBATH/BATHN BA1 .... 100 A3
Worcester Rd *CFTN/FAIL* BS8 .... 6 A1
  KGWD/HNM BS15 .... 68 D1 ⬛
Worcester Ter *CFTN/FAIL* BS8 .... 6 A1
Wordsworth Rd *CLVDN* BS21 .... 70 E1 ⬛
  HORF/LLZ BS7 .... 33 F8
  WSM BS23 .... 117 F3 ⬛
World's End La *KEYN* BS31 .... 81 J6
Worlebury Cl *MTN/WRL* BS22 .. 105 G2 ⬛
Worlebury Hill Rd
  MTN/WRL BS22 .... 105 H2
  WSM BS23 .... 104 E3
Worlebury Park Rd
  MTN/WRL BS22 .... 105 F2
Worle Ct *MTN/WRL* BS22 .... 106 A2
Worrall Rd *CFTN/FAIL* BS8 .... 2 E7
Worrel's La *MANG/FISH* BS16 .... 41 J5
Worsley St *EVILLE/WHL* BS5 .... 9 G2
Worsted Ct *TRWBR* BA14 .... 125 G7 ⬛
Worth Cl *KGWD/HNM* BS15 .... 69 F4 ⬛
Worthing Rd *BRSTK/PCHW* BS34.. 29 J7
Worthy La *WSM* BS23 .... 16 E2 ⬛
Worthy PI *WSM* BS23 .... 16 E2 ⬛
Worthy Rd *AVONM* BS11 .... 36 E1
The Worthys *ALMDB* BS32 .... 41 F2
Wotton Rd *YATE/CS* BS37 .... 33 F3
Wrangle Farm Gn
  CLVDN BS21 .... 71 G1 ⬛
Wraxall Gv
  BMSTRD/HC/WWD BS13............ 77 H3
Wraxall HI *NAIL* BS48 .... 62 C5
Wraxall Rd *KGWD/HNM* BS15 .... 69 G4
  OLD/WMLY/WICK BS30 .... 69 G4
Wrenbert Rd *MANG/FISH* BS16.... 54 C4
Wren Cl *MTN/WRL* BS22 .... 105 J5
Wren Ct *TRWBR* BA14 .... 124 D6
Wren Dr *MANG/FISH* BS16 .... 53 K3
Wrington Cl *BRSTK/PCHW* BS34.... 40 B1
Wrington Crs
  BMSTRD/HC/WWD BS13............ 10 A9
Wrington HI
  BLAG/CWMG/WR BS40 .... 88 D6
Wrington La *YTN/CONG* BS49........ 87 H1
Wrington Md *YTN/CONG* BS49 .... 87 H7

Wrington Rd *YTN/CONG* BS49 .... 109 J1
Wroughton Dr
  BMSTRD/HC/WWD BS13............ 78 B7
Wroughton Gdns
  BMSTRD/HC/WWD BS13............ 78 B7 ⬛
Wroxham Dr
  BRSTK/PCHW BS34 .... 30 B7 ⬛
Wyatt Av
  BMSTRD/HC/WWD BS13............ 77 H6
Wyatt Cl
  BMSTRD/HC/WWD BS13............ 77 H6
Wyatt's Cl *NAIL* BS48 .... 73 H1
Wychwood *KGWD/HNM* BS15 .... 68 D4
Wyck Beck Rd
  HNBRY/STHM BS10............ 38 D4
Wycliffe Rd
  HNLZ/SM/SNYPK/WT BS9............ 51 K2
Wycombe Gv
  BRSG/KWL/STAPK BS4............ 13 G4
Wye Ct *THNB/SVB* BS35 .... 19 H5
Wye Croft Cl *HNBRY/STHM* BS10.. 39 G5
Wyedale Av
  HNLZ/SM/SNYPK/WT BS9............ 50 D2
Wyke Rd *TRWBR* BA14 .... 125 G2
Wykis Ct *KGWD/HNM* BS15 .... 68 E5 ⬛
Wyllie Ct *MTN/WRL* BS22 .... 84 B7 ⬛
Wymbush Crs
  BMSTRD/HC/WWD BS13............ 78 A6
Wymbush Gdns
  BMSTRD/HC/WWD BS13............ 78 A6 ⬛
Wyndham Crs
  BRSG/KWL/STAPK BS4............ 9 M9
  PTSHD/EG BS20 .... 49 H5
Wyndham Wy *PTSHD/EG* BS20 .... 47 J4
Wynsome St *TRWBR* BA14 .... 130 B4
The Wynstones
  KGWD/HNM BS15 .... 68 C3
Wynter Cl *MTN/WRL* BS22 .... 106 B2
Yadley Cl *WNSC* BS25 .... 120 C7
Yanel La *WNSC* BS25 .... 120 E1
Yanleigh Cl
  BMSTRD/HC/WWD BS13............ 76 E5
Yanley La *LGASH* BS41 .... 76 D3
Yarbury Wy
  OMX/HUT/LCK BS24 .... 106 C4
Yarnbrook Rd *TRWBR* BA14 .... 131 J4
Yate Rd *YATE/CS* BS37 .... 32 E3
Yelverton Rd
  BRSG/KWL/STAPK BS4............ 13 J6
Yeo Bank La *CLVDN* BS21 .... 85 F3
Yeo Cl *WSM* BS23 .... 17 J8
Yeolands Dr *CLVDN* BS21 .... 70 D2
Yeomans Cl
  HNLZ/SM/SNYPK/WT BS9............ 51 F4 ⬛
Yeomanside Cl *HGRV/WHIT* BS14.. 79 G6
Yeoman Wy *TRWBR* BA14 .... 124 E7
Yeomead *NAIL* BS48 .... 61 K7
Yeomeads *LGASH* BS41 .... 76 B2
Yeo Moor *CLVDN* BS21 .... 71 G1
Yeoward Rd *CLVDN* BS21 .... 71 G2
Yeo Wy *CLVDN* BS21 .... 70 D1
Yerbury St *TRWBR* BA14 .... 125 F5
Yewcroft Cl *HGRV/WHIT* BS14 .... 78 E7
Yew Tree Cl *NAIL* BS48 .... 73 G2 ⬛
Yew Tree Dr *KGWD/HNM* BS15 .... 55 F6
Yew Tree Gdns *NAIL* BS48 .... 73 G2 ⬛
  PTSHD/EG BS20 .... 49 J5 ⬛
  WNSC BS25 .... 120 D2 ⬛
Yew Tree La *CLVDN* BS21 .... 85 J3
Yew Tree Pk *YTN/CONG* BS49 .... 109 G2
Yomede Pk
  CBATH/BATHN BA1 .... 98 D5 ⬛
York Av *HORF/LLZ* BS7 .... 3 M2
York Buildings *TRWBR* BA14.... 125 F5 ⬛
York Cl *BRSTK/PCHW* BS34 .... 40 C4
  FRCTL/WBN BS36............ 42 A7
  MTN/WRL BS22 .... 106 B1 ⬛
  YATE/CS BS37 .... 34 B3
York Gdns *CFTN/FAIL* BS8 .... 65 H4
  FRCTL/WBN BS36............ 32 A7
York PI *CBRIS/FH* BS1............ 6 E5
  CFTN/FAIL BS8 .... 6 C3
York Rd *BMSTR* BS3 .... 7 J8
  EVILLE/WHL BS5............ 4 E8
  MANG/FISH BS16 .... 54 E5
  RDLND/MONT BS6 .... 3 K7
York St *CBATH/BATHN* BA1 .... 15 G7 ⬛
  CBRISNE BS2............ 3 M6
  CFTN/FAIL BS8 .... 2 B5 ⬛
  EVILLE/WHL BS5............ 8 F3
  WSM BS23............ 16 D3
Youngs Ct *MANG/FISH* BS16 .... 55 H1 ⬛
Youngwood La *NAIL* BS48 .... 73 G5
Zetland Rd *RDLND/MONT* BS6 .... 3 G6
Zig Zag *CLVDN* BS21 .... 59 F6

Index - featured places

Abbotswood Infant School
  YATE/CS BS37............ 44 A2
Abbotswood Surgery
  YATE/CS BS37............ 44 A1
ABC Cinema
  CBATH/BATHN BA1 .... 14 F6
ABC Cinema
  CFTN/FAIL BS8 .... 2 C9
Adam Gallery
  CBATH/BATHN BA1 .... 14 F6
Adcroft Surgery
  TRWBR BA14 .... 125 F4
Air Balloon Hill Junior &
Infant School
  EVILLE/WHL BS5............ 68 A3
Allen School House
  OLD/WMLY/WICK BS30 .... 69 G5
All Saints Exhibition Centre
  CBRIS/FH BS1............ 7 H3
Almondsbury Business Centre
  ALMDB BS32............ 30 C4
Almondsbury C of E VC Primary
School
  ALMDB BS32............ 29 K3

Almondsbury Surgery
  ALMDB BS32............ 29 K2
Almondsbury Town
Football Club
  ALMDB BS32............ 29 K3
Amberley House School
  CFTN/FAIL BS8 .... 2 B1
Ambulance Station
  BATHSE BA2............ 15 H1
Amelia Nutt Clinic
  BMSTRD/HC/WWD BS13............ 77 H7
AMF Bowling
  WSM BS23 .... 16 C4
Amphitheatre
  CBRIS/FH BS1............ 6 F6
Anchor Business Centre
  CFTN/FAIL BS8 .... 2 C8
Antrim Gallery
  CBATH/BATHN BA1 .... 15 G1
Aretians RFC Clubhouse
  BRSTK/PCHW BS34 .... 40 A1
Army Training Corps
  CLVDN BS21 .... 58 E6

Arnolfini Gallery
  CBRIS/FH BS1............ 7 G6
Arts Centre Cinema
  CBRISNE BS2............ 3 H9
Ashbrooke House School
  WSM BS23............ 16 D5
Ashcombe CP School
  WSM BS23............ 17 K3
Ashley Down Junior School
  HORF/LLZ BS7............ 52 C4
Ashley Down OB Rugby Club
  HORF/LLZ BS7............ 53 F1
Ashley Trading Estate
  CBRISNE BS2............ 3 M6
Ashmead Business Park
  KEYN BS31............ 81 H6
Ashton Gate Primary School
  BMSTR BS3............ 6 B9
Ashton Park School
  BMSTR BS3............ 65 G7
Ashton Vale Primary School
  BMSTR BS3............ 77 H1

Assembly Rooms
Museum of Costume
  CBATH/BATHN BA1 .... 14 F4
Avlon Works
  HNBRY/STHM BS10............ 27 J4
Avonbank Industrial Centre
  AVONM BS12............ 49 H2
Avonbridge Trading Estate
  AVONM BS11............ 49 H1
Avon Business Park
  MANG/FISH BS16............ 5 M3
Avon County Council
  BMSTR BS3............ 11 K4
Avondale Business Centre
  MANG/FISH BS16............ 54 C7
Avon Gorge Industrial Estate
  AVONM BS11............ 49 J2
Avonmouth C of E School
  AVONM BS11............ 49 J1
Avonmouth Group Practice
Health Centre
Doctors Surgery
  AVONM BS11............ 49 H1

Avonmouth Medical Centre
  AVONM BS11............ 49 H1
Avon Primary School
  AVONM BS11............ 49 K1
Avon Riverside Estate
  AVONM BS11............ 49 H2
Avon & Somerset Constabulary
  CBRIS/FH BS1............ 7 H2
Avon Trading Estate
  CBRISNE BS2............ 8 A6
Azure Gallery
  HNLZ/SM/SNYPK/WT BS9............ 51 H2
Backwell C of E VC
Junior School
  NAIL BS48............ 74 C6
Backwell Leisure Centre
  NAIL BS48............ 74 B5
Backwell Medical Centre
  NAIL BS48............ 74 B6
Backwell Rugby Football Club
  NAIL BS48............ 74 A5
Backwell School
  NAIL BS48............ 74 B5

Badminton Road
  Trading Estate
    YATE/CS BS37 .... 33 J6
Badminton School
    HNLZ/SM/SNYPK/WT BS9 .... 51 J4
Badocks Wood Primary School
    HNBRY/STHM BS10 .... 52 A1
Baileys Court Primary School
    ALMDB BS32 .... 40 E2
Balaclava Industrial Estate
    MANG/FISH BS16 .... 5 M4
Bandstand
    CBATH/BATHN BA1 .... 14 D5
Bank Leaze Primary School
    AVONM BS11 .... 37 J6
Bannerman Road
  Primary School
    EVILLE/WHL BS5 .... 4 D8
Banwell CP School
    BNWL BS29 .... 119 J3
Banwell Parish Council
    BNWL BS29 .... 119 J3
Barley Close Primary School
    MANG/FISH BS16 .... 55 C5
Barrow Hospital
    NAIL BS48 .... 76 C5
Barrs Court Primary School
    OLD/WMLY/WICK BS30 .... 69 F5
Barton Hill Primary School
    EVILLE/WHL BS5 .... 8 C4
Barton Hill Trading Estate
    EVILLE/WHL BS5 .... 8 D5
Bath Abbey
    CBATH/BATHN BA1 .... 15 G6
Bathampton Primary School
    BATHSE BA2 .... 100 E2
Bath City Council
    CBATH/BATHN BA1 .... 15 C5
Bath City Council
    CBATH/BATHN BA1 .... 99 F5
Bath City Football Club
    BATHSE BA2 .... 98 E6
The Bath Clinic
    BATHSE BA2 .... 112 D3
Bath College of Higher
  Education
    CBATH/BATHN BA1 .... 14 C1
Bath County Court
    CBATH/BATHN BA1 .... 15 G7
Bath Cricket Club
    BATHSE BA2 .... 15 H7
Batheaston Medical Centre
    CBATH/BATHN BA1 .... 101 F1
Bathford C of E VC
  Primary School
    CBATH/BATHN BA1 .... 101 H2
Bath Galleries
    CBATH/BATHN BA1 .... 15 C5
Bath Golf Club
    BATHSE BA2 .... 100 C6
Bath Media College
    CBATH/BATHN BA1 .... 14 F5
Bath Natural Health Clinic
    CBATH/BATHN BA1 .... 14 D6
Bath & North East
  Somerset Council
    CBATH/BATHN BA1 .... 14 F6
Bath & North East
  Somerset Council
    RDSTK/MIDN BA3 .... 126 B4
Bath Postal Museum
    CBATH/BATHN BA1 .... 14 F5
Bath Rugby Club
    BATHSE BA2 .... 15 H6
Bath Spa University College
    BATHSE BA2 .... 97 J7
Bath & Sports Leisure Centre
    BATHSE BA2 .... 15 H6
Bath University
    BATHSE BA2 .... 100 D6
Bathwick St Marys C of E
  Primary School
    BATHSE BA2 .... 15 L3
Baytree School
    MTN/WRL BS22 .... 105 J4
Beacon Rise Junior School
    KGWD/HNM BS15 .... 68 D4
Beazer Garden Maze
    BATHSE BA2 .... 15 H6
Beckett Primary School
    MTN/WRL BS22 .... 106 B3
Bedminster Down School
    BMSTRD/HC/WWD BS13 .... 77 H4
Beechen Cliff Boys School
    BATHSE BA2 .... 111 K1
Beeches Trading Estate
    YATE/CS BS37 .... 33 H5
The Beehive Surgery
    BATHSE BA2 .... 110 D1
Beehive Trading Estate
    EVILLE/WHL BS5 .... 9 K3
Begbrook Primary School
    MANG/FISH BS16 .... 53 K3
Birchills Trading Estate
    BRSG/KWL/STAPK BS4 .... 13 L5
Birdwell Primary School
    LGASH BS41 .... 76 C5
Bishop Road Primary School
    HORF/LLZ BS7 .... 3 H1
Bishopston House Clinic
    HORF/LLZ BS7 .... 3 J2
Bishopsworth C of E School
    BMSTRD/HC/WWD BS13 .... 77 H5
Bishopsworth Swimming Pool
    BMSTRD/HC/WWD BS13 .... 77 J5
Blackberry Hill Hospital
    MANG/FISH BS16 .... 53 K4
Blackhorse CP School
    MANG/FISH BS16 .... 55 C1
Blaise Hamlet (NT)
    HNBRY/STHM BS10 .... 38 C5
Bonville Business Centre
    BRSG/KWL/STAPK BS4 .... 13 L3
Book Museum
    CBATH/BATHN BA1 .... 15 H8
Bournville County Junior &
  Infant School
    WSM BS23 .... 17 H8

Bowling Hill Business Park
    YATE/CS BS37 .... 34 D6
Bradford on Avon Hospital
    BOAV BA15 .... 114 E5
Bradford on Avon
  Swimming Pool
    BOAV BA15 .... 114 D7
Bradgate Surgery
    HNBRY/STHM BS10 .... 38 D5
Brentry Hospital
    HNBRY/STHM BS10 .... 38 E6
Brentry Primary School
    HNBRY/STHM BS10 .... 38 E5
Briarwood School
    MANG/FISH BS16 .... 54 B6
Bridge Farm Junior &
  Infant School
    HGRV/WHIT BS14 .... 78 E7
Bridge Road Business Park
    WSM BS23 .... 17 H5
Brimsham Green School
    YATE/CS BS37 .... 34 A3
Brislington Retail Park
    BRSG/KWL/STAPK BS4 .... 13 J6
Brislington School
    BRSG/KWL/STAPK BS4 .... 13 L7
Brislington Trading Estate
    BRSG/KWL/STAPK BS4 .... 13 M4
Bristol Baptist College
    CFTN/FAIL BS8 .... 65 H2
Bristol Business Park
    MANG/FISH BS16 .... 40 E7
Bristol Cathedral
    CBRIS/FH BS1 .... 6 F5
Bristol Cathedral School
    CBRIS/FH BS1 .... 6 E5
Bristol City Council
    AVONM BS11 .... 36 B7
Bristol City Council
    AVONM BS11 .... 37 H7
Bristol City Council
    AVONM BS11 .... 49 K2
Bristol City Council
    AVONM BS11 .... 50 C2
Bristol City Council
    BMSTR BS3 .... 7 J9
Bristol City Council
    BMSTRD/HC/WWD BS13 .... 77 K7
Bristol City Council
    BMSTRD/HC/WWD BS13 .... 93 F1
Bristol City Council
    BRSG/KWL/STAPK BS4 .... 8 F9
Bristol City Council
    BRSG/KWL/STAPK BS4 .... 11 H9
Bristol City Council
    BRSG/KWL/STAPK BS4 .... 12 A8
Bristol City Council
    BRSG/KWL/STAPK BS4 .... 12 C4
Bristol City Council
    BRSG/KWL/STAPK BS4 .... 13 M2
Bristol City Council
    BRSG/KWL/STAPK BS4 .... 78 B4
Bristol City Council
    CBRIS/FH BS1 .... 6 F4
Bristol City Council
    CBRIS/FH BS1 .... 6 F3
Bristol City Council
    CBRIS/FH BS1 .... 6 E4
Bristol City Council
    CBRIS/FH BS1 .... 7 J1
Bristol City Council
    CBRIS/FH BS1 .... 7 J3
Bristol City Council
    CBRIS/FH BS1 .... 7 M6
Bristol City Council
    CBRISNE BS2 .... 3 L8
Bristol City Council
    CBRISNE BS2 .... 3 J9
Bristol City Council
    CFTN/FAIL BS8 .... 2 B5
Bristol City Council
    CFTN/FAIL BS8 .... 6 C3
Bristol City Council
    CFTN/FAIL BS8 .... 6 E2
Bristol City Council
    CFTN/FAIL BS8 .... 6 A6
Bristol City Council
    EVILLE/WHL BS5 .... 4 C5
Bristol City Council
    EVILLE/WHL BS5 .... 8 D3
Bristol City Council
    EVILLE/WHL BS5 .... 9 G2
Bristol City Council
    HGRV/WHIT BS14 .... 12 E7
Bristol City Council
    HNBRY/STHM BS10 .... 38 E5
Bristol City Council
    HNBRY/STHM BS10 .... 51 K1
Bristol City Council
    HNBRY/STHM BS10 .... 52 C3
Bristol City Council
    HORF/LLZ BS7 .... 39 J7
Bristol City Football Club
    BMSTR BS3 .... 65 H7
Bristol Civil Service Sports Club
    HORF/LLZ BS7 .... 52 D3
Bristol Clifton & West of
  England Zoological Society
    CFTN/FAIL BS8 .... 65 H2
Bristol County Court
    CBRISNE BS2 .... 7 G2
Bristol County Sports Club
    CBRIS/FH BS1 .... 6 F3
Bristol Crown Court
    CBRISNE BS2 .... 7 G2
Bristol Dental Hospital
    CBRISNE BS2 .... 7 G2
Bristol General Hospital
    CBRIS/FH BS1 .... 7 H7
Bristol Grammar School
    CFTN/FAIL BS8 .... 6 D2
Bristol Grammar School
    CFTN/FAIL BS8 .... 64 A7
Bristol Harlequins RFC
    BRSG/KWL/STAPK BS4 .... 80 A1
Bristol Ice Rink
    CBRIS/FH BS1 .... 6 F3

Bristol Industrial Museum
    CBRIS/FH BS1 .... 6 F7
Bristol North Baths
    HORF/LLZ BS7 .... 3 H3
Bristol & North Somerset
  Sports Club
    CFTN/FAIL BS8 .... 63 K7
Bristol Old Vic (New Vic
  Theatre & Theatre Royal)
    CBRIS/FH BS1 .... 7 G4
Bristol Old Vic Theatre School
    CFTN/FAIL BS8 .... 2 A7
Bristol Rovers Football Club
    BRSG/KWL/STAPK BS4 .... 13 M5
Bristol Royal Hospital for Sick
  Children
    CFTN/FAIL BS8 .... 6 F2
Bristol Royal Infirmary
    CBRISNE BS2 .... 7 G1
Bristol Rugby Club
    CBATH/BATHN BA1 .... 14 D6
Bristol South Swimming Pool
    BMSTR BS3 .... 6 F9
Bristol Steiner Waldorf School
    CFTN/FAIL BS8 .... 6 C3
Bristol University
    CFTN/FAIL BS8 .... 6 F3
Bristol Vale Trading Estate
    BMSTR BS3 .... 10 D6
British Empire &
  Commonwealth Museum
    CBRIS/FH BS1 .... 7 L6
Broadlands School
    KEYN BS31 .... 80 D5
Broadmead Lane
  Industrial Estate
    KEYN BS31 .... 81 G4
Broadoak Community School
    WSM BS23 .... 116 D3
Broadwalk Shopping Centre
    BRSG/KWL/STAPK BS4 .... 12 C3
Broadway County
  Infant School
    YATE/CS BS37 .... 34 C5
Brockeridge Infant School
    FRCTL/WBN BS36 .... 42 D1
Brock Street Clinic
    CBATH/BATHN BA1 .... 14 E4
Brockway Medical Centre
    NAIL BS48 .... 73 K1
Bromley Heath Infant School
    MANG/FISH BS16 .... 54 E1
Bromley Heath Junior School
    MANG/FISH BS16 .... 54 E1
Brooklea Clinic
    BRSG/KWL/STAPK BS4 .... 9 J7
Broomhill Infant School
    BRSG/KWL/STAPK BS4 .... 13 L1
Broomhill Jm School
    BRSG/KWL/STAPK BS4 .... 13 L1
Bryer Ash Business Park
    TRWBR BA14 .... 124 C5
The Building of Bath Museum
    CBATH/BATHN BA1 .... 14 F4
Burnbush Primary School
    HGRV/WHIT BS14 .... 79 H4
Burnbush School
    HGRV/WHIT BS14 .... 79 H5
Bush Industrial Estate
    EVILLE/WHL BS5 .... 5 G9
The Business Park
    BMSTRD/HC/WWD BS13 .... 93 H1
BW Estates
    OMX/HUT/LCK BS24 .... 117 F3
CAB & Guildhall
    CBRIS/FH BS1 .... 7 H3
Cabot Primary School
    CBRISNE BS2 .... 3 L9
Cabot Tower
    CFTN/FAIL BS8 .... 6 D4
Cadbury Heath CP School
    OLD/WMLY/WICK BS30 .... 69 H4
Cadbury Heath Health Centre
    OLD/WMLY/WICK BS30 .... 69 G5
Callicroft Infant School
    BRSTK/PCHW BS34 .... 29 J7
Callicroft Junior School
    BRSTK/PCHW BS34 .... 29 H7
Camden Works Museum
    CBATH/BATHN BA1 .... 14 F4
Canons House
    CBRIS/FH BS1 .... 6 F6
The Card Gallery
    YATE/CS BS37 .... 34 E6
Carla Trading Estate
    BMSTR BS3 .... 65 H7
Carlyle Business Centre
    CBRISNE BS2 .... 8 B4
Carrick Business Centre
    BRSG/KWL/STAPK BS4 .... 13 K5
Castle Batch Primary School
    MTN/WRL BS22 .... 84 B7
Castle Business Centre
    THNB/SVB BS35 .... 19 G4
Castle CP School
    KEYN BS31 .... 95 J1
Castlemead Shopping Centre
    MTN/WRL BS22 .... 84 B7
Castle Place Leisure Centre
    TRWBR BA14 .... 125 F6
The Castle School
    THNB/SVB BS35 .... 19 G3
Catherine Cottage Surgery
    CBATH/BATHN BA1 .... 14 E4
Central Trading Estate
    CBRISNE BS2 .... 8 C8
Chandag County & Infant School
    KEYN BS31 .... 81 G6
Charborough Road CP School
    BRSTK/PCHW BS34 .... 39 J6
Charlotte Keel Health Clinic
    EVILLE/WHL BS5 .... 4 B8
Chatterton House
    CBRIS/FH BS1 .... 7 J6
Cheddar Grove Primary School
    BMSTRD/HC/WWD BS13 .... 10 B8
Cherry Garden Primary School
    OLD/WMLY/WICK BS30 .... 81 H1

Chesterfield Hospital
    CFTN/FAIL BS8 .... 6 B4
Chester Park Primary School
    MANG/FISH BS16 .... 54 A6
Chinese Medical Centre
    CBATH/BATHN BA1 .... 15 G8
Chipping Edge Estate
    YATE/CS BS37 .... 34 E6
Chipping Sodbury Library
    YATE/CS BS37 .... 34 E6
Chipping Sodbury School
    YATE/CS BS37 .... 34 E7
Christchurch C of E
  Primary School
    CFTN/FAIL BS8 .... 6 A2
Christ Church C of E VC
  Infant School
    MANG/FISH BS16 .... 54 D4
Christchurch Junior School
    MANG/FISH BS16 .... 54 D4
Christchurch Primary School
    BOAV BA15 .... 114 E6
Christchurch VC
  Primary School
    WSM BS23 .... 16 F2
Christ the King RC School
    THNB/SVB BS35 .... 19 H4
Church Farm Business Park
    BATHSE BA2 .... 97 H5
Churchill C of E VC
  Primary School
    WNSC BS25 .... 121 J2
Churchill School
    WNSC BS25 .... 121 G1
Churchill Sports Centre
    WNSC BS25 .... 121 G1
The Church Street Practice
    BOAV BA15 .... 114 D6
City Business Park
    CBRIS/FH BS1 .... 7 H3
City Business Park
    EVILLE/WHL BS5 .... 8 A2
City of Bath College
    CBATH/BATHN BA1 .... 14 F7
City of Bristol College
    BMSTR BS3 .... 11 J4
City of Bristol College
    CBRIS/FH BS1 .... 6 D5
City of Bristol College
    HORF/LLZ BS7 .... 3 M3
City & Port of Bristol Social &
  Sports Club
    AVONM BS11 .... 50 A4
Civic Centre
    KGWD/HNM BS15 .... 68 E2
Civil Service Sports Club
    BATHSE BA2 .... 112 D3
Clandown Junior VC School
    RDSTK/MIDN BA3 .... 127 F1
Claremont Special School
    RDLND/MONT BS6 .... 52 A4
The Clarendon School
    TRWBR BA14 .... 130 D1
Claverham Cricket Club
    YTN/CONG BS49 .... 87 G5
Claverton Manor
  American Museum in Britain
    BATHSE BA2 .... 101 F7
Clevedon Fruit Market
    CLVDN BS21 .... 59 F7
Clevedon Health Centre
    CLVDN BS21 .... 59 G7
Clevedon Hospital
    CLVDN BS21 .... 59 G7
Clevedon School
    CLVDN BS21 .... 59 H5
Clifton Cathedral Church
    CFTN/FAIL BS8 .... 6 B1
Clifton Clinic
    CFTN/FAIL BS8 .... 6 A3
Clifton College
    CFTN/FAIL BS8 .... 65 H2
Clifton College
  Preparatory School
    CFTN/FAIL BS8 .... 65 H1
Clifton College Sports Club
    CFTN/FAIL BS8 .... 64 D3
Clifton Down Shopping Centre
    CFTN/FAIL BS8 .... 2 C8
The Clifton Gallery
    CFTN/FAIL BS8 .... 6 A3
The Clifton Gallery
    CFTN/FAIL BS8 .... 65 H3
Clifton High Junior School
    CFTN/FAIL BS8 .... 6 A2
Clifton High School
    CFTN/FAIL BS8 .... 6 A1
Clifton High School
    CFTN/FAIL BS8 .... 65 H2
Clifton Rugby Club
    HNBRY/STHM BS10 .... 38 C3
Close Farm Surgery
    OLD/WMLY/WICK BS30 .... 69 K5
Club House
    RDSTK/MIDN BA3 .... 126 D7
Clyde House Surgery
    RDLND/MONT BS6 .... 2 D6
Coates Industrial Estate
    NAIL BS48 .... 61 K7
College House
    MANG/FISH BS16 .... 54 D4
College of St Mathias C of E (A)
  Infant School
    MANG/FISH BS16 .... 54 A4
Colston Hall
    CBRIS/FH BS1 .... 7 G3
Colstons Collegiate
  Lower School
    MANG/FISH BS16 .... 53 H4
Colstons Girls School
    RDLND/MONT BS6 .... 3 J7
Colstons Primary School
    RDLND/MONT BS6 .... 2 F4
Colstons School
    MANG/FISH BS16 .... 54 A4
Combe Down House Surgery
    BATHSE BA2 .... 112 B4

Combe Down Infant School
    BATHSE BA2 .... 112 A4
Combe Down Rugby Club
    BATHSE BA2 .... 112 A3
Community Health Authority
    KEYN BS31 .... 80 E5
Community Mental
  Health Centre
    CLVDN BS21 .... 58 E6
The Compton Clinic
    RDLND/MONT BS6 .... 2 B2
Coniston Primary School
    BRSTK/PCHW BS34 .... 29 J6
Connaught Infants &
  Primary School
    BRSG/KWL/STAPK BS4 .... 11 K7
Conygre Medical Centre
    BRSTK/PCHW BS34 .... 39 K5
Corbett House Clinic
    EVILLE/WHL BS5 .... 8 E3
Coroners Court
    CBRISNE BS2 .... 3 J9
Corpus Christi RC VA
  Primary School
    WSM BS23 .... 16 D6
Cossham Memorial Hospital
    KGWD/HNM BS15 .... 54 C7
Cotham Galleries
    RDLND/MONT BS6 .... 2 D8
Cotham Grammar School
    RDLND/MONT BS6 .... 2 F8
Cotham Park Rugby Club
    CFTN/FAIL BS8 .... 64 C4
Cotham Road Surgery
    RDLND/MONT BS6 .... 2 E9
Council Offices
    TRWBR BA14 .... 130 E2
County Primary School
    WNSC BS25 .... 120 E2
Court De Wyck Primary School
    YTN/CONG BS49 .... 87 J3
Courtney Primary School
    KGWD/HNM BS15 .... 69 F3
Courtside Surgery
    YATE/CS BS37 .... 34 B6
The Craft Gallery
    HORF/LLZ BS7 .... 39 J7
Crescent Gallery
    CBATH/BATHN BA1 .... 14 E4
Cribbs Causeway
  Shopping Centre
    BRSTK/PCHW BS34 .... 39 F1
Crockerne Primary School
    PTSHD/EG BS20 .... 49 J6
Crofts End Industrial Estate
    EVILLE/WHL BS5 .... 5 K7
The Cross Bath
    CBATH/BATHN BA1 .... 14 F7
Crossways Junior &
  Infant School
    THNB/SVB BS35 .... 19 J4
Crown Court
    CBRIS/FH BS1 .... 7 H2
Culverhay Boys School
    BATHSE BA2 .... 110 E3
Culverhill School
    YATE/CS BS37 .... 44 A1
Cumberwell Park Golf Club
    BOAV BA15 .... 114 D2
Custom House
    CBRIS/FH BS1 .... 7 H5
Cutlers Brook Junior School
    CBRISNE BS2 .... 4 A6
David Hamiltons Practice
    CFTN/FAIL BS8 .... 2 D8
Dean Lane Family Practice
    BMSTR BS3 .... 6 F8
Deers Wood Primary School
    KGWD/HNM BS15 .... 55 H7
3-D Gallery
    CBRISNE BS2 .... 7 G2
Dixon Business Centre
    BRSG/KWL/STAPK BS4 .... 13 M3
Docks Industrial Estate
    AVONM BS11 .... 27 F7
Dodington Parish Council
    YATE/CS BS37 .... 34 D7
Dodington Park
    YATE/CS BS37 .... 45 K4
Dolphin Shopping Centre
    WSM BS23 .... 16 D4
Downend Cricket Club
    MANG/FISH BS16 .... 54 D3
Downend School
    MANG/FISH BS16 .... 54 E4
Downend Surgery
    MANG/FISH BS16 .... 54 D4
Downland Surgery
    MTN/WRL BS22 .... 106 B3
Downs Fitness & Health Centre
    CFTN/FAIL BS8 .... 2 B6
Dral Health Centre
    CBATH/BATHN BA1 .... 14 F5
Dr Bells C of E School
    MANG/FISH BS16 .... 54 A5
Drove Road Hospital
    WSM BS23 .... 17 G6
Duckmoor Road
  Industrial Estate
    BMSTR BS3 .... 10 A7
Dundry Primary School
    LGASH BS41 .... 92 A2
Dunmail Primary School
    HNBRY/STHM BS10 .... 39 F6
Eagles Wood Business Park
    ALMDB BS32 .... 30 B4
East Clevedon VC
  Primary School
    CLVDN BS21 .... 59 H6
Easton Business Centre
    EVILLE/WHL BS5 .... 4 C9
Easton C E VA Primary School
    EVILLE/WHL BS5 .... 8 B1
Easton Leisure Centre
    EVILLE/WHL BS5 .... 8 B1
Eastpark Trading Estate
    EVILLE/WHL BS5 .... 5 H7

East Twerton Infant School
BATHSE BA2 .... **14** B7
Eastville Health Centre
EVILLE/WHL BS5 .... **4** D6
Elmlea Infant School
HNLZ/SM/SNYPK/WT BS9 ...... **51** H4
Elmlea Junior School
HNLZ/SM/SNYPK/WT BS9 ...... **51** H4
Elm Park School
FRCTL/WBN BS36 .... **41** K2
The Elms Day Hospital
THNB/SVB BS35 .... **19** G4
Embleton Junior School
HNBRY/STHM BS10 .... **38** E7
Exhibition Centre
CBRIS/FH BS1 .... **6** F5
Explore @ Bristol
CBRIS/FH BS1 .... **6** F5
The Eye Clinic
CBRIS/FH BS1 .... **7** J2
Fairfield Grammar School
RDLND/MONT BS6 .... **3** L6
Fairfield School
NAIL BS48 .... **74** C5
Fair Furlong Primary School
BMSTRD/HC/WWD BS13 ...... **77** J7
Fairway Industrial Centre
BRSTK/PCHW BS34 .... **39** J5
Falconride Primary School
KGWD/HNM BS15 .... **68** E1
The Family Practice
RDLND/MONT BS6 .... **2** E9
Family & Youth Court
CBRIS/FH BS1 .... **7** H3
Farleigh College
RDSTK/MIDN BA3 .... **128** D1
Ferry Steps Trading Estate
CBRISNE BS2 .... **8** A8
Filton Avenue Junior School
HORF/LLZ BS7 .... **52** E2
Filton Clinic
HORF/LLZ BS7 .... **39** K6
Filton College
BRSTK/PCHW BS34 .... **39** K4
Filton High School
BRSTK/PCHW BS34 .... **40** C5
Filton Hill CP School
BRSTK/PCHW BS34 .... **40** A4
Filton Park School
BRSTK/PCHW BS34 .... **39** J6
Filton Recreation Centre
BRSTK/PCHW BS34 .... **39** K6
Filton Shield Road School
HORF/LLZ BS7 .... **39** K7
Filton Town Council
BRSTK/PCHW BS34 .... **39** K6
Filwood Swimming Baths
BRSG/KWL/STAPK BS4 ...... **11** K8
Fire Station
CBRIS/FH BS1 .... **7** K4
Fishponds Health Centre
MANG/FISH BS16 .... **54** B5
Fitzmaurice Primary School
BOAV BA15 .... **123** K1
Five C Business Centre
CLVDN BS21 .... **70** D2
Flax Bourton CP School
NAIL BS48 .... **75** F4
The Florence Brown School
BRSG/KWL/STAPK BS4 ...... **11** G8
The Florence Brown School
CBRISNE BS2 .... **7** L2
Flower Gallery
FRCTL/WBN BS36 .... **41** J2
Folk House
CBRIS/FH BS1 .... **6** F3
Fonthill Junior School
HNBRY/STHM BS10 .... **39** H6
Fosseway Junior &
Infant School
BATHSE BA2 .... **111** G4
Foster Almshouses
CBRIS/FH BS1 .... **7** G3
Fouracres Primary School
BMSTRD/HC/WWD BS13 ...... **77** G7
Four Oaks County Infant School
NAIL BS48 .... **73** J1
Frame Gallery
WSM BS23 .... **16** E2
Framing Workshop & Gallery &
Archival Fine Art Print
CBATH/BATHN BA1 .... **15** G4
Frampton Cotterell
C of E School
FRCTL/WBN BS36 .... **32** B7
Frenchay C of E School
MANG/FISH BS16 .... **54** B2
Frenchay Health Authority
MANG/FISH BS16 .... **54** C4
Frenchay Hospital
MANG/FISH BS16 .... **54** B1
Frenchay Village Museum
MANG/FISH BS16 .... **53** K2
Freshford VC Primary School
RDSTK/MIDN BA3 .... **122** B1
Frome Bank Junior School
YATE/CS BS37 .... **34** A4
Fromeside Clinic
MANG/FISH BS16 .... **53** K4
Fulford Special School
BMSTRD/HC/WWD BS13 ...... **78** A7
The Galleries Shopping Centre
CBRIS/FH BS1 .... **7** J2
Gas Works
HNBRY/STHM BS10 .... **27** J7
Gay Elms Junior & Infant School
BMSTRD/HC/WWD BS13 ...... **77** J7
Georgian House
CBRIS/FH BS1 .... **6** E4
Georgian House
CBATH/BATHN BA1 .... **14** D4
Gillies & Partners
CBATH/BATHN BA1 .... **100** A3
Glebe County School
YTN/CONG BS49 .... **109** G1
Glencoe Business Park
WSM BS23 .... **17** K4

Glenfrome Primary School
EVILLE/WHL BS5 .... **4** E2
Gloucestershire
County Council
KGWD/HNM BS15 .... **68** E2
Gloucestershire County
Cricket Club
HORF/LLZ BS7 .... **3** L3
Glynne Wickham
Studio Theatre
CFTN/FAIL BS8 .... **6** E3
Golden Valley Primary School
BATHSE BA2 .... **73** K1
Gordano Rugby Football Club
PTSHD/EG BS20 .... **48** C6
Gordano School
PTSHD/EG BS20 .... **47** G6
Gordon Fraser Gallery
CBATH/BATHN BA1 .... **14** E5
Graham Road Surgery
WSM BS23 .... **16** E4
Granby House Clinic
BMSTR BS3 .... **10** F1
Grand Pier
WSM BS25 .... **16** C3
Grange Road Surgery
BMSTRD/HC/WWD BS13 ...... **77** H6
Great Western Business Park
YATE/CS BS37 .... **33** J4
Green Park Station
CBATH/BATHN BA1 .... **14** E6
Greystoke Business Centre
PTSHD/EG BS20 .... **47** H5
Grimsbury Park School
OLD/WMLY/WICK BS30 ...... **69** H3
Grosvenor Surgery
CBATH/BATHN BA1 .... **15** L1
Grosvenor Surgery
CBATH/BATHN BA1 .... **100** B3
Grove County Junior School
NAIL BS48 .... **73** H3
Grove Industrial Estate
BRSTK/PCHW BS34 .... **40** A1
The Grove Primary School
TRWBR BA14 .... **130** D2
Grove Road Day Hospital
RDLND/MONT BS6 .... **2** D8
Grove Sports Centre
NAIL BS48 .... **73** H3
Gypsy Lane
KEYN BS31 .... **96** C3
Hambrook CP School
MANG/FISH BS16 .... **41** J5
Hambrook Sports Club
MANG/FISH BS16 .... **41** J5
Hampset Cricket Club
BATHSE BA2 .... **111** G3
Hanham Abbots Junior School
KGWD/HNM BS15 .... **68** C6
Hanham Business Park
KGWD/HNM BS15 .... **68** B5
Hanham C of E Primary School
KGWD/HNM BS15 .... **68** B6
Hanham High School
KGWD/HNM BS15 .... **68** C6
Hanham Surgery
KGWD/HNM BS15 .... **68** D6
Hannah More County
Infant School
NAIL BS48 .... **73** H3
Hannah More Primary School
CBRISNE BS2 .... **7** M4
The Happening Art Gallery
RDLND/MONT BS6 .... **2** D8
Hareclive Primary School
BMSTRD/HC/WWD BS13 ...... **78** A7
Hartcliffe Health Centre
BMSTRD/HC/WWD BS13 ...... **78** A7
Hartcliffe School
BMSTRD/HC/WWD BS13 ...... **78** C7
Harveys Wine Museum
CBRIS/FH BS1 .... **6** F4
Haslemere Industrial Estate
AVONM BS11 .... **36** D6
Hawkins Clinic
CBATH/BATHN BA1 .... **14** F6
Hawthorne Industrial Estate
RDSTK/MIDN BA3 .... **126** D5
Hayesfield School
BATHSE BA2 .... **14** B7
Hayward Road
Industrial Estate
MANG/FISH BS16 .... **54** D6
Headley Park Primary School
BMSTRD/HC/WWD BS13 ...... **77** K4
Health & Fitness Club
WSM BS23 .... **16** F5
Heath House Priory Hospital
HORF/LLZ BS7 .... **4** C1
Henbury Court Junior & Primary
School
HNBRY/STHM BS10 .... **38** D7
Henbury Manor School
HNBRY/STHM BS10 .... **38** B6
Henbury Old Boys AFC
HNBRY/STHM BS10 .... **38** B5
Henbury School
HNBRY/STHM BS10 .... **38** B5
The Henbury Surgery
HNBRY/STHM BS10 .... **38** C5
Henbury Swimming Pool
HNBRY/STHM BS10 .... **38** C6
Henfield Business Park
FRCTL/WBN BS36 .... **42** E6
Hengrove School
HGRV/WHIT BS14 .... **79** F4
Henleaze Infant School
RDLND/MONT BS6 .... **52** A4
Heritage Centre
WSM BS23 .... **16** D2
Herschel House Museum
CBATH/BATHN BA1 .... **14** E6
Heywood Health Centre
PTSHD/EG BS20 .... **49** J5
Highbridge Infant School
BMSTRD/HC/WWD BS13 ...... **77** H5
Highcroft Junior School
FRCTL/WBN BS36 .... **32** D7

High Down Infants and
Junior School
PTSHD/EG BS20 .... **46** E5
Hillfields Park Primary School
MANG/FISH BS16 .... **54** C6
Hillside Infant School
MTN/WRL BS22 .... **105** K3
Hilperton Primary School
TRWBR BA14 .... **125** J2
The Hindu Temple
EVILLE/WHL BS5 .... **8** F1
Hippodrome Theatre
CBRIS/FH BS1 .... **7** G4
Holbrook School
TRWBR BA14 .... **131** F1
Holburne Museum &
Crafts Study Centre
BATHSE BA2 .... **15** J4
Holloway Dental Health Centre
HGRV/WHIT BS14 .... **79** J6
Hollywood Bowl
CBRISNE BS2 .... **8** E6
Holy Family RC Primary School
BRSTK/PCHW BS34 .... **30** A7
Holymead Infant School
BRSG/KWL/STAPK BS4 ...... **13** H3
Holymead School
BRSG/KWL/STAPK BS4 ...... **13** G2
Holy Trinity Primary School
ALMDB BS32 .... **30** B5
Homefield Industrial Estate
OMX/HUT/LCK BS24 .... **118** B1
Homeopathic Hospital
CFTN/FAIL BS8 .... **2** E9
Hope House Surgery
RDSTK/MIDN BA3 .... **127** G3
Horfield C of E School
HNBRY/STHM BS10 .... **52** B2
Horfield Health Centre
HORF/LLZ BS7 .... **52** E3
Horfield Sports Centre
HORF/LLZ BS7 .... **52** D2
Hornets Rugby Football Club
WSM BS23 .... **105** H6
Hospital
PTSHD/EG BS20 .... **50** A5
Hot Bath Gallery and
College of Art
CBATH/BATHN BA1 .... **14** F7
Hotspots Indoor Sports Centre
BRSG/KWL/STAPK BS4 ...... **13** L4
Hotwells Primary School
CFTN/FAIL BS8 .... **65** H4
Hutton Moor Leisure Centre
WSM BS23 .... **17** M4
Hutton Primary School
OMX/HUT/LCK BS24 .... **117** K4
Hydro Estate
AVONM BS11 .... **36** C5
Ilminster Avenue Junior School
BRSG/KWL/STAPK BS4 ...... **12** A7
Industrial Estate
BRSG/KWL/STAPK BS4 ...... **13** L5
Industrial Heritage Centre
BATHSE BA2 .... **14** F3
Iron Acton C of E School
YATE/CS BS37 .... **33** F3
John Cabot City
Technology College
KGWD/HNM BS15 .... **68** C3
John Govett Gallery
BOAV BA15 .... **114** D7
The John Milton Health Clinic
HNBRY/STHM BS10 .... **38** D5
The John of Gaunt School
TRWBR BA14 .... **124** D6
Jorrocks Estate
YATE/CS BS37 .... **43** K4
Jubilee Public Baths
BRSG/KWL/STAPK BS4 ...... **12** D4
Kenn Business Park
CLVDN BS21 .... **71** G3
Kennedy Way Surgery
YATE/CS BS37 .... **34** B6
Kewstoke Primary School
MTN/WRL BS22 .... **105** G2
Keynsham County
Primary School
KEYN BS31 .... **80** D6
Keynsham Hospital
KEYN BS31 .... **81** F7
Keynsham Leisure Centre
KEYN BS31 .... **81** F6
Keynsham Rugby Club
KEYN BS31 .... **80** D4
Keynsham Town Football Club
KEYN BS31 .... **80** D4
Kilmersdon Magistrates Court
RDSTK/MIDN BA3 .... **127** F3
Kilmersdon School
RDSTK/MIDN BA3 .... **127** H7
King Edmund
Community School
YATE/CS BS37 .... **34** B6
King Edwards School
BATHSE BA2 .... **15** L4
Kings Business Park
CBRISNE BS2 .... **8** E5
Kings Chase Shopping Centre
KGWD/HNM BS15 .... **68** D2
Kings Court Primary School
YATE/CS BS37 .... **34** B7
Kingsdown Golf Club
COR/BOX SN13 .... **102** C1
Kingsdown Sports Centre
CBRISNE BS2 .... **2** F9
Kingsfield School
KGWD/HNM BS15 .... **69** G2
Kingshill Primary School
NAIL BS48 .... **61** H7
Kingsweston School
AVONM BS11 .... **50** C1
Kingswood Borough Council
MANG/FISH BS16 .... **54** D5
Kingswood District Council
KGWD/HNM BS15 .... **68** D3
Kingswood Health Centre
KGWD/HNM BS15 .... **68** E2

Kingswood Leisure Centre
MANG/FISH BS16 .... **54** D6
Kingswood Preparatory School
CBATH/BATHN BA1 .... **99** H3
Kingswood School
CBATH/BATHN BA1 .... **99** H2
Knowle Junior Mixed School
BRSG/KWL/STAPK BS4 ...... **12** B1
Knowle Park Junior School
BRSG/KWL/STAPK BS4 ...... **12** A5
The Lake Surgery
HNBRY/STHM BS10 .... **51** K2
Lancaster House School
WSM BS23 .... **17** G2
Lansdown Cricket Club
CBATH/BATHN BA1 .... **98** E4
Larkhall Football Club
CBATH/BATHN BA1 .... **100** A1
Larkrise School
TRWBR BA14 .... **125** H5
Lawnwood Road
Industrial Estate
EVILLE/WHL BS5 .... **8** C1
Lawrence Hill Health Centre
CBRISNE BS2 .... **8** B2
Lawrence Hill Industrial Estate
EVILLE/WHL BS5 .... **8** E1
Lawrence Hill Industrial Park
EVILLE/WHL BS5 .... **8** C1
Lawrence Weston School
AVONM BS11 .... **37** J7
Le Coree Gallery
BOAV BA15 .... **114** D7
Leigh Court Business Centre
CFTN/FAIL BS8 .... **50** C7
Leisure Pavillion
WSM BS23 .... **16** B3
Lewis Road Surgery
BMSTRD/HC/WWD BS13 ...... **10** B8
Liberty Industrial Park
BMSTR BS3 .... **10** A4
Lime Grove School
BATHSE BA2 .... **15** J7
Little Stoke Junior School
BRSTK/PCHW BS34 .... **40** C2
Little Theatre
CBATH/BATHN BA1 .... **14** F7
Locking Road Business Park
WSM BS23 .... **17** J4
Lockleaze School
HORF/LLZ BS7 .... **53** G1
The Lodge Park School
CBATH/BATHN BA1 .... **99** F4
Long Ashton Surgery
LGASH BS41 .... **76** B2
Longbrook Trading Estate
BMSTR BS3 .... **65** G7
Longvernal Primary School
RDSTK/MIDN BA3 .... **126** A4
Longwell Green CP School
OLD/WMLY/WICK BS30 ...... **69** F7
Lonsdale Business Centre
KGWD/HNM BS15 .... **54** C7
Lord Chancellors Department
CBRIS/FH BS1 .... **7** H3
Lord Chancellors Department
CFTN/FAIL BS8 .... **65** H3
Lovemead Group Practice
TRWBR BA14 .... **125** F6
Luckwell Road School
BMSTR BS3 .... **10** B2
Lyntony House Reading School
HORF/LLZ BS7 .... **3** H3
Malago Surgery
BMSTR BS3 .... **10** F1
Malago Vale Trading Estate
BMSTR BS3 .... **10** F2
The Mall Gallery
CFTN/FAIL BS8 .... **65** H3
The Mall
BRSTK/PCHW BS34 .... **39** G2
The Maltings Industrial Estate
CBATH/BATHN BA1 .... **98** E5
Mangotsfield School
MANG/FISH BS16 .... **55** H5
Mangotsfield United
Football Club
MANG/FISH BS16 .... **55** H4
Manilla Crescent
WSM BS23 .... **104** B4
Manor Brook School
THNB/SVB BS35 .... **19** H2
Manor C of E School
FRCTL/WBN BS36 .... **42** D2
Manor Farm Associated
Football Club
HNLZ/SM/SNYPK/WT BS9 ...... **50** D4
Margaret Coates
Special School
BATHSE BA2 .... **111** G1
Margaret Stancomb
Infant School
TRWBR BA14 .... **124** E5
Maritime Heritage Centre
CBRIS/FH BS1 .... **6** D6
Marlow Vetinary Surgery
CBATH/BATHN BA1 .... **99** F6
Marlwood School
THNB/SVB BS35 .... **22** E1
Mary Elton Primary School
CLVDN BS21 .... **70** D2
May Park Primary School
EVILLE/WHL BS5 .... **4** F5
The Meadows Primary School
OLD/WMLY/WICK BS30 ...... **81** K3
Mead Vale Primary School
MTN/WRL BS22 .... **105** K4
The Medical Centre
AVONM BS11 .... **37** H7
Meltone Gallery
BATHSE BA2 .... **15** J3
Mendip Green First School
MTN/WRL BS22 .... **105** K4
Mendip Leisure Centre
PTSHD/EG BS20 .... **47** H5
Merrywood School
BRSG/KWL/STAPK BS4 ...... **11** L5

Midland Way Business Park
THNB/SVB BS35 .... **19** G5
Midsomer Norton County
Primary School
RDSTK/MIDN BA3 .... **126** C4
Millpond Primary School
EVILLE/WHL BS5 .... **4** B7
Milson Street Clinic
CBATH/BATHN BA1 .... **14** F5
Milton CP Infant School
MTN/WRL BS22 .... **105** G4
Milton Junior School
MTN/WRL BS22 .... **105** H4
The Milton Surgery
MTN/WRL BS22 .... **17** M1
Minto Road Industrial Centre
CBRISNE BS2 .... **3** M6
Mizzymean Recreation Centre
NAIL BS48 .... **73** H2
Model Yacht Pond
WSM BS24 .... **16** C2
Monks Park School
HORF/LLZ BS7 .... **39** J7
Monks Park Surgery
HORF/LLZ BS7 .... **52** D1
Monkton Combe
Junior School
BATHSE BA2 .... **112** B4
Monkton Combe School
BATHSE BA2 .... **112** D4
Monkton Farleigh
Primary School
BOAV BA15 .... **101** K5
Montpelier Health Centre
RDLND/MONT BS6 .... **3** J7
Moorlands Infant School
BATHSE BA2 .... **111** G1
Moorlands Junior School
BATHSE BA2 .... **111** G2
Mount Zion School
RDLND/MONT BS6 .... **3** G7
Museum
RDSTK/MIDN BA3 .... **127** F6
Museum of Asian Art
CBATH/BATHN BA1 .... **14** F4
Museum of Costume & Fashion
Research Centre
CBATH/BATHN BA1 .... **14** E5
Nailsea Health Centre
NAIL BS48 .... **73** J1
Nailsea School
NAIL BS48 .... **73** J1
Natural Health Clinic
RDLND/MONT BS6 .... **2** D8
Newbridge Industrial Estate
BRSG/KWL/STAPK BS4 ...... **9** G5
Newbridge Junior School
CBATH/BATHN BA1 .... **98** E5
Newbridge St Johns C of E
Infant School
CBATH/BATHN BA1 .... **98** E5
Newbridge Surgery
CBATH/BATHN BA1 .... **98** E5
New Court Surgery
WSM BS23 .... **16** E1
New Fosseway School
HGRV/WHIT BS14 .... **79** F4
New Siblands School
THNB/SVB BS35 .... **19** J4
The New Surgery
BNWL BS29 .... **119** H3
New Theatre Royal
CBATH/BATHN BA1 .... **14** E6
Newton Park College
BATHSE BA2 .... **97** J7
Newtown County
Primary School
TRWBR BA14 .... **124** E6
Northavon Business Centre
YATE/CS BS37 .... **33** K4
North Avon Magistrates Court
YATE/CS BS37 .... **34** B6
North Bradley C of E School
TRWBR BA14 .... **130** E5
North Bristol Rugby
Football Club
ALMDB BS32 .... **29** K4
Northleaze Primary School
LGASH BS41 .... **76** D1
Northridge Business Centre
YATE/CS BS37 .... **33** K5
North Road CP School
YATE/CS BS37 .... **33** J3
North Somerset Council
CLVDN BS21 .... **59** F7
North Somerset Council
NAIL BS48 .... **73** J1
North Somerset Council
WSM BS23 .... **16** C2
North Somerset Council
WSM BS23 .... **17** K4
North Somerset Council
WSM BS23 .... **116** B4
Northville Family Practice
HORF/LLZ BS7 .... **40** A7
North Worle Shopping Centre
MTN/WRL BS22 .... **106** C2
Norton Hill School
RDSTK/MIDN BA3 .... **126** C5
Norton Radstock College
RDSTK/MIDN BA3 .... **126** B4
Norton Radstock College
RDSTK/MIDN BA3 .... **127** G3
Norton Radstock
Town Council
RDSTK/MIDN BA3 .... **127** G3
Novers Hill Trading Estate
BMSTR BS3 .... **10** E6
Novers Lane Jmi School
BRSG/KWL/STAPK BS4 ...... **10** F7
Oakfield Business Park
KGWD/HNM BS15 .... **68** D3
Oatley Trading Estate
KGWD/HNM BS15 .... **68** D1
Odd Down Football Club
BATHSE BA2 .... **111** F5
Odeon Cinema
CBRIS/FH BS1 .... **7** H3

Odeon Cinema
WSM BS23 .... 16 E3
Odeon Theatre
WSM BS23 .... 16 E3
Off Centre Gallery
BMSTR BS3 .... 11 G2
Old Bristolians Sports Club
CFTN/FAIL BS8 .... 64 B6
Oldbury Court Infant School
MANG/FISH BS16 .... 54 C2
Oldbury Court JM School
MANG/FISH BS16 .... 54 C2
Old Culverhaysians RFC
BATHSE BA2 .... 111 F4
Oldfield Old Boys Rugby Club
BATHSE BA2 .... 14 D8
The Oldfield Park Surgery
BATHSE BA2 .... 14 C9
Oldfield School
CBATH/BATHN BA1 .... 98 C3
Old Knightstone Theatre
WSM BS23 .... 16 A1
Oldland Surgery
OLD/WMLY/WICK BS30 .... 69 J7
Oldmixon County
Infant School
OMX/HUT/LCK BS24 .... 117 F4
The Old Surgery
WSM BS23 .... 16 F2
The Open University
CBRIS/FH BS1 .... 7 J5
Optimax Laser Eye Clinic
CBRIS/FH BS1 .... 7 G4
The Orchard Medical Centre
KGWD/HNM BS15 .... 68 D2
The Other Surgery
CFTN/FAIL BS8 .... 2 C8
Our Lady of Lourdes RC School
KGWD/HNM BS15 .... 68 E3
Our Lady of the Rosary RC
Primary School
AVONM BS11 .... 50 C1
Overndale School
YATE/CS BS37 .... 45 K1
Paddingham House
WNSC BS25 .... 120 E6
Paragon School
BATHSE BA2 .... 111 K2
Parish Wharf Leisure Centre
PTSHD/EG BS20 .... 47 J3
Park House Clinic
RDSTK/MIDN BA3 .... 126 B5
Park Preparatory
School for Boys
CBATH/BATHN BA1 .... 99 F4
The Park School
KGWD/HNM BS15 .... 68 E2
Parkside Infant School
CBATH/BATHN BA1 .... 14 E5
Parkwall CP School
OLD/WMLY/WICK BS30 .... 69 G6
Parkway Trading Estate
RDLND/MONT BS6 .... 3 M5
Parnall Road Industrial Estate
MANG/FISH BS16 .... 54 A6
Parochial Junior School
TRWBR BA14 .... 125 F4
Parson Street Primary School
BMSTR BS3 .... 10 D4
Patchway C of E
Primary School
BRSTK/PCHW BS34 .... 30 B6
Patchway Health Clinic
BRSTK/PCHW BS34 .... 29 K7
Patchway High School
ALMDB BS32 .... 30 A6
Patchway Town Council
BRSTK/PCHW BS34 .... 29 J7
Patchway Trading Estate
BRSTK/PCHW BS34 .... 29 G7
Paulton Memorial Hospital
PLTN/PENS BS39 .... 126 A1
Pavilion
BATHSE BA2 .... 15 H6
Pavilion
CBATH/BATHN BA1 .... 14 E5
Pavillion
BATHSE BA2 .... 15 H7
Paxcroft Primary School
TRWBR BA14 .... 125 H5
Pembroke Road Surgery
CFTN/FAIL BS8 .... 2 A8
Pen Park School
HNBRY/STHM BS10 .... 39 G6
Perry Court Junior &
Infant School
HGRV/WHIT BS14 .... 78 C5
Petherton Road Infant School
HGRV/WHIT BS14 .... 12 C9
Philback Works
HNBRY/STHM BS10 .... 27 G7
Phoenix Business Park
BMSTR BS3 .... 10 B4
Phoenix NHS Trust
KGWD/HNM BS15 .... 68 C6
The Picture House
CBRIS/FH BS1 .... 7 J1
Pilning CP School
THNB/SVB BS35 .... 28 B1
Pines Way Industrial Estate
BATHSE BA2 .... 14 D7
Pixash Business Centre
KEYN BS31 .... 81 H6
Playhouse Theatre
WSM BS23 .... 16 D1
The Podium Shopping
Cente and Library
CBATH/BATHN BA1 .... 15 G6
Portbury Sawmills
Industrial Estate
PTSHD/EG BS20 .... 49 F2
Portbury VA Primary School
PTSHD/EG BS20 .... 48 E6
Portishead CP School
PTSHD/EG BS20 .... 47 G4
Portishead Health Centre
PTSHD/EG BS20 .... 47 H4

Portishead & North
Weston Town Council
PTSHD/EG BS20 .... 47 H4
Portrait Gallery
HORF/LLZ BS7 .... 39 J7
Portview Trading Estate
AVONM BS11 .... 49 H1
Portway School
AVONM BS11 .... 50 A2
Portway Trading Estate
AVONM BS11 .... 49 J2
The Practice
CFTN/FAIL BS8 .... 6 D3
Prim School
THNB/SVB BS35 .... 19 G5
Prior Park College
BATHSE BA2 .... 112 B3
The Priory Doctors Surgery
BRSG/KWL/STAPK BS4 .... 12 D4
Priory Farm Trading Estate
PTSHD/EG BS20 .... 48 D6
Priory School
MTN/WRL BS22 .... 106 C2
Pucklechurch C of E
Primary School
MANG/FISH BS16 .... 56 E3
QEH Sports Club
CFTN/FAIL BS8 .... 63 K7
QEH Theatre
CFTN/FAIL BS8 .... 6 C3
Quakers Friars
CBRIS/FH BS1 .... 7 K2
Queen Elizabeth Hospital
CFTN/FAIL BS8 .... 6 D3
Radstock County Infant
School
RDSTK/MIDN BA3 .... 127 G2
Radstock St Nicholas
Infant School
RDSTK/MIDN BA3 .... 127 G3
Radstock St Nicholas
Junior School
RDSTK/MIDN BA3 .... 127 G3
Radstock Town Football Club
RDSTK/MIDN BA3 .... 127 H3
Ralph Allen School
BATHSE BA2 .... 112 D3
Rangeworthy C of E
Primary School
YATE/CS BS37 .... 25 G5
Ravenswood School
NAIL BS48 .... 61 H7
Raysfield Infant School
YATE/CS BS37 .... 34 C7
Raysfield Junior School
YATE/CS BS37 .... 34 C7
Redfield Edge Primary School
OLD/WMLY/WICK BS30 .... 69 K6
Redfield Leisure Centre
EVILLE/WHL BS5 .... 8 F1
Redgrave Theatre
CFTN/FAIL BS8 .... 65 H2
Redhouse Primary School
BMSTRD/HC/WWD BS13 .... 77 J6
Redland High Junior School
RDLND/MONT BS6 .... 2 F5
Redland High School
RDLND/MONT BS6 .... 2 F5
Redland High School
Sixth Form Centre
RDLND/MONT BS6 .... 2 E5
Red Maids Junior School
HNLZ/SM/SNYPK/WT BS9 .... 51 J3
Red Maids School
HNLZ/SM/SNYPK/WT BS9 .... 51 J3
Register Office
CBRIS/FH BS1 .... 7 J2
Registry Office
CBATH/BATHN BA1 .... 14 E5
The Ridge Junior School
YATE/CS BS37 .... 34 C5
Ridgeway Industrial Centre
EVILLE/WHL BS5 .... 5 J6
Ridings High School
FRCTL/WBN BS36 .... 41 J2
Riverbank Medical Centre
MTN/WRL BS22 .... 106 C2
Riverside Business Park
BRSG/KWL/STAPK BS4 .... 9 H5
Riverside Leisure Park
CBRISNE BS2 .... 3 M9
Riverside Surgery
BRSG/KWL/STAPK BS4 .... 13 L1
Robin Cousins Sports Centre
AVONM BS11 .... 49 J1
Rockingham Works
AVONM BS11 .... 36 E3
Rode Methodist VC First School
RDSTK/MIDN BA3 .... 128 E7
Rodford CP School
YATE/CS BS37 .... 44 A1
Rodford Infant School
YATE/CS BS37 .... 43 K1
Roman Baths and Pump Rooms
CBATH/BATHN BA1 .... 15 G7
Romney Avenue Junior
Mixed School
HORF/LLZ BS7 .... 53 F3
Rooksmoor Gallery
CBATH/BATHN BA1 .... 14 E4
The Rostra Gallery
CBATH/BATHN BA1 .... 14 F5
The Royal High School
CBATH/BATHN BA1 .... 14 E2
The Royal High School
CBATH/BATHN BA1 .... 99 J2
Royal National Hospital for
Rheumatic Diseases
CBATH/BATHN BA1 .... 14 F6
Royal Navy & Royal Marines
CBRIS/FH BS1 .... 7 G3
Royal United Hospital
CBATH/BATHN BA1 .... 98 E4
Royal West of England
Academy
CFTN/FAIL BS8 .... 6 D2
Royce Clinic
TRWBR BA14 .... 125 G4

RPS Octagon Galleries
CBATH/BATHN BA1 .... 14 F5
RSPCA & Dogs Home
BRSG/KWL/STAPK BS4 .... 7 M8
Russell Town Avenue
Industrial Centre
EVILLE/WHL BS5 .... 8 E2
Rydal School
CLVDN BS21 .... 59 F6
St Andrews C of E VA
Primary School
CBATH/BATHN BA1 .... 14 E3
St Andrews C of E VC
Primary School
WUE GL12 .... 21 H4
St Andrews Trading Estate
AVONM BS11 .... 36 D6
St Andrews VC Junior School
YTN/CONG BS49 .... 109 F1
St Annes C of E Primary School
OLD/WMLY/WICK BS30 .... 69 J7
St Annes Junior Mixed School
BRSG/KWL/STAPK BS4 .... 9 G6
St Annes Park JMI School
BRSG/KWL/STAPK BS4 .... 9 K5
St Annes Primary School
OMX/HUT/LCK BS24 .... 85 J7
St Apollonias Surgery
KEYN BS31 .... 80 E5
St Augustine of Canterbury RC
Primary School
MANG/FISH BS16 .... 54 E2
St Augustines RC School
TRWBR BA14 .... 124 D6
St Barnabas C of E V C
Junior Mixed Infant School
RDLND/MONT BS6 .... 3 L7
St Barnabas C of E VC
Primary School
PTSHD/EG BS20 .... 47 F4
St Bedes RC School
AVONM BS11 .... 37 H6
St Benedicts RC Primary School
RDSTK/MIDN BA3 .... 126 D6
St Bernadette RC School
HGRV/WHIT BS14 .... 79 C5
St Bernadettes RC
Primary School
HGRV/WHIT BS14 .... 79 F5
St Bernards RC
Primary School
AVONM BS11 .... 50 A3
St Bonaventures RC School
HORF/LLZ BS7 .... 2 F2
St Brandons School
CLVDN BS21 .... 58 E7
St Brendans Sixth
Form College
BRSG/KWL/STAPK BS4 .... 13 M6
St Brendans Trading Estate
AVONM BS11 .... 36 C6
St Catherines Industrial Estate
BMSTR BS3 .... 11 H1
St Chads Surgery
RDSTK/MIDN BA3 .... 126 C4
St Francis RC School
NAIL BS48 .... 73 K2
St Gabriels Business Park
EVILLE/WHL BS5 .... 4 C9
St George Health Centre
KGWD/HNM BS15 .... 68 A2
St George School
EVILLE/WHL BS5 .... 8 E1
St Georges Industrial Estate
AVONM BS11 .... 36 C5
St Georges Primary School
CFTN/FAIL BS8 .... 6 D5
St Gloucester Co
THNB/SVB BS35 .... 19 F4
St Gregorys RC School
BATHSE BA2 .... 111 G5
St Helens C of E
Primary School
THNB/SVB BS35 .... 23 F2
St James's Gallery
CBATH/BATHN BA1 .... 14 E4
St James Surgery
CBATH/BATHN BA1 .... 14 E3
St Johns Church &
Old City Gate
CBRIS/FH BS1 .... 7 H3
St Johns C of E
Primary School
KEYN BS31 .... 80 E6
St Johns C of E VC
Primary School
CFTN/FAIL BS8 .... 2 B6
St Johns Hospital
TRWBR BA14 .... 130 E1
St Johns Junior School
RDSTK/MIDN BA3 .... 126 A4
St Johns Lane Health Centre
BMSTR BS3 .... 11 J3
St Johns Mead C of E VC
Primary School
YATE/CS BS37 .... 34 E6
St Johns RC Primary School
BATHSE BA2 .... 15 J6
St Johns RC School
TRWBR BA14 .... 124 D6
St John the Evangelist
Primary School
CLVDN BS21 .... 70 E2
St Josephs RC School
MANG/FISH BS16 .... 54 B6
St Josephs RC School
PTSHD/EG BS20 .... 47 F3
St Katherine C of E School
BLAG/CWMG/WR BS40 .... 90 B4
St Katherines School
PTSHD/EG BS20 .... 50 A4
St Laurence School
BOAV BA15 .... 114 D6
St Margarets Surgery
BOAV BA15 .... 114 E4
St Marks C of E School
CBATH/BATHN BA1 .... 100 A2

St Mark's Community Centre
BATHSE BA2 .... 15 G9
St Marks VA Primary School
MTN/WRL BS22 .... 106 A1
St Martins Hospital
BATHSE BA2 .... 111 H4
St Martins Junior School
MTN/WRL BS22 .... 105 J3
St Martins Surgery
BRSG/KWL/STAPK BS4 .... 12 D5
St Mary Redcliffe Primary
School
BMSTR BS3 .... 7 J9
St Mary Redcliffe & Temple
C of E VA School
CBRIS/FH BS1 .... 7 K7
St Marys C of E Primary School
YATE/CS BS37 .... 34 B5
St Marys C of E School
THNB/SVB BS35 .... 19 F3
St Marys Hospital
CFTN/FAIL BS8 .... 6 D3
St Marys RC Infant School
CBATH/BATHN BA1 .... 98 E3
St Marys RC Primary School
RDSTK/MIDN BA3 .... 127 K3
St Mary's Redcliff
CBRIS/FH BS1 .... 7 J6
St Marys Rugby Club
ALMDB BS32 .... 30 E5
St Michael on the Mount C of E
Primary School
CFTN/FAIL BS8 .... 6 F3
St Michaels C of E VC
Primary School
FRCTL/WBN BS36 .... 41 K2
St Michaels Hill Clinic
CBRISNE BS2 .... 6 F2
St Michaels Hospital
CBRISNE BS2 .... 6 F1
St Michaels Primary School
BRSTK/PCHW BS34 .... 40 D3
St Nicholas Chantry
Primary School
CLVDN BS21 .... 59 G6
St Nicholas Market
CBRIS/FH BS1 .... 7 H4
St Nicholas RC Primary School
EVILLE/WHL BS5 .... 7 M1
St Patricks RC School
EVILLE/WHL BS5 .... 9 G2
St Pauls RC Primary School
YATE/CS BS37 .... 34 B7
St Peter & St Paul RC School
RDLND/MONT BS6 .... 2 E9
St Peters C of E VC
Primary School
PTSHD/EG BS20 .... 47 H5
St Philips Junior &
Infant School
BATHSE BA2 .... 111 G3
St Pius X RC Primary School
BMSTRD/HC/WWD BS13 .... 77 J6
St Saviours Infant School
CBATH/BATHN BA1 .... 100 A2
St Saviours Junior School
CBATH/BATHN BA1 .... 100 A2
St Stephens Business Centre
OLD/WMLY/WICK BS30 .... 69 J5
St Stephens C of E VC
Junior School
KGWD/HNM BS15 .... 54 D7
St Teresas Private Hospital
BATHSE BA2 .... 97 J4
St Teresas RC School
HORF/LLZ BS7 .... 39 H7
St Thomas More RC School
HORF/LLZ BS7 .... 4 B3
St Ursulas High School
HNLZ/SM/SNYPK/WT BS9 .... 51 J3
St Vincents Trading Estate
CBRISNE BS2 .... 8 F5
Sally Lunn's House
CBATH/BATHN BA1 .... 15 G7
Saltford Primary School
KEYN BS31 .... 97 F2
Salvation Army
BMSTR BS3 .... 6 F9
Salvation Army
CBATH/BATHN BA1 .... 14 E7
Salvation Army
WSM BS23 .... 16 D4
Sampson House Business Park
HNBRY/STHM BS10 .... 38 A1
Samuel Whites Infant School
KGWD/HNM BS15 .... 68 C5
Saracens Rugby Club
HNBRY/STHM BS10 .... 38 C3
Satellite Business Park
EVILLE/WHL BS5 .... 9 H3
Saville Court Business Centre
CFTN/FAIL BS8 .... 6 A3
Sawclose Health Clinic
CBATH/BATHN BA1 .... 14 F6
Scotch Horn Community &
Sports Centre
NAIL BS48 .... 73 K1
Sea Life Centre
WSM BS23 .... 16 C5
Sea Mills Infant School
HNLZ/SM/SNYPK/WT BS9 .... 50 E2
Sea Mills Junior School
HNLZ/SM/SNYPK/WT BS9 .... 50 D4
Sea Mills Surgery
HNLZ/SM/SNYPK/WT BS9 .... 50 D4
Sefton Park Infants School
HORF/LLZ BS7 .... 3 L3
Severn Beach CP School
THNB/SVB BS35 .... 27 H1
Severnside Trading Estate
AVONM BS11 .... 36 D3
Severnside Works
HNBRY/STHM BS10 .... 27 H5
Sheene Court Industrial Estate
BMSTR BS3 .... 10 E2
Sheilding Schools
THNB/SVB BS35 .... 19 F4

Shipham C of E VC
First School
WNSC BS25 .... 121 H6
Shirehampton Baths
AVONM BS11 .... 50 A3
Shirehampton Cricket Club
AVONM BS11 .... 50 B2
Shirehampton Health Centre
AVONM BS11 .... 50 A3
Shirehampton Infant School
AVONM BS11 .... 49 K3
Shirehampton Junior School
AVONM BS11 .... 49 K3
Showcase Cinema Bristol
CBRISNE BS2 .... 8 E6
Sidcot School
WNSC BS25 .... 120 E7
Sikh Temple
EVILLE/WHL BS5 .... 4 E3
Silverhill School
FRCTL/WBN BS36 .... 41 K1
Simplex Trading Estate
OLD/WMLY/WICK BS30 .... 69 K6
Sir Bernard Lovell School
OLD/WMLY/WICK BS30 .... 69 J6
The Sisters of the Temple
CFTN/FAIL BS8 .... 65 H3
Sneyd Park Surgery
HNLZ/SM/SNYPK/WT BS9 .... 51 G6
Soaphouse Industrial Estate
EVILLE/WHL BS5 .... 5 J9
The Soga Gallery
CFTN/FAIL BS8 .... 6 A4
Somerton House Surgery
RDSTK/MIDN BA3 .... 126 B4
Somervale School
RDSTK/MIDN BA3 .... 126 B4
Soundwell College
CBRISNE BS2 .... 8 B4
Soundwell College
KGWD/HNM BS15 .... 54 E7
South Bristol College
BMSTRD/HC/WWD BS13 .... 78 B7
Southdown Junior School
BATHSE BA2 .... 110 E2
Southfield Road Trading Estate
NAIL BS48 .... 61 K7
Southgate Shopping Centre
CBATH/BATHN BA1 .... 15 G7
South Gloucestershire Council
BRSTK/PCHW BS34 .... 29 K3
South Gloucestershire Council
BRSTK/PCHW BS34 .... 40 A4
South Gloucestershire Council
MANG/FISH BS16 .... 55 H3
South Gloucestershire Council
THNB/SVB BS35 .... 28 A2
South Gloucestershire Council
YATE/CS BS37 .... 33 K3
Southmead Health Centre
HNBRY/STHM BS10 .... 39 F4
Southmead Health Services
NHS Trust
HNBRY/STHM BS10 .... 52 B1
South Street Primary School
BMSTR BS3 .... 10 D2
South View Business Centre
MANG/FISH BS16 .... 54 E4
South View Business Park
MANG/FISH BS16 .... 54 E4
Southville Primary School
BMSTR BS3 .... 6 D9
Southville Surgery
BMSTR BS3 .... 6 F7
South Wansdyke
Sports Centre
RDSTK/MIDN BA3 .... 126 C5
Southwick C of E
Primary School
TRWBR BA14 .... 130 A3
Sovereign Shopping Centre
WSM BS23 .... 16 D2
Speedwell Industrial Estate
CLVDN BS21 .... 70 E1
Speedwell School
EVILLE/WHL BS5 .... 68 A1
Speedwell Swimming Baths
EVILLE/WHL BS5 .... 5 M6
Springfield School
RDLND/MONT BS6 .... 3 K6
Springwater Park Trading Estate
EVILLE/WHL BS5 .... 9 J3
Ss Great Britain
CBRIS/FH BS1 .... 6 D6
Stafford Business Centre
WSM BS23 .... 17 G3
The Stafford Clinic
WSM BS23 .... 16 D9
Stanbridge CP School
MANG/FISH BS16 .... 55 F3
Stanley Court Surgery
RDSTK/MIDN BA3 .... 126 C3
Staple Hill Primary School
MANG/FISH BS16 .... 54 D5
Staverton C of E School
TRWBR BA14 .... 125 F1
Steps Gallery
CBRIS/FH BS1 .... 7 G3
Sterling College International
CBATH/BATHN BA1 .... 15 G3
Stockwood Green
Primary School
HGRV/WHIT BS14 .... 79 J7
Stoke Bishop C of E
Primary School
HNLZ/SM/SNYPK/WT BS9 .... 51 F3
Stoke Gifford Medical Centre
BRSTK/PCHW BS34 .... 40 D4
Stoke Lodge Infant School
BRSTK/PCHW BS34 .... 30 E1
Stokes Medical Centre
BRSTK/PCHW BS34 .... 40 D1
Stoke View Business Park
MANG/FISH BS16 .... 5 L2
Stonar School
MELK SN12 .... 103 J4
Stonehill Business Centre
OLD/WMLY/WICK BS30 .... 68 E6

Storybox Theatre
  YTN/CONG BS49 .... **87** K4
Stover Trading Estate
  YATE/CS BS37 .... **33** J6
Stroud College
  YATE/CS BS37 .... **34** B6
Stuckeys Furniture Gallery
  HNLZ/SM/SNYPK/WT BS9 .... **2** A5
Stuckleys Pine Gallery
  HORF/LLZ BS7 .... **52** C4
Studley Green Primary School
  TRWBR BA14 .... **130** C1
Summerfield School
  CBATH/BATHN BA1 .... **14** A1
Summerhill Infant School
  EVILLE/WHL BS5 .... **9** K1
Sun Life Sports Club
  HNBRY/STHM BS10 .... **38** C4
Sunnyside Farm Trading Estate
  PTSHD/EG BS20 .... **49** J7
Sussex Place Surgery
  RDLND/MONT BS6 .... **3** M6
Swimming Pool
  PTSHD/EG BS20 .... **47** G1
Temple County Primary School
  KEYN BS31 .... **81** F5
Temple House Doctors Surgery
  KEYN BS31 .... **80** E6
Temple Trading Estate
  CBRISNE BS2 .... **8** D6
Teyfant Primary School
  BMSTRD/HC/WWD BS13 .... **78** C7
Thornbury Health Centre
  THNB/SVB BS35 .... **19** H4
Thornbury Hospital
  THNB/SVB BS35 .... **19** H4
Thornbury Leisure Centre
  THNB/SVB BS35 .... **19** G6
Tickenham School
  CLVDN BS21 .... **60** D6
Time Machine Museum
  WSM BS23 .... **16** E2
Tockington Manor School
  ALMDB BS32 .... **22** B4
Toll House Clinic
  YATE/CS BS37 .... **35** F6
Totterdown Bridge Estate
  CBRISNE BS2 .... **8** B8
Trimbridge Galleries
  CBATH/BATHN BA1 .... **14** F6
Trinity College
  HNLZ/SM/SNYPK/WT BS9 .... **51** G5
Tropicana Leisure Complex
  WSM BS23 .... **16** C6
Trowbridge College
  TRWBR BA14 .... **130** C1
Trowbridge & District Hospital
  TRWBR BA14 .... **124** E4
Trowbridge Mosque
  TRWBR BA14 .... **125** F7
Trowbridge Rugby
  Football Club
  TRWBR BA14 .... **125** J6
TT Trading Estate
  YATE/CS BS37 .... **35** F6
Twerton C of E Junior School
  BATHSE BA2 .... **98** D6

Twerton Infant School
  BATHSE BA2 .... **98** C7
Two Mile Hill Junior &
  Infant School
  KGWD/HNM BS15 .... **68** B2
Twyford House Cricket Club
  AVONM BS11 .... **50** B2
Tyning Junior & Mixed School
  HGRV/WHIT BS14 .... **78** E4
The Tynings CP School
  MANG/FISH BS16 .... **54** E5
United Bristol Healthcare
  NHS Trust
  CBRIS/FH BS1 .... **7** H2
University of Bristol
  CBRIS/FH BS1 .... **6** F3
University of Bristol
  CBRISNE BS2 .... **6** F1
University of Bristol
  CFTN/FAIL BS8 .... **6** E1
University of Bristol
  CFTN/FAIL BS8 .... **6** B4
University of Bristol
  HNLZ/SM/SNYPK/WT BS9 .... **51** G5
University of Bristol Childrens
  Hospital
  CFTN/FAIL BS8 .... **6** F1
University of the
  West of England
  CBRIS/FH BS1 .... **7** H4
University of the
  West of England
  MANG/FISH BS16 .... **53** J4
University of the
  West of England Bristol
  BMSTR BS3 .... **65** G5
University of the
  West of England Bristol
  MANG/FISH BS16 .... **40** C7
University of the
  West of England Bristol
  MANG/FISH BS16 .... **54** A4
University of the
  West of England Bristol
  RDLND/MONT BS6 .... **2** C4
Uphill CP School
  WSM BS23 .... **116** C4
Upper Horfield Primary School
  HORF/LLZ BS7 .... **52** E1
Victoria Art Gallery
  CBATH/BATHN BA1 .... **15** G6
Victoria Park County
  Infant School
  BMSTR BS3 .... **11** J2
Victoria Rooms
  CFTN/FAIL BS8 .... **6** C2
The Village Surgery
  MTN/WRL BS22 .... **105** K3
Vines Industrial Estate
  NAIL BS48 .... **62** A7
Wadehurst Industrial Park
  CBRISNE BS2 .... **8** B3
Walcot Infant School
  CBATH/BATHN BA1 .... **15** H2
Walliscote Primary School
  WSM BS23 .... **16** E4

Wallis Estate
  CBRISNE BS2 .... **4** A4
Wansdyke Business Centre
  BATHSE BA2 .... **111** G1
Wansdyke District Council
  RDSTK/MIDN BA3 .... **126** E3
Wansdyke School
  BATHSE BA2 .... **111** H5
Wansdyke School
  HGRV/WHIT BS14 .... **78** D7
Warmley C of E School
  OLD/WMLY/WICK BS30 .... **69** J4
Waterloo Galleries
  WSM BS23 .... **16** D2
Watershed Arts Complex
  CBRIS/FH BS1 .... **7** G5
Waycroft Primary School
  HGRV/WHIT BS14 .... **79** J6
Wellesley CP School
  YATE/CS BS37 .... **44** A2
Wellsway School
  KEYN BS31 .... **81** G6
Welton CP School
  RDSTK/MIDN BA3 .... **126** D3
Welton Rovers Football Club
  RDSTK/MIDN BA3 .... **126** C3
West Ashton Primary School
  TRWBR BA14 .... **131** K3
Westbury Bazaar & Gallery
  HNLZ/SM/SNYPK/WT BS9 .... **51** J2
Westbury-on-trym C of E
  Primary School
  HNLZ/SM/SNYPK/WT BS9 .... **51** J2
Westbury on Trym Practice
  HNLZ/SM/SNYPK/WT BS9 .... **51** H3
Westbury Park School
  RDLND/MONT BS6 .... **2** C3
Westcliff College of Further
  Education
  WSM BS23 .... **104** A4
Westfield CP School
  RDSTK/MIDN BA3 .... **126** D5
Westfield Surgery
  RDSTK/MIDN BA3 .... **127** F4
Westhaven School
  WSM BS23 .... **116** B4
Westlands Sports Club
  OMX/HUT/LCK BS24 .... **117** F2
West Leigh County
  Infant School
  NAIL BS48 .... **74** A5
Weston All Saints C of E
  Junior & Infant School
  CBATH/BATHN BA1 .... **98** D2
Weston Area Health Trust
  WSM BS23 .... **116** D4
Weston Business Park
  BNWL BS29 .... **119** F3
Weston College
  WSM BS23 .... **16** C1
Weston County Infant School
  CBATH/BATHN BA1 .... **98** D2
Weston Park Primary School
  AVONM BS11 .... **50** B1
Weston St Johns
  Associated Football Club
  WSM BS23 .... **116** E3

Weston Sixth Form College
  WSM BS23 .... **116** D4
Weston-Super-Mare AFC
  WSM BS23 .... **17** K7
Weston-Super-Mare Borough
  Employees Sports Club
  WSM BS23 .... **17** G4
Weston-Super-Mare
  County Court
  WSM BS23 .... **16** D3
Weston-Super-Mare
  Cricket Club
  WSM BS23 .... **116** D3
Weston-Super-Mare
  General Hospital
  WSM BS23 .... **116** D4
Weston-Super-Mare
  Rugby Football Club
  WSM BS23 .... **16** F5
Westpoint Trading Estate
  KGWD/HNM BS15 .... **68** D3
West Town Lane Junior School
  BRSG/KWL/STAPK BS4 .... **12** F6
West Walk Surgery
  YATE/CS BS37 .... **34** B6
Westwing School
  THNB/SVB BS35 .... **18** D5
Westwood with Iford School
  BOAV BA15 .... **123** F3
Whitchuch Health Centre
  HGRV/WHIT BS14 .... **78** E6
Whitchurch Parish Council
  HGRV/WHIT BS14 .... **79** G7
Whitchurch Primary School
  HGRV/WHIT BS14 .... **79** G7
Whitefield Fishponds School
  MANG/FISH BS16 .... **5** L1
Whitehall Primary &
  Infant School
  EVILLE/WHL BS5 .... **5** G8
Whitehall Trading Estate
  EVILLE/WHL BS5 .... **4** E9
Whiteladies Medical Group
  CFTN/FAIL BS8 .... **2** B8
Widbrook Medical Practice
  TRWBR BA14 .... **124** C6
Widcombe C of E
  Junior & Infant School
  BATHSE BA2 .... **15** J8
Widcombe Surgery
  BATHSE BA2 .... **15** H9
Wildscreen @ Bristol
  CBRIS/FH BS1 .... **6** F5
William Budd Health Centre
  BRSG/KWL/STAPK BS4 .... **11** H8
Willow Green Infant School
  CBRISNE BS2 .... **4** B5
Wilverley Trading Estate
  BRSG/KWL/STAPK BS4 .... **13** J5
Wincombe Trading Estate
  BRSG/KWL/STAPK BS4 .... **7** M8
Windmill Farm Business Centre
  BMSTR BS3 .... **7** C9
Windmill Hill City Farm
  BMSTR BS3 .... **7** H9
Window Arts Centre
  CBATH/BATHN BA1 .... **14** F7

Windwhistle CP School
  WSM BS23 .... **116** E3
Winford School
  BLAG/CWMG/WR BS40 .... **91** G5
Wingfield Primary School
  TRWBR BA14 .... **129** J1
Winscombe Cricket Club
  WNSC BS25 .... **120** D7
Winscombe & Sandford
  Parish Council
  WNSC BS25 .... **120** C6
Winscombe Woodborough
  Primary School
  WNSC BS25 .... **120** D5
Winsley C of E School
  BOAV BA15 .... **113** K6
Withywood School
  BMSTRD/HC/WWD BS13 .... **77** J6
Wood Road Industrial Centre
  KGWD/HNM BS15 .... **68** D2
Woodspring District Council
  MTN/WRL BS22 .... **105** K3
Woodstock Special School
  KGWD/HNM BS15 .... **68** E3
Worleburygolf Course
  MTN/WRL BS22 .... **105** G2
Worlebury School
  MTN/WRL BS22 .... **105** G3
Worle Health Centre
  MTN/WRL BS22 .... **105** K3
Worle School
  MTN/WRL BS22 .... **105** K4
Wraxall School
  NAIL BS48 .... **62** C6
Writhlington School
  RDSTK/MIDN BA3 .... **127** J4
Wyncroft School
  WSM BS23 .... **16** C9
Wyvern School
  WSM BS23 .... **17** H7
Yate Leisure Centre
  YATE/CS BS37 .... **34** B5
Yate Town Council
  YATE/CS BS37 .... **34** B5
Yate Town Football Club
  YATE/CS BS37 .... **33** J4
Yatton Family Practice
  YTN/CONG BS49 .... **86** E5
Yatton Infant School
  YTN/CONG BS49 .... **87** F4
Yatton Junior School
  YTN/CONG BS49 .... **87** F4
Yatton Parish Council
  YTN/CONG BS49 .... **87** G5
Yeo Moor Junior &
  Infant School
  CLVDN BS21 .... **71** G1
YHA
  CBRIS/FH BS1 .... **7** G6
YMCA
  BRSG/KWL/STAPK BS4 .... **7** M9
YMCA
  CBATH/BATHN BA1 .... **15** G5
Zhong Yi Clinic
  CFTN/FAIL BS8 .... **2** D8

Page 14

F6
1 Barton St
2 Beauford Sq
3 Bridewell La
4 Harington Pl
5 Kingsmead Sq
6 Kingsmead St
7 Old Bond St
8 Parsonage La
9 Princes St
10 Queen St
11 Quiet St
12 St John's Pl
13 Saw Cl
14 Trim Br
15 Trim St
16 Westgate Buildings
17 Westgate St

Page 15

G6
1 Abbey Rd
2 Boat Stall La
3 Cheap St
4 Grand Pde
5 Green St
6 High St
7 New Bond St
8 Northgate St
9 Northumberland Pl
10 Orange Gv
11 Spring Gardens Rd
12 Union St
13 Upper Borough Walls

G7
1 Abbeygate St
2 Abbey Gn
3 Amery La
4 Church St
5 Henry St
6 Kingston Rd
7 Manvers St
8 New Orchard St
9 Pierrepont St
10 Pierrepont St
11 Southgate
12 Stall St
13 Swallow St
14 Terrace Wk
15 York St

Page 30

C5
1 Boursland Cl
2 Campion Dr
3 Foxborough Gdns
4 Perrys Lea
5 Primrose Cl
6 Teal Cl

Page 34

D6
1 Cherry Rd
2 Chestnut Dr
3 Meadow Rd
4 The Parade
5 River Rd
6 Streamside Rd
7 Wistaria Av

Page 42

A7
1 Chantry La
2 Chepstow Pk
3 Goodwood Gdns
4 Haydock Cl
5 Plumpton Ct
6 Redcar Ct
7 Sedgefield Gdns
8 Wetherby Ct
9 Wincanton Cl

Page 51

F4
1 Ellbridge Cl
2 Halwyn Cl
3 Yeomans Cl

J7
1 Anglesea Pl
2 Belgrave Hl
3 Highland Crs
4 Highland Sq
5 Hughenden Rd
6 Mornington Rd
7 Normanton Rd
8 Quarry Steps
9 Redland Ter
10 Richmond Cl
11 St Vincent's Hl
12 Westbury Rd
13 York St

K3
1 Blandford Cl
2 Grange Cl North
3 Waterford Rd

K7
1 East Shrubbery
2 Evans Rd
3 Hartington Pk
4 Luccombe Hl
5 Shrubbery Cottages
6 West Shrubbery
7 Woodland Ter

Page 52

A3
1 Croft Vw

D1
1 St Aldwyn's Cl

D2
1 Caine Rd

D3
1 Crofton Av

D4
1 Draycott Rd
2 Uphill Rd

D6
1 Hopetoun Rd
2 Osborne Rd
3 St Bartholomew's Rd

D7
1 Ashley Court Rd
2 Ashley Grove Rd
3 Ashley Pde
4 Cumberland Gv
5 Fairlawn Rd
6 Falkland Rd
7 Milverton Gdns
8 Old Ashley Hl
9 Richmond Av
10 Richmond Rd
11 St Andrew's Rd
12 St Werburgh's Rd
13 Sommerville Rd South
14 York St

E1
1 Austen Gv
2 Cropthorne Rd South
3 St Gregory's Wk
4 Thackeray Wk

E2
1 Masefield Wy
2 Rose Mead
3 Shearmore Cl
4 Taunton Wk

E7
1 Boucher Pl
2 Boyce Dr
3 Cleave St
4 Dorset Gv
5 Durham Rd
6 Hereford Rd
7 John St
8 Lancaster Rd
9 Lynmouth Rd
10 Merstham Rd
11 Norman Rd
12 Ryland St
13 Seddon Rd
14 Stafford Rd
15 Tewkesbury Rd
16 Treefield Rd
17 Trentham Cl
18 Warminster Rd
19 Weedon Cl
20 York St

Page 53

G7
1 Apsley St
2 Argyle St
3 Bay Gdns
4 Berkeley Av
5 Boswell St
6 Caraway Gdns
7 Coombe Rd
8 Coriander Wk
9 East Park Dr
10 Fountaine Ct
11 Freeland Buildings
12 Juniper Ct
13 St Leonard's Rd

H3
1 Bryansons Cl
2 Countess Wk
3 Princess Gdns

J4
1 Blackberry Av
2 Cromwells Hide
3 Frome Pl
4 Glenside Pk
5 Kite Hay Cl
6 Lark's Fld
7 Pennyroyal Gv
8 Spires Vw

K2
1 Broadways Dr

K3
1 Curlew Cl
2 Lapwing Gdns
3 Ronald Rd
4 Whinchat Gdns
5 Witherlies Rd

K5
1 Adelaide Pl
2 Albert Ter
3 Featherstone Rd
4 Langdale Rd
5 Wharf Rd

K6
1 Balaclava Rd
2 Drummond Rd
3 Halstock Av
4 Lodore Rd
5 Midland Ter
6 Stoke View Rd

K7
1 Irena Rd
2 Madeline Rd

Page 54

A2
1 Blenman Cl
2 Probyn Cl
3 Scott Lawrence Cl
4 Stourden Cl

A4
1 Claverham Rd
2 College Av
3 Guinea La

A5
1 Hinton Rd
2 Hockey's La

A6
1 Acton Rd
2 Ivy La
3 Justice Rd
4 Poplar Pl

A7
1 Dean's Dr

B2
1 Churchside

B3
1 Lanaway Rd
2 Little Hayes
3 Oldbury Court Dr

B4
1 Cunningham Gdns

B5
1 Bridges Ct
2 Chasefield La
3 Daws Ct
4 Parkhurst Av
5 Vicars Cl

B6
1 Fillwood Ct
2 William St

B7
1 Forest Wk
2 Lyncombe Wk

C1
1 Beckspool Rd

C2
1 Quarry Rd
2 Tuckett La

C3
1 Bracey Dr
2 Bridges Dr
3 Grangewood Cl
4 Shimsey Cl
5 Urfords Dr

C4
1 Pemberton Ct

C5
1 Edgeware Rd

C6
1 Acacia Cl
2 The Chase
3 Glendale
4 Glenwood
5 The Greenway
6 Market Sq
7 Quadrant East
8 The Rosery

C7
1 Coulson Wk
2 Henshaw Cl
3 Welton Wk
4 Wentforth Dr
5 Willow Gv
6 Woodland Cl

D1
1 Bromley Heath Rd
2 Pilgrims Wy
3 Quaker's Cl
4 Scantleberry Cl

D2
1 Cleeve Wood Rd
2 Heath Cl

D3
1 Chestnut Rd
2 Conifer Cl
3 Edmund Cl

D4
1 Christchurch Av
2 Christchurch La
3 Downend Park Rd
4 Nelson Rd
5 Tyler's La

D5
1 Alexandra Cl
2 Kensington Rd
3 Nelson Rd
4 North Vw
5 Pendennis Av

D7
1 Norman Gv
2 Wellington Rd
3 Whitfield Cl
4 The Wickets
5 Woodland Av

E1
1 Sandholme Cl
2 Sandringham Pk

E2
1 Oakdale Ct

E3
1 Buckingham Pl
2 Westerleigh Rd
3 Woodlands

E4
1 Clarence Gdns
2 Heathcote Rd

E5
1 Byron Pl
2 Eastleigh Cl
3 Fiennes Cl
4 Irving Cl
5 James Cl
6 Saunders Rd
7 Shipman Ct
8 Teewell Cl

E6
1 Gladstone Dr
2 Gloucester Rd
3 St Stephens Cl
4 Wiltshire Pl
5 Woodchester

E7
1 Blackthorn Wk
2 Deerhurst
3 Frys Hl
4 Pembroke Rd
5 Tyndale Rd

Page 55

F3
1 Stanbridge Cl
2 Woodhall Cl

Page 65

H4
1 Albemarle Rw
2 Cornwallis Av
3 Cumberland Pl
4 Dowry Sq
5 Freeland Pl
6 Glendale
7 Hopechapel Hl
8 Hotwell Rd
9 Joy Hl
10 North Green St
11 Oxford Pl
12 The Paragon
13 Royal York Crs
14 South Green St
15 Victoria Ter
16 Windsor Ter

J4
1 Ambra V
2 Ambra V South
3 Ambra V West
4 Camden Ter
5 Clifton Hl
6 Clifton Vale Cl
7 Cliftonwood Ter
8 Dowry Rd
9 Polygon Rd
10 Royal York Vls
11 St Vincent's Rd
12 Saville Pl

J6
1 Ashton Gate Ter
2 Baynton Rd
3 Leigh St
4 North Rd
5 St Francis Rd
6 Wells St

K2
1 Alma Road Av
2 Melrose Av
3 Oakfield Pl
4 Westbourne Pl

K4
1 Bellevue Cottages
2 Cliftonwood Crs
3 Gasferry Rd
4 Glentworth Rd
5 Gorse La
6 John Carr's Ter
7 St Edward's Rd
8 Southernhay
9 Southernhay Av

K7
1 Crowther St
2 Dartmoor St
3 Dorset St
4 Jasper St
5 Lindrea St
6 Martin St
7 The Nursery
8 Parker St
9 Pembery Rd
10 Stanley St North
11 Thistle St
12 Upper Sydney St

Page 66

A3
1 Berkeley Av
2 Berkeley Sq
3 Lodge St
4 Lodge St
5 Old Park Hl
6 Park La
7 Park Street Av
8 Royal Fort Rd
9 There-and-back-again La

A4
1 Bigwood La
2 Brandon Steep
3 Charlotte St South
4 College Sq
5 Culver St
6 Denmark Av
7 Frogmore St
8 Gaunt's La
9 Hobb's La
10 Lower College St
11 Lower Lamb St
12 Orchard Av
13 Orchard La
14 Orchard St
15 Partition St
16 Unity St
17 Upper Wells St
18 York Pl

A6
1 Argyle St
2 Dean St
3 Fairfield Rd
4 Kingston Rd
5 Merrywood Cl
6 Morley Rd
7 Mount Pleasant Ter
8 Murray St
9 Summer St

B1
1 Arley Cottages
2 Arley Pk
3 Elmgrove Pk
4 Fremantle La
5 Fremantle Rd
6 St Matthew's Av
7 Southfield Rd
8 Victoria Gdns
9 Winsley Rd

B2
1 Barton St
2 Cherry La
3 Clevedon Ter
4 Cottage Pl
5 Earl St
6 Henrietta St
7 Hillgrove St North
8 King Sq
9 King Square Av
10 Lower Gay St
11 Montague Hl
12 Montague Hill South
13 Montague St
14 Princess Rw
15 Spring Hl
16 Terrell St
17 Whitson St

B3
1 All Saints' St
2 Bell La
3 Blackfriars
4 Bridewell St
5 Cannon St
6 Christmas St
7 Fiennes St
8 High St
9 Host St
10 Lewins Mead
11 Nelson St
12 Newmarket Av
13 Pithay
14 Pithay Ct
15 Quay St
16 St Stephen's St
17 Silver St
18 Union St

B4
1 All Saints' La
2 Assembly Rooms La
3 Bridge St
4 Broad Quay
5 Clare St
6 Coronation Pl
7 Crow La
8 High St
9 King William Av
10 Marsh St
11 Middle Av
12 Queen Square Av
13 Rackhay
14 St Stephen's Av
15 Telephone Av

B6
1 Bedminster Pl
2 Boot La
3 Brook Rd
4 Clarke St
5 Dean Crs
6 Leicester St
7 Lombard St
8 Regent Rd
9 St Paul's Rd
10 Southville Pl
11 Whitehouse La

C1
1 Armidale Av
2 Barnabas St
3 Bath Buildings
4 Dalrymple Rd
5 Drummond Rd
6 Elmgrove Av
7 Luxton St
8 Owen St
9 Pountney Dr
10 Thomson Rd
11 Vining Wk
12 Westbourne Rd
13 Woodborough St

C3
1 Callowhill Ct
2 George Whitefield Ct
3 Hanover Ct
4 Marybush La
5 Meadow St
6 Merchant St
7 Old King Street Ct
8 Philadelphia Ct
9 Quakers' Friars
10 Wellington Ct
11 Whippington Ct

C6
1 Church St
2 Ferry St
3 Long Rw
4 Narrow Pln
5 St Thomas St East
6 Three Queens' La
7 Tower St

C7
1 Almorah Rd
2 Newport St
3 Orwell St
4 Paultow Av

D1
1 Albany Rd
2 Albert Pk
3 Ashfield Pl
4 Brook La
5 Cairns' Crs
6 Corey Cl
7 Franklyn La
8 London Rd
9 Tudor Rd
10 Winkworth Pl

D2
1 Beggarswell Cl
2 Charlotte St
3 Cheapside
4 East St
5 Elton St
6 Eugene St
7 Frome St
8 Wilson Pl

D3
1 Asher La
2 David St
3 Eyer's La
4 Gloucester La
5 Hawkins St
6 Redcross St
7 St Matthias Pk
8 Tucker St
9 Waterloo St
10 Willway St

D4
1 Broad Pln
2 Louisa St
3 Midland St
4 New Kingsley Rd
5 New Thomas St
6 Providence Pl
7 Straight St

D5
1 Chatterton Rd
2 Chatterton St
3 Lower Station Approach Rd

D6
1 Bellevue Ter
2 Bushy Pk
3 Cheapside St
4 Dunmore St
5 Higham St
6 Vernon St

D7
1 Merioneth St
2 Monmouth St
3 Montgomery St
4 Nottingham St

E1
1 Ashley Grove Rd
2 Baptist St
3 Barker Wk
4 Bean St
5 Blenheim St
6 Byron St
7 Conduit Pl
8 Dermot St
9 Gable Rd
10 Highett Dr
11 Kensington Pk
12 Lower Ashley Rd
13 Newfoundland St
14 Oxford Pl
15 Pennywell Rd
16 Rosebery Av
17 Summers Rd
18 Waverley St

E3
1 Armoury Sq
2 Ashman Ct
3 Bates Cl
4 Beaufort St
5 Beaumont St
6 Beaumont Ter
7 Clark St
8 Durbin Wk
9 Hamilton Rd
10 Harleston St
11 Perry St
12 Robinson St
13 St Gabriel's Rd
14 Webb St
15 Winsford St

E4
1 Barton V
2 Dings Wk
3 Firestone Rd
4 Queen Victoria St
5 William St

E5
1 Victoria Rd

E6
1 Angers Rd
2 Firfield St
3 Fitzroy St
4 Fredrick St
5 Highgrove St
6 Hillside St
7 Kingstree St

B7
1 Bathwell Rd
2 Clyde Ter
3 Fairfoot Rd
4 Fordell Pl
5 Goolden St
6 Knowle Rd
7 Vale St

Page 67

F1
1 Chapel Rd
2 Church Av
3 Graham Rd
4 Greenbank Av West
5 Henrietta St
6 Lawrence Av
7 Moorhill St
8 Normandy Rd
9 Northcote St
10 St Mark's Ter
11 St Nicholas Pk
12 Warwick Av
13 Warwick Rd
14 Woodborough St

F2
1 Abraham Cl
2 Adelaide Pl
3 All Hallows Rd
4 Brighton Pk
5 Cattybrook St
6 Clayton St
7 Combfactory La
8 Eastbourne Rd
9 Elmgrove Av
10 Luxton St
11 Owen St
12 Pountney Dr
13 Thomson Rd
14 Tyndall Rd
15 Vining Wk
16 Westbourne Rd
17 Windsor Gv

F3
1 Arthur Skemp Cl
2 Atchley St
3 Bright St
4 Charlton St
5 Church St
6 Earl Russell Wy
7 Ernest Barker Cl
8 Morton St
9 Payne Dr
10 Robert St
11 Strawbridge Rd
12 William Mason Cl

J4
1 Holy Well Cl
2 Roegate Dr
3 Whiteway Cl

J5
1 The Beeches

K1
1 Dragon Wk
2 Emra Cl
3 Fernhurst Rd
4 Whitewood Rd

K2
1 Albert Gv
2 Bruton Cl
3 Orchard Rd
4 Park St

Page 70

E2
1 Summerhill Ter

K2
1 Angels Gnd
2 Avonside Wy
3 Barton Cl
4 Celia Ter
5 Cousins Ms
6 Coventry Wk
7 Crew's Hole Rd
8 Elizabeths Ms
9 Quayside La
10 Riverside Wk
11 St Georges Av

K5
1 Abbey Ct
2 Chelmsford Wk
3 Davies Dr
4 Stockwood Ms

K7
1 Millbrook Av
2 St Helier Av

Page 68

B7
1 Rowan Wy
2 Sycamore Cl

C5
1 Avonlea
2 Briarfield Av
3 Creswicke Av
4 Hunters Cl
5 Laburnum Rd
6 Lower Chapel La
7 Martins Cl

D1
1 Brighton Rd
2 Chesham Wy
3 Gladstone Rd
4 Hampton St
5 Kennington Av
6 Kimberley Rd
7 Morley Ter
8 Wesley Hl
9 Worcester Rd

E1
1 Collingwood Av
2 Frys Hl
3 Holly Crs
4 Runnymede

E3
1 Bellevue Rd
2 Berkeley Rd

E4
1 Emfield Rd
2 Granny's La
3 High Elm
4 Kemble Cl

Page 69

C4
1 Brake Cl
2 Bredon Cl
3 Gee Moors
4 Kingsleigh Ct
5 Kingsleigh Gdns
6 Ladd Cl
7 Norton Cl
8 Penard Wy
9 Shilton Cl
10 Woodstock Rd

F6
1 Alwins Ct
2 Bramley Ct
3 Britten Ct
4 Drummond Ct
5 Dudley Ct
6 Frampton Ct
7 Godfrey Ct
8 Greve Ct
9 Harris Ct
10 Hicks Ct
11 Laphams Ct
12 Logus Ct
13 Lynch Ct
14 Miles Ct
15 Park Farm Ct
16 Pippin Ct
17 Press Moor Dr
18 Stibbs Ct
19 Tindell Ct
20 Turners Ct
21 Woodington Ct

G5
1 Betjeman Ct
2 Churchill Ct
3 Coronation Cl
4 Dylan Thomas Ct
5 Earlstone Crs
6 Henry Williamson Ct
7 Laurie Lee Ct

G7
1 Bakersfield
2 Beaumont Cl
3 Fairoaks
4 Penngrove
5 Redwood Cl
6 Rutherford Cl
7 Springville Cl

J5
1 The Dell
2 Makin Cl
3 Neads Dr

J6
1 Brendon Cl
2 Hawkins Cl

J7
1 Brookfield Wk
2 Chequers Cl
3 The Clamp
4 The Croft

K4
1 Ashcombe Crs
2 Coniston Cl
3 Haweswater Cl
4 Mitchell Wk
5 Ullswater Cl

K5
1 Hardwick Cl
2 Samuel Wright Cl
3 Summerhayes

K6
1 Batley Ct
2 Lovell Av
3 North Cft

Page 99

H7
1 Cheltenham St
2 Hayden Cl
3 Junction Av
4 Westmoreland Rd
5 Westmoreland Station Rd
6 Westmoreland St

Page 71

F1
1 Churchill St
2 Coleridge Vale Rd East
3 Elm Tree Rd
4 Hillview Av
5 Kingsley Rd
6 Melbourne Ter
7 New Rd

F2
1 Closemead
2 Corner Cft
3 Dawes Cl
4 Leach Cl
5 Newlands Gn
6 Orchard Rd
7 The Paddock
8 Pedder Rd
9 Stonebridge
10 Tone Rd

Page 73

G2
1 Chantry Cl
2 Chapel Barton
3 Elm Cl
4 Goss Cl
5 Goss Vw
6 May Tree Cl
7 Yew Tree Cl
8 Yew Tree Gdns

Page 74

A1
1 Birch Dene
2 The Birches
3 Cerney Gdns
4 Chesterton Dr
5 Chestnut Cha
6 Coates Gv
7 The Oaks
8 Redwood Cl
9 Rowan Cl
10 Sawyers Cl

A2
1 Cairn Cl
2 Cleeve Pl
3 Cricklade Ct
4 Falmouth Cl
5 Gleneagles Cl
6 Kemble Cl
7 St Agnes Cl
8 St Andrews Cl
9 St Ives Cl
10 Sherston Cl
11 Sunningdale Cl
12 Truro Rd
13 Vynes Cl
14 Woodford Cl

Page 77

H5
1 Costiland Dr
2 Marlepit Gv
3 Sandburrows Wk
4 Spartley Wk

K1
1 Bedminster Down Rd
2 Brighton Ter
3 Churchlands Rd
4 Derry Rd
5 Hardy Rd
6 Harptree Gv
7 Hengaston St
8 Highridge Rd
9 Osborne Ter
10 Parade South
11 Temple St
12 Trafalgar Ter
13 Winterstoke Cl

K6
1 Farmwell Cl
2 Flowerwell Rd
3 Fulford Rd
4 Fulford Wk
5 Gander Cl
6 Gatehouse Ct
7 Lyveden Gdns
8 Vigor Rd
9 Whitland Av

Page 78

B5
1 Elgar Cl
2 Inns Court Dr
3 Stainer Cl
4 Travers Cl
5 Wilbye Gv

D3
1 Barnstaple Rd
2 Corsley Wk
3 Dunster Rd
4 Hartcliffe Wk
5 Neston Wk

E1
1 Stoneleigh Wk

E2
1 Green Wk
2 Greenwood Rd
3 Preston Wk
4 The Square
5 Teignmouth Cl

E4
1 Parsons Paddock
2 Portmeirion Cl

Page 79

F3
1 Allanmead Rd
2 Drayton Cl
3 Edgewood Cl

F7
1 Foxcombe Rd

H4
1 Fontmell Ct
2 Hanford Ct
3 Morden Wk
4 Roundmoor Gdns

K1
1 Clothier Rd

K2
1 Emery Rd

K5
1 Cogsall Rd
2 Holsom Rd
3 Swane Rd

K6
1 Cantell Gv
2 Warren Gdns

K1
1 Blake End
2 Collingwood Cl
3 The Dell
4 Frobisher Ct
5 Harwood Gdns
6 Jellicoe Ct
7 The Lindens
8 Mountbatten Cl
9 Nelson Ct
10 Ramsay Cl
11 Tovey Cl
12 Willowdown

K3
1 Deacons Cl
2 Hawthorn Hl
3 Hill Rd East
4 Lawrence Close Ms
5 Martins Gv
6 Nutwell Sq

K4
1 Bunting Cl
2 Linnet Cl
3 Mayfield Av
4 Nightingale Cl
5 Nutwell Rd

K5
1 Artemesia Av
2 Bailey Cl
3 Falcon Crs
4 Finch Cl
5 Greengage Cl
6 Lombardy Cl
7 Magpie Cl
8 Merlin Cl
9 Sutton Cl
10 Swan Cl
11 Thrush Cl
12 Wagtail Gdns

K6
1 Damson Rd
2 Magnolia Cl

Page 106

C5
1 Atholl Cl
2 Constable Dr
3 Gainsborough Dr
4 Gleneagles Cl
5 Kielder Dr
6 Landseer Cl
7 Lynch Cl
8 Meadowbank
9 Reubens Ct
10 St Andrews Cl
11 Turnbury Cl
12 Turner Ct

A4
1 Bittern Cl
2 Blueberry Wy
3 Cormorant Cl
4 Curlew Gdns
5 Downs Cl
6 Lark Rd
7 Swift Cl
8 Teal Cl

B2
1 Becket Dr
2 Bishop Av
3 Blythe Gdns
4 Gilbervn Dr
5 Hogarth Ms
6 The Larches
7 Lester Dr
8 Parsons Gn
9 St Michael's Av
10 Torrington Cl
11 Vicarage Cl
12 Wentworth Cl

C1
1 Austen Cl
2 Denning Ct
3 Fenners
4 The Fielders
5 Gill Ms
6 Goddard Dr
7 Kent Wy
8 Longdown Dr
9 Marindrin Dr
10 Portishead Ct
11 Sadbury Cl
12 The Saffrons
13 Saxby Cl
14 Spinners End
15 Taylor Ct
16 Tremlett Ms
17 Wainwright Cl
18 Wellard Cl

C3
1 Griffin Cl
2 Thorn Cl

C4
1 Collett Cl
2 Ellis Pk
3 Hawksworth Cl
4 Jesmond Rd

Page 104

C5
1 Cambridge Pl
2 Connaught Pl
3 Grove Rd
4 High St
5 Knightstone Rd
6 Market La
7 Old Post Office La
8 St Margaret's Ter
9 Victoria Pl
10 Wadham St
11 West St

D5
1 Albert Quadrant
2 Burlington St
3 Edinburgh Pl
4 Gerard Rd
5 Glebe Rd
6 Hans Price Cl
7 Hopkins St
8 King's La
9 Longton Grove Rd
10 Orchard Pl
11 Poplar Pl
12 Prospect Pl
13 Tivoli La
14 Victoria Quadrant
15 Worthy La

Page 105

F5
1 Maple Cl
2 Summerlands Cl
3 Sycamore Cl

H5
1 Saxon Rd